Contemporary Issues in Bioethics

Beauchamp / Walter

THOMSON
WADSWORTH

Australia · Canada · Mexico · Singapore · Spain · United Kingdom · United States

Contemporary Issues in Bioethics
Beauchamp / Walter

Executive Editors:
Michele Baird, Maureen Staudt &
Michael Stranz

Project Development Manager:
Linda de Stefano

Marketing Coordinators:
Lindsay Annett and Sara Mercurio

**Production/Manufacturing
Supervisor:**
Donna M. Brown

Pre-Media Services Supervisor:
Dan Plofchan

Rights and Permissions Specialists:
Kalina Hintz and Bahman Naraghi

Cover Image
Getty Images*

www.thomsonrights.com
The Adaptable Courseware Program
consists of products and additions to
existing Thomson products that are
produced from camera-ready copy.
Peer review, class testing, and
accuracy are primarily the responsibility
of the author(s).

ISBN 0-495-20887-6

International Divisions List

Asia (Including India):
Thomson Learning
(a division of Thomson Asia Pte Ltd)
5 Shenton Way #01-01
UIC Building
Singapore 068808
Tel: (65) 6410-1200
Fax: (65) 6410-1208

Australia/New Zealand:
Thomson Learning Australia
102 Dodds Street
Southbank, Victoria 3006
Australia

Latin America:
Thomson Learning
Seneca 53
Colonia Polano
11560 Mexico, D.F., Mexico
Tel (525) 281-2906
Fax (525) 281-2656

Canada:
Thomson Nelson
1120 Birchmount Road
Toronto, Ontario
Canada M1K 5G4
Tel (416) 752-9100
Fax (416) 752-8102

UK/Europe/Middle East/Africa:
Thomson Learning
High Holborn House
50-51 Bedford Row
London, WC1R 4L$
United Kingdom
Tel 44 (020) 7067-2500
Fax 44 (020) 7067-2600

Spain (Includes Portugal):
Thomson Paraninfo
Calle Magallanes 25
28015 Madrid
España
Tel 34 (0)91 446-3350
Fax 34 (0)91 445-6218

Contents

INTRODUCTION TO ETHICS

1.
Ethical Theory and Bioethics

The moral problems discussed in this book have emerged from professional practice in the fields of clinical medicine, biomedical research, nursing, public health, and the social and behavioral sciences. The goal of this first chapter is to provide a basis in language, norms, and theory sufficient for reading and criticizing the selections in the later chapters.

Everyone is aware that ethics in the biomedical professions has had a distinguished history. Among the most influential sources of medical and nursing ethics are its traditions: the concepts, practices, and norms that have long guided conduct in these fields. The history and precise character of these traditions may be the logical starting point in reflecting on professional ethics, but great traditions such as Hippocratic ethics often fail to provide a comprehensive, unbiased, and adequately justified ethics. Indeed, the history of medical ethics over the last two thousand years is a particularly disappointing history from the perspective of today's concerns in bioethics about the rights of patients and research subjects.

Prior to the early 1970s, there was no firm ground in which a commitment to principles outside of Hippocratic medical ethics could take root and flourish. Particular ethical codes written for the medical, nursing, and research professions had always been written by their own members to govern their own conduct. To consult persons outside the profession was thought not only unnecessary, but dangerous. This conception has collapsed in the face of the pressures of the modern world. Such a professional morality has been judged not adequately comprehensive, coherent, or sensitive to conflicts of interest. The birth of bioethics occurred as a result of an increasing awareness that this older ethic had become obsolete.

FUNDAMENTAL PROBLEMS

THE STUDY OF MORALITY

Some Basic Concepts and Definitions. The field of ethics includes the study of social morality as well as philosophical reflection on its norms and practices. The terms *ethical theory* and *moral philosophy* refer exclusively to philosophical reflection on morality. The term *morality,* by contrast, refers to traditions of belief about right and wrong human conduct. Morality is a social institution with a history and a code of learnable rules. Moral standards and responsibilities predate us and are transmitted across generations. Like political constitutions and languages, morality exists before we are instructed in its relevant rules, and thus it has a transindividual status as a body of guidelines for action.

Since virtually everyone grows up with a basic understanding of the institution of morality, its norms are readily understood. All persons who are serious about living a moral life already grasp the core dimensions of morality. They know not to lie, not to steal property, to keep promises, to respect the rights of others, not to kill or cause harm to innocent persons, and the like. Individuals do not create these moral norms, and morality therefore cannot be purely a personal policy or code. The core parts of morality exist before their acceptance by individuals, who learn about moral responsibilities and moral ideals as they grow up.

Individuals also eventually learn to distinguish the general morality that holds for all persons—sometimes called the common morality (see later)—from rules that bind only members of special groups, such as physicians. We learn moral rules alongside other important social rules, which is one reason it later becomes difficult to distinguish the two. For example, we are constantly reminded in our early years that we must observe social rules of etiquette, such as saying "Please" when we want something and "Thank you" when we receive it, as well as more specific rules, such as "A judge is addressed as 'Judge.'" We are also taught rules of prudence, including "Don't touch a hot stove," together with rules of housekeeping, dressing, and the like.

Morality enters the picture when certain actions ought or ought not to be performed because of the considerable impact these actions can be expected to have on the interests of other people. We first learn maxims such as "Keep your promises" and "Respect the rights of others." These are elementary instructions in morality; they express what society expects of us and of everyone in terms of taking the interests of other people into account. We thus learn about moral instructions and expectations, and gradually we come to understand morality as a set of normative standards about doing good, avoiding harm, respecting others, keeping promises, and acting fairly. We also absorb standards of character and moral excellence.

The Common Morality. The set of norms that all morally serious persons share is the *common morality*. This morality binds all persons in all places. In recent years, the favored category to represent this universal core of morality in public discourse has been human rights, but moral obligation and moral virtue are no less vital parts of the common morality. The norms in the common morality do not deviate from what every morally serious person already knows. Every such person believes that we should not lie to others, should keep our promises, should take account of the well-being of others, and should treat them fairly. This background in morality is the raw data for theory and is why we can speak of the origins of moral principles as located in the common morality that we all already share.

A distinction is needed, however, between morality in the narrow sense and morality in the broad sense. The universal principles of the common morality comprise only a narrow range or skeleton of a well-developed body of moral standards. *Morality in the narrow sense* is comprised of universal principles, whereas *morality in the broad* (full-bodied) *sense* includes divergent moral norms, obligations, ideals, and attitudes that spring from particular cultures, religions, and institutions. For example, different standards of allocating resources for health care and different standards of giving to charitable causes are parts of morality in the broad sense. A pluralism of judgments and practices is the inevitable outcome of historical developments in cultures, moral disagreement and resolution, and the formulation of complex institutional and public policies.

Sometimes persons who suppose that they speak with an authoritative moral voice operate under the false belief that they have the force of the common morality (that is, universal morality) behind them. The particular moral viewpoints that such persons represent may be acceptable and even praiseworthy, but they also may not bind other persons or communities. For example, persons who believe that scarce medical resources such as transplantable organs should be distributed by lottery rather than by medical need may have very good moral reasons for their views, but they cannot claim the force of the common morality for those views.

A theory of common morality does not hold that all *customary* moralities qualify as part of the *common* morality; and use of the common morality in moral reasoning need not lead to conclusions that are socially received. An important function of the general norms in the common morality is to provide a basis for the evaluation and criticism of groups or communities whose customary moral viewpoints are in some respects deficient. Critical reflection may ultimately vindicate moral judgments that at the outset were not widely shared.

Four Approaches to the Study of Ethics. Morality can be studied and developed in a variety of ways. In particular, four ways of either studying moral beliefs or doing moral philosophy appear prominently in the literature of ethics. Two of these approaches describe and analyze morality without taking moral positions, and these approaches are therefore called *nonnormative*. Two other approaches do involve taking moral positions and are therefore called *normative*. These four approaches can be grouped as follows:

A. *Nonnormative approaches*
   1. Descriptive ethics
   2. Metaethics
B. *Normative approaches*
   3. General normative ethics
   4. Practical normative ethics

It would be a mistake to regard these categories as expressing rigid, sharply differentiated approaches. They are often undertaken at the same time, and they overlap in goal and content. Nonetheless, when understood as broad polar contrasts exemplifying models of inquiry, these distinctions are important.

First among the two nonnormative fields of inquiry into morality is *descriptive ethics,* or the factual description and explanation of moral behavior and beliefs. Anthropologists, sociologists, and historians who study moral behavior employ this approach when they explore how moral attitudes, codes, and beliefs differ from person to person and from society to society. Their works often dwell in detail on matters such as professional codes and practices, codes of honor, and rules governing permissible killing in a society. Although philosophers do not typically engage in descriptive ethics in their work, some have combined descriptive ethics with philosophical ethics—for example, by analyzing the ethical practices of Native American tribes or researching Nazi experimentation during World War II.

The second nonnormative field, *metaethics,* involves analysis of the meanings of central terms in ethics, such as *right, obligation, good, virtue,* and *responsibility.* The proper analysis of the term *morality* and the distinction between the moral and the nonmoral are typical metaethical problems. Crucial terms in bioethics, including *physician-assisted suicide, informed consent,* and *universal access* to health care, can be and should be given careful conceptual attention, and they are so treated in various chapters in this volume. (Descriptive ethics and metaethics may not be the only forms of nonnormative inquiry. In recent years there has been an active discussion of the biological bases of moral behavior and of the ways in which humans do and do not differ from animals.)

General normative ethics attempts to formulate and defend basic principles and virtues governing the moral life. Ideally, any ethical theory will provide a system of moral principles or virtues and reasons for adopting them and will defend claims about the range of their applicability. In the course of this chapter the most prominent of these theories will be examined, as will various principles of respect for autonomy, justice, and beneficence that have played a major role in some of these theories.

General normative theories are sometimes used to justify positions on particular moral problems such as abortion, euthanasia, the distribution of health care, and research involving human subjects. Usually, however, no direct move can be made from theory or principles to particular judgments, and theory and principles therefore typically only *facilitate* the development of policies, action guides, or judgments. In general, the attempts to delineate practical action guides are referred to as *practical ethics* (B.4 in the outline).

Substantially the same general ethical theories and principles apply to problems across different professional fields and in areas beyond professional ethics as well. One might appeal to principles of justice, for example, in order to illuminate and resolve issues of taxation, health care distribution, criminal punishment, and affirmative action in hiring. Similarly, principles of veracity (truthfulness) are invoked to discuss secrecy and deception in international politics, misleading advertisements in business ethics, balanced reporting in journalistic ethics, and the disclosure of the nature and extent of an illness to a patient in medical ethics.

MORAL DILEMMAS AND DISAGREEMENTS

In the teaching of ethics, moral problems are often examined through cases—in particular, law cases, clinical cases, and public policy cases. These cases, which appear in virtually every chapter in this book, vividly display dilemmas and disagreements that require students to identify and grapple with real moral problems.

Moral Dilemmas. In a case presented in Chapter 3, two judges became entangled in apparent moral disagreement when confronted with a murder trial. A woman named Tarasoff had been killed by a man who previously had confided to a therapist his intention to kill her as soon as she returned home from a summer vacation. Owing to obligations of confidentiality between patient and physician, a psychologist and a consulting psychiatrist did not report the threat to the woman or to her family, though they did make one unsuccessful attempt to commit the man to a mental hospital.

One judge held that the therapist could not escape liability: "When a therapist determines, or pursuant to the standards of his profession should determine, that his patient presents a serious danger of violence to another, he incurs an obligation to use reasonable care to protect the intended victim against such danger." Notification of police and direct warnings to the family were mentioned as possible instances of due care. The judge argued that although medical confidentiality must generally be observed by physicians, it was overridden in this case by an obligation to the possible victim and to the "public interest in safety from violent assault."

In the minority opinion, a second judge stated his firm disagreement. He argued that a patient's rights are violated when rules of confidentiality are not observed, that psychiatric treatment would be frustrated by nonobservance, and that patients would subsequently lose confidence in psychiatrists and would fail to provide full disclosures. He also suggested that violent assaults would actually increase because mentally ill persons would be discouraged from seeking psychiatric aid.[1]

The Tarasoff case is an instance of a moral dilemma because strong moral reasons support the rival conclusions of the two judges. The most difficult and recalcitrant moral controversies that we encounter in this volume generally have at least some dilemmatic features. They may even involve what Guido Calabresi has called "tragic choices." Everyone who has been faced with a difficult decision—such as whether to have an abortion, to have a pet "put to sleep," or to commit a family member to a mental institution—knows through deep anguish what is meant by a dilemma.

Dilemmas occur whenever good reasons for mutually exclusive alternatives can be cited; if any one set of reasons is acted upon, events will result that are desirable in some respects but undesirable in others. Here an agent morally ought to do one thing and also morally ought to do another thing, but the agent is precluded by circumstances from doing both. Although the moral reasons behind each alternative are good reasons, neither set of reasons clearly outweighs the other. Parties on both sides of dilemmatic disagreements thus can *correctly* present moral reasons in support of their competing conclusions. The reasons behind each alternative are good and weighty, and neither set of reasons is obviously the best set. Most moral dilemmas therefore present a need to balance rival claims in untidy circumstances.

One possible response to the problem of public moral dilemmas and disputes is that we do not have and are not likely ever to have a single theory or method for resolving public disagreements. In any pluralistic culture there may be many sources of moral value and consequently a pluralism of moral points of view on many issues: bluffing in business deals, providing national health insurance to all citizens, involuntarily committing the mentally disturbed, civil disobedience in pursuit of justice, and so on. If this response is correct, we can understand why there seem to be intractable moral dilemmas and controversies both inside and outside professional philosophy. However, there also are ways to alleviate at least some dilemmas and disagreements, as we shall now see.

The Resolution of Moral Disagreements. No single set of considerations is an entirely reliable method for resolving disagreement and controversy, but several methods for dealing constructively with moral disagreements have been employed in the past. Each deserves recognition as a method of constructively contending with disagreement.

1. *Obtaining Objective Information.* First, many moral disagreements can be at least facilitated by obtaining factual information concerning points of moral controversy. It has often been assumed that moral disputes are produced solely by differences over moral principles or their interpretation and application, rather than by a lack of information. However, disputes over what morally ought or ought not to be done often have nonmoral elements as central ingredients. For example, debates about the justice of government allocation of health dollars to preventive and educational strategies have often bogged down over factual issues of whether these strategies actually function to prevent illness and promote health.

In some cases new information facilitates negotiation and compromise. New information about the alleged dangers involved in certain kinds of scientific research, for instance, have turned public controversies regarding the risks of science and the rights of scientific researchers in unanticipated directions. In several controversies over research with a high level of uncertainty, it has been feared that the research might create an irreversible and dangerous situation (for example, by releasing an organism of pathogenic capability that known antibodies would be unable to combat and that could produce widespread contagion).

Controversies about sweetening agents for drinks, toxic substances in the workplace, pesticides in agriculture, radiation therapies, and vaccine dissemination, among others, have been laced with issues of both values and facts. Current controversies over whether there should be compulsory screening for AIDS sometimes turn chiefly on factual claims about how much can be learned by screening, how many persons are threatened, whether health education campaigns can successfully teach safe sex practices, and the like.

The arguments used by disagreeing parties in these cases sometimes turn on a dispute about liberty or justice and therefore sometimes are primarily normative, but they may also rest on purely factual disagreements. New information may have only a limited bearing on the resolution of some of these controversies, whereas in others it may have a direct and almost overpowering influence. The problem is that rarely, if ever, is all the information obtained that would be sufficient to settle factual disagreements.

2. *Providing Definitional Clarity.* Second, controversies have been calmed by reaching conceptual or definitional agreement over the language used by disputing parties. Controversies over the morality of euthanasia, for example, are often needlessly entangled because disputing parties use different senses of the term and have invested heavily in their particular definitions. For example, it may be that one party equates euthanasia with mercy killing and another party equates it with voluntarily elected natural death. Some even hold that euthanasia is by definition *nonvoluntary* mercy killing. Any resulting moral controversy over the concept *euthanasia* is ensnared in terminological problems, rendering it doubtful that the parties are even discussing the same problem. Fortunately, conceptual analysis does often facilitate discussion of issues, and many essays in this volume dwell at some length on conceptual analysis.

3. *Adopting a Code.* Third, resolution of moral problems can be facilitated if disputing parties can come to agreement on a common set of moral guidelines. If this method requires a complete shift from one starkly different moral point of view to another, disputes will virtually never be eased. Differences that divide persons at the level of their most cherished principles are deep divisions, and conversions are infrequent. Various forms of discussion and negotiation can, however, lead to the adoption of a new or changed moral framework that can serve as a common basis for discussion.

For example, a national commission appointed to study ethical issues in research involving human subjects unanimously adopted a common framework of moral principles. These principles provided a general background for deliberation about particular problems. Commissioners utilized three moral principles: respect for persons, beneficence, and justice. The principles were then used, along with other considerations, to justify a position on a wide range of moral problems that confronted the commission.[2] This common framework of principles facilitated discussion of controversies and opened up avenues of agreement that might otherwise not have been spotted.

Virtually every professional association in medicine and nursing has a code of ethics, and the reason for the existence of these codes is to give guidance in a circumstance of uncertainty or dispute. Their rules apply to all persons in the relevant professional roles in medicine, nursing, and research and often help resolve charges of unprofessional or unethical conduct. These codes are very general and cannot be expected to cover every possible case, but agreed-upon general principles do provide an important starting point.

4. *Using Examples and Counterexamples.* Fourth, resolution of moral controversies can be aided by a constructive method of example and opposed counterexample. Cases or examples favorable to one point of view are brought forward, and counterexamples to these cases are thrown up against the examples and claims of the first. This form of debate occurred when the commission mentioned in the preceding section considered the level of risk that can justifiably be permitted in scientific research involving children as subjects, where no therapeutic benefit is offered to the child. On the basis of principles of acceptable risk used in their own previous deliberations, commissioners were at first inclined to accept the view that only low-risk or *minimal-risk* procedures could be justified in the case of children (where *minimal risk* refers analogically to the level of risk present in standard medical examinations of patients). Examples from the history of medicine were cited that revealed how certain significant diagnostic, therapeutic, and preventive advances in medicine would have been unlikely, or at least slowed, unless procedures

that posed a higher level of risk had been employed. Counterexamples of overzealous researchers who placed children at too much risk were then thrown up against these examples, and the debate continued in this way for several months.

Eventually a majority of commissioners abandoned their original view that nontherapeutic research involving more than minimal risk was unjustified. The majority accepted the position that a higher level of risk can be justified by the benefits provided to other children, as when a group of terminally ill children become subjects of research in the hope that something will be learned about their disease that can be applied to other children. Once a consensus on this issue crystallized, resolution was achieved on the primary moral controversy about the involvement of children as research subjects (although two commissioners never agreed).

5. *Analyzing Arguments*. Fifth and finally, one of the most important methods of philosophical inquiry is the exposing of inadequacies, gaps, fallacies, and unexpected consequences of an argument. If an argument rests on accepting two incoherent points of view, then pointing out the incoherence will require a change in the argument. There are many subtle ways of attacking an argument. For example, in Chapters 4–5 there are discussions of the nature of "persons" dealing with problems of the right to die and euthanasia. Some writers on these topics have not appreciated that their arguments about persons were so broad that they carried important but unnoticed implications for both infants and animals. Their arguments implicitly provided reasons they had not noticed for denying rights to infants (rights that adults have), or for granting (or denying) the same rights to fetuses that infants have, and in some cases for granting (or denying) the same rights to animals that infants have.

It may, of course, be correct to hold that infants have fewer rights than adults, or that fetuses and animals should be granted the same rights as infants. The point is that if a moral argument leads to conclusions that a proponent is not prepared to defend and did not previously anticipate, the argument will have to be changed, and this process may reduce the distance between the parties who were initially in disagreement. This style of argument may be supplemented by one or more of the other four ways of reducing moral disagreement. Much of the work published in journals takes the form of attacking arguments, using counterexamples, and proposing alternative principles.

To accept this ideal of criticism is not to assume that conflicts can always be eliminated. The moral life will always be plagued by forms of conflict and incoherence. Our pragmatic goal should be a method that helps in a circumstance of disagreement, not a method that will always eradicate problems. We need not claim that moral disagreements can always be resolved, or even that every rational person must accept the same method for approaching problems. However, if something is to be done to alleviate disagreement, a resolution is more likely to occur if the methods outlined in this section are used.

THE PROBLEM OF RELATIVISM

The fact of moral disagreement and the idea of a universal common morality raise questions about whether moral judgments can be reached impartially and hold for everyone, or instead lead to an inescapable relativism.

Cultural Relativism. Relativists have often appealed to anthropological data indicating that moral rightness and wrongness vary from place to place and that there are no absolute or universal moral standards that could apply to all persons at all times. They maintain that rightness is contingent on cultural beliefs and that the concepts of rightness and wrongness are meaningless apart from the specific contexts in which they arise. The claim is that patterns of culture can only be understood as unique wholes and that moral beliefs are closely connected in a culture.

Although it is certainly true that many cultural practices and individual beliefs vary, it does not follow that morally serious people disagree about the moral standards that were described earlier in this chapter as norms in the common morality. Two cultures may agree about these norms and yet disagree about how to apply them in particular situations or practices. The two cultures may even agree on all the basic principles of morality yet disagree about how to live by these principles in particular circumstances.

For example, if personal payments for special services are common in one culture and punishable as bribery in another, then it is undeniable that these customs are different, but it does not follow that the moral principles underlying the customs are relative. One culture may exhibit a belief that practices of grease payments produce a social good by eliminating government interference and by lowering the salaries paid to functionaries, while the people of another culture may believe that the overall social good is best promoted by eliminating all special favors. Both justifications rest on an appraisal of the overall social good, but the people of the two cultures apply this principle in disparate and apparently competing ways.

This possibility suggests that a basic or fundamental conflict between cultural values can only occur if apparent cultural disagreements about proper principles or rules occur at the level of ultimate moral principles. Otherwise, the apparent disagreements can be understood in terms of, and perhaps be arbitrated by, appeal to deeper shared values. If a moral conflict were truly fundamental, then the conflict could not be removed even if there were perfect agreement about the facts of a case, about the concepts involved, and about background beliefs.

We need, then, to distinguish *relativism of judgments* from *relativism of standards:* Different judgments may rely upon the same general standards for their justification. Relativism of judgment is so pervasive in human social life that it would be foolish to deny it. When people differ about whether one policy for keeping hospital information confidential is more acceptable than another, they differ in their judgments, but they need not have different moral standards of confidentiality. They may hold the same moral standard on protecting confidentiality but differ over how to implement that standard.

Showing the falsity of a relativism of standards is more than we can hope to achieve here, but we can show how difficult it would be to show that it is true. Suppose, for the sake of argument, that disagreement exists at the deepest level of moral belief; that is, suppose that two cultures disagree on basic or fundamental norms. It does not follow even from a relativity of *standards* that there is no ultimate norm or set of norms in which everyone *ought* to believe. Consider an analogy to religious disagreement: From the fact that people have incompatible religious or atheistic beliefs, it does not follow that there is no single correct set of religious or atheistic propositions. Nothing more than skepticism is justified by the facts about religion that are adduced by anthropology; and, similarly, nothing more than this skepticism would be justified if fundamental conflicts of social belief were discovered in ethics.

Normative Relativism. Consider now a second type of relativism. Some relativists interpret "What is right at one place or time may be wrong at another" to mean that *it is right* in one context to act in a way that *it is wrong* to act in another. This thesis is normative, because it makes a value judgment; it delineates *which standards or norms correctly determine right and wrong behavior.* One form of this normative relativism asserts that one ought to do what one's society determines to be right (a group or social form of normative relativism), and a second form holds that one ought to do what one personally believes is right (an individual form of normative relativism).

This normative position has sometimes crudely been translated as "Anything is right or wrong whenever some individual or some group judges that it is right or wrong." However, less crude formulations of the position can be given, and more or less plausible examples can be adduced. One can hold the view, for example, that in order to be right something must be conscientiously and not merely customarily believed. Alternatively, it might be formulated as the view that whatever is believed to be right is right if it is part of a well-formed traditional moral code of rules in a society—for example, a medical code of ethics developed by a professional society.

The evident inconsistency of this form of relativism with many of our most cherished moral beliefs is one major reason to be doubtful of it. No general theory of normative relativism is likely to convince us that a belief is acceptable merely because others believe it in a certain way, although that is exactly the commitment of this theory. At least some moral views seem relatively more enlightened, no matter how great the variability of beliefs. The idea that practices such as slavery cannot be evaluated across cultures by some common standard seems morally unacceptable, not morally enlightened. It is one thing to suggest that such beliefs might be *excused*, still another to suggest that they are *right*.

We can evaluate this second form of relativism by focusing on (1) the objectivity of morals within cultures, and (2) the stultifying consequences of a serious commitment to moral relativism. (The first focus provides an argument against *individual* relativism and the second provides an argument against a *cultural* source of relativism.)

We noted previously that morality is concerned with practices of right and wrong transmitted within cultures from one generation to another. The terms of social life are set by these practices, whose rules are pervasively acknowledged and shared in that culture. Within the culture, then, a significant measure of moral agreement (objectivity) exists, and morality cannot be modified through a person's individual preferences.

For example, a hospital corporation cannot develop its professional ethics in any way it wishes. No hospital chain can draw up a code that brushes aside the need for confidentiality of patient information or that permits surgeons to proceed without adequate consents from patients, and a physician cannot make up his or her individual "code" of medical ethics. If codes deviate significantly from standard or accepted rules, they will rightly be rejected as subjective and mistaken.

Room for invention or alteration in morality is therefore restricted by the broader understanding of social morality. Beliefs cannot become *moral* standards simply because an individual so labels them. Because individual (normative) relativism claims that moral standards can be invented or labeled, the theory seems *factually* mistaken. This critique of *individual* relativism does not count against *cultural* relativism, however, because a cultural relativist could easily accept this critique. Our discussion needs to shift, then, to a second argument, which is directed at cultural forms of normative relativism.

The problem is this: In circumstances of disagreement, moral reflection is needed to resolve moral issues whether or not people accept different norms. When two parties argue about a serious, divisive, and contested moral issue—for example, conflicts of interest—most of us think that some fair and justified compromise may be reached despite the differences of belief causing the dispute. People seldom infer from the mere fact of a conflict between beliefs that there is no way to judge one view as correct or as better argued or fairer minded than the other. The more implausible the position advanced by one party, the more convinced others become that some views are mistaken or require supplementation.

People seldom conclude, then, that there is not a better and worse ethical perspective or a more reasonable form of negotiation. If cultural normative relativists deny the acceptability of these beliefs, they seem to give up too early on the possibility that moral agreement may be achieved.

THE ACCEPTABILITY OF MORAL DIVERSITY AND MORAL DISAGREEMENT

Even conscientious and reasonable moral agents who work diligently at moral reasoning sometimes disagree with other equally conscientious persons. They may disagree about whether disclosure to a fragile patient is appropriate, whether religious values about brain death have a central place in secular ethics, whether physician-assisted suicide should be legalized, and hundreds of other issues in bioethics. Such disagreement does not indicate moral ignorance or moral defect. We simply lack a single, entirely reliable way to resolve all disagreements.

This fact returns us to the questions about morality in the particular (or broad) sense that opened this chapter. Neither morality nor ethical theory has the resources to provide a single solution to every moral problem. Moral disagreement can emerge because of (1) factual disagreements (for example, about the level of suffering that an action will cause), (2) scope disagreements about who should be protected by a moral norm (for example, whether fetuses or animals are protected), (3) disagreements about which norms are relevant in the circumstances, (4) disagreements about appropriate specifications, (5) disagreements about the weight of the relevant norms in the circumstances, (6) disagreements about appropriate forms of balancing, (7) the presence of a genuine moral dilemma, and (8) insufficient information or evidence.

Different parties may emphasize different principles or assign different weights to principles even when they do not disagree over which principles are relevant. Such disagreement may persist even among morally serious persons who conform to all the demands that morality makes upon them. Moreover, when evidence is incomplete and different sets of evidence are available to different parties, one individual or group may be justified in reaching a conclusion that another individual or group is justified in rejecting. Even when both parties have incorrect beliefs, each party may be justified in holding those beliefs. We cannot hold persons to a higher standard in practice than to make judgments conscientiously in light of the relevant norms and the available and relevant evidence.

These facts about the moral life sometimes discourage those who must deal with practical problems, but the phenomenon of reasoned moral disagreement provides no basis for skepticism about morality or about moral thinking. Indeed, it offers a reason for taking morality seriously and using the best tools that we have to carry our moral projects as far as we can. We should not forget that we frequently obtain near complete agreement in our moral judgments and that we have the universal basis for morality considered earlier in this chapter.

When disagreements arise, a moral agent can—and often should—defend his or her decision without disparaging or reproaching others who reach different decisions. Recognition of legitimate diversity (by contrast to moral violations that call for criticism) is exceedingly important when we evaluate the actions of others. What one person does may not be what other persons should do even when they face the same problem. Similarly, what one institution or government should do may not be what another institution or government should do. From this perspective, individuals and societies legitimately construct different requirements that comprise part of the moral life (consistent with what we have called morality in the broad sense), and we may not be able to judge one as better than another.[3]

MORAL JUSTIFICATION

Typically we have no difficulty in deciding whether and how to act morally. We make moral judgments through a mix of appeals to rules, paradigm cases, role models, and the like. These moral beacons work well as long as we are not asked to deliberate about or justify our judgments. However, when we experience moral doubt or uncertainty, we are led to moral deliberation, and often from there to a need to justify our beliefs. As we deliberate, we usually consider which among the possible courses of action is morally justified—that is, which has the strongest moral reasons behind it. The reasons we finally accept express the conditions under which we believe some course of action is morally justified.

The objective of justification is to establish one's case by presenting a sufficient set of reasons for belief and action. Not all reasons, however, are good reasons, and even good reasons are not always sufficient for justification. There is, then, a need to distinguish a reason's *relevance* to a moral judgment from its final *adequacy* for that judgment; and also to distinguish an *attempted* justification from a *successful* justification. For example, a good reason for involuntarily committing certain mentally ill persons to institutions is that they present a clear and present danger to other persons. By contrast, a reason for commitment that is sometimes offered as a good reason, but that many people consider a bad reason (because it involves a deprivation of liberty), is that some mentally ill persons present a clear and present danger to themselves or that they require treatment for a serious mental disorder.

If someone holds that involuntary commitment on grounds of danger to self is a good reason and is solely sufficient to justify commitment, that person should be able to give some account of why this reason is good and sufficient. That is, the person should be able to give further justifying reasons for the belief that the reason offered is good and sufficient. The person might refer, for example, to the dire consequences for the mentally ill that will occur if no one intervenes. The person might also invoke certain principles about the moral importance of caring for the needs of the mentally ill. In short, the person is expected to give a set of reasons that amounts to an argued defense of his or her perspective. These appeals are usually either to a coherent group of moral principles or to consequences of actions, and they form the substantive basis of justification.

Many philosophers now defend the view that the relationship between general moral norms and particular moral judgments is bilateral (neither a unilateral "application" of general norms nor a unilateral abstraction from particular case judgments). John Rawls's celebrated account of *reflective equilibrium* has been the most influential model in this literature. In developing and refining a system of ethics, he argues, it is appropriate to start with the broadest possible set of *considered judgments* (see later) about a subject and to erect a provisional set of principles that reflects them. Reflective equilibrium views investigation in ethics (and theory construction) as a reflective testing of moral principles, theoretical postulates, and other relevant moral beliefs to render them as coherent as possible. Starting with paradigms of what is morally right or wrong, one searches for principles that are consistent with these paradigms as well as one another. Such principles and considered judgments are taken, as Rawls puts it, "provisionally as fixed points," but also as "liable to revision."

Considered judgments is a technical term referring to judgments in which moral beliefs and capacities are most likely to be presented without a distorting bias. Examples are judgments about the wrongness of racial discrimination, religious intolerance, and predatory sexual behavior. The goal of reflective equilibrium is to match, prune, and adjust considered judgments and principles so that they form a coherent moral outlook. This model demands the best approximation to full coherence under the assumption of a never-ending search for consistency and unanticipated situations. From this perspective, ethical theories and individual moral outlooks are never complete, always stand to be informed by practical contexts, and must be tested for adequacy by their practical implications.

Although the justification of particular moral *judgments* is often the issue, philosophers are as also concerned with the justification of general ethical *theories*. Which theory, we can now ask, is the best theory? Or do all theories fail tests for considered judgments and coherence?

TYPES OF ETHICAL THEORY

Many writers in bioethics believe that we would justifiably have more confidence in our individual and communal moral judgments if only we could justify them on the basis of a comprehensive ethical theory. The ambition of such an ethical theory is to provide an adequate normative framework for processing, and hopefully resolving, moral problems.

To deal with these issues, the reader should be prepared not only to understand ethical theory but also to make some assessment of its value for bioethics. Our objective in this section is not to show how ethical theory actually can resolve problems in health care, but only to present several influential types of ethical theory. These theories should be situated under the category that we earlier called general normative ethics. We will concentrate on utilitarianism, Kantianism, virtue (or character) ethics, the ethics of care, and casuistry. Some knowledge of these theories is indispensable for reflective study in bioethics because a sizable part of the field's literature draws on methods and conclusions found in these theories.

UTILITARIAN THEORIES

Utilitarianism is rooted in the thesis that an action or practice is right (when compared to any alternative action or practice) if it leads to the greatest possible balance of good consequences or to the least possible balance of bad consequences in the world as a whole. Utilitarians hold that there is one and only one basic principle of ethics: the principle of utility. This principle asserts that we ought always to produce the maximal balance of good consequences over bad consequences. The classical origins of this theory are found in the writings of Jeremy Bentham (1748–1832) and John Stuart Mill (1806–1873).

Utilitarians invite us to consider the larger objective or function of morality as a social institution, where *morality* is understood to include our shared rules of justice and other principles of the moral life. The point of the institution of morality, they insist, is to promote human welfare by minimizing harms and maximizing benefits: There would be no point in having moral codes unless they served this purpose. Utilitarians thus see moral rules as the means to the fulfilment of individual needs as well as to the achievement of broad social goals.

Mill's Utilitarianism. In several types of ethical theory, classic works of enduring influence form the basis for development of the theory. The most influential exposition of utilitarianism is John Stuart Mill's book *Utilitarianism* (1863). In this work Mill refers to the principle of utility as the Greatest Happiness Principle: "Actions are right in proportion as they tend to promote happiness, wrong as they tend to produce the reverse of happiness, i.e., pleasure or absence of pain." Mill's view seems to be that the purpose of morality is to tap natural human sympathies so as to benefit others while at the same time controlling unsympathetic attitudes that cause harm to others. The principle of utility is conceived as the best means to these basic human goals.

For Mill and other utilitarians, moral theory is grounded in a theory of the general goals of life, which they conceive as the pursuit of pleasure and the avoidance of pain. The production of pleasure and pain assumes moral and not merely personal significance when the consequences of our actions affect the pleasurable or painful states of others. Moral rules and moral and legal institutions, as they see it, must be grounded in a general theory of value, and morally good actions are alone determined by these final values.

Essential Features of Utilitarianism. Several essential features of utilitarianism may be extracted from the reasoning of Mill and other utilitarians. In particular, four conditions must be satisfied in order to qualify as a utilitarian theory.

1. The Principle of Utility: Maximize the Good. First, actors are obliged to maximize the good: We ought always to produce the greatest possible balance of value over disvalue (or the least possible balance of disvalue, if only bad results can be achieved). But what is the good or the valuable? This question takes us to the second condition.

2. A Theory of Value: The Standard of Goodness. The goodness or badness of consequences is to be measured by items that count as the primary goods or utilities. Various theories of value (or theories of the good) held by utilitarians point to (1) happiness, (2) the satisfaction of desires and aims, and (3) the attainment of such conditions or states of affairs as autonomy, understanding, various kinds of functioning, achievement, and deep personal relationships.

Many utilitarians agree that ultimately we ought to look to the production of *agent-neutral* or intrinsic values, those that do not vary from person to person. That is, what is good in itself, not merely what is good as a means to something else, ought to be produced. Bentham and Mill are hedonists; they believe that only pleasure or happiness (which are synonymous terms in this context) can be intrinsically good. Pluralistic utilitarian philosophers, by contrast, believe that no single goal or state constitutes the good and that many values besides happiness possess intrinsic worth—for example, the values of friendship, knowledge, love, personal achievement, culture, freedom, and liberties can all qualify.

Both the hedonistic and the pluralistic approaches have seemed to some recent philosophers relatively problematic for purposes of objectively aggregating widely different interests in order to determine where maximal value, and therefore right action, lies. Many utilitarians interpret the good as that which is *subjectively* desired or wanted. The satisfaction of desires or wants is seen as the goal of our moral actions. To maximize an individual's utility is to maximize what he or she has chosen or would choose from the available alternatives.

3. Consequentialism. Whatever its value theory, any utilitarian theory decides which actions are right entirely by reference to the *consequences* of the actions, rather than by reference to any intrinsic moral features the actions may have, such as truthfulness or fidelity. Here the utilitarian need not demand that all future consequences or even all avoidable consequences be anticipated. A utilitarian demands only that we take account of what can reasonably be expected to produce the greatest balance of good or least balance of harm. In judging the *agent* of the action, we should assess whether the agent conscientiously attempts to produce the best utilitarian outcome.

4. Impartiality (Universalism). Finally, in the utilitarian approach all parties affected by an action must receive *impartial consideration*. Utilitarianism thus stands in sharp contrast to egoism, which proposes maximizing consequences for oneself rather than for all parties affected by an action. In seeking a blinded impartiality, utilitarianism aligns good and mature moral judgment with moral distance from the choices to be made.

Act and Rule Utilitarianism. Utilitarian moral philosophers are conventionally divided into several types, and it is best to think of "utilitarianism" as a label designating a family of theories that use a consequentialist principle. A significant dispute has arisen among utilitarians over whether the principle of utility is to be applied to *particular acts* in particular circumstances or to *rules of conduct* that determine which acts are right and wrong. For the *rule utilitarian,* actions are justified by appeal to rules such as "Don't deceive" and "Don't break promises." These rules, in turn, are justified by appeal to the principle of utility. An *act utilitarian* simply justifies actions directly by appeal to the principle of utility. Act utilitarianism is thus characterized as a "direct" or "extreme" theory because the act utilitarian directly asks, "What good and evil consequences will result directly from this action in this circumstance?"—not "What good and evil consequences will result generally from this sort of action?"

Consider the following case, which occurred in the state of Kansas and which anticipates some issues about euthanasia encountered in Chapter 4. An elderly woman lay ill and dying. Her suffering came to be too much for her and her faithful husband of fifty-four years to endure, so she requested that he kill her. Stricken with grief and unable to bring himself to perform the act, the husband hired another man to kill his wife. An act utilitarian might reason that *in this case* hiring another to kill the woman was justified, although *in general* we would not permit persons to perform such actions. After all, only this woman and her husband were directly affected, and relief of her pain was the main issue. It would be unfortunate, the act utilitarian might reason, if our "rules" against killing failed to allow for selective killings in extenuating circumstances, because it is extremely difficult to generalize from case to case. The jury, as it turned out, convicted the husband of murder, and he was sentenced to twenty-five years in prison. An act utilitarian might maintain that a *rigid* application of rules inevitably leads to injustices and that rule utilitarianism cannot escape this problem of an undue rigidity of rules.

Many philosophers object vigorously to act utilitarianism, charging its exponents with basing morality on mere expediency. On act-utilitarian grounds, they say, it is desirable for a physician to kill babies with many kinds of birth defects if the death of the child would relieve the family and society of a burden and inconvenience and would lead to the greatest good for the greatest number. Many opponents of act utilitarianism have thus argued that strict rules, which cannot be set aside for the sake of convenience, must be maintained. Many of these apparently desirable rules can be justified by the principle of utility, so utilitarianism need not be abandoned if act utilitarianism is judged unworthy.

Rule utilitarians hold that rules have a central position in morality and cannot be compromised in particular situations. Compromise threatens the rules themselves. The rules' effectiveness is judged by determining whether the observance of a given rule would maximize social utility better than would any substitute rule (or having no rule). Utilitarian rules are, in theory, firm and protective of all classes of individuals, just as human rights firmly protect all individuals regardless of social convenience and momentary need.

Nonetheless, we can ask whether rule-utilitarian theories offer anything more than act utilitarianism. Dilemmas often arise that involve conflicts among moral rules—for example, rules of confidentiality conflict with rules protecting individual welfare, as in the Tarasoff case. If there are no rules to resolve these conflicts, perhaps the rule utilitarian cannot be distinguished from the act utilitarian.

KANTIAN THEORIES

We have seen that utilitarianism conceives the moral life in terms of intrinsic value and the means to produce this value. A second type of theory departs significantly from this approach. Often called *deontological* (i.e., a theory that some features of actions other than or in addition to consequences make actions obligatory), this type is now increasingly called *Kantian*, because of its origins in the theory of Immanuel Kant (1724–1804).

Duty from Rules of Reason. Kant believed that an act is morally praiseworthy only if done neither for self-interested reasons nor as the result of a natural disposition, but rather from *duty*. That is, the person's motive for acting must be a recognition of the act as resting on duty. It is not good enough, in Kant's view, that one merely performs the morally correct action, because one could perform one's duty for self-interested reasons having nothing to do with morality. For example, if an employer discloses a health hazard to an employee only because he or she fears a lawsuit, and not because of a belief in the importance of truth telling, then this employer acts rightly but deserves no moral credit for the action.

Kant tries to establish the ultimate basis for the validity of moral rules in pure reason, not in intuition, conscience, or utility. He thinks all considerations of utility and self-interest secondary, because the moral worth of an agent's action depends exclusively on the moral acceptability of the rule on the basis of which the person is acting. An action has moral worth only when performed by an agent who possesses a good will, and a person has a good will only if moral duty based on a universally valid rule is the sole motive for the action. Morality, then, provides a rational framework of principles and rules that constrain and guide everyone, without regard to their personal goals and interests.

Kant's supreme principle, *the categorial imperative,* also called *the moral law,* is expressed in several ways in his writings. His first formulation may be roughly paraphrased in this way: "Always act in such a way that you can will that everyone act in the same manner in similar situations." Kant's view is that wrongful practices, such as lying, theft, cheating, and failure to help someone in distress when you can easily do so, involve a kind of contradiction. Consider the example of cheating on exams. If everyone behaved as the cheater did, exams would not serve their essential function of testing mastery of relevant material, in which case there would effectively be no such thing as an exam. But cheating presupposes the background institution of taking exams, so the cheater cannot consistently will that everyone act as she does.

The categorical imperative is categorical, Kant says, because it admits of no exceptions and is absolutely binding. It is imperative because it gives instruction about how one must act. Kant clarifies this basic moral law by drawing a distinction between a categorical imperative and a *hypothetical imperative*. A hypothetical imperative takes the form, "If I want to achieve such and such a valued end, then I must do so and so." These prescriptions—so reminiscent of utilitarian thinking—tell us what we must do, provided that we already have certain desires, interests, or goals. An example is, "If you want to regain your health, then you must take this medication," or "If you want to improve infant mortality rates, then you must improve your hospital facilities." These imperatives are not commanded for their own sake. They are commanded as means to an end that has already been willed or accepted. Hypothetical imperatives are not moral imperatives in Kant's philosophy because moral imperatives tell us what must be done independently of our goals or desires.

Kant emphasizes the notion of *rule as universal law*. Rules that determine duty are made correct by their universality, that is, the fact that they apply to everyone. This criterion of universality offers some worthwhile lessons for bioethics. Some of the clearest cases of immoral behavior involve a person's trying to make a unique exception of himself or herself purely for personal reasons. This conduct could not be made universal, or the rules presupposed by the idea of "being an exception" would be destroyed. If carried out consistently by others, this conduct would violate the rules presupposed by the system of morality, thereby rendering the system inconsistent—that is, having inconsistent rules of operation.

Kant's view is that wrongful practices, including invasion of privacy, theft, and manipulative suppression of information, are "contradictory"; that is, they are not consistent with the very duties they presuppose. In cases of lying, for example, the universalization of rules that allow lying would entitle everyone to lie to you, just as you would be entitled to lie to them. Such rules are inconsistent with the practice of truth telling that they presuppose. Similarly, fraud in research is inconsistent with the practice of publishing the truth. All such practices are inconsistent with a rule or practice that they presuppose.

The Requirement to Never Treat Persons as Means. A second formulation of Kant's categorical imperative—one more frequently invoked in medical ethics—may be paraphrased in this way: "Treat every person as an end and never solely as a means."[4] This principle requires us to treat persons as having their own established goals. Deceiving prospective subjects in order to get them to consent to participate in nontherapeutic research is one example of a violation of this principle.

It has commonly been said that Kant is here arguing that we can never treat another as a means to our ends. This interpretation, however, misrepresents his views. He argues only that we must not treat another *exclusively* as a means to our own ends. When adult human research subjects are asked to volunteer, for example, they are treated as a means to a researcher's ends. However, they are not exclusively used for others' purposes, because they do not become mere servants or objects. Their consent justifies using them as means to the end of research.

Kant's imperative demands only that persons in such situations be treated with the respect and moral dignity to which all persons are always entitled, including the times when they are used as means to the ends of others. To treat persons merely as means, strictly speaking, is to disregard their personhood by exploiting or otherwise using them without regard to their own thoughts, interests, and needs. It involves a failure to acknowledge that every person has a worth and dignity equal to that of every other person and that this worth and dignity cannot be compromised for utilitarian or any other reasons.

CONTEMPORARY CHALLENGES TO THE TRADITIONAL THEORIES

Thus far we have treated only two types of theory: utilitarianism and Kantianism. These theories combine a variety of moral considerations into a surprisingly systematized framework, centered around a single major principle. Much is attractive in these theories, and they have been the dominant models in ethical theory throughout much of the twentieth century. During the 1970s and much of the 1980s, utilitarian and deontological approaches exerted enormous influence on the literature and discourse of bioethics.

Although utilitarian and deontological arguments or patterns of reasoning are still common today, the theories themselves now hold a much diminished stature in the field. The reasons for the demotion of utilitarian and single-principle deontological theories concern the disadvantages of any approach that attempts to characterize the entire domain of morality with one supreme principle. Three disadvantages are especially worthy of note. First, there is a problem of authority. Despite myriad attempts by philosophers in recent centuries to justify the claim that some principle is morally authoritative—that is, correctly regarded as the supreme moral principle—no such effort at justification has persuaded a majority of philosophers or other thoughtful people that either the principle or the moral system is as authoritative as the common morality that supplies its roots. Thus to attempt to illuminate problems in bioethics with a single-principle theory has struck many as misguided as well as presumptuous or dogmatic.

Second, even if an individual working in this field is convinced that some such theory is correct (authoritative), he or she needs to deal responsibly with the fact that many other morally serious individuals do not share this theory and give it little or no authority. Thus, problems of how to communicate and negotiate in the midst of disagreement do not favor appeals to rigid theories or inflexible principles, which can generate a gridlock of conflicting principled positions, rendering moral discussion hostile and alienating.

Third, there is the problem that a highly general principle is indeterminate in many contexts in which one might try to apply it. That is, the content of the principle itself does not always identify a unique course of action as right. It has increasingly become apparent that single-principle theories are significantly incomplete, frequently depending on independent moral considerations with the help of which the theories can serve as effective guides to action.

Much recent philosophical writing has focused on weaknesses in utilitarian and Kantian theories and on ways in which the two types of theory actually affirm some broader and less controversial conception of the moral life. Critics of utilitarian and Kantian models believe that the contrast between the two "types of theory" has been overestimated and that they do not merit the attention they have received and the lofty position they have occupied. Three accounts have been popular in bioethics as replacements for, or perhaps supplements to, utilitarian and Kantian theories. They are (1) virtue theory (which is character based), (2) the ethics of care (which is relationship based), and (3) casuistry (which is case based). These are the topics of the next three sections.

VIRTUE ETHICS

In discussing utilitarian and Kantian theories, we have looked chiefly at obligations and rights. Beyond obligations and rights, we often reflect on the agents who perform actions, have motives, and follow principles. Here we commonly make judgments about good and evil character in persons; virtue ethics gives good character a preeminent place.

Virtue ethics descends from the classical Greek tradition represented by Plato and Aristotle. Here the cultivation of virtuous traits of character is viewed as morality's primary function. Moral virtues are understood as morally praiseworthy character traits, such as courage, compassion, sincerity, reliability, and industry. In virtue ethics, the primary concern is with what sort of person is ideal, while action is considered to have secondary importance. People are viewed as acquiring virtues much as they do skills such as carpentry, playing an instrument, or cooking. They become just by performing just actions and become temperate by performing temperate actions. Virtuous character is cultivated and made a part of the individual, much like a language or tradition.

However, an ethics of virtue is more than habitual training. One must also have a correct *motivational structure*. A conscientious person, for example, not only has a disposition to act conscientiously, but a morally appropriate desire to be conscientious. The person characteristically has a moral concern and reservation about acting in a way that would not be conscientious.

Imagine a Kantian who always performs his or her obligation because it is an obligation but intensely dislikes having to allow the interests of others to be of importance. Such a person does not cherish, feel congenial toward, or think fondly of others, and respects them only because obligation requires it. This person can, on a theory of moral obligation such as Kant's (or Mill's), perform a morally right action, have an ingrained disposition to perform that action, and act with obligation as the foremost motive. It is possible (1) to be disposed to do what is right, (2) to intend to do it, and (3) to do it while also (4) yearning to be able to avoid doing it. If the motive is improper, a vital moral ingredient is missing, and if a person *characteristically* lacks this motivational structure, a necessary condition of virtuous character is absent.

Consider a physician who meets his moral obligations because they are his obligations and yet has underlying motives that raise questions of character. This physician detests his job and hates having to spend time with every patient who comes through the door. He cares not about being of service to people or creating a better environment in the office. All he wants to do is make money, avoid malpractice suits, and meet his obligations. Although this man never acts immorally from the perspective of duty, something in his character is deeply defective morally. The admirable compassion and dedication guiding the lives of many health professionals is absent in this person, who merely engages in rule-following behavior.

Virtue ethics may seem only of intellectual interest, but it has practical value in that a morally good person with right desires or motives is more likely to understand what should be done, to perform required acts, and to form moral ideals than is a morally bad or indifferent person. A trusted person has an ingrained motivation and desire to do what is right and to care about whether it is done. Whenever the feelings, concerns, and attitudes of others are the morally relevant matters, rules and principles are not as likely as human warmth and sensitivity to lead a person to notice what should be done. From this perspective, virtue ethics is at least as fundamental in the moral life as principles of basic obligation.

We also often morally evaluate a person's emotional responses—which tend to reflect one's character—even where no particular action is called for. One might admire a social worker's genuine sorrow at the news that another social worker's patient committed suicide; her expression of sorrow reflects her caring and sympathy. Moreover, in practice, well-established virtues may prove at least as important as mastery of principles, rules, and other action guides. For example, it may be the case that being truthful, compassionate, perceptive, diligent, and so forth is a more reliable basis for good medical practice than knowledge of the principles and rules of bioethics.

A proponent of character ethics need not claim that analysis of the virtues subverts or discredits ethical principles, rules, or theories. It is enough to argue that ethical theory is more complete if the virtues are included and that moral motives deserve to be at center stage in a way some leading traditional theories have inadequately appreciated. It is not difficult to see the compatibility of virtue ethics and duty ethics.

Indeed, it is doubtful that virtue can be adequately conceptualized without some background assumptions about right action. For example, seeing truthfulness as a virtue seems inseparable from seeing truth telling as a prima facie obligation. If we ask why one should generally be truthful, it seems evasive to say, "Because virtuous people are that way." A more adequate response would show how truthfulness displays respect for people's autonomy, tends to promote certain benefits, and ordinarily avoids certain kinds of harm.

THE ETHICS OF CARE

Related to virtue ethics in some respects is a relatively new body of moral reflection often called the "ethics of care." This theory develops some of the themes in virtue ethics about the centrality of character, but the ethics of care focuses on a set of character traits that people all deeply value in close personal relationships: sympathy, compassion, fidelity, love, friendship, and the like. Noticeably absent are universal moral rules and impartial utilitarian calculations such as those espoused by Kant and Mill.

To understand this approach, consider the traditional theories' criterion of impartiality in moral judgment. This criterion of distanced fairness and treating similar cases similarly makes eminently good sense for courts, but does it make good sense of intimate moral relationships? The care perspective views this criterion as cutting away too much of morality in order to get to a standpoint of detached fairness. Lost in the traditional *detachment* of impartiality is *attachment*—that which we care about most and which is closest to us. In seeking blindness, we may be made blind and indifferent to the special needs of others. So, although impartiality is a moral virtue in some contexts, it may be a moral vice in others. The care perspective is especially important for roles such as parent, friend, physician, and nurse, where contextual response, attentiveness to subtle clues, and discernment are likely to be more important morally than impartial treatment.

Being cautious about abstract principles of obligation—the instruments of impartiality—is also characteristic of the ethics of care. Defenders of the ethics of care find principles often to be irrelevant, vacuous, or ineffectual in the moral life. A defender of principles could say that principles of care, compassion, and kindness structure our understanding of when it is appropriate to respond in caring, compassionate, and kind ways, but there is something hollow about this claim. It seems to best capture our moral experience to say that we rely on our emotions, our capacity for sympathy, our sense of friendship, and our knowledge of how caring people behave.

Exponents of the ethics of care have also criticized the autonomous, unified, rational beings that typify both the Kantian and the utilitarian conception of the moral self. They argue that moral decisions often require a sensitivity to the situation as well as an awareness of the beliefs, feelings, attitudes, and concerns of each of the individuals involved and of the relationships of those individuals to one another.

Additional reasons exist for thinking that a morality centered on care and concern cannot be squeezed into a morality of rules. For example, it seems very difficult to express the responsibilities of a health care professional adequately through principles and rules. We can generalize about how caring physicians and nurses respond in encounters with patients, but these generalizations do not amount to principles, nor will such generalizations be subtle enough to give sound guidance for the next patient. Each situation calls for a different set of responses, and behavior that in one context is caring seems to intrude on privacy or be offensive in another context.

A morality centered on care and concern can potentially serve health care ethics in a constructive and balanced fashion, because it is close to the processes of reason and feeling exhibited in clinical contexts. Disclosures, discussions, and decision making in health care typically become a family affair, with support from a health care team. The ethics of care maintains that many human relationships in health care and research involve persons who are vulnerable, dependent, ill, and frail and that the desirable moral response is attached attentiveness to needs, not detached respect for rights. Feeling for and being immersed in the other person establish vital aspects of the moral relationship. Accordingly, this approach features responsibilities and forms of empathy that a rights-based account may ignore in the attempt to protect persons from invasion by others.

Part II

JUSTICE AND AUTONOMY IN HEALTH CARE

2.

Justice in Access to Health Care

INTRODUCTION

Health care costs have continued to rise dramatically for several decades. These costs have been studied by government agencies worldwide. Many have concluded that their payment policies fuel unacceptable increases in expenditures for health care services. The basic *economic problem* is how to control costs and efficiently distribute resources in order to satisfy human needs and desires. The basic *ethical problem* is how to structure a health care system that fairly distributes resources and provides equitable access to health care. These economic and ethical problems are intertwined in the formation of health policy.

The proper role of government lies at the center of these health policy discussions. It is widely agreed that government is constituted to protect citizens against risks from the environment, risks from external invasion, risks from crime, risks from fire, risks from highway accidents, and the like. But the idea that certain kinds of health care should be similarly provided as a government service is more controversial, and even if it is agreed in a country that the government has an obligation to provide health care, there seem to be severe limits on what government can and should do.

THE ALLOCATION OF HEALTH CARE RESOURCES

Public health policies allocate resources, as do private sector policies such as health insurance provided as an employee benefit. To *allocate* is to distribute goods, services, or financial resources according to a system or principle. The distribution scheme need not be established or controlled by governments. For example, charitable organizations often distribute health care and the free market distributes health care goods and services through exchanges made by free agents acting in their own interests.

When a decision is social or governmental, in contrast to individual, decisions fall into two broad types: macroallocation and microallocation. In *macroallocation,* social decisions are made about how much will be expended for health care resources as well as how it will be distributed. These decisions are taken by legislatures, health organizations, private foundations, and health insurance companies. At the *microallocation* level, decisions are made by specific institutions or health professionals about who shall obtain available resources—for example, which of several potential patients will be admitted to the last available bed in the intensive care unit. This chapter emphasizes issues of fairness in systems of macroallocation.

Two primary considerations are involved in macroallocation decisions about health care and research: (1) What percentage of the total available resources should be allotted to biomedicine, an area that must compete for funding with other social projects such as defense, education, and transportation? (2) How much budgeted to biomedicine should go to each specific area—for example, how much to cancer research, to preventive medicine, and to the production of technology for treatment facilities? An example of the second problem is whether funding for *preventive* medicine should take priority over funding for *crisis* medicine. The prevention of disease by improvements in unsanitary environments and dissemination of health information is often cheaper and more efficient in raising health levels and saving lives than are kidney dialysis, heart transplantation, and intensive care units. From another perspective, however, a concentrated preventive approach seems morally unsatisfactory if it leads to the neglect of sick and injured persons who could directly benefit from available resources.

These problems of macroallocation are handled differently by competing systems of distribution. Which is the fairest?

DISTRIBUTIVE JUSTICE IN REDISTRIBUTING RESOURCES

In Chapter 1 we surveyed competing theories of justice. We will now examine how these same theories might be used to gauge the justice of health care systems, including macroallocation decisions.

Egalitarian Theory. In Chapter 1 we noted that John Rawls's *A Theory of Justice* has been a particularly influential work on social justice in the egalitarian tradition. Rawls argues that a social arrangement is a communal effort to advance the good of all in the society. Because inequalities of birth, historical circumstance, and natural endowment are undeserved, persons in a cooperative society should aim to make the unequal situation of naturally disadvantaged members more equal. Evening out disabilities in this way, Rawls claims, is a fundamental part of our shared conception of justice. His recognition of a positive societal obligation to eliminate or reduce barriers that prevent fair opportunity and that correct or compensate for various disadvantages has clear implications for discussions of justice in health care. Indeed, Rawls's analysis of justice has deeply influenced the articles in this chapter by Norman Daniels and Robert Veatch.

In his first article in this chapter, Daniels addresses the question, "Is there a right to health care?" He proposes that we conceptualize this right as a requirement of justice and then considers how we might interpret the commitments of various theories of justice to health care rights. He interprets Rawls's theory, in particular, as an account of protecting equality of opportunity; and he uses this theory it to clarify the many complexities surrounding the idea of a right to health care.

Veatch begins with a somewhat different interpretation of Rawls and egalitarian theory. He argues that those individuals who are worst off in a society (that is, are at the minimum level) should be guaranteed access to a certain level of health care. In this way, the society improves the conditions of the least fortunate by increasing the level of care available to them.

Utilitarian Theory. One need not be an egalitarian to believe in an equitable social system that redistributes resources to improve the health care needs of all citizens. Utilitarians believe that society has obligations to assist its members by preventing harms such as sickness. In the distribution of health care, utilitarians commonly view justice as involving tradeoffs and partial allocations that strike a balance. In devising a system of public funding for health care, we must balance public and private benefit, predicted cost savings, the probability of failure, the magnitude of risks, and the like. In his essay, Daniels considers whether utilitarians can provide a basis for recognizing rights to health care, and, if so, what the scope of utilitarian rights would be.

Although no author in this chapter explicitly defends a utilitarian system of distribution for health care, it is worth noting that many governments around the world adopt roughly a utilitarian approach to health policy. Their policies reflect the view that gov-

ernment has an obligation to maximize social resources in determining how best to relieve suffering and prevent premature death. This general utilitarian outlook can be and
has been implemented in more than one way. Some utilitarians endorse a system of universal access to health care; others argue for a two-tiered system of health care in which
persons are free to purchase more than can be provided by a public scheme of health insurance. Both approaches are utilitarian because the fundamental goal is to maximize social welfare.

Libertarian Theory. A perennial problem associated with the distribution of health
care is whether *justice requires* that societies adopt an explicit distribution plan for health
care. Robert Nozick has raised the following question about our shared conception of
justice:

Hearing the term "distribution," most people presume that some thing or mechanism uses some
principle or criterion to give out a supply of things. . . . So it is an open question, at least, whether
*re*distribution [of resources] should take place; whether we should do again what has already been
done once.[1]

In Chapter 1 we examine the libertarian theory of justice, for which Nozick is a spokesperson. Proponents of this theory reject the conclusion that egalitarian and utilitarian patterns
of distribution represent an appropriate normative ideal for distributing health care. People may be equal in many morally significant respects, they say, but *justice* does not demand the collection and redistribution of economic resources that are required to fund
government-distributed health care goods and services. For a libertarian, just distributions
flow from free market procedures of acquiring property and legitimately transferring that
property. A libertarian therefore prefers a system in which health care insurance is privately and voluntarily purchased by individual or group initiative. In this system no one
has had property coercively extracted by the state in order to benefit someone else.

A libertarian theory is defended in this chapter by H. Tristram Engelhardt, Jr., who relies on the principle of rights of free choice rather than a substantive principle of justice.
Engelhardt argues that a theory of justice should work to protect our right not to be coerced; it should not propound a doctrine intended to distribute resources with a particular outcome. Use of the tax code to effect social goals such as saving lives with advanced
medical technologies is a matter of social *choice,* not social justice. Some disadvantages
created by ill health, Engelhardt argues, are merely *unfortunate,* whereas injury and illness caused by another person are correctly viewed as *unfair.* From this perspective, one
will call a halt to the demands of justice where one draws the distinction between the unfair (and therefore obligatory in justice to correct) and the merely unfortunate.

THE RIGHT TO HEALTH CARE

These debates about justice and fair macroallocation have implications for the idea of a
right to health care. If this right exists, national allocations for health care would presumably be based (as Daniels notes) on demands of justice, not merely on charity, compassion, or benevolence. In this context a "right" is understood as an *entitlement* to some
measure of health care; rights are contrasted with privileges, ideals, and acts of charity.

In many nations there is a firmly established legal right to health care goods and services for all citizens. The legal situation in the United States, by contrast, involves entitlements for a few, but not for most. In 1965 Congress created Medicare to provide coverage for health care costs in populations that could not afford adequate coverage,

especially the elderly. Medicare conferred a right to health care on a particularly vulnerable population and thereby stimulated discussion of whether all citizens have, or at least should have, a right to health care under similar conditions of need.

There is, then, no *legal* basis to support entitlements to health care in the United States, but this fact does not mean there is no *moral* basis. As noted previously, Daniels's concern is with a moral right to health care and how it might be implemented in health policy; he is not concerned with whether the law provides an entitlement, only with whether it should provide such an entitlement. His Rawlsian account also does not give individuals a right to have all their health care needs met. Instead, he outlines how a health care system can be constructed to protect equality of opportunity through entitlements to certain kinds of health care services. Daniels argues that any social system that denies access to services that promote normal functioning does an injustice to those who cannot obtain the services.

It is often asked whether moral arguments like that proposed by Daniels can support what has been called a right to a "decent minimum" of health care. Proponents of a right of this description (Daniels being an apparent example) assert that each person should have equal access to an adequate (though not maximal) level or "tier" of health care for all available types of services. The distribution proceeds on the basis of need, and needs are met by fair access to adequate services. Better services, such as luxury hospital rooms and expensive but optional dental work, can then be made available for purchase at personal expense by those who are able to and wish to do so.

Allen Buchanan argues (in his article in the first section of this chapter) that we have no *right* to this decent minimum of care but that there is nonetheless a social *obligation* to provide this level of care to the needy. By contrast, Engelhardt concludes that there is no right and no social obligation, although a society may *freely choose* to enact such a policy. From his perspective and Buchanan's, if needs are unfortunate they may be ameliorated by benevolence or compassion, but only if they are unfair does the obligation of justice justify compensation to the disadvantaged by using state force to tax and redistribute resources.

Veatch defends a different conclusion. He defends a right even stronger than the right to a decent minimum. He proposes the distribution of health care based on the individual's health care needs using the yardstick of an "equal right to health care." The result is that "people have a right to needed health care to provide an opportunity for a level of health equal as far as possible to the health of other people." This application of the principle of justice to health care would result in a health care delivery system with only one class of services available rather than a two-tiered system.

Even if one does not support either moral rights to health care or political obligations to supply it, one can still support legal entitlements to health care on grounds of charity, beneficence, or a sense of moral excellence in a community. Appeals other than those to moral *rights* can therefore be used to defend public distributions that confer legal rights, as Buchanan argues in his essay.

MANAGED CARE AND ACCESS TO CARE

It is difficult to predict the outcome of the spirited debate in the United States about health care reform, but it is virtually certain that changes will occur in forms of access to care and in the system of managed care. Of special interest is how to arrange insurance and manage care so that all subscribers have access to it at an affordable price. Many ethical issues derive from unequal resources, unequal access to care, and incentives in the system to reduce costs.

Several obstacles stand in the way of a more efficient, fair, and comprehensive system of access to health care in the United States. Roughly 40 million U.S. citizens (including 8.5 million children, or approximately 14 percent of the total population), annually lack all health care insurance, largely because of the high cost of health insurance and a system in which access is generally obtained through an employer-based health plan. (Roughly 64 percent of the U.S. population is covered by a health plan related to employment.) Despite the fact that approximately 14 percent of the gross national product is spent annually for health care in the United States, the poor and the uninsured often cannot afford or find access to even minimally adequate care. Even counting the existing Medicaid program, approximately 30 percent of all poor people have no health insurance of any type.

Many U.S. citizens are uninsurable because they cannot pass physical examinations, present the kind of medical histories required for insurance, or are excluded because of their occupation. There is also a problem of underinsurance for over 20 million U.S. citizens. Costs require limiting coverage even in employer-based plans, and exclusionary clauses often deny access for types of treatment as well as for specific diseases, injuries, or organ systems. A few people are uninsured at times and underinsured at other times. They experience gaps in insurance coverage that cannot be bridged because they move quickly from job to job or suffer from temporary but lengthy layoffs. More than a million laborers lose their insurance for some period of time during the year while they are unemployed, and more than one-quarter of the entire U.S. population changes insurance, with a resulting coverage gap, during the course of each year.

The problem of rising costs and underinsurance afflicts many countries other than the United States. Most countries are now facing problems of serious undercoverage for their citizens. Each country is adjusting its system to meet the problems of health care costs and distribution, and each faces somewhat different issues. In the United States, concern has recently been focused primarily on managed care—the system that was introduced to provide health insurance together with delivery of care for specific populations of enrollees and in which clinical decision making is designed to control costs and boost efficiency and productivity. Managed competition among providers of care adds another dimension in which the system of health care is cost driven.

Managed care was originally devised to provide greater availability of care, but it was quickly noticed that there is potentially a deep conflict between the goal of reducing costs and the traditional ethics of medicine. Everyone lauds the prevention of unnecessary care, but a cost-driven system is by definition not a patient-centered system. A core worry is that managed care creates a situation of physicians with a divided loyalty: Loyalty to institutional goals of economic efficiency competes with loyalty to the patient. This divided loyalty may function to undermine trust in physicians if they cannot be relied on to act in the best interests of patients. If physicians cannot profess fidelity to the patient above other interests, a pivotal principle of traditional medical ethics has been lost.

Some systems of managed care heighten this concern through a structure of financial incentives that links remuneration or job security for physicians to efficiency and productivity, as determined by managed care institutions. This system has been criticized for prematurely discharging hospital patients, ordering cheaper but less effective drugs and devices, postponing expensive medical tests, not providing experimental treatments that constitute last-chance treatments for some patients, using less skilled physicians for some services, disallowing or discontinuing coverage for very sick patients, and the like.

Each author in the second section of this chapter deals with some of these questions about managed care. In the first article, Lawrence Gostin is concerned with a recent overemphasis on the economic effects of health care. He thinks that this concern is in part responsible for the turn to market theory and managed care. Gostin thinks that cost concerns have caused many to overlook even more fundamental values of maintaining the health of individuals and populations. His thesis is that the failure to provide universal coverage in the United States through reasonable levels of resource allocation itself has adverse effects on the economy, American business, and American health. He thinks that these adverse effects are as high or higher under the present system than they would be under a system in which the government assured universal coverage.

In the second selection in this section, Madison Powers focuses on this country's embrace of managed care in the absence of the kind of systematic and comprehensive health care reform endorsed by Gostin. Powers argues that what survives of the traditional free market system in the United States is managed care, but he thinks it shows no promise of either managed competition or universal access. He argues that this system works against the public interest, for two reasons. First, the system of incentives does not promote medical innovation, and this loss does not seem to be offset by a substantial increase of equity in the distribution of health care. Second, managed care plans are not structured to address needs for long-term accountability (e.g., responsibility for the lifetime health outcomes of the population served). In effect, Powers finds that the current system of diverse managed care plans does not face up to the most important moral and political questions of an efficient and just system of health care.

In the final essay in this section, Allen Buchanan considers three common moral criticisms of managed-care organizations, each of which he thinks misses the one truly significant problem of managed care. The three criticisms of managed-care organizations are: (1) that they "skim the cream" of the healthiest patient populations while denying access to other populations; (2) that, through rationing, they deprive patients of care to which they are entitled; and (3) that, through rationing, they interfere with physicians' fulfillment of the fiduciary obligation to provide the best care to each patient. Buchanan finds each criticism misconceived. The first criticism wrongly assumes that the system of health care insurance has ever been structured so that it creates obligations to cover less healthy groups of persons; and the second and third wrongly assume that the U.S. health care system provides clear standards of care so that we can objectively say that they are violated by the rules and procedures that have been adopted by managed-care organizations. Finally, the central criticism that Buchanan thinks ought to be directed at managed care is that it operates within a health care system in which no connection has been or can be made between rationing and the basic requirements of justice.

If Buchanan is right, rationing itself has become a central topic in the quest for a just health care system.

RATIONING

In the face of rising costs of health care and other welfare needs such as education and environmental protection, it has become apparent that governments and their citizens cannot afford all medically beneficial resources. It appears inevitable that limits must be placed how much is spent for health care. That is, rationing seems inevitable. But what does it mean to ration, and how can we do so in a manner that does not discriminate against the sick and the poor?

Unfortunately, the term *rationing* has acquired more than one meaning in discussions of the allocation of health care. This term often suggests financially stringent and medically extenuating circumstances in which some persons receive care and others are excluded from care. However, the original meaning of *rationing* did not suggest austerity, emergency, or exclusion. It meant a form of allowance, share, or portion, as when food is divided into rations in the military. Only recently has this term been tied to limited resources, the setting of priorities in the health care budget, and the inclusion of some to the exclusion of others.

Rationing has come to have at least three meanings, all centered on the notion of a *limiting of resources*. The first sense is "denial as a result of lack of resources." In a market economy, for example, many types of health care are to some extent rationed by ability to pay. A good or service is limited to those persons who can pay for it. A second sense is "limited as a result of a government determination of an allowance or allotment" (i.e., some individuals are denied access to some good or service beyond an allotment amount). This is limitation through social policy rather than through market ceilings. Rationing gasoline and certain types of food during a war is a well-known example, and health care could be structured to follow this same pattern. A third sense combines the first two: An allowance or allotment is determined and distributed equitably, and only those who can afford additional goods are not denied access beyond the allotted amount. In this third sense, public policy fixes an allowance, but those who can afford additional units are not denied access beyond the allowance.

The article by Peter A. Ubel and Susan Dorr Goold in this section deals in a nuanced way with how best to define this troublesome term. They note that this term generally carries a negative connotation in the United States, suggesting crisis decisions carrying potentially tragic consequences. Ubel and Goold explore the most significant definitions of *rationing* and provide a schematic way of understanding these definitions. Some definitions turn on whether mechanisms of rationing are both explicit and implicit, how the scarcity of resources is understood, and the nature of the services that are denied. Ubel and Goold themselves argue for a broad interpretation of rationing encompassing any explicit or implicit measure that causes or allows persons to go without beneficial health care services. They maintain that this broad sense has advantages over other definitions, the most important advantage being that it points directly to the frequency with which patients are allowed to go without beneficial health care services because of their cost.

If poor insurance coverage and inability to pay are ways of eliminating those who are uninsured from access to health care, then much of the U.S. health care system involves rationing by level of personal resources. However, many other forms of rationing are also already in place, including forms of government reimbursement to hospitals, various forms of cost containment, restriction of the elderly to certain forms of care, and methods for disseminating new medical technologies.

A closely watched attempt to implement a policy of rationing has taken place for more than a decade in the state of Oregon. Faced with skyrocketing costs and a restive population demanding more efficient and fairer access to quality health care, Oregon established a state committee in 1989 charged to rank hundreds of medical procedures for Medicaid, from most to least important, based in part on data about quality of well-being. State officials sought to extend coverage to a larger percentage of its citizens through its allocated Medicaid funds, and to do so both efficiently and fairly. The goal was to fund as many top priority–ranked services as possible.

The Oregon plan was implemented for its Medicaid population in 1994. By 2000 it had expanded health care coverage to well over 100,000 additional Oregonians, decreased the percentage of the uninsured, and reduced cost shifting. Although such outcomes make it appear that the Oregon system has been a major success, the plan does also explicitly deny health services to thousands of Oregonians. Moreover, ethical issues of fairness and comprehensiveness in coverage have long been raised about it. Problems of rationing stemming from the Oregon plan—but not limited to that plan—are treated in the selections by Daniels and Leonard M. Fleck. Daniels discusses troublesome questions about fairness that would have to be addressed in any system of rationing. He focuses on four general rationing problems that he thinks remain unresolved in bioethics and that also have plagued Oregon's rationing plan. In the course of a reply to Daniels, Fleck argues in the third selection that our national efforts at health reform ought to be informed by several lessons learned from Oregon. Specifically, he thinks that we can learn that rationing is inevitable and that it must be public and visible. The kind of hidden rationing that occurs in the present system therefore must be eliminated.

T.L.B.

NOTE

1. Robert Nozick, *Anarchy, State, and Utopia* (New York: Basic Books, 1974), pp. 149–50.

Just Health Care and the Right to Health Care

NORMAN DANIELS

Is There a Right to Health Care and, If So, What Does It Encompass?

Norman Daniels is Goldthwaite Professor of Philosophy at Tufts University and professor of medical ethics at Tufts Medical School. He has written widely in the philosophy of science, ethics, political and social philosophy, and medical ethics. Among his books are Seeking Fair Treatment: From the AIDS Epidemic to National Health Care Reform *(Oxford) and (with Donald Light and Ronald Caplan)* Benchmarks of Fairness for Health Care Reform *(Oxford). He is currently working on* Just Health, *a substantial revision and expansion of his earlier book* Just Health Care.

IS THERE A RIGHT TO HEALTH CARE?

LEGAL VS. MORAL RIGHTS TO HEALTH CARE

One way to answer this question is to adopt the stance of legal positivists, who claim that there are no rights except those that are embodied in actual institutions through law. We would then be able to reply that in nearly every advanced industrial democracy in the

world, there is a right to health care, since institutions exist in them that assure everyone access to needed services regardless of ability to pay. The notable exception is the United States, where many poor and near poor people have no insurance coverage for, and thus no assured access to, medically necessary services, although by law they cannot be denied emergency services.

The legal right to health care is embodied in a wide variety of types of health-care systems. These range from national health services, where the government is the provider of services, as in Great Britain, to pub-

From Norman Daniels, "Is there a right to healthcare and, if so, what does it encompass?" in *A Companion to Bioethics*, eds. Helga Kuhse and Peter Singer, Blackwell Publishers © 1998, pp. 316–25. Reprinted by permission.

lic insurance schemes, where the government finances services, as in Canada, to mixed public and private insurance schemes, as in Germany and the Netherlands. Despite these differences in the design of systems, there is a broad overlap in the scope or content of the legal right to health care in these countries. Most cover "medically necessary" services, including a broad range or preventive, curative, rehabilitative and long-term care for physical and mental diseases, disorders and disabilities. Most exclude uses of medical technologies that enhance otherwise normal functioning or appearance, such as purely cosmetic surgery. The legal rights vary in significant ways, however, for example, in the degree to which they cover new reproductive technologies, or in the types of mental health and long-term care services that are offered.

In the context of rising costs and the rapid dissemination of new technologies, there is growing debate in many countries about how to set limits on the scope of a right to health care. This debate about the scope of rights to health care pushes moral deliberation about such a right into the forefront, even where a legal right is recognized. Legal entitlements, most people believe, should reflect what society is morally obliged to provide by way of medical services. What, then, is the basis and scope of a moral right to health care?

POSITIVE VS. NEGATIVE RIGHTS

A right to health care is a *positive* as opposed to a *negative* right. Put quite simply, a positive right requires others to do something beneficial or enabling for right-bearers, whereas a negative right requires others to refrain from doing something, usually harmful or restrictive, to right-bearers. To say that others are required to do something or to refrain from doing something is to say they must so act or refrain even if they could produce more good or improve the world by not doing so (Thomson, 1990). For example, a negative right to free expression requires others to refrain from censuring the expression of the right-bearer even if censuring this speech would make a better world. Some public-health measures that protect people against interference with their health, such as environmental protections that protect people against polluters of air, water and food sources, might be construed as requirements of a negative right. More generally, however, a right to health care imposes an obligation on others to assist the right-bearers in obtaining needed and appropriate services. Specifically, claiming a right to health care includes these other

claims: society has the duty to its members to allocate an adequate share of its total resources to health-related needs; society has the duty to provide a just allocation of different types of health care services, taking into account the competing claims of different types of health-care needs; each person is entitled to a fair share of such services, where a "fair share" includes an answer to the question, who should pay for the services? (Daniels, 1985). Health-care rights thus form a part of a broader family of positive 'welfare' rights that includes rights to education and to income support. Because positive rights require other people to contribute their resources or skills to benefit right-bearers, rather than merely refraining from interfering with them, they have often been thought more difficult to justify than negative rights, and their scope and limits have been harder to characterize.

THEORIES OF JUSTICE AND RIGHTS TO HEALTH CARE

If we are to think of a right to health care as a requirement of justice, then we should look to more general theories of justice as a way to specify the scope and limits of that right. On some theories of justice, however, there is little basis for requiring people to assist others by meeting their health care or other needs. Libertarians, for example, believe that fundamental rights to property, including rights to personal assets, such as talents and skills, are violated if society coerces individuals into providing "needed" resources or skills (Nozick, 1974). Libertarians generally recognize an "imperfect" duty to act beneficently or charitably, but this duty involves discretion. It can be discharged in different ways that are matters of choice. People denied charity have no right to it and have no complaint against people who act charitably in other ways. Though some have argued that the difficulty of coordinating the delivery of charitable assistance might justify coercive measures (Buchanan, 1984), and others have tried to show that even libertarians must recognize some forms of welfare rights (Sterba, 1985), most libertarians resist any weakening of the property rights at the core of their view (Brennan and Friedman, 1981).

A spectre sometimes raised by libertarians against the idea of a right to health care is that such a right is a "bottomless pit." Since new technologies continuously expand the scope of "medical needs," a right to health care would give rise to unlimited claims on the resources of others (Fried, 1969; Engelhardt, 1986).

Protecting such an expansive right to health care would thus not be compatible with the function of a libertarian "minimal state" to assure the non-violation of rights to liberty and property.

Though there remains controversy about whether utilitarians can provide a basis for recognizing true moral rights, there are strong utilitarian arguments in favour of governments assuring access to at least some broad range of effective medical services. Preventing or curing disease or disability reduces suffering and enables people to function in ways that contribute to aggregate welfare. In addition, knowing that health-care services are available increases personal security and strengthens the ties of community. Utilitarians can also justify redistributing the burden of delivering these benefits to society as a whole, citing the decreasing marginal utility of money to support progressive financing of health-care services (Brandt, 1979).

Beneath these quite general arguments, however, there lies a more specific controversy about the scope of utilitarian entitlements to health care. There seems to be little utilitarian justification for investing resources in health care if those resources would produce more net welfare when invested in other things, yet many people believe they have moral obligations to assist others with their health-care needs even at a net cost in utility. For example, some highly expensive and effective medical treatments that most people believe should be offered to people might not be "cost beneficial" and thus not defensible on utilitarian grounds. Similarly, many forms of long-term care, especially for those who cannot be restored to productive social activity, are also difficult to defend on utilitarian grounds, yet we insist our health-care systems are obliged to provide such services.

Lack of moral acceptance of the distributive implications of utilitarianism makes many uncomfortable with the use of methods, such as cost-effectiveness analysis, that are intended to guide decisions about resource allocation in health care. For example, an assumption of cost-effectiveness analysis is that a unit of health benefit, such as a quality-adjusted life year (QALY), is of equal value or importance regardless of where it is distributed. But this assumption does not capture the concerns many people have about how much priority to give to the sickest patients, or when aggregating modest benefits to large numbers of people it outweighs the moral importance of delivering more significant benefits to fewer people (Nord, 1993; Daniels, 1993).

Two points about a utilitarian framework for a right to health care are worth noting. Recognizing a right to health care is compatible with recognizing limits on entitlements that result from resource scarcity and the fact that there are competing uses of those resources. Consequently, recognizing a right to health care need not open a bottomless pit. Second, just what entitlements to services follow from a right to health care cannot be specified outside the context of a *system* properly designed to deliver health care in a way that promotes aggregate utility. For the utilitarian, entitlements are *system-relative*. The same two points apply to other accounts of the foundations and limits of a right to health care.

Because many people reject the utilitarian rationales for health care (and other welfare) rights, theorists have explored other ways to ground such rights. Some claim that these rights are presupposed as enabling conditions for the exercise of other rights or liberties, or as practical presuppositions of all views of justice (Braybrooke, 1987) or as a way of avoiding vulnerability and exploitation (Goodin, 1988). One approach that has been developed in some detail views a right to health care as a special case of a right to equality of opportunity (Daniels, 1985). This approach shows how the most important contractarian theory of justice, Rawls' (1971) account of justice as fairness, can be extended to the problem of health care, since that theory gives prominence to a principle protecting equality of opportunity (Rawls, 1993). Without endorsing that account here, we shall use it to illustrate further the complexity surrounding the concept of a right to health care.

EQUAL OPPORTUNITY AND A RIGHT TO HEALTH CARE

The central observation underlying this account of a right to health care is that disease and disability restrict the range of opportunities that would otherwise be open to individuals. This is true whether they shorten our lives or impair our ability to function, including through pain and suffering. Health care in all its forms, whether public health or medical, preventive or acute or chronic, aims to keep people functioning as close to normally as possible. Since we are complex social creatures, our normal functional capabilities include our capabilities for emotional and cognitive functioning and not just physical capabilities.

Health care thus preserves for us the range of opportunities we would have, were we not ill or disabled, given our talents and skills.

The significant contribution health care makes to protecting the range of opportunities open to individuals is nevertheless *limited* in two important ways. It is limited because other things, such as the distribution of wealth and income and education, also profoundly affect equality of opportunity. It is also limited because health care, by restricting its aim to protecting normal functioning, leaves the normal distribution of talents and skills unmodified. It aims to help us function as "normal" competitors, not strictly equal ones.

Some argue that an equal opportunity account of health care should abandon the limit set by a focus on normal functioning (see Arneson, 1988; G. A. Cohen, 1989; Sen, 1992). They claim our concerns about equality, including equality of opportunity, require us to use health-care technologies whenever doing so would equalize opportunity for welfare or equalizes capabilities. For example, if through medical intervention we can "enhance" the otherwise normal capabilities of those who are at a competitive disadvantage, then our commitment to equality of opportunity requires us to do so. Obviously, this version of an equal opportunity account would vastly expand the moral requirements on medicine, yielding a right to health care much more expansive than any now embodied in actual systems and, arguably, one that would make administration of a health-care system unwieldy (Sabin and Daniels, 1994).

This expansive version of the appeal to equal opportunity ignores an important fact about justice: our concern for equality must be reconciled with considerations of liberty and efficiency in arriving at the overall requirements of justice (see Sen, 1992; Cohen, 1995; Daniels, 1996). Such a reconciliation seems to underlie the limits we commonly accept when we appeal to equality of opportunity. We generally believe that rights to equal opportunity are violated only if unfair social practices or preventable or curable diseases or disabilities interfere with the pursuit of reasonable plans of life within our society by making us lose competitive advantage. We accept, however, the fact that the natural distribution of talents and skills, working in an efficient market for them, will both enhance the social product and lead to inequalities in social outcomes. A just society will try to mitigate the effects of these inequalities in competitive advantage in others ways than by eliminating all eliminable differences in capabilities. For example, on Rawls' account, transfers that make the worst off as well off as they can be mitigate the effects on equality of allowing the natural distribution of talents and skills to enhance productivity. In what follows, the account of a right to health care rests on a more limited appeal to equal opportunity, one that takes the maintenance of normal functioning as a reasonable limit.

WHAT DOES A RIGHT TO HEALTH CARE INCLUDE?

SYSTEM-RELATIVE ENTITLEMENTS

By making the right to health care a special case of rights to equality of opportunity, we arrive at a reasonable, albeit incomplete and imperfect, way of restricting its scope while still recognizing its importance. The account does not give individuals a basic right to have all of their health-care needs met. At the same time, there are social obligations to design a health-care system that protects opportunity through an appropriate set of health-care services. If social obligations to provide appropriate health care are not met, then individuals are definitely wronged. For example, if people are denied access—because of discrimination or inability to pay—to a basic tier of services adequate to protect normal functioning, injustice is done to them. If the basic tier available to people omits important categories of services without consideration of their effects on normal functioning, for example, whole categories of mental health or long-term care or preventive services, their rights are violated.

Still, not every medical need gives rise to an entitlement to services. The scope and limits of rights to health care, that is, the entitlements they actually carry with them, will be relative to certain facts about a given system. For example, a health-care system can protect opportunity only within the limits imposed by resource scarcity and technological development within a society. We cannot make a direct inference from the fact that an individual has a right to health care to the conclusion that this person is entitled to some specific health-care service, even if the service would meet a health-care need. Rather the individual is entitled to a specific service only if, in the light of facts about a society's technological capabilities and resource limitations, it should be a part of a system that appropriately protects fair equality of opportunity. The equal opportunity account of a right to health care, like the utilitarian account, makes entitlements to health care system-relative.

EFFECTIVE TREATMENT OF DISEASE AND DISABILITY

The health care we have strongest claim to is care that effectively promotes normal functioning by reducing the impact of disease and disability, thus protecting the range of opportunities that would otherwise be open to us. Just what counts as "effective," however? And what should we do about hard cases on the boundary between treatment of disease or disability and enhancement of capabilities?

It is a common feature of public and private insurance systems to limit care to treatments that are not "experimental" and have some "proven effectiveness." Unfortunately, many services that count as standard treatment have little direct evidence about outcomes to support their use (Hadorn, 1992). They are often just customary treatment. Furthermore, it is often controversial just when new treatments or technologies should count as "safe and efficacious." What counts as "reasonably effective" is then a matter of judgement and depends on the kind of condition and the consequences of not correcting it. We might, for example, want to lower our standards for effectiveness when we face a treatment of last resort, or raise them if resource scarcity is very great. On the other hand, we do not owe people a chance to obtain miracles through whatever unproven procedures they prefer to try.

By focusing a right to health care on the maintenance of normal functioning, a line is drawn between uses of medical technologies that count as legitimate "treatments" and those that we may want but which do not meet our "health-care needs." Although we may want medical services that can enhance our appearance, like cosmetic (as opposed to reconstructive) plastic surgery, or that can optimize our otherwise normal functioning, like some forms of counselling or some uses of Prozac, we do not truly need these services to maintain normal functioning. We are obliged to help others achieve normal functioning, but we do not "owe" each other whatever it takes to make us more beautiful or strong or completely happy (Daniels, 1985).

Though this line is widely used in both public and private insurance practices, it leaves us with hard cases. Some of the hardest issues involve reproductive technologies. Abortion, where there is no preventive or therapeutic need, does not count as "treatment" because an unwanted pregnancy is not a disease or disability. Some nevertheless insist that requirements of justice, including a right to control one's body, means that non-therapeutic abortion should be included as an entitlement in a health-care system. Some national health-insurance schemes do not cover infertility services. Yet infertility is a departure from normal functioning, even if some people never want to bear children. Controversy may remain about how much social obligation we have to correct this form of impaired opportunity, especially where the costs of some interventions, such as *in vitro* fertilization, are high and their effectiveness is modest. Different societies will judge this question differently, in part because they may place different values on the rearing of biologically related children or on the experience of childbearing.

Hard cases involve non-reproductive technologies as well. In the United States, for example, many insurers will cover growth hormone treatment only for children deficient in growth hormone, not for those who are equally short but without any pathology. Yet the children denied therapy will suffer just as much as those who are eligible. Similar difficulties are involved in drawing a line between covered and non-covered uses of mental health services (Sabin and Daniels, 1994). As in the cases of reproductive technologies, there is room for different societies to "construct" the concept of mental disorder somewhat differently, with resulting variation in decisions about insurance coverage.

RIGHTS AND LIMITS ON EFFECTIVE TREATMENTS

Even when some health-care service is reasonably effective at meeting a medical need, not all such needs are equally important. When a disease or disability has little impact on the range of opportunities open to someone, it is not as morally important to treat as other conditions that more seriously impair opportunity. The effect on opportunity thus gives us some guidance in thinking about resource allocation priorities.

Unfortunately, the impact on our range of opportunities gives only a crude and incomplete measure of the importance or priority we should give to a need or service. In making decisions about priorities for purposes of resource allocation in health care, we face difficult questions about distributive fairness that are not answered by this measure of importance. For example, we must sometimes make a choice between investing in a technology that delivers a significant benefit to few people or one that delivers a more modest benefit to a larger number of people. Sometimes we must make a choice between investing in a service that helps the sickest, most impaired patients or one that helps those whose functioning is less impaired. Sometimes we must decide between the fairness of giving a scarce resource to those who derive the largest benefit or giving a broader range of people some chance at getting a benefit. In all of these cases, we lack clear principles for deciding how to make our choices, and the account of a right to health care we are discussing does not provide those principles either (Daniels, 1993). Some methodologies, like cost-effectiveness analysis, are intended to help us make appropriate resource allocation decisions in these kinds of cases. But these methodologies may themselves embody controversial moral assumptions about distributive fairness. This means they cannot serve as decision procedures for making these choices and can at best serve as aids to decision-makers who must be explicit about the moral reasoning that determines the distributive choices they make (Gold et al., 1996).

In any health-care system, then, some choices will have to be made by a fair, publicly accountable, decision-making process. Just what constitutes a fair decision-making procedure for resolving moral disputes about health care entitlements is itself a matter of controversy. It is a problem that has been addressed little in the literature. Our rights are not violated, however, if the choices that are made through fair decision-making procedures turn out to be ones that do not happen to meet our personal needs, but instead meet needs of others that are judged more important (Daniels and Sabin, 1997).

HOW EQUAL MUST OUR RIGHTS TO HEALTH CARE BE?

How equal must our rights to health care be? Specifically, must everyone receive exactly the same kinds of health-care services and coverage, or is fairness in health care compatible with a "tiered" system? Around the world, even countries that offer universal health insurance differ in their answers to this question. In Canada and Norway, for example, no supplementary insurance is permitted. Everyone is served solely by the national health-insurance schemes, though people who seek additional services or more rapid service may go elsewhere, as some Canadians do by crossing the border. In Britain, supplementary private insurance allows about 10 per cent of the population to gain quicker access to services for which there is ex-

tensive queuing in the public system. Basing a right to health care on an obligation to protect equality of opportunity is compatible with the sort of tiering the British have, but it does not require it, and it imposes some constraints on the kind of tiering allowed.

The primary social obligation is to assure everyone access to a tier of services that effectively promotes normal functioning and thus protects equality of opportunity. Since health care is not the only important good, resources to be invested in the basic tier are appropriately and reasonably limited, for example, by democratic decisions about how much to invest in education or job training as opposed to health care. Because of their very high "opportunity costs," there will be some beneficial medical services that it will be reasonable not to provide in the basic tier, or to provide only on a limited basis, for example, with queuing. To say that these services have "high opportunity costs" means that providing them consumes resources that would produce greater health benefits and protect opportunity more if used in other ways.

In a society that permits significant income and wealth inequalities, some people will want to buy coverage for these additional services. Why not let them? After all, we allow people to use their after-tax income and wealth as they see fit to pursue the "quality of life" and opportunities they prefer. The rich can buy special security systems for their homes. They can buy safer cars. They can buy private schooling for their children. Why not allow them to buy supplementary health care for their families?

One objection to allowing a supplementary tier is that its existence might undermine the basic tier either economically or politically. It might attract better-quality providers away from the basic tier, or raise costs in the basic tier, reducing the ability of society to meet its social obligations. The supplementary tier might undermine political support for the basic tier, for example, by undercutting the social solidarity needed if people are to remain committed to protecting opportunity for all. These objections are serious, and where a supplementary tier undermines the basic tier in either way, economically or politically, priority must be given to protecting the basic tier. In principle, however, it seems possible to design a system in which the supplementary tier does not undermine the basic one. If that can be done, then a system that permits tiering avoids restricting liberty in ways that some find seriously objectionable.

A second objection is not to tiering itself but to the structure of inequality that results. Compare two scenarios. In one, most people are adequately served by the basic tier and only the best-off groups in society have the means and see the need to purchase supplementary insurance. That is the case in Great Britain. In the other, the basic tier serves only the poorest groups in society and most other people buy supplementary insurance. The Oregon plan to expand Medicaid eligibility partly through rationing the services it covers has aspects of this structure of inequality, since most people are covered by plans that avoid these restrictions (Daniels, 1991). The first scenario seems preferable to the second on grounds of fairness. In the second, the poorest groups can complain that they are left behind by others in society even in the protection of their health. In the first, the majority has less grounds for reasonable resentment or regret.

If the basic tier is not undermined by higher tiers, and if the structure of the inequality that results is not objectionable, then it is difficult to see why some tiering should not be allowed. There is a basic conflict here between concerns about equality and concerns about liberty, between wanting to make sure everyone is treated properly with regard to health care and wanting to give people the liberty to use their resources (after tax) to improve their lives as they see fit. In practice, the crucial constraint on the liberty we allow people seems to depend on the magnitude of the benefit available in the supplementary tier and unavailable in the basic tier. Highly visible forms of saving lives and improving function would be difficult to exclude from the basic tier while we make them available in a supplementary tier. In principle, however, some forms of tiering will not be unfair even when they involve medical benefits not available to everyone.

REFERENCES

Arneson, Richard (1988). Equality and equal opportunity for welfare. *Philosophical Studies*, 54, 79–95.

Brandt, Richard (1979). *A Theory of the Good and the Right*. Oxford: Oxford University Press.

Braybrooke, David (1987). *Meeting Needs*. Princeton, NJ: Princeton University Press.

Brennan, Geoffrey and Friedman, David (1981). A libertarian perspective on welfare. In Peter G. Brown, Conrad Johnson and Paul Vernier (eds). *Income Support: Conceptual and policy issues*. Totowa, NJ: Rowman and Littlefield.

Buchanan, Allen (1984). The right to a decent minimum of health care. *Philosophy and Public Affairs*, 13, 55–78.

Cohen, G. A. (1989). On the currency of egalitarian justice. *Ethics*, 99, 906–44.

Cohen, Joshua (1995). Amartya Sen: *Inequality Reexamined*. *Journal of Philosophy*, 92/5, 275–88.

Daniels, N. (1985). *Just Health Care*. Cambridge: Cambridge University Press.

——— (1991). Is the Oregon rationing plan fair? *Journal of the American Medical Association*, 265, 2232–5.

——— (1993). Rationing fairly: programmatic considerations. *Bioethics*, 7, 224–33.

——— (1996). *Justice and Justification: reflective equilibrium in theory and practice*. Cambridge: Cambridge University Press.

Daniels, N. and Sabin, J. (1997). Limits to health care: fair procedures, democratic deliberation, and the legitimacy problem for insurers. *Philosophy and Public Affairs*, 26/4, 303–50.

Engelhardt, H. Tristram (1986). *The Foundations of Bioethics*. Oxford: Oxford University Press.

Fried, Charles (1969). *An Anatomy of Value*. Cambridge, MA: Harvard University Press.

Gold, Marthe, Siegel, Joanna, Russell, Louise, and Weinstein, Milton (eds) (1996). *Cost-Effectiveness in Health and Medicine: recommendations of the Panel on Cost-Effectiveness in Health and Medicine*. New York: Oxford University Press.

Goodin, Robert (1988). *Reasons for Welfare*. Princeton, NJ: Princeton University Press.

Hadorn, David (ed.) (1992). *Basic Benefits and Clinical Guidelines*. Boulder, CO: Westview Press.

Nord, Eric (1993). The relevance of health state after treatment in prioritizing between different patients. *Journal of Medical Ethics*, 19, 37–42.

Nozick, R. (1974). *Anarchy, State, and Utopia*. New York: Basic Books.

Rawls, J. (1971). *A Theory of Justice*. Cambridge, MA: Harvard University Press.

——— (1993). *Political Liberalism*. New York: Columbia University Press.

Sabin, James and Daniels, Norman (1994). Determining "medical necessity" in mental health practice. *Hastings Center Report*, 24/6, 5–13.

Sen, Amartya (1992). *Inequality Reexamined*. Cambridge, MA: Harvard University Press.

Sterba, James (1985). From liberty to welfare. *Social Theory and Practice*, 11, 285–305.

Thomson, Judith (1990). *The Realm of Rights*. Cambridge, MA: Harvard University Press.

ROBERT M. VEATCH

Justice, the Basic Social Contract, and Health Care

Robert M. Veatch is professor of medical ethics and the former director of the Kennedy Institute of Ethics at Georgetown University. His recent books include *The Basics of Bioethics, Case Studies in Pharmacy Ethics,* and the second editions of *Case Studies in Nursing Ethics, Cross Cultural Perspectives in Medical Ethics,* and *Transplant Ethics.* His current research focuses on the history of professional medical ethics and its relation to philosophical and religious ethics.

The principle that each person's welfare should count equally is crucial if the community generated is to be a moral community. The moral community is one of impartiality. If the community employed an impartial perspective to draw up the basic principles or practices for the society, the principles would be generated without reference to individual talents, skills, abilities, or good fortune. Another way of formulating this condition is to say that the basic principles or practices established must meet the test of reversibility. That is, they must be acceptable to one standing on either the giving or the receiving end of a transaction.[1] The general notion is that the contractors must take equal account of all persons. . . .

The most intriguing contractual theory of ethics that makes this commitment to impartiality or reversibility is that espoused by John Rawls.[2] In his version of social contract theory, Rawls asks us to envision ourselves in what he calls the original position. He does not pretend that such a position exists or ever could exist. Rather, it is a device for making "vivid to ourselves the restrictions that it seems reasonable to impose on arguments for principles of justice, and therefore on these principles themselves."[3] The restrictions on the original position are that no one should be advantaged or disadvantaged in the choice of principles either by natural fortune or social circumstances. Persons in the

original position are equal. To help us imagine such a situation, he asks us to impose what he calls a "veil of ignorance," under which "no one knows his place in society, his class position or social status, nor does any one know his fortune in the distribution of natural assets and abilities, his intelligence, strength, and the like."[4]

From that position one can derive impartially a set of principles or practices that provide the moral foundations for a society. Even if we cannot discover a universal basis for ethical decisions, perhaps we can create a community that accepts rules such as respect for freedom and the impartial consideration of interests; that is, one that adopts the moral point of view and thereby provides a common foundation for deciding what is ethical. Those who take this view believe it possible to generate some commonly agreed upon principles or practices for a society. The creation of a contractual framework could then provide a basis for making medical ethical decisions that would be commonly recognized as legitimate. . . .

There is . . . a moral community constituted symbolically by the metaphor of the contract or covenant. There is a convergence between the vision of people coming together to discover a preexisting moral order—an order that takes equally into account the welfare of all—and the vision of people coming together to invent a moral order that as well takes equally into account the welfare of all. The members of the moral community thus generated are bound together by bonds of mutual loyalty and trust. There is a fundamental equality and reciprocity in the relationship,

From *A Theory of Medical Ethics,* © 1981. Reprinted by permission of the Kennedy Institute of Ethics.

something missing in the philanthropic condescension of professional code ethics. . . .

THE MAXIMIN THEORY

Some say that reasonable people considering alternative policies or principles for a society would not opt to maximize the aggregate benefits that exist in the society. Rather, they say that at least for basic social practices that determine the welfare of members of the moral community, they would opt for a strategy that attempts to assure fundamentally that the least well off person would do as well as possible. . . .

The implication is that those having the greatest burden have some claim on the society independent of whether responding to their needs is the most efficient way of producing the greatest net aggregate benefit. Holders of this view say that the commitment of a principle of justice is to maximize not net aggregate benefit, but the position of the least advantaged members of the society. If the principle of justice is a right-making characteristic of actions, a principle that reasonable people would accept as part of the basic social contract independent of the principle of beneficence, it probably incorporated some moral notion that the distribution of benefits and burdens counts as well as the aggregate amount of them. One plausible alternative is to concentrate, insofar as we are concerned about justice, on the welfare of the least well off. This is part of those principles of justice defended by Rawls as derived from his version of social contract theory. . . .

Since Rawls's scheme is designed to provide insights into only the basic practices and social institutions, it is very hard to discern what the implications are for specific problems of resource distribution such as the allocation of health care resources. Some have argued that no direct implications can be read from the Rawlsian principles. That seems, however, to overstate the case. At the least, basic social practices and institutional arrangements must be subject to the test of the principles of justice.

It appears, then, that this view will not justify inequalities in the basic health care institutions and practices simply because they produce the greatest net aggregate benefit. Its notion of justice, concentrating on improving the lot of the least advantaged, is much more egalitarian in this sense than the utilitarian system. It would distribute health care resources to the least well off rather than just on the aggregate amount of benefit.

There is no obvious reason why our hypothetical contractors articulating the basic principles for a society would favor a principle that maximized aggregate utility any more than one that maximized minimum utility. Our contract model, as an epistemological device for discovering the basic principles, views them, after all, as committed to the moral point of view, as evaluating equally the welfare of each individual from a veil of ignorance, to use the Rawlsian language. This perspective retains the notion of individuals as identifiable, unique personalities, as noncommensurable human beings, rather than simply as components of an aggregate mass. Faced with a forced choice, it seems plausible that one would opt for maximizing the welfare of individuals, especially the least well-off individuals, rather than maximizing the aggregate.

Nevertheless, the interpretation of justice that attempts to maximize the minimum position in the society (and is hence sometimes called the "maximin" position), still permits inequalities and even labels them as just. What, for example, of basic health care institutional arrangements that systematically single out elites with unique natural talents for developing medical skill and services and gives these individuals high salaries as incentives to serve the interests of the least well off? What if a special health care system were institutionalized to make sure these people were always in the best of health, were cared for first in catastrophies, and were inconvenienced least by the normal bureaucratic nuisances of a health care system?

It is conceivable that such an institutional arrangement would be favored by reasonable people taking the moral point of view. They could justify the special gains that would come to the elites by the improved chances thus created for the rest of the population (who would not have as great a gain as the favored ones, but would at least be better off than if the elite were not so favored). The benefits, in lesser amounts, would trickle down in this plan to the consumers of health care so that all, or at least the least advantaged, would gain. The gap between the elite of the health profession and the masses could potentially increase by such a social arrangement, but at least all would be better off in absolute terms.

So it is conceivable that reasonable people considering equally both the health professionals and the masses would favor such an arrangement, but it is not obvious. Critics of the Rawlsian principles of justice say that in some cases alternative principles of distribution would be preferred. Brian Barry, for example, argues that rational choosers would look not just at the welfare of the least advantaged, but also at the average or aggregate welfare of alternative policies.[5] On the other hand, Barry and many others suggest that in some circumstances, rational choosers might opt for the principle that would maximize equality of outcome.[6] At most, considering the institutionalization of advantages for a health care elite, they would be supported as a prudent sacrifice of the demands of justice in order to serve some other justifiable moral end.

From this perspective, favoring elites with special monetary and social incentives in order to benefit the poor might be a prudent compromise.[7] It might mediate between the demands that see justice as requiring equality of outcome (subject to numerous qualifications) and the demands of the principle of beneficence requiring maximum efficiency in producing good consequences. If that is the case, though, then there is still a fourth interpretation of the principle of justice that must be considered, one that is more radically egalitarian than the maximin strategy.

THE EGALITARIAN THEORY

Those who see the maximin strategy as a compromise between the concern for justice and the concern for efficient production of good consequences must feel that justice requires a stricter focus on equality than the maximin understanding of the principle of justice. The maximin principle is concerned about the distribution of benefits. It justifies inequalities only if they benefit the least well off. But it does justify inequalities—and it does so in the name of justice.

Rawls recognizes that there is an important difference between a right action and a just or a fair action. Fairness is a principle applying to individuals along with beneficence, noninjury, mutual respect, and fidelity. The list is not far removed from the basic principles I have identified. But, given this important difference between what is right in this full, inclusive sense and what is fair, if one is convinced that incentives and advantages for medical elites are justified, why would one claim that the justification is one based on the principle of fairness? One might instead maintain that they are right on balance because they are a necessary compromise with the principle of fairness (or justice) in order to promote efficiently the welfare of a disadvantaged group. It is to be assumed, given the range of basic principles in an ethical system, that conflicts will often emerge so that one principle will be sacrificed, upon occasion, for the sake of another.

The egalitarian understanding of the principle of justice is one that sees justice as requiring (subject to certain important qualifications) equality of net welfare for individuals.[8] . . .

Everyone, according to the principle of egalitarian justice, ought to end up over a lifetime with an equal amount of net welfare (or, as we shall see shortly, a chance for that welfare). Some may have a great deal of benefit offset by large amounts of unhappiness or disutility, while others will have relatively less of both. What we would call "just" under this principle is a basic social practice or policy that contributes to the same extent to greater equality of outcome (subject to restrictions to be discussed). I am suggesting that reasonable people who are committed to a contract model for discovering, inventing, or otherwise articulating the basic principles will want to add to their list the notion that one of the right-making characteristics of a society would be the equality of welfare among the members of the moral community.

THE EQUALITY OF PERSONS

The choice of this interpretation of the principle of justice will depend upon how the contractors understand the commitment to the moral point of view—the commitment to impartiality that takes the point of view of all equally into account. We certainly are not asserting the equality of ability or even the equality of the merit of individual claims. . . .

If this is what is meant by the moral point of view, taking into account equally the individuality of each member of the community, then in addition to the right-making characteristics or principles of beneficence, promise keeping, autonomy, truth telling, and avoiding killing, the principle of justice as equality of net welfare must be added to the list. The principle might be articulated as affirming that people have a claim on having the total net welfare in their lives equal insofar as possible to the welfare in the lives of others.

Of course, no reasonable person, even an egalitarian, is going to insist upon or even desire that all the features of people's lives be identical.[9] It seems obvious that the most that anyone would want is that the total net welfare for each person be comparable. . . .

If this egalitarian understanding of the principle of justice would be acceptable to reasonable people taking the moral point of view, it provides a solution to the dilemma of the tension between focusing exclusively on the patient and opening the doors to considerations of social consequences such as in classical utilitarianism. The principle of justice provides another basis for taking into account a limited set of impacts on certain other parties. If the distribution of benefits as well as the aggregate amount is morally relevant, then certain impacts on other parties may be morally more relevant than others. A benefit that accrues to a person who is or predictably will be in a least well-off group would count as a consideration of justice while a benefit of equal size that accrued to other persons not in the least well-off group would not. The hypothetical benefits of a Nazi-type experiment would not accrue to a least well-off group (while the harms of the experiment presumably would). They are thus morally different from, in fact diametrically opposed to, a redistribution scheme that produced benefits for only the least advantaged group.

EQUALITY AND ENVY

Critics of the egalitarian view of justice have argued that the only way to account for such a position is by attributing it to a psychology of envy.[10] Freud accounted for a sense of justice in this way.[11] They feel the only conceivable reason to strive for equality is the psychological explanation that the less well off envy the better off, and they hold that contractors take that psychological fact into account. Since they believe that envy is not an adequate justification for a commitment to equal outcome, they opt instead for an alternative theory of justice. . . .

The egalitarian holds that there is something fundamentally wrong with gross inequalities, with gross differences in net welfare. The problem is encountered when people of unequal means must interact, say, when representatives of an impoverished community apply to an elite foundation for funds to support a neighborhood health program. There is no way that real communication can take place between the elites of the foundation and the members of the low-income community. It is not simply that the poor envy the foundation executives or that the executives feel resentful of the poor. Rather, as anyone who has been in such a relationship knows, the sense of community is fractured. Not only do the less well off feel that they cannot express themselves with self-respect, but the elites realize that there is no way the messages they receive can be disentangled from the status and welfare differentials. Neither can engage in any true interaction. A moral relationship is virtually impossible. . . .

It turns out that incorporating health care into this system of total welfare will be extremely difficult. Let us begin, temporarily, therefore, by considering a simpler system dealing only with food, clothing, and shelter. Fairness could mean, according to the egalitarian formula, that each person had to have an equal amount of each of these. No reasonable person, however, would find that necessary or attractive. Rather, what the egalitarian has in mind with his concept of justice is that the net of welfare, summed across all three of these goods, be as similar as possible. We could arbitrarily fix the amount of resources in each category, but nothing seems wrong with permitting people to trade some food for clothing, or clothing for shelter. If one person preferred a large house and minimal food and could find someone with the opposite tastes, nothing seems wrong with permitting a trade. The assumption is that the need of people for food, clothing, and shelter is about the same in everybody and that marginal utilities in the trades will be about the same. If so, then permitting people to trade around would increase the welfare of each person without radically distorting the equality of net overall welfare. Up to this point, then, the egalitarian principle of justice says that it is just (though not necessarily right) to strive in social practices for equality of net welfare. . . .

For health care and education, however, the situation is much different. Here it is reasonable to assume that human needs vary enormously. Nothing could be more foolish than to distribute health care or even the money for health care equally. The result would be unequal overall well-being for those who were unfortunate in the natural lottery for health, objectively much worse off than others. If the goal of justice is to produce a chance for equal, objective net welfare, then the starting point for consideration of health care distribution should be the need for it. Education (or the resources to buy education) initially would be distributed in the same way. The amount added to the resources for food, clothing, and shelter should then be in proportion to an "unhealthiness status index" plus another amount proportional to an "educational needs index."

However, that proposal raises two additional questions: Should people be permitted to use the resources set aside for health care in some other way? And who should bear the responsibility if people have an opportunity to be healthy and do not take advantage of it?

Even for the egalitarian it is not obvious why society ought to strive for an equal right to health care. Certainly it ought not to be interested in obtaining the same amount of health care for everyone. To do so would require forcing those in need of great amounts of care to go without or those who have the good fortune to be healthy to consume uselessly. But it is not even obvious that we should end up with a right to health care equal in proportion to need, though that is the conclusion that many, especially egalitarians, are reaching. . . .

Is there any reason to believe that health care is any more basic than, say, food or protection from the elements? All are absolutely essential to human survival, at least up to some minimum for subsistence. All are necessary conditions for the exercise of liberty, self-respect, or any other functioning as part of the human moral community. Furthermore, while the bare minimum of health care is as necessary as food and shelter, in all cases these may not really be "necessities" at the margin. If trades are to be tolerated between marginal food and clothing, is there any reason why someone placing relatively low value on health care should not be permitted to trade, say, his annual checkups for someone else's monthly allotment of steak dinners? Or, if we shall make trading easier by distributing money fairly rather than distributing rations of these specific goods, is there any reason why, based on an "unhealthiness index," we could not distribute a fair portion of funds for health care as well as for other necessities? Individuals could then buy the health care (or health care insurance) that they need, employing individual discretion about where their limit for health care is in comparison with steak dinners. Those at a high health risk would be charged high amounts for health care (or high premiums for insurance), but those costs would be exactly offset by the money supplement based on the index.

Perhaps we cannot make a case for equal access to health care on the basis that it is more fundamental than other goods. There may still be reasons, though, why reasonable people would structure the basic institutions of society to provide a right to equal health care in the sense I am using the term, that is a right equal in proportion to need.

Our response will depend somewhat upon whether we are planning a health care distribution for a just world or one with the present inequities in the distribution of net welfare. . . .

But obviously we do not live in a perfectly just world. The problem becomes more complex. How do we arrange the health care system, which all would agree is fundamental to human well-being at least at some basic level, in order to get as close as possible to equality of welfare as the outcome? Pragmatic considerations may, at this point, override the abstract, theoretical argument allowing trades of health care for other goods even at the margin.

Often defenders of free-market and partial free-market solutions to the allocation of health care resources assume that if fixed in-kind services such as health care are not distributed, money will be. . . .

There is a more subtle case for an equal right to health care (in proportion to need) in an unfair world. Bargaining strengths are likely to be very unequal in a world where resources are distributed unfairly. Those with great resources, perhaps because of natural talents or naturally occurring good health or both, are in an invincible position. The needy, for example those with little earning power because of congenital health problems, may be forced to use what resources they have in order to buy immediate necessities, withholding on health care investment; particularly preventive health care and health insurance, while gambling that they will be able to survive without those services.

It is not clear what our moral response should be to those forced into this position of bargainers from weakness. If the just principle of distribution were Pareto optimality (where bargains were acceptable, regardless of the weaknesses of the parties, provided all gained in the transaction), we would accept the fact that some would bargain from weakness and be forced to trade their long-term health care needs for short-term necessities. If the principle of justice that reasonable people would accept taking the moral point of view, however, is something like the maximin position or the egalitarian position, then perhaps such trades of health care should be prohibited. The answer will depend on how one should behave in planning social policies in an unjust world. The fact that resources are not distributed fairly generates pressures on the least well off (assuming they act rationally) to make choices they would not have to make in a more fair world. If unfairness in the general distribution of resources is a given, we are forced into a choice between two unattractive options: We could opt for the rule that will permit the least well off to maximize their position under the existing conditions or we could pick the rule that would arrange resources as closely as possible to the way they would be arranged in a just world. In our present, unjust society distributing health care equally is a closer approximation to the way it would be distributed in a just society than giving a general resource like money or permitting trades. . . .

I see justice not just as a way to efficiently improve the lot of the least well off by permitting them trades (even though those trades end up increasing the gap between the haves and the have-nots). That might be efficient and might preserve autonomy, but it would not be justice. If I were an original contractor I would cast my vote in favor of the egalitarian principle of justice, applying it so that there would be a right to health care equal in proportion to health care need. The principle of justice for health care could, then, be stated as follows: People have a right to needed health care to provide an opportunity for a level of health equal as far as possible to the health of other people.

The principle of justice for health care is a pragmatic derivative from the general principle of justice requiring equality of objective net welfare. The result would be a uniform health care system with one class of service available for all. Practical problems would still exist, especially at the margins. The principle, for example, does not establish what percentage of total resources would go for health care. The goal would be to arrange resources so that health care needs would, in general, be met about as well as other needs. This means that a society would rather arbitrarily set some fixed amount of the total resources for health care. Every nation currently spends somewhere between five and ten percent of its gross national product (GNP) in this area, with the wealthier societies opting for the higher percentages. Presumably the arbitrary choice would fall in that range.

With such a budget fixed, reasonable people will come together to decide what health care services can be covered under it. The task will not be as great as it seems. The vast majority of services will easily be sorted into or out of the health care system. Only a small percentage at the margin will be the cause of any real debate. The choice will at times be arbitrary, but the standard applied will at least be clear. People should have services necessary to give them a chance to be as close as possible to being as healthy as other people. Those choices will be made while striving to emulate the position of original contractors taking the moral point of view. The decision-making panels will not differ in task greatly from the decision makers who currently sort health care services in and out of insurance coverage lists. However, panels will be committed to a principle of justice and will take the moral point of view, whereas the self-interested insurers try to maximize profits or efficiency or a bargaining position against weak, unorganized consumers.

NOTES

1. Kurt Baier, *The Moral Point of View: A Rational Basis of Ethics* (New York: Random House, 1965), p. 108.

2. John Rawls, *A Theory of Justice* (Cambridge, Mass.: Harvard University Press, 1971).

3. Ibid., p. 18.

4. Ibid., p. 12; cf. pp. 136–42.

5. Brian Barry, *The Liberal Theory of Justice: A Critical Examination of the Principal Doctrines in "A Theory of Justice" by John Rawls* (Oxford: Clarendon Press, 1973), p. 109; see also Robert L. Cunningham, "Justice: Efficiency or Fairness?" *Personalist* 52 (Spring 1971): 253–81.

6. Barry, *The Liberal Theory;* idem. "Reflections on 'Justice as Fairness,'" in Justice and Equality, ed. H. Bedau (Englewood Cliffs, N.J.: Prentice-Hall, 1971), pp. 103–115; Bernard Williams, "The Idea of Equality," reprinted in Bedau, *Justice and Equality*, pp. 116–137; Christopher Ake, "Justice as Equality," *Philosophy and Public Affairs* 5 (Fall 1975): 69–89; Robert M. Veatch, "What Is 'Just' Health Care Delivery?" in *Ethics and Health Policy*, ed. R. M. Veatch and R. Branson (Cambridge, Mass.: Ballinger, 1976), pp. 127–153.

7. Barry, "Reflections," p. 113.

8. See Ake, "Justice as Equality," for a careful development of the notion.

9. Hugo A. Bedau, "Radical Egalitarianism," in *Justice and Equality*, ed. H. A. Bedau, p. 168.

10. Rawls, *A Theory of Justice*, p. 538, note 9.

11. Sigmund Freud, *Group Psychology and the Analysis of the Ego*, rev. ed., trans. James Strachey (London: Hogarth Press, 1959), pp. 51f. (as cited in Rawls, *A Theory of Justice*, p. 439).

ALLEN E. BUCHANAN

The Right to a Decent Minimum of Health Care

Allen Buchanan is professor of philosophy at Duke University. He publishes
mainly in bioethics and political philosophy and currently serves as a member of
the Advisory Council for the Human Genome Research Institute on goals and
funding priorities for genomic research. Among his books are *Ethics, Efficiency, and
the Market* (1985) and (with Dan Brock) *Deciding for Others: The Ethics of Surrogate
Decision Making* (1989).

THE ASSUMPTION THAT THERE IS A RIGHT
TO A DECENT MINIMUM

A consensus that there is (at least) a right to a decent
minimum of health care pervades recent policy debates and much of the philosophical literature on
health care. Disagreement centers on two issues. Is
there a more extensive right than the right to a decent
minimum of health care? What is included in the decent minimum to which there is a right?

PRELIMINARY CLARIFICATION
OF THE CONCEPT

Different theories of distributive justice may yield different answers both to the question "Is there a right to
a decent minimum?" and to the question "What com-
prises the decent minimum?" The justification a particular theory provides for the claim that there is a
right to a decent minimum must at least cohere with
the justifications it provides for other right-claims.
Moreover, the character of this justification will determine, at least in part, the way in which the decent
minimum is specified, since it will include an account
of the nature and significance of health-care needs. To
the extent that the concept of a decent minimum is
theory-dependent, then, it would be naive to assume
that a mere analysis of the concept of a decent minimum would tell us whether there is such a right and
what its content is. Nonetheless, before we proceed to
an examination of various theoretical attempts to

ground and specify a right to a decent minimum, a
preliminary analysis will be helpful.

Sometimes the notion of a decent minimum is applied not to health care but to health itself, the claim
being that everyone is entitled to some minimal level,
or welfare floor, of health. I shall not explore this variant of the decent minimum idea because I think its
implausibility is obvious. The main difficulty is that
assuring any significant level of health for all is simply not within the domain of social control. If the alleged right is understood instead as the right to everything which can be done to achieve some significant
level of health for all, then the claim that there is such
a right becomes implausible simply because it ignores
the fact that in circumstances of scarcity the total social expenditure on health must be constrained by the
need to allocate resources for other goods.

Though the concept of a right is complex and controversial, for our purposes a partial sketch will do. To
say that person A has a right to something, X, is first
of all to say that A is entitled to X, that X is due to
him or her. This is not equivalent to saying that if A
were granted X it would be a good thing, even a morally
good thing, or that X is desired by or desirable for A.
Second, it is usually held that valid right-claims, at
least in the case of basic rights, may be backed by
sanctions, including coercion if necessary (unless doing so would produce extremely great disutility or
grave moral evil), and that (except in such highly exceptional circumstances) failure of an appropriate authority to apply the needed sanctions is itself an injustice. Recent rights-theorists have also emphasized a

From President's Commission, *Securing Access to Health Care*,
vol. 2. Washington, DC: U.S. Government Printing Office, 1983.

third feature of rights, or at least of basic rights or rights in the strict sense: valid right-claims "trump" appeals to what would maximize utility, whether it be the utility of the right-holder, or social utility. In other words, if A has a right to X, then the mere fact that infringing A's right would maximize overall utility or even A's utility is not itself a sufficient reason for infringing it.[1] Finally, a universal (or general) right is one which applies to all persons, not just to certain individuals or classes because of their involvement in special actions, relationships, or agreements.

The second feature—enforceability—is of crucial importance for those who assume or argue that there is a universal right to a decent minimum of health care. For, once it is granted that there is such a right and that such a right may be enforced (absent any extremely weighty reason against enforcement), the claim that there is a universal right provides the moral basis for using the coercive power of the state to assure a decent minimum for all. Indeed, the surprising absence of attempts to justify a coercively backed decent minimum policy by arguments that do *not* aim at establishing a universal right suggests the following hypothesis: advocates of a coercively backed decent minimum have operated on the assumption that such a policy must be based on a universal right to a decent minimum. The chief aim of this article is to show that this assumption is false.

I think it is fair to say that many who confidently assume there is a (universal) right to a decent minimum of health care have failed to appreciate the significance of the first feature of our sketch of the concept of a right. It is crucial to observe that the claim that there is a right to a decent minimum is much stronger than the claim that everyone *ought* to have access to such a minimum, or that if they did it would be a good thing, or that any society which is capable, without great sacrifice, of providing a decent minimum but fails to do so is deeply morally defective. None of the latter assertions implies the existence of a right, if this is understood as a moral entitlement which ought to be established by the coercive power of the state if necessary. . . .

THE ATTRACTIONS OF THE IDEA OF A DECENT MINIMUM

There are at least three features widely associated with the idea of a right to a decent minimum which, together with the facile consensus that vagueness pro-motes, help explain its popularity over competing conceptions of the right to health care. First, it is usually, and quite reasonably, assumed that the idea of a decent minimum is to be understood in a society-relative sense. Surely it is plausible to assume that, as with other rights to goods or services, the content of the right must depend upon the resources available in a given society and perhaps also upon a certain consensus of expectations among its members. So the first advantage of the idea of a decent minimum, as it is usually understood, is that it allows us to adjust the level of services to be provided as a matter of right to relevant social conditions and also allows for the possibility that as a society becomes more affluent the floor provided by the decent minimum should be raised.

Second, the idea of a decent minimum avoids the excesses of what has been called the strong equal access principle, while still acknowledging a substantive universal right. According to the strong equal access principle, everyone has an equal right to the best health-care services available. Aside from the weakness of the justifications offered in support of it, the most implausible feature of the strong equal access principle is that it forces us to choose between two unpalatable alternatives. We can either set the publicly guaranteed level of health care lower than the level that is technically possible or we can set it as high as is technically possible. In the former case, we shall be committed to the uncomfortable conclusion that no matter how many resources have been expended to guarantee equal access to that level, individuals are forbidden to spend any of their resources for services not available to all. Granted that individuals are allowed to spend their after-tax incomes on more frivolous items, why shouldn't they be allowed to spend it on health? If the answer is that they should be so allowed, as long as this does not interfere with the provision of an adequate package of health-care services for everyone, then we have retreated from the strong equal access principle to something very like the principle of a decent minimum. If, on the other hand, we set the level of services guaranteed for all so high as to eliminate the problem of persons seeking extra care beyond this level, this would produce a huge drain on total resources, foreclosing opportunities for producing important goods other than health care.

So both the recognition that health care must compete with other goods and the conviction that beyond some less than maximal level of publicly guaranteed services individuals should be free to purchase additional services point toward a more limited right than the strong access principle asserts. Thus, the endorsement of a right to a decent minimum may be more of a recognition of the implausibility of the stronger right to equal access than a sign of any definite position on the content of the right to health care.

A third attraction of the idea of a decent minimum is that since the right to health care must be limited in scope (to avoid the consequences of a strong equal access right), it should be limited to the "most basic" services, those normally "adequate" for health, or for a "decent" or "tolerable" life. However, although this aspect of the idea of a decent minimum is useful because it calls attention to the fact that health-care needs are heterogeneous and must be assigned some order of priority, it does not itself provide any basis for determining which are most important.

THE NEED FOR A SUPPORTING THEORY

In spite of these attractions, the concept of a right to a decent minimum of health care is inadequate as a moral basis for a coercively backed decent minimum policy in the absence of a coherent and defensible theory of justice. Indeed, when taken together they do not even imply that there is a right to a decent minimum. Rather, they only support the weaker conditional claim that if there is a right to health care, then it is one that is more limited than a right of strong equal access, and is one whose content depends upon available resources and some scheme of priorities which shows certain health services to be more basic than others. It appears, then, that a theoretical grounding for the right to a decent minimum of health care is indispensable. . . .

My suggestion is that the combined weight of arguments from special (as opposed to universal) rights to health care, harm-prevention, prudential arguments of the sort used to justify public health measures, and two arguments that show that effective charity shares features of public goods (in the technical sense) is sufficient to do the work of an alleged universal right to a decent minimum of health care.

ARGUMENTS FROM SPECIAL RIGHTS

The right-claim we have been examining (and find unsupported) has been a *universal* right-claim: one that attributes the same right to all persons. *Special* right-claims, in contrast, restrict the right in question to certain individuals or groups.

There are at least three types of arguments that can

be given for special rights to health care. First, there are arguments from the requirements of rectifying past or present institutional injustices. It can be argued, for example, that American blacks and native Americans are entitled to a certain core set of health-care services owing to their history of unjust treatment by government or other social institutions, on the grounds that these injustices have directly or indirectly had detrimental effects on the health of the groups in question. Second, there are arguments from the requirements of compensation to those who have suffered unjust harm or who have been unjustly exposed to health risks by the assignable actions of private individuals or corporations—for instance, those who have suffered neurological damage from the effects of chemical pollutants.

Third, a strong moral case can be made for special rights to health care for those who have undergone exceptional sacrifices for the good of society as a whole—in particular those whose health has been adversely affected through military service. The most obvious candidates for such compensatory special rights are soldiers wounded in combat.

ARGUMENTS FROM THE PREVENTION OF HARM

The content of the right to a decent minimum is typically understood as being more extensive than those traditional public health services that are usually justified on the grounds that they are required to protect the citizenry from certain harms arising from the interactions of persons living together in large numbers. Yet such services have been a major factor—if not *the* major factor—in reducing morbidity and mortality rates. Examples include sanitation and immunization. The moral justification of such measures, which constitute an important element in a decent minimum of health care, rests upon the widely accepted Harm (Prevention) Principle, not upon a right to health care.

The Harm Prevention argument for traditional public health services, however, may be elaborated in a way that brings them closer to arguments for a universal right to health care. With some plausibility one might contend that once the case has been made for expending public resources on public health measures, there is a moral (and perhaps Constitutional) obligation to achieve some standard of *equal protection* from the harms these measures are designed to prevent. Such an argument, if it could be made out, would imply that the availability of basic public health services should not vary greatly across different racial, ethnic, or geographic groups within the country.

PRUDENTIAL ARGUMENTS

Prudent arguments for health-care services typically emphasize benefits rather than the prevention of harm. It has often been argued, in particular, that the availability of certain basic forms of health care make for a more productive labor force or improve the fitness of the citizenry for national defense. This type of argument, too, does not assume that individuals have moral rights (whether special or universal) to the services in question.

It seems very likely that the combined scope of the various special health-care rights discussed above, when taken together with harm prevention and prudential arguments for basic health services and an argument from equal protection through public health measures, would do a great deal toward satisfying the health-care needs which those who advocate a universal right to a decent minimum are most concerned about. In other words, once the strength of a more pluralistic approach is appreciated, we may come to question the popular dogma that policy initiatives designed to achieve a decent minimum of health care for all must be grounded in a universal moral right to a decent minimum. This suggestion is worth considering because it again brings home the importance of the methodological difficulty encountered earlier. Even if, for instance, there is wide consensus on the considered judgment that the lower health prospects of inner city blacks are not only morally unacceptable but an injustice, it does not follow that this injustice consists of the infringement of a universal right to a decent minimum of health care. Instead, the injustice might lie in the failure to rectify past injustices or in the failure to achieve public health arrangements that meet a reasonable standard of equal protection for all.

TWO ARGUMENTS FOR ENFORCED BENEFICENCE

The pluralistic moral case for a legal entitlement to a decent minimum of health care (in the absence of a universal moral right) may be strengthened further by nonrights-based arguments from the principle of beneficence.[2] The possibility of making out such arguments depends upon the assumption that some principles may be justifiably enforced even if they are not principles specifying valid right-claims. There is at least one widely recognized class of such principles requiring contribution to the production of "public goods" in the technical sense (for example, tax laws requiring contribution to national defense). It is characteristic of public goods that each individual has an incentive to withhold his contribution to the collective goal even though the net result is that the goal will not be achieved. Enforcement of a principle requiring all individuals to contribute to the goal is necessary to overcome the individual's incentive to withhold contribution by imposing penalties for his own failure to contribute and by assuring him that others will contribute. There is a special subclass of principles whose enforcement is justified not only by the need to overcome the individual's incentive to withhold compliance with the principle but also to ensure that individuals' efforts are appropriately *coordinated*. For example, enforcing the rule of the road to drive only on the right not only ensures a joint effort toward the goal of safe driving but also coordinates individuals' efforts so as to make the attainment of that goal possible. Indeed, in the case of the 'rule of the road' a certain kind of coordinated joint effort is the public good whose attainment justifies enforcement. But regardless of whether the production of a public good requires the solution of a coordination problem or not, there may be no *right* that is the correlative of the coercively backed obligation specified by the principle. There are two arguments for enforced beneficence, and they each depend upon both the idea of coordination and on certain aspects of the concept of a public good.

Both arguments begin with an assumption reasonable libertarians accept: there is a basic moral obligation of charity or beneficence to those in need. In a society that has the resources and technical knowledge to improve health or at least to ameliorate important health defects, the application of this requirement of beneficence includes the provision of resources for at least certain forms of health care. If we are sincere, we will be concerned with the efficacy of our charitable or beneficent impulses. It is all well and good for the libertarian to say that voluntary giving *can* replace the existing array of government entitlement programs, but this *possibility* will be cold comfort to the needy if, for any of several reasons, voluntary giving falters.

Social critics on the left often argue that in a highly competitive acquisitive society such as ours it is naive to think that the sense of beneficence will win out over the urgent promptings of self-interest. One need not argue, however, that voluntary giving fails from weakness of the will. Instead one can argue that even if each individual recognizes a moral duty to contribute to the aid of others and is motivationally capable of acting on that duty, some important forms of beneficence will not be forthcoming because each individual will rationally conclude that he should not contribute.

Many important forms of health care, especially those involving large-scale capital investment for technology, cannot be provided except through the contributions of large numbers of persons. This is also true of the most important forms of medical research. But if so, then the beneficent individual will not be able to act effectively, in isolation. What is needed is a coordinated joint effort.

First argument. There are many ways in which I might help others in need. Granted the importance of health, providing a decent minimum of health care for all, through large-scale collective efforts, will be a more important form of beneficence than the various charitable acts A, B, and C, which I might perform *independently,* that is, whose success does not depend upon the contributions of others. Nonetheless, if I am rationally beneficent I will reason as follows: either enough others will contribute to the decent minimum project to achieve this goal, even if I do not contribute to it; or not enough others will contribute to achieve a decent minimum, even if I do contribute. In either case, my contribution will be wasted. In other words, granted the scale of the investment required and the virtually negligible size of my own contribution, I can disregard the minute possibility that my contribution might make the difference between success and failure. But if so, then the rationally beneficent thing for me to do is not to waste my contribution on the project of ensuring a decent minimum but instead to undertake an independent act of beneficence; A, B, or C—where I know my efforts will be needed and efficacious. But if everyone, or even many people, reason in this way, then what we each recognize as the most effective form of beneficence will not come about. Enforcement of a principle requiring contributions to ensuring a decent minimum is needed.

The first argument is of the same form as standard public goods arguments for enforced contributions to national defense, energy conservation, and many other goods, with this exception. In standard public goods arguments, it is usually assumed that the individual's incentive for not contributing is self-interest and that it is in his interest not to contribute because he will be able to partake of the good, if it is produced, even if he does not contribute. In the case at hand, however, the individual's incentive for not contributing is not self-interest, but rather his desire to maximize the good he can do for others with a given amount of his resources. Thus if he contributes but the goal of achieving a decent minimum for all would have been achieved without his contribution, then he has still failed to use his resources in a maximally beneficent way relative to the options of either contributing or not to the joint project, even though the goal of achieving a decent minimum is attained. The rationally beneficent thing to do, then, is not to contribute, even though the result of everyone's acting in a rationally beneficent way will be a relatively ineffective patchwork of small-scale individual acts of beneficence rather than a large-scale, coordinated effort.

Second argument. I believe that ensuring a decent minimum of health care for all is more important than projects A, B, or C, and I am willing to contribute to the decent minimum project, but only if I have assurance that enough others will contribute to achieve the threshold of investment necessary for success. Unless I have this assurance, I will conclude that it is less than rational—and perhaps even morally irresponsible—to contribute my resources to the decent minimum project. For my contribution will be wasted if not enough others contribute. If I lack assurance of sufficient contributions by others, the rationally beneficent thing for me to do is to expend my "beneficence budget" on some less-than-optimal project A, B, or C, whose success does not depend on the contribution of others. But without enforcement, I cannot be assured that enough others will contribute, and if others reason as I do, then what we all believe to be the most effective form of beneficence will not be forthcoming. Others may fail to contribute either because the promptings of self-interest overpower their sense of beneficence, or because they reason as I did in the First Argument, or for some other reason.

Both arguments conclude that an enforced decent minimum principle is needed to achieve coordinated joint effort. However, there is this difference. The Second Argument focuses on the *assurance problem,* while the first does not. In the Second Argument all that is needed is the assumption that rational beneficence requires assurance that enough others will contribute. In the First Argument the individual's reason for not contributing is not that he lacks assurance that enough others will contribute, but rather that it is better for him not to contribute regardless of whether others do or not.

Neither argument depends on an assumption of conflict between the individual's moral motivation of beneficence and his inclination of self-interest. Instead the difficulty is that in the absence of enforcement, individuals who strive to make their beneficence most effective will thereby fail to benefit the needy as much as they might.

A standard response to those paradoxes of rationality known as public goods problems is to introduce a coercive mechanism which attaches penalties to noncontribution and thereby provides each individual with the assurance that enough others will reciprocate so that his contribution will not be wasted and an effective incentive for him to contribute even if he has reason to believe that enough others will contribute to achieve the goal without his contribution. My suggestion is that the same type of argument that is widely

accepted as a justification for enforced principles requiring contributions toward familiar public goods provides support for a coercively backed principle specifying a certain list of health programs for the needy and requiring those who possess the needed resources to contribute to the establishment of such programs, even if the needy have no *right* to the services those programs provide. Such an arrangement would serve a dual function: it would coordinate charitable efforts by focusing them on one set of services among the indefinitely large constellation of possible expressions of beneficence, and it would ensure that the decision to allocate resources to these services will become effective. . . .

NOTES

1. Ronald Dworkin, *Taking Rights Seriously* (Cambridge, MA: Harvard University Press, 1977), pp. 184–205.

2. For an exploration of various arguments for a duty of beneficence and an examination of the relationship between justice and beneficence, in general and in health care, see Allen E. Buchanan, "Philosophical Foundations of Beneficence," *Beneficence and Health Care*, ed. Earl E. Shelp (Dordrecht, Holland: Reidel Publishing Co., 1982).

H . T R I S T R A M   E N G E L H A R D T ,   J R .

Rights to Health Care, Social Justice, and Fairness in Health Care Allocations: Frustrations in the Face of Finitude

H. Tristram Engelhardt, Jr., is a professor of bioethics, medicine, and community medicine at the Baylor College of Medicine. His areas of scholarship are bioethics, philosophy of medicine, and continental philosophy. Among his books are *Foundations of Bioethics* (Oxford) and *Bioethics and Secular Humanism* (Trinity Press International).

The imposition of a single-tier, all-encompassing health care system is morally unjustifiable. It is a coercive act of totalitarian ideological zeal, which fails to recognize the diversity of moral visions that frame interests in health care, the secular moral limits of state authority, and the authority of individuals over

themselves and their own property. It is an act of secular immorality.

A basic human secular moral right to health care does not exist—not even to a "decent minimum of health care." Such rights must be created.

The difficulty with supposed right to health care, as well as with many claims regarding justice or fairness in access to health care, should be apparent. Since the secular moral authority for common action is derived from permission or consent, it is difficult (indeed, for a large-scale society, materially impossi-

From *Foundations of Bioethics*, 2d ed., by H. Tristram Engelhardt, Jr. Reprinted by permission of Oxford University Press, 1996.

ble) to gain moral legitimacy for the thoroughgoing imposition on health care of one among the many views of beneficence and justice. There are, after all, as many accounts of beneficence, justice, and fairness as there are major religions.

Most significantly, there is a tension between the foundations of general secular morality and the various particular positive claims founded in particular visions of beneficence and justice. It is materially impossible both to respect the freedom of all and to achieve their long-range best interests. . . .

Rights to health care constitute claims on services and goods. Unlike rights to forbearance, which require others to refrain from interfering, which show the unity of the authority to use others, rights to beneficence are rights grounded in particular theories or accounts of the good. For general authority, they require others to participate actively in a particular understanding of the good life or justice. Without an appeal to the principle of permission, to advance such rights is to claim that one may press others into labor or confiscate their property. Rights to health care, unless they are derived from special contractual agreements, depend on particular understandings of beneficence rather than on authorizing permission. They may therefore conflict with the decisions of individuals who may not wish to participate in, and may indeed be morally opposed to, realizing a particular system of health care. Individuals always have the secular moral authority to use their own resources in ways that collide with fashionable understandings of justice or the prevailing consensus regarding fairness.

HEALTH CARE POLICY: THE IDEOLOGY OF EQUAL, OPTIMAL CARE

It is fashionable to affirm an impossible commitment in health care delivery, as, for example, in the following four widely embraced health care policy goals, which are at loggerheads:

1. The best possible care is to be provided for all.
2. Equal care should be guaranteed.
3. Freedom of choice on the part of health care provider and consumer should be maintained.
4. Health care costs are to be contained.

One cannot provide the best possible health care for all and contain health care costs. One cannot provide equal health care for all and respect the freedom of individuals peaceably to pursue with others their own visions of health care or to use their own resources

and energies as they decide. For that matter, one cannot maintain freedom in the choice of health care services while containing the costs of health care. One may also not be able to provide all with equal health care that is at the same time the very best care because of limits on the resources themselves. That few openly address these foundational moral tensions at the roots of contemporary health care policy suggests that the problems are shrouded in a collective illusion, a false consciousness, an established ideology within which certain facts are politically unacceptable.

These difficulties spring not only from a conflict between freedom and beneficence, but from a tension among competing views of what it means to pursue and achieve the good in health care (e.g., is it more important to provide equal care to all or the best possible health care to the least-well-off class?). . . .

Only a prevailing collective illusion can account for the assumption in U.S. policy that health care may be provided (1) while containing costs (2) without setting a price on saving lives and preventing suffering when using communal funds and at the same time (3) ignoring the morally unavoidable inequalities due to private resources and human freedom. This false consciousness shaped the deceptions central to the Clinton health care proposal, as it was introduced in 1994. It was advanced to support a health care system purportedly able to provide all with (1) the best of care and (2) equal care, while achieving (3) cost containment, and still (4) allowing those who wish the liberty to purchase fee-for-service health care.[1] While not acknowledging the presence of rationing, the proposal required silent rationing in order to contain costs by limiting access to high-cost, low-yield treatments that a National Health Board would exclude from the "guaranteed benefit package."[2] In addition, it advanced mechanisms to slow technological innovation so as further to reduce the visibility of rationing choices.[3] One does not have to ration that which is not available. There has been a failure to acknowledge the moral inevitability of inequalities in health care due to the limits of secular governmental authority, human freedom, and the existence of private property, however little that may be. There was also the failure to acknowledge the need to ration health care within communal programs if costs are to be contained. It has been ideologically unacceptable to recognize these circumstances. . . .

JUSTICE, FREEDOM, AND INEQUALITY

Interests in justice as beneficence are motivated in part by inequalities and in part by needs. That some have so little while others have so much properly evokes moral concerns of beneficence. Still, . . . the moral authority to use force to set such inequalities aside is limited. These limitations are in part due to the circumstance that the resources one could use to aid those in need are already owned by other people. One must establish whether and when inequalities and needs generate rights or claims against others.

THE NATURAL AND SOCIAL LOTTERIES

"Natural lottery" is used to identify changes in fortune that result from natural forces, not directly from the actions of persons. The natural lottery shapes the distribution of both naturally and socially conditioned assets. The natural lottery contrasts with the social lottery, which is used to identify changes in fortune that are not the result of natural forces but the actions of persons. The social lottery shapes the distribution of social and natural assets. The natural and social lotteries, along with one's own free decisions, determine the distribution of natural and social assets. The social lottery is termed a lottery, though it is the outcome of personal actions, because of the complex and unpredictable interplay of personal choices and because of the unpredictable character of the outcomes, which do not conform to an ideal pattern, and because the outcomes are the results of social forces, not the immediate choices of those subject to them.

All individuals are exposed to the vicissitudes of nature. Some are born healthy and by luck remain so for a long life, free of disease and major suffering. Others are born with serious congenital or genetic diseases, others contract serious crippling fatal illnesses early in life, and yet others are injured and maimed. Those who win the natural lottery will for most of their lives not be in need of medical care. They will live full lives and die painless and peaceful deaths. Those who lost the natural lottery will be in need of health care to blunt their sufferings and, where possible, to cure their diseases and to restore function. There will be a spectrum of losses, ranging from minor problems such as having teeth with cavities to major tragedies such as developing childhood leukemia, inheriting Huntington's chorea, or developing amyelotrophic lateral sclerosis.

These tragic outcomes are the deliverances of nature, for which no one, without some special view of accountability or responsibility, is responsible (unless, that is, one recognizes them as the results of the Fall or as divine chastisements). The circumstance that individuals are injured by hurricanes, storms, and earthquakes is often simply no one's fault. When no one is to blame, no one may be charged with the responsibility of making whole those who lose the natural lottery on the ground of accountability for the harm. One will need an argument dependent on a particular sense of fairness to show that the readers of this volume should submit to the forcible redistribution of their resources to provide health care for those injured by nature. It may very well be unfeeling, unsympathetic, or uncharitable not to provide such help. One may face eternal hellfires for failing to provide aid.[4] But it is another thing to show in general secular moral terms that individuals owe others such help in a way that would morally authorize state force to redistribute their private resources and energies or to constrain their free choices with others. To be in dire need does not by itself create a secular moral right to be rescued from that need. The natural lottery creates inequalities and places individuals at disadvantage without creating a straightforward secular moral obligation on the part of others to aid those in need.

Individuals differ in their resources not simply because of outcomes of the natural lottery, but also due to the actions of others. Some deny themselves immediate pleasures in order to accumulate wealth or to leave inheritances; through a complex web of love, affection, and mutual interest, individuals convey resources, one to another, so that those who are favored prosper and those who are ignored languish. Some as a consequence grow wealthy and others grow poor, not through anyone's malevolent actions or omissions, but simply because they were not favored by the love, friendship, collegiality, and associations through which fortunes develop and individuals prosper. In such cases there will be neither fairness nor unfairness, but simply good and bad fortune.

In addition, some will be advantaged or disadvantaged, made rich, poor, ill, diseased, deformed, or disabled because of the malevolent and blameworthy actions and omissions of others. Such will be unfair circumstances, which just and beneficent states should try to prevent and to rectify through legitimate police protection, forced restitution, and charitable programs. Insofar as an injured party has a claim against an injurer to be made whole, not against society, the outcome is unfortunate from the perspective of society's obligations and obligations of innocent citizens to make restitution. Restitution is owed by the injurer, not society or others. There will be outcomes of the social lottery that are on the one hand blameworthy in the sense of resulting from the culpable actions of others, though on the other hand a society has no obligation to rectify them. The social lottery includes the exposure to the immoral and unjust actions of others. Again, one will need an argument dependent on a particular sense of fairness to show that the readers of this volume should submit to the forcible redistribution of their resources to provide health care to those injured by others.

When individuals come to purchase health care, some who lose the natural lottery will be able at least in part to compensate for those losses through their winnings at the social lottery. They will be able to afford expensive health care needed to restore health and to regain function. On the other hand, those who lose in both the natural and the social lottery will be in need of health care, but without the resources to acquire it.

THE RICH AND THE POOR:
DIFFERENCES IN ENTITLEMENTS

If one owns property by virtue of just acquisition or just transfer, then one's title to that property will not be undercut by the tragedies and needs of others. One will simply own one's property. On the other hand, if one owns property because such ownership is justified within a system that ensures a beneficent distribution of goods (e.g., the achievement of the greatest balance of benefits over harms for the greatest number or the greatest advantage for the least-well-off class), one's ownership will be affected by the needs of others. . . . Property is in part privately owned in a strong sense that cannot be undercut by the needs of others. In addition, all have a general right to the fruits of the earth, which constitutes the basis for a form of taxation as rent to provide fungible payments to individuals, whether or not they are in need. Finally, there are likely to be resources held in common by groups that may establish bases for their distribution to meet health care concerns. The first two forms of entitlement or ownership exist unconstrained by medical or other needs. The last form of entitlement or ownership, through the decision of a community, may be conditioned by need.

The existence of any amount of private resources can be the basis for inequalities that secular moral authority may not set aside. Insofar as people own things, they will have a right to them, even if others need them. Because the presence of permission is cardinal, the test of whether one must transfer one's goods to others will not be whether such a redistribution will not prove onerous or excessive for the person subjected to the distribution, but whether the resources belong to that individual. Consider that you may be reading this book next to a person in great need. The test of whether a third person may take resources from you to help that individual in need will not be whether you will suffer from the transfer, but rather whether you have consented—at least this is the case if the principle of permission functions in general secular morality. . . . The principle of permission is the source of authority when moral strangers collaborate, because they do not share a common understanding of fairness or of the good. As a consequence, goal-oriented approaches to the just distribution of resources must be restricted to commonly owned goods, where there is authority to create programs for their use.

Therefore, one must qualify the conclusions of the 1983 American President's Commission for the Study of Ethical Problems that suggest that excessive burdens should determine the amount of tax persons should pay to sustain an adequate level of health care for those in need.[5] Further, one will have strong grounds for morally condemning systems that attempt to impose an all-encompassing health care plan that would require "equality of care [in the sense of avoiding] the creation of a tiered system [by] providing care based only on differences of need, not individual or group characteristics."[6] Those who are rich are always at secular moral liberty to purchase more and better health care.

DRAWING THE LINE BETWEEN
THE UNFORTUNATE AND THE UNFAIR

How one regards the moral significance of the natural and social lotteries and the moral force of private ownership will determine how one draws the line between circumstances that are simply unfortunate and those that are unfortunate and in addition unfair in the sense of constituting a claim on the resources of others.

Life in general, and health care in particular, reveal circumstances of enormous tragedy, suffering, and deprivation. The pains and sufferings of illness, disability, and disease, as well as the limitations of deformity, call on the sympathy of all to provide aid and give comfort. Injuries, disabilities, and diseases due to the forces of nature are unfortunate. Injuries, disabilities, and diseases due to the unconsented-to actions of others are unfair. Still, outcomes of the unfair actions of others are not necessarily society's fault and are in this sense unfortunate. The horrible injuries that come every night to the emergency rooms of major hospitals may be someone's fault, even if they are not the fault of society, much less that of uninvolved citizens. Such outcomes, though unfair with regard to the relationship of the injured with the injurer, may be simply unfortunate with respect to society and other citizens (and may licitly be financially exploited). One is thus faced with distinguishing the difficult line between acts of God, as well as immoral acts of individuals that do not constitute a basis for societal retribution on the one hand, and injuries that provide such a basis on the other.

A line must be created between those losses that will be made whole through public funds and those that will not. Such a line was drawn in 1980 by Patricia Harris, the then secretary of the Department of Health, Education, and Welfare, when she ruled that heart transplantations should be considered experimental and therefore not reimbursable through Medicare.[7] To be in need of a heart transplant and not have the funds available would be an unfortunate circumstance but not unfair. One was not eligible for a heart transplant even if another person had intentionally damaged one's heart. From a moral point of view, things would have been different if the federal government had in some culpable fashion injured one's heart. So, too, if promises of treatment had been made. For example, to suffer from appendicitis or pneumonia and not as a qualifying patient receive treatment guaranteed through a particular governmental or private insurance system would be unfair, not simply unfortunate.

Drawing the line between the unfair and the unfortunate is unavoidable because it is impossible in general secular moral terms to translate all needs into rights, into claims against the resources of others. One must with care decide where the line is to be drawn. To distinguish needs from mere desires, one must endorse one among the many competing visions of morality and human flourishing. One is forced to draw a line between those needs (or desires) that constitute claims on the aid of others and those that do not. The

line distinguishing unfortunate from unfair circumstances justifies by default certain social and economic inequalities in the sense of determining who, if any one, is obliged in general secular immorality to remedy such circumstances or achieve equality. Is the request of an individual to have life extended through a heart transplant at great cost, and perhaps only for a few years, a desire for an inordinate extension of life? Or is it a need to be secure against a premature death? . . . Outside a particular view of the good life, needs do not create rights to the services or goods of others.[8] Indeed, outside of a particular moral vision there is no canonical means for distinguishing desires from needs.

There is a practical difficulty in regarding major losses at the natural and social lotteries as generating claims to health care: attempts to restore health indefinitely can deplete societal resources in the pursuit of ever-more incremental extensions of life of marginal quality. A relatively limited amount of food and shelter is required to preserve the lives of individuals. But an indefinite amount of resources can in medicine be committed to the further preservation of human life, the marginal postponement of death, and the marginal alleviation of human suffering and disability. Losses at the natural lottery with regard to health can consume major resources with little return. Often one can only purchase a little relief, and that only at great costs. Still, more decisive than the problem of avoiding the possibly overwhelming costs involved in satisfying certain health care desires (e.g., postponing death for a while through the use of critical care) is the problem of selecting the correct content-full account of justice in order canonically to distinguish between needs and desires and to translate needs into rights.

BEYOND EQUALITY: AN EGALITARIANISM
OF ALTRUISM VERSUS AN EGALITARIANISM OF ENVY

The equal distribution of health care is itself problematic, a circumstance recognized in *Securing Access to Health Care*, the 1983 report of the President's Commission.[9] The difficulties are multiple:

1. Although in theory, at least, one can envisage providing all with equal levels of decent shelter, one cannot restore all to or preserve all in an equal state of health. Many health needs cannot be satisfied in the same way one can address most needs for food and shelter.

2. If one provided all with the same amount of

funds to purchase health care or the same amount of services, the amount provided would be far too much for some and much too little for others who could have benefited from more investment in treatment and research.

3. If one attempts to provide equal health care in the sense of allowing individuals to select health care only from a predetermined list of available therapies, or through some managed health care plan such as accountable (to the government) health care plans or regional health alliances, which would be provided to all so as to prevent the rich from having access to better health care than the poor, one would have immorally confiscated private property and have restricted the freedom of individuals to join in voluntary relationships and associations.

That some are fortunate in having more resources is neither more nor less arbitrary or unfair than some having better health, better looks, or more talents. In any event, the translation of unfortunate circumstances into unfair circumstances, other than with regard to violations of the principle of permission, requires the imposition of a particular vision of beneficence or justice.

The pursuit of equality faces both moral and practical difficulties. If significant restrictions were placed on the ability to purchase special treatment with one's resources, one would need not only to anticipate that a black market would inevitably develop in health care services, but also acknowledge that such a black market would be a special bastion of liberty and freedom of association justified in general secular moral terms. . . .

CONFLICTING MODELS OF JUSTICE: FROM CONTENT TO PROCEDURE

John Rawls's *A Theory of Justice* and Robert Nozick's *Anarchy, State, and Utopia* offer contrasting understandings of what should count as justice or fairness. They sustain differing suggestions regarding the nature of justice in health care. They provide a contrast between justice as primarily structural, a pattern of distributions that is amenable to rational disclosure, versus justice as primarily procedural, a matter of fair negotiation.[10] In *A Theory of Justice* Rawls forwards an expository device of an ahistorical perspective from which to discover the proper pattern for the distribution of resources, and therefore presumably for the distribution of health care resources. In this under-

standing, it is assumed that societally based entitlements have moral priority. Nozick, in contrast, advances a historical account of just distributions within which justice depends on what individuals have agreed to do with and for each other. Nozick holds that individually based entitlements are morally prior to societally based entitlements. In contrast with Rawls, who argues that one can discover a proper pattern for the allocation of resources, Nozick argues that such a pattern cannot be discovered and that instead one can only identify the characteristics of a just process for fashioning rights to health care. . . .

The differences between Nozick of *Anarchy, State, and Utopia* and Rawls of *A Theory of Justice* express themselves in different accounts of entitlements and ownership, and in different understandings of non-principled fortune and misfortune. For Rawls, one has justifiable title to goods if such a title is part of a system that ensures the greatest benefit to the least advantaged, consistent with a just-savings principle, and with offices and positions open to all under conditions of fair equality and opportunity, and where each person has an equal right to the most extensive total system of equal basic liberties compatible with a similar system of liberty for all. In contrast, for Nozick, one simply owns things: "Things come into the world already attached to people having entitlements over them."[11] If one really owns things, there will be freedom-based limitations on principles of distributive justice. One may not use people or the property without their permission or authorization. The needs of others will not erase one's property rights. The readers of this book should consider that they may be wearing wedding rings or other jewelry not essential to their lives, which could be sold to buy antibiotics to save identifiable lives in the third world. Those who keep such baubles may in part be acting in agreement with Nozick's account and claiming that "it is my right to keep my wedding ring for myself, even though the proceeds from its sale could save the lives of individuals in dire need."

Nozick's account requires a distinction between someone's secular moral rights and what is right, good, or proper to do. At times, selling some (perhaps all) of one's property to support the health care of those in need will be the right thing to do, even though one has a secular moral right to refuse to sell. This contrast derives from the distinction Nozick makes between *freedom as a side constraint*, as the very condition for the possibility of a secular moral community, and *freedom as one value among others*. This contrast can be understood as a distinction between those claims of justice based on the very possibility of a moral community, versus those claims of justice that turn on interests in particular goods and values, albeit interests recognized in the original position. . . .

This contrast between Rawls and Nozick can be appreciated more generally as a contrast between two quite different principles of justice, each of which has strikingly different implications for the allocation of health care resources.

1. Freedom- or permission-based justice is concerned with distributions of goods made in accord with the notion of the secular moral community as a peaceable social structure binding moral strangers, members of diverse concrete moral communities. Such justice will therefore require the consent of the individuals involved in a historical nexus of justice-regarding institutions understood in conformity with the principle of permission. The principle of beneficence may be pursued only within constraints set by the principle of permission.

2. Goals-based justice is concerned with the achievement of the good of individuals in society, where the pursuit of beneficence is not constrained by a strong principle of permission, but driven by some particular understanding of morality, justice, or fairness. Such justice will vary in substance as one attempts, for example, to (a) give each person an equal share; (b) give each person what that person needs; (c) give each person a distribution as a part of a system designed to achieve the greatest balance of benefits over harms for the greatest number of persons; (d) give each person a distribution as a part of a system designed to maximize the advantage of the least-well-off class with conditions of equal liberty for all and of fair opportunity.

Allocations of health care in accord with freedom- or permission-based justice must occur within the constraint to respect the free choices of persons, including their exercise of their property rights. Allocations of health care in accord with goals-based justice will need to establish what it means to provide a just pattern of health care, and what constitutes true needs,

not mere desires, and how to rank the various health goals among themselves and in comparison with non-health goals. Such approaches to justice in health care will require a way of ahistorically discovering the proper pattern for the distribution of resources.

Permission-based and goals-based approaches to justice in health care contrast because they offer competing interpretations of the maxim, "Justitia est constans et perpetua voluntas jus suum cuique tribuens" (Justice is the constant and perpetual will to render everyone his due).[12] A permission-based approach holds that justice is first and foremost giving to each the right to be respected as a free individual as the source of secular moral authority, in the disposition of personal services and private goods: that which is due *(ius)* to individuals is respect of their authority over themselves and their possessions. In contrast, a goals-based approach holds that justice is receiving a share of the goods, which is fair by an appeal to a set of ahistorical criteria specifying what a fair share should be, that is, what share is due to each individual. Since there are various senses of a fair share (e.g., an equal share, a share in accordance with the system that maximizes the balance of benefits over harms, etc.), there will be various competing senses of justice in health care under the rubric of goals-based justice. . . .

THE MORAL INEVITABILITY OF A MULTITIER HEALTH CARE SYSTEM

. . . In the face of unavoidable tragedies and contrary moral intuitions, a multitiered system of health care is in many respects a compromise. On the one hand, it provides some amount of health care for all, while on the other hand allowing those with resources to purchase additional or better services. It can endorse the use of communal resources for the provision of a decent minimal or basic amount of health care for all, while acknowledging the existence of private resources at the disposal of some individuals to purchase better basic as well as luxury care. While the propensity to seek more than equal treatment for oneself or loved ones is made into a vicious disposition in an egalitarian system, a multitier system allows for the expression of individual love and the pursuit of private advantage, though still supporting a general social sympathy for those in need. Whereas an egalitarian system must suppress the widespread human inclination to devote private resources to the purchase of the best care for those whom one loves, a multitier system can recognize a legitimate place for the expression of such inclinations. A multitier system

(1) should support individual providers and consumers against attempts to interfere in their free association and their use of their own resources, though (2) it may allow positive rights to health care to be created for individuals who have not been advantaged by the social lottery.

The serious task is to decide how to define and provide a decent minimum or basic level of care as a floor of support for all members of society, while allowing money and free choice to fashion special tiers of services for the affluent. In addressing this general issue of defining what is to be meant by a decent minimum basic level or a minimum adequate amount of health care, the American President's Commission in 1983 suggested that in great measure content is to be created rather than discovered by democratic processes, as well as by the forces of the market. "In a democracy, the appropriate values to be assigned to the consequences of policies must ultimately be determined by people expressing their values through social and political processes as well as in the marketplace."[13] The Commission, however, also suggested that the concept of adequacy could in part be discovered by an appeal to that amount of care that would meet the standards of sound medical practice. "Adequacy does require that everyone receive care that meets standards of sound medical practice."[14] But what one means by "sound medical practice" is itself dependent on particular understandings within particular cultures. Criteria for sound medical practice are as much created as discovered. The moral inevitability of multiple tiers of care brings with it multiple standards of proper or sound medical practice and undermines the moral plausibility of various obiter dicta concerning the centralized allocation of medical resources. . . .

Concepts of adequate care are not discoverable outside of particular views of the good life and of proper medical practice. In nations encompassing diverse moral communities, an understanding of what one will mean by an adequate level or a decent minimum of health care will need to be fashioned, if it can indeed be agreed to, through open discussion and by fair negotiation. . . .

NOTES

1. The White House Domestic Policy Council, *The President's Health Security Plan* (New York: Times Books, 1993).

2. The White House Domestic Policy Council, *The President's Health Security Plan*, p. 43.

3. Innovation would be discouraged as drug prices are subject to review as reasonable. The White House Domestic Policy Council, *The President's Health Security Plan*, p. 45.

4. In considering how to respond to the plight of the impecunious, one might consider the story Jesus tells of the rich man who fails to give alms to "a certain beggar named Lazarus, full of sores, who was laid at his gate, desiring to be fed with the crumbs which fell from the rich man's table" (Luke 16:20–21). The rich man, who was not forthcoming with alms, was condemned eternally to a hell of excruciating torment.

5. President's Commission for the Study of Ethical Problems in Medicine and Biomedical and Behavioral Research, *Securing Access to Health Care* (Washington, D.C.: U.S. Government Printing Office, 1983), vol. 1, pp. 43–46.

6. The White House Domestic Policy Council, "Ethical Foundations of Health Reform," in *The President's Health Security Plan*, p. 11.

7. H. Newman, "Exclusion of Heart Transplantation Procedures from Medicare Coverage." *Federal Register* 45 (Aug. 6, 1980): 52296. See also H. Newman, "Medicare Program: Solicitation of Hospitals and Medical Centers to Participate in a Study of Heart Transplants," *Federal Register* 46 (Jan. 22, 1981): 7072–75.

8. The reader should understand that the author holds that almsgiving is one of the proper responses to human suffering (in addition to being an appropriate expression of repentance, an act of repentance to which surely the author is obligated). It is just that the author acknowledges the limited secular moral authority of the state to compel charity coercively.

9. President's Commission, *Securing Access to Health Care*, vol. 1, pp. 18–19.

10. John Rawls, *A Theory of Justice* (Cambridge, Mass.: Harvard University Press, 1971), and Robert Nozick, *Anarchy, State, and Utopia* (New York: Basic Books, 1974).

11. Nozick, *Anarchy, State, and Utopia*, p. 160.

12. Flavius Petrus Sabbatius Justinianus, *The Institutes of Justinian*, trans. Thomas C. Sandars (1922; repr. Westport, Conn,: Greenwood Press, 1970), 1.1, p. 5.

13. President's Commission, *Securing Access to Health Care*, vol. 1, p. 37.

14. Ibid.

Managed Care and Access to Care

LAWRENCE O. GOSTIN

Securing Health or Just Health Care? The Effect of the Health Care System on the Health of America

Lawrence Gostin is professor of law at Georgetown University and professor of public health at the Johns Hopkins University. He is also director of the Center for Law and the Public's Health and editor of the Health Law and Ethics section of the *Journal of the American Medical Association*. His latest book is *Public Health Law: Power, Duty, Restraint* (University of California Press and the Milbank Memorial Fund).

. . . Given the emphasis on financial costs and personal burdens, it is not surprising that political debate and academic discourse on health care reform focused so intensely on market structures and the economic effects on major segments of commercial society. Consequently, the linguistics of health care reform was market-oriented: managed competition, small and large insurance markets, employer mandates, tax credits and other market incentives. The overarching concern was the economic impact on the predominate players in the market: large employers, small businesses, insurers, and health care providers.

Manifestly, the effects of reform on the buying and selling of health care as a commodity, and its economic effects on American business (including the business of health care) are weighty concerns. It is not misguided, then, that so much focus was placed on the effects of health care reform on the economy. Yet, it is striking that so little attention was given to a still more fundamental value—the effect of the health care system on the health of individuals and populations. It is my thesis that promotion of the health of the population is the most important objective of health care reform; that reasonable levels of resource allocation are warranted to achieve this purpose; and that the adverse effects on the economy, American business, and citizens are as high, or higher, under the status quo

than they would be if government assured universal coverage for health care. . . .

I. THE PREEMINENCE OF THE VALUE OF HEALTH

. . . In this article, I make no claim to a right to health. The government cannot be expected to take responsibility for assuring the health of each member of the population, and the concept of a right to health is too broad to have legal meaning. Nor do I claim a constitutional right to any level of health care that a person may want. An unfettered constitutional right to health care is not currently tenable. Further, the government could not be expected to respond to all demands and preferences for health care, irrespective of the cost or effectiveness.

My claim is simply that the prevention of disease or disability and the promotion of health, within reasonable resource constraints, provides the preeminent justification for the government to act for the welfare of society. In determining the allocation of resources in society, the transcending public value must be based upon improved health outcomes for the population, based upon objective measures of morbidity and mortality. Despite marked increases in spending for personal medical services and advances in bio-medical technology, the decade 1980–90 showed little improvement in numerous objective health indicators such as maternal and child health, nutrition, sexually transmitted diseases, and occupational health and safety. Health promotion is measured not only by in-

From *Saint Louis University Law Journal* 39, no. 1 (Fall 1994), 7–43. Reprinted by permission.

creased longevity or life extension. Rather, health promotion is measured by improvement in the quality of life, "compression" of morbidity and suffering, and extension of active or well-functioning life expectancy.

The very purpose of government is to attain through collective action human goods that individuals acting alone could not realistically achieve. Chief among those human goods is the assurance of the conditions under which people can be healthy. While the government cannot assure health, it can, within the reasonable limits of its resources, organize its activities in ways that best prevent illness and disability, and promote health among its population. . . .

II. THE IMPORTANCE OF UNIVERSAL ACCESS TO HEALTH CARE SERVICES

It is not necessary to demonstrate which is the more fundamental governmental activity—public health or personal medical services. What is important is that both are essential to the health of individuals and populations, and both systems are functioning badly. Consequently, an assessment of the inadequacies in the personal health care system shows many people receiving insufficient and inequitable access to medical services.

Most countries with advanced economies in the world concentrate their resources in one health insurance system that provides universal coverage to their populations.[1] The United States, however, provides a fragmented array of private and public programs that results in a substantial portion of the population without health insurance coverage or with highly inadequate coverage. The American public, while purporting to support universal coverage,[2] appears highly ambivalent about whether health insurance is a social good, of which the costs should be borne collectively, or an economic enterprise that effectively should be governed by market forces.[3]

Whatever vision of health care that the public may prefer, the system itself has become market-oriented. By the nature of markets those who are unable or unwilling to pay the price of the commodity are left out. Not being included in a commodities market that trades in durable goods and services may be justified on economic grounds, but exclusion from the market in health care presents profoundly different considerations.

The number and profile of those who have been left out of the health insurance market, juxtaposed with current national health expenditures, is illumi-

nating. The United States spent approximately $900 billion dollars on health care in 1993.[4] This represented approximately 14% of the nation's gross domestic product.[5] Health care expenditures are expected to reach $1.7 trillion, between 16% and 18% of the gross domestic product, by the end of the decade if effective controls are not instituted.[6]

Despite the inordinate national expenditures on health care, many Americans lack health insurance. At any given time during the last year, approximately 37 to 40 million people were without health insurance,[7] about 15–18% of all children and adults.[8] While different methods of counting the uninsured have allowed critics of health care reform to obfuscate its true dimensions, any dispassionate assessment reveals a considerable and enduring national problem.[9] Thus, while the census reported 33.5 million uninsured in 1992 based on monthly averages, others calculated that 50[10] to 58 million[11] lacked health insurance for at least one month in that year.

It is suggested by market-oriented analysts that the alleged 37 million uninsured is a "big lie"[12] that "wilts under analysis."[13] These analysts claim that the chronically uninsured amount to fewer than 10 million, and that the number of uninsured persons could be reduced dramatically by introducing medical savings accounts.[14] These claims are based on data suggesting that the median spell length of persons without insurance is six months, and that 70% of all spells end within nine months.[15] However, a deeper examination of the pool of uninsured persons demonstrates the intransigence and severity of the problem. At least 28% of all uninsured spells last for more than one year, and 15–18% last more than two years. For over 20 million people in 1993, being without health insurance was not a temporary or transient phase in their lives.[16] Professor Swartz, the scholar who originally reported these insurance data, concludes that the point-in-time estimate of 37 million uninsured actually refers to at least 21 million long-term uninsured plus nearly 16 million with spells lasting less than one year.[17] . . .

The uninsured are not the only persons in the population with difficulties in obtaining access to health care. An additional 20 million people are thought to be underinsured. Under-insurance is a concept that is hard to define or quantify. Persons may have inadequate access to health care because of insufficient overall insurance coverage (e.g., capitations on coverage based on limits on cost or hospital stays);

exemptions for certain conditions (e.g., pre-existing coverage, waiting periods, mental health or childbirth services); or low reimbursement schedules for the payment of physicians, which results in denials of service (e.g., Medicaid patients in certain geographic areas or seeking certain kinds of services). . . .

The demographics of the uninsured population reveal the deep interconnections between the absence of health insurance and socio-economic status, race, and age. The uninsured population is disproportionately poor or near-poor, African-American or Hispanic, young, and unemployed.[18] . . .

There is certainly an inter-connectedness to each of the primary barriers to access—financial, structural, personal and cultural. It is clear, however, that without dismantling financial barriers, access to health care will continue to be highly adequate; the Institute of Medicine recently "reaffirmed that lack of health care coverage is, to a great extent, a good proxy for access."[19]

It is commonly believed that patients without health insurance are not so much denied access, but are diverted to emergency rooms and other public clinics for their care. It is, therefore, important to inquire whether the absence of insurance leads to delayed or insufficient access of such seriousness that it actually affects health outcomes. The data show that lack of access is closely associated not only with under-utilization of services but, more importantly, with poorer health outcomes.[20] Although health insurance coverage is not the sole determinant of health status, it is a key factor. . . .

Those who reject the view that health is the foremost objective of a health care system may instead prefer to focus attention to the finance system, administrative efficiency, or a favorable cost-benefit ratio. Health care is only one of many possible goods that government can provide. It is, therefore, not unreasonable to suggest that if health care could be provided more efficiently and less expensively, government could spend on other worthwhile social programs such as housing, poverty, hunger, or education.

As explained previously, the expenditure on health care in the United States represents approximately 14% of the nation's gross domestic product.[21] Health care expenditures are expected to reach $1.7 trillion, between sixteen and eighteen percent of the gross domestic product, by the end of the decade if effective controls are not instituted.[22] These figures stand in stark contrast to the percentage of the gross national product (GNP) that is devoted to health care in countries that offer their citizens virtually universal health coverage such as Canada, Germany, Great Britain, and Japan; these countries devote from 5.8% to 8.7% of their GNP to health care.[23] In 1990, while the United Kingdom, Japan, and Germany spent between $909 and $1,287 on each person for health care, the United States spent $2,566;[24] for every $1 per capita spent in England, the United States spends $3 per capita.[25] The high per capita expenditures on health care in the United States relative to other countries is not all spent on personal care services. It is estimated that 19% to 24% of health care expenditures goes toward administrative expenses, including those of the nation's insurance companies.[26]

In summary, whether the U.S. health care system is measured in terms of infant mortality or life expectancy, utilization rates, or cost effectiveness, it appears to lag well behind other developed countries in North America and Europe.

III. INEQUITABLE ACCESS TO HEALTH CARE

There is another perspective on how to measure the quality of a health care system. All else held constant, it is possible to argue that if health care resources are distributed equitably, the system provides consistent and fair benefits for all citizens. Some may even be willing to sacrifice certain benefits of health care to achieve greater equity. If a society does very well in health outcomes for some of its citizens, say those who are in higher socioeconomic classes and within majority racial populations, and others do very poorly, is that society worth emulating? Under Rawlsian theory, if individuals could not pre-determine whether they would be born into a favored or the disfavored class, most people would choose to be in a country that provides roughly equal access to health care for all classes.[27] . . .

A. SCRUTINY OF THE "EQUITY" PRINCIPLE

Before examining the substantial disparities in access to health care and health status among various classes in the United States, it is necessary to ask two inter-related questions: what ethical values support the claim of equity in the distribution of health services, and what exactly is the equity claim being made? To many, it is not intuitively obvious that equity is a principle that deserves general recognition in society. Americans are prepared to tolerate significant and pervasive inequalities in wealth and in the distribution of most social goods. A theory of equity in health care must provide an account of why health care deserves special treatment, unless the advocate is prepared to defend a considerably broader view of distributive justice for all goods and services.

One theory of equity in health care . . . relies on the special importance of health care in providing a necessary condition for the fulfillment of human opportunity. Professor Daniels observes that pain and disability, limitation of function, and premature loss of life all restrict human opportunities.[28] If it is accepted that a certain level of health services is a precondition to affording human beings reasonable life opportunities, then some equitable access to those services is warranted.

Government is prepared to provide a public education to all children of school age. Access to education is presumably justified by the importance of education in furnishing fair opportunities for all children, irrespective of their social or economic class. Like education, a certain level of health care is essential to a person's ability to pursue life's opportunities on some roughly equitable basis. Health care, at least in some fundamental ways, is as important to equal opportunity as education. While health care does not provide opportunities by facilitating basic knowledge and skill, it does so by enabling the person to function mentally and physically in the application of that knowledge and skill.

More equitable access to health care is supported by collective, as well as individual goods. Health care does not only enable individuals to gain life opportunities for themselves, it also allows individuals to contribute to society. A healthy population, like an educated population, is much more likely to be socially and economically productive, and less dependent. A multi-tiered system of health care, in which those in the lower tiers receive clearly inferior and lower-quality services, perpetuates inequalities among individuals and groups. These inequalities occur not only in attaining health but, indirectly, in attaining status, acceptance, and livelihood in society. As various inequalities among individuals and groups expand, society must deal with the consequences of social unrest, alienation, and dissatisfaction. Strikingly disparate standards of health care for different social, economic and racial groups, then, is unjust for individuals who lose indispensable life opportunities and harmful for society generally which loses much productive activity and risks greater disaffection among major segments of the population.

Professor Daniels makes the following claim to equity in health care: "*if* an acceptable theory of justice includes a principle providing for fair equality of opportunity, then health care institutions should be among those governed by it."[29] But to suggest that health care institutions ought to be governed by the principle of fair equality of opportunity, is not the same as stating precisely the claim being made. For reasons explained earlier, no claim to health, let alone equal health, is feasible since the vast variabilities in health are to a great extent biologically, socially, and behaviorally determined. Nor do I make a claim for *equal* health care or even equal access to health care. Such a claim would not only require a fundamental redistribution of health care resources, but also would require restrictions on discretionary spending. Very few health care systems in developed countries restrict access to private health insurers, providers, and technology for people who can afford them, irrespective of the fact that these amenities are effectively inaccessible to the poor or near poor. Even in education, families are not restricted in their access to private educational opportunities of many kinds that are of better quality than public education. Nor is public education itself equal in quality, but is often superior in more affluent neighborhoods.

Rather than defending the broad re-distributive agenda implied in the principle of *equality* so that health care must be the same, I urge the modest claim of greater *equity,* so that health care is distributed more fairly. I do not even expect society to achieve anywhere near complete equity in the sense that health care is distributed in a totally impartial or unbiased way. But it is reasonable to expect society to set a goal of a more equitable system by reducing inordinately wide disparities in health care. The claim of equitable or fair access applies especially to those health services that most effectively help prevent illness, disease, disability, and premature death, and which best care for and treat persons in ill-health.

B. DISPARITIES IN ACCESS TO HEALTH CARE AMONG POPULATIONS

Access to health care is measured by the use of health services, the quality of those services, and health outcomes. The test of equity involves a determination of whether there are systematic differences in access, and whether these differences result from financial or other barriers to health care. Using these objective measures of equitable access to health care, researchers have been able to demonstrate persistent and sometimes remarkable differences among groups in the United States.

There is a powerful and growing literature on inequitable access to health care. On each of the three dimensions just discussed—use, quality, and health outcomes—considerable data exist to demonstrate significant differences among groups based upon their personal, social, and economic status. The disparities in access to care are particularly sharp and enduring for persons with low socioeconomic status (the poor or near poor, the uninsured, and those in public programs such as Medicaid) and persons in minority racial and ethnic groups.

The relationships between low socioeconomic status and poor health are deep and enduring. In 1991, there were 35.7 million persons below the official poverty level,[30] accounting for 14.2% of the population.[31] If alternative methods of valuation were used that excluded non-cash benefits such as Medicaid and food stamps, there would have been 54.8 million persons in official poverty, accounting for 21.8% of the population.[32] From 1977 to 1990, the poorest 20% of the population suffered a 15% loss in real income, while the wealthiest one percent had a 110% after-tax rise in income.[33] . . .

The subgroups that are over-represented in the poverty population are precisely those groups that are most affected by lack of health insurance and poor health. In 1991, nearly one-third (32.7%) of all African-Americans and more than one quarter of Hispanics (28.7%) were living under the poverty line.[34] One half of the nation's poor were either children or the elderly.[35] One-fourth of all children and one half of all African-American children were below the poverty line.[36]

Health disparities between poor people and those with higher incomes are almost universal for all dimensions of health. . . .

The association between economic disadvantage and ill-health is manifested most strongly in strikingly poor pregnancy outcomes (e.g., prematurity, low birth weight, birth defects) and higher infant mortality; the limitations in life activities due to ill health; and elevated mortality rates. Low income people have death rates that are twice the rates for people with incomes above the poverty level.

Compared to other groups in society, African-Americans and other racial and ethnic minorities are three times more likely to live in poverty and to lack health insurance. They also are subject to discrimination in health care. The effects of these burdens are borne out by poorer utilization of services, outcomes, and health status "virtually across the board." . . .

IV. HEALTH CARE AND MARKETS

• • •

A. THE APPLICABILITY OF MARKET THEORY TO HEALTH CARE

Competition is widely thought to be an effective mechanism for lowering the price and increasing the quality of goods and services in the marketplace. The question, however, is whether competition is an appropriate theory, or the marketplace is the appropriate approach, to the cost effective allocation of health care services. Competition in health care can occur at least on two levels—health care plans can compete for subscribers, and individual providers can compete in offering service to patients. Each level of competition presents its own set of opportunities for reducing cost and its own set of theoretical and practical problems.

Competition among health care plans, which is the organizing theory behind managed competition, is vehemently put forward as a strategy for cost containment. Managed competition remains a proposal constructed in theory, not practice. No health care system outside of the United States has demonstrated the worth of managed competition in promoting quality and constraining medical inflation.

The theory of managed competition assumes that a sufficient number of health care plans exist to sustain competition in the market. A study by one of managed competition's original proponents suggests that populations large enough to support three or more competing health plans exist only in middle-sized to large metropolitan areas.[37] Professor Kronick and his colleagues assume that a minimum of three competing health plans is necessary for the system to work effectively, however, no empirical evidence exists to rely on this number to foster competition. Would players in the market truly compete or would they collude to maintain prices? What economic conditions and/or antitrust arrangements would have to exist to ensure genuine competition? . . .

Predicting the economic effects of managed competition on national health spending is fraught with complexity. Managed competition is not based on empirical evidence, and since the elements of proposals are diverse, it is exceedingly difficult to determine the probable economic effects. Estimates of the economic impact of managed competition on national health care expenditures vary significantly, "rang[ing] from *increased spending* of $47.9 billion in 1993 to *decreased spending* of $21.8 billion in 1994."[38] Given the totality of the evidence, competition among health care plans has theoretical potential for impeding the rise in health care spending, but the potential is unproven and would be unlikely to produce significant reductions in national health expenditures.

Would greater competition among health care plans help achieve the primary good of increased access or equity? Managed competition theorists argue that the savings from their program might be used to fund subsidies for increased access, but no assurance exists as to when, or if, savings would occur. Even if savings do occur, much of the economic benefit will accrue to the private sector; it is unclear to what extent, if any, government would benefit or whether government would use any cost savings to subsidize health care for the poor. Competition at the level of the health plan, in and of itself, promises little to increase access to health services for the currently uninsured or under-insured.

Competition can also occur at the level of the individual provider who competes in offering services to patients. The implicit assumption behind competition is that consumers purchase health care in the same way they buy durable goods or personal services. Good reasons exist, however, for believing that consumers view health care rather differently than most other goods and services. Health services are unique because they can relieve unremitting pain or suffering, restore normal functioning, or prevent premature death. If a medical service could provide a small chance of an improved quality of life or a longer life, most people would be prepared to pay an inordinate price for the service. It is precisely because health is a preeminent human value that markets cannot determine the worth of medical services to individuals in need of care.

Additionally, when persons become ill they are more appropriately seen in the subservient position of a patient rather than of an educated consumer. Patients who are suffering seldom are able to make the clear-headed economic judgments society expects of consumers in the marketplace. They are unable to accurately assess the quality of the "product" or to make reasoned judgments about alternatives.

Even if it were accurately assumed that the market would behave as theorized when buying and selling health services, the result of a well functioning market would be the opposite of that which is desirable. The essential characteristic of the marketplace is that it allocates goods and services on the basis of the ability to pay rather than on the basis of the need for the service. The market, therefore, excludes those who are unable to afford the service being sold. Seen in this way, it is not surprising that the U.S. health care system has exhibited two notable trends, both harmful to the social fabric—steadily increasing prices and greater numbers of persons unable to afford medical services. If it is true that health care is a precious and sought after commodity, the demand for services would be expected to rise. As demand increases, so should price. It would be similarly expected that individuals in poorer income groups would have a decreasing ability to purchase the product as the price rises. Since poverty is often associated with poorer health for a variety of environmental, nutritional and behavioral reasons, those who need the service most would be least likely to afford access.

Free market scholars acknowledge that the market has not worked efficiently. Rather than abandoning the idea, they choose to "fix" the health services market through greater deregulation. The results of these efforts, however, are likely to exacerbate existing problems precisely because inaccessibility and inequity are inherent concerns with competition in all markets. . . .

At least from the time of President Truman to the present day, reform of the health care system at the national level has been very much a part of the public and scholarly discourse in the United States. Yet comprehensive reform of the health care system has become, for now and the immediate future, unattainable. The country appears caught in a paradox. We value the choice and quality in the current health care system, but recognize the harm to the economy of escalating costs and the harm to the social fabric from inadequate access and inequitable distribution of services. . . .

Those in our society who tolerate significant numbers of their fellow men, women, and children going without health care coverage have a burden of carefully explaining the values that underlie their position and demonstrating why they take precedence over the health of the wider community.

NOTES

1. John K. Iglehart, *The American Health Care System,* 326 NEW ENGL. J. MED. 962, 962 (1992).

2. *See, e.g.,* Robert J. Blendon et al., *The American Public and the Critical Choices for Health Reform,* 271 JAMA 1540 (1994).

3. Iglehart, *supra* note 1, at 962.

4. *See* Sally T. Burner et al., *National Health Expenditures Projections Through 2030,* 11 HEALTH CARE FINANCE REV. at 1, 14, 20 (1992) (estimates).

5. OFFICE OF TECHNOLOGY ASSESSMENT, U.S. CONGRESS, UNDERSTANDING ESTIMATES OF NATIONAL HEALTH EXPENDITURES UNDER HEALTH REFORM 1 (1994) [hereinafter UNDERSTANDING ESTIMATES].

6. *See id.* at 1–3 (figures 1–2); Sally T. Sonnenfield et al., *Projections of National Health Expenditures Through the Year 2000,* HEALTH CARE FINANCE REV., Fall 1991, at 1, 4, 22. *See also* CONGRESSIONAL BUDGET OFFICE, PROJECTIONS OF NATIONAL HEALTH EXPENDITURES 14 (1992) [hereinafter HEALTH EXPENDITURES] (table).

7. Sarah C. Snyder, *Who Are the Medically Uninsured in the United States?,* STAT. BULL., 20, 21 (1994) (38.9 million had no private or public health insurance during 1992); BNA, *Number of Uninsured Persons Increases to 36.6 million in 1991,* Daily Labor Rep., Jan. 12, 1993, *available in* LEXIS, BNA Library, DLABRT File.

8. Emily Friedman, *The Uninsured: From Dilemma to Crisis,* 265 JAMA 2491, 2491 (1991).

9. *See How Many Americans Are Uninsured?,* 111 ARCHIVES OF OPHTHALMOLOGY 309, 309 (1993) (number of uninsured Americans varies with the method of surveying, giving a variety of numbers).

10. BUREAU OF THE CENSUS, U.S. DEP'T OF COMMERCE, HEALTH INSURANCE COVERAGE: 1987-1990: SELECTED DATA FROM THE SURVEY OF INCOME AND PROGRAM PARTICIPATION 3 (1992); Friedman, *supra* note 59, at 2491 (noting that 63.6 million lacked insurance for at least one month from 1986 to 1988).

11. FAMILIES USA FOUNDATION, HALF OF US: FAMILIES PRICED OUT OF HEALTH PROTECTION 3 (1993).

12. Alan Reynolds, *Another Big Lie,* FORBES, June 22, 1992, at 241, 241.

13. *Medical Reform Simplified,* Wall St. J., Oct. 18, 1993, at A16.

14. See id.

15. Katherine Swartz & Timothy McBride, *Spells with Health Insurance: Distributions of Durations and Their Link to Point-in-Time Estimates of the Uninsured,* 27 INQUIRY 281, 283 (1990).

16. Katherine Swartz, *Dynamics of People Without Health Insurance: Don't Let the Numbers Fool You,* 271 JAMA 64, 65 (1994) (estimating that at least 21 million people were uninsured all of 1992).

17. Id..

18. Howard E. Freeman et al., Abstract, *Uninsured Working-age Adults: Characteristics and Consequences,* 265 JAMA 2474, 2474 (1991) (noting that "the uninsured are most likely to be poor or near poor, Hispanic, young, unmarried and unemployed.")

19. *See* COMMISSION ON MONITORING ACCESS TO PERSONAL HEALTH CARE SERVICES, INSTITUTE OF MEDICINE, ACCESS TO HEALTH CARE IN AMERICA 2 (Michael Millman ed., 1993) at 17 (hereinafter ACCESS TO HEALTH CARE) (noting that population-based strategies in such areas as the environment, pollutants, health education, occupational health, and injury control could potentially "save more lives and have a greater impact on quality of life than programs to extend health services.").

20. Id. at 3 (indicators that measure health outcomes suggest that low income persons with no health insurance experience profoundly different health outcomes).

21. UNDERSTANDING ESTIMATES, *supra* note 5, at 1.

22. Id. at 1–3 (figures 1–2); Sally T. Sonnenfield, *supra* note 6 at 1, 4, 22. *See also* HEALTH EXPENDITURES, *supra* note 6, at 14 (table).

23. George J. Schieber et al., *Health Care Systems in Twenty-Four Countries,* 10 HEALTH AFF. 22, 24 (Fall 1991). *See* Timothy S. Jost & Sandra J. Tanenbaum, *Selling Cost Containment,* 19 Am. J. L., & Med. 95, 96–97 (1993).

24. *See generally* ORGANIZED FOR ECONOMIC AND COMMUNITY DEVELOPMENT, HEALTH DATA: COMPARATIVE ANALYSIS OF HEALTH CARE SYSTEMS (1991) [hereinafter COMPARATIVE ANALYSIS]; William C. Hsiao, *Comparing Health Care Systems: What Nations Can Learn from One Another,* 17 J. Health Pol., Pol'y & L. 613, 626–29 (1992).

25. Victor R. Fuchs, *The Best Health Care System in the World?,* 268 JAMA 916, 917 (1992).

26. Steffie Woolhandler & David U. Himmelstein, *The Deteriorating Administrative Efficiency of the U.S. Health Care System,* 324 NEW ENG. J. MED. 1253, 1255–56 (1991).

27. *See* JOHN RAWLS, A THEORY OF JUSTICE 95–100 (1971).

28. *See generally* Norman Daniels, *Health-Care Needs and Distributive Justice,* 10 PHIL., & PUB. AFF. 146 (1981); Norman Daniels, *Health Care Needs and Distributive Justice,* in IN SEARCH OF EQUITY: HEALTH NEEDS AND THE HEALTH CARE SYSTEM 1 (Ronald Bayer et al. eds., 1983); Norman Daniels, JUST HEALTH CARE (1985).

29. Norman Daniels, *Health Care Needs and Distributive Justice,* in IN SEARCH OF EQUITY: HEALTH NEEDS AND THE HEALTH CARE SYSTEM 115 (Ronald Bayer et al. eds., 1983). (emphasis added).

30. The poverty line was set in 1993 at the low level of $11,890 for a family of three. This leaves many families living just above the poverty line who have difficulty affording housing, food, and clothing. *See* Victor W. Sidel et al., *The Resurgence of Tuberculosis in the United States: Societal Origins and Societal Responses,* 21 J. L., MED. & ETHICS 303, 307 (1993).

31. *See* Eleanor Baugher, *Poverty,* in BUREAU OF THE CENSUS, U.S. DEP'T OF COMMERCE, POPULATION PROFILE OF THE UNITED STATES 1993, at 28 (1994).

32. Id. at 29.

33. Sidel, *supra* note 30, at 308 (citing STEFFIE WOOLHANDLER & DAVID U. HIMMELSTEIN, THE NATIONAL HEALTH PROGRAM CHARTBOOK 24 (1992)).

34. BUREAU OF THE CENSUS, U.S. DEP'T OF COMMERCE, POPULATION PROFILE OF THE UNITED STATES 1993, at 29 (1994).

35. Id.

36. Sidel, *supra* note 30, at 307.

37. Richard Kronick et al., *The Marketplace in Health Care Reform: The Demographic Limitations of Managed Competition,* 328 NEW ENG. J. MED. 148 (1993).

38. OFFICE OF TECHNOLOGY ASSESSMENT, U.S. CONGRESS, AN INCONSISTENT PICTURE: A COMPILATION OF ANALYSES OF ECONOMIC IMPACTS OF COMPETING APPROACHES TO HEALTH CARE REFORM BY EXPERTS AND STAKEHOLDERS 34 (1993) (emphasis added).

MADISON POWERS

Managed Care: How Economic Incentive Reforms Went Wrong

Madison Powers is a lawyer with a doctorate in philosophy from University College, Oxford. His research interests include political and legal philosophy, especially issues of distributive justice. Dr. Powers has taught at the Vanderbilt School of Law and the Johns Hopkins School of Public Health; he is currently director and senior research scholar at the Kennedy Institute of Ethics at Georgetown University. He is coeditor, with Ruth Faden and Gail Geller, of *AIDS, Women and the Next Generation* (Oxford). With Ruth Faden he is now completing a book entitled *The Job of Justice.*

MANAGED CARE AND INCENTIVE REFORM

In May 1991, *Journal of the American Medical Association* editor George Lundberg noted that an "aura of inevitability is upon us." What seemed inevitable to Lundberg and to almost every other knowledgeable observer at the time was the enactment of comprehensive national health care reform. The next two years were remarkable for the degree of political consensus that emerged on both the nature of the problem and the preferred solution. Surveys of both patients and physicians identified the two main deficiencies in the American health care system as uncontrollable costs and lack of universal access (Harvey 1990 and 1991). Economists Alain Enthoven and Richard Kronick (1991) labeled the problem as the "paradox of excess and deprivation."

Indeed, virtually all major parties to the debate accepted the premise that the twin problems of access and costs needed to be addressed in tandem. The Pepper Commission, for example, opined that political success in the battle for universal access required effective mechanisms for controlling costs (Rockefeller 1991). Health economists warned that universal access would remain an elusive goal without significant cost savings.

The available policy options were limited. The publicly financed and administered systems of Canada and Europe had demonstrated an ability to control costs and provide universal access. These systems provide health care to all, and they operate within the constraints of a fixed sum of money to be allocated for the benefit of an entire population. Setting a global budget or cap on aggregate expenditure made cost a primary consideration for health care decision makers. Implicit in a cost-driven system are the assumptions that not all beneficial care can be provided and that, accordingly, tradeoffs are necessary.

The incentive structure governing the United States health care system at the time was just the opposite. Fee-for-service medicine, combined with indemnity health insurance, virtually guaranteed that considerations of potential medical benefit would eclipse cost considerations. Rapid innovations in technology fueled increased demand for costly new services and whatever was perceived to be the latest and the best had a way of becoming the standard of medical care. The result was inadequate incentives for curbing the public appetite for expensive medical care, even when expected medical gains were modest or unproven.

Despite their successes, the centralized tax-based systems of Europe and Canada found little support among American political leaders. The consensus was that a distinctively American solution was needed, one built upon the existing mechanisms of private insurance companies, employer-provided health benefits, and the decentralized web of health care providers

From *Kennedy Institute of Ethics Journal* 7, no. 4 (1997), 353–360. Copyright © 1997 by The Johns Hopkins University Press. Reprinted by permission.

already in place. Presidential candidate Bill Clinton made health care reform a centerpiece of his campaign, and by late September 1992, he had embraced the key concepts of managed care and managed competition championed by the health economists in the Jackson Hole Group and by many of the nation's business leaders (Skocpol 1996).

Managed care arrangements were meant to control costs by mimicking a key component of European models. Like publicly controlled health authorities in Europe, managed care organizations (MCOs) would have the responsibility for maintaining the health of a defined population, and individual treatment decisions would be made within budget constraints that limit the total resources available for services for everyone in the plan.

Managed care alone, however, was not viewed as the complete solution. Instead of relying on global budgets set directly by the state, a managed competition model would make room for MCOs to compete for the business of cost-conscious consumers. Although specific plans differed in important respects, the main outlines of the theory were widely accepted. MCOs would put together an integrated system of health care providers and medical facilities needed for an efficient provision of services to its enrollees for a fixed per capita annual premium. Individuals would have a choice among managed care plans, and their choices would be based on price and quality of care. Employers and other sponsoring organizations—health care alliances, as they were called under the Clinton plan—would function as "market makers" (Newman 1995). They would perform an initial screening of the plans to be made available to their employees or members. All three parties—consumers, providers, and employers—would have powerful economic incentives for cost containment.

The goal of universal access would be achieved by a combination of legal requirements mandating employer-sponsored insurance and government financing for those not covered by employer sponsors. Under some managed competition proposals, additional fiscal discipline would be achieved by instituting global budgets for all sponsored plans operating in each geographic region. Employers and other health care purchasing alliances therefore would negotiate prices for health care with integrated MCOs under conditions in which aggregate expenditures either were capped by government regulation or by economic pressure that would keep expenditures within a targeted level (Enthoven 1993).

Managed competition, however, never became a reality. The Clinton legislation stalled, and public support for reform eroded (Skocpol 1996). Nonetheless, managed care—without managed competition, employer mandates, or universal access—grew by leaps and bounds in the 1990s. In the place of Enthoven's "set of economic principles which aim to focus incentives for these organizations to do the right thing" (Newman 1995), managed care developed into a system of incentives that bear faint resemblance to those Enthoven and others favored as a means of solving problems of access and cost control.

In the following sections, I identify two problems inherent in the incentive structure of MCOs developed without comprehensive health care reform, and I show how these incentives work against the public interest.

THE EQUITY-INNOVATION TRADEOFF

A central aim of managed care is to create greater downward pressure on medical costs by slowing the pace of medical innovation, especially the incorporation of high-cost, high-technology medical interventions into clinical practice. Those who worry that quality of care may be reduced too much will ask what benefit society gets in return for such a sharp reduction?

On the European model, the nature of the bargain is well understood. Tradeoffs in medical innovation and quality of care are usually made for the sake of greater equity (Reinhardt 1994). Cost savings derived from limiting expensive treatments are used to provide medical benefits for others in the population. Because the dominant incentive in public systems is the need for maintaining a broad political constituency, distributive principles resulting in the paradox of excess and deprivation are politically unpalatable. As one British physician puts it, the consensus on the appropriate tradeoffs is "bread for all before caviar for some" (Shaw 1994).

However, downward pressures on medical innovation exerted by MCOs result from very different incentives, and they involve a very different kind of tradeoff. Most MCOs are accountable first and foremost to their shareholders or governing boards. Because greater profit, or competitive advantage, not greater equity in the distribution of medical care, is the dominant incentive for MCOs, cost savings that lessen quality of care are not directly connected to a need to serve the public interest in greater equity of access.

Moreover, while uncontrollable health care costs virtually guarantee that many people will lack adequate access to health care, no knowledgeable observer thinks that the savings can lower insurance prices enough to make health care affordable to all. Indeed, nothing in the new medical marketplace offers incentives for MCOs to open their doors to the medically most expensive members of society. In fact, the intense competitive atmosphere increases market incentives for MCOs to exclude more costly enrollees from their plans. A recent study funded by the Robert Wood Johnson Foundation, for example, estimates that increasingly fierce competition in health care over the next few years will cause the number of uninsured Americans to rise from the current level of 40 million (already 6 to 9 million more than at the time of the Clinton health reform debate in 1992–93) to 67 million (Robert Wood Johnson Foundation 1996).

From a societal perspective, managed care does not serve an important element of the public interest as long as large (perhaps even larger) segments of the population lack health care even after costs have been cut and the pressure for medical innovation has been dampened. A system of managed care by itself provides no reliable mechanism for ensuring that potential sacrifices of innovation are offset by gains in equity. In short, bringing the medical arms race to an end does not guarantee how the peace dividend will be spent.

Some observers, however, may be less pessimistic, arguing that MCOs will respond to increased consumer demand for higher quality health care. They predict that quality, measured in terms of the richness of plan benefits, will join price as an important desideratum in choice of health plans, and they might point to increased marketing of plans offering direct access to medical specialists and other expanded consumer choices—e.g., point of service options—as evidence of the existence of strong market incentives for maintaining and improving quality of care.

Presently, however, there is little incentive for considerations of quality of care to figure in health plan purchase decisions. Most Americans get health coverage as a benefit of employment, and surveys of benefits managers reveal that most employers are interested chiefly in cost savings, not quality and that there are severe obstacles to assessment of differences in quality of care (Jensen et al. 1997). More importantly, most employees lack significant choice among health plans, and the trend is toward employers offering less choice among health plans. Roughly half of American workers have only one option and another quarter have only two (Etheredge, Jones, and Lewin 1996, p. 94). Absent legislation or a resurgence of the labor movement, this situation is unlikely to change. Employer incentives to cut down on costly negotiations and administrative overhead, and to deliver a large pool of enrollees to one MCO in return for substantial premium savings, are just too strong to resist.

Even if the optimists are right in supposing that there are enough available incentives to limit some of the erosion of quality of care, there may be negative implications for equity. Where the vast majority of employees once had a range of health care options, now only the more fortunate have such choices. Those who continue to have choices tend to be persons with superior bargaining position in the workplace. Thus, any change in consumer behavior toward more quality-based choice among plans is likely to come at the price of greater stratification between the health care haves and the health care have-nots.

To summarize the first dilemma of managed care: Where medical innovation is a casualty of managed care, there is little reason to expect that sacrifice will be offset by greater equity. Not only can we expect that some will continue to have caviar before there is bread for all, many of those who have had bread can expect less in the future. Managed care, divorced from its theoretical roots in a comprehensive approach to the problems of access and cost control, offers sacrifice without the promise of greater equity in return.

LONG-TERM ACCOUNTABILITY

A second problem inherent in the incentive structure of MCOs developed without comprehensive health care reform is the failure of such MCOs to address the problem of long-term accountability. Public plans in Europe operate with the expectation that they will have financial responsibility for the lifetime health outcomes of the population they serve. This expectation puts plan managers in a position to make rational and fair decisions about which treatments get priority, whether prevention will be preferred over acute care, how much, if any, to spend for research or the clinical application of new therapies, whether the claims of the young or the old are most pressing, and the like.

In the United States, however, most MCOs have no reason to expect enrollees to be their responsibility for more than a few years. People move in and out of plans, often because employers shift to new plans for reasons of cost (Jensen et al. 1997). This expectation of short-term responsibility, coupled with the ability to limit the coverage of those who enter the plan after leaving other MCOs, limits the incentives for plan managers to invest resources sufficient to maintain the long-term health of their enrollees. Hence, they lack the responsibility for making the hard choices that European plan managers must shoulder.

A more significant contributor to the long-term accountability problem is the role of Medicare and other programs for elderly health care in affecting the incentives surrounding MCO decisions. As long as MCOs can turn the burden of expensive senior care over to Medicare, the long-term care program under Medicaid, or another MCO carved out for seniors only, neither MCO plan managers concerned with their pre-65-year-old population, nor individuals concerned about prudent use of resources over their own lifetimes, nor the social institutions charged with making collective social policy are required to address questions of fair allocation among the generations.

The current arrangement is the antithesis of what proponents of managed competition advocated. The aim was to make individuals more cost-conscious consumers by forcing them to set priorities for their own care over the course of their lifetimes. The expectation was that people would forgo marginally beneficial care now provided near the end of life or in old age and that consumer demand in turn would make public and private institutional decision makers more accountable for the long-term health outcomes of the populations they serve. However, the current system of market segregation, or population-specific carve-out arrangements based on age, undermines any efforts to encourage individuals or institutional decision makers to think seriously about health care priorities over a complete lifetime.

CONCLUSION

What we are left with after the failure of the Clinton plan are small scale or incremental proposals either for preserving quality and innovation in medical care or for curbing some of the most unpopular (although not necessarily for worst) inequities of managed care. These approaches merely put off facing up to the moral and political questions raised by the equity/innovation tradeoff and long-term accountability problems.

The managed competition approach, whatever its shortcomings (and I think there are many), was a significant attempt to devise a comprehensive American alternative to European methods of addressing the twin problems of access and cost control. In its stead we have managed care, stripped of its central role for consumer choice and its commitment to universal coverage. Managed care alone, however, was never envisioned either as the right way to control costs or as a solution to the problem of access. Reformers sought to change the structure of incentives by giving individual consumers enhanced choice among competing plans and by removing market incentives for excluding persons from insurance coverage. In the present managed care environment, however, the problem of access has only worsened, and the role of consumer choice as a vehicle for controlling cost and ensuring quality of care is on its way to extinction. Individual consumers now have decreased ability to choose among competing plans or to disenroll from plans if they become dissatisfied with price, coverage, or quality of care. The kinds of incentives dominating the new medical marketplace are not what the reformers had in mind.

REFERENCES

Enthoven, Alain. 1993. The History and Principles of Managed Competition. *Health Affairs* 12: 24–46.

———, and Kronick, Richard. 1991. Universal Health Insurance Through Incentives Reform. *Journal of the American Medical Association* 265: 2532–36.

Etheredge, Lynn; Jones, Stanley; and Lewin, Lawrence. 1996. What Is Driving Health System Change? *Health Affairs* 15: 93–103.

Harvey, L. K. 1990 and 1991. *AMA Survey of Public and Physician's Opinions on Health Care Issues.* Chicago: American Medical Association.

Jensen, Gail; Morrisey, Michael; Gaffney, Shannon; and Liston, Derek. 1997. The New Dominance of Managed Care: Insurance Trends in the 1990s. *Health Affairs* 16: 125–35.

Lundberg, George. 1991. National Health Care Reform: An Aura of Inevitability is Upon Us. *Journal of the American Medical Association* 265: 2566–67.

Newman, Penny. 1995. Interview with Alain Enthoven: Is There Convergence between Britain and the United States in the Organization of Health Services? *British Medical Journal* 310: 1652–55.

Reinhardt, Uwe. 1994. Managed Competition in Health Care Reform: Just Another Dream, or the Perfect Solution? *Journal of Law, Medicine & Ethics* 22: 106–20.

Robert Wood Johnson Foundation. 1996. *Advances: The Quarterly Journal of the Robert Wood Johnson Foundation* (Issue no. 1).

Rockefeller, Jay. 1991. A Call for Action: The Pepper Commission's Blueprint for Health Care Reform. *Journal of the American Medical Association* 265:2507–10.

Shaw, A. B. 1994. In Defense of Ageism. *Journal of Medical Ethics* 20: 188–91.

Skocpol, Theda. 1996. *Boomerang: The Health Security Effort and the Anti-Government Turn in U.S. Politics.* New York: W. W. Norton.

ALLEN BUCHANAN

Managed Care: Rationing without Justice, But Not Unjustly

ETHICAL CRITICISMS OF MANAGED CARE

Managed care, the latest manifestation of efforts to privatize health care, is often passionately criticized on *ethical* grounds. The ethical criticisms most frequently voiced are these: (1) by "skimming the cream" of the patient population, managed care organizations fail to discharge their obligations to improve (or at least to not worsen) the access problem; (2) in order to contain costs, managed care organizations engage in rationing techniques that withhold some types of beneficial care and that reduce the quality of care, depriving patients of care to which they are entitled; and (3) by pressuring physicians to ration care, managed care organizations interfere with physicians fulfilling their professional fiduciary obligation to provide the best care for each patient (Council 1995; Emanuel and Dubler 1995; Rodwin 1993: 135–153; Spece, Shimm, and Buchanan 1996: 1–11).

I shall argue that each of these allegations is radically misconceived. The first criticism is misconceived because it rests on a false assumption: that the health care system within which managed care operates includes a workable division of responsibility for achieving access to care for all, and that this division of responsibility assigns obligations concerning access to managed care organizations. The second and third criticisms are misguided because they wrongly assume that we in the United States have taken the first step toward ensuring equitable access to care for all, namely, articulating a standard for what counts as the "adequate level" or "decent minimum" of care to which all are entitled. Because the current U.S. system provides no basis for assigning obligations concerning access to managed care organizations, these organizations cannot be said to violate any obligations

when they act in ways that reduce access. Because no authoritative standard has been determined for what constitutes the types and quality of care to which everyone could be said to be entitled, complaints that patients are treated unethically when they are denied care or when they receive care of less than the highest quality are groundless. Because there is no authoritative standard for the care to which everyone is entitled, there is no benchmark for determining what the physician's fiduciary obligation to the patient is, once we acknowledge that in any system in which resources are not infinite, physicians cannot be expected to provide all of the highest quality care that is of any net benefit.

The three misguided criticisms stated above obscure the most fundamental ethical flaw of managed care: the fact that it operates in an institutional setting in which no connection can be made between the activity of rationing and the requirements of justice.

WHAT MANAGED CARE IS

For our purposes a simple characterization of managed care will suffice. A managed care organization *combines* health care *insurance* and the *delivery* of a broad range of integrated health care services for *populations* of plan enrollees, financing the services *prospectively* from a predicted, limited budget. At present the following cost-containment techniques are often identified with managed care: (1) payment limits (e.g., diagnosis-related grouping [DRGs] for Medicare hospital fees); (2) requirement of preauthorization for certain services (e.g., surgeries); (3) the use of primary care physicians as "gatekeepers" to control referral to specialists; (4) so-called "deskilling" (using less highly trained providers for certain services than was customary during the premanaged care, third-party fee-for-service era); and (5) financial incentives for physicians to limit

From *Journal of Health Politics, Policy and Law,* 23, no. 4 (August 1998), 617–634. Copyright © 1998 by Duke University Press. All rights reserved. Reprinted by permission.

utilization of care (e.g., year-end bonuses or hold-backs of payments that physicians receive only if they do not exceed specified utilization limits). . . .

WHY MANAGED CARE ORGANIZATIONS HAVE NO OBLIGATIONS OF JUSTICE TO ENSURE ACCESS

Although they seem oblivious to the fact, those who currently criticize managed care organizations for marketing strategies and benefit designs that "skim the cream" of the patient population and exclude those with costly health conditions are simply repeating a fundamental mistake that the opponents of the first wave of privatization made a decade ago. In the mid-1980s, privatization of health care in the United States took the form of the rapid growth of for-profit hospitals. Critics complained that for-profit hospitals were shunning uninsured or underinsured patients and that this had the effect of dumping such patients on already financially precarious public hospitals, thereby worsening the access problem.

That such behavior on the part of for-profits has made it harder for public hospitals to serve the medically indigent is probably true. But it does not follow that in behaving in this way, for-profit hospitals are violating their obligations to help ensure access to care. They would only be guilty of violating obligations to help ensure access if they had such obligations, but they do not.

To understand why they do not, it is important to draw a distinction between two models for how access to a decent minimum or adequate level of health care for all might be achieved through the combined operation of the private sector and government entities (Buchanan 1992: 235–250). According to the first model, a private health care insurance market is expected to provide adequate care at affordable prices for a substantial portion (perhaps even a majority) of the total population, and government recognizes and acts on a commitment to fill whatever gaps in access remain. Private commercial entities, whether they are for-profit hospitals or managed care organizations, have no obligations to help ensure access. They are under no obligation to provide care that is not profitable for them to provide.

According to the second model, there is an institutionally prescribed *division of obligations to secure access* between the private and public sectors. Political processes at the highest level assign private-sector

entities determinate obligations regarding access. In the first model, the role of government is to fill whatever gaps in access remain after the market has done its job, but commercial entities in the private sector have no obligations regarding access. In the second model, private-sector entities are not simply agents in the market; they have special obligations to act in ways they would not act if they simply acted as agents in the market.

Those who charge that managed care organizations are violating ethical obligations when they engage in practices that exclude especially costly patients from coverage altogether (and thereby increase the financial strain on public providers) are implicitly assuming that in doing so, these organizations are not bearing their fair share of the burden of securing access for all. But this last assumption would only be true if the United States had adopted the second model, that is, if it actually had an institutional division of labor that assigned obligations concerning access to private commercial entities. It does not. Nor does it have a government that is willing to play the gap-filling role required by the first model (nor, apparently, is there a majority of citizens that is willing and able to demand that their representatives act so as to make government play that role).

In the absence of a political assignment of obligations to private-sector entities such as for-profit hospitals or managed care organizations, there is no more reason to assume that such entities have obligations regarding access than there is to assume that grocers have obligations to supply the poor with food or that home builders are obligated to furnish free housing (Brock and Buchanan 1986: 224–249). It will not do to say that health care is unique. Food and shelter are also essential for life. . . .

It should be clear at this point that the chief *conceptual* mistake that prevents the U.S. public and policy makers from dealing with the primary access problem (and from even framing the ethical issues of managed care in a coherent and fruitful way) is that we overlook the unpleasant fact that our system is neither an instance of model one nor of model two. My point is not that we have an access problem due to a purely conceptual mistake. Rather, what I am suggesting is that this conceptual mistake aids and abets both our unwillingness to confront the primary access problem and our confusion about what the real ethical problems of current arrangements are. This is nowhere clearer than in the muddled terms with which the debate over rationing in managed care is framed.

The lack of (1) a societal agreement on what the entitlement to health care includes and of (2) concrete institutional arrangements for seeing that all have access to a decent minimum of care through the combined operations of the private and public sectors (the implementation of either model one or model two of a mixed private-public system) undercuts the very assumptions under which the current ethical debate about rationing in managed care is conducted. This fundamental point will become clearer as we examine the controversy over rationing in managed care. . . .

WHY THE DENIAL OF CARE IN MANAGED CARE IS NOT SUBSTANTIVELY UNJUST

There are three chief ways in which rationing practices may be unethical. Rationing practices are (1) *contractually unjust* if they violate the special rights of enrollees that are generated through the contract offering the plan. Rationing practices are (2) *procedurally unjust* if there is discrimination (say, on the basis of sex or race), if the rules for limiting care are applied inconsistently, or if there are no reasonable institutional mechanisms for informing patients that rationing choices are being made and giving them opportunities to appeal decisions they believe to be unfair. Rationing practices are (3) *substantively unjust* if the principles of rationing upon which they rely are themselves unjust, even when applied consistently, without discrimination, and under conditions of adequate disclosure and due process.

Sometimes the complaint about managed care rationing practices is that they are contractually or procedurally unjust, but often it is stated or implied that they are substantively unjust. For example, there has been considerable public outrage (and several lawsuits) in response to the fact that some patients who might have benefited from autologous bone marrow transplant have been denied this treatment for breast cancer by their HMOs. In some cases, the complaint has been that denial of such care violates contractually generated rights. However, even here there is often the suggestion that contractual language concerning the provision of "comprehensive care" is to be interpreted ultimately by reference to the notion of an adequate level or decent minimum of care to which the individual is supposed to be entitled. The complaint about denial of care is then based on the assumption that the care denied falls within the adequate level or decent minimum to which each individual is entitled and that ultimately defines the "comprehensive care" that HMOs promise to deliver.

If such complaints about denial of care are understood as charges of substantive injustice, as opposed to procedural or contractual injustice, then they must rest upon an assumption that the form of treatment being denied is included in the array of services to which the individual is entitled, independently of the particular nature of the plan contract. But we have already seen that at present in the United States there is no authoritative standard for defining the scope of this entitlement. For this reason an individual who is denied some service cannot plausibly argue that the rationing practice of the organization commits an injustice by excluding a service that ought to be immune from exclusion. In the absence of an authoritative determination of what is included in the adequate level or decent minimum, virtually *no* service is in principle immune from exclusion.

It would be quite different if there were an authoritative political determination or even a rough but deep societal consensus on what the adequate level or decent minimum includes. Then disputes about whether a particular service may be denied would in principle be resolvable. But in the United States we have not settled on a standard because we have not been forced to do so as a prerequisite of trying to implement a commitment to provide universal access. Yet in the absence of a societal agreement about what services the individual is entitled to, we cannot say that a managed care organization rations unfairly when it refuses to pay for a particular form of care (unless doing so is contractually or procedurally unjust). So, unless they are construed narrowly as disagreements about contractual rights or procedural injustice, charges that managed care wrongs patients by denying certain services are simply muddled. . . .

The further we proceed into the "managed care revolution," the less convincing it is to claim that enrollees have a reasonable expectation that there will be no limits on care. If contracts and policies are reasonably clear, if rationing policies are applied in a nondiscriminatory way, if marketing does not misrepresent coverage, and if a reasonable person should know that managed care means limits, there is no basis for inferring that injustice has occurred simply because a patient does not get some beneficial care or receives care of less than the highest quality. Efforts at ethical reform within the managed care system should focus on procedural and contractual injustices and on educating patients so that their expectations are realistic, not based on imagined substantive injustices.

WHY THE REDUCTION ON QUALITY OF CARE IN MANAGED CARE IS NOT IN ITSELF UNETHICAL

The situation is similar in the case of allegations that managed care is undermining the *quality* of care. The lack of an institutional commitment to securing access to an adequate level of care for all deprives us of any rational basis for saying that anyone is *wronged* by reductions in quality for the sake of cost containment, so long as contractual rights are respected and procedural justice is observed. For example, frequently there are complaints that managed care organizations are reducing the quality of care by so-called de-skilling—using less highly trained individuals to perform certain services (e.g., having nurses do some tasks physicians have customarily performed or using social workers to do what psychiatrists used to do). Or, to take another common example, there are complaints that some HMOs are using cheaper medications that have more side effects or that are less efficacious than the best drugs available for the condition in question (e.g., using older generation tricyclic antidepressants rather than the newer serotonin-uptake inhibitors).

Using a drug that is less efficacious or that has more side effects or using a provider with lesser skills may indeed reduce the quality of care. But it does not follow that there is anything unjust or in any way unethical about doing so. Rationing practices that reduce quality of care are only unethical if they are contractually unjust, procedurally unjust, or substantively unjust. Suppose for a moment that neither of our two examples of rationing-produced reductions in care quality involve violations of contractual obligations or of the requirements of procedural justice. Is there anything unethical per se about reducing quality to reduce costs?

The answer must be no, unless one of two assumptions is granted: (1) that every patient is entitled to the highest quality care that is technically feasible, regardless of cost; or (2) that these particular reductions in quality result in the care provided falling below the level of quality that is included in the adequate level or decent minimum of care to which every individual is entitled.

At this stage of the debate over health care costs,

the falsity of the first assumption should be obvious to everyone. Providing the highest quality of care for everyone all the time is neither politically feasible nor required by any reasonable theory of just health care. Only if one denies that resources are scarce (or fails to understand that there are other goods in life besides health care) would one assume that everyone is entitled to the highest quality of care that is technically feasible, without regard to cost.

So if lower quality care is substantively unjust, it must be because it falls below the adequate level or decent minimum of care to which all are entitled. But as we have already seen, there is no societal consensus on what this is and political processes have yielded no authoritative determination of it. Of course, there may be some services that are so inexpensive and so efficacious in preventing or curing serious diseases that we can assume that they would be included in any reasonable societal consensus. But many reductions in quality wrought by managed care organizations will not fall within this uncontroversial core. For these latter quality reductions, there is no basis for saying that the organizations that effect them are acting wrongly, or that their enrollees are being deprived of something to which they are entitled.

WHY THE DENIAL OF CARE AND LOWER QUALITY ARE NOT INCOMPATIBLE WITH ETHICAL BEHAVIOR ON THE PART OF PROVIDERS

It is often said that participation in the rationing practices of managed care is incompatible with ethical behavior on the part of physicians (and nurses, etc.). The most vigorous critics seem to assume that it is unethical for physicians to provide anything other than all services that are expected to be of any benefit for the patient at the highest level of quality that is technically feasible.

This assumption, however, is indefensible. In any system, but especially in a system in which coverage is primarily financed by private employers, there must be limits on which services are provided and on the quality with which they are delivered. It is simply wishful thinking to assume that cost containment in managed care can succeed in controlling health care costs without having a negative impact on coverage and quality. (It is worth noting that some managed care organizations have explicitly acknowledged that reductions in quality are sometimes justified by emphasizing that they seek to maximize *value*, where value is understood as a function of quality and cost.)

So, in itself the fact that managed care rationing denies services and lowers quality provides no basis for saying that these organizations are requiring physicians to act unethically. In the absence of an authoritative standard for what counts as adequate care, such behavior on the part of physicians would only be unethical if physicians were obligated to provide all beneficial care and to provide only care of the highest quality. Of course, some assume that physicians have this obligation simply by virtue of being medical professionals. But if a realistic appreciation of the need to control costs in health care is to count for anything, such an understanding of the role of physicians must be rejected. There is every reason to believe that effective cost containment can only be achieved if physicians refrain from insisting on the highest quality care that is expected to be of any benefit, regardless of costs and regardless of the ratio of costs to benefits.

If this is so, then the alternatives are stark but simple: Either we hold fast to the assumption that medical professionalism is incompatible with physicians providing anything less than the highest quality care in every case, but must conclude that a system that effectively controls costs has no place for medical professionals; or we rethink our conception of medical professionalism to make room for the idea that providing less than the highest quality of care is sometimes acceptable.

The former alternative is unacceptable. There is no reason why cost control in our health care system should be held hostage to an indefensible "essentialist" conception of medical professionalism that, in effect, says that a physician cannot be a true physician or an ethical physician unless he ignores the fact that resources are scarce. None of this is to deny that physicians face serious ethical challenges in managed care. It is only to reject the groundless claim that whenever physicians do not provide all beneficial care or provide less than the highest quality care, they act wrongly. Once this point is appreciated, it becomes clear just how debilitating the absence of a standard for adequate care is. In the absence of such a standard for what patients are entitled to there is no answer to the question, "Which denials of care and how much reduction in quality is acceptable?" And there is no answer to the question: "When does the physician's participation in efforts at cost containment violate his or her fiduciary obligation to the patient?"

A disclaimer is in order at this point. My contention is not that no standards of ethical behavior apply to the actions of physicians in managed care, nor that everything physicians are asked to do by managed care organizations is ethically permissible. I have only argued that the fact that physicians do not provide potentially beneficial care, or that they provide care that is not of the highest quality, does not in itself constitute a breach of their obligations. There are other ways that physicians can go wrong ethically in the managed care environment, however. For example, if physicians encourage their patients to believe that they are acting solely as advocates for the patient's best interests, but in fact make decisions that do not maximize the patient's interests, then they act wrongly. Similarly, given the pervasive and long-standing cultural expectation that physicians are to give their patients all reasonable information about alternatives for treatment, "gag clauses" that prohibit physicians from informing their patients of potentially beneficial treatments available elsewhere that are not provided by the patient's managed care organization are unethical.

THE POVERTY OF ETHICAL THEORY

At this point it might be objected that even if there is no societal consensus or authoritative political determination of what constitutes an adequate level of care, and no existing institutional division of responsibilities for access, an appropriate conception of the moral right to health care can tell us what we need to know. The problem, however, is that no available general ethical theory or theory of justice in health care can in itself tell us what the appropriate division of labor between private and public entities for securing equitable access to health care is in a particular society at a particular point in its history. Empirical premises are needed—premises predicting what will actually work and which concrete institutional arrangements will effectively implement the right to health care, as the various theories understand this right. Moreover, there is no reason to believe that there is only one set of institutional arrangements that would secure access for all. What is needed is not only a conception of justice but also a political choice among the feasible alternatives for implementing it (White 1995: 290–291; Health Care Study Group 1994).

Similarly, no available general ethical theory or theory of justice in health care by itself can tell us what the concrete *content* of the right to health care is for a particular society at a particular time. With the exception of libertarian theories (which deny that there is a right to health care), the most influential theories of distributive justice converge on the notion that the right to health care is a limited right—a right to a decent minimum or adequate level of care, not a right to all care that would be of any benefit (President's Commission 1983; Buchanan 1996: 349–351). However, none of these theories seems capable of articulating the content of this right with sufficient specificity to provide a basis for saying which denials of care and which reductions in quality of care fall below the adequate level, even if we could assume that we actually have an institutional division of obligations that assigns managed care organizations the task of providing an adequate level of care to their enrollees.

This point about the limitations of ethical theory can best be illustrated by reference to what many believe is the most thoroughly developed account of justice in health care, Norman Daniels's adaptation of Rawls's theory. According to Daniels, the right to health care is based on the right to equal opportunity. The distinctive contribution to equal opportunity that health care makes is to prevent, restore, or compensate for adverse departures from "normal species functioning" (Daniels 1985: 26–31). Daniels's theory does give us some guidance in prioritizing various health care services: generally speaking, those that are more effective in addressing the more serious adverse departures from normal species functioning are more important.

However, as I argued some time ago, and as Daniels now acknowledges, neither his theory of justice in health care nor Rawls's general theory of distributive justice can tell us how to prioritize among the needs of different individuals (Buchanan 1983; Daniels 1993). For example, these theories provide no answer to the question, "Should we devote all or most of our health care resources to attempts to improve the conditions of those who are farthest from normal species functioning, or should some resources also be allocated for those whose departures from normal species functioning are not so serious?" In short, even the most systematic and best thought-out theory of the right to health care does not provide an answer to the question, "What is included in the adequate level or decent minimum of care to which all are entitled?"

It seems likely that ethical theory alone will not be able to provide a substantive account of what health care everyone is entitled to. Some ethical theories, such as Daniels's, may provide useful guidance on how to formulate an adequate level or decent minimum of care, but how generous the entitlement should be depends in part on the available resources in the society in question, and perhaps even on how much health care is generally valued compared to other goods. Above all, it is clear that in any pluralistic society there will be disagreements about the proper content of the right to health care that can only be resolved ultimately by procedurally just, democratic political processes, not by abstract theory. . . .

THE ILLUSION OF TECHNIQUE

In spite of the ethical complaints, managed care finds a number of supporters because it holds the promise of a technocratic solution to the problem of providing affordable, high-quality care. Managed care is not just a change in the structure of health care organizations—it is an effort to reshape the very way in which medicine is practiced, making it more scientific by fostering greater reliance on population-based outcome studies to determine which treatment modalities are most effective. However, no amount of outcome data and no improvements in the efficiency of the organization and delivery of care can answer the question, "What is the decent minimum of care to which all are entitled?" This is an unavoidably ethical question. At most, reasoning about efficiency can tell us how best to achieve the decent minimum for all and can help us make informed judgments about how generous the minimum should be, in light of trade-offs for other socially desirable goods for which the same resources might be used.

Furthermore, to the extent that its techniques are rooted in cost-benefit or cost-effectiveness methodologies and focus on the health of populations, managed care is likely to exhibit an uncritical and unarticulated bias toward purely consequentialist (utilitarian) decision making. But purely consequentialist decision making can only reveal what maximizes utility for a given group (whether it is society as a whole or the enrollees of a managed care organization); and maximizing utility for the group may come at the price of depriving some individuals of even the most basic goods. The enthusiasm for technique that characterizes managed care thus not only fails to address the fundamental issue of what the standard for care should be; it may even encourage modes of reasoning that tacitly legitimate rationing practices that compromise the commitment to treating each individual as a legitimate subject of entitlements.

CONCLUSION

I began this essay by noting that the problems of managed care seem to have eclipsed the primary access problem in the United States—the fact that over 40 million people lack health insurance (along with at least another 20 million who are radically underinsured). Before we become excessively preoccupied with the ethical dilemmas of managed care, we should pause to note that all the parties to the controversy over managed care are the "haves"—the insured population that worries about denial of beneficial care, the payers who want to control costs, and the providers who fear losing their professional autonomy and forfeiting patient trust. Conspicuously absent from this triad are the millions of uninsured. If my analysis is correct, the "haves" cannot so easily escape the "have nots"—that is, the ethics of managed care will remain a confused muddle of blame-shifting until the primary access problem is addressed. For until a societal consensus emerges on what forms of health care at what level of quality all are entitled to, and until an authoritative and realistic division of responsibilities for access is institutionalized in our mixed private-public system, the ethical debate about rationing and quality of care *in* managed care will continue to be confused and sterile. . . .

What is most ethically problematic about managed care is not that it denies beneficial care, reduces quality, and pressures physicians to act as rationers. What is most ethically problematic about managed care is the system of which it is a part, for whose most basic ethical flaw it provides, and can provide, no remedy.

REFERENCES

Brock, Dan W., and Allen Buchanan. 1986. Ethical Issues in For-Profit Health Care. In *For-Profit Enterprise in Health Care*, ed. Bradford H. Gray. Washington, DC: National Academy.

Buchanan, Allen. 1983. The Right to a "Decent Minimum" of Health Care. *Philosophy and Public Affairs* 13(2):55–78.

———. 1992. Private and Public Responsibilities in the U.S. Health Care System. In *Changing to National Health Care*, ed. Robert P. Huefner and Margaret P. Battin. Salt Lake City: University of Utah Press.

———. 1996. Health Care Delivery and Resource Allocation. In *Medical Ethics*, 2d ed., ed. Robert M. Veatch. Boston: Bartlett and Jones.

Council on Ethical and Judicial Affairs, American Medical Association. 1995. Ethical Issues in Managed Care. *Journal of the American Medical Association* 273(4):330–335.

Daniels, Norman. 1985. *Just Health Care.* Cambridge: Cambridge University Press.

———. 1986. Why Saying No to Patients in the United States Is So Hard. *New England Journal of Medicine* 314(21): 1380–1383.

———. 1993. Rationing Fairly: Programmatic Considerations. *Bioethics* 7(2–3):224–233.

Emanuel, Ezekiel J., and Nancy Neveloff Dubler. 1995. Preserving the Physician-Patient Relationship in the Era of Managed Care. *Journal of the American Medical Association* 273(4):323–329.

Health Care Study Group. 1994. Understanding the Choices in Health Care Reform. *Journal of Health Politics, Policy and Law* 19(3):499–541.

President's Commission for the Study of Ethical Problems in Medicine and Biomedical and Behavioral Research. 1983. *Securing Access to Health Care,* vol. 2. Washington, DC: U.S. Government Printing Office.

Rodwin, Marc. 1983. *Medicine, Money, and Morals: Physicians' Conflicts of Interest.* New York: Oxford University Press.

Spece, Roy G., Jr., David S. Shimm, and Allen Buchanan, eds. 1996. *Conflicts of Interest in Clinical Practice and Research.* New York: Oxford University Press.

White, Joseph. 1995. *Competing Solutions: American Health Care Proposals and International Experience.* Washington, DC: Brookings Institution.

Rationing

PETER A. UBEL AND SUSAN DORR GOOLD

"Rationing" Health Care: Not All Definitions Are Created Equal

Peter Ubel is a member of the faculty of the University of Pennsylvania's Division of General Internal Medicine. His research interests focus on the allocation of scarce health care resources and on the psychology of moral decision making. His book *Pricing Life: Why It's Time for Health Care Rationing* was published by MIT Press.

Susan Dorr Goold teaches internal medicine and is associate director for Ethics and Health Policy in the Program in Society and Medicine at the University of Michigan Medical School. Dr. Goold's research interests include ethics and managed care, finances and the doctor-patient relationship, and allocating scarce medical resources. She has published on limiting treatment, cost-utility analysis, bedside rationing, and organizational ethics consultation.

Despite consensus among most experts that health care costs need to be contained, there is great controversy about whether it is ever acceptable to ration health care. Part of this controversy results from disagreement about whether health care costs can be adequately contained by eliminating waste, rather than by rationing health care. Another part of this controversy, however, may arise from disagreement about what it means to ration health care. To the extent that this is true, people may have similar views about what health care services ought to be offered to patients, while vehemently disagreeing about the appropriateness of rationing. . . .

In this article, we explore various definitions of health care rationing and provide a simple schematic to understand and categorize these definitions. We argue that not all these definitions are equally acceptable. Instead, we favor a broad interpretation of health care rationing, whereby rationing encompasses any explicit or implicit measures that allow people to go without beneficial health care services. We argue that

From *Archives of Internal Medicine* 158 (Feb. 9 1998), 209–214. Footnotes renumbered.

this broad view of health care rationing has several advantages, most important being that it highlights the frequency with which we allow patients to go without beneficial health care services because of their cost.

DEFINITIONS OF RATIONING

. . . Rationing definitions differ in several ways. First, they differ according to whether something has to be explicit to qualify as rationing. Some argue that rationing includes only conscious decisions taken at an administrative level that make a service unavailable to some people. In contrast, others say that nonexplicit mechanisms, such as allocating goods by the free market, also qualify as rationing.

Second, they differ according to whether a resource must be absolutely scarce before its distribution qualifies as rationing. Some people think rationing is limited to the distribution of absolutely scarce resources, such as transplantable organs, while others think rationing can also refer to the allocation of nonscarce resources, such as access to subspecialists or prescriptions for expensive medicines.

Third, they differ according to whether rationing

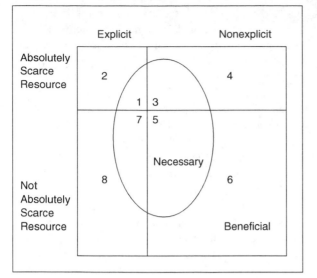

Distinctions among rationing definitions. The vertical line separates medical services that are being limited explicitly versus those limited nonexplicitly. The horizontal line separates absolutely scarce resource from those not absolutely scarce.

only involves limits on necessary services, or whether limits on any beneficial services qualify as health care rationing. By some definitions, rationing only involves withholding necessary medical services, such as dialysis for patients with end-stage renal disease. By other definitions, rationing also includes withholding beneficial (but unnecessary) services, such as the low-osmolar contrast agent described earlier.

The **figure** captures these 3 distinctions among rationing definitions. In the figure, the vertical line separates medical services that are being limited explicitly vs those that are being limited nonexplicitly. This line is to the left of the midpoint to suggest that more services are withheld nonexplicitly than explicitly, although the exact ratio of explicit-to-nonexplicit limitations is not represented. The horizontal line separates absolutely scarce resources from those that are not absolutely scarce. The horizontal line is above the midpoint of the diagram to suggest that few resources are absolutely scarce, although the exact ratio of scarce-to-nonscarce resources is not represented. Finally, within the figure is a circle. Inside the circle are those health care services believed to be necessary; outside the circle are those health care services that are believed to be beneficial but not necessary.

The figure is helpful in illustrating differences among various definitions of health care rationing.

For example, the view that rationing only includes the explicit distribution of absolutely scarce and necessary resources, such as life-saving transplantations, is represented by section 1 of the figure. The slightly less restrictive view, that rationing includes explicit distribution of absolutely scarce resources that are either necessary or beneficial, is represented by sections 1 and 2. And our view, that rationing includes any mechanism that allows people to go without beneficial health care services, is represented by sections 1 through 8. Nevertheless, as we discuss later, the 8 areas delineated by this figure are not always distinct from each other. Instead, the lines between absolutely scarce and not absolutely scarce, between explicit and nonexplicit, and between necessary and beneficial are often fuzzy.

NOT ALL DEFINITIONS ARE CREATED EQUAL
. . . In the context of health care, the term *rationing* has gained largely negative connotations in this country. When politicians say a health care policy is an example of rationing they are not intending to compliment their opponents. *Health care rationing* is a morally charged term, suggesting difficult decisions with potentially tragic consequences. An ideal definition of rationing should recognize these powerful moral connotations. With this in mind, it is worthwhile to explore various definitions of rationing to see which are best at framing the difficult moral challenges facing our health care system.

IS HEALTH CARE RATIONING LIMITED TO EXPLICIT MECHANISMS?
Some authors define rationing as the explicit denial of health care services to people who could benefit from them. By this view, rationing involves explicit decisions about how many health care goods and what type of health care goods people will receive. This definition is reminiscent of U.S. government practices during World War II, when it limited the amount of gasoline and aluminum foil, for example, that people received.

It is important to understand that, according to this definition, the explicit denial of health care services to people is not merely an example of rationing, but it is the only example of rationing. That is, for something to qualify as rationing it must involve the explicit denial of health care services to people who could benefit from them.

There is little doubt that explicitly denying health

care services to people qualifies as rationing. What is in question is whether it encompasses all of rationing. To an economist, who would view rationing broadly to include any mechanisms that limit how many goods people receive, society rations BMW cars by requiring people to pay for them. According to the explicit definition of rationing, limiting the availability of health care services by ability to pay is not an example of rationing.

If common usage were determining the best definition of health care rationing, the explicit view of rationing would win out over the economists' broader view of rationing. People do not generally think that BMW cars are rationed by ability to pay. However, people do not think about health care the way they think about automobiles or videocassette recorders. Suppose, for example, that a health care policy made life-saving bypass surgery available only to those able to pay for it. It is likely that most people would consider this policy to be an example of health care rationing. People do not think about health care goods the same way they think about other goods. Some health care services are necessary and vitally important in a way that BMWs and videocassette recorders are not.

In summary, explicit programs to deny health care services to people are appropriately classified as rationing. But, when thinking about health care rationing, we should not limit it only to such explicit mechanisms. Some health care services are so important that limiting their distribution by ability to pay can result in a type of deprivation and hardship commonly associated with rationing. Furthermore, by only calling rationing that which is explicit, one is encouraging the development and use of implicit mechanisms, or hidden rationing. Since openness (or publicity) is a vital criterion for fairness, explicit mechanisms may be preferable. Thus, while explicit mechanisms to distribute health care resources are examples of health care rationing, they are not the only things that qualify as health care rationing. Implicit mechanisms, such as market mechanisms that influence the availability of health care resources, are also examples of health care rationing.

DOES HEALTH CARE RATIONING OCCUR ONLY WHEN RESOURCES ARE ABSOLUTELY SCARCE?

Some people limit the meaning of health care rationing to apply to the distribution of scarce resources,

such as organ transplantations. For example, Evans[1] distinguishes between allocation and rationing. By allocation, he refers to aggregate level decisions about what type and amount of health care resources to make available, such as the number of intensive care beds or magnetic resonance imaging (MRI) scanners. By rationing, in contrast, he refers to "the process by which criteria are applied to selectively discriminate among patients who are eligible for resources that had been previously allocated to various programs."

By this view, rationing involves divvying up the health care pie, whereas allocation involves deciding how many pies to bake.

Evans' distinction between allocation and rationing is reminiscent of the distinction by Calabresi and Bobbit[2] between "first-order" and "second-order" tragic choices. Their book, *Tragic Choices,* explores the painful choices that become necessary when goods are scarce. First-order tragic choices determine how much of a particular item will be available, for example, the number of dialysis machines in the United States. Second-order tragic choices involve deciding who should receive available resources. . . .

By calling both first-order and second-order decisions tragic choices, Calabresi and Bobbit are able to highlight the moral significance of both kinds of decisions. Evans' distinction between allocation and rationing suggests a stronger separation than exists. Even Calabresi and Bobbitt admit that their distinction between first- and second-order decisions is an oversimplification. Rather, there are multiple levels of rationing decisions, and influence can travel from higher levels to lower levels or vice versa. Higher level decisions generally affect more people than lower level ones. For example, a public policy decision to base health care on a free market has a huge effect on almost everyone, and a corresponding decision to link health insurance with employment has a large effect on unemployed people, who have less insurance than others. At a lower level, a managed care organization's decision not to hire a pediatric surgeon would mainly affect children in the plan who need surgery, although it may free up more resources for other patients in the managed care plan. At the lowest level, a decision by a physician that a specific health care resource is not medically necessary would primarily affect the individual patient in question. But even these lowest level decisions influence, in a small way, higher levels. The number of MRIs available to physicians, for example, influences their decisions about who needs an MRI, while physicians' collective decisions about who needs an MRI influence higher level decisions about whether to purchase additional MRIs. All these decisions, whether implicit or explicit, whether involving absolutely scarce resources or relatively scarce resources, have important implications for health care rationing. All layers may involve tragic choices.

IMPLICATIONS FOR WHETHER HEALTH CARE RATIONING INVOLVES WITHHOLDING OR DISTRIBUTING SERVICES

If health care rationing occurred only when resources were absolutely scarce, then rationing would not primarily involve the withholding of these resources, but would involve the distribution of these scarce resources to those who could benefit from them. Some people would get the scarce resources and others would not. In such a scenario, it would make sense to talk about the resource being rationed to some people and rationed from others. . . .

In situations where resources are not absolutely scarce, health care rationing generally involves the withholding of services from patients. For example, if a physician decides not to order an MRI scan for a patient because the benefits are not worth the cost of an MRI, that MRI scan has been rationed from the patient. In contrast, if a physician decides to order an MRI scan for the patient because it is the most beneficial thing to do, it is not an example of health care rationing; the physician did not ration the MRI scan to the patient. Instead, there was no rationing in this case, because the patient received the most beneficial thing available. This decision may have rationing implications; the cost of the MRI may make fewer resources available for other patients. But unless this relationship between using one resource to the detriment of another is fairly direct, it makes little sense to describe this physician's decision to order an MRI scan as an example of rationing.

In summary, while it makes sense in some contexts to talk about rationing health care to patients rather than from patients, in most contexts, and in most discussions of health care rationing, attention is focused on withholding resources from patients. Thus, our discussion focuses on definitions of health care rationing that center on allowing patients to go without health care resources.

DOES HEALTH CARE RATIONING OCCUR ONLY WHEN WITHHELD SERVICES ARE NECESSARY?

. . . The phrase "beneficial health care service" does not have the strong implications that "necessary health care service" does for resource allocation decisions. Necessary services seem, almost by definition, to be necessary. We must provide them. Beneficial services, on the other hand, do not have to be provided. In fact, most people are probably willing to admit that cosmetic surgery is beneficial for fashion models while not wanting to make it part of any basic benefits package.

Determining which health care services are beneficial also requires difficult value judgments. For example, how do we decide when an unproved but theoretically promising treatment is beneficial? Nevertheless, determinations of which services are beneficial are less value laden than are the determinations of which services are necessary, because they do not involve cost-worthiness judgments. If yearly Pap smears bring more medical benefit than Pap smears every 3 years, then yearly Pap smears are beneficial, regardless of their financial cost. Expert panels deciding which necessary services to include in a basic benefits package must decide whether the additional costs of yearly Pap smears are justified. In contrast, panels deciding whether the intervention is beneficial do not have to make such cost-worthiness judgments. For this reason, some argue that decisions about determining basic benefits packages should not be made by expert panels, but instead by more representative bodies.

A great advantage of defining rationing as the withholding of beneficial services is that it will point out that it is no longer possible, if it ever was, to offer people every potentially beneficial medical service. Instead, determinations of which services are beneficial will often identify beneficial services that are unaffordable. Difficult judgments about whether to offer these benefits will no longer be made to look like scientific judgments about whether the benefits are truly necessary. Instead, people will recognize the need to make value judgments about whether specific beneficial services can be offered to everyone.

In addition, by equating rationing with the withholding of any beneficial medical service, we can use the word's negative connotations to draw attention to difficult moral decisions about which benefits are worth pursuing. By focusing attention on our inability to offer beneficial services to all who need them, we can highlight morally questionable health care policies that create inequitable access to beneficial health care. For example, it is not difficult to convince the public that allowing millions of people to be uninsured or underinsured is an example health care rationing. . . .

People do not like rationing. They should not like a health care system that allows so many people to live without adequate insurance. By equating rationing with the withholding of beneficial care, we can highlight the terrible consequences of having so many uninsured and underinsured people.

CHOOSING A BROAD DEFINITION OF HEALTH CARE RATIONING

We content that health care rationing is best defined as implicitly or explicitly allowing people to go without beneficial health care services. By arguing for this broad definition of health care rationing, we do not suggest that there is only 1 meaning of the term *health care rationing*. Instead, we argue that a broad definition of health care rationing is a more useful starting point for debates about health care policy and health care priority setting. . . .

As mentioned earlier, the dividing lines illustrated in the figure, between absolutely scarce and nonscarce resources, between explicitly and implicitly withheld resources, and between necessary and beneficial resources, are not nearly as sharp as the figure suggests. Where, for example, is the line between beneficial and necessary health care services? Given the fuzziness of these distinctions, it seems arbitrary to limit rationing to any of the narrow definitions that rely on maintaining these distinctions. Instead, a broad definition of rationing, by acknowledging the arbitrariness of these distinctions, focuses our attention less on distinctions and more on whether particular health care services are appropriate to withhold from patients. While we could debate whether cosmetic surgery is necessary or beneficial, it is much more important to decide whether all patients who want a specific type of cosmetic surgery should receive it.

Our broad definition of rationing will include many occurrences that do not strike most people as morally problematic and will include others where it is clearly wrong to withhold services from patients. It will force people to deal with the gray areas in moral debates about what patients ought to receive and what they should be allowed to live without. This broad definition of rationing forces us to deal with the moral issues in their full and troubling complexity.

By choosing this broad definition of health care rationing, we create room for many types of rationing, a number of which are suggested by the distinctions discussed earlier. For example, there is explicit rationing and implicit rationing, rationing of absolutely scarce resources and of fiscally scarce resources, and rationing of necessary resources and of beneficial but unnecessary resources. Similarly, it is highly likely that there are more and less justifiable types of rationing. By this broad definition of health care rationing, rationing is not defined as de facto inappropriate. Indeed, a major advantage of this broad view of rationing is that it forces us to decide when it is acceptable to allow particular patients to go without beneficial health care services.

It should be understood that this broad view of rationing is not without problems. There is no consensus, for example, about what constitutes beneficial health care. As discussed earlier, some of this debate occurs because many health care services have not been studied enough to show whether they are beneficial. Other parts of this debate occur because of more irresolvable controversies. What should we do, for example, about therapies that are beneficial for some subgroups of patients but, when used in aggregate, are not beneficial? These issues are beyond the scope of this article, but are clearly where much of the debate about health care policy ought to focus.

REFERENCES

1. Evans RW. Health care technology and the inevitability of resource allocation and rationing decisions. *JAMA* 1983;249: 2208–2219.

2. Calabresi G, Bobbit P. *Tragic Choices: the Conflicts Society Confronts in the Allocation of Tragically Scarce Resources.* New York, NY: WW Norton & Co Inc; 1978.

NORMAN DANIELS

Rationing Fairly: Programmatic Considerations

Despite its necessity, rationing raises troublesome questions about fairness. We ration in situations in which losers, as well as winners, have plausible claims to have their needs met. When we knowingly and deliberately refrain from meeting some legitimate needs, we had better have justification for the distributive choices we make. Not surprisingly, health planners and legislators appeal to bioethicists for help, asking what justice requires here. Can we help them? I think we are not ready to yet, and I will support this claim by noting four general rationing problems that we remain unsure how to solve, illustrating how they plague Oregon's rationing plan.

Before turning to the four problems, I want to make several preliminary remarks. First, philosophers (including me) have traditionally underestimated the importance of rationing, thinking of it as a peripheral, not central problem. Since we simply cannot afford, for example, to educate, treat medically, or protect legally people in all the ways their needs for these goods require or the accepted distributive principles seem to demand, rationing is clearly pervasive, not peripheral.

Rationing decisions share three key features. First, the goods we often must provide—legal services, health care, educational benefits—are not divisible without loss of benefit, unlike money. We thus cannot avoid unequal or "lumpy" distributions. Meeting the educational, health care or legal needs of some people, for example, will mean that the requirements of others will go unsatisfied. Second, when we ration, we deny benefits to some individuals who can plausibly claim they are owed them in principle. They can cite an accepted principle of distributive justice that governs their situation and should protect them. Third,

From *Bioethics* 7 (1993), 224–233. Copyright © 1993 Basil Blackwell Ltd. Reprinted by permission.

the general distributive principles appealed to by claimants as well as by rationers do not by themselves provide adequate reasons for choosing among claimants: they are too schematic. This point was driven home to me by the way in which my "fair equality of opportunity" account of just health care (Daniels 1985, 1988) fails to yield specific solutions to the rationing problems I shall survey. Finally, even the best work in the general theory of justice has not squarely faced the problems raised by the indeterminacy of distributive principles. Rawls (1971), for example, suggests that the problem of fleshing out the content of principles of distributive justice is ultimately procedural, falling to the legislature. Perhaps, but the claim that we must in general turn to a fair democratic procedure should not be an assumption, but the conclusion, either of a general argument or of a failed search for appropriate moral constraints on rationing. If however, there are substantive principles governing rationing, then the theory of justice is incomplete in a way we have not noticed. This point cuts across the debates between proponents of "local justice" (Walzer 1983; Elster 1992) and "global justice" (Rawls 1971; Gauthier 1986), and between liberalism and communitarianism (cf. Emanuel 1991; Daniels 1992).

FOUR UNSOLVED RATIONING PROBLEMS: ILLUSTRATIONS FROM OREGON

THE FAIR CHANCES/BEST OUTCOMES PROBLEM

Before seeing how the fair chances/best outcomes problem arises in Oregon's macrorationing plan, consider its more familiar microrationing form: Which of several equally needy individuals should get a scarce resource, such as a heart transplant? Suppose, for example, that Alice and Betty are the same age, have waited on queue the same time, and that each will live only one week without a transplant. With the transplant, however, Alice is expected to live two years and Betty twenty. Who should get the transplant (cf. Kamm 1989)? Giving priority to producing best outcomes, a priority built into some point systems for awarding organs, would mean that Betty gets the organ and Alice dies (assuming persistent scarcity of organs, as Brock (1988) notes). But Alice might complain, "Why should I give up my only chance at survival—and two years of survival is not insignificant—just because Betty has a chance to longer? It is not fair that I give up everything that is valuable to me just so Betty can have more of what is valuable to her." Alice demands a lottery that gives her an equal chance with Betty.

Some people agree with Alice's complaint and agree with her demand for a lottery. Few would agree with her, however, if she had very little chance at survival; more would agree if her outcomes were only somewhat worse than Betty's. Still, at the level of intuitions, there is much disagreement about when and how much to favor best outcomes. Brock (1988), like Broome (1987), proposes breaking this deadlock by giving Alice and Betty chances proportional to the benefits they can get (e.g., by assigning Alice one side of a ten sided die). Kamm (1989, 1993) notes that Brock's proposal must be amended once we allow differences in urgency or need among patients. She favors assigning multiplicative weights to the degree of need or urgency. Then, the neediest might end up with no chance to receive a transplant if their outcomes were very poor, but, compared to Brock's "proportional chances" proposal, they would have greater opportunity to get an organ if their outcomes were reasonably high. Both Brock's and Kamm's suggestions seem ad hoc. That there is some force to each of Alice's and Betty's demands does not, as Brock would have it, mean the force is clearly equal; similarly, assigning weights to more factors, as Kamm does, seems to add an element of precision lacking in our intuitions about these cases. Our intuitions may fall short of giving us clear, orderly principles here.

We might try to break the deadlock at the level of intuitions by appealing to more theoretical considerations. For example, we might respond to Alice that she already has lost a "natural" lottery; she might have been the one with twenty years expected survival, but it turned out to be Betty instead. After the fact, however, Alice is unlikely to agree that there were no prior differences in access to care and so on.

To undercut Alice's demand for a new lottery, we would have to persuade her that the proper perspective for everyone to adopt is *ex ante*, not *ex post* information about her condition (cf. Menzel 1989). But what should Alice know about herself *ex ante*? If Alice knows about her family history of heart disease, she might well not favor giving complete priority to best outcomes. Perhaps Alice should agree it is reasonable to adopt more radical *ex ante* position, one that denies her all information about herself, a thick "veil of ignorance." Controversy persists. Behind such a veil, some would argue that it would be irrational to forego the greater expected payoff that would result from giving priority to best outcomes. Citing Rawls's adoption of a maximin strategy, Kamm (1993) argues against such "gambling" behind the veil. Alternatively, she appeals to Scanlon (1982): if Alice would "reasonably regret" losing to Betty, then she should not be held to a scheme that favors best outcomes. Unclear about our intuitions, we are also stymied by a controversy at the deepest theoretical levels.

The best outcomes problem arises in macrorationing as well. Consider HSS Secretary Louis Sullivan's (1992) recent refusal to grant a Medicaid waiver to Oregon's rationing plan. Sullivan's main criticism of the Oregon plan is that in preferring treatments that provide greater net benefits the plan discriminates against the disabled. The clearest example of such discrimination would be this: Two groups of patients, both in need of a treatment that can give them a net benefit of a given magnitude; because one group has a disability, e.g., difficulty walking, that would not be affected by the treatment, we deny them the treatment. Neither Sullivan nor the NLC give an example, even hypothetical, of how this situation could arise in the Oregon scheme. The denial of coverage for aggressive treatment of very low birthweight (<500 gr) neonates, which they do cite as an example of discrimination, is not an appropriate example, because the denial is premised on the lack of benefit produced by aggressive treatment of such neonates.

Consider an example suggestive of the Oregon scheme. Suppose two treatments, T1 and T2, can benefit different groups of patients, G1 and G2 as follows. T1 preserves life for G1's (or provides some other major benefit), but it does not restore a particular function, such as walking, to G1s. T2 not only preserves life for G2s (or provides some other major benefit), but it also enables them to walk again. The Oregon Health Service Commission ranks T2 as a more important service than T1 because it produces a greater net benefit (I ignore the OTA (1991) argument that net benefit is not a major contributor to rank). Sullivan says that it is discriminatory to deny G1s T1, even though a single person would clearly consider relative benefit in deciding between T1 and T2.

The Sullivan/NLCMDD objection can, with charity, be interpreted as a version of Alice's complaint that favoring best outcomes denies her a fair chance at a benefit. Interpreted this way, the Sullivan/NLCMDD objection is that we cannot rule out giving G1s any chance at the benefit treatment would bring them simply because G2s would benefit more from the use of our limited resources. In effect, they seem to be saying we should give no weight to best outcomes. As I noted earlier, this extreme position does not seem to match our intuitions in the microrationing case. But neither does the alternative extreme position, that we must always give priority to better outcomes. The point is that a rationing approach that ranks services by net benefit, whether it turns out to be Oregon's scheme or simply Hadorn's (1991) alternative proposal, thus carries with it unsolved moral issues. To justify ranking by net benefit we must be prepared to address those underlying issues.

THE PRIORITIES PROBLEM

Oregon's (intended) methodology of ranking by net benefit also ignores the moral issues I group here as the priorities problem. Suppose that two treatment condition pairs give equal net benefits. (Remember, this [does] not generally mean they produce the same health outcomes, only the same net benefits). Then the OHSC should rank them equal in importance. But now suppose that people with C1 are more seriously impaired by their disease or disability than people with C2. Though T1 and T2 produce equivalent net gains in benefit, people with C2 will end up better off than people with C1, since they started out better off. Nothing in the method of ranking treatment/condition pairs by net benefit responds to this difference between C1s and C2s. Nevertheless, most of us would judge it more important to give services to C1s than it is to give them to C2s under these conditions. We feel at least some inclination to help those worse off than those better off. For example, if C1s after treatment were no better off than C2s before treatment, we are more strongly inclined to give priority to the worse off. Our concern to respect that priority might decline if the effect of treating C1s but not C2s is that C1s end up better off than C2s. How troubled we would be by this outcome might depend on how great the

new equality turned out to be, or on how significant the residual impairment of C2s was.

Suppose now that there is greater net benefit from giving T2 to C2s than there is from giving T1 to C1s. If C1s are sufficiently worse off to start with than T2s, and if C1s end up worse off or not significantly better off than C2s, then our concern about priorities may compel us to forego the greater net benefit that results from giving T2 to C2s. But how much priority we give to the worst off still remains unclear. If we can only give a very modest improvement to the worst off, but we must forego a very significant improvement to those initially better off, then we may overrule our concern for the worst off. Our intuitions do not pull us toward a strict priority for the worst off.

Just what the structure of our concern about priority is, however, remains unclear. The unsolved priorities problem not only affects a methodology that ranks by net benefit or by net QLY's. It affects cost/benefit and cost/effectiveness rankings, including Eddy's (1991a) "willingness to pay" methodology. So too does the aggregation problem, to which I now briefly turn.

THE AGGREGATION PROBLEM

In June of 1990, the Oregon Health Services Commission released a list of treatment/condition pairs ranked by a cost/benefit calculation. Critics were quick to seize on rankings that seemed completely counterintuitive. For example, as Hadorn noted (1991), toothcapping was ranked higher than appendectomy. The reason was simple: an appendectomy cost about $4,000, many times the cost of capping a tooth. Simply aggregating the net medical benefit of many capped teeth yielded a net benefit greater than that produced by one appendectomy.

Eddy (1991b) points out that our intuitions in these cases are largely based on comparing treatment/condition pairs for their importance on a one:one basis. One appendectomy is more important than one toothcapping because it saves a life rather than merely reduces pain and preserves dental function. But our intuitions are much less developed when it comes to making one:many comparisons (though we can establish indifference curves that capture trades we are willing to make; cf. Nord 1992). When does saving more lives through one technology mean we should forego saving fewer through another? The complex debate about whether "numbers count" has a bearing on rationing problems. How many legs should we be willing to forego saving in order to save one life? How many eyes? How many teeth? Can we aggregate *any* small benefits, or only those that are in some clear way significant, when we want to weigh these benefits against clearly significant benefits (e.g. saving a life) to a few? Kamm (1987, 1993) argues persuasively that we should not favor saving one life and curing a sore throat over saving a different life, because curing a sore throat is not a "competitor" with saving a life. She also argues that benefits that someone is morally not required to sacrifice in order to save another's life also have significant standing and can be aggregated. If we are not required to sacrifice an arm in order to save someone's life, then we can aggregate arms saved and weigh them against lives saved. She suggests that our judgments about aggregation differ if we are in contexts where saving lives rather than inducing harms (positive vs. negative duties) are at issue.

Kamm shows that we are not straightforward aggregators of all benefits and that our moral views are both complex and difficult to explicate in terms of well-ordered principles. These views are not compatible with the straightforward aggregation (sum ranking) that is presupposed by the dominant methodologies derived from welfare economics. Yet we do permit, indeed require, some forms of aggregation. Our philosophical task is to specify which principles governing aggregation have the strongest justification. If it appears there is no plausible, principled account of aggregation, then we have strong reason to rely instead on fair procedures and an obligation to give any of them.

THE DEMOCRACY PROBLEM

When Sullivan rejected Oregon's application for a Medicaid waiver, he complained that the methodology for assessing net medical benefit drew on biased or discriminatory public attitudes toward disabilities. Adapting Kaplan's (Kaplan and Anderson 1990) "quality of wellbeing" scale for use in measuring the benefit of medical treatments, Oregon surveyed residents, asking them to judge on a scale of 0 (death) to 100 (perfect health) what the impact would be of having to live the rest of one's life with some physical or mental impairment or symptom; for example, wearing eyeglasses was rated 95 out of 100, for a weighting of −0.05. Many of these judgments seem downright

bizarre, whether or not they reflect bias. For example, having to wear eyeglasses was rated slightly worse than the −0.046 weighting assigned to not being able to drive a car or use public transportation or the −0.049 assigned to having to stay at a hospital or nursing home. Other weightings clearly reflected cultural attitudes and possibly bias: having trouble with drugs or alcohol was given the second most negative weighting (−0.455) of all conditions, much worse than, for example, having a bad burn over large areas of your body (−0.372) or being so impaired that one needs help to eat or go to the bathroom (−0.106). Having to use a walker or wheelchair under your own control was weighted as much worse (−0.373) than having losses of consciousness from seizures, blackouts or coma (−0.114).

Claiming that people who experience a disabling condition, like being unable to walk, tend to give less negative ratings to them than people who have experienced them, Sullivan argued Oregon was likely to underestimate the benefit of a treatment that left people with such disabilities. Excluding such treatments would thus be the result of public bias.[1] His complaint carries over to other methodologies, e.g., Eddy's (1991) willingness-to-pay approach and the use of QLY's in cost-effectiveness or cost-benefit analyses.

Sullivan's complaint raises an interesting question: Whose judgments about the effects of a condition should be used? Those who do not have a disabling condition may suffer from cultural biases, overestimating the impact of disability. But those who have the condition may rate it as less serious because they have modified their preferences, goals, and values in order to make a "healthy adjustment" to their condition. Their overall dissatisfaction—tapped by these methodologies—may not reflect the impact that would be captured by a measure more directly attuned to the range of capabilities they retain. Still, insisting on the more objective measure has a high political cost and may even seem paternalistic.

Sullivan simply assumes that we must give priority to the judgments made by those experiencing the condition, but that is not so obvious. Clearly, there is something attractive about the idea, embedded in all these methodologies, of assessing the relative impact of conditions on people by asking them what they think about that impact (cf. Menzel 1992). Should we give people what they actually want? Or should we give them what they should want, correcting for various defects in their judgment? What corrections to expressed preferences are plausible?

The democracy problem arises at another level in procedures that purport to be directly democratic. The Oregon plan called for the OHSC to respect "community values" in its ranking of services. Because prevention and family planning services were frequently discussed in community meetings, the OHSC assigned the categories including those services very high ranking. Consequently, in Oregon, vasectomies are ranked more important than hip replacements. Remember the priority and aggregation problems: it would seem more important to restore mobility to someone who cannot walk than to improve the convenience of birth control through vasectomy in several people. But, assuming that the Commissioners properly interpreted the wishes of Oregonians, that is not what Oregonians wanted the rankings to be. Should we treat this as error? Or must we abide by whatever the democratic process yields?

Thus far I have characterized the problem of democracy as a problem of error: a fair democratic process, or a methodology that rests in part on expressions of preferences, leads to judgments that deviate from either intuitive or theoretically based judgments about the relative importance of certain health outcomes or services. The problem is how much weight to give the intuitive or theoretically based judgments as opposed to the expressed preferences. The point should be put in another way as well. Should we in the end think of the democratic process as a matter of pure procedural justice? If so, then we have no way to correct the judgment made through the process, for what it determines to be fair is what counts as fair. Or should we really consider the democratic process as an impure and imperfect form of procedural justice? Then it is one that can be corrected by appeal to some prior notion of what constitutes a fair outcome of rationing. I suggest that we do not yet know the answer to this question, and we will not be able to answer it until we work harder at providing a theory of rationing.

CONCLUSION

I conclude with a plea against provincialism. The four problems I illustrated have their analogues in the rationing of goods other than health care. To flesh out a principle that says "people are equal before the law" will involve decisions about how to allocate legal services among all people who can make plausible claims to need them by citing that principle. Similarly, to give content to a principle that assumes equal educational opportunity will involve decisions about re-source allocation very much like those involved in rationing health care. Being provincial about health care rationing will prevent us from seeing the relationships among these rationing problems. Conversely, a rationing theory will have greater force if it derives from consideration of common types of problems that are independent of the kinds of goods whose distribution is in question. I am suggesting that exploring a theory of rationing in this way is a prolegomenon to serious work in "applied ethics."

REFERENCES

Brock, Dan. 1988. "Ethical Issues in Recipient Selection for Organ Transplantation." In D. Mathieu (ed.) *Organ Substitution Technology: Ethical, Legal, and Public Policy Issues.* Boulder: Westview. pp. 86–99.

Broome, John. 1987. "Fairness and the Random Distribution of Goods." (Unpublished manuscript.)

Capron, Alexander. 1992. "Oregon's Disability: Principles or Politics?" *Hastings Center Report* 22: 6 (November-December): 18–20.

Daniels, Norman. 1985. *Just Health Care.* Cambridge: Cambridge University Press.

Daniels, Norman. 1988. *Am I My Parents' Keeper? An Essay on Justice Between the Young and the Old.* New York: Oxford University Press.

Daniels, Norman. 1992. "Liberalism and Medical Ethics," *Hastings Center Report.* 22: 6 (November-December): 41–3.

Eddy, D. 1991a. "Rationing by Patient Choice," *JAMA* 265: 1 (January 2): 105–08.

Eddy, D. 1991b. "Oregon's Methods: Did Cost-Effectiveness Analysis Fail?" *JAMA* 266: 15 (October 16): 2135–41.

Elster, John. 1992. *Local Justice: How Institutions Allocate Scarce Goods and Necessary Burdens.* New York: Russel Sage.

Emanuel, Ezekiel. 1991. *The Ends of Human Life: Medical Ethics in a Liberal Polity.* Cambridge, MA: Harvard University Press.

Gauthier, D. 1986. *Morals By Agreement.* Oxford: Oxford University Press.

Hadorn, David. 1992. "The Problem of Discrimination in Health Care Priority Setting," *JAMA* 268: 11 (16 September): 1454–59.

Kamm, Frances. 1987. "Choosing Between People: Commonsense Morality and Doctors' Choices," *Bioethics* 1: 255–71.

Kamm, Frances. 1989. "The Report of the US Task Force on Organ Transplantation: Criticisms and Alternatives," *Mount Sinai Journal of Medicine* 56: 207–20.

Kamm, Frances. 1993. *Morality and Mortality,* Vol. 1. Oxford: Oxford University Press.

Kaplan, R.M. Anderson, J.P. 1990. "The General Health Policy Model: An Integrated Approach." In B. Spilker (ed.) *Quality of Life Assessments in Clinical Trials.* New York: Raven Press.

Menzel, Paul. 1989. *Strong Medicine.* New York: Oxford University Press.

Menzel, Paul. 1992. "Oregon's Denial: Disabilities and Quality of Life," *Hastings Center Report* 22: 6 (November-December): 21–25.

National Legal Center for the Medically Dependent and Disabled. 1991. Letter to Representative Christopher H. Smith.

Nord, Eric. 1992. "The Relevance of Health State After Treatment in Prioritising Between Different Patients," *Journal of Medical Ethics*. (forthcoming).

Office of Technology Assessment. 1991. *Evaluation of the Oregon Medicaid Proposal*. U.S. Congress (final draft in press).

Oregon Health Services Commission. 1991. *Prioritization of Health Services: A Report to the Governor and Legislature*.

Rawls, John. 1971. *A Theory of Justice*. Cambridge, MA: Harvard University Press.

Scanlon, Thomas. 1982. "Contractualism and Utilitarianism." In Amartya Sen and Bernard Williams, eds. *Utilitarianism and Beyond*, pp. 103–28. Cambridge: Cambridge University Press.

Sullivan, Louis. 1992. Press Release (August 3, 1992). Health and Human Services Press Office.

Walzer, Michael. 1983. *Spheres of Justice*. New York: Basic.

NOTE

1. The OTA (1991) notes that men gave dismenorhea a greater negative weight than women. The effect of this weighting is that greater net benefit, and thus higher rank accrues to treating dismenorhea if we include the judgments of men than if we counted only the judgments of women.

LEONARD M. FLECK

Just Caring: Oregon, Health Care Rationing, and Informed Democratic Deliberation

Leonard M. Fleck is currently professor of philosophy and medical ethics at Michigan State University. Dr. Fleck's main areas of teaching and research are medical ethics, health care policy, and social and political philosophy. His most recent major research project has been the book *Just Caring: The Moral and Political Challenges of Health Reform and Health Care Rationing*.

What does it mean to be a just and caring society when we have only limited resources and virtually unlimited health care needs that must be met? This is the problem of health care rationing. This is *the* central problem of health reform for the foreseeable future. Oregon has taken the lead in addressing this problem. Health care rationing is a ubiquitous phenomenon, though few recognize that, because rationing is accomplished for the most part in invisible ways that effectively hide the practice from critical scrutiny.

What is distinctive of Oregon is that its citizens chose to make explicit, visible, systematic rationing decisions that would be a product of democratic deliberations that were morally and rationally justifiable. For its efforts Oregon has been subjected to intense moral and political criticism, claiming that it is the politically weak, sick poor who will bear the burden of health care rationing. . . .

From *Journal of Medicine and Philosophy* 19 (1994), 367–388. Copyright © Swets & Zeitlinger Publishers. Used with permission.

I. IS THE OREGON RATIONING PLAN FAIR?

We begin with two preliminary claims. First, the problems of health reform in general, and health care rationing in particular, are fundamentally moral and political problems, and only secondarily economic or organizational problems. . . . Health care services are not simply commodities in the market, like VCRs, that can be justifiably distributed in accord with individual ability to pay. As Daniels has argued, access to needed and effective health care is essential to protecting fair equality of opportunity in our society. Thus, health care ought to be thought of as a public good, as a public interest, and hence, as a legitimate object of public policy.

Our second preliminary claim is that *justice*, not beneficence, is the fundamental moral value that ought to govern the debates about health reform options. . . . What I have in mind is a Rawlsian, moderately egalitarian contractarian conception of justice congruent with our liberal democratic commitments. . . (Rawls, 1993). However, there are morally distinctive features of health care that require the articulation of a conception of "health care justice" (Fleck, 1989b). In this essay our goal is to articulate some considered judgments of just health care rationing.

Oregon sought to achieve two health policy objectives simultaneously: (1) expand access to needed health care for the uninsured, and (2) control health care costs for the state. . . . What is noteworthy is that these policies were justified by a very explicit appeal to moral principles. John Kitzhaber, physician-president of the Oregon Senate, has listed eight publicly approved principles behind this legislation (Kitzhaber, 1990). The first of these required "universal access for the state's citizens to a basic level of health care" while the fourth asserted that it is "the obligation of society to provide sufficient resources to finance a basic level of care for those who cannot pay for it themselves" (Kitzhaber, 1990).

Note that it is not *equal access* to health care that Oregon feels morally obligated to guarantee to the poor and uninsured. For Oregon the poor and uninsured do not have a moral claim to a middle class standard of care, but to *basic care*. There are *limits* to society's obligation to assure access to needed health care because, according to Oregon's eighth principle, "allocations for health care must be part of a broader allocation policy which recognizes that health can only be maintained if investments in a number of related areas are balanced" (Kitzhaber, 1990). These include housing, education, and highways, all of which are important public goods, all of which have legitimate claims on public resources, but none of which have unlimited claims on these resources. Granting this, how can we determine fairly and rationally what will count as basic health care that must be guaranteed to all citizens?

Oregon's response to our question was that there was no perfectly objective, uniquely rational, or indisputably fair way of answering it. At bottom, however, this was a process question that would have to be resolved through open, democratic dialogue whose outcome would be shaped both by social value judgments and medical information. The goal of the dialogue would be a prioritization of health services, a ranking of 709 medical-condition/treatment pairs, from those that were most effective in addressing a given medical problem and yielding substantial benefit at a reasonable cost, to those that were marginally effective at best and yielded only small benefits at often unreasonable costs.

Though the public dialogue initially shaped this prioritization process, the ultimate responsibility for

the final rankings fell to a Commission comprised of eleven individuals. Then the legislature chose a funding level. The legislature was barred from tinkering with the rankings. All the services above that line constituted the basic package of health services guaranteed to all citizens in Oregon; the services below the line would not be funded. Morally speaking, services below the line did not represent futile or medically inappropriate or non-beneficial care. Rather, they represented marginally beneficial care, where the benefits were very uncertain or relatively small, especially in relationship to costs. This is health care rationing.

The well-known case of Coby Howard put a human face on the practice of rationing. Howard's death came about when it did and as it did because of a deliberate social choice not to fund bone marrow transplants. Middle class children in Oregon in the same medical circumstances as Coby did receive bone marrow transplants paid for by their parents' health insurance. Is it morally right that middle class children should have an opportunity for survival denied to poor *children?* . . .

II. THE INESCAPABILITY OF HEALTH CARE RATIONING

It is by now a truism that escalating health care costs are socially problematic. However, rising costs do not, of themselves, yield the conclusion that rationing is necessary, morally or politically, as a policy response. There are compelling reasons for resisting rationing as a cost containment strategy if there are other viable cost containment approaches. Rationing seems morally objectionable because: (1) needed, potentially beneficial health care is directly denied an identifiable individual; (2) the denial of these benefits is coercively imposed, not freely chosen; (3) the benefits that they are denied may be very substantial, such as life itself, and often irreplaceable and uncompensatable; (4) the individuals denied these benefits are sick and vulnerable; (5) the denial of benefits to individuals will appear to be arbitrary because the primary reason for the denial will be economic; (6) the ultimate source of the rationing decision disadvantaging this individual will be government, and government is supposed to protect equally the rights of all; and (7) the proximate source of the rationing decision will often be an individual's personal physician, ideally a loyal and uncompromised advocate for that individual.

The above paragraph represents the first premise in the anti-rationing argument. The second premise is that there are alternative ways of effectively controlling health costs that do not have the morally objectionable features associated with rationing. The unholy trinity of waste, fraud, and abuse are usually cited, and proposed remedies include: more effective utilization review (Angell, 1985), better technology assessment, banning self-referral by physicians (Rodwin, 1993), and reducing administrative waste (Himmelstein and Woolhandler, 1994). This list fairly represents premise two in the anti-rationing argument, which concludes that rationing is unnecessary given all these morally legitimate, barely tried alternatives to health care cost containment.

Note that critics of rationing construe the concept very narrowly. The most critical defining features seem to be that an identified individual is denied needed health care through a coercive government policy, and this seems to violate the social values of compassion and respect for individual liberty.

One implication of this narrow construal of rationing is that it will appear to be conceptually inappropriate to speak of "rationing by ability to pay." Markets distribute by ability to pay, but this seems to be done in a wholly impartial, mechanical manner that is wholly indifferent to the welfare of any identified individual. However, this is a dodge. One of the features of markets is that they do diffuse responsibility for bad outcomes, often creating the impression that these outcomes are a product of chance and the workings of specific markets. . . .

Angell (1985), Brown (1991) and Relman (1991a; 1991b) imagine that more rational and efficient overall management of health care system and the use of health services will result in cost containment without rationing. Health planning, technology assessment, utilization review and practice protocols are recommended to control health costs without the objectionable moral consequences associated with rationing. Yet all these cost containment methods will in various circumstances result in "preventable" deaths and harms. But these deaths and harms will be mixed so thoroughly with non-preventable, natural deaths and harms from assorted medical problems that they will all appear equally fated and equally unfortunate, whereas death or harm to someone like Coby Howard that is the product of an explicit rationing decision will appear to be uncaring and unjust and preventable.

Is this in fact a morally correct judgment? I do not believe it is.

Implicit rationing is, first, a pervasive feature of our approaches to health care cost containment, and it is at least as morally problematic as Oregon's explicit approach to health care rationing. Second, that there are *identifiable* individuals who are the "victims" of health care rationing is morally and conceptually irrelevant. Here I disagree with Hadorn (1991b). What is conceptually essential to rationing is that someone makes a judgment regarding kinds of health care that are judged to be non-costworthy and marginally beneficial. Once that judgment is made there will always be individuals who will bear the consequences of that decision. Third, there is nothing intrinsically immoral about any rationing decision. The real moral question is whether a particular individual has a just claim to the health care that he will be denied. But, fourth, what is presumptively morally problematic about *implicit* forms of rationing is that all manner of arbitrary, discriminatory, and clearly unjust rationing decisions can be effectively hidden from moral scrutiny by anyone, including the individuals who are the victims of these choices. Hence, for its commitment to explicit rationing Oregon deserves moral commendation, not condemnation. Fifth, Oregon did make a moral mistake in the Coby Howard case, for it represented piecemeal, uncoordinated rationing, which will always be morally difficult to justify. Oregon's subsequent efforts at rationing and priority setting in a more comprehensive, rational, systematic fashion are immune to such criticism. But the many forms of implicit rationing that are pervasive features of most of our current approaches to health care cost containment continue to be morally objectionable because they are piecemeal and uncoordinated. This reflects our highly fragmented approach to health care financing, which both permits and encourages irresponsible cost-shifting. . . .

III. OREGON AND HEALTH CARE RATIONING: KEY MORAL LESSONS

We will draw eleven key moral lessons from Oregon's experience with health care rationing, explicate them, then respond to the moral criticisms directed at Oregon's efforts.

Lesson One: Rationing decisions made in a piecemeal, uncoordinated fashion are very likely to be arbitrary and unjust. Fair rationing decisions must be a product of comprehensive, systematic, rational deliberation. This is the main lesson of the Coby Howard case. Rationing decisions always imply trade-offs. Health resources will be denied to some health needs because there are other health needs that have a stronger just claim to those resources. When rationing is done systematically and explicitly, then we know what trade-offs we have endorsed, and those trade-offs are open to rational and moral assessment.

Lesson Two: Rationing decisions made publicly are open to critical assessment and correction, and are more likely to be just. Oregon was not the first state to permit the denial of life-sustaining medical care to a Medicaid patient. This is surely a routine occurrence in Medicaid programs and for patients who are without health insurance (Hadley, 1991; Lurie, 1984). But denials are effected subtly and are essentially hidden from the public scrutiny, as well as scrutiny by the patient himself which means there is ample opportunity for invidious discrimination.

Lesson Three: The whole process of health reform and health rationing must be guided by explicit moral considerations, such as health care justice, and only secondarily be economic or managerial or organizational considerations. There are thousands of children and adults like Coby Howard, whose lives are threatened by a deadly illness and whose lives could be prolonged if they had access to some expensive life-prolonging medical technology, such as a bone marrow transplant. Whether they have a just claim to that technology will not be settled by an economic equation or organizational theory or more clinical data. We need to address that issue directly as a moral problem. Further, allocational problems caused by advancing medical technology are not an oddity in our health care system; they are at the heart of twentieth-century technological medicine.

Lesson Four: Fair rationing decisions ought to be a product of informed democratic decisionmaking processes that include all who will be affected by the decision.

Lesson Five: If all who will be affected by rationing decisions have a fair opportunity to shape these decisions, then these rationing decisions will be freely self-imposed, which is an essential feature of just rationing decisions.

Lesson Six: Stable community membership over the course of a life is essential to preserving the fairness of the rationing process. Individuals cannot have the option of enjoying the benefits of health reform in a given community only to exit the community when the burdens of rationing fall upon them.

Lessons four through six comprise our "principle of community" for health care rationing. All of us as citizens must take responsibility for health reform; experts alone will not do. Expert knowledge is essential for intelligent rationing decisions, but expert knowledge is not a suitable replacement for public moral judgment and public moral responsibility for fair rationing judgments.

Moreover, rationing decisions are more likely to be fair if they are decisions that are self-imposed rather than being imposed by some (healthy individuals) on others (sick and vulnerable individuals). Note that for a liberal society embedded in this principle of community must be a principle of autonomy with respect to health care rationing: just rationing decisions must be freely self-imposed. These two principles must be inextricably linked with one another as a practical matter and as a moral matter. . . .

What the Oregon approach recognizes is that a budget for meeting health needs must be communally agreed to. As noted earlier, there is no perfectly objective way of identifying health needs because there are value considerations necessarily bound up with that determination, and because emerging medical technologies are constantly adding "new" health needs. This means there is no perfectly objective way of determining that communal health budget. That will require a balancing judgment that takes into account other important social needs. In a democratic society all should have the opportunity to participate in the making of that balancing judgment since all will be affected by the results of that judgment.

In order for such impartial circumstances to yield actually fair health priorities and rationing protocols all who have a voice in shaping those protocols and priorities must be ongoing members of that community so that all are more or less equally at risk of having to accept the burdens of rationing. . . .

Lesson Seven: Justice requires that there be limits that health care makes on total societal resources, and that these limits be expressed in the form of hard budgets. The moral virtue of hard budgets is that they make clear and visible the trade-offs that must be made among competing health needs.

Lesson Eight: Hard budgets give structure and coherence to a process of prioritizing health needs/services. A process of prioritizing that is explicit, rationally determined, and freely agreed to protects fairness against special pleading.

Lesson Nine: Those who are least well off healthwise have presumptively stronger moral claims to needed health resources so long as they are able to benefit sufficiently from those resources, and so long as their health needs are fairly judged as being of sufficiently high priority from the larger social perspective embodied in the prioritization process. No individual has a right to unlimited health care; and no individual has a moral right to have their health needs met at the expense of the more just (higher priority) health claims of others.

Lesson Ten: Physicians are more likely to protect their own moral integrity as loyal advocates of their patients' best interests and as fair rationers of societal resources if they make their rationing decisions within the framework of a fixed global budget and a system of health priorities that have been freely agreed to by all who are part of that health care system. This is the perspective that allows physicians to be just and compassionate to patients over the course of their life.

Lesson Eleven: Equity and efficiency must be achieved together. We will not have fair or effective or affordable or stable health reform if we attempt to maximize either of these social values at the expense of the other.

Oregon is less than a perfect exemplar of the moral lessons regarding just health care rationing sketched above. The most frequently voiced criticism of Oregon is that the poor were exploited to achieve health reform. That is, Oregon committed itself to achieving nearly universal access to health care and hoped to pay for it by imposing a rationing system on the poor, that is, those who were least well off. The objective was clearly laudable, but the means to the objective were unjust (Daniels, 1991, p. 2232). I have defended Oregon on this point at some length (Fleck, 1990c). I argue that this policy choice must be assessed from the perspective of non-ideal justice. More precisely, Oregon can justifiably argue that the poor as a class are better off under the reform proposal than they are under the current Medicaid program, which covers only 58% of the poor. All the poor can now be assured access to a basic package of health services. It is also morally relevant that rational poor persons, suitably informed, would autonomously choose this reform package over the current Medicaid program.

Daniels readily concedes that Oregon has achieved a more equitable health care system. However, he adds that "even greater reductions in inequality are possible if other groups sacrifice instead of Medicaid recipients. It is unfair for current Medicaid recipients to bear a burden that others could bear much better, especially since inequality would then be even further reduced" (1991, pp. 2232–33). Better-off Oregonians, for example, could pay more taxes in support of the Medicaid program. Indeed, an actual attempt was made to cover all state employees with the same benefit package and rationing protocols as the Medicaid population, but that measure was soundly defeated in the state legislature. Morally, this outcome is bothersome. Moreover, it is not consistent with the principle of community discussed above, since it appears that the healthy and powerful are imposing rationing protocols on the sick and poor, who are not in a fair bargaining position. . . .

IV. JUSTICE, RATIONING, AND DEMOCRATIC DELIBERATION

We now turn to a consideration of rational democratic deliberation as an approach to health care rationing. There are two criticisms of this process I will address. First, the poor were not fairly represented in the democratic forums in Oregon integral to priority-setting and were the ones who ended up having to bear the risks and burdens of rationing. Prima facie, this looks like a morally insensitive middle class majority imposing its will on the politically weak, sick poor.

This first criticism can be addressed if the following conditions are met: (1) We must all belong to one or another Accountable Health Plan. . . . Alternatively, we must all belong to the same single-payer health care system, where "all belong" means that there is no potentially morally objectionable sorting of individuals according to socio-economic status or health status. (2) Belonging to the plan must mean that there is a single health budget to purchase all health services for plan members. (3) We must know the budget cannot cover all likely demands for health services. (4) We must limit demands on the budget through a priority-setting process and mutually agreed upon rationing protocols that apply equally to all members of the plan. (5) We must be largely ignorant of our future health care needs, which is largely true for most of us most of the time. If these conditions are met, then the likelihood is that the rationing protocols and health priorities that emerge from a rationally informed process of democratic deliberation will be "just enough" or "fair enough." This is to concede that there will be future individuals who will die "prematurely" because they will have been denied the only medical intervention that promised them some additional opportunity for prolonged life for no better reason than that it was the informed and impartial judgment of the community that the benefits promised by these interventions were too small, too costly, and too uncertain. The essential fairness of the process is secure because any member of that community, given the right circumstances, could be the individual denied particular interventions.

A second critical objection is the democracy problem (Daniels, 1993). Democracy is about respecting expressed preferences. Daniels points out that Oregonians in community meetings were very concerned about assured access to family planning services. As a result vasectomies were rated more highly in the priority setting process than hip replacements for the elderly. Daniels asks whether we must abide by whatever the democratic process yields? If we see this as a matter of pure procedural justice, then there is no correcting of results that seem counter-intuitive. But if it can be corrected by an appeal to some prior notion of what counts as a fair rationing outcome, then we might wonder what the point of the democratic process is.

Yet another rationing problem is the "fair chances/best outcome" problem (Daniels, 1993, p. 225), which I see as related to the democracy problem. Daniels borrows the following example from Frances Kamm (1989). Alice and Betty are both in need of a liver transplant; both are the same age and have waited the same period of time for a transplant; both will be dead in a week without the transplant. With the transplant Alice will live only two years while Betty will live twenty. Who should get the transplant? We get the best outcome, maximum number of quality-adjusted life years saved, by saving Betty. But Alice wants a lottery, in effect arguing that each has an equal right to life, however long the rest of their life might be. Both have reasonable and morally compelling considerations on their side. Oregon's democratic deliberations favored the net benefit approach. The critical issue is whether Alice has a moral right to be aggrieved as this result. Has she been harmed in

a morally significant sense, and does this undermine the moral authority of the democratic deliberative process for yielding just results?

In responding I want to sketch a somewhat idealized version of just rational democratic deliberation. We begin with the assumption that no matter how fine-grained a conception of health care justice we develop, it will never be fine-grained enough to generate a uniquely correct complete set of just rationing protocols. There are innumerable reasonable, morally permissible trade-offs that might be made in articulating some set of rationing protocols. I will refer to this moral space as "the domain of the just democratic decisionmaking." Again, within this space we have no reason to believe that we could identify something that could justifiably be called the "most just" set of rationing protocols possible for our society. Many possible trade-off patterns will be "just enough," all things considered, especially when we recall that there are other values besides justice that are a legitimate part of the overall moral equation.

There are two critical conditions that elicit and justify the need for a democratic deliberative process of decisionmaking. The first is that we cannot simply allow individual liberty to resolve this particular rationing decision. For if we did allow medical or administrative or consumer discretion to be ultimately determinative, the result would be the potential for arbitrary or discriminatory results that would be unjust. . . .

Our second condition for appealing to the rational democratic deliberative process is that there are these plural choice possibilities, all of which have prima facie moral and political legitimacy, but none of which are unequivocally superior from a moral, political, or rational perspective. This is the situation we are faced with regard to Alice and Betty. A good case can be made for going with a decision rule that might favor a lottery in this situation, or going with net benefits. There are any number of very complex decisions rules we might adopt, especially if we vary morally relevant case facts, such as the ages of the individuals, the gap between likelihood of survival for each, morally permissible quality of life consideration, and so on. What is morally important is that whatever decision rule we adopt through the democratic deliberative process is one that is applied consistently over time to all members of that society/health plan. So long as that decision rule is in place and was, in fact, approved by both Alice and Betty (or their democratic representatives) at some prior point in time when they did not know that their future medical circumstances, neither one will have just cause for moral complaint, no matter what the outcome. Again, one of the other assumptions we have to work with is that individual participants in this democratic process are ongoing members of this community so that the trade-offs they agree to, some specific distribution of benefits and burdens, or benefits and risks, is a distribution that they are imposing on themselves. That is, in many cases of rationing, say, with reference to the health care needs of the elderly (our future elderly selves), the distribution of benefits and burdens do not occur simultaneously with respect to any individual. It would clearly be unfair for a younger individual to derive the benefits of rationing health care for the elderly, then have the option of exiting that health plan as an older person to escape the risks/burdens of rationing for the elderly.

Two other large points must be made with respect to understanding the moral and political legitimacy of rational democratic decisionmaking. The first is that this "democratic space" should be thought of as being bounded and structured by principles of health care justice. These principles have emerged and will emerge through the same process of moral discourse that has generated medical ethics as we know it today. These principles should be thought of as having a status akin to constitutional principles, which is to say that any proposed rationing protocol that violated one of these principles would have to be rejected.

Among such principles, I would include: (1) a Publicity Principle, aimed at eliminating invisible rationing; (2) a Fair Equality of Opportunity Principle; (3) an Equality Principle, the intent of which is to assure each citizen equal moral consideration; (4) an Autonomy Principle: (5) a Just Maximizing Principle; (6) Need-Identification Principles, to distinguish health needs from health preferences; (7) Priority-Setting Principles; and (8) a Neutrality Principle aimed at protecting the liberal character of our society with respect to choosing health services in our benefit package. . . .

In concluding, Oregon failed to meet important requirements of just democratic decisionmaking. But it was an instructive failure. Oregon should not be thought of as being morally culpable for its failures; we however, would be morally culpable if we failed to learn the lessons of Oregon.

REFERENCES

Aaron, H.: 1992, "The Oregon experiment," in *Rationing America's Medical Care: The Oregon Plan and Beyond,* M. Strosberg *et al.* (eds.), The Brookings Institution, Washington, D.C., pp. 107–11.

Angell, M.: 1985, "Cost containment and the physician," *Journal of the American Medical Association* 254, 1203–07.

Brown, L.: 1991, "The national politics of Oregon's rationing plan," *Health Affairs* 10 (Summer), 28–51.

Daniels, N.: 1991, "Is the Oregon rationing plan fair?" *Journal of the American Medical Association* 265, 2232–35.

Daniels, N.: 1993, "Rationing fairly: programmatic considerations," *Bioethics* 7, 224–33.

Fleck, L. M.: 1990c, "The Oregon medicaid experiment: is it just enough?" *Business and Professional Ethics Journal* 9 (Fall) 201–17.

Hadley, J. et al.: 1991, "Comparison of uninsured and privately insured hospital patients: condition on admission, resource use, and outcome," *Journal of the American Medical Association* 265, 274–78.

Hadorn, D. C.: 1991a, "Oregon priority-seeting exercise: quality of life and public policy," *The Hastings Center Report* 19 (May/June), S11–16.

Hadorn, D. C.: 1991b, "Setting health care priorities in Oregon: cost-effectiveness meets the rule of rescue," *Journal of the American Medical Association* 265, 2218–25.

Himmelstein, D. U. and Woolhandler, S.: 1994, *The National Health Program Book: A Source Guide for Advocates,* Common Courage Press, Monroe, Maine.

Kamm, F.: 1993, *Morality, Mortality: Death and Whom to Save From It,* Volume 1, Oxford University Press, Oxford, England.

Kitzhaber, J.: 1990, "Rationing health care: the Oregon model," *The Center Report,* The Center for Public Policy and contemporary Issues (Denver) 2 (Winter), 3–4.

Lurie, N. *et al.*: 1984, "Termination from Medi-Cal—does it affect health?" *The New England Journal of Medicine* 311, 480–84.

Oregon Health Services Commission: 1991, *Prioritization of Health Services: A Report to the Governor and the Legislature,* Salem, Oregon.

Rawls, J.: 1993, *Political Liberalism,* Columbia University Press, New York.

Relman, A.: 1991a, "Is rationing inevitable?" *The New England Journal of Medicine* 322, 1809–10.

Relman, A.: 1991b, "The trouble with rationing," *The New England Journal of Medicine* 323, 911–12.

Rodwin, M.: 1993, *Money, Medicine, and Morals,* Oxford University Press, Oxford, England.

SUGGESTED READINGS FOR CHAPTER 2

Acheson, Sir Donald (Chairperson). *Independent Inquiry into Inequalities in Health: Report.* London: The Stationery Office, published for the Department of Health, 1998.

American Journal of Bioethics 1 (Spring 2001). Special issue on "Justice, Health, and Healthcare."

Benatar, Solomon R. "Health Care Reform in the New South Africa." *New England Journal of Medicine* 336 (March 20, 1997), 891–95.

Bodenheimer, Thomas. "The Oregon Health Plan—Lessons for the Nation." *New England Journal of Medicine* 337, nos. 9, 10 (1997), 651–56, 720–24.

Bole, Thomas J., and Bondeson, William B., eds. *Rights to Health Care.* Boston: Kluwer, 1991.

Brock, Dan W. "Justice, Health Care, and the Elderly." *Philosophy & Public Affairs* 18 (1989), 297–312.

———. "Justice and the ADA: Does Prioritizing and Rationing Health Care Discriminate against the Disabled?" *Social Philosophy and Policy* 12 (1995), 159–85.

Buchanan, Allen. "Health-Care Delivery and Resource Allocation." In Robert M. Veatch, ed., *Medical Ethics,* 2d ed. Boston: Jones and Bartlett, 1997, 321–61.

———. "Trust in Managed Care Organizations." *Kennedy Institute of Ethics Journal* 10 (2000), 189–212.

Callahan, Daniel. "Managed Care and the Goals of Medicine." *Journal of American Geriatrics Society* 46 (March 1998), 385–88.

———. *Setting Limits: Medical Goals in an Aging Society.* New York: Simon & Schuster, 1987.

———. *What Kind of Life: The Limits of Medical Progress.* New York: Simon & Schuster, 1990.

Chapman, Audrey R., ed. *Health Care Reform: A Human Rights Approach.* Washington, DC: Georgetown University, 1994.

Churchill, Larry M. *Self-Interest and Universal Health Care: Why Well-Insured Americans Should Support Coverage for Everyone.* Cambridge, MA: Harvard University Press, 1994.

Daniels, Norman. *Just Health Care.* New York: Cambridge University Press, 1985.

———. *Justice and Justification: Reflective Equilibrium in Theory and Practice.* New York: Cambridge University Press, 1997.

———. "National Health-Care Reform." In Robert M. Veatch, ed., *Medical Ethics,* 2d ed. Boston: Jones and Bartlett, 1997, 415–41.

———. "Rationing Fairly: Programmatic Considerations." *Bioethics* 7 (1993), 224–33.

———. *Seeking Fair Treatment: From the AIDS Epidemic to National Health Care Reform.* New York: Oxford University Press, 1995.

Daniels, Norman, Kennedy, Bruce P., and Kawachi, Ichiro. "Why Justice Is Good for Our Health: The Social Determinants of Health Inequalities." *Daedalus* 128 (Fall 1999): 215–25.

Daniels, Norman, Light, Donald W., and Caplan, Ronald L. *Benchmarks of Fairness for Health Care Reform.* New York: Oxford University Press, 1996.

Daniels, Norman, and Sabin, James E. "Closure, Fair Procedures, and Setting Limits within Managed Care Organizations." *Journal of the American Geriatrics Society* 46 (1998), 351–54.

———. "Last Chance Therapies and Managed Care." *Hastings Center Report* 28 (March/Apr. 1998), 27–41.

DeGrazia, David. "Why the United States Should Adopt a Single-Payer System of Health Care Finance." *Kennedy Institute of Ethics Journal* 6 (1996), 145–60.

Dougherty, Charles J. "And Still the Only Advanced Nation without Universal Health Coverage." *Hastings Center Report* 27 (July-August 1997), 39–41.

———. *Back to Reform: Values, Markets, and the Health Care System.* New York: Oxford University Press, 1996.

Elster, Jon. *Local Justice: How Institutions Allocate Scarce Goods and Necessary Burdens.* New York: Russell Sage Foundation, 1992.

Emanuel, Ezekiel J. *The Ends of Human Life: Medical Ethics in a Liberal Polity.* Cambridge, MA: Harvard University Press, 1991.

———, and Dubler, Nancy N. "Preserving the Physician-Patient Relationship in the Era of Managed Care." *Journal of the American Medical Association* 273 (1995), 323–29.

Engelhardt, H. Tristram. "Freedom and Moral Diversity: The Moral Failures of Health Care in the Welfare State." *Social Philosophy & Policy* 14 (1997), 180–96.

Epstein, Richard. *Mortal Peril: Our Inalienable Right to Health Care?* Reading, MA: Addison-Wesley, 1997.

Fleck, Leonard M. "Justice, HMOs, and the Invisible Rationing of Health Care Resources." *Bioethics* 4 (1990), 97–120.

Goold, Susan D. "Allocating Health Care: Cost-Utility Analysis, Informed Democratic Decision Making, or the Veil of Ignorance?" *Journal of Health Politics, Policy, and Law* 21 (1996), 69–98.

Hall, Mark A. *Making Medical Spending Decisions: The Law, Ethics, and Economics of Rationing Mechanisms.* New York: Oxford University Press, 1997.

———. "The Problem with Rule-Based Rationing." *The Journal of Medicine and Philosophy* 19 (1994), 315–32.

Health Affairs 10 (1991). Special issue on "Rationing."

Journal of the American Geriatrics Society 40 (1992). Special issue on "Ethics and Rationing."

Journal of Health Politics, Policy and Law 24 (February 1999). "Special Reports from the Field on The Oregon Plan."

Journal of Medicine and Philosophy 19 (August 1994). Special issue on the "Oregon Health Plan."

Journal of Medicine and Philosophy 26 (April 2001). Special issue on "Children and a Fair Share of Health and Dental Care."

Kitzhaber, John A. "The Oregon Health Plan: A Process for Reform." *Annals of Emergency Medicine* 23 (February 1994), 330–33.

Mechanic, David. "Dilemmas in Rationing Health Care Services: The Case for Implicit Rationing." *British Medical Journal* 310 (1995), 1655–59.

Menzel, Paul T. "Equality, Autonomy, and Efficiency: What Health Care System Should We Have?" *Journal of Medicine & Philosophy* 17 (1992), 33–57.

———. *Strong Medicine: The Ethical Rationing of Health Care.* New York: Oxford University Press, 1990.

Moreno, Jonathan D. "Recapturing Justice in the Managed Care Era." *Cambridge Quarterly of Healthcare Ethics* 5 (1996), 493–99.

Nord, Erik. *Cost-Value Analysis in Health Care: Making Sense Out of QALYs.* Cambridge: Cambridge University Press, 1999.

Nord, Erik, et al. "Incorporating Societal Concerns for Fairness in Numerical Valuations of Health Programmes." *Health Economics* 8 (1999), 25–39.

Orentlicher, David. "Destructuring Disability: Rationing of Health Care and Unfair Discrimination against the Sick." *Harvard Civil Rights-Civil Liberties Law Review* 31 (1996): 49–87.

———. "Health Care Reform and the Patient-Physician Relationship." *Health Matrix: Journal of Law-Medicine* 5 (1995), 141–80.

Patrick, Donald L., and Erickson, Pennifer. *Health Status and Health Policy.* New York: Oxford University Press, 1993.

Pellegrino, Edmund. "Managed Care and Managed Competition: Some Ethical Reflections." *Calyx* 4 (Fall 1994): 1–5.

Powers, Madison. "Justice and the Market for Health Insurance." *Kennedy Institute of Ethics Journal* 1 (1991), 307–23.

———, and Faden, Ruth. "Inequalities in Health, Inequalities in Health Care: Four Generations of Discussion about Justice and Cost-Effectiveness Analysis." *Kennedy Institute of Ethics Journal* 10 (June 2000), 109–27.

President's Commission for the Study of Ethical Problems in Medicine and Biomedical and Behavioral Research. *Securing Access to Health Care.* Vols. 1–3. Washington, DC: U.S. Government Printing Office, 1983.

Rawls, John. *The Law of Peoples.* Cambridge, MA: Harvard University Press, 1999.

Reinhardt, Uwe E. "Reforming the Health Care System: The Universal Dilemma." *American Journal of Law and Medicine* 19 (1993), 21–36.

Relman, Arnold S. "The Trouble with Rationing." *New England Journal of Medicine* 323 (September 27, 1990), 911–13.

Ubel, Peter A. "The Challenge of Measuring Community Values in Ways Appropriate for Setting Health Care Priorities." *Kennedy Institute of Ethics Journal* 9 (1999): 263–84.

Veatch, Robert M. "Single Payers and Multiple Lists: Must Everyone Get the Same Coverage in a Universal Health Plan?" *Kennedy Institute of Ethics Journal* 7 (1997), 153–69.

Weinstein, Milton C., and Stason, William B. "Allocating Resources: The Case of Hypertension." *Hastings Center Report* 7 (October 1977), 24–29.

World Health Organization. *The World Health Report 2000—Health Systems: Improving Performance.* Geneva: World Health Organization, 2000.

Yarborough, Mark. "The Private Health Insurance Industry: The Real Barrier to Healthcare Access?" *Cambridge Quarterly of Healthcare Ethics* 3 (1994), 99–107.

BIBLIOGRAPHIES AND REFERENCE WORKS

Curran, William J., et al. *Health Care Law and Ethics.* New York: Aspen Law & Business, Inc., 1998. (Includes bibliographical references.)

Becker, Lawrence, and Charlotte Becker, eds. *Encyclopedia of Ethics,* New York: Garland, 1992.

Leatt, Peggy, et al. *Perspectives on Physician Involvement in Resource Allocation and Utilization Management: An Annotated Bibliography.* Toronto: University of Toronto, 1991.

Lineback, Richard H., ed. *Philosopher's Index.* Vols. 1–. Bowling Green, OH: Philosophy Documentation Center, Bowling Green State University. Issued quarterly. Also CD Rom.

National Library of Medicine (NLM) Gateway. http://gateway. nlm.nih.gov.

Reich, Warren, ed. *Encyclopedia of Bioethics,* 2d ed., New York: Macmillan, 1995.

Walters, LeRoy, and Kahn, Tamar Joy, eds. *Bibliography of Bioethics.* Vols. 1–. New York: Free Press. Issued annually.

3.
Autonomy Rights and Medical Information

INTRODUCTION

The problems investigated in this chapter are (1) the conditions under which patients and related parties should have control over medical information and decisionmaking, and (2) how health professionals should manage and protect medical information.

MEDICAL CONFIDENTIALITY

The section on medical confidentiality in this chapter provides a strong link to traditional medical ethics, where rules of confidentiality have played a significant role since the Hippocratic Oath. There the physician vows: "What I may see or hear in the course of treatment or even outside of the treatment in regard to the life of men . . . I will keep to myself."

In the first selection in this chapter, Mark Siegler questions whether the tradition of confidentiality has been reduced to a "decrepit" concept of more symbolic than real value. Siegler maintains that traditional medical confidentiality has been systematically compromised in the course of modern bureaucratic health care and data storage systems that allow informational access to a large number of persons. He argues that infringements of confidentiality have become routine events in medical practice—the rule rather than the exception.

Siegler's article raises the question of whether medical confidentiality is an especially strict duty, a relic of the past, or a requirement in need of reconstruction. In addressing this question, we can begin by asking what would justify a practice of maintaining medical confidentiality in a profession in which access to vital information may mean the difference between life and death. Two general types of justification have been proposed for the confidentiality principle. The first type of justification appeals to the principle of respect for autonomy. The argument is that the health professional does not show proper respect for the patient's autonomy and privacy if he or she does not uphold the confidentiality of the professional-patient relationship. A variant of this approach asserts that there is an implied promise of confidentiality inherent in the professional-patient relationship, whether the professional explicitly recognizes the promise or not. In the absence of an explicit acknowledgment that confidentiality does *not* hold, the patient would always be entitled to assume that it does hold.

A second justification is that confidentiality should be maintained because it is a necessary condition of properly doing the work of a physician (or nurse or hospital). If confidentiality were ignored in medical practice, patients would be unwilling to reveal sensitive information to health professionals. This unwillingness would render diagnosis and cure more difficult and, in the long run, would be detrimental to the health of patients. The assumption is that the physician-patient relationship rests on a basis of trust that would be imperiled if physicians were not under an obligation to maintain confidence.

The second justification appeals to the positive *consequences* of confidentiality, whereas the first looks to a moral violation that would be wrong irrespective of the kinds of consequences envisaged in the second. That is, the first justification maintains that breaches of trust, broken promises, and failures to keep contractual obligations are themselves wrong, whereas the second looks not at what is intrinsically wrong but instead at whether the balance of the consequences supports maintaining confidentiality.

The second justification has been at the center of recent controversy about confidentiality. Its consequentialist commitments require that we compare the benefits of keeping confidences with the benefits of revealing confidential information in circumstances in which the information is desperately needed by another party. If through this comparison it turns out that there is an overriding duty to warn persons who might be seriously harmed if confidentiality were maintained, then confidentiality is not an absolute duty. Yet many have long held that confidentiality is an absolute duty.

A now classic case of conflict between the obligation of confidentiality and the obligation to protect others from harm occurred in *Tarasoff v. Regents of the University of California* (the second selection in this chapter). In this case a patient confided to his psychologist that he intended to kill a third party. The psychologist then faced the choice of preserving the confidentiality of the patient or of infringing his right of confidentiality to warn a young woman that her life might be in danger. The court finds that health care professionals have a duty to weigh a peril to the public that a patient discloses in confidence against the duty of maintaining confidentiality. But how is the one duty to be weighed against the other? How can we be confident that warning potential victims of a dangerous patient's disclosures will not undermine the benefits of a medical system that motivates disturbed individuals to seek help? As the *Tarasoff* opinion itself indicates, it is difficult to verify which alternative produces a better outcome for society.

One way out of this problem is to take the first justification very seriously and allow rights of patient autonomy to override the utilitarian social benefits of disclosing confidential information. There is a loss, however, by giving such stringent weight to rights of autonomy: The benefits of disclosure under desperate circumstances are lost if we allow no violations of confidentiality whatever. For example, physicians would not be able to report contagious diseases, child abuse, gunshot wounds, epilepsy (to a motor vehicle department), and the like.

To meet this challenge, perhaps one could support a *firm* rule of confidentiality without supporting an *absolute* rule. Using this approach, one could recognize a range of exceptions under which disclosure of clearly confidential information is permitted. One example of this problem is found in the contemporary discussion of the conditions under which confidential information about AIDS patients may be disclosed, especially when the disclosure constitutes a warning to persons such as health professionals of imminent danger.

Morton Winston considers a range of problems about AIDS and the limits of medical confidentiality in the final article in this section. He notes that rights of autonomy can often be limited by the *harm principle,* which requires persons to refrain from causing preventable wrongful harm to innocent others. This principle has special force when persons are vulnerable and dependent upon others. Winston uses these premises to argue that breaches of confidentiality can be justified in a range of cases in which each of the following conditions is satisfied: (1) persons would be placed at risk of contracting AIDS, (2) carriers will not freely disclose their status, and (3) the identity and status of the carrier is known to a health professional.

Not all examples of the problem of confidentiality are so dramatic or socially significant as those discussed in the Tarasoff case and the Winston article. More troublesome and pervasive problems concern how much of a patient's medical record can be fed into a widely accessed "public" data bank, how much information about a patient's genetic makeup may be revealed to a sexual partner if there is a substantial likelihood of the couple's producing genetically handicapped children, what information employers and insurance companies should and should not receive, and to whom in a family the full range of test results in genetic screening should be disclosed. These are some of the many issues about confidentiality currently under discussion.

TRUTH TELLING AND THE DISCLOSURE OF BAD NEWS

In modern medicine the nature and quality of the physician-patient relationship varies with prior contact, the mental or physical state of the patient, the manner in which the physician relates to the family, and problems in patient-family interactions. The patient's right to know the truth and the physician's obligation to tell it are contingent on these and other factors in the relationship.

Most writers in the history of medical ethics have held that departures from the general principle of truth telling are justified when information disclosure itself carries serious risks for patients. They view truth telling as limited by the Hippocratic principle that they should do no harm to patients in difficult circumstances by revealing upsetting conditions. If disclosure of a diagnosis of cancer, for example, would cause the patient anxiety or lead to an act of self-destruction, they believe that medical ethics requires that the physician carefully monitor and, at times, withhold the information that could cause additional harm. A common thesis is that in cases in which risks of harm from nondisclosure are low and benefits of nondisclosure to the patient are substantial, a physician may legitimately deceive or underdisclose the truth, and sometimes lie.

Deception is sometimes said to be easier to justify than blatant lying, because deception does not necessarily threaten the relationship of trust. Underdisclosure and nondisclosure are also thought to be more easily justified than lying. Those who share this perspective argue that it is important not to conflate duties, not to lie, not to deceive, and to disclose as if they were a single duty of veracity.

These justifications of nondisclosure seem especially plausible in cases in which bad news must be delivered to fragile patients or to strangers. Nevertheless, almost all authorities now agree that there is a strong duty of veracity in medicine because of respect for autonomous patients. Can these views about justified disclosure and justified nondisclosure be rendered consistent?

In the first essay in this chapter, David Thomasma explains both why truth telling is important and when truth telling rules might plausibly be overridden in the clinical setting. Thomasma defends the controversial thesis that "truth is a secondary good . . . [and] other primary values take precedence over the truth." Moreover, he says, "the only values that can trump the truth are recipient survival, community survival, and the ability to absorb the full impact of the truth at a particular time."

Using a very different analysis, Garry Sigman and colleagues analyze cases in which parents of children and adolescents request nondisclosure of a diagnosis. They use a case study to help identify specific clinical factors that are important when deciding whether to make truthful disclosures to children after their parents object to the disclosures. They analyze disclosure duties, disease specific factors, patient factors, and family factors—arguing for a context specific approach to truth telling in which lying to the patient and hiding information may occasionally be justified in light of all the factors at work.

Despite the mitigating conditions mentioned by Thomasma and Sigman and colleagues, many writers in contemporary bioethics believe that all intentional suppression of pertinent information violates a patient's autonomy rights and violates the fundamental duties of the health professional. Here the duty of veracity is derived from obligations of respect for the autonomy of persons. This thesis has been especially prominent in the recent literature on informed consent.

INFORMED CONSENT

It is now widely believed that the physician has a moral obligation not only to tell patients the truth, but also to help them decide important matters that affect their health. This ability to make an educated decision is dependent upon the availability of truthful information and the patient's capacity to handle the information. For this reason it is often said that before a physician performs a medical procedure on a competent patient, he or she has an obligation to obtain the patient's informed consent and to engage in mutual decision making with the patient.

The history of informed consent is not ancient. Prior to the 1950s, there was no firm ground in which a commitment to informed consent could take root. This is not to say that there is no relevant history of the physician's management of medical information in the encounter with patients. However, with few exceptions, no serious consideration was given to issues of either consent or self-determination by patients and research subjects. Proper principles, practices, and virtues of "truthfulness" in disclosure were occasionally discussed, but the perspective was largely one of how to make disclosures without harming patients by revealing their condition too abruptly and starkly.

Because of the vagueness that surrounds the term *informed consent*, some writers have been interested in analyzing the concept so that its meaning is as clear as possible. If overdemanding criteria such as "full disclosure and complete understanding" are adopted, an informed consent becomes impossible to obtain. Conversely, if underdemanding criteria such as "the patient signed the form" are used, an informed consent becomes too easy to obtain and the term loses all moral significance. Many interactions between a physician and a patient or an investigator and a subject that have been called informed consents have been so labelled only because they rest on underdemanding criteria; they are inappropriately referred to as informed consents. For example, a physician's truthful disclosure to a patient has often been declared the essence of informed consent, as if a patient's silence following disclosure could add up to an informed consent.

Jay Katz has been at the forefront of this effort to analyze the concept of informed consent. He argues that *informed consent* and *shared decision making* should be treated as virtually synonymous terms. His basic moral conviction is that the primary goal of informed consent in medical care and in research is to enable potential subjects and patients to make autonomous decisions about whether to grant or refuse authorization for medical and research interventions.

Ruth Faden and Tom Beauchamp agree that there is a historical relationship between shared decision making and informed consent but believe it is confusing to treat them as *synonymous.* They argue that decision making should be distinguished from a subject's or patient's act of knowledgeably *authorizing* the intervention, that is, giving an informed consent. The essence of an informed consent, on this analysis, is an autonomous authorization. Such an authorization requires more than merely acquiescing in, yielding to, or complying with an arrangement or a proposal made by a physician or investigator.

One crucial question addressed in the articles on informed consent in this chapter is whether a valid informed consent can be given if a patient or subject does *not* autonomously authorize an intervention. The authors in this chapter all appear to answer "No" to this question. Yet most of the "consents" obtained in health care institutions at the present time probably do not constitute autonomous authorizations, in the sense of autonomy discussed in Chapter 1. That is, it is doubtful that a patient substantially understands the circumstances, makes a decision absent coercion, and intentionally authorizes a professional to proceed with a medical or research intervention. This situation opens up a range of questions about the validity of the practices of consent currently at work in contemporary medicine and research.

Another problem addressed in these articles concerns adequate standards of disclosure in informed consent contexts. Legal history reveals an evolving doctrine of informed consent from a 1767 case to the 1972 *Canterbury v. Spence* case (and its aftermath). *Canterbury* was the first and most influential of the recent landmark informed consent cases. In *Canterbury,* surgery on the patient's back and a subsequent accident in the hospital led to further injuries and unexpected paralysis, the possibility of which had not yet been disclosed. Judge Spottswood Robinson's opinion focuses on the needs of the reasonable person and the right to self-determination. As for sufficiency of information, the court holds: "The patient's right of self-decision shapes the boundaries of the duty to reveal. That right can be effectively exercised only if the patient possesses enough information to enable an intelligent choice." Katz delivers a blistering attack on the development of these standards in the precedent legal cases, especially *Canterbury.*

Many have challenged whether any legal standard could be adequate for clinical ethics (as distinct from a standard in law), since the law is almost uniformly directed at adequate *disclosures.* In recent bioethics the focus on informed consent has turned somewhat away from disclosure duties and more toward the quality of understanding and consent in the patient. Much has been made of Katz's claim that the key to effective communication is to invite participation by patients or subjects in an exchange of information and dialogue. Asking questions, eliciting the concerns and interests of the patient or subject, and establishing a climate that encourages the patient or subject to ask questions seems to be more important for medical ethics than the full body of requirements of disclosed information in law.

In the final selection in this section, Robert Levine discusses why the Western model of informed consent is unsuitable in much of the remainder of the world, where he thinks the concept of "person" differs substantially from that in Western societies. Levine concludes that we would be better off if we used a procedural solution to these problems when they are encountered rather than insisting on rules of obtaining consent. Levine's treatment also suggests how we might handle the growing problem of cultural diversity in Western nations when patients from non-Western countries present to health professionals.

REFUSAL OF TREATMENT

The subject of the fourth section of this chapter is refusal of treatment by a patient or a duly authorized representative of the patient (when a patient is incompetent or seriously ill). The major question is, "Under what conditions, if any, is it permissible for patients, health professionals, and surrogate decision makers to forgo treatment with the foreknowledge that there may be serious health consequences for the patient (such as death or disability)?"

It is now generally agreed, in both law and ethics, that a competent patient has an autonomy right to forgo treatment at any time, including the right to refuse medical nutrition and hydration. Indeed, refusals in medical settings have a moral power lacking in mere requests for assistance: A physician is morally and legally required to comply with a refusal. However, competent persons sometimes exercise their rights in a way inconsistent with the beliefs of other members of their family or inconsistent with the commitments of a health care institution—a problem that arises in this chapter in the case of Elizabeth Bouvia. She suffered from cerebral palsy that left her with virtually no motor function in her limbs or skeletal muscles, but she was unaffected cognitively. The court asserts that patients like Bouvia have a moral and constitutional right to refuse treatment even if its exercise creates a "life-threatening condition" of which physicians disapprove and consider against standards of practice.

Several celebrated legal cases have centered on whether formerly competent patients have some kind of right to refuse treatment despite their present incompetence. Among the best known cases, and the only one to reach the U.S. Supreme Court, is that of Nancy Cruzan. The 25-year-old Ms. Cruzan was in a persistent vegetative state for over three years. Her parents then petitioned for permission to remove the feeding tube, knowing that, by doing so, their daughter would die. A lower court's authorization of termination of treatment was reversed by the Missouri Supreme Court, which ruled that no one may order an end to life-sustaining treatment for an incompetent person in the absence of a valid living will or clear and convincing evidence of the patient's wishes.

This decision was appealed to the U.S. Supreme Court, which handed down its decision in 1990. The majority opinion—the second selection in this section—holds that a state may constitutionally require "clear and convincing evidence" whenever surrogates claim to represent a patient's autonomous wishes about continuing or refusing life-sustaining treatment. The majority insists that its findings rest on a judgment by society that it is better to err in preserving life in a vegetative state than to err through a decision that leads directly to death. The dissenting justices express a particularly vigorous disagreement with this majority opinion. Justices Brennan, Marshall, and Blackmun find that "Nancy Cruzan has a fundamental right to be free of unwanted artificial nutrition and hydration"—a direct challenge to the line of argument in the majority opinion.

Whether the Court's opinion is adequate to protect the autonomy interests of patients is still under discussion. One of the major issues raised by *Cruzan* is whether a protected autonomy interest in refusing medical treatment can be meaningfully exercised only by competent patients or also by incompetent patients, either through their surrogates or through some forms of advance directive to health care authorities. These questions have fostered an active discussion of the role of advance directives in health care—our final topic in this chapter.

ADVANCE DIRECTIVES

In an advance directive—a device intended to implement patients' rights of autonomy— a person, while competent, either writes a directive for health care professionals or selects a surrogate to make decisions about treatments during periods of incompetence. Two types of advance directive have been recognized: *living wills,* which are substantive directives regarding medical procedures that should be provided or forgone in specific circumstances, and *durable powers of attorney* (DPA) for health care. A durable power of attorney is a legal document in which one person assigns another person as authority to perform specified actions on behalf of the signer.

Both kinds of advance directive can reduce stress for individuals, families, and health professionals who fear wrong outcomes or decisions, but they also generate practical and moral problems. First, relatively few persons compose them or leave explicit instructions. Second, a designated decision maker might be unavailable when needed, might be incompetent to make good decisions for the patient, or might have a conflict of interest. Third, laws often severely restrict the use of advance directives. For example, advance directives have legal effect in some states if and only if the patient is terminally ill and death is imminent. But decisions must be made in some cases when death is not imminent or the medical condition cannot appropriately be described as a terminal illness. Fourth, in the case of living wills, individuals have difficulty in specifying decisions or guidelines that adequately anticipate the full range of medical situations that might occur. The directive given may provide no basis for health professionals to overturn instructions that turn out not to be in the patient's best medical interest, although the patient could not have reasonably anticipated this circumstance while competent. Surrogate decision makers also make decisions with which physicians sharply disagree.

Despite these problems, the advance directive is widely recognized as a promising and valid way for competent persons to exercise their autonomy. On December 1, 1991, the Patient Self-Determination Act—a federal law known as PSDA—went into effect in the United States. This law requires health care facilities certified by Medicare or Medicaid to notify competent adult patients of their right to accept or refuse medical treatment and their right to execute an advance directive. This law gave powerful legal effect to advance directives in the United States.

The intent of this law—and of almost all rules and regulations pertaining to advance directives—is to allow patients to take control of their medical fate, on the grounds that their interests will ultimately be best served by making their own decisions, rather than having the decisions made for them. In their article in this chapter, Linda Emanuel and colleagues attempt to provide a practically oriented set of basic steps and skills for advance care planning. Their model of advance care planning *as a process* should be viewed as augmenting and updating (rather than replacing) executed advance directive forms. They identify several steps of providing information, facilitating discussion, recording statements, reviewing directives, and implementing decisions. They argue that their model will minimize risks and maximize benefits for patients and health professionals alike.

In the final article in this chapter, Ben A. Rich assesses advance directives as a form of anticipatory decision making that moves "beyond informed consent and refusal." Rich distinguishes between and assesses oral directives, living wills, and the durable power of attorney. He points to several flaws and limitations in these forms of advance planning, especially living wills and durable powers of attorney. He also discusses why there has been so much physician inattention to advance directives. Rich concludes that it is not the concept of advance directives that is flawed, but rather "our fledgling efforts at crafting them." He provides some reasons for optimism that "the next generation of advance directives will succeed where the others have failed."

T.L.B.

The Confidentiality of Medical Information

MARK SIEGLER

Confidentiality in Medicine—A Decrepit Concept

Mark Siegler, MD, is director of the MacLean Center for Clinical Medical Ethics and a professor in the Department of Medicine at the University of Chicago. With Albert Jonsen and William Winslade, he published *Clinical Ethics,* which is widely consulted by health professionals. Among his many articles in bioethics are "The External Control of Private Medical Decisions: A Major Change in the Doctor-Patient Relationship," *Journal of American Geriatrics Society* and a collaboration entitled "A Procedure for Balancing the Rights of Patients and the Responsibilities of Physicians," *The Law-Medicine Relation: A Philosophical Exploration.*

Medical confidentiality, as it has traditionally been understood by patients and doctors, no longer exists. This ancient medical principle, which has been included in every physician's oath and code of ethics since Hippocratic times, has become old, worn-out, and useless; it is a decrepit concept. Efforts to preserve it appear doomed to failure and often give rise to more problems than solutions. Psychiatrists have tacitly acknowledged the impossibility of ensuring the confidentiality of medical records by choosing to establish a separate, more secret record. The following case illustrates how the confidentiality principle is compromised systematically in the course of routine medical care.

A patient of mine with mild chronic obstructive pulmonary disease was transferred from the surgical intensive-care unit to a surgical nursing floor two days after an elective cholecystectomy. On the day of transfer, the patient saw a respiratory therapist writing in his medical chart (the therapist was recording the results of an arterial blood gas analysis) and became concerned about the confidentiality of his hospital records. The patient threatened to leave the hospital prematurely unless I could guarantee that the confidentiality of his hospital record would be respected.

This patient's complaint prompted me to enumerate the number of persons who had both access to his hospital record and a reason to examine it. I was amazed to learn that at least 25 and possibly as many as 100 health professionals and administrative personnel at our university hospital had access to the patient's record and that all of them had a legitimate need, indeed a professional responsibility, to open and use that chart. These persons included 6 attending physicians (the primary physician, the surgeon, the pulmonary consultant, and others); 12 house officers (medical, surgical, intensive-care unit, and "covering" house staff); 20 nursing personnel (on three shifts); 6 respiratory therapists; 3 nutritionists; 2 clinical pharmacists; 15 students (from medicine, nursing, respiratory therapy, and clinical pharmacy); 4 unit secretaries; 4 hospital financial officers; and 4 chart reviewers (utilization review, quality assurance review, tissue review, and insurance auditor). It is of interest that this patient's problem was straightforward, and he therefore did not require many other technical and support services that the modern hospital provides. For example, he did not need multiple consultants and fellows, such specialized procedures as dialysis, or social workers, chaplains, physical therapists, occupational therapists, and the like.

Upon completing my survey I reported to the patient that I estimated that at least 75 health professionals and hospital personnel had access to his medical record. I suggested to the patient that these people were all involved in providing or supporting his health care services. They were, I assured him, working for him. Despite my reassurances the patient was obviously distressed and retorted, "I always believed that medical confidentiality was part of a doctor's code of ethics. Perhaps you should tell me just what you people mean by 'confidentiality'!"

TWO ASPECTS OF MEDICAL CONFIDENTIALITY

CONFIDENTIALITY AND THIRD-PARTY INTERESTS

Previous discussions of medical confidentiality usually have focused on the tension between a physician's responsibility to keep information divulged by patients secret and a physician's legal and moral duty, on occasion, to reveal such confidences to third parties, such as families, employers, public-health authorities, or police authorities. In all these instances, the central question relates to the stringency of the physician's obligation to maintain patient confidentiality when the health, well-being, and safety of identifiable others or of society in general would be threatened by a failure to reveal information about the patient. The tension in such cases is between the good of the patient and the good of others.

CONFIDENTIALITY AND THE PATIENT'S INTEREST

As the example above illustrates, further challenges to confidentiality arise because the patient's personal interest in maintaining confidentiality comes into conflict with his personal interest in receiving the best possible health care. Modern high-technology health care is available principally in hospitals (often, teaching hospitals), requires many trained and specialized workers (a "health-care team"), and is very costly. The existence of such teams means that information that previously had been held in confidence by an individual physician will now necessarily be disseminated to many members of the team. Furthermore, since health-care teams are expensive and few patients can afford to pay such costs directly, it becomes essential to grant access to the patient's medical record to persons who are responsible for obtaining third-party payment. These persons include chart reviewers, financial officers, insurance auditors, and quality-of-care assessors. Finally, as medicine expands from a narrow, disease-based model to a model that encompasses psychological, social, and economic problems, not only will the size of the health-care team

and medical costs increase, but more sensitive information (such as one's personal habits and financial condition) will now be included in the medical record and will no longer be confidential.

The point I wish to establish is that hospital medicine, the rise of health-care teams, the existence of third-party insurance programs, and the expanding limits of medicine will appear to be responses to the wishes of people for better and more comprehensive medical care. But each of these developments necessarily modifies our traditional understanding of medical confidentiality.

THE ROLE OF CONFIDENTIALITY IN MEDICINE

Confidentiality serves a dual purpose in medicine. In the first place, it acknowledges respect for the patient's sense of individuality and privacy. The patient's most personal physical and psychological secrets are kept confidential in order to decrease a sense of shame and vulnerability. Secondly, confidentiality is important in improving the patient's health care—a basic goal of medicine. The promise of confidentiality permits people to trust (i.e., have confidence) that information revealed to a physician in the course of a medical encounter will not be disseminated further. In this way patients are encouraged to communicate honestly and forthrightly with their doctors. This bond of trust between patient and doctor is vitally important both in the diagnostic process (which relies on an accurate history) and subsequently in the treatment phase, which often depends as much on the patient's trust in the physician as it does on medications and surgery. These two important functions of confidentiality are as important now as they were in the past. They will not be supplanted entirely either by improvements in medical technology or by recent changes in relations between some patients and doctors toward a rights-based, consumerist model.

POSSIBLE SOLUTIONS TO THE CONFIDENTIALITY PROBLEM

First of all, in all nonbureaucratic, noninstitutional medical encounters—that is, in the millions of doctor–patient encounters that take place in physician's offices, where more privacy can be preserved— meticulous care should be taken to guarantee that patients' medical and personal information will be kept confidential.

Secondly, in such settings as hospitals or large-scale group practices, where many persons have opportunities to examine the medical record, we should aim to provide access only to those who have "a need to know." This could be accomplished through such administrative changes as dividing the entire record into several sections—for example, a medical and financial section—and permitting only health professionals access to the medical information.

The approach favored by many psychiatrists—that of keeping a psychiatric record separate from the general medical record—is an understandable strategy but one that is not entirely satisfactory and that should not be generalized. The keeping of separate psychiatric records implies that psychiatry and medicine are different undertakings and thus drives deeper the wedge between them and between physical and psychological illness. Furthermore, it is often vitally important for internists or surgeons to know that a patient is being seen by a psychiatrist or is taking a particular medication. When separate records are kept, this information may not be available. Finally, if generalized, the practice of keeping a separate psychiatric record could lead to the unacceptable consequence of having a separate record for each type of medical problem.

Patients should be informed about what is meant by "medical confidentiality." We should establish the distinction between information about the patient that generally will be kept confidential regardless of the interest of third parties and information that will be exchanged among members of the health-care team in order to provide care for the patient. Patients should be made aware of the large number of persons in the modern hospital who require access to the medical record in order to serve the patient's medical and financial interests.

Finally, at some point most patients should have an opportunity to review their medical record and to make informed choices about whether their entire record is to be available to everyone or whether certain portions of the record are privileged and should be accessible only to their principal physician or to others designated explicitly by the patient. This approach would rely on traditional informed-consent procedural standards and might permit the patient to balance the personal value of medical confidentiality against the personal value of high-technology, team health care. There is no reason that the same procedure should not be used with psychiatric records instead of the arbitrary system now employed, in which everything related to psychiatry is kept secret.

AFTERTHOUGHT: CONFIDENTIALITY AND INDISCRETION

There is one additional aspect of confidentiality that is rarely included in discussions of the subject. I am referring here to the wanton, often inadvertent, but avoidable exchanges of confidential information that occur frequently in hospital rooms, elevators, cafeterias, doctors' offices, and at cocktail parties. Of course, as more people have access to medical information about the patient the potential for this irresponsible abuse of confidentiality increases geometrically.

Such mundane breaches of confidentiality are probably of greater concern to most patients than the broader issues of whether their medical records may be entered into a computerized data bank or whether a respiratory therapist is reviewing the results of an arterial blood gas determination. Somehow, privacy is violated and a sense of shame is heightened when intimate secrets are revealed to people one knows or is close to—friends, neighbors, acquaintances, or hospital roommates—rather than when they are disclosed to an anonymous bureaucrat sitting at a computer terminal in a distant city or to a health professional who is acting in an official capacity.

I suspect that the principles of medical confidentiality, particularly those reflected in most medical codes of ethics, were designed principally to prevent just this sort of embarrassing personal indiscretion rather than to maintain (for social, political, or economic reasons) the absolute secrecy of doctor–patient communications. In this regard, it is worth noting that Percival's Code of Medical Ethics (1803) includes the following admonition: "Patients should be interrogated concerning their complaint in a tone of voice which cannot be overheard."* We in the medical profession frequently neglect these simple courtesies.

CONCLUSION

The principle of medical confidentiality described in medical codes of ethics and still believed in by patients no longer exists. In this respect, it is a decrepit concept. Rather than perpetuate the myth of confidentiality and invest energy vainly to preserve it, the public and the profession would be better served if they devoted their attention to determining which aspects of the original principle of confidentiality are worth retaining. Efforts could then be directed to salvaging those.

*Leake C. D., ed. Percival's medical ethics. Baltimore: Williams & Wilkins, 1927.

CALIFORNIA SUPREME COURT

Tarasoff v. Regents of the University of California

TOBRINER, Justice

On October 27, 1969, Prosenjit Poddar killed Tatiana Tarasoff. Plaintiffs, Tatiana's parents, allege that two months earlier Poddar confided his intention to kill Tatiana to Dr. Lawrence Moore, a psychologist employed by the Cowell Memorial Hospital at the University of California at Berkeley. They allege that on Moore's request, the campus police briefly detained Poddar, but released him when he appeared rational. They further claim that Dr. Harvey Powelson, Moore's superior, then directed that no further action be taken to detain Poddar. No one warned plaintiffs of Tatiana's peril. . . .

We shall explain that defendant therapists cannot escape liability merely because Tatiana herself was not their patient. When a therapist determines, or pursuant to the standards of his profession should determine, that his patient presents a serious danger of violence to another, he incurs an obligation to use reasonable care to protect the intended victim against such danger. The discharge of this duty may require the therapist to take one or more of various steps, depending upon the nature of the case. Thus it may call for him to warn the intended victim or others likely to apprise the victim of the danger, to notify the police, or to take whatever other steps are reasonably necessary under the circumstances. . . .

1. PLAINTIFFS' COMPLAINTS

Plaintiffs, Tatiana's mother and father, filed separate but virtually identical second amended complaints. The issue before us on this appeal is whether those complaints now state, or can be amended to state,

From 131 *California Reporter* 14. Decided July 1, 1976. All footnotes and numerous references in the text of the decision and a dissent have been omitted.

causes of action against defendants. We therefore begin by setting forth the pertinent allegations of the complaints.

Plaintiffs' first cause of action, entitled "Failure to Detain a Dangerous Patient," alleges that on August 20, 1969, Poddar was a voluntary outpatient receiving therapy at Cowell Memorial Hospital. Poddar informed Moore, his therapist, that he was going to kill an unnamed girl, readily identifiable as Tatiana, when she returned home from spending the summer in Brazil. Moore, with the concurrence of Dr. Gold, who had initially examined Poddar, and Dr. Yandell, assistant to the director of the department of psychiatry, decided that Poddar should be committed for observation in a mental hospital. Moore orally notified Officers Atkinson and Teel of the campus police that he would request commitment. He then sent a letter to Police Chief William Beall requesting the assistance of the police department in securing Poddar's confinement.

Officers Atkinson, Brownrigg, and Halleran took Poddar into custody, but, satisfied that Poddar was rational, released him on his promise to stay away from Tatiana. Powelson, director of the department of psychiatry at Cowell Memorial Hospital, then asked the police to return Moore's letter, directed that all copies of the letter and notes that Moore had taken as therapist be destroyed, and "ordered no action to place Prosenjit Poddar in 72-hour treatment and evaluation facility."

Plaintiffs' second cause of action, entitled "Failure to Warn On a Dangerous Patient," incorporates the allegations of the first cause of action, but adds the assertion that defendants negligently permitted Poddar to be released from police custody without "notifying the parents of Tatiana Tarasoff that their daughter was in grave danger from Prosenjit Poddar." Poddar persuaded Tatiana's brother to share an apartment with him near Tatiana's residence; shortly after her return from Brazil, Poddar went to her residence and killed her. . . .

2. PLAINTIFFS CAN STATE A CAUSE OF ACTION AGAINST DEFENDANT THERAPISTS FOR NEGLIGENT FAILURE TO PROTECT TATIANA

The second cause of action can be amended to allege that Tatiana's death proximately resulted from defendants' negligent failure to warn Tatiana or others likely to apprise her of her danger. Plaintiffs contend that as amended, such allegations of negligence and proximate causation, with resulting damages, establish a cause of action. Defendants, however, contend that in the circumstances of the present case they owed no duty of care to Tatiana or her parents and that, in the absence of such duty, they were free to act in careless disregard of Tatiana's life and safety. . . .

In the landmark case of *Rowland v. Christian* (1968), Justice Peters recognized that liability should be imposed "for an injury occasioned to another by his want of ordinary care or skill" as expressed in section 1714 of the Civil Code. Thus, Justice Peters, quoting from *Heaven v. Pender* (1883) stated: " 'whenever one person is by circumstances placed in such a position with regard to another . . . that if he did not use ordinary care and skill in his own conduct . . . he would cause danger of injury to the person or property of the other, a duty arises to use ordinary care and skill to avoid such danger.' "

We depart from "this fundamental principle" only upon the "balancing of a number of considerations"; major ones "are the foreseeability of harm to the plaintiff, the degree of certainty that the plaintiff suffered injury, the closeness of the connection between the defendant's conduct and the injury suffered, the moral blame attached to the defendant's conduct, the policy of preventing future harm, the extent of the burden to the defendant and consequences to the community of imposing a duty to exercise care with resulting liability for breach, and the availability, cost and prevalence of insurance for the risk involved."

The most important of these considerations in establishing duty is foreseeability. As a general principle, a "defendant owes a duty of care to all persons who are foreseeably endangered by his conduct, with respect to all risks which make the conduct unreasonably dangerous."

As we shall explain, however, when the avoidance of foreseeable harm requires a defendant to control the conduct of another person, or to warn of such conduct, the common law has traditionally imposed liability only if the defendant bears some special relationship to the dangerous person or to the potential victim. Since the relationship between a therapist and his patient satisfies this requirement, we need not here decide whether foreseeability alone is sufficient to create a duty to exercise reasonable care to protect a potential victim of another's conduct. . . .

A relationship of defendant therapists to either Tatiana or Poddar will suffice to establish a duty of care; as explained in section 315 of the Restatement Second of Torts, a duty of care may arise from either "(a) a special relation . . . between the actor and the third person which imposes a duty upon the actor to control the third person's conduct, or (b) a special relation . . . between the actor and the other which gives to the other a right of protection." . . .

The courts hold that a doctor is liable to persons infected by his patient if he negligently fails to diagnose a contagious disease, or, having diagnosed the illness, fails to warn members of the patient's family.

Since it involved a dangerous mental patient, the decision in *Merchants Nat. Bank & Trust Co. of Fargo v. United States* (1967) comes closer to the issue. The Veterans Administration arranged for the patient to work on a local farm, but did not inform the farmer of the man's background. The farmer consequently permitted the patient to come and go freely during non-working hours; the patient borrowed a car, drove to his wife's residence and killed her. Notwithstanding the lack of any "special relationship" between the Veterans Administration and the wife, the court found the Veterans Administration liable for the wrongful death of the wife.

In their summary of the relevant rulings Fleming and Maximov conclude that the "case law should dispel any notion that to impose on the therapists a duty to take precautions for the safety of persons threatened by a patient, where due care so requires, is in any way opposed to contemporary ground rules on the duty relationship. On the contrary, there now seems to be sufficient authority to support the conclusion that by entering into a doctor-patient relationship the therapist becomes sufficiently involved to assume some responsibility for the safety, not only of the patient himself, but also of any third person whom the doctor knows to be threatened by the patient." (Fleming & Maximov, *The Patient or His Victim: The Therapist's Dilemma* [1974] 62 Cal.L.Rev. 1025, 1030.)

Defendants contend, however, that imposition of a duty to exercise reasonable care to protect third persons is unworkable because therapists cannot accurately predict whether or not a patient will resort to violence. In support of this argument amicus representing the American Psychiatric Association and other professional societies cites numerous articles which indicate that therapists, in the present state of the art, are unable reliably to predict violent acts; their forecasts, amicus claims, tend consistently to over-predict violence, and indeed are more often wrong than right. Since predictions of violence are often erroneous, amicus concludes, the courts should not render rulings that predicate the liability of therapists upon the validity of such predictions. . . .

We recognize the difficulty that a therapist encounters in attempting to forecast whether a patient presents a serious danger of violence. Obviously we do not require that the therapist, in making that determination, render a perfect performance; the therapist need only exercise "that reasonable degree of skill, knowledge, and care ordinarily possessed and exercised by members of [that professional specialty] under similar circumstances." Within the broad range of reasonable practice and treatment in which professional opinion and judgment may differ, the therapist is free to exercise his or her own best judgment without liability; proof, aided by hindsight, that he or she judged wrongly is insufficient to establish negligence.

In the instant case, however, the pleadings do not raise any question as to failure of defendant therapists to predict that Poddar presented a serious danger of violence. On the contrary, the present complaints allege that defendant therapists did in fact predict that Poddar would kill, but were negligent in failing to warn.

Amicus contends, however, that even when a therapist does in fact predict that a patient poses a serious danger of violence to others, the therapist should be absolved of any responsibility for failing to act to protect the potential victim. In our view, however, once a therapist does in fact determine, or under applicable professional standards reasonably should have determined, that a patient poses a serious danger of violence to others, he bears a duty to exercise reasonable care to protect the foreseeable victim of that danger.

While the discharge of this duty of due care will necessarily vary with the facts of each case, in each instance the adequacy of the therapist's conduct must be measured against the traditional negligence standard of the rendition of reasonable care under the circumstances. As explained in Fleming and Maximov, *The Patient or His Victim: The Therapist's Dilemma* (1974) 62 Cal.L.Rev. 1025, 1967: ". . . the ultimate question of resolving the tension between the conflicting interests of patient and potential victim is one of social policy, not professional expertise. . . . In sum, the therapist owes a legal duty not only to his patient, but also to his patient's would-be victim and is subject in both respects to scrutiny by judge and jury." . . .

The risk that unnecessary warning may be given is a reasonable price to pay for the lives of possible victims that may be saved. We could hesitate to hold that the therapist who is aware that his patient expects to attempt to assassinate the President of the United States would not be obligated to warn the authorities because the therapist cannot predict with accuracy that his patient will commit the crime.

Defendants further argue that free and open communication is essential to psychotherapy, that "Unless a patient . . . is assured that . . . information [revealed to him] can and will be held in utmost confidence, he will be reluctant to make the full disclosure upon which diagnosis and treatment . . . depends." The giving of a warning, defendants contend, constitutes a breach of trust which entails the revelation of confidential communications.

We recognize the public interest in supporting effective treatment of mental illness and in protecting the rights of patients to privacy, and the consequent public importance of safeguarding the confidential character of psychotherapeutic communication. Against this interest, however, we must weigh the public interest in safety from violent assault. . . .

We realize that the open and confidential character of psychotherapeutic dialogue encourages patients to express threats of violence, few of which are ever executed. Certainly a therapist should not be encouraged routinely to reveal such threats; such disclosures could seriously disrupt the patient's relationship with his therapist and with the persons threatened. To the contrary, the therapist's obligations to his patient require that he not disclose a confidence unless such disclosure is necessary to avert danger to others, and even then that he do so discretely, and in a fashion that would preserve the privacy of his patient to the fullest extent compatible with the prevention of the threatened danger.

The revelation of a communication under the above circumstances is not a breach of trust or a violation of professional ethics; as stated in the Principles of Medical Ethics of the American Medical Association (1957), section 9: "A physician may not reveal the confidence entrusted to him in the course of medical attendance . . . *unless he is required to do so by law or unless it becomes necessary in order to protect the welfare of the individual or of the community.*" (Emphasis added.) We conclude that the public policy favoring protection of the confidential character of patient–psychotherapist communications must yield to the extent to which disclosure is essential to avert danger to others. The protective privilege ends where the public peril begins. . . .

For the foregoing reasons, we find that plaintiffs' complaints can be amended to state a cause of action against defendants Moore, Powelson, Gold, and Yandell and against the Regents as their employer, for breach of a duty to exercise reasonable care to protect Tatiana.

• • •

CLARK, Justice (dissenting).

Until today's majority opinion, both legal and medical authorities have agreed that confidentiality is essential to effectively treat the mentally ill, and that imposing a duty on doctors to disclose patient threats to potential victims would greatly impair treatment. Further, recognizing that effective treatment and society's safety are necessarily intertwined, the Legislature has already decided effective and confidential treatment is preferred over imposition of a duty to warn.

The issue of whether effective treatment for the mentally ill should be sacrificed to a system of warnings is, in my opinion, properly one for the Legislature, and we are bound by its judgment. Moreover, even in the absence of clear legislative direction, we must reach the same conclusion because imposing the majority's new duty is certain to result in a net increase in violence. . . .

Overwhelming policy considerations weigh against imposing a duty on psychotherapists to warn a potential victim against harm. While offering virtually no benefit to society, such a duty will frustrate psychiatric treatment, invade fundamental patient rights and increase violence.

The importance of psychiatric treatment and its need for confidentiality have been recognized by this court. "It is clearly recognized that the very practice of psychiatry vitally depends upon the reputation in the community that the psychiatrist will not tell." (Slovenko, *Psychiatry and a Second Look at the Medical Privilege* (1960) 6 Wayne L.Rev. 175, 188.)

Assurance of confidentiality is important for three reasons.

DETERRENCE FROM TREATMENT

First, without substantial assurance of confidentiality, those requiring treatment will be deterred from seeking assistance. It remains an unfortunate fact in our society that people seeking psychiatric guidance tend to become stigmatized. Apprehension of such stigma—apparently increased by the propensity of people considering treatment to see themselves in the worst possible light—creates a well-recognized reluctance to seek aid. This reluctance is alleviated by the psychiatrist's assurance of confidentiality.

FULL DISCLOSURE

Second, the guarantee of confidentiality is essential in eliciting the full disclosure necessary for effective treatment. The psychiatric patient approaches treatment with conscious and unconscious inhibitions against revealing his innermost thoughts. "Every person, however well-motivated, has to overcome resistances to therapeutic exploration. These resistances seek support from every possible source and the possibility of disclosure would easily be employed in the service of resistance." (Goldstein & Katz, 36 Conn. Bar J. 175, 179.) Until a patient can trust his psychiatrist not to violate their confidential relationship, "the unconscious psychological control mechanism of repression will prevent the recall of past experiences." (Butler, *Psychotherapy and Griswold: Is Confidentiality a Privilege or a Right?* (1971) 3 Conn.L.Rev. 599, 604.)

SUCCESSFUL TREATMENT

Third, even if the patient fully discloses his thoughts, assurance that the confidential relationship will not be breached is necessary to maintain his trust in his psychiatrist—the very means by which treatment is effected. "[T]he essence of much psychotherapy is the contribution of trust in the external world and ultimately in the self, modelled upon the trusting relationship established during therapy." (Dawidoff, *The Malpractice of Psychiatrists,* 1966 Duke L.J. 696, 704.) Patients will be helped only if they can form a trusting relationship with the psychiatrist. All authorities appear to agree that if the trust relationship cannot be developed because of collusive communication between the psychiatrist and others, treatment will be frustrated.

Given the importance of confidentiality to the practice of psychiatry, it becomes clear the duty to warn imposed by the majority will cripple the use and effectiveness of psychiatry. Many people, potentially violent—yet susceptible to treatment—will be deterred from seeking it; those seeking it will be inhibited from making revelations necessary to effective treatment; and, forcing the psychiatrist to violate the patient's trust will destroy the interpersonal relationship by which treatment is effected.

VIOLENCE AND CIVIL COMMITMENT

By imposing a duty to warn, the majority contributes to the danger to society of violence by the mentally ill and greatly increases the risk of civil commitment—the total deprivation of liberty—of those who should not be confined. The impairment of treatment and risk of improper commitment resulting from the new duty to warn will not be limited to a few patients but will extend to a large number of the mentally ill. Although under existing psychiatric procedures only a relatively few receiving treatment will ever present

a risk of violence, the number making threats is huge, and it is the latter group—not just the former—whose treatment will be impaired and whose risk of commitment will be increased.

Both the legal and psychiatric communities recognize that the process of determining potential violence in a patient is far from exact, being fraught with complexity and uncertainty. In fact precision has not even been attained in predicting who of those having already committed violent acts will again become violent, a task recognized to be of much simpler proportions.

This predictive uncertainty means that the number of disclosures will necessarily be large. As noted above, psychiatric patients are encouraged to discuss all thoughts of violence, and they often express such thoughts. However, unlike this court, the psychiatrist does not enjoy the benefit of overwhelming hindsight in seeing which few, if any, of his patients will ultimately become violent. Now, confronted by the majority's new duty, the psychiatrist must instantaneously calculate potential violence from each patient on each visit. The difficulties researchers have encountered in accurately predicting violence will be heightened for the practicing psychiatrist dealing for brief periods in his office with heretofore nonviolent patients. And, given the decision not to warn or commit must always be made at the psychiatrist's civil peril, one can expect most doubts will be resolved in favor of the psychiatrist protecting himself.

MORTON E. WINSTON

AIDS, Confidentiality, and The Right to Know

Morton Winston is professor of philosophy at the College of New Jersey. His work has focused on applied ethics, human rights, cognitive science, and philosophy of the mind. He is also a former chair of the board of directors of Amnesty International. Recently he coauthored *Society, Ethics, and Technology* (Wadsworth) as well as *Global Ethics: Human Rights and Responsibilities* (University of Pennsylvania).

In June of 1987, a young woman who was nine months pregnant was shot with an arrow fired from a hunting bow on a Baltimore street by a man who was engaged in an argument with another person. Emergency workers from the city fire fighting unit were called to the scene, administered resuscitation to the profusely bleeding woman and took her to a local hospital where she died shortly afterwards. Her child, delivered by emergency Caesarian section, died the next day.

This tragedy would have been quickly forgotten as yet another incident of random urban violence if it had not been later learned that the woman was infected with the AIDS virus. A nurse at the hospital decided on her own initiative that the rescue workers who had brought the woman to the emergency room should be informed that they had been exposed to HIV-infected blood and contacted them directly. Several days after this story hit the newspapers two state legislators introduced a bill adding AIDS to the list of diseases that hospitals would be required to inform workers about. A hospital spokeswoman was quoted in the newspaper as opposing the proposed legislation on the grounds that it would violate patient confidentiality and that, "People taking care of patients should assume that everyone is a potential AIDS patient and take precautions. The burden is on you to take care of yourself.[1]"

This case, and others like it, raises difficult and weighty ethical and public policy issues. What are the limits of medical confidentiality? Who, if anyone, has

a right to know that they may have been exposed to AIDS or other dangerous infectious diseases? Whose responsibility is it to inform the sexual contacts of AIDS patients or others who may have been exposed to the infection? Can public health policies be framed which will effectively prevent the spread of the epidemic while also protecting the civil and human rights of its victims?

I. THE LIMITS OF CONFIDENTIALITY

The rule of medical confidentiality enjoins physicians, nurses, and health care workers from revealing to third parties information about a patient obtained in the course of medical treatment. The rule protecting a patient's secrets is firmly entrenched in medical practice, in medical education, and receives explicit mention in all major medical oaths and codes of medical ethics. Sissela Bok has argued that the ethical justification for confidentiality rests on four arguments.[2]

The first and most powerful justification for the rule of confidentiality derives from the individual's right, flowing from autonomy, to control personal information and to protect privacy. The right of individuals to control access to sensitive information about themselves is particularly important in cases where revelation of such information would subject the individual to invidious discrimination, deprivation of rights, or physical or emotional harm. Since persons who are HIV-infected or who have AIDS or ARC (AIDS-Related Complex), are often subjected to discrimination, loss of employment, refusal of housing and insurance, many physicians believe that the confidentiality of HIV antibody test results and diagnoses

From *Public Affairs Quarterly* 2, no. 2 (April 1988), 91–104. Footnotes renumbered.

of AIDS should be safeguarded under all circumstances. Since many infected persons and AIDS patients are members of groups which have traditionally been subject to discrimination or social disapproval—homosexuals, drug users, or prostitutes—the protection of confidentiality of patients who belong to these groups is especially indicated.

The second and third arguments for confidentiality concern the special moral relationship which exists between physicians and their patients. Medical practice requires that patients reveal intimate personal secrets to their physicians, and that physicians live up to the trust that is required on the part of patients to reveal such information; to fail to do so would violate the physician's duty of fidelity. Additionally, since medical practice is normally conducted under a tacit promise of confidentiality, physicians would violate this expectation by revealing their patients' secrets.

The fourth argument for confidentiality is based on utilitarian or broadly pragmatic considerations. Without a guarantee of confidentiality, potential patients in need of medical care would be deterred from seeking medical assistance from fear that sensitive personal information will be revealed to third parties thereby exposing the individual to the risk of unjust discrimination or other harm. Many physicians who work with AIDS patients find such pragmatic arguments particularly compelling, believing, perhaps correctly, that breaches of medical confidentiality concerning antibody status or a diagnosis of AIDS, would have a "chilling effect" preventing people in high-risk groups from seeking voluntary antibody testing and counselling. . . .

Bok believes that confidentiality is at best a prima facie obligation, one that while generally justified, can be overridden in certain situations by more compelling moral obligations. Among the situations which license breaches of confidentiality Bok cites are: cases involving a minor child or incompetent patient who would be harmed if sensitive information were not disclosed to a parent or guardian, cases involving threats of violence against identifiable third parties, cases involving contagious sexually transmitted diseases, and other cases where identifiable third parties would be harmed or placed at risk unknowingly by failure to disclose information known to a physician obtained through therapeutic communication.

In general, personal autonomy, and the derivative right of individuals to control personal information, is limited by the "Harm Principle" [HP], which requires moral agents to refrain from acts and omissions which would foreseeably result in preventable wrongful harm to innocent others. Bok argues that when HP (or a related ethical principle which I will discuss shortly) comes into play, "the prima facie premises supporting confidentiality are overridden" . . .[3] If this argument is correct, then the strict observance of confidentiality cannot be ethically justified in all cases, and physicians and nurses who invoke the rule of confidentiality in order to justify their not disclosing information concerning threats or risks to innocent third parties, may be guilt of negligence.

Before accepting this conclusion, however, it is necessary that we clarify the force of HP in the context of the ethics of AIDS, and refine the analysis of the conditions under which breaches of confidentiality pertaining to a patient's antibody status or a diagnosis of AIDS may be ethically justifiable.

II. VULNERABILITY, DISEASE CONTROL, AND DISCRIMINATION

Defenders of HP typically hold that all moral agents have a general moral obligation with respect to all moral patients to (a) avoid harm, (b) prevent or protect against harm, and (c) remove harm. One problem with HP is that not all acts and omissions which result in harm to others appear to be wrong. For instance, if I buy the last pint of Haagen-Daz coffee ice cream in the store, then I have, in some sense, harmed the next customer who wants to buy this good. Similarly, if one baseball team defeats another, then they have harmed the other team. But neither of these cases represent *wrongful* harms. Why then are some harms wrongful and others not?

Robert Goodin has recently developed a theory which provides at least a partial answer to this question. According to Goodin, the duty to protect against harm tends to arise most strongly in contexts in which someone is specially dependent on others or in some way specially vulnerable to their choices and actions.[4] He dubs this the Vulnerability Principle [VP]. Vulnerability, implying risk or susceptibility to harm, should be understood in a relational sense: being vulnerable to another is a condition which involves both a relative inability of the vulnerable party to protect themselves from harm or risk, and a correlative ability of another individual to act (or refrain from actions) which would foreseeably place the vulnerable party in a position of harm or risk or remove them from such a position. . . .

The Vulnerability Principle is related to the Harm Principle in giving a more precise analysis of the circumstances in which a strict duty to protect others arises. For example, under HP it might be thought that individuals, qua moral agents, have a duty to insure that persons be inoculated against contagious, preventable diseases, such as polio. However, while we have no strong obligations under HP to ensure that other adults have been inoculated, we *do* have a strong general obligation under VP to see to it that all young children are inoculated, and I have a special duty as a parent to see that my own children are inoculated. Children, as a class, are especially vulnerable and lack the ability to protect themselves. Being a parent *intensifies* the duty to prevent harm to children, by focusing the duty to protect the vulnerable on individuals who are specially responsible for the care of children. For other adults, on the other hand, I have no strong duty to protect, since I may generally assume that mature moral agents have both the ability and the responsibility to protect themselves.

Viewed in this light, the remarks quoted earlier by the hospital spokeswoman take on new meaning and relevance. She argued that it is the responsibility of health care workers to protect themselves by taking appropriate infection control measures in situations in which they may be exposed to blood infected with HIV. This argument might be a good one if people who occupy these professional roles are trained in such measures and are equipped to use them when appropriate. If they were so equipped, then in the Baltimore case, the nurse who later informed the rescue workers of the patient's antibody status was *not* specially responsible to prevent harm; the paramedics were responsible for their own safety.

The main problem with this argument is that it is not always possible to assume that emergency workers and others who provide direct care to AIDS patients or HIV-infected individuals are properly trained and equipped in infection control, nor, even if they are, that it is always feasible for them to employ these procedures in emergency situations. The scene of an emergency is not a controlled environment, and while emergency and public safety workers may take precautions such as wearing gloves and masks, these measures can be rendered ineffective, say, if a glove is torn and the worker cut while wrestling someone from a mass of twisted metal that was a car. While *post hoc* notification of the antibody status of people whom public safety workers have handled may not prevent them from contracting infection, it can alert them to the need to be tested, and thus can prevent them from spreading the infection (if they are in fact infected) to others, e.g. their spouses.

Health care workers, public safety workers, paramedics, and others who come into direct contact with blood which may be infected with the AIDS virus represent a class of persons for whom the Vulnerability Principle suggests a special "duty to protect" is appropriate. It is appropriate in these cases because such workers are routinely exposed to blood in the course of their professional activities, and exposure to infected blood is one way in which people can become infected with the AIDS virus. Such workers could protect themselves by simply refusing to handle anyone whom they suspected of harboring the infection. Doing this, however, would mean violating their professional responsibility to provide care. Hence, morally, they can only protect themselves by reducing their risk of exposure, in this case, by employing infection control measures and being careful. In this respect, health care workers, whether they work inside or outside of the hospital, are in a relevantly different moral situation than ordinary people who are not routinely exposed to blood and who have no special duty to provide care, and this makes them specially vulnerable. It thus appears that the nurse who informed the emergency workers of their risk of exposure did the right thing in informing them, since in doing so she was discharging a duty to protect the vulnerable.

But do similar conclusions follow with respect to "ordinary" persons who need not expose themselves to infection in the course of their professional activities? Consider the case in which a patient who is known to have a positive antibody status informs his physician that he does not intend to break off having sexual relations and that he will not tell his fiancée that he is infected with the AIDS virus.

In this case, we have a known, unsuspecting party, the fiancée, who will be placed at risk by failure to discharge a duty to protect. The fiancée is vulnerable in this case to the infected patient, since it is primarily *his* actions or omissions which place her at risk. According to HP + VP, the patient has a strong special responsibility to protect those with whom he has or will have sexual relations against infection. There are a number of ways in which he can discharge this duty. For instance, he can break off the relationship, abstain from sexual intercourse, practice "safe sex," or he can inform his fiancée of his antibody status.

This last option protects the fiancée by alerting her to the need to protect herself. But does the physician in this case also have a special responsibility to protect the fiancée?

She does, in this case, if she has good reason to believe that her patient will not discharge his responsibility to protect his fiancée or inform her of his positive antibody status. Since the physician possesses the information which would alert her patient's fiancée to a special need to protect herself, and the only other person who has this information will not reveal it, the fiancée is specially dependent upon the physician's choices and actions. Were she to fail to attempt to persuade her patient to reveal the information, or if he still refused to do so, to see to it that the patient's fiancée was informed, she would be acting in complicity with a patient who was violating his duty to prevent harm, and so would also be acting unethically under the Vulnerability Principle.

It thus appears that the rule of confidentiality protecting a patient's HIV antibody status cannot be regarded as absolute. There are several sorts of cases where HP + VP override the rule of confidentiality. However, finding there are justified exceptions to a generally justified rule of practice does not allow for unrestricted disclosure of antibody status to all and sundry. The basic question which must be answered in considering revealing confidential information concerning a patient's HIV antibody status is: *Is the individual to be notified someone who is specially vulnerable? That is, are they someone who faces a significant risk of exposure to the infection, and, will revealing confidential information to them assist them in reducing this risk to themselves or others?*

Answering this question is not always going to be easy, and applying HP + VP and balancing its claims against those of confidentiality will require an extraordinary degree of moral sensitivity and discretion. Because the rule of confidentiality describes a valid prima facie moral responsibility of physicians, the burden of proof must always fall on those who would violate it in order to accommodate the claims of an opposing ethical principle. Perhaps this is why physicians tend to assume that if the rule of confidentiality is not absolute, it might as well be treated as such. Physicians, nurses, and others who are privy to information about patients' antibody status, by and large, are likely to lack the relevant degree of ethical sensitivity to discriminate the cases in which confidentiality can be justifiably violated from those where it cannot. So if we must err, the argument goes, it is better to err on the side of confidentiality.

Aside from underestimating the moral sensitivity of members of these professional groups, this argument fails to take into account that there are two ways of erring—one can err by wrongfully disclosing confidential information to those who have no right to know it, and one can err by failing to disclose confidential information to those who do have a right to know it. The harm that can result from errors of the first kind are often significant, and sometimes irreparable. But so are the harms that result from errors of the second kind. While the burden of proof should be placed on those who would breach the prima facie rule of confidentiality, it should sometimes be possible for persons to satisfy this burden and act in accordance with HP + VP without moral fault.

The strength of conviction with which many physicians in the forefront of AIDS research and treatment argue for the protection of confidentiality can be explained partly by recognizing that they view themselves as having a special responsibility to prevent harm to AIDS patients. The harm which they seek to prevent, however, is not only harm to their patient's health. It is also social harm caused by discrimination that these physicians are trying to prevent. This is yet a different application of HP + VP in the context of AIDS which merits close attention. . . .

Medical personnel and public health authorities who take the position that confidentiality is absolute in order to shield their patients from discrimination, will increasingly find themselves in the uncomfortable position of being accomplices to the irresponsible behavior of known noncompliant positives. What is needed, then, is a finely drawn public policy that includes strong and effective anti-discrimination standards, a public education program which encourages individual and professional responsibility, and a set of clear effective guidelines for public health authorities concerning when and to whom confidential information necessary for disease control and the protection of those at risk may be revealed.

III. WHO HAS A RIGHT TO KNOW?

The Vulnerability Principle suggests that breaches of confidentiality may be justified in cases where the following conditions obtain: (1) there is an identifiable person or an identifiable group of people who are "at risk" of contracting AIDS from a known carrier,

(2) the carrier has not or will not disclose his/her antibody status to those persons whom he/she has placed or will place at risk, and (3) the identity of the carrier and his/her antibody status is known to a physician, nurse, health care worker, public health authority, or another person privileged to this information. It is justifiable, under these circumstances, to reveal information which might enable others to identify an AIDS patient or HIV-infected person. Revelation of confidential information is justified under this rule by the fact that others are vulnerable to infection, or may be unknowingly infecting others, and the information to be revealed may serve as an effective means of protecting those at risk.

NOTES

1. *The Baltimore Sun*, June 11, 1987, p. D1.
2. Sissela Bok, *Secrets: On the Ethics of Concealment and Revelation* (New York: Vintage Books, 1983); Chapter IX.
3. Bok, Op. Cit., pp. 129–130.
4. Robert E. Goodin, *Protecting the Vulnerable: A Reanalysis of Our Social Responsibilities* (Chicago: The University of Chicago Press, 1985).

Truth Telling and Disclosing Bad News

DAVID C. THOMASMA

Telling the Truth to Patients: A Clinical Ethics Exploration

David Thomasma was professor of medical ethics in the Neiswanger Institute for Bioethics and Health Policy at Loyola University Chicago Medical Center, where until recently he directed the Medical Humanities Program. His many publications focused heavily on the Doctor-Patient Relationship. His collaborations with Dr. Ed Pellegrino long produced several books, including *For the Patient's Good: The Restoration of Beneficence in Health Care* (Oxford).

REASONS FOR TELLING THE TRUTH

... In all human relationships, the truth is told for a myriad of reasons. A summary of the prominent reasons are that it is a right, a utility, and a kindness.

It is a right to be told the truth because respect for the person demands it. As Kant argued, human society would soon collapse without truth telling, because it is the basis of interpersonal trust, covenants, contracts, and promises.

The truth is a utility as well, because persons need to make informed judgments about their actions. It is a mark of maturity that individuals advance and grow morally by becoming more and more self-aware of their needs, their motives, and their limitations. All these steps toward maturity require honest and forthright communication, first from parents and later also from siblings, friends, lovers, spouses, children, colleagues, co-workers, and caregivers.[1]

Finally, it is a kindness to be told the truth, a kindness rooted in virtue precisely because persons to whom lies are told will of necessity withdraw from important, sometimes life-sustaining and life-saving relationships. Similarly, those who tell lies poison not only their relationships but themselves, rendering themselves incapable of virtue and moral growth.[2] ...

From *Cambridge Quarterly of Healthcare Ethics* 3 (1994), 375–82. Copyright © 1994 Cambridge University Press. Reprinted with the permission of Cambridge University Press.

. . . Not all of us act rationally and autonomously at all times. Sometimes we are under sufficient stress that others must act to protect us from harm. This is called necessary paternalism. Should we become seriously ill, others must step in and rescue us if we are incapable of doing it ourselves. . . .

IN GENERAL RELATIONSHIPS

In each of the three main reasons why the truth must be told, as a right, a utility, and a kindness, lurk values that may from time to time become more important than the truth. When this occurs, the rule of truth telling is trumped, that is, overridden by a temporarily more important principle. The ultimate value in all instances is the survival of the community and/or the well-being of the individual. Does this mean for paternalistic reasons, without the person's consent, the right to the truth, the utility, and the kindness, can be shunted aside? The answer is "yes." The truth in a relationship responds to a multivariate complexity of values, the context for which helps determine which values in that relationship should predominate.

Nothing I have said thus far suggests that the truth may be treated in a cavalier fashion or that it can be withheld from those who deserve it for frivolous reasons. The only values that can trump the truth are recipient survival, community survival, and the ability to absorb the full impact of the truth at a particular time. All these are only temporary trump cards in any event. They only can be played under certain limited conditions because respect for persons is a foundational value in all relationships.

IN HEALTHCARE RELATIONSHIPS

It is time to look more carefully at one particular form of human relationship, the relationship between the doctor and the patient or sometimes between other healthcare providers and the patient.

Early in the 1960s, studies were done that revealed the majority of physicians would not disclose a diagnosis of cancer to a patient. Reasons cited were mostly those that derived from nonmaleficence. Physicians were concerned that such a diagnosis might disturb the equanimity of a patient and might lead to desperate acts. Primarily physicians did not want to destroy their patients' hope. By the middle 1970s, however, repeat studies brought to light a radical shift in physician attitudes. Unlike earlier views, physicians now emphasized patient autonomy and informed consent over paternalism. In the doctor–patient relation, this meant the majority of physicians stressed the patient's right to full disclosure of diagnosis and prognosis.

One might be tempted to ascribe this shift of attitudes to the growing patients' rights and autonomy movements in the philosophy of medicine and in public affairs. No doubt some of the change can be attributed to this movement. But also treatment interventions for cancer led to greater optimism about modalities that could offer some hope to patients. Thus, to offer them full disclosure of their diagnosis no longer was equivalent to a death sentence. Former powerlessness of the healer was supplanted with technological and pharmaceutical potentialities.

A more philosophical analysis of the reasons for a shift comes from a consideration of the goal of medicine. The goal of all healthcare relations is to receive/provide help for an illness such that no further harm is done to the patient, especially in that patient's vulnerable state.[3] The vulnerability arises because of increased dependency. Presumably, the doctor will not take advantage of this vulnerable condition by adding to it through inappropriate use of power or the lack of compassion. Instead, the vulnerable person should be assisted back to a state of human equality, if possible, free from the prior dependency.[4]

First, the goal of the healthcare giver–patient relation is essentially to restore the patient's autonomy. Thus, respect for the right of the patient to the truth is measured against this goal. If nothing toward that goal can be gained by telling the truth at a particular time, still it must be told for other reasons. Yet, if the truth would impair the restoration of autonomy, then it may be withheld on grounds of potential harm. Thus the goal of the healing relationship enters into the calculus of values that are to be protected.

Second, most healthcare relationships of an interventionist character are temporary, whereas relationships involving primary care, prevention, and chronic or dying care are more permanent. These differences also have a bearing on truth telling. During a short encounter with healthcare strangers, patients and healthcare providers will of necessity require the truth more readily than during a long-term relation among near friends. In the short term, decisions, often dramatically important ones, need to be made in a compressed period. There is less opportunity to maneuver or delay for other reasons, even if there are concerns about the truth's impact on the person.

Over a longer period, the truth may be withheld for

compassionate reasons more readily. Here, the patient and physician or nurse know one another. They are more likely to have shared some of their values. In this context, it is more justifiable to withhold the truth temporarily in favor of more important long-term values, which are known in the relationship.

Finally, the goal of healthcare relations is treatment of an illness. An illness is far broader than its subset, disease. Illness can be viewed as a disturbance in the life of an individual, perhaps due to many non-medical factors. A disease, by contrast, is a medically caused event that may respond to more intervention-ist strategies.[5]

Helping one through an illness is a far greater personal task than doing so for a disease. A greater, more enduring bond is formed. The strength of this bond may justify withholding the truth as well, although in the end "the truth will always out."

CLINICAL CASE CATEGORIES

The general principles about truth telling have been reviewed, as well as possible modifications formed from the particularities of the healthcare professional–patient relationship. Now I turn to some contemporary examples of how clinical ethics might analyze the hierarchy of values surrounding truth telling.

There are at least five clinical case categories in which truth telling becomes problematic: intervention cases, long-term care cases, cases of dying patients, prevention cases, and nonintervention cases.

INTERVENTION CASES

Of all clinically difficult times to tell the truth, two typical cases stand out. The first usually involves a mother of advanced age with cancer. The family might beg the surgeon not to tell her what has been discovered for fear that "Mom might just go off the deep end." The movie *Dad,* starring Jack Lemmon, had as its centerpiece the notion that Dad could not tolerate the idea of cancer. Once told, he went into a psychotic shock that ruptured standard relationships with the doctors, the hospital, and the family. However, because this diagnosis requires patient participation for chemotherapeutic interventions and the time is short, the truth must be faced directly. Only if there is not to be intervention might one withhold the truth from the patient for a while, at the family's request, until the patient is able to cope with the reality. A contract about the time allowed before telling the truth might be a good idea.

The second case is that of ambiguous genitalia. A woman, 19 years old, comes for a checkup because she plans to get married and has not yet had a period. She is very mildly retarded. It turns out that she has no vagina, uterus, or ovaries but does have an unde-scended testicle in her abdomen. She is actually a he. Should she be told this fundamental truth about her-self? Those who argue for the truth do so on grounds that she will eventually find out, and more of her sub-sequent life will have been ruined by the lies and disingenuousness of others. Those who argue against the truth usually prevail. National standards exist in this regard. The young woman is told that she has something like a "gonadal mass" in her abdomen that might turn into cancer if not removed, and an opera-tion is performed. She is assisted to remain a female.

More complicated still is a case of a young His-panic woman, a trauma accident victim, who is grad-ually coming out of a coma. She responds only to commands such as "move your toes." Because she is now incompetent, her mother and father are making all care decisions in her case. Her boyfriend is a wel-come addition to the large, extended family. However, the physicians discover that she is pregnant. The fetus is about 5 weeks old. Eventually, if she does not re-cover, her surrogate decision makers will have to be told about the pregnancy, because they will be in-volved in the terrible decisions about continuing the life of the fetus even if it is a risk to the mother's re-covery from the coma. This revelation will almost certainly disrupt current family relationships and the role of the boyfriend. Further, if the mother is incom-petent to decide, should not the boyfriend, as pre-sumed father, have a say in the decision about his own child?

In this case, revelation of the truth must be care-fully managed. The pregnancy should be revealed only on a "need to know" basis, that is, only when the survival of the young woman becomes critical. She is still progressing moderately towards a stable state.

LONG-TERM CASES

Rehabilitation medicine provides one problem of truth telling in this category. If a young man has been par-alyzed by a football accident, his recovery to some level of function will depend upon holding out hope. As he struggles to strengthen himself, the motivation might be a hope that caregivers know to be false, that he may someday be able to walk again. Yet this false-hood is not corrected, lest he slip into despair. Hence, because this is a long-term relationship, the truth will be gradually discovered by the patient under the aegis of encouragement by his physical therapists, nurses, and physicians, who enter his life as near friends.

CASES OF DYING PATIENTS

Sometimes, during the dying process, the patient asks directly, "Doctor, am I dying?" Physicians are frequently reluctant to "play God" and tell the patient how many days or months or years they have left. This reluctance sometimes bleeds over into a less-than-forthright answer to the question just asked. A surgeon with whom I make rounds once answered this question posed by a terminally ill cancer patient by telling her that she did not have to worry about her insurance running out!

Yet in every case of dying patients, the truth can be gradually revealed such that the patient learns about dying even before the family or others who are resisting telling the truth. Sometimes, without directly saying "you are dying," we are able to use interpretative truth and comfort the patient. If a car driver who has been in an accident and is dying asks about other family members in the car who are already dead, there is no necessity to tell him the truth. Instead, he can be told that "they are being cared for" and that the important thing right now is that he be comfortable and not in pain. One avoids the awful truth because he may feel responsible and guilt ridden during his own dying hours if he knew that the rest of his family were already dead.

PREVENTION CASES

A good example of problems associated with truth telling in preventive medicine might come from screening. The high prevalence of prostate cancer among men over 50 years old may suggest the utility of cancer screening. An annual checkup for men over 40 years old is recommended. Latent and asymptomatic prostate cancer is often clinically unsuspected and is present in approximately 30% of men over 50 years of age. If screening were to take place, about 16.5 million men in the United States alone would be diagnosed with prostate cancer, or about 2.4 million men each year. As of now, only 120,000 cases are newly diagnosed each year. Thus, as Timothy Moon noted in a recent sketch of the disease, "a majority of patients with prostate cancer that is not clinically diagnosed will experience a benign course throughout their lifetime."[6]

The high incidence of prostate cancer coupled with a very low malignant potential would entail a whole host of problems if subjected to screening. Detection would force patients and physicians to make very difficult and life-altering treatment decisions. Among them are removal of the gland (with impotence a possible outcome), radiation treatment, and most effective of all, surgical removal of the gonads (orchiectomy). But why consider these rather violent interventions if the probable outcome of neglect will overwhelmingly be benign? For this reason the U.S. Preventive Services Task Force does not recommend either for or against screening for prostate cancer.[7] Quality-of-life issues would take precedence over the need to know.

NONINTERVENTION CASES

This last example more closely approximates the kind of information one might receive as a result of gene mapping. This information could tell you of the likelihood or probability of encountering a number of diseases through genetic heritage, for example, adult onset or type II diabetes, but could not offer major interventions for most of them (unlike a probability for diabetes).

Some evidence exists from recent studies that the principle of truth telling now predominates in the doctor–patient relationship. Doctors were asked about revealing diagnosis for Huntington's disease and multiple sclerosis, neither of which is subject to a cure at present. An overwhelming majority would consider full disclosure. This means that, even in the face of diseases for which we have no cure, truth telling seems to take precedence over protecting the patient from imagined harms.

The question of full disclosure acquires greater poignancy in today's medicine, especially with respect to Alzheimer's disease and genetic disorders that may be diagnosed in utero. There are times when our own scientific endeavors lack a sufficient conceptual and cultural framework around which to assemble facts. The facts can overwhelm us without such conceptual frameworks. The future of genetics poses just such a problem. In consideration of the new genetics, this might be the time to stress values over the truth.

CONCLUSION

Truth in the clinical relationship is factored in with knowledge and values.

First, truth is contextual. Its revelation depends

upon the nature of the relationship between the doctor and patient and the duration of that relationship.

Second, truth is a secondary good. Although important, other primary values take precedence over the truth. The most important of these values is survival of the individual and the community. A close second would be preservation of the relationship itself.

Third, truth is essential for healing an illness. It may not be as important for curing a disease. That is why, for example, we might withhold the truth from the woman with ambiguous genitalia, curing her disease (having a gonad) in favor of maintaining her health (being a woman).

Fourth, withholding the truth is only a temporary measure. *In vino, veritas* it is said. The truth will eventually come out, even if in a slip of the tongue. Its revelation, if it is to be controlled, must always aim at the good of the patient for the moment.

At all times, the default mode should be that the truth is told. If, for some important reason, it is not to be immediately revealed in a particular case, a truth-management protocol should be instituted so that all caregivers on the team understand how the truth will eventually be revealed.

NOTES

1. Bok S. *Lying: Moral Choice in Public and Personal Life.* New York: Vintage Books, 1989.

2. Pellegrino E. D., Thomasma D. C. *The Virtues in Medical Practice.* New York: Oxford University Press, 1993.

3. Cassell E. The nature of suffering and the goals of medicine. *New England Journal of Medicine* 1982; 306(11):639–45.

4. See Nordenfelt L., issue editor. Concepts of health and their consequences for health care. *Theoretical Medicine* 1993; 14(4).

5. Moon T. D. Prostate cancer. *Journal of the American Geriatrics Society* 1992; 40:622–7 (quote from 626).

6. See note 5. Moon. 1992; 40:622–7.

GARRY S. SIGMAN, JEROME KRAUT, AND JOHN LA PUMA

Disclosure of a Diagnosis to Children and Adolescents When Parents Object

Garry S. Sigman, MD, practices adolescent medicine at Lutheran General Children's Hospital (Park Ridge, Illinois) and teaches in the Department of Pediatrics at Northwestern University in Chicago. In addition to serving as the director of adolescent medicine programs, he has served on institutional ethics committees. His collaborative publications include "Ethical Issues in Research on Adolescents," *Adolescent Medicine* and "Confidential Health Care for Adolescents," *Journal of Adolescent Health*.

Jerome R. Kraut, MD, is director of the Pediatric Resident Program and an attending physician at the Lutheran General Children's Hospital, Park Ridge, Illinois. He also has served as clinical associate professor of pediatrics at the University of Chicago, Department of Pediatrics, and as lecturer at the Northwestern University School of Medicine. In addition to his service on ethics committees and advisory committees, he has also published several medical works in the field of pediatrics and ethics.

John La Puma, MD, was formerly a clinical associate professor at the University of Chicago and is now professor of nutrition at Kendall College and School of Culinary Arts in Evanston, Illinois. Following a postgraduate fellowship in medical ethics at the University of Chicago, he has published in the fields of medical ethics, alternative medicine, and nutrition. He has served as the national spokesperson for the Harvard DASH (Dietary Approaches to Stop Hypertension) eating plan and is also the founder and executive director of Alternative Medicine Alert.

Parents of children and adolescents occasionally request that the physician not disclose a diagnosis or prognosis to the young patient. Such a request creates an ethical dilemma for the practitioner: the conflict between a duty to respect parents' wishes as well as a duty to tell the truth to the child.

The authority of parents to direct the flow of information to the child and to organize and provide appropriate systems of emotional support is well recognized in pediatric care. Parents are regarded as moral agents for their children; pediatricians perceive that the integrity of the patient's family is necessary to sustain and nurture the child.

Still, parental authority cannot be absolute. A "best interest" standard that extends beyond parents' wishes is recognized in nontreatment decisions in severely ill neonates and children,[1] in relationship to the treatment of children whose parents have religious objection to usual care,[2] and in relationship to the confidential care of adolescents.[3]

Reprinted by permission of the publisher from *American Journal of Diseases of Children* 147 (1993), 764–768. Copyright © 1993, American Medical Association.

Several cases exploring the physicians' duties to tell the truth to children have been reported.[4-6] We attempt to advance the discussion by using an extraordinary case to identify the clinical circumstances that are important in the decision regarding truthful disclosure to children when parents object.

REPORT OF A CASE

The patient, aged 19 years, was first seen by her current physician, a specialist in the treatment of cystic fibrosis (CF) at age 9 years. After a normal pregnancy, labor, and delivery, the newborn developed irritability, vomiting, and frequent foul stools soon after discharge. At age 4 months, failure to thrive prompted a sweat test that was diagnostic for CF.

Both parents were born in Italy and moved to the United States as adults. The father, aged 48 years, owns a barber shop and is a postal worker. The mother, aged 39 years, cares for her family in the home. The now 6-year-old sister does not have CF.

The parents recall feeling devastated when told that CF is a lethal disease that usually results in early death. They said that nothing could be more horrible than their child knowing of her fatal disease. They agreed at the time of diagnosis that they would never tell her or her extended family of her disease and would not allow health care professionals to disclose the diagnosis and prognosis to their daughter. . . .

By age 15, the patient had grown into a normal-appearing teenager who did well in school and had a normal social life and good relationship with her parents. The physician felt increasingly guilty about participation in the nondisclosure, not because the patient was asking questions (she was not), but simply because she was getting older. In another conference, he and the social worker tried again to convince the parents to change their minds. The parents remained committed to their decision and made it clear that it was not negotiable. The parents agreed to counseling but did not see the benefits of telling their daughter her diagnosis and refused to make that a goal of counseling. They did not follow through with this treatment. . . .

Just after her 18th birthday, the patient developed another pulmonary exacerbation and was seen in the office prior to hospitalization. The physician explained the secrecy oath and the diagnosis and prognosis to the patient, with her parents present. Her mother tried to remove her daughter from the office, but the father gently calmed the mother and allowed the first discussion their daughter ever had about her disease. She reacted calmly and asked questions.

After the session the patient said that she had no idea that she had CF and had not felt the need to question her parents or physician. She thought she had allergies, asthma, and "weak lungs." The patient denied any anger toward her parents or the physician about the secrecy. She has had no further admissions, is doing well to date, understands her disease, and is involved in self-care . . .

ANALYZING DISCLOSURE DUTIES

If there is a moral justification for lying to the patient, or willfully hiding the truth, it must have a strength that overrides the principle of veracity, derived from basic human respect.[7(p31)] People deserve to be told the truth; and circumstances must be morally persuasive when considering deviating from this basic moral duty.

Physician factors, disease-specific factors, patient factors, and family factors are each important in the decision regarding disclosure to pediatric patients (see the table). The strength of the individual factors will ultimately determine the "right" action for the physician regarding disclosure. The factors' relative importance is not implied by their order in the text; all or one may be important in individual cases. Indeed, the relative value of each clinical factor will be different in each case; each clinical decision is context specific. Decisions about disclosure must be made by consid-

Clinical Factors to Be Considered Regarding Truthful Disclosure to Pediatric Patients

Physician factors
  Personal value system
  Societal, legal, and economic influences on medical
    decision making
  Professional codes of behavior

Disease-specific factors
  Natural history of disease
  Factors relating to provision of care
  Public health considerations

Patient factors
  Development and maturation
  Personality traits
  Psychiatric risk factors and symptoms

Family factors
  Cultural considerations
  Family dynamics and support mechanisms
  Family dysfunction and disease

ering the specific details of the case; they are decisions that must be made by a particular physician, regarding a particular disease, for and with a particular child from a particular family.

PHYSICIAN FACTORS

Physicians differ in their approaches to disclosure decisions. For example, individual differences exist in physicians' personal value systems. Some physicians view deception as therapeutic and therefore a justifiable alternative in certain clinical settings.[8] For them, truth telling is not a moral imperative, but a virtue with variable consequences for the patient's health.[9] For other physicians, any deception is wrong, no matter what the consequence. These physicians may consider nontruthful disclosure destructive of the physician's effectiveness with patients.[7(p238–241)] Even though they are unable to formally consent, the assent of children in medical decisions is increasingly recognized as morally and clinically important;[10] the lack of truthful disclosure would be antithetical to such a moral stance.

Internal personal values are derived from religious, social, and familial influences and affect physician attitudes regarding physician-assisted suicide,[11] withholding and withdrawing life-sustaining treatment,[12,13] and drug testing.[14] Some physicians find that, despite rational ethical arguments favoring certain decisions, they cannot make them because "it's against my conscience," an expression of personal values.

In addition, societal, economic, and legal phenomena also influence physicians' management of truth-telling dilemmas. Societal movements supporting individual rights and self-determination have become important and current during the last 25 years. Physicians have correspondingly altered their practices in favor of truthful disclosure, in recognition of patients' right of self-determination.[15,16]

Codes of professional behavior might influence physicians' ethical decisions. The American Medical Association's code of professional responsibility is not specific about truthful disclosure of diagnoses, although principle 2 of the preamble states, "A physician shall deal honestly with patients and colleagues."[17] The code's requirement for informed consent might be taken to apply to truthful disclosure, but the code does not address such issues regarding minors whose parents object to disclosure. To the best of our knowledge, the American Academy of Pediatrics has not published policies regarding truthful disclosure.

Suggesting that physicians differ on disclosure does not imply a moral relativism that leaves us unable to resolve any moral dilemmas. It does suggest that the medical profession, instead of mandating by code or standard of practice, has allowed decisions about disclosure to be left to each physician's assessment of the clinical circumstances.

DISEASE-SPECIFIC FACTORS

A strong argument for disclosure exists if a child's knowledge of the disease positively affects its course and prognosis. There are diseases in which self-care and survival would be impossible without a patient's knowledge of the disease and performance of daily self-care. Examples include diabetes mellitus, chronic renal failure, and severe CF.

Considering only physical aspects of disease does not address the question of whether knowing affects adjustment and prognosis. For CF, it appears that psychological adjustment to the disease is adequate for most adolescents and young adults who know their diagnosis and prognosis,[18–20] although gender differences in coping style have been reported. Girls have more difficulty integrating the presence of the disease with their self-concept.[21] Considering only adolescent identity formation and coping considerations, delay in learning of a CF diagnosis in a mild case may not be harmful in certain patients.

In addition, patients must know the facts of their disease to plan their lives. In CF, premature death and infertility (for most) are generally certain. Patients with CF should be made aware of the effects of the disease on reproduction, "when he or she is sexually and emotionally mature."[22] All young people who have a potential desire to procreate and who are sexually active should have access to genetic counseling. These facts about CF strengthen the need for a patient's decision making. A pediatrician might accede to parents who wish to raise a child in a particular way, but not to parents who usurp a child's future life decisions.

As with many chronic diseases, care for patients with CF is provided by a team approach. Nondisclosure, even if justified, cannot be carried out without a significant alteration in the normal patterns of team communication.[23] Such a "conspiracy" may have an effect on collective care givers that negatively impacts on morale and care provision. Medical education as well may be adversely affected if students and residents perceive that lying to the patient is okay as long as the parents insist.

Do patients with chronic diseases do better if they meet and interact with others with the disease? This cannot be empirically studied since this is standard for patients with CF. Nevertheless, a patient unable to attend a special disease of specialty-based clinic might be unable to take advantage of new diagnostic or treatment opportunities that are on the cutting edge.

The duty to disclose to the patient, despite parental objection, increases with the potential threat to the public health. While no such threats exist for CF, the diagnosis for youth who have human immunodeficiency virus infection, for example, cannot be hidden because of the potential for unwitting transmission. This also applies to truthful disclosure of other chronic transmissible infections, such as hepatitis B or genital herpes simplex.

PATIENT FACTORS

The duty to respect a patient by allowing him or her to make decisions is altered by the patient's inability to make such a decision. At young ages, children cannot do so and are dependent; parents are, of necessity, the primary decision makers. A parent's request to shield a young child from specific knowledge is less morally objectionable than such a request for a child or adolescent of greater maturity.

As a child matures, his or her ability and need to understand increases so that surrogate decision makers are less necessary.[24] As maturity progresses, an emerging adult takes on the moral authority to think, speak, and act for himself or herself.[25,26] The patient's advancing maturity confers an increasing duty to value the patient's right to know personal information above a parent's right to control that information.

The desire for self-determination and decision making varies among pediatric patients. These individual differences are a result of developmental maturity, personality factors, and environmental influences. Children differ in regard to the degree of control they believe that they have (and want) over their lives and their illnesses.[27]

Does a physician have a duty to disclose to a mature patient unrequested information? Just as it might be considered paternalistic on the part of parents to require secrecy, it is also paternalistic on the part of physicians to assume that truth is "good for the patient" if it is unrequested. The fact that patients do not ask does not mean that they do not desire more information. Families of patients with chronic diseases

and fatal prognoses sometimes have unspoken agreements of silence about the prognosis; it is taboo to bring the reality of a child's impending death into the open.[28] This is recognized as a family defense mechanism and supports an emotional equilibrium in the family.[29]

An adolescent patient might emerge from a system of overwhelming family secrecy and demonstrate personal needs and desires if given a chance to speak confidentially to care givers. The physician must form a hypothesis about the patient's desire for autonomy in self-care and the ability to cope. It is a physician's duty to ask directly whether more information is requested. If the physician perceives that the patient wishes to achieve more control over decision making, helping the patient to become more autonomous is required. If the patient express no such wishes, the physician can respect the silence and allow others to decide, while making ongoing inquiries of the patient about his or her own desires.[30]

Finally, the patient's mental health must be considered. When a parent fears that the result of a disclosure might cause psychological harm, the physician should carefully consider the (generally remote) possibility of triggering psychiatric symptoms. Suicide has been reported in adolescents with chronic or fatal illnesses, but this is rare. Physicians should consider whether the history and examination demonstrate clinical features that might suggest a high risk for psychiatric symptoms when considering how, when, and whether disclosure should occur.[31]

FAMILY FACTORS

Just as every patient is different, so is every family; cultural backgrounds and beliefs of families differ. Kleinman et al.[32] have written, "Illness behavior is a normative experience governed by cultural rules." Whether disclosure is right for a patient must be interpreted in light of a family's particular cultural background.[33,34] Otherwise, a physician might simply impose his or her own cultural value of "truth" or "autonomy" and thereby breach a boundary of paternalism. He or she might also do harm by upsetting a stable system of social support provided by the family.

The strength and consistency of parental authority differs between families, regardless of how it is derived. Families differ in how, when, and where they make decisions. Physicians must discern and respect unique decision-making practices in families when faced with dilemmas of disclosure and truth telling.

Family psychosocial dysfunction may account for

the request of parents to not disclose a diagnosis. One or both parents may be delusional, guilt ridden, or otherwise unable to cope with a child's chronic illness. Psychiatric or psychological consultation may be helpful to determine whether the potential for harm to the child and the dysfunctional family member exists if their child is given information they wish him or her not to have.

CLINICAL FACTORS AND THE PRESENT CASE
The clinical factors described above apply specifically to the present case as follows:

PHYSICIAN FACTORS

The personal value system of the CF specialist in this case allowed him to care for the patient, even after deciding not to disclose the diagnosis. This decision was based on his belief that as long as the patient's medical needs were being met, the parents had a right to control medical information. No legal requirement mandated disclosure, and none was suggested by a professional code. The physician's personal reservations about adhering to the parents' demands were overridden by other factors.

DISEASE-SPECIFIC FACTORS

At the beginning of the patient's disease course, prognosis and care needs probably were not altered by her ignorance of the diagnosis. In practical terms, the only difference in her therapy would have been attending the CF clinic, taking pancreatic enzymes, and receiving more frequent chest physiotherapy. There will never be full scientific evidence to prove or disprove the long-term effectiveness of chest physiotherapy[35] since it is one of many treatment modalities that cannot be evaluated singly. It is generally accepted as standard therapy, so one must assume that the lack of it was a deficiency in the care of this patient. All other prescribed treatments were faithfully carried out by the parents, including the administration of medications when necessary.

It is not certain that the patient's treatment was of poorer quality than it would have been had she known about her disease. It cannot be shown that she suffered physically or psychologically by not knowing her diagnosis. For her parents, who did not accept the overriding "right" of autonomy and self-determination of their daughter, it was difficult to accept the physician's argument that improved health would likely result if he told the patient her diagnosis. . . .

PATIENT FACTORS
Adolescent development and the maturing of cognitive processes created an increasing responsibility for the physician to seek out the patient's autonomous wishes. Even in her middle and late teenage years, however, she did not demonstrate initiative in discovering more than what she was told. Her lack of curiosity and general acceptance of all medical prescriptions suggested no desire to alter or rebel against the authority of her parents. A striving for independence and self-actualization did not appear as she aged, at least in regard to her medical care. She questioned neither her parents nor the physician.

It is possible that the patient had perceived a "secret" that must not be discussed and wished to respect this boundary. She did not seem to challenge any such "taboo" and did not seem to seek help from the physician in challenging it. The long-term deception may have prevented her from expressing her choices and her physician from discerning them.

In summary, patient factors were significant in the final decision to disclose, but were not compelling early in the physician's involvement with her. Without evidence of patient psychopathology, the physician did not fear harming the patient by disclosure. The secrecy so firmly demanded by the parents prevented the physician from determining or even guessing what information the patient wanted.

FAMILY FACTORS
. . . The patient was aware of and respected a parent-dominated social structure in which parents made all medical and most nonmedical decisions for their children. Beyond the special characteristics of many first-generation Italian families, however, the persistence of the parents' refusal to tell their daughter the truth, the rigidity of their position, and their resistance to change as the daughter matured can be interpreted as an indication of a dysfunctional family process.[36] The parents unfortunately recognized neither a need for therapy nor any dysfunction in themselves or their daughter.

CONCLUSION
. . . The answer to the problem of disclosure depends on the clinical context that defines the patient's best interests and the physician's values and attitudes. Decisions about truth telling are context specific; they should be continually examined as the clinical

situation changes. Patients' needs change with the natural history of their disease and as their developmental capabilities evolve. It is appropriate that models are developed for clinical ethics that embody this evolution.

NOTES

1. Walters J. W. Approaches to ethical decision making in the neonatal intensive care unit. *AJDC*. 1988;142:825–830.

2. Ackerman T. F. The limits of beneficence: Jehovah's Witness and childhood cancer. *Hasting Cent Rep*. 1980;10:13–18.

3. Forman E. N., Ladd R. E. Treating adolescents: when is a child an adult? In: *Ethical Dilemmas in Pediatrics: A Case Study Approach*. New York, NY: Springer Verlag NY Inc; 1991:111–128.

4. Leiken S. L. An ethical issue in pediatric cancer care: nondisclosure of a fatal prognosis. *Pediatr Ann*. 1981;10:37–46.

5. Truth telling in pediatrics. In: Ganos D., Lipson R. E., Warren G., Weil B. J., eds. *Difficult Decisions in Medical Ethics*. New York, NY: Alan R. Liss Inc; 1983:171–196.

6. Higgs, R., ed. A father says, 'Don't tell my son the truth.' *J Med Ethics*. 1985;11:153–158.

7. Bok S. *Lying: Moral Choice in Public and Private Life*. New York, NY: Vintage Books; 1978.

8. Novack D. H., Detering B. J., Arnold R., Forrow L., Ladinsky M., Pezzullo J. C. Physicians' attitudes toward using deception to resolve difficult ethical problems. *JAMA*. 1989;261:2980–2985.

9. Pernick M. S. Childhood death and medical ethics: an historical perspective on truth-telling in pediatrics. In: Ganos D., Lipson R.E., Warren G., Weil B. J., eds. *Difficult Decisions in Medical Ethics*. New York, NY: Alan R. Liss Inc; 1983:173–188.

10. Bartholome W. G. A new understanding of consent in pediatric practice. *Pediatr Ann*. 1989;18:262–265.

11. Klagsbrun S. C. Physician-assisted suicide: a double dilemma. *J Pain Symptom Manage*. 1991;6(special issue):325–328.

12. Paris J., Lantos J. The case of baby L. *N Engl J Med*. 1990;322:1012–1014.

13. Cranford R. E. Helga Wanglie's ventilator. *Hastings Cent Rep*. 1991;21:23–24.

14. Linn L. S., Yager J., Leake B. Professional vs personal factors related to physicians' attitudes toward drug testing. *J Drug Educ*. 1990;20:95–109.

15. Pellegrino E. D., Thomasma D. C. *For the Patient's Good*. New York, NY: Oxford University Press Inc; 1988:4.

16. Novack D. H., Plumer R., Smith R. L., Ochitill H., Morrow G. R., Bennet J. M. Changes in physicians' attitudes toward telling the cancer patient. *JAMA* 1979;241:897–900.

17. American Medical Association. *Principles of Medical Ethics and Current Opinions of the Council on Ethical and Judicial Affairs*. Chicago, Ill: American Medical Association; 1989:ix.

18. Kashani J. H., Barbero G. J., Wifley D. E., Morris D. A., Sheppard J.A. Psychological concomitants of cystic fibrosis in children and adolescents. *Adolescence*. 1988;23:873–880.

19. Mador J. A., Smith D. H. The psychological adaptation of adolescents with cystic fibrosis: a review of the literature. *J Adolesc Health Care*. 1988;10:136–142.

20. Shepard S. L., Hovell M. F., Harwood I. R., et al. A comparative study of the psychosocial assets of adults with cystic fibrosis and their healthy peers. *Chest*. 1990;97:1310–1316.

21. Simmons R., Corey M., Cowen L., Keenan N., Robertson J., Levinson H. Emotional adjustment of early adolescents with cystic fibrosis. *Psychosom Med*. 1985;47:111–122.

22. Levine S. B., Stern R. C. Sexual function in cystic fibrosis. *Chest*. 1982;81:422–428.

23. Matthews L. W., Droter D. Cystic fibrosis: A challenging long-term chronic disease. *Pediatr Clin North Am*. 1984;31:133–151.

24. Moreno J. D. Treating the adolescent patient: an ethical analysis. *J Adolesc Health Care*. 1989;10:454–459.

25. Lantos J. D., Miles S. H. Autonomy in adolescent medicine. *J Adolesc Health Care*. 1989;10:460–466.

26. Chesler M. A., Paris J., Barbarin O. A. 'Telling' the child with cancer: parental choices to share information with ill children. *J Pediatr Psychol*. 1986;2:497–515.

27. Sanger M. S., Sandler-Howard K., Perrin E. C. Concepts of illness and perception of control in healthy children and in children with chronic illnesses. *J Dev Behav Pediatr*. 1988;9:252–256.

28. Bluebond-Langer M. *The Private Worlds of Dying Children*. Princeton, NJ: Princeton University Press; 1978:198–230.

29. Silber T. J. Ethical considerations in the care of the chronically ill adolescent. In: Blum R. W., ed. *Chronic Illness and Disabilities in Childhood and Adolescence*. Philadelphia, Pa: Grune & Stratton; 1984:17–27.

30. Childress J. F. The place of autonomy in bioethics. *Hastings Cent Rep*. 1990;20:12–17.

31. Gunther M. S. Acute-onset serious chronic organic illness in adolescence: some critical issues. *Adolesc Psychiatry*. 1985;12:58–76.

32. Kleinman A. M., Eisenberg L., Good B. Culture, illness and care: clinical lessons from anthropologic and cross-cultural research. *Ann Intern Medical*. 1978;88:251–258.

33. Surbone A. Truth telling to the patient. *JAMA*. 1992;268:1661–1662.

34. Pellegrino E. D. Is truth telling to the patient a cultural artifact? *JAMA*. 1992;268:1734–1735.

35. MacLusky I., Levison H. Cystic fibrosis. In: Chernick V., Kendig E. L., eds. *Kendig's Disorders of the Respiratory Tract in Children*. 5th ed. Philadelphia, Pa: WB Saunders Co; 1990:711.

36. Andolfi M., Angelo C., Menghi P., Nicolo-Carigliano A. M. *Behind the Family Mask: Therapeutic Change in Rigid Family Systems*. New York, NY: Brunner/Mazel Publishers; 1983:13–14.

Informed Consent

CANTERBURY V. SPENCE

United States Court of Appeals

SPOTTSWOOD W. ROBINSON, III, Circuit Judge

Suits charging failure by a physician adequately to disclose the risks and alternatives of proposed treatment are not innovations in American law. They date back a good half-century, and in the last decade they have multiplied rapidly. There is, nonetheless, disagreement among the courts and the commentators on many major questions, and there is no precedent of our own directly in point. For the tools enabling resolution of the issues on this appeal, we are forced to begin at first principles.

The root premise is the concept, fundamental in American jurisprudence, that "[e]very human being of adult years and sound mind has a right to determine what shall be done with his own body. . . ." True consent to what happens to one's self is the informed exercise of a choice, and that entails an opportunity to evaluate knowledgeably the options available and the risks attendant upon each. The average patient has little or no understanding of the medical arts, and ordinarily has only his physician to whom he can look for enlightenment with which to reach an intelligent decision. From these almost axiomatic considerations springs the need, and in turn the requirement, of a reasonable divulgence by physician to patient to make such a decision possible.

• • •

Once the circumstances give rise to a duty on the physician's part to inform his patient, the next inquiry is the scope of the disclosure the physician is legally

No. 22099, U.S. Court of Appeals, District of Columbia Circuit, May 19, 1972. 464 Federal Reporter, 2nd Series, 772.

obliged to make. The courts have frequently confronted this problem, but no uniform standard defining the adequacy of the divulgence emerges from the decisions. Some have said "full" disclosure,[1] a norm we are unwilling to adopt literally. It seems obviously prohibitive and unrealistic to expect physicians to discuss with their patients every risk of proposed treatment—no matter how small or remote—and generally unnecessary from the patient's viewpoint as well. Indeed, the cases speaking in terms of "full" disclosure appear to envision something less than total disclosure,[2] leaving unanswered the question of just how much.

The larger number of courts, as might be expected, have applied tests framed with reference to prevailing fashion within the medical profession. Some have measured the disclosure by "good medical practice," others by what a reasonable practitioner would have bared under the circumstances, and still others by what medical custom in the community would demand. We have explored this rather considerable body of law but are unprepared to follow it. The duty to disclose, we have reasoned, arises from phenomena apart from medical custom and practice. The latter, we think, should no more establish the scope of the duty than its existence. Any definition of scope in terms purely of a professional standard is at odds with the patient's prerogative to decide on projected therapy himself. That prerogative, we have said, is at the very foundation of the duty to disclose, and both the patient's right to know and the physician's correlative obligation to tell him are diluted to the extent that its compass is dictated by the medical profession.

In our view, the patient's right of self-decision shapes the boundaries of the duty to reveal. That right can be effectively exercised only if the patient possesses enough information to enable an intelligent choice. The scope of the physician's communications to the patient, then, must be measured by the patient's need, and that need is the information material to the decision. Thus the test for determining whether a particular peril must be divulged is its materiality to the patient's decision: all risks potentially affecting the decision must be unmasked. And to safeguard the patient's interest in achieving his own determination on treatment, the law must itself set the standard for adequate disclosure.

Optimally for the patient, exposure of a risk would be mandatory whenever the patient would deem it significant to his decision, either singly or in combination with other risks. Such a requirement, however, would summon the physician to second-guess the patient, whose ideas on materiality could hardly be known to the physician. That would make an undue demand upon medical practitioners, whose conduct, like that of others, is to be measured in terms of reasonableness. Consonantly with orthodox negligence doctrine, the physician's liability for nondisclosure is to be determined on the basis of foresight, not hindsight; no less than any other aspect of negligence, the issue of nondisclosure must be approached from the viewpoint of the reasonableness of the physician's divulgence in terms of what he knows or should know to be the patient's informational needs. If, but only if, the fact-finder can say that the physician's communication was unreasonably inadequate is an imposition of liability legally or morally justified.

Of necessity, the content of the disclosure rests in the first instance with the physician. Ordinarily it is only he who is in a position to identify particular dangers; always he must make a judgment, in terms of materiality, as to whether and to what extent revelation to the patient is called for. He cannot know with complete exactitude what the patient would consider important to his decision, but on the basis of his medical training and experience he can sense how the average, reasonable patient expectably would react. Indeed, with knowledge of, or ability to learn, his patient's background and current condition, he is in a position superior to that of most others—attorneys, for example—who are called upon to make judgments on pain of liability in damages for unreasonable miscalculation.

From these considerations we derive the breadth of the disclosure of risks legally to be required. The scope of the standard is not subjective as to either the physician or the patient; it remains objective with due regard for the patient's informational needs and with suitable leeway for the physician's situation. In broad outline, we agreed that "[a] risk is thus material when a reasonable person, in what the physician knows or should know to be the patient's position, would be likely to attach significance to the risk or cluster of risks in deciding whether or not to forgo the proposed therapy."[3]

The topics importantly demanding a communication of information are the inherent and potential hazards of the proposed treatment, the alternatives to that treatment, if any, and the results likely if the patient remains untreated. The factors contributing significance to the dangerousness of a medical technique are, of course, the incidence of injury and the degree of the harm threatened. A very small chance of death or serious disablement may well be significant; a potential disability which dramatically outweighs the potential benefit of the therapy or the detriments of the existing malady may summon discussion with the patient.

There is no bright line separating the significant from the insignificant; the answer in any case must abide a rule of reason. Some dangers—infection, for example—are inherent in any operation; there is no obligation to communicate those of which persons of average sophistication are aware. Even more clearly, the physician bears no responsibility for discussion of hazards the patient has already discovered, or those having no apparent materiality to patients' decision on therapy. The disclosure doctrine, like others marking lines between permissible and impermissible behavior in medical practice, is in essence a requirement of conduct prudent under the circumstances. Whenever nondisclosure of particular risk information is open to debate by reasonable-minded men, the issue is for the finder of the facts.

Two exceptions to the general rule of disclosure have been noted by the courts. Each is in the nature of a physician's privilege not to disclose, and the reasoning underlying them is appealing. Each, indeed, is but a recognition that, as important as is the patient's right to know, it is greatly outweighed by the magnitudinous circumstances giving rise to the privilege. The first comes into play when the patient is unconscious or otherwise incapable of consenting, and harm from a failure to treat is imminent and outweighs any harm threatened by the proposed treatment. When a genuine emergency of that sort arises, it is settled that the impracticality of conferring with the patient dispenses with need for it. Even in situations of that character the physician should, as current law requires, attempt to secure a relative's consent if possible. But if time is too short to accommodate discussion obviously the physician should proceed with the treatment.

The second exception obtains when risk-disclosure poses such a threat of detriment to the patient as to become unfeasible or contraindicated from a medical point of view. It is recognized that patients occasionally become so ill or emotionally distraught on disclosure as to foreclose a rational decision, or complicate or hinder the treatment, or perhaps even pose psychological damage to the patient. Where that is so, the cases have generally held that the physician is armed with a privilege to keep the information from the patient, and we think it clear that portents of that type may justify the physician in action he deems medically warranted. The critical inquiry is whether the physician responded to a sound medical judgment that communication of the risk information would present a threat to the patient's well-being.

The physician's privilege to withhold information for therapeutic reasons must be carefully circumscribed, however, for otherwise it might devour the disclosure rule itself. The privilege does not accept the paternalistic notion that the physician may remain silent simply because divulgence might prompt the patient to forgo therapy the physician feels the patient really needs. That attitude presumes instability or perversity for even the normal patient, and runs counter to the foundation principle that the patient should and ordinarily can make the choice for himself. Nor does the privilege contemplate operation save where the patient's reaction to risk information, as reasonably foreseen by the physician, is menacing. And even in a situation of that kind, disclosure to a close relative with a view to securing consent to the proposed treatment may be the only alternative open to the physician.

NOTES

1. *E.g., Salgo v. Leland Stanford Jr. Univ. Bd. of Trustees*, 154 Cal. App. 2d 560, 317 P.2d 170, 181 (1975); *Woods v. Brumlop, supra* note 13 [in original text], 377 P.2d at 524–525.

2. See, Comment, Informed Consent in Medical Malpractice, 55 Calif. L. Rv. 1396, 1402–03 (1967).

3. Waltz and Scheuneman, Informed Consent to Therapy, 64, Nw. U.L. Rev. 628, 640 (1970).

JAY KATZ

Physicians and Patients: A History of Silence

Jay Katz, MD, is Elizabeth K. Dollard Professor Emeritus of Law, Medicine, and Psychiatry, as well as Harvey L. Karp Professorial Lecturer in Law and Psychoanalysis at Yale Law School. In the field of bioethics, he published two foundational works in the field: the edited work *Experimentation with Human Beings* (Russell Sage Foundation) and the authored work *The Silent World of Doctor and Patient* (Johns Hopkins University Press).

Disclosure and consent, except in the most rudimentary fashion, are obligations alien to medical thinking and practice. Disclosure in medicine has served the function of getting patients to "consent" to what physicians wanted them to agree to in the first place. "Good" patients follow doctor's orders without question.

Reprinted by permission of the author.

Therefore, disclosure becomes relevant only with recalcitrant patients. Since they are "bad" and "ungrateful," one does not need to bother much with them. Hippocrates once said, "Life is short, the Art long, Opportunity fleeting, Experiment treacherous, Judgment difficult. The physician must be ready, not only to do his duty himself, but also to secure the cooperation of the patient, of the attendants and of externals." These were, and still are, the lonely obligations of physicians: to wrestle as best they can with life, art, opportunity, experiment and judgment. Sharing with patients the vagaries of available opportunities, however perilous or safe, or the rationale underlying judgments, however difficult or easy, is not part of the Hippocratic task. For doing that, the Art is too long and Life too short.

Physicians have always maintained that patients are only in need of caring custody. Doctors felt that in order to accomplish that objective they were obligated to attend to their patients' physical and emotional needs and to do so on their own authority, without consulting with their patients about the decisions that needed to be made. Indeed, doctors intuitively believed that such consultations were inimical to good patient care. The idea that patients may also be entitled to liberty, to sharing the burdens of decision with their doctors, was never part of the ethos of medicine. Being unaware of the idea of patient liberty, physicians did not address the possible conflict between notions of custody and liberty. When, however, in recent decades courts were confronted with allegations that professionals had deprived citizen-patients of freedom of choice, the conflict did emerge. Anglo-American law has, at least in theory, a long-standing tradition of preferring liberty over custody; and however much judges tried to sidestep law's preferences and to side with physicians' traditional beliefs, the conflict remained and has ever since begged for a resolution. . . .

The legal doctrine remained limited in scope, in part, because judges believed or wished to believe that their pronouncements on informed consent gave legal force to what good physicians customarily did; therefore they felt that they could defer to the disclosure practices of "reasonable medical practitioners." Judges did not appreciate how deeply rooted the tradition of silence was and thus did not recognize the revolutionary, alien implications of their appeal for patient "self-determination." In fact, precisely because of the appeal's strange and bewildering novelty, physicians misinterpreted it as being more far-reaching than courts intended it to be.

Physicians did not realize how much their opposition to informed consent was influenced by suddenly encountering obligations divorced from their history, their clinical experience, or medical education. Had they appreciated that even the doctrine's modest appeal to patient self-determination represented a radical break with medical practices, as transmitted from teacher to student during more than two thousand years of recorded medical history, they might have been less embarrassed by standing so unpreparedly, so nakedly before this new obligation. They might then perhaps have realized that their silence had been until most recently a historical necessity, dictated not only by the inadequacy of medical knowledge but also by physicians' incapacity to discriminate between therapeutic effectiveness based on their actual physical interventions and benefits that must be ascribed to other causes. They might also have argued that the practice of silence was part of a long and venerable tradition that deserved not to be dismissed lightly. . . .

When I speak of silence I do not mean to suggest that physicians have not talked to their patients at all. Of course, they have conversed with patients about all kinds of matters, but they have not, except inadvertently, employed words to invite patients' participation in sharing the burden of making joint decisions. . . .

Judges have made impassioned pleas for patient self-determination, and then have undercut them by giving physicians considerable latitude to practice according to their own lights, exhorting them only to treat each patient with the utmost care. Judges could readily advance this more limited plea because generally doctors do treat their patients with solicitude. The affirmation of physicians' commitment to patients' physical needs, however, has failed to address physicians' lack of commitment to patients' decision making needs. These tensions have led judges to fashion a doctrine of informed consent that has secured for patients the right to better custody but not to liberty—the right to choose how to be treated. . . .

CANTERBURY V. SPENCE (1972)

Judge Robinson, of the D.C. Court of Appeals, who authored the . . . last landmark informed consent decision, also had good intentions. . . . The lesson to be learned from a study of *Canterbury* [is that]: The strong commitment to self-determination at the beginning of the opinion gets weaker as the opinion moves from jurisprudential theory to the realities of hospital and courtroom life. By the end, the opinion has only obscured the issue it intended to address: the nature of the relationship between the court's doctrine of informed consent, as ultimately construed, and its root premise of self-determination. . . .

Respect for the patient's right of self-determination on particular therapy demands a standard set by law for physicians rather than one which physicians may or may not impose upon themselves.

For this apparently bold move, *Canterbury* has been widely celebrated, as well as followed in many jurisdictions.

The new rule of law laid down in *Canterbury,* however, is far from clear. Judge Robinson, returning to basic principles of expert testimony, simply said that there is "no basis for operation of the special medical standard where the physician's activity does not bring his medical knowledge and skills peculiarly into play," and that ordinarily disclosure is not such a situation. But he left room for such situations by adding: "When medical judgment enters the picture and for that reason the special standard controls, prevailing medical practice must be given its *just due*." He did not spell out the meaning of *"just due."*

Both standards tend to confuse the need for *medical knowledge* to elucidate the risks of and alternatives to a proposed procedure in the light of professional experience with the need for *medical judgment* to establish the limits of appropriate disclosure to patients. The difference is crucial to the clarification of the law of informed consent. In *Natanson* and many subsequent cases, judges lumped the two together uncritically, relying solely on current medical practice to resolve the question of reasonableness of disclosure. In *Canterbury,* the distinction was formally recognized. The plaintiff was required to present expert evidence of the applicable medical knowledge, while the defendant had to raise the issue of medical judgment to limit disclosure in defense. But even *Canterbury* did not undertake a detailed judicial analysis of the nature of medical judgment required, precisely because judges were hesitant to make rules in an area that doctors strongly believed was solely the province of medicine.

In *Canterbury,* Dr. Spence claimed that "communication of that risk (paralysis) to the patient is not good medical practice because it might deter patients from undergoing needed surgery and might produce adverse psychological reactions which could preclude the success of the operation." Such claims will almost invariably be raised by physicians since they are derived from deeply held tenets of medical practice. Judge Robinson's enigmatic phrase of "just due" certainly suggests that the medical professional standard would be applicable in such a case, raising profound questions about the extent to which the novel legal standard has been swallowed up by the traditional and venerable medical standard.

In fact, medical judgment was given its "just due" twice. It could also be invoked under the "therapeutic privilege" not to disclose, which Judge Robinson retained as a defense to disclosure:

It is recognized that patients occasionally become so ill or emotionally distraught on disclosure as to foreclose a rational decision, or complicate or hinder the treatment, or perhaps even pose psychological damage to the patient. . . . The critical inquiry is whether the physician responded to a sound medical judgment that communication of the risk information would present a threat to the patient's well-being.

The therapeutic privilege not to disclose is merely a procedurally different way of invoking the professional standard of care. . . .

Since the court wished to depart from medical custom as the standard, it had to give some indication as to the information it expected physicians to disclose. The court said that "the test for determining whether a particular peril must be divulged is its materiality to the patient's decision: all risks potentially affecting the decision must be unmasked." It added that physicians must similarly disclose alternatives to the proposed treatment and the "results likely if the patient remains untreated."

But then the court chose to adopt an "objective" test for disclosure of risks and alternatives—what a [reasonable] *prudent* person in the patient's position would have decided if suitably informed"—and rejected a "subjective" test of materiality—"what an *individual* patient would have considered a significant risk." In opting for an "objective" standard, self-determination was given unnecessarily short shrift. The whole point of the inquiry was to safeguard the right of *individual* choice, even where it may appear idiosyncratic. Although law generally does not protect a person's right to be unreasonable and requires reasonably prudent conduct where injury to another may occur, it remains ambiguous about the extent to which prudence can be legally enforced where the potential injury is largely confined to the individual decision maker. For example, courts have split on the question of whether society may require the wearing of motorcycle helmets and whether an adult patient may be compelled to undergo unwanted blood transfusions.

The "objective" standard for disclosure contradicts the right of each individual to decide what will be done with his or her body. The belief that there is one "reasonable" or "prudent" response to every situation inviting medical intervention is nonsense, from the point of view of both the physician and the patient. The most cursory examination of medical practices demonstrates that what is reasonable to the internist may appear unreasonable to the surgeon or even to other internists and, more significantly, that the value preferences of physicians may not coincide with those of their patients. For example, doctors generally place a higher value on physical longevity than their patients do. But physical longevity is not the only touchstone of prudence. Why should not informed consent law countenance a wide range of potentially reasonable responses by patients to their medical condition based on other value preferences? . . .

Ascertaining patients' informational needs is difficult. Answers do not lie in guessing or "sensing" patients' particular concerns or in obliterating the "subjective" person in an "objective" mass of persons. The "objective" test of materiality only tempts doctors to introduce their own unwarranted subjectivity into the disclosure process. It would have been far better if the court had not committed itself prematurely to the labels "objective" and "subjective." Instead it should have considered more the patients' plight and required physicians to learn new skills: how to inquire openly about their patients' *individual* informational needs and patients' concerns, doubts, and misconceptions about treatment—its risks, benefits, and alternatives. Safeguarding self-determination requires assessing whether patients' informational needs have been satisfied by asking them whether they understand what has been explained to them. Physicians should not try to "second-guess" patients or "sense" how they will react. Instead, they need to explore what questions require further explanation. Taking such unaccustomed obligations seriously is not easy. . . .

SUMMING UP

The legal life of "informed consent," if quality of human life is measured not merely by improvements in physical custody but also by advancement of liberty, was over almost as soon as it was born. Except for the . . . law promulgated in a handful of jurisdictions and the more generally espoused dicta about "self-determination" and "freedom of choice," this is substantially true. Judges toyed briefly with the idea of patients' right to self-determination and largely cast it aside. . . .

Treatment decisions are extremely complex and require a more sustained dialogue, one in which patients are viewed as participants in medical decisions affecting their lives. This is not the view of most physicians, who believe instead that patients are too ignorant to make decisions on their own behalf, that disclosure increases patients' fears and reinforces "foolish" decisions, and that informing them about the uncertainties of medical interventions in many instances seriously undermines faith so essential to the success of therapy. Therefore, physicians asserted that they must be the ultimate decision makers. Judges did not probe these contentions in depth but were persuaded to refrain from interfering significantly with traditional medical practices.

I have not modified my earlier assessment of law's informed consent vision:

[T]he law of informed consent is substantially mythic and fairy tale-like as far as advancing patients' rights to self-decisionmaking is concerned. It conveys in its dicta about such rights a fairy tale-like optimism about human capacities for "intelligent" choice and for being respectful of other persons' choices; yet in its implementation of dicta, it conveys a mythic pessimism of human capacities to be choice-makers. The resulting tensions have had a significant impact on the law of informed consent which only has made a bow toward a commitment to patients' self-determination, perhaps in an attempt to resolve these tensions by a belief that it is "less important that this commitment be total than that we believe it to be there."

Whether fairy tale and myth can and should be reconciled more satisfactorily with reality remains to be seen. If judges contemplate such a reconciliation, they must acquire first a more profound understanding and appreciation of medicine's vision of patients and professional practice, of the capacities of physicians and patients for autonomous choice, and of the limits of professional knowledge. Such understanding cannot readily be acquired in courts of law, during disputes in which inquiry is generally constrained by claims and counter-claims that seek to assure victory for one side.

The call to liberty, embedded in the doctrine of informed consent, has only created an atmosphere in which freedom has the potential to survive and grow. The doctrine has not as yet provided a meaningful blueprint for implementing patient self-determination.

The message . . . is this: Those committed to greater patient self-determination can, if they look hard enough, find inspiration in the common law of informed consent, and so can those, and more easily, who seek to perpetuate medical paternalism. Those who look for evidence of committed implementation will be sadly disappointed. The legal vision of in-

formed consent, based on *self-determination*, is still largely a mirage. Yet a mirage, since it not only deceives but also can sustain hope, is better than no vision at all. . . .

RUTH R. FADEN AND TOM L. BEAUCHAMP

The Concept of Informed Consent

Ruth R. Faden is Philip Franklin Wagley Professor of Biomedical Ethics and executive director of the Bioethics Institute at the Johns Hopkins University. She is also a senior research scholar at the Kennedy Institute, Georgetown University and former chair of the President's Advisory Committee on Human Radiation Experiments. Among her books are *AIDS, Women and the Next Generation* (Oxford), edited with Gail Geller and Madison Powers, *A History and Theory of Informed Consent* (Oxford), written with Tom Beauchamp, and *HIV, AIDS, and Childbearing* (Oxford), edited with Nancy Kass.

Tom L. Beauchamp is professor of philosophy and senior research scholar at the Kennedy Institute, Georgetown University. He has written widely in applied ethics, concentrating in research ethics and medical ethics, and also specializes in the philosophy of David Hume. Among his books are *Principles of Biomedical Ethics* (Oxford), written with James Childress, and *A History and Theory of Informed Consent* (Oxford), written with Ruth Faden. He has published two volumes in the Clarendon Hume (a critical edition of Hume's *Works*) and is currently working on two more volumes.

What is an informed consent? Answering this question is complicated because there are two common, entrenched, and starkly different meanings of "informed consent." That is, the term is analyzable in two profoundly different ways—not because of mere subtle differences of connotation that appear in different contexts, but because two different *conceptions* of informed consent have emerged from its history and are still at work, however unnoticed, in literature on the subject.

　In one sense, which we label *sense*₁, "informed consent" is analyzable as a particular kind of action

by individual patients and subjects: an autonomous authorization. In the second sense, *sense*₂, informed consent is analyzable in terms of the web of cultural and policy rules and requirements of consent that collectively form the social practice of informed consent in institutional contexts where *groups* of patients and subjects must be treated in accordance with rules, policies, and standard practices. Here, informed consents are not always *autonomous* acts, nor are they always in any meaningful respect *authorizations*.

SENSE₁: INFORMED CONSENT AS AUTONOMOUS AUTHORIZATION

The idea of an informed consent suggests that a patient or subject does more than express agreement with, acquiesce in, yield to, or comply with an

　From *A History and Theory of Informed Consent* by Ruth R. Faden and Tom L. Beauchamp. Copyright © 1986 by Oxford University Press, Inc. Reprinted by permission.

arrangement or a proposal. He or she actively *authorizes* the proposal in the act of consent. John may *assent* to a treatment plan without authorizing it. The assent may be a mere submission to the doctor's authoritative order, in which case John does not call on his own authority in order to give permission, and thus does not authorize the plan. Instead, he acts like a child who submits, yields, or assents to the school principal's spanking and in no way gives permission for or authorizes the spanking. Just as the child merely submits to an authority in a system where the lines of authority are quite clear, so often do patients.

Accordingly, an informed consent in sense$_1$ should be defined as follows: An informed consent is an autonomous action by a subject or a patient that authorizes a professional either to involve the subject in research or to initiate a medical plan for the patient (or both). We can whittle down this definition by saying that an informed consent in sense$_1$ is given if a patient or subject with (1) substantial understanding and (2) in substantial absence of control by others (3) intentionally (4) authorizes a professional (to do intervention I).

All substantially autonomous acts satisfy conditions 1–3; but it does not follow from that analysis alone that all such acts satisfy 4. The fourth condition is what distinguishes informed consent as one *kind* of autonomous action. (Note also that the definition restricts the kinds of authorization to medical and research contexts.) A person whose act satisfies conditions 1–3 but who refuses an intervention gives an *informed refusal*.

The Problem of Shared Decisionmaking. This analysis of informed consent in sense$_1$ is deliberately silent on the question of how the authorizer and agent(s) being authorized *arrive at an agreement* about the performance of "I." Recent commentators on informed consent in clinical medicine, notably Jay Katz and the President's Commission, have tended to equate the idea of informed consent with a model of "shared decisionmaking" between doctor and patient. The President's Commission titles the first chapter of its report on informed consent in the patient-practitioner relationship "Informed Consent as Active, Shared Decision Making," while in Katz's work "the idea of informed consent" and "mutual decisionmaking" are treated as virtually synonymous terms.[1]

There is of course an historical relationship in clinical medicine between medical decisionmaking and informed consent. The emergence of the legal doctrine of informed consent was instrumental in drawing attention to issues of decisionmaking as well as authority in the doctor-patient relationship. Nevertheless, it is a confusion to treat informed consent and shared decisionmaking as anything like *synonymous*. For one thing, informed consent is not restricted to clinical medicine. It is a term that applies equally to biomedical and behavioral research contexts where a model of shared decisionmaking is frequently inappropriate. Even in clinical contexts, the social and psychological dynamics involved in selecting medical interventions should be distinguished from the patient's *authorization*.

We endorse Katz's view that effective communication between professional and patient or subject is often instrumental in obtaining informed consents (sense$_1$), but we resist his conviction that the idea of informed consent entails that the patient and physician "share decisionmaking," or "reason together," or reach a consensus about what is in the patient's best interest. This is a manipulation of the concept from a too singular and defined moral perspective on the practice of medicine that is in effect a moral program for changing the practice. Although the patient and physician *may* reach a decision together, they need not. It is the essence of informed consent in sense$_1$ only that the patient or subject *authorizes autonomously;* it is a matter of indifference where or how the proposal being authorized originates.

For example, one might advocate a model of shared decisionmaking for the doctor-patient relationship without simultaneously advocating that every medical procedure requires the consent of patients. Even relationships characterized by an ample slice of shared decisionmaking, mutual trust, and respect would and should permit many decisions about routine and low-risk aspects of the patient's medical treatment to remain the exclusive province of the physician, and thus some decisions are likely always to remain subject exclusively to the physician's authorization. Moreover, in the uncommon situation, a patient could autonomously authorize the physician to make *all* decisions about medical treatment, thus giving his or her informed consent to an arrangement that scarcely resembles the sharing of decisionmaking between doctor and patient.

Authorization. In authorizing, one both assumes responsibility for what one has authorized and transfers to another one's authority to implement it. There is no informed consent unless one *understands* these features of the act and *intends* to perform that act. That is, one must understand that one is assuming responsibility and warranting another to proceed.

To say that one assumes responsibility does not quite locate the essence of the matter, however, because a *transfer* of responsibility as well as of authority also occurs. The crucial element in an authorization is that the person who authorizes uses whatever right, power, or control he or she possesses in the situation to endow another with the right to act. In so doing, the authorizer assumes some responsibility for the actions taken by the other person. Here one could either authorize *broadly* so that a person can act in accordance with general guidelines, or *narrowly* so as to authorize only a particular, carefully circumscribed procedure.

SENSE$_2$: INFORMED CONSENT AS EFFECTIVE CONSENT

By contrast to sense$_1$, sense$_2$, or *effective* consent, is a policy-oriented sense whose conditions are not derivable solely from analyses of autonomy and authorization, or even from broad notions of respect for autonomy. "Informed consent" in this second sense does not refer to *autonomous* authorization, but to a legally or institutionally *effective* (sometimes misleadingly called *valid*) authorization from a patient or a subject. Such an authorization is "effective" because it has been obtained through procedures that satisfy the rules and requirements defining a specific institutional practice in health care or in research.

The social and legal practice of requiring professionals to obtain informed consent emerged in institutional contexts, where conformity to operative rules was and still is the sole necessary and sufficient condition of informed consent. Any consent is an informed consent in sense$_2$ if it satisfies whatever operative rules apply to the practice of informed consent. Sense$_2$ requirements for informed consent typically do not focus on the autonomy of the act of giving consent (as sense$_1$ does), but rather on regulating the behavior of the *consent-seeker* and on establishing *procedures and rules* for the context of consent. Such requirements of professional behavior and procedure are obviously more readily monitored and enforced by institutions.

However, because formal institutional rules such as federal regulations and hospital policies govern whether an act of authorizing is effective, a patient or

subject can autonomously authorize an intervention, and so give an informed consent in sense$_1$, and yet *not effectively authorize* that intervention in sense$_2$.

Consider the following example. Carol and Martie are nineteen-year-old, identical twins attending the same university. Martie was born with multiple birth defects, and has only one kidney. When both sisters are involved in an automobile accident, Carol is not badly hurt, but her sister is seriously injured. It is quickly determined that Martie desperately needs a kidney transplant. After detailed discussions with the transplant team and with friends, Carol consents to be the donor. There is no question that Carol's authorization of the transplant surgery is substantially autonomous. She is well informed and has long anticipated being in just such a circumstance. She has had ample opportunity over the years to consider what she would do were she faced with such a decision. Unfortunately, Carol's parents, who were in Nepal at the time of the accident, do not approve of her decision. Furious that they were not consulted, they decide to sue the transplant team and the hospital for having performed an unauthorized surgery on their minor daughter. (In this state the legal age to consent to surgical procedures is twenty-one.)

According to our analysis, Carol gave her informed consent in sense$_1$ to the surgery, but she did not give her informed consent in sense$_2$. That is, she autonomously authorized the transplant and thereby gave an informed consent in sense$_1$ but did not give a consent that was effective under the operative legal and institutional policy, which in this case required that the person consenting be a legally authorized agent. Examples of other policies that can define sense$_2$ informed consent (but not sense$_1$) include rules that consent be witnessed by an auditor or that there be a one-day waiting period between solicitation of consent and implementation of the intervention in order for the person's authorization to be effective. Such rules can and do vary, both within the United States by jurisdiction and institution, and across the countries of the world.

Medical and research codes, as well as case law and federal regulations, have developed models of informed consent that are delineated entirely in a sense$_2$ format, although they have sometimes attempted to justify the rules by appeal to something like sense$_1$. For example, disclosure conditions for informed consent are central to the history of "informed consent" in sense$_2$, because disclosure has traditionally been a *necessary* condition of effective informed consent (and sometimes a *sufficient* condition!). The legal doctrine of informed consent is primarily a law of disclosure; satisfaction of disclosure rules virtually consumes "informed consent" in law. This should come as no surprise, because the legal system needs a generally applicable informed consent mechanism by which injury and responsibility can be readily and fairly assessed in court. These disclosure requirements in the legal and regulatory contexts are not conditions of "informed consent" in sense$_1$; indeed disclosure may be entirely irrelevant to giving an informed consent in sense$_1$. If a person has an adequate *understanding* of relevant information without benefit of a disclosure, then it makes no difference whether someone *discloses* that information.

Other sense$_2$ rules besides those of disclosure have been enforced. These include rules requiring evidence of adequate comprehension of information and the aforementioned rules requiring the presence of auditor witnesses and mandatory waiting periods. Sense$_2$ informed consent requirements generally take the form of rules focusing on disclosure, comprehension, the minimization of potentially controlling influences, and competence. These requirements express the present-day mainstream conception in the federal government of the United States. They are also typical of international documents and state regulations, which all reflect a sense$_2$ orientation.

THE RELATIONSHIP BETWEEN SENSE$_1$ AND SENSE$_2$

A sense$_1$ "informed consent" can fail to be an informed consent in sense$_2$ by a lack of conformity to applicable rules and requirements. Similarly, an informed consent in sense$_2$ may not be an informed consent in sense$_1$. The rules and requirements that determine sense$_2$ consents need not result in autonomous authorizations at all in order to qualify as informed consents.

Such peculiarities in informed consent law have led Jay Katz to argue that the legal doctrine of "informed consent" bears a "name" that "promises much more than its construction in case law has delivered." He has argued insightfully that the courts have, in effect, imposed a mere duty to warn on physicians, an obligation confined to risk disclosures and statements of proposed interventions. He maintains that "This judicially imposed obligation must be distinguished from the *idea* of informed consent, namely, that patients have a decisive role to play in the medical decision-making process. The idea of informed consent, though alluded to also in case law, cannot be implemented, as courts have attempted, by only expanding the disclosure requirements." By their actions and declarations, Katz believes, the courts have made informed consent a "cruel hoax" and have allowed "the idea of informed consent . . . to wither on the vine."[2]

The most plausible interpretation of Katz's contentions is through the sense$_1$/sense$_2$ distinction. If a physician obtains a consent under the courts' criteria, then an informed consent (sense$_2$) has been obtained. But it does not follow that the courts are using the *right* standards, or *sufficiently rigorous* standards in light of a stricter autonomy-based model—or "idea" as Katz puts it—of informed consent (sense$_1$).[3] If Katz is correct that the courts have made a mockery of informed consent and of its moral justification in respect for autonomy, then of course his criticisms are thoroughly justified. At the same time, it should be recognized that people can proffer legally or institutionally effective authorizations under prevailing rules even if they fall far short of the standards implicit in sense$_1$.

Despite the differences between sense$_1$ and sense$_2$, a definition of informed consent need not fall into one or the other class of definitions. It may conform to both. Many definitions of informed consent in policy contexts reflect at least a strong and definite reliance on informed consent in sense$_1$. Although the conditions of sense$_1$ are not logically necessary conditions for sense$_2$, we take it as morally axiomatic that they *ought* to serve—and in fact have served—as the benchmark or model against which the moral adequacy of a definition framed for sense$_2$ purposes is to be evaluated. This position is, roughly speaking, Katz's position.

A defense of the moral viewpoint that policies governing informed consent in sense$_2$ *should* be formulated to conform to the standards of informed consent in sense$_1$ is not hard to express. The goal of informed consent in medical care and in research—that is, the purpose behind the obligation to obtain informed consent—is to enable potential subjects and patients to make autonomous decisions about whether to grant or refuse authorization for medical and research interventions. Accordingly, embedded in the reason for having the social institution of informed consent is the idea that institutional requirements for informed consent in sense$_2$ *should* be intended to maximize the likelihood that the conditions of informed consent in sense$_1$ will be satisfied.

A major problem at the policy level, where rules and requirements must be developed and applied in the aggregate, is the following: The obligations imposed to enable patients and subjects to make authorization decisions must be evaluated not only in terms of the demands of a set of abstract conditions of "true" or sense$_1$ informed consent, but also in terms of the impact of imposing such obligations or requirements on various institutions with their concrete concerns and priorities. One must take account of what is fair and reasonable to require of health care professionals and researchers, the effect of alternative consent requirements on efficiency and effectiveness in the delivery of health care and the advancement of science, and—particularly in medical care—the effect of requirements on the welfare of patients. Also relevant are considerations peculiar to the particular social context, such as proof, precedent, or liability theory in case law, or regulatory authority and due process in the development of federal regulations and IRB consent policies.

Moreover, at the sense$_2$ level, one must resolve not only which requirements will define effective consent; one must also settle on the rules stipulating the conditions under which effective consents must be obtained. In some cases, hard decisions must be made about whether requirements of informed consent (in sense$_2$) should be imposed at all, even though informed consent (in sense$_1$) *could* realistically and meaningfully be obtained in the circumstances and could serve as a model for institutional rules. For example, should there be any consent requirements in the cases of minimal risk medical procedures and research activities?

This need to balance is not a problem for informed consent in sense$_1$, which is not policy oriented. Thus, it is possible to have a *morally acceptable* set of requirements for informed consent in sense$_2$ that deviates considerably from the conditions of informed consent in sense$_1$. However, the burden of moral proof rests with those who defend such deviations since the primary moral justification of the obligation to obtain informed consent is respect for autonomous action.

NOTES

1. President's Commission, *Making Health Care Decisions*, Vol. 1, 15 and Jay Katz, *The Silent World of Doctor and Patient* (New York: The Free Press, 1984), 87 and "The Regulation of Human Research—Reflections and Proposals," *Clinical Research* 21 (1973): 758–91. Katz does not provide a sustained analysis of joint or shared decisionmaking, and it is unclear precisely how he would relate this notion to informed consent.

2. Jay Katz, "Disclosure and Consent," in A. Milunsky and G. Annas, eds., *Genetics and the Law II* (New York: Plenum Press, 1980), 122, 128.

3. We have already noted that Katz's "idea" of informed consent—as the active involvement of patients in the medical decisionmaking process—is different from our sense$_1$.

R O B E R T   J .   L E V I N E

Informed Consent: Some Challenges to the Universal Validity of the Western Model

Robert J. Levine, MD, is professor of medicine, lecturer in pharmacology, and chairman of the Human Investigation Committee (an IRB) at the Yale University School of Medicine. He has served as president of the American Society of Law, Medicine, and Ethics and as a fellow at both the Hastings Center and the American College of Physicians. Dr. Levine's focus in bioethics is research ethics. His works include "The Need to Revise the Declaration of Helsinki" (*New England Journal of Medicine*), "Ethics of Clinical Trials: Do They Help the Patient?" (*Cancer*), and the influential textbook *Ethics and Regulation of Clinical Research* (Urban & Schwarzenberg).

INFORMED CONSENT

Informed consent holds a central place in the ethical justification of research involving human subjects. This position is signaled by the fact that it is the first-stated and, by far, the longest principle of the Nuremberg Code.[1]

I. The voluntary consent of the human subject is absolutely essential. This means that the person involved should have the legal capacity to give consent; should be so situated as to be able to exercise free power of choice, without the intervention of any element of force, fraud, deceit, duress, overreaching, or other ulterior form of constraint or coercion; and should have sufficient knowledge and comprehension of the elements of the subject matter involved as to enable him to make an understanding and enlightened decision. This latter element requires that before the acceptance of an affirmative decision by the experimental subject there should be made known to him the nature, duration, and purpose of the experiment; the method and means by which it is to be conducted; all inconveniences and hazards reasonably to be expected; and the effects upon his health or person which may possibly come from his participation in the experiment. . . .

The Nuremberg Code identifies four attributes of consent without which consent cannot be considered

From *Law, Medicine, and Health Care* 19(1991), 207–13. Reprinted with permission of the American Society of Law, Medicine & Ethics.

valid: consent must be "voluntary," "legally competent," "informed," and "comprehending." These four attributes stand essentially unchanged to this day. Although there has been extensive commentary on the meaning of each of these attributes and how they are to be interpreted in specific contexts, there has been no authoritative agreement reached that any of them may be omitted or that there should be any additional attribute elevated to the status of the original four. . . .

The National Commission grounded the requirement for informed consent in the ethical principle of respect for persons which it defined as follows:

Respect for persons incorporates at least two basic ethical convictions: First, that individuals should be treated as autonomous agents, and second, that persons with diminished autonomy and thus in need of protection are entitled to such protections.

The National Commission defined an "autonomous person" as ". . . an individual capable of deliberation about personal goals and of acting under the direction of such deliberation." To show respect for autonomous persons requires that we leave them alone, even to the point of allowing them to choose activities that might be harmful, unless they agree or consent that we may do otherwise. We are not to touch them or to encroach upon their private spaces unless such touching or encroachment is in accord with their wishes. Our actions should be designed to affirm their authority and enhance their capacity to be self-determining; we are not to obstruct their actions unless they are clearly detrimental to others. We show disrespect for autonomous persons when we either repudiate their considered judgments or deny them the freedom to act on those judgments in the absence of compelling reasons to do so.

The National Commission's discussion of an autonomous person is consistent with the prevailing perception of the nature of the "moral agent" in Western civilization. A moral agent is an individual who is capable of forming a rational plan of life, capable of rational deliberation about alternative plans of action with the aim of making choices that are compatible with his or her life plan and who assumes responsibility for the consequences of his or her choices.

Although the National Commission did not cite either of the following sources as authoritative in developing its definition of respect for persons, it is clear to this observer that they found them influential: The first is the statement of the principle of respect for persons as articulated by the German philosopher, Immanuel Kant: "So act as to treat humanity, whether in thine own person or in that of any other, in every case as an end withal, never as a means only." A second influential statement is that of the American judge, Benjamin Cardozo: "Every human being of adult years and sound mind has the right to determine what will be done with his own body . . ."

. . . In the actual process of negotiating informed consent and in the reviews of plans for informed consent conducted by Institutional Review Boards (IRBs), there is a tendency to concentrate on the information to be presented to the prospective subject. Among the IRB's principal concerns are the following questions: Is there a full statement of each of the elements of informed consent? Is the information presented in a style of language that one could expect the prospective subject to understand? Implicit in this is a vision of informed consent as a two step process. First, information is presented to the subject by the investigator. Secondly, the subject satisfies himself or herself that he or she understands, and based upon this understanding either agrees or refuses to participate in the research project. . . .

In the paper I presented at an earlier CIOMS conference[2] I concluded:

This brief survey of descriptions of relationships between health professionals and patients in three disparate cultures leads me to conclude that the informed consent standards of the Declaration of Helsinki are not universally valid. Imposition of these standards as they are now written will not accomplish their purposes; i.e., they will not guide physicians in their efforts to show respect for persons because they do not reflect adequately the views held in these cultures of the nature of the person in his or her relationship to society.

This conclusion was based on a review of observations of the doctor–patient relationship, subject–investigator relationship and perspectives on the nature of disease in three cultures: Western Africa, China, and a Central American Mayan Indian culture.

The concept of personhood as it exists in various cultures has been addressed in an excellent paper by Willy De Craemer.[3] De Craemer is a cross-cultural sociologist with extensive experience in the field in, among other places, Central Africa and Japan.

In this paper he makes it clear that the Western vision of the person is a minority viewpoint in the world. The majority viewpoint manifest in most other societies, both technologically developing (e.g., Central Africa) and technologically developed (e.g., Japan), does not reflect the American perspective of radical individualism. . . .

Although I commend to the readers' attention De Craemer's entire essay, I shall here excerpt some passages from his description of the Japanese vision of the person. I do this because Japan is unquestionably a highly developed society technologically as well as in other respects. Thus, it is less easy to dismiss its vision of the person as exotic, as could be done with some of the examples examined in my earlier paper: . . .

The special status that the Japanese accord to human relationships, with its emphasis on the empathic and solidary interdependence of many individuals, rather than on the autonomous independence of the individual person, includes within it several other core attributes. To begin with, the kind of reciprocity (*on*) that underlies human relationships means that both concretely and symbolically what anthropologist Marcel Mauss . . . termed "the theme of the gift" is one of its dominant motifs. A continuous, gift-exchange-structured flow of material and nonmaterial "goods" and "services" takes place between the members of the enclosed human nexus to which each individual belongs. Through a never-ending process of mutual giving, receiving, and repaying . . . a web of relations develops that binds donors and recipients together in diffuse, deeply personal, and overlapping creditor-debtor ways. Generalized benevolence is involved, but so is generalized obligation, both of which take into account another crucial parameter of Japanese culture: the importance attached to status, rank, and hierarchical order in interpersonal relationships, and to . . . "proper-place occupancy" within them. The triple obligation to give, receive, and repay are tightly regulated by this status-formalism and sense of propriety. . . .

It is not difficult to imagine how a research ethics committee in the Western world—particularly in the United States—would evaluate the custom of exchange of gifts—both material and immaterial—in a system that recognized the legitimacy of "status, rank, and hierarchical order." Attention would soon be focused on the problems of "conflicts of interest." Questions would be raised as to whether consent would be invalidated by "undue inducement," or what the Nuremberg Code calls "other ulterior form(s) of constraint or coercion." In my views, it is impossible to evaluate the meaning of cash payments, provision of free services, and other "inducements" without a full appreciation of the cultural significance of such matters.

It is against this backdrop that I have been asked by the CIOMS Conference Programme Committee to "provide a definition [of informed consent] which is widely applicable to different countries and cultures." Given that the purpose of informed consent is to show respect for persons, in recognition of the vastly different perspectives of the nature of "person," I cannot do this. Since I cannot provide a substantive definition of informed consent, I shall suggest a procedural approach to dealing with the problem.

As an American I am firmly committed to the Western vision of the person and deeply influenced by my experience with the American variant of this vision. . . .

Thus, it would not be prudent to trust an American to provide a universally applicable definition of informed consent. I suggest further, that it would not be prudent to rely on any person situated in any culture to provide a universally applicable definition of informed consent.

Before proceeding, I wish to comment on the continuing controversy on the topic of ethical justification of research that crosses national boundaries. There are those who contend that all research, wherever it is conducted, should be justified according to universally applicable standards; I refer to them as "univer-

salists." Those opposed to the universalist position, whom I call "pluralists," accept some standards as universal, but argue that other standards must be adapted to accommodate the mores of particular cultures. Pluralists commonly refer to the universalist position as "ethical imperialism," while universalists often call that of their opponents, "ethical relativism."

Universalists correctly point out that most therapeutic innovations are developed in industrialized nations. Investigators from these countries may go to technologically developing countries to test their innovations for various reasons; some of these reasons are good and some of them are not (e.g., to save money and to take advantage of the less complex and sophisticated regulatory systems typical to technologically developing countries). Moreover, universalists observe that, once the innovations have been proved safe and effective, economic factors often limit their availability to citizens of the country in which they were tested. Requiring investigators to conform to the ethical standards of their own country when conducting research abroad is one way to restrain exploitation of this type. Universalists also point to the Declaration of Helsinki as a widely accepted universal standard for biomedical research that has been endorsed by most countries, including those labeled "technologically developing." This gives weight to their claim that research must be conducted according to universal principles. Furthermore, the complex regulations characteristic of technologically developed countries are, in general, patterned after the Declaration of Helsinki.

Marcia Angell, in a particularly incisive exposition of the universalists' position, suggests this analogy[4]

Does apartheid offend universal standards of justice, or does it instead simply represent the South African custom that should be seen as morally neutral? If the latter view is accepted, then ethical principles are not much more than a description of the mores of a society. I believe they must have more meaning than that. There must be a core of human rights that we would wish to see honored universally, despite local variations in their superficial aspects . . . The force of local custom or law cannot justify abuses of certain fundamental rights, and the right of self-determination, on which the doctrine of informed consent is based, is one of them.

Pluralists join with universalists in condemning economic exploitation of technologically developing countries and their citizens.[5] Unlike the universalists, however, they see the imposition of ethical standards for the conduct of research by a powerful country on a developing country as another form of exploitation. In their view, it is tantamount to saying, "No, you may not participate in this development of technology, no matter how much you desire it, unless you permit us to replace your ethical standards with our own." Pluralists call attention to the fact that the Declaration of Helsinki, although widely endorsed by the nations of the world, reflects a uniquely Western view of the nature of the person; as such it does not adequately guide investigators in ways to show respect for all persons in the world.

An example of pluralism may be found in the diversity of national policies regarding blind HIV-seroprevalence studies. The United States Centers for Disease Control are now conducting anonymous tests of leftover blood drawn for other purposes without notification in studies designed to "determine the level of HIV-seroprevalence in a nationwide sample of hospital patients and clients at family planning, sexually transmitted disease, tuberculosis, and drug treatment clinics. . . ." No personal identifiers are kept.[6] Although there seems to be widespread agreement among US commentators that such anonymous testing without notification is ethically justified, different judgments have been reached in other countries, most notably in the United Kingdom and in the Netherlands.[7] Who is to say which of these nations has the correct ethical perspective that should be made part of the "universal standard?"

The legitimacy of the pluralists' position is recognized implicitly in U.S. policy on whether research subjects are required to be informed of the results of HIV antibody testing.[8] In general, this policy requires that all individuals "whose test results are associated with personal identifiers must be informed of their own test results . . . individuals may not be given the option 'not to know' the result. . . ." This policy permits several narrowly defined exceptions. One of these provides that research "conducted at foreign sites should be carefully evaluated to account for cultural norms, the health resource capability and official health policies of the host country." Then "the reviewing IRB must consider if any modification to the policy is significantly justified by the risk/benefit evaluation of the research."

WHO/CIOMS Proposed International Guidelines provide specific guidance for the conduct of research in which an investigator or an institution in a technologically developed country serves as the "external sponsor" of research conducted in a technologically developing "host country."[9] In my judgment these guidelines strike a sensitive balance between the universalist and pluralist perspectives. They require that "the research protocol should be submitted to ethical review by the initiating agency. The ethical standards applied should be no less exacting than they would be for research carried out within the initiating country" (Article 28). They also provide for accommodation to the mores of the culture within the "host country." For example:

Where individual members of a community do not have the necessary awareness of the implications of participation in an experiment to give adequately informed consent directly to the investigators, it is desirable that the decision whether or not to participate should be elicited through the intermediary of a trusted community leader. (Article 15).

The conduct of research involving human subjects must not violate any universally applicable ethical standards. Although I endorse certain forms of cultural relativism, there are limits to how much cultural relativism ought to be tolerated. Certain behaviors ought to be condemned by the world community even though they are sponsored by a nation's leaders and seem to have wide support of its citizens. For example, the Nuremberg tribunal appealed to universally valid principles in order to determine the guilt of the physicians (war criminals) who had conducted research according to standards approved by their nation's leaders.

I suggest that the principle of respect for persons is one of the universally applicable ethical standards. It is universally applicable when stated at the level of formality employed by Immanuel Kant: "So act as to treat humanity, whether in thine own person or in that of any other, in every case as an end withal, never as a means only." The key concept is that persons are never to be treated only or merely as means to another's ends. When one goes beyond this level of formality or abstraction, the principle begins to lose its universality. When one restates the principle of respect for persons in a form that reflects a peculiarly Western view of the person, it begins to lose its relevance to some people in Central Africa, Japan, Central America, and so on.

The Conference Programme Committee asked me to address the problem "of obtaining consent in cultures where non-dominant persons traditionally do not give consent, such as a wife." Having subscribed to the Western vision of the meaning of person, I believe that all persons should be treated as autonomous agents, wives included. Thus, I believe that we should show respect for wives in the context of research by soliciting their informed consent. But, if this is not permitted within a particular culture, would I exclude wives from participation in research?

Not necessarily. If there is a strong possibility either that the wife could benefit from participation in the research or that the class of women of which she is a representative could benefit (and there is a reasonable balance of risks and potential benefits), I would offer her an opportunity to participate. To do otherwise would not accomplish anything of value (e.g., her entitlement to self-determination); it would merely deprive her of a chance to secure the benefits of participation in the research. I would, of course, offer her an opportunity to decline participation, understanding that in some cultures she would consider such refusal "unthinkable."

. . . Finally, the Conference Programme Committee has asked me to consider "the special problems of obtaining consent when populations are uneducated or illiterate." Lack of education in and of itself presents no problems that are unfamiliar to those experienced with negotiating informed consent with prospective subjects. These are barriers to comprehension which are not generally insurmountable. Greater problems are presented by those who hold beliefs about health and illness that are inconsistent with the concepts of Western medicine. It may, for example, be difficult to explain the purpose of vaccination to a person who believes that disease is caused by forces that Western civilization dismisses as supernatural or magical.[10] The meaning of such familiar (in the Western world) procedures as blood-letting may be vastly different and very disturbing in some societies.[11] Problems with such explanations can, I believe, be dealt with best by local ethical review committees.

Illiteracy, in and of itself, presents no problems to the process of informed consent which, when conducted properly, entails talking rather than reading. Rather, it presents problems with the documentation of informed consent. The process of informed consent, designed to show respect for persons, fosters their interests by empowering them to pursue and protect their own interests. The consent form, by contrast, is an instrument designed to protect the interests of investigators and their institutions and to defend them against civil or criminal liability. If it is necessary to have such protection of investigators, subjects may be asked to make their mark on a consent document and a witness may be required to countersign and attest to the fact that the subject received the information.

A PROCEDURAL RESOLUTION

In "Proposal Guidelines for International Testing of Vaccines and Drugs Against HIV Infection and AIDS" (hereafter referred to as "Proposed HIV Guidelines"), reference is made to an ethical review system.[12] This system is based on that set forth in the WHO/CIOMS Proposed International Guidelines for Biomedical Research Involving Human Subjects. In the Proposed HIV Guidelines, there are suggestions for divisions of responsibility for ethical review. Here I shall elaborate how responsibilities should be divided for determining the adequacy of informed consent procedures.

This proposal presupposes the existence of an international standard for informed consent. I suggest that the standards for informed consent as set forth in the WHO/CIOMS Proposed International Guidelines and as elaborated in the Proposed HIV Guidelines, be recognized as the international standard for informed consent.

1. All plans to conduct research involving human subjects should be reviewed and approved by a research ethics committee (REC). Ideally the REC should be based in the community in which the research is to be conducted. However, as noted in CIOMS/WHO Proposed International Guidelines, under some circumstances regional or national committees may be adequate for these purposes. In such cases it is essential that regional or national committees have as members or consultants individuals who are highly familiar with the customs of the community in which the research is to be done.

The authority of the REC to approve research should be limited to proposals in which the plans for informed consent conform either to the international standard or to a modification of the international standard that has been authorized by a national ethical review body.

2. Proposals to employ consent procedures that do not conform to the international standard should be justified by the researcher and submitted for review and approval by a national ethical review body. Earlier in this paper I identified some conditions or

circumstances that could justify such omissions or modifications.

The role of the national ethical review body is to authorize consent procedures that deviate from the international standard. The responsibility for review and approval of the entire protocol (with the modified consent procedure) remains with the REC. Specific details of consent procedures that conform to the international standard or to a modified version of the international standard approved by the national ethical review body should be reviewed and approved by the local ethical review committee.

3. There should be established an international ethical review body to provide advice, consultation and guidance to national ethical review bodies when such is requested by the latter.

4. In the case of externally sponsored research: Ethical review should be conducted in the initiating country. Although it may and should provide advice to the host country, its approval should be based on its finding that plans for informed consent are consistent with the international standard. If there has been a modification of consent procedures approved by the national ethical review body in the host country, the initiating country may either endorse the modification or seek consultation with the international review body.

NOTES

1. Reprinted in R. J. Levine: *Ethics and Regulation of Clinical Research.* Urban & Schwarzenberg, Baltimore & Munich, Second Edition, 1986.

2. R. J. Levine, "Validity of Consent Procedures in Technologically Developing Countries". In: *Human Experimentation and Medical Ethics.* Ed. by Z. Bankowski and N. Howard-Jones, Council for International Organizations of Medical Sciences, Geneva, 1982, pp. 16–30.

3. W. De Craemer, "A Cross-Cultural Perspective on Personhood," *Milbank Memorial Fund Quarterly* 61:19–34, Winter 1983.

4. M. Angell, "Ethical Imperialism? Ethics in International Collaborative Clinical Research." *New England Journal of Medicine* 319:1081–1083, 1988.

5. M. Barry, "Ethical Considerations of Human Investigation in Developing Countries: The AIDS Dilemma." *New England Journal of Medicine* 319:1083–1086, 1988; N. A. Christakis, "Responding to a Pandemic: International Interests in AIDS Control." *Daedalus* 118 (No. 2):113–114, 1989; and N. A. Christakis, "Ethical Design of an AIDS Vaccine Trial in Africa." *Hastings Center Report* 18 (No. 3):31–37, June/July, 1988.

6. M. Pappaioanou et al., "The Family of HIV Seroprevalence Studies: Objectives, Methods and Uses of Sentinel Surveillance in the United States." *Public Health Reports* 105(2):113–119, 1990.

7. R. Bayer, L. H. Lumey, and L. Wan, "The American, British and Dutch Responses to Unlinked Anonymous HIV Seroprevalence Studies: An International Comparison." *AIDS* 4:283–290, 1990, reprinted in this issue of *Law, Medicine and Health Care*, 19:3–4.

8. R. E. Windom, Assistant Secretary for Health, policy on informing those tested about HIV serostatus, letter to PHS agency heads, Washington, DC, May 9, 1988.

9. Proposed International Guidelines for Biomedical Research Involving Human Subjects, A Joint Project of the World Health Organization and the Council for International Organizations of Medical Sciences, CIOMS, Geneva, 1982.

10. See De Craemer, *supra* note 3 and Levine, *supra* note 2.

11. A. J. Hall, "Public Health Trials in West Africa: Logistics and Ethics," *IRB: A Review of Human Subjects Research* 11 (No. 5):8–10, Sept/Oct 1989. See also Christakis, *supra* note 5.

12. R. J. Levine, and W. K. Mariner, "Proposed Guidelines for International Testing of Vaccines and Drugs Against HIV Infection and AIDS," prepared at the request of WHO, Global Programme on AIDS and submitted January 5, 1990.

Refusal of Treatment

CALIFORNIA COURT OF APPEALS, SECOND DISTRICT

Bouvia v. Superior Court

OPINION AND ORDER FOR A PEREMPTORY WRIT OF MANDATE

BEACH, Associate Justice

Petitioner, Elizabeth Bouvia, a patient in a public hospital seeks the removal from her body of a nasogastric tube inserted and maintained against her will and without her consent by physicians who so placed it for the purpose of keeping her alive through involuntary forced feeding. . . .

The trial court denied petitioner's request for the immediate relief she sought. It concluded that leaving the tube in place was necessary to prolong petitioner's life, and that it would, in fact, do so. With the tube in place petitioner probably will survive the time required to prepare for trial, a trial itself and an appeal, if one proved necessary. The real party physicians also assert, and the trial court agreed, that physically petitioner tolerates the tube reasonably well and thus is not in great physical discomfort. . . .

FACTUAL BACKGROUND

Petitioner is a 28-year-old woman. Since birth she has been afflicted with and suffered from severe cerebral palsy. She is quadriplegic. She is now a patient at a public hospital maintained by one of the real parties in interest, the County of Los Angeles. . . . Petitioner's physical handicaps of palsy and quadriplegia have progressed to the point where she is completely bedridden. Except for a few fingers of one hand and some slight head and facial movements, she is immobile. She is physically helpless and wholly unable to

care for herself. She is totally dependent upon others for all of her needs. These include feeding, washing, cleaning, toileting, turning, and helping her with elimination and other bodily functions. She cannot stand or sit upright in bed or in a wheelchair. She lies flat in bed and must do so the rest of her life. She suffers also from degenerative and severely crippling arthritis. She is in continual pain. Another tube permanently attached to her chest automatically injects her with periodic doses of morphine which relieves some, but not all of her physical pain and discomfort.

She is intelligent, very mentally competent. She earned a college degree. She was married but her husband has left her. She suffered a miscarriage. She lived with her parents until her father told her that they could no longer care for her. She has stayed intermittently with friends and at public facilities. A search for a permanent place to live where she might receive the constant care which she needs has been unsuccessful. She is without financial means to support herself and, therefore, must accept public assistance for medical and other care.

She has on several occasions expressed the desire to die. In 1983 she sought the right to be cared for in a public hospital in Riverside County while she intentionally "starved herself to death." A court in that county denied her judicial assistance to accomplish that goal. She later abandoned an appeal from that ruling. Thereafter, friends took her to several different facilities, both public and private, arriving finally at her present location. . . .

Petitioner must be spoon fed in order to eat. Her present medical and dietary staff have determined that she is not consuming a sufficient amount of nutrients. Petitioner stops eating when she feels she cannot

Reprinted from the *California Reporter,* 225 Cal.Rptr. 297 (Cal. App. 2 Dist.).

orally swallow more, without nausea and vomiting. As she cannot now retain solids, she is fed soft liquid-like food. Because of her previously announced resolve to starve herself, the medical staff feared her weight loss might reach a life-threatening level. Her weight since admission to real parties' facility seems to hover between 65 and 70 pounds. Accordingly, they inserted the subject tube against her will and contrary to her express written instruction. . . .

THE RIGHT TO REFUSE MEDICAL TREATMENT

"[A] person of adult years and in sound mind has the right, in the exercise of control over his own body, to determine whether or not to submit to lawful medical treatment." (*Cobbs v. Grant* (1972) 8 Cal.3d 229, 242, 104 Cal.Rptr. 505, 502 P.2d 1.) It follows that such a patient has the right to refuse *any* medical treatment, even that which may save or prolong her life. (*Barber v. Superior Court* (1983) 147 Cal. App.3d 1006, 195 Cal.Rptr. 484; *Bartling v. Superior Court* (1984) 163 Cal.App.3d 186, 209 Cal.Rptr. 220.) In our view the foregoing authorities are dispositive of the case at bench. Nonetheless, the County and its medical staff contend that for reasons unique to this case, Elizabeth Bouvia may not exercise the right available to others. Accordingly, we again briefly discuss the rule in the light of real parties' contentions.

The right to refuse medical treatment is basic and fundamental. It is recognized as a part of the right of privacy protected by both the state and federal constitutions. . . . Its exercise requires no one's approval. It is not merely one vote subject to being overridden by medical opinion.

In *Barber v. Superior Court, supra,* 147 Cal.App.3d 1006, 195 Cal.Rptr. 484, we considered this same issue although in a different context. Writing on behalf of this division, Justice Compton thoroughly analyzed and reviewed the issue of withdrawal of life-support systems beginning with the seminal case of the *Matter of Quinlan* (N.J. 1976) 355 A.2d 647, *cert. den.* 429 U.S. 922, 97 S.Ct. 319, 50 L.Ed.2d 289, and continuing on to the then recent enactment of the California Natural Death Act (Health & Saf. Code. §§ 7185–7195). His opinion clearly and repeatedly stresses the fundamental underpinning of its conclusion, i.e., the patient's right to decide: 147 Cal.App.3d at page 1015, 195 Cal.Rptr. 484, "In this state a clearly recognized legal right to control one's own medical treatment predated the Natural Death Act. A long line of cases, approved by the Supreme Court in *Cobbs v. Grant* (1972) 8 Cal.3d 229 [104 Cal.Rptr. 505, 502 P.2d 1] . . . have held that where a doctor performs treatment in the absence of an informed consent, there is an actionable battery. The obvious corollary to this principle is that *"a competent adult patient has the legal right to refuse medical treatment."* . . .

Bartling v. Superior Court, supra, 163 Cal.App.3d 186, 209 Cal.Rptr. 220, was factually much like the case at bench. Although not totally identical in all respects, the issue there centered on the same question here present: i.e., "May the patient refuse even life continuing treatment?" Justice Hastings, writing for another division of this court, explained: "In this case we are called upon to decide whether a competent adult patient, with serious illness which are probably incurable but have not been diagnosed as terminal, has the right, over the objection of his physicians and the hospital, to have life-support equipment disconnected despite the fact that withdrawal of such devices will surely hasten his death." (At p. 189, 209 Cal.Rptr. 220.) . . .

The description of Mr. Bartling's condition fits that of Elizabeth Bouvia. The holding of that case applies here and compels real parties to respect her decision even though she is not "terminally" ill. . . .

THE CLAIMED EXCEPTIONS TO THE PATIENT'S RIGHT TO CHOOSE ARE INAPPLICABLE

. . . At bench the trial court concluded that with sufficient feeding petitioner could live an additional 15 to 20 years; therefore, the preservation of petitioner's life for that period outweighed her right to decide. In so holding the trial court mistakenly attached undue importance to the *amount of time* possibly available to petitioner, and failed to give equal weight and consideration for the *quality* of that life; an equal, if not more significant, consideration.

All decisions permitting cessation of medical treatment or life-support procedures to some degree hastened the arrival of death. In part, at least, this was permitted because the quality of life during the time remaining in those cases had been terribly diminished. In Elizabeth Bouvia's view, the quality of her life has been diminished to the point of hopelessness, uselessness, unenjoyability and frustration. She, as the patient, lying helplessly in bed, unable to care for herself, may consider her existence meaningless. . . .

Here Elizabeth Bouvia's decision to forego medical treatment or life-support through a mechanical means belongs to her. It is not a medical decision for her physicians to make. Neither is it a legal question whose soundness is to be resolved by lawyers or judges. It is not a conditional right subject to approval by ethics committees or courts of law. It is a moral and philosophical decision that, being a competent adult, is hers alone. . . .

Here, if force fed, petitioner faces 15 to 20 years of a painful existence, endurable only by the constant administrations of morphine. Her condition is irreversible. There is no cure for her palsy or arthritis. Petitioner would have to be fed, cleaned, turned, bedded, toileted by others for 15 to 20 years! Although alert, bright, sensitive, perhaps even brave and feisty, she must lie immobile, unable to exist except through physical acts of others. Her mind and spirit may be free to take great flights but she herself is imprisoned and must lie physically helpless subject to the ignominy, embarrassment, humiliation, and dehumanizing aspects created by her helplessness. We do not believe it is the policy of this State that all and every life must be preserved against the will of the sufferer. It is incongruous, if not monstrous, for medical practitioners to assert their right to preserve a life that someone else must live, or, more accurately, endure, for "15 to 20 years." We cannot conceive it to be the policy of this State to inflict such an ordeal upon anyone.

It is, therefore, immaterial that the removal of the nasogastric tube will hasten or cause Bouvia's eventual death. Being competent she has the right to live out the remainder of her natural life in dignity and peace. It is precisely the aim and purpose of the many decisions upholding the withdrawal of life-support systems to accord and provide a large measure of dignity, respect and comfort as possible to every patient for the remainder of his days, whatever be their number. This goal is not to hasten death, though its earlier arrival may be an expected and understood likelihood. . . .

It is not necessary to here define or dwell at length upon what constitutes suicide. Our Supreme Court dealt with the matter in the case of *In re Joseph G.* (1983) 34 Cal.3d 429, 194 Cal.Rptr. 163, 667 P.2d 1176, wherein declaring that the State has an interest in preserving and recognizing the sanctity of life, it observed that it is a crime to aid in suicide. But it is significant that the instances and the means there discussed all involved affirmative, assertive, proximate, direct conduct such as furnishing a gun, poison, knife, or other instrumentality or usable means by which an-

other could physically and immediately inflict some death-producing injury upon himself. Such situations are far different than the mere presence of a doctor during the exercise of his patient's constitutional rights.

This is the teaching of *Bartling* and *Barber*. No criminal or civil liability attaches to honoring a competent, informed patient's refusal of medical service.

We do not purport to establish what will constitute proper medical practice in all other cases or even other aspects of the care to be provided petitioner. We hold only that her right to refuse medical treatment even of the life-sustaining variety, entitles her to the immediate removal of the nasogastric tube that has been involuntarily inserted into her body. The hospital and medical staff are still free to perform a substantial, if not the greater part of their duty, i.e., that of trying to alleviate Bouvia's pain and suffering.

Petitioner is without means to go to a private hospital and, apparently, real parties' hospital as a public facility was required to accept her. Having done so it may not deny her relief from pain and suffering merely because she has chosen to exercise her fundamental right to protect what little privacy remains to her. . . .

IT IS ORDERED

Let a peremptory writ of mandate issue commanding the Los Angeles Superior Court immediately upon receipt thereof, to make and enter a new and different order granting Elizabeth Bouvia's request for a preliminary injunction, and the relief prayed for therein; in particular to make an order (1) directing real parties in interest forthwith to remove the nasogastric tube from petitioner, Elizabeth Bouvia's, body, and (2) prohibiting any and all of the real parties in interest from replacing or aiding in replacing said tube or any other or similar device in or on petitioner without her consent. . . .

COMPTON, ASSOCIATE JUSTICE, CONCURRING OPINION

I have no doubt that Elizabeth Bouvia wants to die; and if she had the full use of even one hand, could probably find a way to end her life—in a word—commit suicide. In order to seek the assistance which she needs in ending her life by the only means she sees available—starvation—she has had to stultify her position before this court by disavowing her desire to end her life in such a fashion and proclaiming that she will eat all that she can physically tolerate. Even the majority opinion here must necessarily "dance" around the issue.

Elizabeth apparently has made a conscious and informed choice that she prefers death to continued existence in her helpless and, to her, intolerable condition. I believe she has an absolute right to effectuate that decision. This state and the medical profession instead of frustrating her desire, should be attempting to relieve her suffering by permitting and in fact assisting her to die with ease and dignity. The fact that she is forced to suffer the ordeal of self-starvation to achieve her objective is in itself inhumane.

The right to die is an integral part of our right to control our own destinies so long as the rights of others are not affected. That right should, in my opinion, include the ability to enlist assistance from others, including the medical profession, in making death as painless and quick as possible. . . .

UNITED STATES SUPREME COURT

Cruzan v. Director, Missouri Department of Health

ARGUED DECEMBER 6, 1989.
DECIDED JUNE 25, 1990.

OPINION OF THE COURT

CHIEF JUSTICE REHNQUIST delivered the opinion of the Court.

Petitioner Nancy Beth Cruzan was rendered incompetent as a result of severe injuries sustained during an automobile accident. Co-petitioners Lester and Joyce Cruzan, Nancy's parents and co-guardians, sought a court order directing the withdrawal of their daughter's artificial feeding and hydration equipment after it became apparent that she had virtually no chance of recovering her cognitive faculties. The Supreme Court of Missouri held that because there was no clear and convincing evidence of Nancy's desire to have life-sustaining treatment withdrawn under such circumstances, her parents lacked authority to effectuate such a request. . . .

She now lies in a Missouri state hospital in what is commonly referred to as a persistent vegetative state: generally, a condition in which a person exhibits motor reflexes but evinces no indications of significant cognitive function. The State of Missouri is bearing the cost of her care.

From *United States [Supreme Court] Reports* 497 (1990), 261–357 (excerpts). Footnotes and some references omitted.

After it had become apparent that Nancy Cruzan had virtually no chance of regaining her mental facilities her parents asked hospital employees to terminate the artificial nutrition and hydration procedures. All agree that such a removal would cause her death. The employees refused to honor the request without court approval. The parents then sought and received authorization from the state trial court for termination. The court found that a person in Nancy's condition had a fundamental right under the State and Federal Constitutions to refuse or direct the withdrawal of "death prolonging procedures." App to Pet for Cert A99. The court also found that Nancy's "expressed thoughts at age twenty-five in somewhat serious conversation with a housemate friend that if sick or injured she would not wish to continue her life unless she could live at least halfway normally suggest that given her present condition she would not wish to continue with her nutrition and hydration." Id., at A97–A98.

The Supreme Court of Missouri reversed by a divided vote. The court recognized a right to refuse treatment embodied in the common-law doctrine of informed consent, but expressed skepticism about the application of that doctrine in the circumstances of this case. *Cruzan v. Harmon*, 760 SW2d 408, 416–417 (Mo 1988) (en banc). The court also declined to read a broad right of privacy into the State Constitution which would "support the right of a person to refuse medical treatment in every circumstance," and expressed doubt as to whether such a right existed under the United States Constitution. Id., at 417–418. It then decided that the Missouri Living Will statue, Mo Rev Stat § 459.010 et seq. (1986), embodied a state policy strongly favoring the preservation of life. 760 SW2d, at 419–420. The court found that Cruzan's statements to her roommate regarding her desire to live or die under certain conditions were "unreliable for the purpose of determining her intent," id., at 424, "and thus insufficient to support the co-guardians claim to exercise substituted judgment on Nancy's behalf." Id., at 426. It rejected the argument that Cruzan's parents were entitled to order the termination of her medical treatment, concluding that "no person can assume that choice for an incompetent in the absence of the formalities required under Missouri's Living Will statutes or the clear and convincing, inherently reliable evidence absent here." Id., at 425. The court also expressed its view that "[b]road policy questions bearing on life and death are more properly addressed by representative assemblies" than judicial bodies. Id., at 426. . . .

The common-law doctrine of informed consent is viewed as generally encompassing the right of a competent individual to refuse medical treatment. Beyond that, [court] decisions demonstrate both similarity and diversity in their approach to decision of what all agree is a perplexing question with unusual strong moral and ethical overtones. State courts have available to them for decision a number of sources—state constitutions, statutes, and common law—which are not available to us. In this Court, the question is simply and starkly whether the United States Constitution prohibits Missouri from choosing the rule of decision which it did. This is the first case in which we have been squarely presented with the issue of whether the United States Constitution grants what is in common parlance referred to as a "right to die." . . .

The Fourteenth Amendment provides that no State shall "deprive any person of life, liberty, or property, without due process of law." The principle that a competent person has a constitutionally protected liberty interest in refusing unwanted medical treatment may be inferred from our prior decisions. . . .

But determining that a person has a "liberty interest" under the Due Process Clause does not end the inquiry; "whether respondent's constitutional rights have been violated must be determined by balancing his liberty interests against the relevant state interests." *Youngberg v. Romeo,* 457 US 307, 321 (1982). See also *Mills v. Rogers,* 457 US 291, 299 (1982).

Petitioners insist that under the general holdings of our cases, the forced administration of life-sustaining medical treatment, and even of artificially delivered food and water essential to life, would implicate a competent person's liberty interest. . . . The dramatic consequences involved in refusal of treatment would inform the inquiry as to whether the deprivation of the interest is constitutionally permissible. But for purposes of this case, we assume that the United States Constitution would grant a competent person a constitutionally protected right to refuse lifesaving hydration and nutrition.

Petitioners go on to assert that an incompetent person should possess the same right in this respect as is possessed by a competent person. . . .

The difficulty with petitioners' claim is that in a sense it begs the question: an incompetent person is not able to make an informed and voluntary choice to exercise a hypothetical right to refuse treatment or any other right. Such a "right" must be exercised for her, if at all, by some sort of surrogate. Here, Missouri has in effect recognized that under certain circumstances a surrogate may act for the patient in electing to have hydration and nutrition withdrawn in such a way as to cause death, but it has established a procedural safeguard to assure that the action of the surrogate conforms as best it may to the wishes expressed by the patient while competent. Missouri requires that evidence of the incompetent's wishes as to the withdrawal of treatment be proved by clear and convincing evidence. The question, then, is whether the United States Constitution forbids the establishment of this procedural requirement by the State. We hold that it does not.

Whether or not Missouri's clear and convincing evidence requirement comports with the United States Constitution depends in part on what interests the State may properly seek to protect in this situation. Missouri relies on its interest in the protection and preservation of human life, and there can be no gainsaying this interest. . . .

But in the context presented here, a State has more particular interests at stake. The choice between life and death is a deeply personal decision of obvious and overwhelming finality. We believe Missouri may legitimately seek to safeguard the personal element of this choice through the imposition of heightened evidentiary requirements. It cannot be disputed that the

Due Process Clause protects an interest in life as well as an interest in refusing life-sustaining medical treatment. Not all incompetent patients will have loved ones available to serve as surrogate decision makers. And even where family members are present "[t]here will, of course, be some unfortunate situations in which family members will not act to protect a patient." . . . Finally, we think a State may properly decline to make judgments about the "quality" of life that a particular individual may enjoy, and simply assert an unqualified interest in the preservation of human life to be weighed against the constitutionally protected interests of the individual.

In our view, Missouri has permissibly sought to advance these interests through the adoption of a "clear and convincing" standard of proof to govern such proceedings. "The function of a standard of proof, as that concept is embodied in the Due Process Clause and in the realm of factfinding, is to 'instruct the factfinder concerning the degree of confidence our society thinks he should have in the correctness of factual conclusions for a particular type of adjudication.' " . . .

There is no doubt that statutes requiring wills to be in writing, and statutes of frauds which require that a contract to make a will be in writing, on occasion frustrate the effectuation of the intent of a particular decedent, just as Missouri's requirement of proof in this case may have frustrated the effectuation of the not-fully-expressed desires of Nancy Cruzan. But the Constitution does not require general rules to work faultlessly; no general rule can. . . .

The Supreme Court of Missouri held that in this case the testimony adduced at trial did not amount to clear and convincing proof of the patient's desire to have hydration and nutrition withdrawn. In so doing, it reversed a decision of the Missouri trial court which had found that the evidence "suggest[ed]" Nancy Cruzan would not have desired to continue such measures, App to Pet for Cert A98, but which had not adopted the standard of "clear and convincing evidence" enunciated by the Supreme Court. The testimony adduced at trial consisted primarily of Nancy Cruzan's statements made to a housemate about a year before her accident that she would not want to live should she face life as a "vegetable," and other observations to the same effect. The observations did not deal in terms with withdrawal of medical treatment or of hydration and nutrition. We cannot say that the Supreme Court of Missouri committed constitutional error in reaching the conclusion that it did. . . .

No doubt is engendered by anything in this record but that Nancy Cruzan's mother and father are loving and caring parents. If the States were required by the United States Constitution to repose a right of "substituted judgment" with anyone, the Cruzans would surely qualify. But we do not think the Due Process Clause requires the State to repose judgment on these matters with anyone but the patient herself. Close family members may have a strong feeling—a feeling not at all ignoble or unworthy, but not entirely disinterested, either—that they do not wish to witness the continuation of the life of a loved one which they regard as hopeless, meaningless, and even degrading. But there is no automatic assurance that the view of close family members will necessarily be the same as the patient's would have been had she been confronted with the prospect of her situation while competent. All of the reasons previously discussed for allowing Missouri to require clear and convincing evidence of the patient's wishes lead us to conclude that the State may choose to defer only to those wishes, rather than confide the decision to close family members.

The judgment of the Supreme Court of Missouri is affirmed.

SEPARATE OPINIONS

JUSTICE O'CONNOR, concurring.

[T]he Court does not today decide the issue whether a State must also give effect to the decisions of a surrogate decisionmaker. . . . In my view, such a duty may well be constitutionally required to protect the patient's liberty interest in refusing medical treatment. Few individuals provide explicit oral or written instructions regarding their intent to refuse medical treatment should they become incompetent. States which decline to consider any evidence other than such instructions may frequently fail to honor a patient's intent. Such failures might be avoided if the State considered an equally probative source of evidence: the patient's appointment of a proxy to make health care decisions on her behalf. Delegating the authority to make medical decisions to a family member or friend is becoming a common method of planning for the future. . . .

Today's decision, holding only that the Constitution permits a State to require clear and convincing evidence of Nancy Cruzan's desire to have artificial hydration and nutrition withdrawn, does not preclude a future determination that the Constitution requires the States to implement the decisions of a patient's duly appointed surrogate. Nor does it prevent States from developing other approaches for protecting an incompetent individual's liberty interest in refusing medical treatment. As is evident from the Court's survey of state court decisions . . . no national consensus has yet emerged on the best solution for this difficult and sensitive problem. Today we decide only that one State's practice does not violate the Constitution; the more challenging task of crafting appropriate procedures for safeguarding incompetents' liberty interests is entrusted to the "laboratory" of the States, *New State Ice Co. v. Liebmann,* 285 US 262, 311 (1932) (Brandeis, J., dissenting), in the first instance.

Justice Brennan, with whom Justice Marshall and Justice Blackmun join, dissenting.

A grown woman at the time of the accident, Nancy had previously expressed her wish to forgo continuing medical care under circumstances such as these. Her family and her friends are convinced that this is what she would want. A guardian ad litem appointed by the trial court is also convinced that this is what Nancy would want. See 760 SW2d at 444 (Higgins, J., dissenting from denial of rehearing). Yet the Missouri Supreme Court, alone among state courts deciding such a question, has determined that an irreversibly vegetative patient will remain a passive prisoner of medical technology—for Nancy, perhaps for the next 30 years. . . . Because I believe that Nancy Cruzan has a fundamental right to be free of unwanted artificial nutrition and hydration, which right is not outweighed by any interests of the State, and because I find that the improperly biased procedural obstacles imposed by the Missouri Supreme Court impermissibly burden that right, I respectfully dissent. Nancy Cruzan is entitled to choose to die with dignity. . . .

I

. . . The right to be free from medical attention without consent, to determine what shall be done with one's own body, *is* deeply rooted in this Nation's traditions, as the majority acknowledges. . . . This right has long been "firmly entrenched in American tort law" and is securely grounded in the earliest common law. . . . " 'Anglo-American law starts with the premise of thoroughgoing self determination. It follows that each man is considered to be master of his

own body, and he may, if he be of sound mind, expressly prohibit the performance of lifesaving surgery, or other medical treatment.' " *Natanson v. Kline,* 186 Kan 393, 406–407, 350 P2d 1093, 1104 (1960). . . .

No material distinction can be drawn between the treatment to which Nancy Cruzan continues to be subject—artificial nutrition and hydration—and any other medical treatment. . . .

Artificial delivery of food and water is regarded as medical treatment by the medical profession and the Federal Government. According to the American Academy of Neurology, "[t]he artificial provision of nutrition and hydration is a form of medical treatment . . . analogous to other forms of life-sustaining treatment, such as the use of the respirator. When a patient is unconscious, both a respirator and an artificial feeding device serve to support or replace normal bodily functions that are compromised as a result of the patient's illness." . . .

II

A

The right to be free from unwanted medical attention is a right to evaluate the potential benefit of treatment and its possible consequences according to one's own values and to make a personal decision whether to subject oneself to the intrusion. For a patient like Nancy Cruzan, the sole benefit of medical treatment is being kept metabolically alive. . . .

There are also affirmative reasons why someone like Nancy might choose to forgo artificial nutrition and hydration under these circumstances. Dying is personal. And it is profound. For many, the thought of an ignoble end, steeped in decay, is abhorrent. A quiet, proud death, bodily integrity intact, is a matter of extreme consequence. "In certain, thankfully rare, circumstances the burden of maintaining the corporeal existence degrades the very humanity it was meant to serve." *Brophy v. New England Sinai Hospital, Inc.* 398 Mass 417, 434, 497 NE2d 626, 635–636 (1986). . . .

Such conditions are, for many, humiliating to contemplate, as is visiting a prolonged and anguished vigil on one's parents, spouse, and children. A long, drawn-out death can have a debilitating effect on family members. . . .

B

Although the right to be free of unwanted medical intervention, like other constitutionally protected interests, may not be absolute, no State interest could outweigh the rights of an individual in Nancy Cruzan's position. Whatever a State's possible interests in mandating life-support treatment under other circumstances, there is no good to be obtained here by Missouri's insistence that Nancy Cruzan remain on life-support systems if it is indeed her wish not to do so. Missouri does not claim, nor could it, that society as a whole will be benefited by Nancy's receiving medical treatment. No third party's situation will be improved and no harm to others will be averted. Cf, nn 6 and 8, supra.

The only state interest asserted here is a general interest in the preservation of life. But the State has no legitimate general interest in someone's life, completely abstracted from the interest of the person living that life, that could outweigh the person's choice to avoid medical treatment. . . . Thus, the State's general interest in life must accede to Nancy Cruzan's particularized and intense interest in self-determination in her choice of medical treatment. There is simply nothing legitimately within the State's purview to be gained by superseding her decision. . . .

III

Missouri may constitutionally impose only those procedural requirements that serve to enhance the accuracy of a determination of Nancy Cruzan's wishes or are at least consistent with an accurate determination. The Missouri "safeguard" that the Court upholds today does not meet that standard. The determination needed in this context is whether the incompetent person would choose to live in a persistent vegetative state on life-support or to avoid this medical treatment. Missouri's rule of decision imposes a markedly asymmetrical evidentiary burden. Only evidence of specific statements of treatment choice made by the patient when competent is admissible to support a finding that the patient, now in a persistent vegetative state, would wish to avoid further medical treatment. Moreover, this evidence must be clear and convincing. No proof is required to support a finding that the incompetent person would wish to continue treatment. . . .

Even more than its heightened evidentiary standard, the Missouri court's categorical exclusion of relevant evidence dispenses with any semblance of accurate factfinding. The court adverted to no evidence supporting its decision, but held that no clear and convincing, inherently reliable evidence had been pre-

sented to show that Nancy would want to avoid further treatment. In doing so, the court failed to consider statements Nancy had made to family members and a close friend. The court also failed to consider testimony from Nancy's mother and sister that they were certain that Nancy would want to discontinue artificial nutrition and hydration, even after the court found that Nancy's family was loving and without malignant motive. See 760 SW2d, at 412. The court also failed to consider the conclusions of the guardian ad litem, appointed by the trial court, that there was clear and convincing evidence that Nancy would want to discontinue medical treatment and that this was in her best interests. Id., at 444 (Higgins, J., dissenting from denial of rehearing); Brief for Respondent Guardian Ad Litem 2–3. The court did not specifically define what kind of evidence it would consider clear and convincing, but its general discussion suggests that only a living will or equivalently formal directive from the patient when competent would meet this standard. Seed 760 SW2d, at 424–425. . . .

The Missouri Court's disdain for Nancy's statements in serious conversations not long before her accident, for the opinions of Nancy's family and friends as to her values, beliefs and certain choice, and even for the opinion of an outside objective factfinder appointed by the State evinces a disdain for Nancy Cruzan's own right to choose. The rules by which an incompetent person's wishes are determined must represent every effort to determine those wishes. The rule that the Missouri court adopted and that this Court upholds, however, skews the result away from a determination that as accurately as possible reflects the individual's own preferences and beliefs. It is a rule that transforms human beings into passive subjects of medical technology. . . .

That Missouri and this Court may truly be motivated only by concern for incompetent patients makes no matter. As one of our most prominent jurists warned us decades ago: "Experience should teach us to be most on our guard to protect liberty when the government's purposes are beneficent. . . . The greatest dangers to liberty lurk in insidious encroachment by men of zeal, well meaning but without understanding." *Olmstead v. United States,* 277 US 438, 479 (1928) (Brandeis, J., dissenting).

I respectfully dissent.

Advance Directives

LINDA A. EMANUEL, MARION DANIS, ROBERT A. PEARLMAN, AND PETER A. SINGER

Advance Care Planning as a Process: Structuring the Discussions in Practice

Linda A. Emanuel, MD, is professor of medicine at Northwestern University Medical School as well as the founder and principal of the Education for Physicians in End-of-Life Care (EPEC) Project. She trained at Cambridge University, University College–Oxford, and Harvard Medical School. She also pursued studies in both medical and professional ethics. Former Vice President of Ethics Standards and head of the Institute for Ethics at the American Medical Association, she has published extensively in the field of bioethics, with particular attention to end-of-life care, the doctor-patient relationship, academic integrity, and organizational ethics.

Marion Danis, MD, is chief of the Bioethics Consultation Service and head of the Section on Ethics and Health Policy in the Department of Clinical Bioethics in the Clinical Center of the National Institutes of Health. In this position, she has focused on the connection between ethical values and health policy. Some of her other articles on advanced directives include "Following Advance Directives," *Hastings Center Report* and "A Prospective Study of Advance Directives for Life-Sustaining Care," *New England Journal of Medicine*.

Robert A. Pearlman, MD, is located at the VA Puget Sound Health Care System, where he has served as chair of the Ethics Advisory Committee. He is also a professor of medicine, specializing in geriatric medicine and gerontology, at the University of Washington School of Medicine as well as adjunct professor in the program in Medical History and Ethics at the University of Washington. He has published extensively on issues of consent, advance care planning, the quality of life, and empirical research in clinical ethics.

Peter A. Singer, MD, holds the Sun Life Chair in Bioethics at the University of Toronto and is director of the University of Toronto Joint Centre for Bioethics. He is professor in the Department of Medicine and is extensively involved in bioethics in Canada. In addition to his longstanding interests in advance directives, he has worked on problems of euthanasia and physician-assisted suicide, global health ethics, and research ethics.

From *The American Geriatrics Society* 43 (1995), 440–446.
Reprinted by permission.

The structured discussion should be aimed at framing the issues, and tentatively identifying wishes. It need not aim to resolve all issues or come to final determination of all prior wishes. Neither should it aim to be a deep personal revelation seeking perfect knowledge of the patient's core self; this is unrealistic and unnecessary. Nevertheless, this step is the core of all advanced planning processes.

The skills required of the professional for this stage are those of communicating pertinent medical understanding and of supportive elicitation of the patient's wishes, as in most ideal informed consent discussions. Specific training sessions may be needed to acquire the information, skills, and judgment involved in this critical part of the process of advance plan-ning because, unlike most medical decisions, in this case patients' preferences are cast forward into future scenarios.

Initial Decisions about the Mode of Advance Planning. An early part of the discussion may focus on whether proxy designation, instructional directives, or both are most suitable for the particular patient. Most patients should be advised to combine the two forms of planning so that the proxy may be guided by the patient's stated prior wishes. Thus, the conversation might continue as follows:

"Ms/r. X, I suggest we start by considering a few examples as a way of getting to know your thinking. I will use examples that I use for everyone."

If, in the physician's judgment, a particular patient proves not competent to make prior directives, he or she might nevertheless be competent to designate a proxy decision-maker. In such a case the conversation might go rather differently. For example, the physician might proceed as follows:

"These decisions may be hard to think about when they are not even relevant right now. You have had a long and trusting relationship with Ms/r. Y. You might even have had discussions like this before with her/him. Would you want to give Ms/r. Y, or someone else you trust, the authority to make decisions for you in case of need?"

Understanding the Patient's Goals for Treatment in a Range of Scenarios. When instructional directives are suitable, we believe that the physician should help the patient articulate abstract values, goals of treatment, and concrete examples of treatment prefer-

ences in order to provide all the major components of decision-making. Discussions can be well structured by going through an illustrative predrafted document together; this approach can prevent long confusing and overwhelming encounters. With such structuring, this portion of advance planning can be informative, accessible to patients with a wide range of educational levels, and still quite brief. Many documents that can be used for structuring discussions are available; however, a properly validated document should be chosen to maximize the chance that patients are accurately representing their wishes.

Scenarios representative of the range of prognosis and of the range of disability usually encountered in circumstances of incompetence should be presented to the patient. The physician might start like this:

"So, let's try to imagine several circumstances. We will go through four and then perhaps another one or two. First imagine you were in a coma with no awareness. Assume there was a chance that you might wake up and be yourself again, but it wasn't likely. Some people would want us to withdraw treatment and let them die, others would want us to attempt everything possible, and yet others would want us to try to restore health but stop treatment and allow death if it was not working. What do you think you would want?"

After a standard set of scenarios, tailored scenarios can be considered. When a patient has a serious diagnosis with a predictable outcome involving incompetence that is not covered in the standard document, the physician might continue:

"We should also consider the situations that your particular illness can cause; that way you can be sure we will do what you want. For sure, all people are different and you may never face these circumstances. Nevertheless, let's imagine . . ."

While illness scenarios may be difficult for people to imagine, we suggest that preferences arrived at without illness scenarios are unlikely to be accurate or realistic wishes; a treatment preference without a specified illness circumstance is meaningless.

A patient considering illness scenarios also may be able to articulate which states, if any, are greatly feared and/or are felt to be *worse than death* for them. So, for example, the physician may go on:

"People often think about circumstances they have seen someone in or heard about in the news. Some may seem worse than death. Do you have such concerns?"

When a range of scenarios have been considered it

is often possible to go back and identify the scenario(s) in which the patient's goals changed from "treat" to "don't treat." This can provide a useful personal threshold to guide the physician and proxy later. The physician may also use it to check back at the time with the patient that his or her wishes are properly reflected, saying, for example:

"Well, we've gone through several scenarios now. It seems to me that you feel particularly strongly about . . . Indeed, you move from wanting intervention to wanting to be allowed to die in peace at the point when . . . Do I speak for you correctly if I say that your personal threshold for deciding to let go is . . . ?"

Raising Specific Examples and Asking About General Values. In any scenario after the patient's response about goals, specific examples may be used:

"So, let us take an example to be sure I understand you, not only in general but also in specific. Say you were in a coma with a very small chance of recovery, and you had pneumonia; to cure the pneumonia we would have to put you on a breathing machine. Would you want us to use the breathing machine and try to cure; allow the pneumonia to cause death; or perhaps try the treatment, withdrawing the breathing machine if you did not get better?"

Checking and specifying a patient's views by providing concrete examples may be a useful way to reduce the incidence of clinically unrealistic choices by patients. So, for example, a patient who declines intubation but wants resuscitation may need more information on resuscitation and a suggestion as to how his or her wishes may be translated into a clinically reasonable decision.

The preceding discussion about goals for treatment and specific choices may be usefully combined with an open ended question about the patient's reasons for particular decisions and the *values* that pertain to such decisions.

"I think you have given a good picture of particular decisions you would want. Can you also say something about the values or beliefs that you hold? Understanding your more general views can be an important part of getting specific decisions right."

Patients' statements might refer to their wish to act in accord with the positions of their religious denomination, or to their views on the sanctity of life or dignity of death, or they might articulate their disposition to take a chance or to favor a secure choice.

Including the Proxy. The proxy, if already known at this point, should be encouraged to attend this discussion. Much understanding of the patient's wishes can be gained from hearing this part of the process. The clinician can guide the proxy to adopt a listening role; the proxy may ask clarifying questions but should avoid biasing the patient's expressions. Sometimes the proxy can be following the conversation with a predrafted document in hand, noting down the patient's statements. The ground can be set for future discussions between any of the patient, physician, and proxy. The proxy becomes part of the working team, and future interactions between proxy and physician, if the patient does become incompetent, are likely to go more smoothly than they might without such prior discussions.

At this stage, the advance directive should be, at most, pencilled in. The tentative draft can be taken home by the patient for further reflection and review with other involved parties, such as the proxy, family, friends, or pastor. This step can be a useful mechanism for dealing with difference among the parties ahead of time. The structured discussion should be brief and followed by a subsequent meeting when a directive may be finalized. Physicians will initially take longer in these interviews, but with training in the requisite skills and with experience, time will be reduced.

COMPLETING AN ADVISORY DIRECTIVE AND RECORDING IT

. . . The professional's main required skill here is to ascertain whether the patient has reached resolution and is ready to articulate well considered preferences. Any facet of the first two steps not yet complete should be completed at this step. Even if a patient has reached resolution, there should be a reminder that advance directives can be revised if his/her wishes are changed. If the proxy has not been present at previous stages, the physician should particularly encourage the proxy to enter the process at this point. The proxy should again be encouraged to adopt a listening and clarifying role, avoiding undue influence on the patient. It can be helpful for the physician to co-sign the document at this stage to endorse physician involvement and to document the primary physician for ease of future follow up.

REVIEWING AND UPDATING DIRECTIVES

Along with other regular check-ups and screening tests, patients should be told to expect periodic review of their directives. The clinician may re-introduce the topic.

"Ms/r. X, a year has gone by since we completed your advance care plans, and in that time a lot has happened. People do sometimes change their wishes so let's review the wishes you wrote down a year ago."

Competent people are often known to change their minds about all matters, whether they are of great import or not. Reasonable but imperfect consistency has also been found in advance planning decisions by competent individuals. Physicians should be aware of this and should review directives with the patient periodically. Physicians should check which decisions a patient maintains and which are changed. Changed positions should prompt the physician to pay particular attention to the source of change; some changes will be well reasoned, and others will be markers for misunderstandings that need to be clarified. Some people will be generally changeable; the physician should address this observation to the patient, inquiring after the reason. If supportive guidance and education do not permit the patient to reach reasonable stability in his or her advance directives, more emphasis must be placed on proxy decision-making for the patient. The physician will often be able to come to this decision jointly with the patient and proxy:

"Your choices changed on several decisions both times when we reviewed your statement, even though we have discussed the issues a lot. You have already said that you want Ms/r. Y to be your proxy. Would you prefer to give these decisions over to Ms/r. Y to decide according to what she/he thinks would be in your best interests?"

Some changed decisions may occur after the onset of incompetence. There is continuing debate on how to deal with such circumstances. The physician should be careful to evaluate the exact nature of the patient's incompetence; some patients will be globally incompetent while others will be competent to make some decisions and incompetent for other decisions. The role of the proxy and possibly a further adjudicating party may be crucial in such circumstances.

The skills that physicians require for this portion of advance planning are not as yet matched by detailed understanding of how patients might make or can be encouraged to make valid and enduring decisions, or the type of circumstances that tend to prompt changes. It is reasonable to expect that researchers will continue to study how best to elicit patient's enduring and valid wishes.

APPLICATION OF PRIOR DIRECTIVES
TO ACTUAL CIRCUMSTANCES

Clinicians will require both interpersonal and interpretive skills in this difficult final step. Patients will often end up in need of decisions that are not accurately specified in their advance directive. The physicians and proxy, then, must work from the information they have to make a good guess as to what the patient would have wanted. Knowledge of the patient's values, goals, choices in a range of scenarios, and thresholds for withholding or withdrawing specific interventions can all be helpful. Choices in scenarios can often provide very accurate predictors.

The spirit as much as the letter of the directive should be the focus of the physician and the proxy. Documents that are given as an advisory statement rather than a legal imperative are less likely to lead to blind application of irrelevant decisions. So, for example, if a patient has a poorly drafted document stating only that he or she does not want to be on a respirator, the physicians should try to clarify what circumstances this preference applies to; the patient may have intended the statement to apply to circumstances of hopeless prognosis, but may actually be facing a reversible life threatening illness. The physicians and proxy would need to "override" the simple statement in order to honor the true wishes of the patient in such a case; they would be interpreting simple statements to match presumed true wishes, not trumping the patient's wishes. The full responsibility of this interpretive process and the risks of misusing it in parentalistic judgments should be clear to the physician and proxy.

When the physician writes orders for the incompetent patient's care they should be as detailed as the advance directive permits. Thus a "Do Not Resuscitate" order can usually be supplemented with orders such as "evaluate and treat infection," "do not intubate," "provide full comfort care," and so forth. They can be gathered together in a series of orders altogether intended to translate the directive into doctors orders. Life threatening illness often prompts a change in health care facility or attending physician and will, therefore, entail transfer of advance directives from the physician who has guided the process to a new physician. At a minimum, physicians, patients, proxies, and institutions should all be aware of the need to transfer advance care documents with the patient to the new facility and physician. However, transmittal of accurate portrayals of a patient's wishes will rarely be adequately completed by simply passing on a document; whenever possible, the earlier physician should remain available as a key resource as the patient's prior wishes are brought to bear on specific decisions. It is likely that the physician and proxy who have undertaken the entire process of advance planning with the patient will have a more accurate sense of the patient's actual wishes than those who were simply presented with a document after patient incompetence has already occurred. Those who attempt substituted judgments in the absence of specific patient guidance are known to have discrepancies in their decisions compared with the wishes of the patient, and it is reasonable to assume that explicit communication on the matter should reduce the gap.

Decision-making, especially when there is a proxy involved, is a collaborative matter. The physician and the proxy have distinct roles that should be understood. The physician's role is to diagnose the condition and convey information, opinions, and judgment, and then to discuss them with the proxy, as would ordinarily occur with the patient. The proxy's role is to attempt substituted judgments and speak for the patient wherever possible, or to make best interest judgments as a second best approach if there is no way of surmising what the patient would have wanted. Unless the patient or the local state statutes say otherwise, the proxy should take on the "voice" of the patient and assume equal levels of authority—nor more or less—that would have been the patient's.

FURTHER CONCERNS

ARE ADVANCED DIRECTIVES FOR EVERYONE?

Time constraints and other practical considerations may lead physicians to target their sicker and older patients. However, younger and healthier patients are often quite interested in the approach. Furthermore, advance planning for those who suffer an accident or sudden illness may be most helpful. Advance planning may be considered as a branch of preventive medicine.

There will be a proportion of patients who should not be advised to undertake advance care planning. For example, there are people with no one they wish to choose as a proxy who also have limited ability to imagine future hypothetical situations. Others might find the notion so dissonant with the type of care re-

lationship they want that they do not wish to consider the process. This latter group of patients should still have sufficient discussion to permit understanding of how decisions get made in the absence of directives. For example, the different powers of proxy and next of kin should be clear, as should the occasional role of a guardian ad lidum, and the limited ability of substituted decisions to match the patient's prior wishes in the absence of guidance from the patient. Neither physician nor patient should allow themselves the assumption that this is a topic they need not even raise. If the patient and physician are explicitly content with the hitherto more traditional approaches to decision-making at the end of life, this is acceptable.

A considerable proportion of people have no primary care physician or health professional, and the only educational materials that reach them will be through the public media. Some of these people are able to have a physician; they should seek out a physician for the purposes of advance planning if they wish to undertake it. They should be aware that many directives are highly dependent on medical knowledge and understanding of the individual patient's medical circumstances; decisions made in the absence of medical expertise may be inaccurate reflections of the person's true preferences.

People who face limited access to the health care system should not be discouraged from advance care planning if they are inclined toward it. However, people who complete directives without talking to a physician should be encouraged to discuss their views in as much depth as possible with their next-of-kin or proxy so that ultimately someone will be able to discuss with a physician how the patient's known prior wishes relate to actual circumstances and treatment decisions. Publicly provided information or work sheets to guide persons and their proxy in such discussions can be helpful.

WHEN AND WHERE SHOULD ADVANCE DIRECTIVES BE DISCUSSED?

Advanced care planning should ideally be initiated in the outpatient setting, where such discussions are known to be well received. Then, when the topic is raised on admission to the hospital, as required by the Patient Self Determination Act, it is likely to be less threatening. Inquiry can be continued to an indepth inpatient discussion in selected cases. For example, it is appropriate with patients who are at risk of needing life-sustaining intervention soon, and discussions in this setting can be well conducted, providing guidance and welcome coordination of goals and expectations for all concerned. Although judgment of need for such intervention is known to be difficult, physicians may be guided in part by published criteria. For those with a completed directive, review during an admission may also be advisable. Other patients with a good prognosis who want to complete directives should first be advised of the merits of deferring the process to an outpatient setting. While there is little data on the question, we fear that those patients who complete directives for the first time in the hospital setting risk making more unstable decisions because of the emotional turbulence of the moment. For those who do complete a directive for the first time during hospital admission, review of the directives after health has stabilized may be particularly important.

TIME CONSTRAINTS

No step in the process of advance care planning needs to take longer than standard doctor-patient encounters. Furthermore, advance care planning probably reduces difficult and time-consuming decisions made in the absence of such planning and should, therefore, be understood as a wise investment of time. Like any other clinical process, skill and experience will make the planning process more time-efficient.

WHAT IS THE ROLE FOR NONPHYSICIAN HEALTHCARE PROFESSIONALS?

Decision-making for incompetent patients has always been among the central tasks of the physician. We regard the facilitation of a structured discussion as the central step in the process of advance planning and, therefore, as particularly dependent on physician involvement. Nevertheless, time constraints and the different communication styles of physicians will make it inevitable that some, and perhaps many, physicians will not include all the steps of advance planning in the routine activities that are the core of good doctoring. Thus, there is likely to be a need for other healthcare professionals to engage in the process of advance planning. Some facilities may form interdisciplinary source groups or consult services that will be available to physicians or patients who seek extra help. Other facilities may train nursing staff in advance planning. Social workers may have a role in facilitating communication around these difficult concepts. However, we view it as essential that the physician, who must ultimately take responsibility for life-sustaining treatment decisions, communicate with the patient at some point and at least check with the patient for possible misunderstandings' unrealistic expectations, or wishes for treatment that the physician would find contrary to standards of medical practice or contrary to his or her conscience. Omission of this step risks discovery of advance directives which have internal inconsistencies or other major problems when it is too late to correct the problem. If the physician cannot participate in this step of advance planning, then another appropriate point may be at the next step of completing a signed advisory statement.

HELPING PROXIES UNDERSTAND THEIR ROLE

The proxy will need to distinguish his or her emotional and personal motives from concerns appropriate to their role as a proxy. Some will have emotional connections with the patient or personal views of their own that will drive them toward more aggressive intervention; others may have monetary or other concerns which may cause a conflict of interest and motivate them toward less aggressive intervention than the patient would have wanted. The physician should be sensitive to these and related possibilities and be able to help the proxy disentangle and understand the relevant motivations, both during the planning process and when making actual decisions. Complex or destructive cases may require further professional counseling and support. Together, the physician and proxy should deliberate the various therapeutic options available. The goal is to avoid any need for one party to assert authority over the other and to achieve consensus instead.

RISKS OF PLACING THE ADVANCE DIRECTIVE IN THE PATIENT'S CHART

Concerns have arisen about how to record the statement in such a fashion that it is least likely to result in inappropriate care and most likely to be available when it becomes relevant. Advance directives placed in hospital records may run the same risk as "Do Not Resuscitate" orders, which are known to sometimes result in inappropriate cessation of other therapies. Education of health professionals on the matter is clearly necessary. Detailed doctors orders can help too. In addition, sections in the medical records for advance directives may be prominently stamped with a statement to the effect that prior directives are (1) intended as an extension of patient autonomy beyond *wishlessness,* (2) may be for the purposes of requesting as well as declining treatment, and (3) have no relevance to care before incompetence.

Copies of the advisory statement and statutory document are best kept not only by the physician but also the proxy and any other person likely to be in early contact in the event of changed medical circumstances. The physician's copy should be recorded as part of the patient's medical records.

DEALING WITH LEGAL CONCERNS

Advance planning statements with physicians should be considered as advisory statements rather than adversarial challenges. (We use the term "advisory statement" in order to distinguish planning devices from narrower statutory documents, which have different legal purposes.) Physicians should make it clear to patients that the advisory statement is the area where medical counsel is most relevant and that the advisory statement is one of the best means of expressing their wishes. An advisory statement can be considered a portrait of a patient's wishes, a profile that should be interpreted to fit with whatever circumstances ultimately pertain. Such a statement can be interpreted with the flexibility needed to meet the complexities of medical decision-making and uncertainties of human decision-making.

Clinicians should be reassured that it has been well argued that such advisory statements will be honored under Common, Statutory, or Constitutional Law, even if they are not part of a statutory document. We nevertheless urge health care professionals to be less concerned with legal issues and more concerned with the medical task of translating a patient's deepest wishes into sound medical decisions. Usually, an advisory statement does not need to raise legal issues because its primary purpose is to provide a valid description of the patient's wishes. However, points of legal concern such as whether living will and proxy statutes in other states are significantly different, may require legal expertise; in such a case the physician should avoid offering unauthorized legal advice and refer to a lawyer.

Physicians may encourage simultaneous use of statutory documents, i.e., predrafted statements designed for specific state statutes, because this is what gives physicians most legal immunity from prosecution when the physician carries out the patient's or proxy's directions. Some statutory documents may contain an advisory section. If not, the advisory and statutory documents may be combined or filed together.

BEN A. RICH

Advance Directives: The Next Generation

Ben A. Rich teaches in the Bioethics Program at the University of California–Davis Medical Center. He is also visiting professor at the U.C. Davis School of Law. As a lawyer, he specialized in litigation and health law. Later in his career he focused his interests on bioethics. He has published numerous works on pain management and advance directives, including *Strange Bedfellows: How Medical Jurisprudence has Influenced Medical Ethics and Medical Practice* (Kluwer Academic/Plenum Publishers).

PROSPECTIVE AUTONOMY AND THE RECOGNITION OF ADVANCE DIRECTIVES

• • •

BEYOND INFORMED CONSENT AND REFUSAL

The doctrine of informed consent, in respecting the individual autonomy of the patient, presupposes that the person has present decisional capacity. Thus, the circumstances of diagnosis, prognosis, and proposed treatment are directly and immediately confronting the patient and are ripe for decisionmaking. When the patient gives or refuses consent to a recommended procedure or a course of treatment, it is one that is deemed by the physician to be appropriate given the patient's present and/or immediately anticipated circumstances. While there is always a certain amount of speculation or uncertainty involved, it is probably as low as it ever will be.

When, on the other hand, a healthy person states preferences for treatment or nontreatment of a hypothetical condition that might arise during some possible future period of decisional incapacity, the level of potential uncertainty is greatly increased. The question then arises whether the uncertainty is so great that, as a matter of ethics, law, and public policy, it is reasonable to honor such declarations. Perhaps we can best consider this question in the context of a few

judicial decisions involving oral directives. In doing so, we also can begin to appreciate why a movement in support of statutorily recognized written directives developed.

ORAL DIRECTIVES

It is not uncommon for people, when reflecting upon serious illness or disabling injury, to share with relatives and close friends their views on how they would wish to be cared for under such circumstances. If, at some future time, the individual does become a victim of such an illness or disability, and is also decisionally incapacitated, then the concern is whether the person, when making those statements, actually intended such expressions to dictate subsequent treatment or nontreatment.

The case of *In re Eichner*[1] presented such a scenario. Brother Fox, the member of a Catholic religious order, had discussed the highly publicized case of Karen Ann Quinlan with other members of the order. He indicated that he did not wish to have his life sustained if he were to become, as she was, permanently unconscious. Some years later, during a surgical procedure, Brother Fox suffered cardiac arrest. Although he was resuscitated, he remained in a persistent vegetative state with no reasonable prospect of regaining consciousness. Father Eichner, acting on behalf of Brother Fox, petitioned the court for an order directing the hospital to remove all life support.

The testimony was uncontroverted that Brother Fox, in his prior statements, had fortuitously addressed precisely the medical contingency that had now be-fallen him—permanent unconsciousness, which might be prolonged indefinitely through medical interven-tions. The decision of the court turned upon the seri-ousness with which Brother Fox had made the state-ment. The continuum along which such statements run appears to be that of "casual remarks" at one end and "solemn pronouncements" at the other. The court concluded that Brother Fox's statements constituted solemn pronouncements, and therefore met the clear and convincing evidence standard applied in such cases.[2] . . .

[In *In re Martin*,][3] Michael Martin had a tremen-dous fear of becoming and remaining severely debil-itated and disabled, regardless of whether it was men-tal, physical, or both. He discussed this profound concern on several occasions with his wife, indicating that he would not wish to have his life sustained by medical interventions if he were incapable of per-forming various functions such as walking, convers-ing with others, dressing and bathing himself, or tend-ing to his basic needs. For example, after a conversation about frail and demented patients in long-term care facilities who were completely depen-dent upon others, Michael Martin's wife quoted him as saying: "I would never want to live like that. Please don't ever let me exist that way because those people don't even have their dignity."[4] On another occasion, after viewing the motion picture "Brian's Song," the story of an athlete with a terminal illness, Michael Martin said to his wife: "If I ever get sick don't put me on any machines to keep me going if there is no hope of getting better." He then said to her, in an ob-vious effort to emphasize the point, that if she ever did that to him: "I'll always haunt you, Mary."[5] On still another occasion, Michael Martin, who was an avid hunter, indicated to his wife that, if he were to become the victim of a hunting accident in which he was seriously and permanently injured, so that he would never again be the same person, then he would not want to go on living. To further reinforce his point, he said to his wife: "Mary, promise me you wouldn't let me live like that if I can't be the person I am right now, because if you do, believe me I'll haunt you every day of your life."[6]

Within months after the last in a series of conver-sations of this nature with his wife, Michael Martin sustained grave injuries in an automobile accident. As a result of these injuries, he was rendered decisionally incapacitated, unable to walk or talk, and dependent upon a colostomy tube for elimination and a gastros-tomy tube for nutrition and hydration. His wife was appointed his guardian, and respecting his repeatedly expressed views, she sought to have his life-sustain-ing interventions withdrawn. The ethics committee of the institution where he was being treated reviewed the case and concluded that withdrawing his nutri-tional support was both medically and ethically ap-propriate, but suggested that prior judicial authoriza-tion should be obtained.[7] When Mary Martin filed a petition in the probate court requesting such autho-rization, Michael Martin's mother and sister opposed the petition and sought to have Mary removed as Michael's guardian. Remarkably, the probate court ruled that, although clear and convincing evidence had been presented that Michael's present condition was one in which he had indicated he would not wish to have his life maintained, his wishes could not be considered because they were never expressed in writ-ing. The court also declined to remove Mary as Michael's guardian.[8]

Following the remand by the appellate court for additional evidentiary proceedings, the trial court found that nutritional support could be withdrawn by the guardian based upon the clear and convincing ev-idence that Michael's present, irreversible condition was one in which he had indicated he would not wish to be maintained. The appellate court affirmed, based upon the determination that Michael Martin's present condition fell within the parameters that he had de-scribed when competent.

The Michigan Supreme Court, in a fashion remi-niscent of the Missouri Supreme Court in the case of Nancy Cruzan,[9] disagreed on the weight and suffi-ciency of the evidence as determined by the trial court, and reversed on the grounds that the majority was not satisfied that the evidence in the record is "so clear, direct, weighty and convincing as to enable [the fact finder] to come to a clear conviction, without hesi-tancy, of the truth of the precise facts in issue."[10] The majority cites with favor the following language from the brief filed by the respondents regarding the vari-ous remarks made by Michael Martin:

[the remarks] were remote in time and place from his present circumstances. At the time the remarks were sup-posedly made, Michael was young and healthy. The re-marks were general, vague and casual, because Mr. Martin was not presently experiencing and likely had never experienced the form of "helplessness" he supposedly disliked, and thus he could not bring to bear his specific views about specific circumstances of which he was intimately knowledgeable. Not being informed by his actual experience, Michael's purported remarks thus were "no different than those that many of us might make after witnessing an agonizing death of another."[11]

The implications of this proposition for the exercise of prospective autonomy are immense and profoundly negative. A few of them are discussed here. First, young and healthy persons would be precluded from issuing directives (that such courts will honor) refusing treatment in the event of grave and permanent injury because (1) they have never experienced life under such circumstances, and (2) the occurrence of such catastrophic illness or injury may come years later. Second, and more significant, no competent person may ever prospectively decline treatment for a future period of incompetence because the person will have no first-hand experience of what life is like as an incompetent individual. Their refusal, from this point of view, is fatally uninformed and therefore need not be respected. Followed to its natural conclusion, 20 years of public policy in support of advance care planning would be completely annihilated.

Because Michigan, like New York, is one of the few jurisdictions that refuses to apply a best interests approach in the absence (real or purported) of clear and convincing evidence, there was no basis upon which the petitioner could argue for withdrawal of nutritional support. Again echoing the Missouri Supreme Court in *Cruzan,* the Michigan Supreme Court asserted: "Our determination is consistent with the furtherance of this state's interest in preserving the sanctity of life and does not abridge Mr. Martin's right to refuse life-sustaining medical treatment."[12] This facile and self-serving observation by the court to the contrary notwithstanding, the conclusion for the citizens of Michigan is inescapable: if you wish your views on withholding or withdrawing life-sustaining treatment to overcome the almost insurmountable burdens imposed by the clear and convincing evidence standard (as interpreted by the state's highest court) and the state's strong interest in preserving the sanctity of life (regardless of its quality or the disproportion between the burdens and benefits of continued existence to the individual), then you must express those views in a formal written directive. Furthermore, do not just state your views so that anyone can understand them, state them so that no one can misunderstand them.

Cases such as those considered in this section help to explain why citizens concerned about their ability to exercise a purported right to prospective autonomy turned to the state legislatures for redress.

THE LIVING WILL

The first type of written advance directive to be recognized by law was the living will. It is the most well known, to the extent that it has (problematically) become in common parlance a generic term for any type of directive. A living will is usually a declaration that, under certain medical conditions, the declarant would not wish to have his or her life sustained through major medical interventions such as artificial respiration, nutrition or hydration, or cardiopulmonary resuscitation. Living wills were designed to prevent the use of medical technology that could not cure disease or reverse an ultimately terminal condition, and thus might reasonably be viewed as merely prolonging the dying process rather than saving life.

What is both interesting and ironic about living wills is that the most significant impetus for their development came from highly publicized cases such as that of Karen Ann Quinlan, a woman in her early twenties whose life was sustained for years while she remained in a persistent vegetative state (PVS) with no hope of recovery to a competent, sapient state.[13] Many of the people who executed living wills believed that, in so doing, they were ensuring they would avoid Karen Quinlan's fate. However, many state living will statutes require, before the will can take effect, that an attending and one other physician certify in writing not only that the patient is unconscious, comatose, or otherwise decisionally incapacitated, but also that the patient's condition is terminal (that is, will result in the patient's death within six months). Many physicians do not consider a PVS to be terminal, because with proper care, such patients may live for many years. Thus, the fate worse than death, which those executing living wills sought to avoid (being kept alive biologically with no hope of regaining consciousness), was something from which those directives could not protect them.

The other ironic aspect of the *Quinlan* case as an impetus for the use of living wills is that, as previously noted, Quinlan was a very young and otherwise healthy woman when she entered a PVS. Yet it is rarely the case that people in their twenties or even thirties execute living wills. Similarly, even those physicians who have become proponents of living wills acknowledge that they do not make a practice of discussing these instruments with their young, healthy patients, even though they are perhaps most at risk of severe brain injury through trauma.

Another difficulty with the terminal illness requirement is that it means different things to different physicians. If the statute recognizing living wills defines terminal condition, then it may characterize it as an irreversible condition from which the patient will die in six months. Medicine is not good at making such predictions except for patients who are only a few hours or at most a few days away from death, regardless of the medical interventions they receive. This is another fact confirmed by SUPPORT. If the statute does not define terminal illness in terms of a maximum life expectancy, then there is likely to be wide variation among physicians as to when they would be willing to certify in writing that a condition is terminal. A conservative view may reject the terminal label until death is imminent (a matter of hours), thereby essentially nullifying the living will. A liberal view may take the position that any irreversible condition that ultimately will result in the patient's death should be deemed a terminal condition, including a PVS.

The other common limitation of living will statutes is that certain types of interventions are specifically excluded. The Missouri living will statute, which was discussed by the Missouri Supreme Court (with highly questionable relevance) in the *Cruzan* case, provides a dramatic example. One of the dissenting judges in that case described the Missouri Living Will Act as "a fraud on Missourians who believe we have been given a right to execute a living will, and to die naturally, respectably, and in peace."[14] The Missouri Living Will Act excludes from the phrase "death-prolonging procedure" comfort care, artificial nutrition and hydration, or the administration of any medication (presumably even antibiotics in the case of pneumonia). Even statutes that do not completely exclude certain procedures from the ambit of living will declarations may, as is the case in Colorado, require that declarants specifically state that they do not wish to receive artificial nutrition and hydration if they are decisionally incapacitated and suffering from a terminal condition.

The primary purpose of this type of advance directive is the designation of a particular individual as the attorney-in-fact for the making of surrogate health care decisions. To be valid, a health care power of attorney need not contain any indication of the person's views about life, death, life-sustaining medical interventions, or other information that might be informative and helpful to the designated surrogate or treating physicians. There seems to be an assumption, which may not necessarily be accurate, that the person executing the health care power of attorney has made his or her wishes with regard to various forms of treatment, and the medical interventions they might entail, known to the attorney-in-fact and perhaps the individual's primary care physician as well. Such an assumption may be nothing more than wishful thinking, however.

In many states, the health care power of attorney constitutes a means by which to avoid the serious limitations that characterize the living will. Typically, the statutes recognizing this form of directive require only the decisional incapacity of the patient in order for the power of attorney to take effect. Similarly, most statutes do not single out any particular intervention (such as artificial nutrition and hydration), which the attorney-in-fact may not reject or reject only when certain conditions have been met. Consequently, the attorney-in-fact has the same, virtually unlimited, authority to reject any or all medical procedures, including those necessary to sustain the life of the patient, as the patient has when competent.

Although the durable power of attorney for health care can be viewed as a significant improvement on the living will in terms of the exercise of prospective autonomy, use of this form of directive carries potential risks for the declarant. An often-repeated critique of advance directives generally, which was noted in *Martin,* is that no one who is competent and reasonably healthy can anticipate accurately how he or she might feel about major medical interventions, especially potentially life-saving ones, during a later period of incompetence and grave illness. To the extent that this critique is valid, it can be asserted even more strongly with regard to a surrogate decisionmaker. Particularly in those situations in which the document contains no personal statement, and the declarant and the attorney-in-fact have not had extensive discussions on this subject, there exists a considerable risk that the surrogate, in making health care decisions for the incompetent patient, will project his or her own views onto the patient. Indeed, health care professionals often (wittingly or unwittingly) encourage such behaviors on the part of surrogates by posing the critical question to them in terms such as: "What do you want us to do for the patient?" rather than using the more appropriate phraseology: "Knowing the patient as you do, what do you believe that he/she would want us to do under the circumstances as we have described them?"

When the person executing the durable power of attorney provides explicit indications of the kinds of interventions he or she would wish to receive in particular situations, as well as those the person would not wish, an objective standard can be said to have been applied by the attorney-in-fact acting as the duly appointed surrogate decisionmaker. However, when explicit indications are not provided in the durable power, and the author simply trusts that the designated attorney-in-fact will know the right thing to do, then a subjective standard will have to be applied. The practice of referring to the standard of decisionmaking under these circumstances as one of "substituted judgment" can be misleading. Courts using such terminology state that the surrogate substitutes his or her judgment for that of the incompetent patient. Typically, however, when a person designates another to be a health care proxy, it is not because that person has demonstrated a capacity to make good decisions in general. Rather, the proxy is selected because he or she knows the patient well, and based upon that familiarity will be in the best position to know, or at least intuit, what the now incompetent patient would decide if he or she were still competent and had been apprised fully of the circumstances.

A person who wishes to create a durable power of attorney for health care that provides the designated proxy (attorney-in-fact), and the health care professionals with whom the proxy will interact on behalf of the incompetent patient, with reasonably explicit guidance on the values and preferences that should inform the decisionmaking process, must expend some significant amount of time and effort. Personal views and wishes on these matters must be assessed accurately and clearly expressed in the directive as well as in discussions with the individual's primary care physician, designated attorney-in-fact, and one or more alternate surrogates in the event that the primary surrogate is no longer available at the critical time. The more out of the mainstream the patient's views

are with regard to desired treatment or nontreatment during grave or terminal illness, the greater will be the need to document those views. Otherwise, physicians responsible for the incompetent patient's care reasonably may believe that the proxy is not acting in good faith and in pursuit of the patient's best interests.

A health care proxy document that is neither too general nor too specific presents a genuine challenge in draftsmanship. If too general, then the document will not provide the attorney-in-fact with sufficient guidance or documentation of views that may have been previously expressed in conversation. If too specific, then the document may be viewed as addressing only the situations actually mentioned, thereby suggesting that any other circumstance, no matter how similar, was not intended to be governed by it. One solution for the version that errs on the side of specificity is to include the phrase "by way of example and not limitation" in conjunction with the discussion of particular medical conditions or interventions. Another solution is to utilize one of the next generation of advance care planning documents discussed later in this article. . . .

• • •

CONCLUSION

A common explanation for physician inattention to advance directives is the lack of time and reimbursement for such discussions. However, in the era of cost containment, such an attitude is counterproductive. Most patients who engage in advance care planning choose to limit care at the end of life rather than demand care that would be described as "futile." Thus, the time spent in assisting patients in carefully and clearly constraining the use of heroic measures in their care ultimately will produce significant reductions in the cost of care, not to mention stress and anxiety on the part of caregivers. A health care system that seeks to contain costs and minimize inappropriate care (which certainly should include within its ambit care the patient would not want) has every reason to embrace wholeheartedly all forms of advance care planning.

Patients, physicians, hospitals, and health plans all can benefit immensely from the utilization of some combination of health care proxies, medical directives, and a values history. The emphasis should be upon the creation of a clear, cogent, yet concise record of patient wishes and preferences, including the identity of surrogate decisionmakers. In addition to the tangible benefits discussed, engaging in the process of creating and reviewing the next generation of directives offers the intangible benefit of countering the increasingly common patient perception that physicians are cold, impersonal, and more interested in moving on to the next case than in relating to them as a unique individual.

As we move into our new millennium, we would do well to learn from the past, lest we repeat it. It is not the concept of advance directives that is flawed and unworkable, but merely our fledgling efforts at crafting them. The next generation of advance directives will succeed where the others have failed. They will do so, in significant part, because they remedy the fatal flaw of the earlier versions—removal of the physician from a fundamental aspect of the professional relationship, which is to provide guidance, counsel, and moral support in planning for care at the end of life.

NOTES

1. 420 N.E.2d 64 (N.Y. 1981).
2. *Id.* at 72.
3. *In re* Martin, 538 N.W.2d 399 (Mich. 1995).
4. *Id.* at 412.
5. *Id.*
6. *Id.*
7. *Id.* at 402.
8. *Id.* at 403.
9. Cruzan v. Harmon, 760 S.W.2d 408 (Mo. 1988) (en banc).
10. *Martin,* 538 N.W.2d at 413.
11. *Id.* at 411.
12. *Id.* at 413.
13. *In re* Quinlan, 355 A.2d 647 (N.J. 1976).
14. *Cruzan,* 760 S.W.2d at 442 (Welliver, J., dissenting).

SUGGESTED READINGS FOR CHAPTER 3

CONFIDENTIALITY

Bayer, Ronald, and Toomey, Kathleen E. "HIV Prevention and the Two Faces of Partner Notification." *American Journal of Public Health* 82 (August 1992), 1158–64.

Beauchamp, Tom L., and Childress, James F. *Principles of Biomedical Ethics,* 5th ed. New York: Oxford University Press, 2001, chaps. 3 and 7.

Beck, James C., ed. *Confidentiality versus the Duty to Protect: Foreseeable Harm in the Practice of Psychiatry.* Washington, DC: American Psychiatry Press, 1990.

Black, Sir Douglas. "Absolute Confidentiality?" In Raanan Gillon, ed. *Principles of Health Care Ethics.* London: John Wiley & Sons, 1994.

Bok, Sissela. *Secrets: On the Ethics of Concealment and Revelation.* New York: Pantheon Books, 1983.

Gostin, Lawrence O. "Genetic Privacy." *Journal of Law, Medicine & Ethics* 23 (1995), 320–30.

———. "Health Information Privacy." *Cornell Law Review* 80 (1995), 451–528.

——— et al. "Privacy and Security of Personal Information in a New Health Care System." *Journal of the American Medical Association* 270 (November 24, 1993), 2487–93.

Hall, Robert. "Confidentiality as an Organizational Ethics Issue." *The Journal of Clinical Ethics* 10 (Fall 1999), 230–36.

Kottow, Michael H. "Medical Confidentiality: An Intransigent and Absolute Obligation." *Journal of Medical Ethics* 12 (1986), 117–22.

Powers, Madison. "Privacy and the Control of Genetic Information." In Mark S. Frankel and Albert Teich, eds. *The Genetic Frontier: Ethics, Law, and Policy.* Washington: AAAS, 1994, 77–100.

Roback, Howard B., et al. "Confidentiality Dilemmas in Group Psychotherapy with Substance-Dependent Physicians." *American Journal of Psychiatry* 153 (1996), 1250–60.

TRUTH TELLING AND THE MANAGEMENT OF BAD NEWS

Akabayashi, A., et al. "Truth Telling in the Case of a Pessimistic Diagnosis in Japan." *The Lancet* 354 (October 1999), 1263.

Asai, Atsushi. "Should Physicians Tell Patients the Truth?" *Western Journal of Medicine* 163 (1995), 36–39.

Bok, Sissela. *Lying: Moral Choice in Public and Private Life.* New York: Pantheon Books, 1978.

Buckman, R. F. *How to Break Bad News.* Baltimore: Johns Hopkins University Press, 1992.

Burack, Jeffrey H., Back, Anthony L., and Pearlman, Robert A. "Provoking Nonepileptic Seizures: The Ethics of Deceptive Diagnostic Testing." *Hastings Center Report* 27 (July-August 1997), 24–33.

Cabot, Richard C. "The Use of Truth and Falsehood in Medicine," as edited by Jay Katz from the 1909 version. *Connecticut Medicine* 42 (1978), 189–94.

Erde, Edmund L., Drickamer, Margaret A., and Lachs, Mark S. "Should Patients with Alzheimer's Disease Be Told Their Diagnosis?" *New England Journal of Medicine* 326 (April 1992), 947–51.

Fallowfield, L. "Giving Sad and Bad News." *The Lancet* 341 (February 1993), 476–78.

Gillon, Raanan. "Is There an Important Moral Distinction for Medical Ethics between Lying and Other Forms of Deception?" *Journal of Medical Ethics* 19 (1993), 131–32.

Jackson, Jennifer. "Telling the Truth." *Journal of Medical Ethics* 17 (1991), 5–9.

Orona, Celia J., Koenig, Barbara A., and Davis, Anne J. "Cultural Aspects of Nondisclosure." *Cambridge Quarterly of Healthcare Ethics* 3 (1994), 338–46.

Potter, Nancy. "Discretionary Power, Lies, and Broken Trust." *Theoretical Medicine* 17 (1996), 329–52.

Ptacek, J. T., and Eberhardt, Tara L. "Breaking Bad News: A Review of the Literature." *Journal of the American Medical Association* 276 (August 14, 1996), 496–502.

INFORMED CONSENT

American Psychiatric Association. Council on Psychiatry and Law. "American Psychiatric Association Resource Document on Principles of Informed Consent in Psychiatry." *Journal of the*

American Society of Human Genetics. "ASHG Report: Statement on Informed Consent for Genetic Research." *American Journal of Human Genetics* 59 (1996), 471–74.

Beauchamp, Tom L., and Childress, James F. *Principles of Biomedical Ethics*, 5th ed. New York: Oxford University Press, 2001, chap. 3.

Berg, Jessica W., Applebaum, Paul S., Lidz, Charles W., and Parker, Lisa S. *Informed Consent: Legal Theory and Clinical Practice*, 2d ed. New York: Oxford University Press, 2001.

Bok, Sissela. "Shading the Truth in Seeking Informed Consent." *Kennedy Institute of Ethics Journal* 5 (1995), 1–17.

Buchanan, Allen E., and Brock, Dan W. *Deciding for Others: The Ethics of Surrogate Decision Making.* Cambridge: Cambridge University Press, 1989.

Cocking, Dean, and Oakley, Justin. "Medical Experimentation, Informed Consent and Using People." *Bioethics* 8 (1994), 293–311.

Faden, Ruth R. "Informed Consent and Clinical Research." *Kennedy Institute of Ethics Journal* 6 (1996), 356–59.

————, and Beauchamp, Tom L. *A History and Theory of Informed Consent.* New York: Oxford University Press, 1986.

Geller, Gail, Strauss, Misha, Bernhardt, Barbara A., and Holtzman, Neil A. " 'Decoding' Informed Consent: Insights from Women Regarding Breast Cancer Susceptibility Testing." *Hastings Center Report* 27 (March-April 1997), 28–33.

Gostin, Lawrence O. "Informed Consent, Cultural Sensitivity, and Respect for Persons." *Journal of American Medical Association* 274 (September 13, 1995), 844–45.

Gunderson, Martin, Mayo, David, and Rhame, Frank. "Routine HIV Testing of Hospital Patients and Pregnant Women: Informed Consent in the Real World." *Kennedy Institute of Ethics Journal* 6 (1996), 161–82.

Hewlett, Sarah. "Consent to Clinical Research—Adequately Voluntary or Substantially Influenced?" *Journal of Medical Ethics* 22 (1996), 232–37.

Howe, Edmund G. "Leaving Laputa: What Doctors Aren't Taught about Informed Consent." *The Journal of Clinical Ethics* 11 (Spring 2000), 3–13.

Katz, Jay. *The Silent World of Doctor and Patient.* New York: Free Press, 1984.

Kondo, Douglas G., Bishop, F. Marian, and Jacobson, Jay A. "Residents' and Patients' Perspectives on Informed Consent in Primary Care Clinics." *The Journal of Clinical Ethics* 11 (Spring 2000), 39–48.

Meisel, Alan. "The Legal Consensus about Forgoing Life-Sustaining Treatment: Its Status and its Prospects." *Kennedy Institute of Ethics Journal* 2 (1992): 309–345.

Meisel, Alan, and Kuczewski, Mark. "Legal and Ethical Myths About Informed Consent." *Archives of Internal Medicine* 156 (December 1996), 2521–26.

Veatch, Robert M. "Abandoning Informed Consent." *Hastings Center Report* 25 (March-April 1995), 5–12.

White, Becky Cox, and Zimbelman, Joe. "Abandoning Informed Consent: An Idea Whose Time Has Not Yet Come." *Journal of Medicine and Philosophy* 23 (1998), 477–99.

REFUSAL OF TREATMENT

Beauchamp, Tom L., and Veatch, Robert, eds. *Ethical Issues in Death and Dying.* Upper Saddle River, NJ: Prentice-Hall, 1996.

DeGrazia, David. "On the Right of 'Nondangerous' Incompetent

Patients to Leave Psychiatric Units Against Medical Advice." *Contemporary Philosophy* 14 (September 1992), 1–5.

Elliston, Sarah. "If You Know What's Good For You: Refusal of Consent to Medical Treatment by Children." In Sheila A. M. McLean, ed. *Contemporary Issues in Law, Medicine and Ethics.* Brookfield, VT: Dartmouth, 1996, 29–55.

Gostin, Lawrence O. "Life and Death Choices after *Cruzan.*" *Law, Medicine & Health Care* 19 (1991), 9–12.

Hewson, Barbara. "The Law on Managing Patients Who Deliberately Harm Themselves and Refuse Treatment." *British Medical Journal* 319 (October 1999), 905–07.

Kliever, Lonnie D., ed. *Dax's Case: Essays in Medical Ethics and Human Meaning.* Dallas, TX: Southern Methodist University Press, 1989.

Powell, Tia, and Lowenstein, Bruce. "Refusing Life-Sustaining Treatment after Catastrophic Injury: Ethical Implications." *Journal of Law, Medicine and Ethics* 24 (Spring 1996), 54–61.

President's Commission for the Study of Ethical Problems in Medicine and Biomedical and Behavioral Research. *Deciding to Forego Life-Sustaining Treatment.* Washington, DC: U.S. Government Printing Office, 1983.

Ross, Lainie Friedman. *Children, Families, and Health Care Decision Making.* New York: Oxford University Press, 1998.

Sullivan, Mark D., and Youngner, Stuart J. "Depression, Competence, and The Right to Refuse Lifesaving Medical Treatment." *American Journal of Psychiatry* 151 (July 1994), 971–78.

Wear, A. N., and Brahams, D. "To Treat or Not to Treat: The Legal, Ethical and Therapeutic Implications of Treatment Refusal." *Journal of Medical Ethics* 17 (September 1991), 131–35.

Weir, Robert F., and Peters, Charles. "Affirming the Decisions Adolescents Make about Life and Death." *Hastings Center Report* 27 (November-December 1997), 29–40.

Youngner, Stuart J. "Competence To Refuse Life-Sustaining Treatment." In Maurice D. Steinberg, and Stuart J. Youngner, eds. *End-of-Life Decisions: A Psychosocial Perspective.* Washington, DC: American Psychiatric Press, 1998, 19–54.

ADVANCE DIRECTIVES

Ackerman, Terrence F. "Forsaking the Spirit for the Letter of the Law: Advance Directives in Nursing Homes." *Journal of the American Geriatrics Society* 45 (1997), 114–16.

Bradley, Elizabeth H., and Rizzo, John A. "Public Information and Private Search: Evaluating the Patient Self-Determination Act." *Journal of Health Politics, Policy and Law* 24 (April 1999), 239–73.

Brock, Dan W. "A Proposal for The Use of Advance Directives in the Treatment of Incompetent Mentally Ill Persons." *Bioethics* 7 (April 1993), 247–56.

————. "What Is the Moral Authority of Family Members to Act as Surrogates for Incompetent Patients?" *Milbank Quarterly* 74 (1996), 599–618.

Celesia, Gastone G. "Persistent Vegetative State: Clinical and Ethical Issues." *Theoretical Medicine* 18 (1997), 221–36.

Dresser, Rebecca. "Confronting the 'Near Irrelevance' of Advance Directives." *Journal of Clinical Ethics* 5 (1994), 55–56.

Engel, John D., et al. "The Patient Self-Determination Act and Advance Directives: Snapshots of Activities in a Tertiary Health Care Center." *Journal of Medical Humanities* 18 (1997), 193–208.

King, Nancy. *Making Sense of Advance Directives.* Dordrecht: Kluwer Academic Publishers, 1991.

May, Thomas. "Reassessing the Reliability of Advance Directives." *Cambridge Quarterly of Healthcare Ethics* 6 (1997), 325–38.

Olick, Robert S. *Taking Advance Directives Seriously: Prospective Autonomy and Decisions Near the End of Life.* Washington: Georgetown University Press, 2001.

Ritchie, Janet, Sklar, Ron, and Steiner, Warren. "Advance Directives in Psychiatry: Resolving Issues of Autonomy and Competence." *International Journal of Law and Psychiatry* 21 (1998), 245–60.

Sehgal, A., et al. "How Strictly Do Dialysis Patients Want Their Advance Directives Followed?" *Journal of the American Medical Association* 267 (January 1, 1992), 59–63.

Teno, Joan M., and Lynn, Joanne, et al. "Do Formal Advance Directives Affect Resuscitation Decisions and the Use of Resources for Seriously Ill Patients?" *Journal of Clinical Ethics* 5 (1994), 23–30 [with following commentary].

Curran, William J., et al. *Health Care Law and Ethics.* New York: Aspen Law & Business, 1998. [Includes bibliographical references.]

Harman, Laurinda Beebe. *Ethical Challenges in the Management of Health Information.* Gaithersburg, MD: Aspen Publishers, 2001.

Lineback, Richard H., ed. *Philosopher's Index.* Vols. 1–. Bowling Green, OH: Philosophy Documentation Center, Bowling Green State University. Issued quarterly.

National Library of Medicine (NLM) Gateway, http://gateway.nlm.nih.gov.

Reich, Warren, ed. *Encyclopedia of Bioethics.* New York: Macmillan, 1995.

Walters, LeRoy, and Kahn, Tamar Joy, eds. *Bibliography of Bioethics.* Vols. 1–. New York: Free Press. Issued annually.

4.
End-of-Life Decision Making

INTRODUCTION

There is no stronger or more enduring prohibition in medicine than the rule against killing or intentionally causing the death of patients. Yet many writers in bioethics now suggest a need to rethink this prohibition in both law and medicine. This challenge is addressed in the present chapter.

KEY TERMS AND DISTINCTIONS

Physicians and nurses have long worried that if they withdraw treatment and a patient dies, they will be accused of killing the patient and will be subject to criminal liability. A parallel concern exists that patients who refuse life-sustaining treatment are killing themselves and that health professionals assist in the suicide if they acknowledge the refusal. A related concern is that physicians who help patients hasten the time of their deaths are involved either in physician-assisted suicide or euthanasia.

We will later look at the *ethical* issues that surround these worries. However, we need first to define some central terms. What do key words like *killing, letting die, euthanasia,* and *physician-assisted suicide* mean in the context of these controversies?

The Distinction between Killing and Letting Die. In its ordinary language meaning, *killing* is any form of deprivation or destruction of life, including animal and plant life. *Killing* represents a family of ideas whose central condition is direct causation of another's death, whereas *letting die* represents another family of ideas whose central condition is intentional avoidance of causal intervention so that a natural death is caused by disease or injury.

However, this way of distinguishing killing and letting die has problems. A person can be killed, it seems, by intentionally letting him or her die of a "natural" condition of disease when the death should have been prevented by a physician. Is this circumstance a killing, a letting die, or both? Can an act be both? What are we to say about a circumstance in which a physician prescribes a lethal medication at a patient's request, which the patient then voluntarily ingests and dies. Is this a killing, a letting die, or neither?

Even if one can provide a clear distinction between killing and letting die that answers these questions, the term *killing* cannot be said to entail a wrongful act or a crime. Standard justifications of killing, such as killing in self-defense, killing to rescue a person endangered by other persons' immoral acts, and killing by misadventure (accidental, non-negligent killing while engaged in a lawful act), prevent us from prejudging an action as wrong merely because it is a killing. To correctly apply the label *killing* or the label *letting die* to an action will therefore fail to determine whether it is acceptable or unacceptable.

Euthanasia. Euthanasia is the act or practice of ending a person's life in order to release the person from an incurable disease, intolerable suffering, or undignified death. Originally, *euthanasia* was derived from two Greek roots meaning "good death." Today the term is used to refer both to painlessly causing death and to failing to prevent death from natural causes for merciful reasons.

Two main types of euthanasia are commonly distinguished: active euthanasia and passive euthanasia. Using this distinction, four subtypes of euthanasia can be represented schematically as follows:

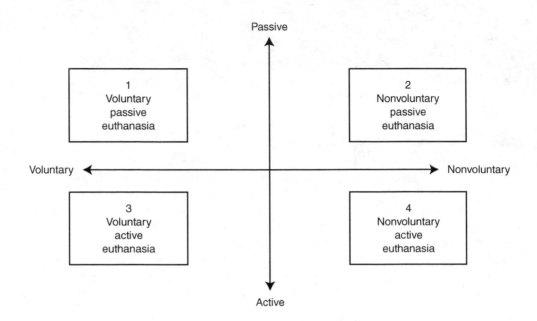

If a person requests the termination of his or her life, the action is called *voluntary euthanasia*. (See the introduction to Dan Brock's essay in this chapter.) If the person is not mentally competent to make an informed request, the action is called *nonvoluntary euthanasia*. Both forms should be distinguished from *involuntary euthanasia*, in which a person capable of making an informed request has not done so. Involuntary euthanasia has been universally condemned and is not under discussion in this chapter. Articles in this chapter are concerned primarily with subtype 3: *voluntary active euthanasia* (VAE).

Physician-Assisted Suicide. Physician-assisted suicide is a patient's voluntary choice of death (suicide) with the assistance of a physician. Unlike voluntary active euthanasia, physician-assisted suicide does not entail that the person who dies be acutely suffering or terminally ill, though these conditions are usually the reasons for electing suicide. The persons who die are themselves the ultimate cause of death; the physician merely assists.

Physician-assisted suicide can be difficult to distinguish from both treatment withdrawals and physician assistance to control pain. Like suicides, patients who refuse a treatment often *intend* to end their lives because of their grim prospects, not because they seek death as an end in itself. From this perspective, their deaths are self-produced. In other cases, physicians heavily sedate dying patients and the drugs have the *unintended* though *foreseen* effect of causing death. From this perspective, an act of controlling pain causes the death, under the foreknowledge that death might be the outcome.

THE RIGHT TO DIE

Several issues about killing, letting die, and physician-assisted death have been discussed under the general heading of the "right to die"—itself a controversial idea because it implies that there *is* a right to die. But is there a right to die? If so, what is it.

We saw in Chapter 1 that a right is a valid claim to a liberty or to a benefit. The notion of a right to die, in particular, points to a liberty right. It derives historically in the U.S. from a series of landmark "right-to-die" cases dating from *in re Quinlan* (1976). These cases include the Cruzan and Bouvia cases considered previously in Chapter 3 (see pp. 168–171, 171–75). Prior to the Quinlan case, few judicial cases and effectively no public policy set the contours of decision-making rights for seriously ill or injured patients. In *Quinlan*, the New Jersey Supreme Court held that it is permissible for a guardian to direct a physician and hospital to discontinue all extraordinary measures. The court asserted that the patient's rights and autonomous judgment are to prevail over the physician's judgment in decisions at the end of life.

The main ethical issue soon became whether all medical treatments, depending on the circumstances, can be construed as optional: Are artificial nutrition and hydration and all other medical technologies subject to the same standards of evaluation? The answer was decided by increasing the scope of the right to make autonomous choices. These legal developments joined with a developing ethics literature and increased public interest to produce a social consensus in the 1990s: A passive letting die at a patient's or family's request is generally acceptable, but an active hastening of death or killing is not. Accordingly, it became the established rule that there is a right to refuse treatment, but no right to request (or perform) an intentionally hastened death.

Leading legal decisions have raised questions about precisely what one has a right to decide and what one does not have a right to decide in the circumstance of one's own death. Over time, the idea of the right to die has evolved from a recognition of a purely negative right against intrusive medical procedures to a positive right to determine the actual manner of one's dying. From this perspective, the right to die has historically not been one thing, but a gradually developing set of autonomy rights giving patients more control over the dying process.

These developments have led to questions of whether the right to die includes the right to request that physicians assist in one's dying. Many physicians (including Leon Kass in this chapter) have been concerned that an expansive, positive right to die may restructure or redefine the physician's role so that the physician is obligated to assist the patient in committing suicide when requested to do so. Some physicians even worry that what began as an effort to give patients the right to be free from unwanted control by physicians will eventually lead to patients having a right to control physicians. However, proponents of a right to die have always insisted that the right includes only a right to request assistance, not a right to compel it.

The two opening articles in the chapter exhibit the sharply different opinions that surround these questions. F. M. Kamm discusses whether death can be a benefit, whether there is a right to choose the end of one's life, whether a doctor has a duty to relieve suffering even if it foreseeably makes the doctor a killer, and whether a patient can waive the right to live, thereby releasing others from the duty not to kill him or her. Kamm believes that a patient would sometimes do no wrong in intending or causing his or her death. She argues that if it is permissible to treat persons in their best interests when we foresee that the treatment will rapidly cause death, then it is permissible to intentionally kill or assist in killing someone when the death is in the person's best interest. Kamm therefore concludes that both euthanasia and physician-assisted suicide are justified under some circumstances.

In the second essay in this section, Leon Kass raises questions about both the coherence and the consequences of the right to die. Noting that the language of rights was introduced into political discourse by Hobbes and Locke, Kass argues that the right to die betrays the excessive individualism of its intellectual forebears. Kass questions whether the right-to-die notion applies equally well to contexts in which treatment is refused with uncertain consequences and to situations in which treatment is refused in order to achieve the result of the patient's death. He suspects that the right to die is at times cynically asserted on behalf of others by healthy people who fervently hope that the unproductive, the incurable, and the repulsive will die sooner rather than later.

THE LEGAL BACKGROUND IN THE UNITED STATES

It is one thing to attempt to justify particular acts of causing death to seriously ill or injured patients and quite another to justify general practices or social policies. Particular acts of assisted suicide may in some circumstances be humane, compassionate, and in a person's best interest, but a social policy that authorizes such acts in medicine, it is often argued, would weaken moral restraints that we cannot replace, threatening practices that provide a basis of trust between patients and health care professionals. Should we, then, *legalize* physician-assisted death?

The right-to-die movement has exerted pressure to reform current laws so that physicians are allowed to play a more extensive role in facilitating the wishes of patients. A major initiative was accepted by the majority of citizens in the state of Oregon. A ballot measure (Measure 16) was first approved by voters in that state in November 1994. It allows physicians to prescribe lethal drugs for those terminally ill patients who wish to escape unbearable suffering. Under the provisions of the Oregon Death with Dignity Act, which is reprinted in this chapter, physicians are legally allowed to prescribe death-inducing drugs for terminally ill patients (so declared by two physicians) when they wish to escape unbearable suffering. These patients must three times request a physician's prescription for lethal drugs.

This Oregon legislation was upheld as a result of two 1997 U.S. Supreme Court decisions: *Vacco v. Quill* and *Washington v. Glucksberg,* both reprinted in this chapter. The Supreme Court reviewed two decisions in circuit courts (both of which are discussed by John Arras in this chapter). These decisions had endorsed a constitutional right to limited physician-assisted suicide. The decisions of these lower courts were reversed by the Supreme Court, which found that there are no constitutional rights to physician aid in dying, but that each state may set its own policy. By returning the issue to the states, the Supreme Court effectively recognized the legal validity of statutes that allow physician-assisted death as well as those that disallow it.

Chief Justice Rehnquist maintains in these opinions that a doctor may provide "aggressive palliative care" that "hastens a patient's death" if the doctor's intent is "only to ease his patient's pain." This doctor is presumably distinguished from the doctor who has the intention of assisting in a suicide because, according to Justice Rehnquist, doctors involved in physician-assisted suicide "must, necessarily and indubitably, intend primarily that the patient be made dead." The Chief Justice appears to be using intention to distinguish between killing and letting die, while assuming that the former is unwarranted and the latter permissible.

This approach has generated controversy. The doctor who prescribes a fatal medication with the intention of giving the patient the choice of using or not using it need have no ill intention; the physician may even try to convince the patient not to use the medication. The doctor's intention may be a benevolent one of easing the patient's anxiety about a loss of control while giving the patient an option he or she has requested. This raises the question of whether the physician's intention is an important consideration in assessing the morality of the physician's action.

Despite Rehnquist's reservations about physician-assisted suicide, the U.S. Supreme Court decision had the effect of clearing the way for a right to physician-assisted death to be enacted by individual states, which then occurred in Oregon in 1997. The Oregon law appears to reflect the new frontier of issues about whether society should expand autonomy rights to control the moment of death. The cutting edge of the right-to-die movement seems, from this perspective, to have shifted from *refusal* of treatment to *request* for aid. On November 6, 2001, however, U.S. Attorney General John Ashcroft attempted to trump the Oregon law. He issued a directive to the Drug Enforcement Agency to investigate physicians who prescribe federally controlled substances and to revoke their license to prescribe the very drugs used in Oregon. The state of Oregon, in turn, sued the U.S. government. The state challenged Ashcroft's authority to limit the practice of medicine under Oregon law.

The final opinion in this chapter on the legal background is *Wendland v. Wendland,* an opinion of the California Supreme Court. In this case, the Court considered whether a patient's conservator (a person designated to protect the interests of an incompetent) can validly withhold artificial nutrition and hydration from a patient even though the patient is not terminally ill, comatose, or in a persistent vegetative state. The patient, Robert Wendland, sustained a severe injury to the brain that left him conscious but severely disabled, both mentally and physically. He had not left an advance directive or appointed a surrogate decision maker. Wendland's wife proposed to direct his physician to remove his feeding tube and allow him to die, but Wendland's mother and sister objected. They saw the act as *killing* Robert, not *allowing him to die.* A twenty-member hospital ethics committee supported the wife's decision, but without speaking with Robert's mother or sister. The court finds that the conservator may not withhold artificial nutrition and hydration absent a clear and convincing statement by the patient or clear and convincing evidence that the act is in the best interest of the patient.

THE MORAL FOUNDATIONS OF PUBLIC POLICY

The legal developments just examined have encouraged the belief that the most pressing moral questions about physician-assisted death is whether it should be *legalized.* This issue will now be framed in terms of the moral foundations of public policy.

Many who are opposed to the legalization of killing or any form of intentional hastening of death appeal not to the intrinsic moral wrongness of helping someone die, but to the social consequences that would result from a public policy that supports physician-assisted dying. A prominent argument in this discussion is the *slippery slope argument.* It proceeds roughly as follows: Although particular acts of active killing are sometimes morally justified, the social consequences of sanctioning practices of killing would run serious risks of abuse and misuse and, on balance, would cause more harm than benefit. The argument is not that these negative consequences will occur immediately, but that they will grow incrementally over time. Although society might start by carefully restricting the number of patients who qualify for assistance in suicide or homicide, these restrictions would be revised and expanded over time, with an ever-increasing risk of unjustified killing. Unscrupulous persons would learn how to abuse the system, just as they do with methods of tax evasion. Slippery slope arguments are discussed in this chapter by several authors, including Brock, John Arras, and the authors of the articles on the Netherlands (see later).

Supporters of a public policy that permits physician-assisted death argue that there are cases in which respect for the rights of patients obligates society to respect the decisions of those who elect this course. Brock supports this position. He and others note that competent patients have a legal and moral right to refuse treatment that brings about their deaths. Why, then, they ask, should there not be a similar right to arrange for death by an active means? Proponents of assisted death like Brock emphasize circumstances in which a condition has become overwhelmingly burdensome for a patient, pain management for the patient is inadequate, and only a physician seems capable of bringing relief.

Brock argues that the "central ethical argument" for voluntary active euthanasia is that it promotes patient autonomy and well-being in circumstances in which persons have a strong need to be in control of their lives. Brock does not balk at the thesis that euthanasia involves intentionally killing the innocent, but he argues that such killing is justified under certain circumstances. Brock views the argument against euthanasia at the policy level as stronger than the argument against it at the level of individual cases, but he maintains that the objections are unpersuasive at both levels.

In the next selection in this section, Arras considers slippery slope arguments with the intention of showing that the legalization of physician-assisted suicide would pose serious and predictable social harms, but he also allows for democratic deliberation on the issue. The natural home for this sort of discussion he finds in legislatures rather than the courts in which so many discussions of the treatment of the dying have appeared in the past. Arras argues that physician-assisted suicide poses a "tragic choice" for society in that there will be victims of any policy that is ultimately adopted. The best public policy, he suggests, is one that limits social harms by erecting legal barriers to assisted death while vigorously addressing the medical and social problems that prompt requests for an early death.

If dire consequences will flow from the legal legitimation of assisted suicide or voluntary active euthanasia, then it would appear that such practices should be legally prohibited, as Arras recommends. But, Brock and others ask, how accurate is the evidence that such dire consequences will occur? Is there a sufficient reason to think that we cannot provide safeguards and maintain control over a public policy of assisted death?

PHYSICIAN-ASSISTED DEATH IN THE NETHERLANDS

As the controversy over assisted death has increased, its practice in the Netherlands has become ever more closely watched. Many in the Netherlands, both inside and outside the medical profession, believe that physician-administered death (killing) in cases of seriously ill and dying patients can be morally and legally justified. However, opponents of the Dutch system have argued that loose state controls have led to an almost unregulated and dangerous social practice.

Dutch euthanasia practices and reporting requirements are addressed first in this chapter by Henk Jochemsen and John Keown. They discuss statistical findings about current practices and consider whether these findings show that voluntary euthanasia is under effective control in the Netherlands. They conclude that although there has been significant improvement in compliance with reporting and other procedural requirements, the practice of voluntary euthanasia remains beyond effective controls and that safeguards in the Dutch system have largely failed. They are concerned that the situation has led to a precarious slippery slope in which Dutch physicians have failed to act on the promise to involve only last resort cases.

In a response, Johannes J. M. van Delden argues three main points. First, he argues that it is not always inappropriate to use euthanasia when palliative care might have been used instead. Such cases do not provide evidence of a slippery slope, he maintains, because patients made their own autonomous judgments about the best way to end their lives. Second, he argues that no significant data show that a slippery slope has occurred in the Netherlands in the sense that *nonvoluntary* euthanasia has become a threat in the system. Finally, he argues that the Dutch reporting system has now been altered to address problems of underreporting. He agrees that many questions remain about needed reforms, but he thinks that the Dutch are now diligent in addressing these questions.

ALTERNATIVES TO PHYSICIAN-ASSISTED DEATH

The two final articles in this chapter discuss several alternatives to physician-assisted suicide that either increase the range of patient autonomy or offer better end-of-life care. In the first, Bernard Gert, Charles M. Culver, and K. Danner Clouser argue that no patient should feel constrainted by the system to stay alive, because every patient can refuse hydration and nutrition, which will ultimately cause death—a form of *passive* euthanasia. All patients therefore already have the right to control their own destinies, and there is no need to rush to physician-assisted suicide or voluntary *active* euthanasia. These authors maintain that key questions turn on whether a competent patient has rationally refused treatment. What makes something a case of letting a competent person die is the patient's refusal, not an omission by the physician. Therefore, the distinction between killing and letting die should be retained, but should be based on the difference between patients' *requests* and patients' *refusals:* Dying by starvation is, on this analysis, a case of letting die, not of killing, despite the fact that the physician cares for the patient during the dying process.

In the final article in this chapter, Timothy Quill, Bernard Lo, and Dan Brock discuss four options that might be presented to patients, so that they can choose how they will die. These authors argue that both terminal sedation and voluntarily stopping eating and drinking would allow physicians to be responsive to the suffering of certain types of patients, but they argue that these strategies are ethically and clinically far closer to physician-assisted suicide and voluntary active euthanasia than has generally been appreciated. These authors propose safeguards for a system in which patients can choose to die as they wish. They also maintain that explicit public policy allowing these alternatives (rather than leaving them hidden, as is now often the case) would reassure many patients who fear a bad death in their future. Unlike Gert and colleagues, these authors consider physician-assisted suicide as one among the four viable options for patients, the other three being improved palliative care, terminal sedation, and refusal of hydration and nutrition.

Whatever options are made available to patients, it should not be presumed that physicians face large numbers of desperately ill patients who wish to be assisted through voluntary active euthanasia or physician-assisted suicide. Virtually all parties to these controversies believe that pain management has made circumstances at least bearable for many of today's patients, reducing the need for physician-assisted death and increasing the need for adequate medical facilities, training, and hospice programs. Nonetheless, as Quill, Lo, and Brock point out, some patients cannot be satisfactorily relieved and experience intolerable suffering. If physicians can benefit patients of this description in ways other than by palliation, terminal sedation, or the withholding of food and fluids, should they be restricted by law or morals from doing so? This question remains at the center of the contemporary discussion.

T.L.B.

F . M . K A M M

A Right to Choose Death?

Frances Myrna Kamm is professor of philosophy at NYU and of medicine and af-
filiated faculty at the NYU School of Law. She is a member of the editorial boards
of *Utilitas* and *Legal Theory*, and the advisory board of the Routledge International
Library of Philosophy. Her publications include *Creation and Abortion* (1992) and
Morality, Mortality, vols. 1 and 2 (1996).

. . . [T]he debate about the right to choose death may
appear to present a stand-off between people who endorse life's intrinsic value, and those who think life's
value depends on the interests, judgments, and choices
of the person whose life it is.

This picture of irreconcilable moral conflict is, I
believe, too despairing about the powers of moral argument. To make headway, however, we may need to
pay closer attention to the complexities of cases and
the specific moral terrain they occupy: to think about
people on medication, being treated by physicians,
sometimes relying on technical means to stay alive,
trying to decide how to live out what remains of their
lives. I will explore this terrain in *moral*, not legal,
terms: I will be asking you to consult your moral
judgments about cases, and follow out the implications of those judgments. Though this moral argument
bears on constitutional argument and on appropriate
legislation, I will not propose laws or rules for judges,
doctors, or hospital administrators to consult, or worry
about slippery slopes created by legally hard cases.
The moral landscape affords firmer footing, and does
not, I will suggest, permit a blanket ban on euthanasia and physician-assisted suicide: Though both involve intentionally ending human lives, both are sometimes morally permissible. I will conclude by
discussing a different argument for such permissibil-

ity offered by a distinguished group of moral philosophers in a recent amicus brief to the Supreme Court.

I. LOGICAL TROUBLES?

Before getting to the issue of moral permissibility, we
need to overcome a preliminary hurdle. I said that euthanasia and physician-assisted suicide are intended
to benefit the patient. Some may object that these
ideas make no sense. How is it possible for death to
benefit the person who dies? Death eliminates the person—how can we produce a benefit if we eliminate
the potential beneficiary?

To see how, consider the parallel question about
death as a harm: Can a person be harmed by her own
death even though death means that she is no longer
around to suffer the harm? Suppose Schubert's life
would have included even greater musical achievement had he not died so young. Because musical
achievement is an important good, Schubert had a less
good life overall than he would have had if he lived
longer. But living a less good life is a harm. By excluding those achievements, then, Schubert's death
harmed him: it prevented the better life. Now come
back to the original concern about how death might
be a benefit. Suppose a person's life would go on containing only misery and pain with no compensating
goods. That person will be better off living a shorter
life containing fewer such uncompensated-for bad
things rather than a longer one containing more of
them. But living a better life is a benefit. By interfering with the important bads, the person's death benefits him; it prevents the worse life.

From *Boston Review* (Summer 1997), 20–23. An earlier version
of this paper was given as a talk at the Plenary Session of the American Academy of Forensic Sciences in New York, in February 1997.

It is possible, in short, to benefit a person by ending his life. The concept of euthanasia is, therefore, at least not simply logically confused; similarly for the idea that physician-assisted suicide may be aimed at the good of the patient. But conceptual coherence does not imply moral permissibility. So let's turn now to the moral question: Is it ever morally permissible to benefit a person by hastening his death, even when he requests it?

II. A RIGHT TO CHOOSE

Suppose a doctor is treating a terminally ill patient in severe pain. Suppose, too, that the pain can only be managed with morphine, but that giving the morphine is certain to hasten the patient's death. With the patient's consent, the doctor may nevertheless give the morphine. Why so? Because, in this particular case, the greater good for the patient is relief of pain, and the lesser evil is loss of life: after all, the patient is terminally ill, and in severe pain, so life would end soon anyway and is not of very good quality. So the patient is overall benefited by having a shorter pain-free life rather than a longer, even more painful life. (Notice that this could be true even if the morphine put the patient in a deep unconscious state from which he never awoke, so that he never consciously experienced pain-free time.)

In giving morphine to produce pain relief, the doctor foresees with certainty (let's assume) that the patient will die soon. Still, death is a side-effect of the medication, not the doctor's goal or reason for giving it: the doctor, that is, is not *intending* the patient's death, and would give the medication even if he thought death would not result. (If I have a drink to soothe my nerves and foresee a hangover, it does not follow that I intend the hangover.) Because the intended death is not present, we don't yet have a case of euthanasia or physician-assisted suicide. At the same time, in giving morphine for pain relief, the doctor is not simply letting the patient die as the disease runs its course; he administers a drug which causes death. So I think this should be understood as a case of killing, even though the doctor does not intend the death. (In other cases we have no trouble seeing that it is possible to kill without intending death: consider a driver who runs someone over while speeding.)

Now suppose the morphine loses its power to reduce the intensity of the patient's pain, but that administering it would still shorten the patient's life and thus limit the duration of his pain. Suppose, too, that the patient requests the morphine; fully aware of its effects, he wants to take it so that it will end his pain by killing him. In short, we now have a case of *morphine for death* rather than *morphine for pain relief.* Is it still morally permissible to give the morphine? Some people say that we may not kill in this case. They do not deny that relief of pain is still the greater good and death the lesser evil: they know that the consequences are essentially the same as in the case of morphine for pain relief. The problem, they say, lies in a difference of intent. In the case of giving morphine for pain relief, we intend the pain relief, and merely foresee the death; but in the case of giving morphine for death, we intend the death (which is the lesser evil): we would not give the morphine if we did not expect the death. But some people think it is impermissible to act with the intent to produce an evil. They support what is called the *Doctrine of Double Effect,* according to which there is a large moral difference between acting with the foresight that one's conduct will have some evil consequence and acting with the intent to produce that same evil (even as part of or means to a greater good). So whereas killing the patient by giving morphine for pain relief is permissible, killing the patient by giving morphine for death is impermissible.

The distinction between intending an evil and merely foreseeing it sometimes makes a moral difference. But does it provide a reason to refrain from performing euthanasia or assisting in suicide? I think not. On many occasions already, doctors (with a patient's consent) *intend the lesser evil* to a person in order *to produce his own greater good.* For example, a doctor may intentionally amputate a healthy leg (the lesser evil) in order to get at and remove a cancerous tumor, thereby saving the patient's life (the greater good). Or, he may intentionally cause blindness in a patient if seeing would somehow, for example, destroy the patient's brain, or cause him to die. Furthermore, he may intentionally cause someone pain, thereby acting contrary to a duty to relieve suffering, if this helps to save the person's life. The duty to save life sometimes just outweighs the other duty. Why then is it impermissible for doctors to intend death when it is the lesser evil, in order to produce the greater good of no pain; why is it morally wrong to benefit the patient by giving her a shorter, less painful life rather than having her endure a longer, more painful one? Recall that in the case of morphine for pain relief, it was assumed that death would be the lesser evil and pain relief the greater good. That was one reason we could give the morphine. Why is it wrong, then, for doctors sometimes to act against a duty to preserve life in order to relive pain, just as they could sometimes act against a duty not to intend pain in order to save a life?

To summarize, I have constructed a three-step argument for physician-assisted suicide and euthanasia. Assuming patient consent:

1. We may permissibly cause death as a side effect if it relieves pain, because sometimes death is a lesser evil and pain relief a greater good.
2. We may permissibly intend other lesser evils to the patient, for the sake of her greater good.
3. Therefore, when death is a lesser evil, it is sometimes permissible for us to intend death in order to stop pain.

Thus, suppose we accept that it is sometimes permissible to *knowingly* shorten a life by giving pain-relieving medication, and agree, too, that it is sometimes permissible for a doctor to *intend* a lesser evil in order to produce a greater good. How, then, can it be wrong to *intentionally* shorten a life when that will produce the greater good?[1]

I don't expect that everyone will immediately find this argument compelling. I suspect that many—including some who are inclined to agree with the conclusion—will feel that death is different, so to speak. While they agree that we may intend pain, if it is a lesser evil, in order to save a life, they think it is impermissible to intentionally hasten death in order to relieve pain. I will address this concern later. But first I want to add another set of considerations that support euthanasia and physician-assisted suicide.

III. AN ARGUMENT FOR DUTY

According to the three-step argument, a doctor is *permitted* to give morphine for pain relief, even though he knows it will expedite the patient's death, if death is the lesser evil. But I think we can say more. Suppose, as I have stipulated, that giving morphine is the only way for a doctor to relieve a patient's suffering. A doctor, I assume, has a duty to relieve a patient's suffering. I conclude that the doctor has a *duty* to relieve suffering by giving the morphine, if the patient requests this. He cannot refuse to give the morphine on the ground that he will be a killer if he does.

If doctors have a duty to relieve pain, and even being a killer does not override this duty when the pa-

tient requests morphine for pain relief, then perhaps they also have a duty, not merely a permission, to kill their patients, or aid in their being killed, intending their deaths in order to relieve suffering. Now we have a new argument. Assuming patient consent:

1. There is a duty to treat pain even if it foreseeably makes one a killer, when death is the lesser evil and no pain is the greater good.
2. There is a duty to intend the other lesser evils (e.g., amputation) for a patient's own greater good.
3. There is a duty to kill the patient, or assist in his being killed, intending his death when this is the lesser evil and pain relief the greater good.

I think this argument, too, is compelling, but will concentrate here on the case for permissibility.

IV. IS KILLING SPECIAL?

As I indicated earlier, a natural rejoinder to the three-step argument for euthanasia and physician-assisted suicide is to emphasize that "death is different." But how precisely is it different, and why is the difference morally important?

Perhaps it will be said, simply, that the doctor who intends the death of his patient is *killing*. Even if intending a lesser evil for a greater good is often permissible, it might be condemned when it involves killing. Killing, it might be said, is not on a par with other lesser evils.

But this does not suffice to upset the three-step argument. For giving a lethal injection of morphine to relieve pain also involves killing and we approve of giving the morphine. To be sure, a patient's right to life includes a right not to be killed. But that right gives us a protected option whether to live or die, an option with which others cannot legitimately interfere; it does not give one a duty to live. If a patient decides to die, he is waiving his right to live. By waiving his right, he releases others (perhaps a specific other person) from a duty not to kill him, at least insofar as that duty stems from his right to live.[2] The duty not to kill him may also stem from their duty not to harm him, even if he so wishes; but I have stipulated that the doctor is to kill only when death is the lesser evil.

A more compelling version of the objection is, however, waiting in the wings. This one points not merely to the fact of killing, but to intentional killing. It claims that there is something distinctive about intending death, and that this distinction makes a large moral difference. In particular, acting with the intention to bring about death as a lesser evil requires that we treat ourselves or other persons as available to be used for achieving certain goods—in particular, the reduction of suffering. In euthanasia and physician-assisted suicide, we intentionally terminate a being with a rational nature—a being that judges, aims at goals, and evaluates how to act.[3] We have no such intention to use a person as a mere means when we aim at such lesser evils as destruction of a leg. Indeed, one of the things that seems odd about killing someone only if he is capable of voluntarily deciding in a reasonable way to end his life is that one is thereby ensuring that what is destroyed is a reasoning, thinking being, and therefore a being of great worth. This will not be so if the person is unconscious or vegetative or otherwise no longer functioning as a rational being. Obviously, people take control of their lives and devote their rational natures to the pursuit of certain goals within those lives; but, it is claimed, when this is appropriate, they do not aim to interfere with or destroy their personhood but set it in one direction or another.

The idea that there are limits on what we may do to ourselves as persons derives from Immanuel Kant. In his moral writings, Kant said that rational humanity, as embodied in ourselves and others, is—and should be treated as—*an end in itself, and not a mere means* to happiness or other goals. The fact that one is a judging, aiming, evaluating rational agent has worth in itself. To have this value as a person is more like an honor to us (Kant called it "dignity") than a benefit that answers to some interest of ours. Thus my life may have worth, even if my life is not a benefit to me (and my death would benefit me) because goods *other than* being a person are outweighed by bads. The worth of my life is not measured solely by its worth to me in satisfying my desires, or its worth to others in satisfying theirs. According to Kant, then, it is wrong for others to treat me as a mere means for their ends, but equally wrong for me to treat myself as a mere means for my own ends: As others should respect my dignity as a person by not using me merely as a means for their purposes, I should have proper regard for my own dignity as a person, and not simply use myself as a means for my own purposes. But that is precisely what I do when I aim at my own death as a way to eliminate pain. So I ought not to pursue that aim, and therefore ought not to consent to a morphine injection aiming at death, or give one to a patient who has consented.

Before assessing this Kantian argument, I want to justify focusing it on intentional killing rather than other ways of intentionally contributing to a death. Consider a patient who intends his own death and therefore wants life support of any sort removed. Suppose, for the sake of argument, that we disapprove of this intention. Suppose, too, that we disapprove of a doctor's agreeing to remove treatment because he also intends this patient's death. But while we may disapprove of the intentions and conduct, acting on that disapproval would require us to *force* life support on the patient, and he has a right that we not do this. Our opposition to his intentions and the doctor's is trumped by our opposition to forced invasion of the patient. So we permit the patient and doctor to act—to remove treatment—intending death. Consider, in contrast, a patient who intends his own death and, therefore, requests a lethal injection or pills. Suppose, once more, that we disapprove of this intention. Acting on our opposition would require us to refrain from invading him with a lethal injection or refuse the pills. But it seems clear that the right not to be invaded with treatment against one's will is stronger than the right simply to be invaded (with a lethal injection) or given pills. So the fact that we must terminate treatment, even when the patient and doctor intend the patient's death, does not show that it is permissible to kill the patient or assist him in killing when he and his doctor intend his death. Correspondingly, an objection to intentional killing need not imply an objection to terminating treatment for someone who intends his own death.[4]

I turn now to the Kantian-style argument against aiming at one's death (or aiming at another's death with his consent). In assessing this argument, we must distinguish three different ways in which one may treat a person as a mere means:

1. Calculating the worth of living on in a way which gives insufficient weight to the worth of being a person.
2. Treating the nonexistence of persons as a means to a goal (e.g., no pain).
3. Using persons in order to bring about their own end.

The first idea is that being a person has worth in itself and is not merely a means to an overall balance of other goods over evils in the person's life. On this interpretation, we treat persons as a mere means if we give inadequate weight in our decisions to the value of our existence as persons; if we do, then death may seem a lesser evil. But even when there are few goods in life besides the capacity to be a rational agent, the loss of life—and therefore the loss of that capacity—may still be a greater evil than pain.

Though I do not doubt that this idea has force, it can equally well be given as a reason for not terminating a course of treatment, even when one merely foresees one's death. Because this way of treating a person as a mere means does not distinguish the *morality of intending death* from the *morality of merely foreseeing death,* it cannot be used to explain why intentional killing in particular is impermissible.[5] . . .

What, then, about the second and third interpretations of the idea of using persons as mere means? To see the difference between them, consider an analogy: My radio is a device for getting good sounds and filtering out bad sounds. It is a means to a balance of good sounds over bad ones. Suppose it stops performing well, that it only produces static, but cannot be turned off. I can wait until its batteries run down and not replace them, or I can smash it now, thus using the radio itself to stop the noise it produces. Either way, I would see its death as I saw its life, as a means to a better balance of good over bad sounds. While I have always seen my radio as a mere means to an end if I smash it, I use it as a means to its end (termination): This is sense (3).[6] If I let the radio run down, intending its demise, but do not smash it—I see it wasting away and do not replace its parts—then I do not see it as a means to its own end, but I do see *its end as a means* to a better balance of sounds. This is sense (2).

Active suicide is analogous to smashing the radio: the person uses himself as a means to his own death. Some people find this complete taking control of one's life particularly morally inappropriate, perhaps because they think our bodies belong to God and that we have no right to achieve the goal of our own death by manipulating a "tool" that is not ours (or intending that others manipulate it). This objection is not present if—here we have sense (2)—we terminate medical assistance with the intention that the system run down, aiming at its death. For then we achieve the goal of death by interfering with what is ours (the medication), not God's. Here we have another reason why someone may object to killing but not to terminating treatment, even if accompanied by the intention that the system run down; unlike intentional killing, terminating treatment does not involve using persons to bring about their own end. Some say, though, that this way of using persons as means is also more objectionable than merely foreseeing the death. They say that if we terminate medical assistance, intending death, we do not merely treat our life as a means to greater good over bad, but treat *our death (the end of our life)* as a means to greater good over bad.

How much weight, then, should be placed on the second and third senses of "using a person as a means"? Should they really stand in our way? I believe not. It cannot be argued, at least in secular moral terms, that one's body belongs to someone else and that one cannot, therefore, use it as a means to achieve death. Notice also that if your body belonged to someone else, it isn't clear why you should be permitted to use it by administering morphine to stop your pain when you merely foresee that this will destroy the body. We aren't usually permitted to treat other people's property in this way either. Nor does it seem that treating one's death as available for one's purposes (i.e., being rid of pain) is necessarily a morally inappropriate attitude to take to oneself—so long as there is not failure to properly value the importance of just being a person. If this is right, then, at least sometimes, a patient would do no wrong in intending or causing his death. At least sometimes, a doctor who helped him by giving pills would also do no wrong merely because he killed, or assisted killing, aiming at death.

The strongest case for such conduct can be made, I believe, if the overriding aim is to end physical pain. The need to do this may be rare with modern techniques of pain control, but still the patient has a "disjunctive" right: either to adequate pain control or the assistance in suicide of a willing doctor. Psychological suffering which is a reaction to one's knowledge or beliefs about a state of affairs is a weaker case. The test I suggest here is: Would we give a drug to treat psychological suffering if we *foresaw* that it would rapidly kill as a side effect? If not, then giving pills to a patient intending that they kill him in order to end psychological suffering would not be permissible. This same test can be applied to other reasons that might be offered for seeking death by euthanasia or physician-assisted suicide. For example, would we allow a patient to use a drug that will rapidly cause death (rather than a safer one) if it will save him money? If not, then we may not perform euthanasia or physician-assisted suicide to stop the drain on his family finances. Would we give a demented patient a drug that unraveled the tangled neurons that caused his dementia but which we foresaw would rapidly kill him as a side effect? If not, then why should we be permitted to give him pills, intending his death? Of course, the application of this test may yield positive responses rather than negative ones to these questions.

NOTES

1. I first presented this argument in *Creation and Abortion* (New York: Oxford University Press, 1992), pp. 33–35, and again in *Morality, Mortality,* Vol. II (New York: Oxford University Press, 1996), pp. 194–98.

2. Notice that this waiver seems to be morally necessary even when the doctor wishes to give morphine that will kill as a foreseen side effect. This means doctors should get permission for giving the morphine for pain relief as well as for giving it to deliberately kill. (I do not believe they always do so.)

3. We also terminate human life considered independently of whether it is the life of a rational being. It may seem harder to justify destroying a person than a human life that lacks qualities required for personhood—for example, a functioning brain. But I will assume that one could substitute "human life" for "person" in the argument I give against intentional killing and in my response to that argument.

4. In contrast, suppose that a patient who intends his own death is also suffering great pain that only morphine will stop. He asks for the morphine, not because it will stop the pain, but because he knows it will kill him. If it would not kill him, he would not ask for it. Does he have a right that the doctor give him the morphine? If he does, then the doctor is not at liberty to refuse simply because of the *patient's intention,* any more than he could refuse to terminate treatment because of the patient's intention. Indeed we might not be permitted to interfere with the doctor's giving morphine in this case even if he gave it only because *he* intended death. I owe this case to Timothy Hall.

5. Kant thought we had a duty to actively preserve rational humanity and hence we should not too lightly do what we foresee will lead to its end. Still, he allows that we may sometimes engage in conduct though we foresee it will result in our deaths, but we may never aim at our deaths.

6. If I see someone else destroy it and do not interfere, I may be intending its use as a means to its own end, though I do not myself use it.

LEON R. KASS

Is There a Right to Die?

Leon Kass is Addie Clark Harding Professor in the Committee on Social Thought and the College of the University of Chicago. Kass has served as a surgeon for the U.S. Public Health Service and has held positions in the field of medical ethics at the National Academy of Sciences, St. John's College, and the Kennedy Institute of Ethics of Georgetown University. Among his books are *Toward a More Natural Science: Biology and Human Affairs* (1998) and *The Hungry Soul: Eating and the Perfecting of Our Nature* (1994). In August 2001, Kass was named chair of a new Council on Bioethics by President George W. Bush.

It has been fashionable for some time now and in many aspects of American public life for people to demand what they want or need as a matter of rights. During the past few decades we have heard claims of a right to health or health care, a right to education or employment, a right to privacy (embracing also a right to abort or to enjoy pornography, or to commit suicide or sodomy), a right to clean air, a right to dance naked, a right to be born, and a right not to have been born. Most recently we have been presented with the ultimate new rights claim, a "right to die."

This claim has surfaced in the context of changed circumstances and burgeoning concerns regarding the end of life. Thanks in part to the power of medicine to preserve and prolong life, many of us are fated to end our once-flourishing lives in years of debility,

From *Hastings Center Report* 23 (January–February 1993), 34–40, 41–43. Copyright © 1993. Leon R. Kass. Reprinted by permission of the author.

dependence, and disgrace. Thanks to the respirator and other powerful technologies that can, all by themselves, hold comatose and other severely debilitated patients on this side of the line between life and death, many who would be dead are alive only because of sustained mechanical intervention. Of the 2.2 million annual deaths in the United States, 80 percent occur in health care facilities; in roughly 1.5 million of these cases, death is preceded by some explicit decision about stopping or not starting medical treatment. Thus, death in America is not only medically managed, but its timing is also increasingly subject to deliberate choice. It is from this background that the claims of a right to die emerge.

I do not think that the language and approach of rights are well suited either to sound personal decision-making or to sensible public policy in this very difficult and troubling matter. In most of the heartrending end-of-life situations, it is hard enough for practical wisdom to try to figure out what is morally right and humanly good, without having to contend with intransigent and absolute demands of a legal or moral right to die. And, on both philosophical and legal grounds, I am inclined to believe that there can be no such thing as a *right* to die—that the notion is groundless and perhaps even logically incoherent. Even its proponents usually put "right to die" in quotation marks, acknowledging that it is at best a misnomer.

Nevertheless, we cannot simply dismiss this claim, for it raises important and interesting practical and philosophical questions. Practically, a right to die is increasingly asserted and gaining popular strength; increasingly, we see it in print without the quotation marks. The former Euthanasia Society of America, shedding the Nazi-tainted and easily criticized "E" word, changed its name to the more politically correct Society for the Right to Die before becoming Choice In Dying. End-of-life cases coming before the courts, nearly always making their arguments in terms of rights, have gained support for some sort of "right to die." The one case to be decided by a conservative Supreme Court, the *Cruzan* case, has advanced the cause. . . .

The voter initiatives to legalize physician-assisted suicide and euthanasia in Washington and California were narrowly defeated, in part because they were badly drafted laws; yet the proponents of such practices seem to be winning the larger social battle over principle. According to several public opinion polls,

most Americans now believe that "if life is miserable, one has the right to get out, actively and with help if necessary." Though the burden of philosophical proof for establishing new rights (especially one as bizarre as a "right to die") should always fall on the proponents, the social burden of proof has shifted to those who would oppose the voluntary choice of death through assisted suicide. Thus it has become politically necessary—and at the same time exceedingly difficult—to make principled arguments about why doctors must not kill, about why euthanasia is not the proper human response to human finitude, and about why there is no right to die, natural or constitutional. This is not a merely academic matter: our society's willingness and ability to protect vulnerable life hang in the balance.

An examination of "right to die" is even more interesting philosophically. It reveals the dangers and the limits of the liberal—that is, rights-based—political philosophy and jurisprudence to which we Americans are wedded. As the ultimate new right, grounded neither in nature nor in reason, it demonstrates the nihilistic implication of a new ("postliberal") doctrine of rights, rooted in the self-creating will. And as liberal society's response to the bittersweet victories of the medical project to conquer death, it reveals in pure form the tragic meaning of the entire modern project, both scientific and political.

The claim of a right to die is made only in Western liberal societies—not surprisingly, for only in Western liberal societies do human beings look first to the rights of individuals. Also, only here do we find the high-tech medicine capable of keeping people from dying when they might wish. Yet the claim of a right to die is also a profoundly strange claim, especially in a liberal society founded on the primacy of the right to life. We Americans hold as a self-evident truth that governments exist to secure inalienable rights, first of all, to self-preservation; now we are being encouraged to use government to secure a putative right of self-destruction. A "right to die" is surely strange and unprecedented, and hardly innocent. Accordingly, we need to consider carefully what it could possibly mean, why it is being asserted, and whether it really exists—that is, whether it can be given a principled grounding or defense.

A *RIGHT* TO DIE

Though the major ambiguity concerns the substance of the right—namely, to die—we begin by reminding ourselves of what it means, in general, to say that someone has a right to something. I depart for now from the original notion of *natural* rights, and indeed abstract altogether from the question of the source of rights. I focus instead on our contemporary usage, for it is only in contemporary usage that this current claim of a right to die can be understood.

A right, whether legal or moral, is not identical to a need or a desire or an interest or a capacity. I may have both a need and a desire for, and also an interest in, the possessions of another, and the capacity or power to take them by force or stealth—yet I can hardly be said to have a right to them. A right, to begin with, is a species of liberty. Thomas Hobbes, the first teacher of rights, held a right to be a *blameless* liberty. Not everything we are free to do, morally or legally, do we have a right to do: I may be at liberty to wear offensive perfumes or to sass my parents or to engage in unnatural sex, but it does not follow that I have a right to do so. Even the decriminalization of a once-forbidden act does not yet establish a legal right, not even if I can give reasons for doing it. Thus, the freedom to take my life—"I have inclination, means, reasons, opportunity, and you cannot stop me, and it is not against the law"—does not suffice to establish the *right* to take my life. A true right would be at least a blameless or permitted liberty, at best a praiseworthy or even rightful liberty, to do or not to do, without anyone else's interference or opposition.

Historically, the likelihood of outside interference and opposition was in fact the necessary condition for the assertion of rights. Rights were and are, to begin with, *political* creatures, the first principles of liberal politics. The rhetoric of claiming rights, which are in principle always absolute and unconditional, performs an important function of defense, but only because the sphere of life in which they are asserted is limited. Rights are asserted to protect, by deeming them blameless or rightful, certain liberties that others are denying or threatening to curtail. Rights are claimed to defend the safety and dignity of the individual against the dominion of tyrant, king, or prelate, and against those high-minded moralizers and zealous meddlers who seek to save man's soul or to preserve his honor at the cost of his life and liberty.

To these more classical, negative rights against interference with our liberties, modern thought has sought to add certain so-called welfare rights—rights that entitle us to certain opportunities or goods to which, it is argued, we have a rightful claim on others, usually government, to provide. The rhetoric of welfare rights extends the power of absolute and un-

qualified claims beyond the goals of defense against tyranny and beyond the limited sphere of endangered liberties; for these reasons their legitimacy as rights is often questioned. Yet even these ever-expanding lists of rights are not unlimited. I cannot be said to have a right to be loved by those who I hope will love me, or a right to become wise. There are many good things that I may rightfully possess and enjoy, but to which I have no claim if they are lacking. Most generally, then, having a right means having a *justified* claim against others that they act in a fitting manner: either that they refrain from interfering or that they deliver what is justly owed. It goes without saying that the mere assertion of a claim or demand, or the stipulation of a right, is insufficient to establish it; making a claim and actually having a rightful claim to make are not identical. In considering an alleged right to die, we must be careful to look for a *justifiable* liberty or claim, and not merely a desire, interest, power, or demand.

Rights seem to entail obligations: one person's right, whether to noninterference or to some entitled good or service, necessarily implies another person's obligation. It will be important later to consider what obligations on others might be entailed by enshrining a right to die.

A RIGHT *TO DIE*

Taken literally, a right to die would denote merely a right to the inevitable; the certainty of death for all that lives is the touchstone of fated inevitability. Why claim a right to what is not only unavoidable, but is even, generally speaking, an evil? Is death in danger of losing its inevitability? Are we in danger of bodily immortality? Has death, for us, become a good to be claimed rather than an evil to be shunned or conquered?

Not exactly and not yet, though these questions posed by the literal reading of "right to die" are surely germane. They hint at our growing disenchantment with the biomedical project, which seeks, in principle, to prolong life indefinitely. It is the already available means to sustain life for prolonged periods—not indefinitely, but far longer than is in many cases reasonable or desirable—that has made death so untimely late as to seem less than inevitable, that has made death, when it finally does occur, appear to be a blessing.

For we now have medical "treatments" (that is, interventions) that do not treat (that is, cure or ameliorate) specific diseases, but do nothing more than keep people alive by sustaining vital functions. The most notorious such device is the respirator. Others include simple yet still artificial devices for supplying food and water and the kidney dialysis machine for removing wastes. And, in the future, we shall have the artificial heart. These devices, backed by aggressive institutional policies favoring their use, are capable of keeping people alive, even when comatose, often for decades. The "right to die," in today's discourse, often refers to—and certainly is meant to embrace—a right to refuse such life-sustaining medical treatment.

But the "right to die" usually embraces also something more. The ambiguity of the term blurs over the difference in content and intention between the already well-established common-law right to refuse surgery or other unwanted medical treatments and hospitalization and the newly alleged "right to die." The former permits the refusal of therapy, even a respirator, even if it means accepting an increased risk of death. The latter permits the refusal of therapy, such as renal dialysis or the feeding tube, *so that* death *will* occur. The former seems more concerned with choosing how to live while dying; the latter seems mainly concerned with a choice *for death*. In this sense the claimed "right to die" is not a misnomer.

Still less is it a misnomer when we consider that some people who are claiming it demand not merely the discontinuance of treatment but positive assistance in bringing about their deaths. Here the right to die embraces the (welfare!) right to a lethal injection or an overdose of pills administered by oneself, by one's physician, or by someone else. This "right to die" would better be called a right to assisted suicide or a right to be mercifully killed—in short, a right *to become dead*, by assistance if necessary.

This, of course, looks a lot like a claim to a right to commit suicide, which need not have any connection to the problems of dying or medical technology. Some people in fact argue that the "right to die" through euthanasia or medically assisted suicide grows not from a right to refuse medical treatment but rather from this putative right to commit suicide (suicide is now decriminalized in most states). There does seem to be a world of moral difference between submitting to death (when the time has come) and killing yourself (in or out of season), or between permitting to die and causing death. But the boundary becomes fuzzy with the alleged right to refuse food and water, artificially delivered. Though few proponents of a right to die want the taint of a general defense of suicide (which though decriminalized remains in bad odor), they in fact presuppose its permissibility and go well beyond it. They claim not only a right to attempt suicide but a right to succeed, and this means, in practice, a *right to the deadly assistance of others*. It is thus certainly proper to understand the "right to die" in its most radical sense, namely, as a right to become or to be made dead, by whatever means.

This way of putting the matter will not sit well with those who see the right to die less as a matter of life and death, more as a matter of autonomy or dignity. For them the right to die means the right to continue, despite disability, to exercise control over one's own destiny. It means, in one formulation, not the right to become dead, but the right to choose the manner, the timing, and the circumstances of one's death, or the right to choose what one regards as the most humane or dignified way to finish out one's life. Here the right to die means either the right to self-command or the right to death with dignity—claims that would oblige others, at a minimum, to stop interfering, but also, quite commonly, to "assist self-command" or to "provide dignity" by participating in bringing one's life to an end, according to plan. In the end, these proper and high-minded demands for autonomy and dignity turn out in most cases to embrace also a right to become dead, with assistance if necessary.

This analysis of current usage shows why one might be properly confused about the meaning of the term "right to die." In public discourse today, it merges all the aforementioned meanings: right to refuse treatment even if, or so that, death may occur; right to be killed or to become dead; right to control one's own dying; right to die with dignity; right to assistance in death. Some of this confusion inheres in the term; some of it is deliberately fostered by proponents of all these "rights," who hope thereby to gain assent to the more extreme claims by merging them with the more modest ones. Partly for this reason, however, we do well to regard the "right to die" at its most radical—and I will do so in this essay—as a right to become dead, by active means and if necessary with the assistance of others. In this way we take seriously and do justice to the novelty and boldness of the claim, a claim that intends to go beyond both the existing common-law right to refuse unwanted medical treatment and the so-called right to commit suicide all by oneself. (The first right is indisputable, the second, while debatable, will not be contested in this essay.

What concerns us here is those aspects of the "right to die" that go beyond a right to attempt suicide and a right to refuse treatment.)

Having sought to clarify the meaning of "right to die," we face next the even greater confusion about who it is that allegedly has such a right. Is it only those who are "certifiably" terminally ill and irreversibly dying, with or without medical treatment? Also those who are incurably ill and severely incapacitated, although definitely not dying? Everyone, mentally competent or not? Does a senile person have a "right to die" if he is incapable of claiming it for himself? Do I need to be able to claim *and act* on such a right in order to have it, or can proxies be designated to exercise my right to die on my behalf? If the right to die is essentially an expression of my autonomy, how can anyone else exercise it for me?

Equally puzzling is the question, Against whom or what is a right to die being asserted? Is it a liberty right mainly against those officious meddlers who keep me from dying—against those doctors, nurses, hospitals, right-to-life groups, and district attorneys who interfere either with my ability to die (by machinery and hospitalization) or with my ability to gain help in ending my life (by criminal sanctions against assisting suicide)? If it is a right to become dead, is it not also a welfare right claimed against those who do not yet assist—a right demanding also the provision of the poison that I have permission to take? (Compare the liberty right to seek an abortion with the welfare right to obtain one.) Or is it, at bottom, a demand asserted also *against nature,* which has dealt me a bad hand by keeping me alive, beyond my wishes and beneath my dignity, and alas without terminal illness, too senile or enfeebled to make matters right?

The most radical formulations, whether in the form of "a right to become dead" or "a right to control my destiny" or "a right to dignity," are, I am convinced, the complaint of human pride against what our tyrannical tendencies lead us to experience as "cosmic injustice, directed against me." Here the ill-fated demand a right not to be ill-fated; those who want to die, but cannot, claim a right to die, which becomes, as Harvey Mansfield has put it, a tort claim against nature. It thus becomes the business of the well-fated to correct nature's mistreatment of the ill-fated by *making them dead.* Thus would the same act that was only yesterday declared a crime against humanity become a mandated act, not only of compassionate charity but of compensatory justice!

WHY ASSERT A RIGHT TO DIE?

Before proceeding to the more challenging question of the existence and ground of a "right to die," it would be useful briefly to consider why such a right is being asserted, and by whom. Some of the reasons have already been noted in passing:

- fear of prolongation of dying due to medical intervention; hence, a right to refuse treatment or hospitalization, even if death occurs as a result;
- fear of living too long, without fatal illness to carry one off; hence, a right to assisted suicide;
- fear of the degradations of senility and dependence; hence, a right to death with dignity;
- fear of loss of control; hence, a right to choose the time and manner of one's death.

Equally important for many people is the fear of becoming a burden to others—financial, psychic, social. Few parents, however eager or willing they might be to stay alive, are pleased by the prospect that they might thereby destroy their children's and grandchildren's opportunities for happiness. Indeed, my own greatest weakening on the subject of euthanasia is precisely this: I would confess a strong temptation to remove myself from life to spare my children the anguish of years of attending my demented self and the horrible likelihood that they will come, hatefully to themselves, to resent my continued existence. Such reasons in favor of death might even lead me to think I had a *duty* to die—they do not, however, establish for me any right to become dead.[1]

But the advocates of a "right to die" are not always so generous. On the contrary, much dishonesty and mischief are afoot. Many people have seen the advantage of using the language of individual rights, implying voluntary action, to shift the national attitudes regarding life and death, to prepare the way for the practice of terminating "useless" lives.[2]

Many who argue for a right to die mean for people not merely to have it but to exercise it with dispatch, so as to decrease the mounting socioeconomic costs of caring for the irreversibly ill and dying. In fact, most of the people now agitating for a "right to die" are themselves neither ill nor dying. Children looking at parents who are not dying fast enough, hospital administrators and health economists concerned about cost-cutting and waste, doctors disgusted with caring for incurables, people with eugenic or aesthetic interests who are repelled by the prospect of a society in which the young and vigorous expend enormous energy to keep alive the virtually dead—all these want to change our hard-won ethic in favor of life.

But they are either too ashamed or too shrewd to state their true intentions. Much better to trumpet a right to die, and encourage people to exercise it. These advocates understand all too well that the present American climate requires one to talk of rights if one wishes to have one's way in such moral matters. Consider the analogous use of arguments for abortion rights by organizations which hope thereby to get women—especially the poor, the unmarried, and the nonwhite—to exercise their "right to choose," to do their supposed duty toward limiting population growth and the size of the underclass.

This is not to say that all reasons for promoting a "right to die" are suspect. Nor do I mean to suggest that it would never be right or good for someone to elect to die. But it might be dangerous folly to circumvent the grave need for prudence in these matters by substituting the confused yet absolutized principle of a "right to die," especially given the mixed motives and dangerous purposes of some of its proponents.

Truth to tell, public discourse about moral matters in the United States is much impoverished by our eagerness to transform questions of the right and the good into questions about individual rights. Partly, this is a legacy of modern liberalism, the political philosophy on which the genius of the American republic mainly rests. But it is augmented by American self-assertion and individualism, increasingly so in an age when family and other mediating institutions are in decline and the naked individual is left face to face with the bureaucratic state.

But the language of rights gained a tremendous boost from the moral absolutism of the 1960s, with the discovery that the nonnegotiable and absolutized character of all rights claims provides the most durable battering ram against the status quo. Never mind that it fuels resentments and breeds hatreds, that it ignores the consequences to society, or that it short-circuits a political process that is more amenable to working out a balanced view of the common good. Never mind all that: go to court and demand your rights. And the courts have been all too willing to oblige, finding or inventing new rights in the process.

These sociocultural changes, having nothing to do with death and dying, surely are part of the reason we are now confronted with vociferous claims of a right to die. These changes are also part of the reason why, despite its notorious difficulties, a right to die is the leading moral concept advanced to address these most complicated and delicate human matters at the end of life. Yet the reasons for the assertion, even if suspect, do not settle the question of truth, to which, at long last, we finally turn. Let us examine whether philosophically . . . we can truly speak of a right to die.

IS THERE A RIGHT TO DIE?

Philosophically speaking, it makes sense to take our bearings from those great thinkers of modernity who are the originators and most thoughtful exponents of our rights-based thinking. They above all are likely to have understood the purpose, character, grounds, and limits for the assertion of rights. If a newly asserted right, such as the right to die, cannot be established on the natural or rational ground for rights offered by these thinkers, the burden of proof must fall on the proponents of novel rights, to provide a new yet equally solid ground in support of their novel claims.

If we start at the beginning, with the great philosophical teachers of natural rights, the very notion of a right to die would be nonsensical. As we learn from Hobbes and from John Locke, all the rights of man, given by nature, presuppose our self-interested attachment to our own lives. All natural rights trace home to the primary right to life, or better, the right to self-preservation—itself rooted in the powerful, self-loving impulses and passions that seek our own continuance, and asserted first against deadly, oppressive policies or against those who might insist that morality requires me to turn the other cheek when my life is threatened. Mansfield summarizes the classical position elegantly:

> Rights are given to men by nature, but they are needed because men are also subject to nature's improvidence. Since life is in danger, men's equal rights would be to life, to the liberty that protects life, and to the pursuit of the happiness with which life, or a tenuous life, is occupied.
>
> In practice, the pursuit of happiness will be the pursuit of property, for even though property is less valuable than life or liberty, it serves as guard for them. Quite apart from the pleasures of being rich, having secure property shows that one has liberty secure from invasion either by the government or by others; and secure liberty is the best sign of a secure life.[3]

Because death, my extinction, is the evil whose avoidance is the condition of the possibility of my having any and all of my goods, my right to secure my life against death—that is, my rightful liberty to self-preservative conduct—is the bedrock of all other rights and of all politically relevant morality. Even Hans Jonas, writing to defend "the right to die," acknowledges that it stands alone, and concedes that "every other right ever argued, claimed, granted, or denied can be viewed as an extension of this primary right [to life], since every particular right concerns the exercise of some faculty of life, the access to some necessity of life, the satisfaction of some aspiration of life."[4] It is obvious that one cannot found on this rock any right to die or right to become dead. Life loves to live, and it needs all the help it can get.

This is not to say that these early modern thinkers were unaware that men might tire of life or might come to find existence burdensome. But the decline in the will to live did not for them drive out or nullify the right to life, much less lead to a trumping new right, a right to die. For the right to life is a matter of nature, not will. Locke addresses and rejects a natural right to suicide, in his discussion of the state of nature:

> But though this be a state of liberty, yet it is not a state of license; though man in that state has an uncontrollable liberty to dispose of his person or possessions, yet he has not liberty to destroy himself, or so much as any creature in his possession, but where some nobler use than its bare preservation calls for it. The state of nature has a law of nature to govern it, which obliges everyone; and reason, which is that law, teaches all mankind who will but consult it, that, being all equal and independent, no one ought to harm another in his life, health, liberty, or possessions.[5]

Admittedly, the argument here turns explicitly theological—we are said to be our wise Maker's property. But the argument against a man's willful "quitting of his station" seems, for Locke, to be a corollary of the natural inclination and right of self-preservation.

Some try to argue, wrongly in my view, that Locke's teaching on property rests on a principle of self-ownership, which can then be used to justify self-destruction: since I own my body and my life, I may do with them as I please. As this argument has much currency, it is worth examining in greater detail. Locke does indeed say something that seems at first glance to suggest self-ownership:

> Though the earth and all inferior creatures be common to all men, *yet every man has a property in his own person;* this nobody has a right to but himself. The labor of his body and the work of his hands we may say are properly his.[6]

But the context defines and constricts the claim. Unlike the property rights in the fruits of his labor, the property a man has in his own person is inalienable: a man cannot transfer title to himself by selling himself into slavery. The "property in his own person" is less a metaphysical statement declaring self-ownership, more a political statement denying ownership by another. This right removes each and every human being from the commons available to all human beings for appropriation and use. My body and my life are my property *only in the limited sense* that they are *not yours.* They are different from my alienable property—my house, my car, my shoes. My body and my life, while mine to use, are not mine to dispose of. In the deepest sense, my body is nobody's body, not even mine.[7]

Even if one continues, against reason, to hold to strict self-ownership and self-disposability, there is a further argument, one that is decisive. Self-ownership might enable one at most to justify *attempting* suicide; it cannot justify a right to succeed or, more important, a right to the assistance of others. The designated potential assistant-in-death has neither a natural duty nor a natural right to become an actual assistant-in-death, and the liberal state, instituted above all to protect life, can never countenance such a right to kill, even on request. A right to become dead or to be made dead cannot be sustained on classical liberal grounds.

Later thinkers in the liberal tradition, including those who prized freedom above preservation, also make no room for a "right to die." Jean-Jacques Rousseau's complaints about the ills of civil society centered especially and most powerfully on the threats to life and limb from a social order whose main purpose should have been to protect them.[8] And Immanuel Kant, for whom rights are founded not in nature but in reason, holds that the self-willed act of self-destruction is simply self-contradictory.

> It seems absurd that a man can injure himself (*volenti non fit injuria* [Injury cannot happen to one who is willing]). The Stoic therefore considered it a prerogative of his personality as a wise man to walk out of his life with an undisturbed mind whenever he liked (as out of a smoke-filled room), not because he was afflicted by actual or anticipated ills, but simply because he could make use of nothing more in this life. And yet this very courage, this strength of mind—of not fearing death and of knowing of something which man can prize more highly than his life—ought to have been an ever so much greater motive for him not to

destroy himself, a being having such authoritative superiority over the strongest sensible incentives; consequently, it ought to have been a motive for him not to deprive himself of life.

Man cannot deprive himself of his personhood so long as one speaks of duties, thus so long as he lives. That man ought to have the authorization to withdraw himself from all obligation, i.e., to be free to act as if no authorization at all were required for this withdrawal, involves a contradiction. To destroy the subject of morality in his own person is tantamount to obliterating from the world, as far as he can, the very existence of morality itself; but morality is, nevertheless, an end in itself. Accordingly, to dispose of oneself as a mere means to some end of one's own liking is to degrade the humanity in one's person *(homo noumenon),* which, after all, was entrusted to man *(homo phoenomenon)* to preserve.[9]

It is a heavy irony that it should be autonomy, the moral notion that the world owes mainly to Kant, that is now invoked as the justifying ground of a right to die. For Kant, autonomy, which literally means self-legislation, requires acting in accordance with one's true self—that is, with one's rational will determined by a universalizable, that is, rational, maxim. Being autonomous means not being a slave to instinct, impulse, or whim, but rather doing as one ought, as a rational being. But autonomy has now come to mean "doing as you please," compatible no less with self-indulgence than with self-control. Herewith one sees clearly the triumph of the Nietzschean self, who finds reason just as enslaving as blind instinct and who finds his true "self" rather in unconditioned acts of pure creative will.

Yet even in its willful modern meaning, "autonomy" cannot ground a right to die. First, one cannot establish on this basis a right to have *someone else's* assistance in committing suicide—a right, by the way, that would impose an obligation on someone else and thereby restrict *his* autonomy. Second, even if my choice for death were "reasonable" and my chosen assistant freely willing, my autonomy cannot ground *his right* to kill me, and, hence, it cannot ground my right to become dead. Third, a liberty right to an assisted death (that is, a right against interference) can at most approve assisted suicide or euthanasia for the mentally competent and alert—a restriction that would prohibit effecting the deaths of the mentally incompetent or comatose patients who have not left explicit instructions regarding their treatment. It is, by the

way, a long philosophical question whether all such instructions must be obeyed, for the person who gave them long ago may no longer be "the same person" when they become relevant. Can my fifty-three-year-old self truly prescribe today the best interests for my seventy-five-year-old and senile self?

In contrast to arguments presented in recent court cases, it is self-contradictory to assert that a proxy not chosen by the patient can exercise the patient's rights of autonomy. Can a citizen have a right to vote that would be irrevocably exercised "on his behalf," and in the name of his autonomy, by the government?[10] Finally, if autonomy and dignity lie in the free exercise of will and choice, it is at least paradoxical to say that our autonomy licenses an act that puts our autonomy permanently out of business.

It is precisely this paradox that appeals to the Nietzschean creative self, the bearer of so many of this century's "new rights." As Mansfield brilliantly shows, the creative ones are not bound by normality or good sense:

Creative beings are open-ended. They are open-ended in fact and not merely in their formal potentialities. Such beings do not have interests; for who can say what is in the interest of a being that is becoming something unknown? Thus the society of new rights is characterized by a loss of predictability and normality: no one knows what to expect, even from his closest companions.[11]

The most authentic self-creative self revels in the unpredictable, the extreme, the perverse. He does not even flinch before self-contradiction; indeed, he can display the triumph of his will most especially in self-negation. And though it may revolt us, who are we to deny him this form of self-expression? Supremely tolerant of the rights of others to their own eccentricities, we avert our glance and turn the other moral cheek. Here at last is the only possible philosophical ground for a right to die: arbitrary will, backed by moral relativism. Which is to say, no ground at all.

• • •

THE TRAGIC MEANING OF "RIGHT TO DIE"

The claim of a "right to die," asserted especially against physicians bent on prolonging life, clearly exposes certain deep difficulties in the foundations of modern society. Modern liberal, technological society rests especially upon two philosophical pillars raised first in the seventeenth century, at the beginning of the modern era: the preeminence of the human individual, embodied in the doctrine of natural rights as espoused first by Hobbes and Locke; and the idea of mastery of nature, attained through a radically new science of nature as proposed by Francis Bacon and René Descartes.

Both ideas were responses to the perceived partial inhospitality of nature to human need. Both encouraged man's opposition to nature, the first through the flight from the state of nature into civil society for the purpose of safeguarding the precarious rights to life and liberty; the second through the subduing of nature for the purpose of making life longer, healthier, and more commodious. One might even say that it is especially an opposition to death that grounds these twin responses. Politically, the fear of violent death at the hands of warring men requires law and legitimate authority to secure natural rights, especially life. Technologically, the fear of death as such at the hands of unfriendly nature inspires a bolder approach, namely, a scientific medicine to wage war against disease and even against death itself, ultimately with a promise of bodily immortality.

Drunk on its political and scientific successes, modern thought and practice have abandoned the modest and moderate beginnings of political modernity. In civil society the natural rights of self-preservation, secured through active but moderate self-assertion, have given way to the non-natural rights of self-creation and self-expression; the new rights have no connection to nature or to reason, but appear as the rights of the untrammeled will. The "self" that here asserts itself is not a natural self, with the predictable interests given it by a universal human nature with its bodily needs, but a uniquely individuated and self-made self. Its authentic selfhood is demonstrated by its ability to say no to the needs of the body, the rules of society, and the dictates of reason. For such a self, self-negation through suicide and the right to die can be the ultimate form of self-assertion.

In medical science, the unlimited battle against death has found nature unwilling to roll over and play dead. The successes of medicine so far are partial at best and the victory incomplete, to say the least. The welcome triumphs against disease have been purchased at the price of the medicalized dehumanization of the end of life: to put it starkly, once we lick cancer and stroke, we can all live long enough to get Alzheimer's disease. And if the insurance holds out, we can die in the intensive care unit, suitably intubated. Fear of the very medical power we engaged to do battle against death now leads us to demand that it give us poison.

Finally, both the triumph of individualism and our reliance on technology (not only in medicine) and on government to satisfy our new wants-demanded-as-rights have weakened our more natural human associations—especially the family, on which we all need to rely when our pretense to autonomy and mastery is eventually exposed by unavoidable decline. Old age and death have been taken out of the bosom of family life and turned over to state-supported nursing homes and hospitals. Not the clergyman but the doctor (in truth, the nurse) presides over the end of life, in sterile surroundings that make no concessions to our finitude. Both the autonomous will and the will's partner in pride, the death-denying doctor, ignore the unavoidable limits on will and technique that nature insists on. Failure to recognize these limits now threatens the entire venture, for rebellion against the project through a "right to die" will only radicalize its difficulties. Vulnerable life will no longer be protected by the state, medicine will become a death-dealing profession, and isolated individuals will be technically dispatched to avoid the troubles of finding human ways to keep company with them in their time of ultimate need.

• • •

Nothing I have said should be taken to mean that I believe life should be extended under all circumstances and at all costs. Far from it. I continue, with fear and trembling, to defend the practice of allowing to die while opposing the practice of deliberately killing—despite the blurring of this morally bright line implicit in the artificial food and water cases, and despite the slide toward the retailing of death that continues on the sled of a right to refuse treatment. I welcome efforts to give patients as much choice as possible in how they are to live out the end of their lives. I continue to applaud those courageous patients and family members and those conscientious physicians who try prudently to discern, in each case, just what form of treatment or nontreatment is truly good for the patient, even if it embraces an increased likelihood of death. But I continue to insist that we cannot serve the patient's good by deliberately eliminating the patient. And if we have no right to do this to another, we have no right to have others do this to ourselves. There is, when all is said and done, no defensible right to die.

A CODA: ABOUT RIGHTS

The rhetoric of rights still performs today the noble, time-honored function of protecting individual life and liberty, a function now perhaps even more necessary than the originators of such rhetoric could have imagined, given the tyrannical possibilities of the modern bureaucratic and technologically competent state. But with the claim of a "right to die," as with so many of the novel rights being asserted in recent years, we face an extension of this rhetoric into areas where it no longer relates to that protective function, and beyond the limited area of life in which rights claims are clearly appropriate and indeed crucial. As a result, we face a number of serious and potentially dangerous distortions in our thought and in our practice. We distort our understanding of rights and weaken their respect-ability in their proper sphere by allowing them to be invented—without ground in nature or in reason—in response to moral questions that lie outside the limited domain of rights. We distort our understanding of moral deliberation and the moral life by reducing all complicated questions of right and good to questions of individual rights. We subvert the primacy and necessity of prudence by pretending that the assertion of rights will produce the best—and most moral—results. In trying to batter our way through the human condition with the bludgeon of personal rights, we allow ourselves to be deceived about the most fundamental matters: about death and dying, about our unavoidable finitude, and about the sustaining interdependencies of our lives.

Let us, by all means, continue to deliberate about whether and when and why it might make sense for someone to give up on his life, or even actively to choose death. But let us call a halt to all this dangerous thoughtlessness about rights. Let us refuse to talk any longer about a "right to die."

NOTES

1. For my "generosity" to succeed, I would, of course, have to commit suicide without assistance and without anyone's discovering it—i.e., well before I were demented. I would not want my children to believe that I suspected them of being incapable of loving me through my inevitable decline. There is another still more powerful reason for resisting this temptation: is it not unreasonably paternalistic of me to try to order the world so as to free my children from the usual intergenerational experiences, ties, obligations, and burdens? What principle of family life am I enacting and endorsing with my "altruistic suicide"?

2. Here is a recent example from a professor of sociology who objected to my condemnation of Derek Humphry's *Final Exit:*

Is Mr. Kass absolutely opposed to suicide? Would he have dissuaded Hitler? Would he disapprove of suicide by Pol Pot? . . . If we would welcome suicide by certain figures on limited occasions, should we prolong the lives of people who lived useless, degrading or dehumanized lives; who inflicted these indignities upon others; or who led vital lives but were reduced to uselessness and degradation by incurable disease? (*Commentary,* May 1992, p. 12).

3. Harvey C. Mansfield, Jr., "The Old Rights and the New: Responsibility vs. Self-Expression," in *Old Rights and New,* ed. Robert A. Licht (Washington: American Enterprise Institute, 1993), in press.

4. Hans Jonas, "The Right to Die," *Hastings Center Report* 8, no. 4 (1978): 31–36, at 31.

5. John Locke, *Second Treatise on Civil Government,* ch. 2, "Of the State of Nature," para. 6.

6. Locke, *Second Treatise,* ch. 5, "Of Property," para. 27. Emphasis added.

7. Later, in discussing the extent of legislative power, Locke denies to the legislative, though it be the supreme power in every commonwealth, arbitrary power over the individual and, in particular, power to destroy his life. "For nobody can transfer to another more power than he has in himself; and nobody has an absolute arbitrary power over himself or over any other to destroy his own life, or take away the life or property of another." *Second Treatise,* ch. 9, "Of the Extent of the Legislative Power," para. 135. Because the state's power derives from the people's power, the person's lack of arbitrary power over himself is the ground for restricting the state's power to kill him.

8. See, for example, Rousseau, *Discourse on the Origin and Foundations of Inequality among Men,* note 9, especially paragraphs four and five.

9. Immanuel Kant, *The Metaphysical Principles of Virtue,* trans. James Ellington (Indianapolis: Bobbs-Merrill, 1964), pp. 83–84. My purpose in citing Kant here is not to defend Kantian morality—and I am not myself a Kantian—but simply to show that the thinker who thought most deeply about rights in relation to *reason* and *autonomy* would have found the idea of a "right to die" utterly indefensible on these grounds.

10. The attempt to ground a right to die in the so-called right to privacy fails for the same reasons. A right to make independent judgments regarding one's body in one's private sphere, free of governmental inference, cannot be the basis of the right of someone else, appointed by or protected by government, to put an end to one's bodily life.

11. Mansfield, "The Old Rights and the New." This permanent instability of "the self" defeats the main benefit of a rights-based politics, which knows how to respect individual rights precisely because they are understood to be rooted in a common human nature, with reliable common interests, both natural and rational. The self-determining self, because it is variable, also turns out to be an embarrassment for attempts to respect prior acts of self-determination, as in the case of living wills. For if the "self" is truly constantly being recreated, there is no reason to honor today "its" prescriptions of yesterday, for the two selves are not the same.

The Legal Background in the United States

The Oregon Death with Dignity Act

ALLOWS TERMINALLY ILL ADULTS TO OBTAIN PRESCRIPTION FOR LETHAL DRUGS

Question. Shall law allow terminally ill adult patients voluntary informed choice to obtain physician's prescription for drugs to end life?

Summary. Adopts law. Allows terminally ill adult Oregon residents voluntary informed choice to obtain physician's prescription for drugs to end life. Removes criminal penalties for qualifying physician-assisted suicide. Applies when physicians predict patient's death within 6 months. Requires:

15-day waiting period;

2 oral, 1 written request;

second physician's opinion;

counseling if either physician believes patient has mental disorder, impaired judgment from depression.

Person has choice whether to notify next of kin. Health care providers immune from civil, criminal liability for good faith compliance. . . .

SECTION 2: WRITTEN REQUEST FOR MEDICATION TO END ONE'S LIFE IN A HUMANE AND DIGNIFIED MANNER

§ 2.01 WHO MAY INITIATE A WRITTEN REQUEST FOR MEDICATION

An adult who is capable, is a resident of Oregon, and has been determined by the attending physician and consulting physician to be suffering from a terminal disease, and who has voluntarily expressed his or her wish to die, may make a written request for medication for the purpose of ending his or her life in a humane and dignified manner in accordance with this Act. . . .

SECTION 3: SAFEGUARDS

§ 3.01 ATTENDING PHYSICIAN RESPONSIBILITIES

The attending physician shall:

1. Make the initial determination of whether a patient has a terminal disease, is capable, and has made the request voluntarily;
2. Inform the patient of:
   (a) his or her medical diagnosis;
   (b) his or her prognosis;
   (c) the potential risks associated with taking the medication to be prescribed;
   (d) the probable result of taking the medication to be prescribed;
   (e) the feasible alternatives, including, but not limited to, comfort care, hospice care and pain control.
3. Refer the patient to a consulting physician for medical confirmation of the diagnosis, and for a determination that the patient is capable and acting voluntarily;
4. Refer the patient for counseling if appropriate pursuant to Section 3.03;
5. Request that the patient notify next of kin;
6. Inform the patient that he or she has an opportunity to rescind the request at any time and in any manner, and offer the patient an opportunity to rescind at the end of the 15-day waiting period pursuant to Section 3.06;
7. Verify, immediately prior to writing the prescription for medication under this Act, that the patient is making an informed decision;
8. Fulfill the medical record documentation requirements of Section 3.09;
9. Ensure that all appropriate steps are carried out in accordance with this Act prior to writing a prescription for medication to enable a qualified patient to end his or her life in a humane and dignified manner.

§ 3.02 CONSULTING PHYSICIAN CONFIRMATION

Before a patient is qualified under this Act, a consulting physician shall examine the patient and his or her relevant medical records and confirm, in writing, the attending physician's diagnosis that the patient is suffering from a terminal disease, and verify that the patient is capable, is acting voluntarily and has made an informed decision.

§ 3.03 COUNSELING REFERRAL

If in the opinion of the attending physician or the consulting physician a patient may be suffering from a psychiatric or psychological disorder, or depression causing impaired judgment, either physician shall refer the patient for counseling. No medication to end a patient's life in a humane and dignified manner shall be prescribed until the person performing the counseling determines that the patient is not suffering from a psychiatric or psychological disorder, or depression causing impaired judgment.

§ 3.04 INFORMED DECISION

No person shall receive a prescription for medication to end his or her life in a humane and dignified manner unless he or she has made an informed decision as defined in Section 1.01(7). Immediately prior to writing a prescription for medication under this Act, the attending physician shall verify that the patient is making an informed decision.

§ 3.05 FAMILY NOTIFICATION

The attending physician shall ask the patient to notify next of kin of his or her request for medication pursuant to this Act. A patient who declines or is unable to notify next of kin shall not have his or her request denied for that reason.

§ 3.06 WRITTEN AND ORAL REQUESTS

In order to receive a prescription for medication to end his or her life in a humane and dignified manner, a qualified patient shall have made an oral request and a written request, and reiterate the oral request to his or her attending physician no less than fifteen (15) days after making the initial oral request. At the time the qualified patient makes his or her second oral request, the attending physician shall offer the patient an opportunity to rescind the request.

§ 3.07 RIGHT TO RESCIND REQUEST

A patient may rescind his or her request at any time and in any manner without regard to his or her mental state. No prescription for medication under this Act may be written without the attending physician

offering the qualified patient an opportunity to rescind the request.

§ 3.08 WAITING PERIODS

No less than fifteen (15) days shall elapse between the patient's initial oral request and the writing of a prescription under this Act. No less than 48 hours shall elapse between the patient's written request and the writing of a prescription under the Act.

§ 3.09 MEDICAL RECORD DOCUMENTATION REQUIREMENTS

The following shall be documented or filed in the patient's medical record:

1. All oral requests by a patient for medication to end his or her life in a humane and dignified manner;
2. All written requests by a patient for medication to end his or her life in a humane and dignified manner;
3. The attending physician's diagnosis and prognosis, determination that the patient is capable, acting voluntarily and has made an informed decision;
4. The consulting physician's diagnosis and prognosis, and verification that the patient is capable, acting voluntarily and has made an informed decision;
5. A report of the outcome and determinations made during counseling, if performed;
6. The attending physician's offer to the patient to rescind his or her request at the time of the patient's second oral request pursuant to Section 3.06; and
7. A note by the attending physician indicating that all requirements under this Act have been met and indicating the steps taken to carry out the request, including a notation of the medication prescribed.

§ 3.10 RESIDENCY REQUIREMENTS

Only requests made by Oregon residents, under this Act, shall be granted.

§ 3.11 REPORTING REQUIREMENTS

1. The Health Division shall annually review a sample of records maintained pursuant to this Act.
2. The Health Division shall make rules to facili-

tate the collection of information regarding compliance with this Act. The information collected shall not be a public record and may not be made available for inspection by the public.

3. The Health Division shall generate and make available to the public an annual statistical report of information collected under Section 3.11(2) of this Act.

§ 3.12 EFFECT ON CONSTRUCTION OF WILLS, CONTRACTS, AND STATUTES

1. No provision in a contract, will or other agreement, whether written or oral, to the extent the provision would affect whether a person may make or rescind a request for medication to end his or her life in a humane and dignified manner, shall be valid.

2. No obligation owing under any currently existing contract shall be conditioned or affected by the making or rescinding of a request, by a person, for medication to end his or her life in a humane and dignified manner.

§ 3.13 INSURANCE OR ANNUITY POLICIES

The sale, procurement, or issuance of any life, health, or accident insurance or annuity policy or the rate charged for any policy shall not be conditioned upon or affected by the making or rescinding of a request, by a person, for medication to end his or her life in a humane and dignified manner. Neither shall a qualified patient's act of ingesting medication to end his her life in a humane and dignified manner have an effect upon a life, health, or accident insurance or annuity policy.

§ 3.14 CONSTRUCTION OF ACT

Nothing in this Act shall be construed to authorize a physician or any other person to end a patient's life by lethal injection, mercy killing or active euthanasia. Actions taken in accordance with this Act shall not, for any purpose, constitute suicide, assisted suicide, mercy killing or homicide, under the law.

SECTION 4: IMMUNITIES AND LIABILITIES

§ 4.01 IMMUNITIES

Except as provided in Section 4.02:

1. No person shall be subject to civil or criminal liability or professional disciplinary action for participating in good faith compliance with this Act. This includes being present when a qualified patient takes the prescribed medication to end his or her life in a humane and dignified manner.

2. No professional organization or association, or health care provider, may subject a person to censure, discipline, suspension, loss of license, loss of privileges, loss of membership or other penalty for participating or refusing to participate in good faith compliance with this Act.

3. No request by a patient for or provision by an attending physician of medication in good faith compliance with the provisions of this Act shall constitute neglect for any purpose of law or provide the sole basis for the appointment of a guardian or conservator.

4. No health care provider shall be under any duty, whether by contract, by statute or by any other legal requirement to participate in the provision to a qualified patient of medication to end his or her life in a humane and dignified manner. If a health care provider is unable or unwilling to carry out a patient's request under this Act, and the patient transfers his or her care to a new health care provider, the prior health care provider shall transfer, upon request, a copy of the patient's relevant medical records to the new health care provider.

§ 4.02 LIABILITIES

1. A person who without authorization of the patient willfully alters or forges a request for medication or conceals or destroys a rescission of that request with the intent or effect of causing the patient's death shall be guilty of a Class A felony.

2. A person who coerces or exerts undue influence on a patient to request medication for the purpose of ending the patient's life, or to destroy a rescission of such a request, shall be guilty of a Class A felony. . . .

SECTION 6: FORM OF THE REQUEST

§ 6.01 FORM OF THE REQUEST

A request for medication as authorized by this act shall be in substantially the [boxed] form.

REQUEST FOR MEDICATION TO END MY LIFE IN A HUMANE AND DIGNIFIED MANNER

I, _____, am an adult of sound mind.

I am suffering from _____, which my attending physician has determined is a terminal disease and which has been medically confirmed by a consulting physician.

I have been fully informed of my diagnosis, prognosis, the nature of medication to be prescribed and potential associated risks, the expected result, and the feasible alternatives, including comfort care, hospice care and pain control.

I request that my attending physician prescribe medication that will end my life in a humane and dignified manner.

INITIAL ONE:

_____ I have informed my family of my decision and taken their opinions into consideration.

_____ I have decided not to inform my family of my decision.

_____ I have no family to inform of my decision.

I understand that I have the right to rescind this request at any time.

I understand the full import of this request and I expect to die when I take the medication to be prescribed.

I make this request voluntarily and without reservation, and I accept full moral responsibility for my actions.

Signed: _____

Dated: _____

DECLARATION OF WITNESSES

We declare that the person signing this request:

    (a) Is personally known to us or has provided proof of identity;

    (b) Signed this request in our presence;

    (c) Appears to be of sound mind and not under duress, fraud or undue influence;

    (d) Is not a patient for whom either of us is attending physician.

_____Witness 1/Date

_____Witness 2/Date

NOTE: one witness shall not be a relative (by blood, marriage or adoption) of the person signing this request, shall not be entitled to any portion of the person's estate upon death and shall not own, operate or be employed at a health care facility where the person is a patient or resident. If the patient is an inpatient at a health care facility, one of the witnesses shall be an individual designated by the facility.

UNITED STATES SUPREME COURT

Dennis C. Vacco, Attorney General of New York, et al., Petitioners v. Timothy E. Quill et al.

On Writ of Certiorari to the United States Court of Appeals for the Second Circuit

CHIEF JUSTICE REHNQUIST delivered the opinion of the Court.

In New York, as in most States, it is a crime to aid another to commit or attempt suicide, but patients may refuse even lifesaving medical treatment. The question presented by this case is whether New York's prohibition on assisting suicide therefore violates the Equal Protection Clause of the Fourteenth Amendment. We hold that it does not. . . .

The Equal Protection Clause commands that no State shall "deny to any person within its jurisdiction the equal protection of the laws." This provision creates no substantive rights. . . . Instead, it embodies a general rule that States must treat like cases alike but may treat unlike cases accordingly. . . .

On their faces, neither New York's ban on assisting suicide nor its statutes permitting patients to refuse medical treatment treat anyone differently than anyone else or draw any distinction between persons. *Everyone,* regardless of physical condition, is entitled, if competent, to refuse unwanted lifesaving medical treatment; *no one* is permitted to assist a suicide. Generally speaking, laws that apply evenhandedly to all "unquestionably comply" with the Equal Protection Clause. . . .

The Court of Appeals, however, concluded that some terminally ill people—those who are on life-support systems—are treated differently than those

521 U.S. 793; 117 S. Ct. 2293; 138 L. Ed. 2d 834; 1997 U.S. LEXIS 4038; 65 U.S.L.W. 4695; 97 Cal. Daily Op. Service 5027; 97 Daily Journal DAR 8122; 11 Fla. L. Weekly Fed. S 174

who are not, in that the former may "hasten death" by ending treatment, but the latter may not "hasten death" through physician-assisted suicide. 80 F. 3d, at 729. This conclusion depends on the submission that ending or refusing lifesaving medical treatment "is nothing more nor less than assisted suicide." *Ibid.* Unlike the Court of Appeals, we think the distinction between assisting suicide and withdrawing life-sustaining treatment, a distinction widely recognized and endorsed in the medical profession and in our legal traditions, is both important and logical; it is certainly rational. . . .

The distinction comports with fundamental legal principles of causation and intent. First, when a patient refuses life-sustaining medical treatment, he dies from an underlying fatal disease of pathology; but if a patient ingests lethal medication prescribed by a physician, he is killed by that medication. . . .

Furthermore, a physician who withdraws, or honors a patient's refusal to begin, life-sustaining medical treatment purposefully intends, or may so intend, only to respect his patient's wishes and "to cease doing useless and futile or degrading things to the patient when [the patient] no longer stands to benefit from them." Assisted Suicide in the United States, Hearing before the Subcommittee on the Constitution of the House Committee on the Judiciary, 104th Cong., 2d Sess., 368 (1996) (testimony of Dr. Leon R. Kass). The same is true when a doctor provides aggressive palliative care; in some cases, painkilling drugs may hasten a patient's death, but the physician's purpose and intent is, or may be, only to ease his patient's pain. A doctor who assists a suicide, however, "must, necessarily and indubitably, intend primarily that the patient be made dead." *Id.*, at 367. Similarly, a patient who commits suicide with a doctor's aid necessarily has the specific intent to end his or her own life, while a patient who refuses or discontinues treatment might not. . . .

The law has long used actors' intent or purpose to distinguish between two acts that may have the same result. See, *e.g., United States v. Bailey,* 444 U.S. 394, 403–406 (1980) ("[T]he . . . common law of homicide often distinguishes . . . between a person who knows that another person will be killed as the result of his conduct and a person who acts with the specific purpose of taking another's life"). . . . M. Hale, 1 Pleas of the Crown 412 (1847) ("If A., with an intent to prevent gangrene beginning in his hand doth without any advice cut off his hand, by which he dies, he is not thereby *felo de se* for tho it was a voluntary act, yet it was not with an intent to kill himself"). Put differently, the law distinguishes actions taken "because of" a given end from actions taken "in spite of" their unintended but foreseen consequences. *Feeney,* 442 U.S., at 279; *Compassion in Dying v. Washington,* 79 F. 3d 790, 858 (CA9 1996) (Kleinfeld, J., dissenting) ("When General Eisenhower ordered American soldiers onto the beaches of Normandy, he knew that he was sending many American soldiers to certain death. . . . His purpose, though, was to . . . liberate Europe from the Nazis").

Given these general principles, it is not surprising that many courts, including New York courts, have carefully distinguished refusing life-sustaining treatment from suicide. See, *e.g., Fosmire v. Nicoleau,* 75 N.Y. 2d 218, 227, and n. 2, 551 N.E. 2d 77, 82, and n. 2 (1990) ("[M]erely declining medical . . . care is not considered a suicidal act").[1] In fact, the first state-court decision explicitly to authorize withdrawing lifesaving treatment noted the "real distinction between the self-infliction of deadly harm and a self-determination against artificial life support." *In re Quinlan,* 70 N.J. 10, 43, 52. . . .

Similarly, the overwhelming majority of state legislatures have drawn a clear line between assisting suicide and withdrawing or permitting the refusal of unwanted lifesaving medical treatment by prohibiting the former and permitting the latter. And "nearly all states expressly disapprove of suicide and assisted suicide either in statutes dealing with durable powers of attorney in health-care situations, or in 'living will'

statutes." *Kevorkian,* 447 Mich., at 478–479, and nn. 53–54, 527 N.W 2d, at 731–732, and nn. 53–54. Thus, even as the States move to protect and promote patients' dignity at the end of life, they remain opposed to physician-assisted suicide. . . .

This Court has also recognized, at least implicitly, the distinction between letting a patient die and making that patient die. In *Cruzan v. Director, Mo. Dept. of Health,* 497 U.S. 261, 278 (1990), we concluded that "[t]he principle that a competent person has a constitutionally protected liberty interest in refusing unwanted medical treatment may be inferred from our prior decisions," and we assumed the existence of such a right for purposes of that case, *id.*, at 279. But our assumption of a right to refuse treatment was grounded not, as the Court of Appeals supposed, on the proposition that patients have a general and abstract "right to hasten death," 80 F, 3d at 727–728, but on well established, traditional rights to bodily integrity and freedom from unwanted touching, *Cruzan,* 497 U.S., at 278–279; *id.*, at 287–288. (O'CONNOR, J., concurring). In fact, we observed that "the majority of States in this country have laws imposing criminal penalties on one who assists another to commit suicide." *Id.*, at 280. *Cruzan* therefore provides no support for the notion that refusing life-sustaining medical treatment is "nothing more nor less than suicide."

For all these reasons, we disagree with respondents' claim that the distinction between refusing lifesaving medical treatment and assisted suicide is "arbitrary" and "irrational." Brief for Respondents 44. Granted, in some cases, the line between the two may not be clear, but certainty is not required, even were it possible. Logic and contemporary practice support New York's judgment that the two acts are different, and New York may therefore, consistent with the Constitution, treat them differently. By permitting everyone to refuse unwanted medical treatment while prohibiting anyone from assisting a suicide, New York law follows a longstanding and rational distinction.

New York's reasons for recognizing and acting on this distinction—including prohibiting intentional killing and preserving life; preventing suicide; maintaining physicians' role as their patients' healers; protecting vulnerable people from indifference, prejudice, and psychological and financial pressure to end their lives; and avoiding a possible slide towards euthanasia—are discussed in greater detail in our opinion in *Glucksberg, ante.* These valid and important public interests easily satisfy the constitutional requirement that a legislative classification bear a rational relation to some legitimate end.

The judgment of the Court of Appeals is reversed.

It is so ordered.

NOTE

1. Thus, the Second Circuit erred in reading New York law as creating a "right to hasten death"; instead, the authorities cited by

the court recognize a right to refuse treatment, and nowhere equate the exercise of this right with suicide. *Schloendorff v. Society of New York Hospital,* 211 N.Y. 125, 129–130, 105 N.E. 92, 93 (1914), which contains Justice Cardozo's famous statement that "[e]very human being of adult years and sound mind has a right to determine what shall be done with his own body," was simply an informed-consent case. . . .

UNITED STATES SUPREME COURT

Washington, et al., Petitioners v. Harold Glucksberg et al.

On Writ of Certiorari to the United States Court of Appeals for the Ninth Circuit

CHIEF JUSTICE REHNQUIST delivered the opinion of the Court.

The question presented in this case is whether Washington's prohibition against "caus[ing]" or "aid[ing]" a suicide offends the Fourteenth Amendment to the United States Constitution. We hold that it does not. . . .

In almost every State—indeed, in almost every western democracy—it is a crime to assist a suicide. The States' assisted-suicide bans are not innovations. Rather, they are longstanding expressions of the States' commitment to the protection and preservation of all human life. . . . Indeed, opposition to and condemnation of suicide—and, therefore, of assisting suicide—are consistent and enduring themes of our philosophical, legal, and cultural heritages. . . .

Because of advances in medicine and technology, Americans today are increasingly likely to die in institutions, from chronic illnesses. President's

521 U.S. 702; 117 S. Ct. 2258; 117 S. Ct. 2302; 138 L. Ed. 2d 772; 1997 U.S. LEXIS 4039; 65 U.S.L.W. 4669; 97 Cal. Daily Op. Service 5008; 97 Daily Journal DAR 8150; 11 Fla. L. Weekly Fed. S 190

Comm'n for the Study of Ethical Problems in Medicine and Biomedical and Behavioral Research, Deciding to Forego Life-Sustaining Treatment 16–18 (1983). Public concern and democratic action are therefore sharply focused on how best to protect dignity and independence at the end of life, with the result that there have been many significant changes in state laws and in the attitudes these laws reflect. . . .

Thus, the States are currently engaged in serious, thoughtful examinations of physician-assisted suicide and other similar issues. For example, New York State's Task Force on Life and the Law—an ongoing, blue-ribbon commission composed of doctors, ethicists, lawyers, religious leaders, and interested laymen—was convened in 1984 and commissioned with "a broad mandate to recommend public policy on issues raised by medical advances." New York Task Force vii. . . .

Attitudes toward suicide itself have changed . . . but our laws have consistently condemned, and continue to prohibit, assisting suicide. Despite changes in medical technology and notwithstanding an increased emphasis on the importance of end-of-life decision-making, we have not retreated from this prohibition. Against this backdrop of history, tradition, and practice, we now turn to respondents' constitutional claim.

II

The Due Process Clause guarantees more than fair process, and the liberty" it protects includes more than the absence of physical restraint. . . . The Clause also provides heightened protection against government interference with certain fundamental rights and liberty interests. . . . We have . . . assumed, and strongly suggested, that the Due Process Clause protects the traditional right to refuse unwanted lifesaving medical treatment. *Cruzan*, 497 U.S., at 278–279.

But we "ha[ve] always been reluctant to expand the concept of substantive due process because guideposts for responsible decisionmaking in this unchartered area are scarce and open-ended." *Collins*, 503 U.S., at 125. By extending constitutional protection to an asserted right or liberty interest, we, to a great extent, place the matter outside the arena of public debate and legislative action. . . .

Our established method of substantive-due-process analysis has two primary features: First, we have regularly observed that the Due Process Clause specially protects those fundamental rights and liberties which are, objectively, "deeply rooted in this Nation's history and tradition," *id.*, at 503 (plurality opinion); . . . Second, we have required in substantive-due-process cases a "careful description" of the asserted fundamental liberty interest. . . .

The Washington statute at issue in this case prohibits "aid[ing] another person to attempt suicide," Wash. Rev. Code §9A.36.060(1) (1994), and, thus, the question before us is whether the "liberty" specially protected by the Due Process Clause includes a right to commit suicide which itself includes a right to assistance in doing so.

We now inquire whether this asserted right has any place in our Nation's traditions. Here, as discussed above . . . we are confronted with a consistent and almost universal tradition that has long rejected the asserted right . . .

Respondents contend, however, that the liberty interest they assert *is* consistent with this Court's substantive-due-process line of cases, if not with this Nation's history and practice. Pointing to *Casey* and *Cruzan*, respondents read our jurisprudence in this area as reflecting a general tradition of "self-sovereignty," Brief of Respondents 12, and as teaching that the "liberty" protected by the Due Process Clause includes "basic and intimate exercises of personal autonomy," *id.*, at 10; see *Casey*, 505 U.S., at 847 ("It is a promise of the Constitution that there is a realm of personal liberty which the government may not enter"). According to respondents, our liberty jurisprudence, and the broad, individualistic principles it reflects, protects the "liberty of competent, terminally ill adults to make end-of-life decisions free of undue government interference." Brief for Respondents 10. . . .

The decision to commit suicide with the assistance of another may be just as personal and profound as the decision to refuse unwanted medical treatment, but it has never enjoyed similar legal protection. Indeed, the two acts are widely and reasonably regarded as quite distinct. See *Quill v. Vacco, post*, at 5–13. In *Cruzan* itself, we recognized that most States outlawed assisted suicide—and even more do today—and we certainly gave no intimation that the right to refuse unwanted medical treatment could be somehow transmuted into a right to assistance in committing suicide. 497 U.S., at 280. . . .

[O]ur decisions lead us to conclude that the asserted "right" to assistance in committing suicide is not a fundamental liberty interest protected by the Due Process Clause. The Constitution also requires, however, that Washington's assisted-suicide ban be rationally related to legitimate government interests. . . . This requirement is unquestionably met here. As the court below recognized, 79 F. 3d, at 816–817,[1] Washington's assisted-suicide ban implicates a number of state interests.[2] . . .

First, Washington has an "unqualified interest in the preservation of human life." *Cruzan*, 497 U.S., at 282. The State's prohibition on assisted suicide, like all homicide laws, both reflects and advances its commitment to this interest. . . .

The State also has an interest in protecting the integrity and ethics of the medical profession. In contrast to the Court of Appeals' conclusion that "the integrity of the medical profession would [not] be threatened in any way by [physician-assisted suicide]," 79 F. 3d, at 827, the American Medical Association, like many other medical and physicians' groups, has concluded that "[p]hysician-assisted suicide is fundamentally incompatible with the physician's role as healer." American Medical Association, Code of Ethics §2.211 (1994); see Council on Ethical and Judicial Affairs, Decisions Near the End of Life, 267 JAMA 2229, 2233 (1992) ("[T]he societal risks of involving physicians in medical interventions to cause patients' deaths is too great"); New York Task Force 103–109 (discussing physicians' views). And physician-assisted suicide could, it is argued, undermine the trust that is essential to the doctor–patient relationship by blurring the time-honored line between healing and harming. . . .

Next, the State has an interest in protecting vulnerable groups—including the poor, the elderly, and disabled persons—from abuse, neglect, and mistakes. The Court of Appeals dismissed the State's concern that disadvantaged persons might be pressured into physician-assisted suicide as "ludicrous on its face." 79 F. 3d, at 825. We have recognized, however, the real risk of subtle coercion and undue influence in end-of-life situations. *Cruzan*, 497 U.S., at 281. Similarly, the New York Task Force warned that "[l]egalizing physician-assisted suicide would pose profound risks to many individuals who are ill and vulnerable. . . . The risk of harm is greatest for the many individuals in our society whose autonomy and well-being are already compromised by poverty, lack of access to good medical care, advanced age, or membership in a stigmatized social group." New York Task Force 120. . . .

Finally, the State may fear that permitting assisted suicide will start it down the path to voluntary and perhaps even involuntary euthanasia. . . .

We need not weigh exactly the relative strengths of these various interests. They are unquestionably important and legitimate, and Washington's ban on assisted suicide is at least reasonably related to their promotion and protection. We therefore hold that Wash. Rev. Code §9A.36.060(1) (1994) does not violate the Fourteenth Amendment, either on its face or "as applied to competent, terminally ill adults who wish to hasten their deaths by obtaining medication prescribed by their doctors." 79 F. 3d, at 838.

• • •

Throughout the Nation, Americans are engaged in an earnest and profound debate about the morality, legality, and practicality of physician-assisted suicide. Our holding permits this debate to continue, as it should in a democratic society. The decision of the en banc Court of Appeals is reversed, and the case is remanded for further proceedings consistent with this opinion.

It is so ordered.

JUSTICE STEVENS, concurring in the judgments. . . .

A State, like Washington, that has authorized the death penalty and thereby has concluded that the sanctity of human life does not require that it always be preserved, must acknowledge that there are situations in which an interest in hastening death is legitimate. Indeed, not only is that interest sometimes legitimate, I am also convinced that there are times when it is entitled to constitutional protection.

• • •

The state interests supporting a general rule banning the practice of physician-assisted suicide do not have the same force in all cases. . . . That interest not only justifies—it commands—maximum protection of every individual's interest in remaining alive, which in turn commands the same protection for decisions about whether to commence or to terminate life-support systems or to administer pain medication that may hasten death. Properly viewed, however, this interest is not a collective interest that should always outweigh the interests of a person who because of pain, incapacity, or sedation finds her life intolerable, but rather, an aspect of individual freedom. . . .

Although as a general matter the State's interest in the contributions each person may make to society outweighs the person's interest in ending her life, this interest does not have the same force for a terminally ill patient faced not with the choice of whether to live, only of how to die. Allowing the individual, rather than the State, to make judgments " 'about the "quality" of life that a particular individual may enjoy.'" *ante,* at 25 (quoting *Cruzan*, 497 U.S., at 282), does not mean that the lives of terminally-ill, disabled people have less value than the lives of those who are healthy, see *ante,* at 28. Rather, it gives proper recognition to the individual's interest in choosing a final chapter that accords with her life story, rather than one that demeans her values and poisons memories of her. . . .

Similarly, the State's legitimate interests in preventing suicide, protecting the vulnerable from coercion and abuse, and preventing euthanasia are less significant in this context. I agree that the State has a compelling interest in preventing persons from committing suicide because of depression, or coercion by third parties. But the State's legitimate interest in preventing abuse does not apply to an individual who is not victimized by abuse, who is not suffering from depression, and who makes a rational and voluntary decision to seek assistance in dying. . . .

Relatedly, the State and *amici* express the concern that patients whose physical pain is inadequately treated will be more likely to request assisted suicide. Encouraging the development and ensuring the availability of adequate pain treatment is of utmost importance; palliative care, however, cannot alleviate all pain and suffering. . . . An individual adequately informed of the care alternatives thus might make a rational choice for assisted suicide. For such an individual, the State's interest in preventing potential abuse and mistake is only minimally implicated.

The final major interest asserted by the State is its interest in preserving the traditional integrity of the medical profession. The fear is that a rule permitting physicians to assist in suicide is inconsistent with the perception that they serve their patients solely as healers. But for some patients, it would be a physician's refusal to dispense medication to ease their suffering and make their death tolerable and dignified that would be inconsistent with the healing role. . . . For doctors who have long-standing relationships with their patients, who have given their patients advice on alternative treatments, who are attentive to their patient's individualized needs, and who are knowledgeable about pain symptom management and palliative care options, see Quill, Death and Dignity, A Case of Individualized Decision Making, 324 New England J. of Med. 691–694 (1991), heeding a patient's desire to assist in her suicide would not serve to harm the physician–patient relationship. Furthermore, because physicians are already involved in making decisions that hasten the death of terminally ill patients—through termination of life support, withholding of medical treatment, and terminal sedation—there is in fact significant tension between the traditional view of the physician's role and the actual practice in a growing number of cases. . . .

I agree that the distinction between permitting death to ensue from an underlying fatal disease and causing it to occur by the administration of medication or other means provides a constitutionally sufficient basis for the State's classification. Unlike the Court, however, . . . I am not persuaded that in all cases there will in fact be a significant difference between the intent of the physicians, the patients or the families in the two situations.

There may be little distinction between the intent of a terminally-ill patient who decides to remove her life-support and one who seeks the assistance of a doctor in ending her life; in both situations, the patient is seeking to hasten a certain, impending death. The doctor's intent might also be the same in prescribing lethal medication as it is in terminating life support. A doctor who fails to administer medical treatment to one who is dying from a disease could be doing so with an intent to harm or kill that patient. Conversely, a doctor who prescribes lethal medication does not necessarily intend the patient's death—rather that doctor may seek simply to ease the patient's suffering and to comply with her wishes. The illusory character of any differences in intent or causation is confirmed by the fact that the American Medical Association unequivocally endorses the practice of terminal sedation—the administration of sufficient dosages of pain-killing medication to terminally ill patients to protect them from excruciating pain even when it is clear that the time of death will be advanced. The purpose of terminal sedation is to ease the suffering of the patient and comply with her wishes, and the actual cause of death is the administration of heavy doses of lethal sedatives. This same intent and causation may exist when a doctor complies with a patient's request for lethal medication to hasten her death.

Thus, although the differences the majority notes in causation and intent between terminating life-support and assisting in suicide support the Court's rejection of the respondents' facial challenge, these distinctions may be inapplicable to particular terminally ill patients and their doctors. Our holding today in *Vacco v. Quill* that the Equal Protection Clause is not violated by New York's classification, just like our holding in *Washington v. Glucksberg* that the Washington statue is not invalid on its face, does not foreclose the possibility that some applications of the New York statute may impose an intolerable intrusion on the patient's freedom.

There remains room for vigorous debate about the outcome of particular cases that are not necessarily resolved by the opinions announced today. How such cases may be decided will depend on their specific facts. In my judgment, however, it is clear that the so-called "unqualified interest in the preservation of human life," *Cruzan*, 497 U.S., at 282, *Glucksberg, ante*, at 24, is not itself sufficient to outweigh the interest in liberty that may justify the only possible means of preserving a dying patient's dignity and alleviating her intolerable suffering. . . .

JUSTICE O'CONNOR, concurring.*

Death will be different for each of us. For many, the last days will be spent in physical pain and perhaps the despair that accompanies physical deterioration and a loss of control of basic bodily and mental functions. Some will seek medication to alleviate that pain and other symptoms.

The Court frames the issues in this case as whether the Due Process Clause of the Constitution protects a "right to commit suicide, which itself includes a right to assistance in doing so," . . . and concludes that our Nation's history, legal traditions, and practices do not support the existence of such a right. I join the Court's opinions because I agree that there is no generalized right to "commit suicide." But respondents urge us to address the narrower question whether a mentally competent person who is experiencing great suffering has a constitutionally cognizable interest in controlling the circumstances of his or her imminent death. I see no need to reach that question in the context of the facial challenges to the New York and Washington laws at issue here. . . . The parties and *amici* agree that in these States a patient who is suffering from a terminal illness and who is experiencing great pain has no legal barriers to obtaining medication, from qualified physicians, to alleviate that suffering, even to the point of causing unconsciousness and hastening death. . . . In this light, even assuming that we would recognize such an interest, I agree that the State's interests in protecting those who are not truly competent or facing imminent death, or those whose decisions to hasten death would not truly be voluntary, are sufficiently weighty to justify a prohibition against physician-assisted suicide. . . .

Every one of us at some point may be affected by our own or a family member's terminal illness. There is no reason to think the democratic process will not strike the proper balance between the interests of terminally ill, mentally competent individuals who would seek to end their suffering and the State's interests in protecting those who might seek to end life mistakenly or under pressure. As the Court recognizes, States are presently undertaking extensive and serious evaluation of physician-assisted suicide and other related issues. . . . In such circumstances, "the . . . challenging task of crafting appropriate procedures for safeguarding . . . liberty interests is entrusted to the 'laboratory' of the States . . . in the first instance." *Cruzan v. Director, Mo. Dept. of Health*, 497 U.S. 261, 292 (1990) (O'CONNOR, J., concurring) (citing *New State Ice Co. v. Liebmann*, 285 U.S. 262, 311 (1932)).

In sum, there is no need to address the question whether suffering patients have a constitutionally cognizable interest in obtaining relief from the suffering that they may experience in the last days of their lives. There is no dispute that dying patients in Washington and New York can obtain palliative care, even when doing so would hasten their deaths. The difficulty in defining terminal illness and the risk that a dying patient's request for assistance in ending his or her life might not be truly voluntary justifies the prohibitions on assisted suicide we uphold here.

NOTES

1. The court identified and discussed six state interests: (1) preserving life; (2) preventing suicide; (3) avoiding the involvement of third parties and use of arbitrary, unfair, or undue influence; (4) protecting family members and loved ones; (5) protecting the integrity of the medical profession; and (6) avoiding future movement toward euthanasia and other abuses. 79 F. 3d, at 816–832.

2. Respondents also admit the existence of these interests, Brief for Respondents 28–39, but contend that Washington could better promote and protect them through regulation, rather than prohibition, of physician-assisted suicide. Our inquiry, however, is limited to the question whether the State's prohibition is rationally related to legitimate state interests.

*JUSTICE GINSBURG concurs in the Court's judgments substantially for the reasons stated in this opinion. JUSTICE BREYER joins this opinion except insofar as it joins the opinion of the Court.

THE SUPREME COURT OF CALIFORNIA

Rose Wendland v. Florence Wendland et al.

In this case we consider whether a conservator of the person may withhold artificial nutrition and hydration from a conscious conservatee who is not terminally ill, comatose, or in a persistent vegetative state, and who has not left formal instructions for health care or appointed an agent or surrogate for health care decisions. Interpreting Probate Code section 2355 in light of the relevant provisions of the California Constitution, we conclude a conservator may not withhold artificial nutrition and hydration from such a person absent clear and convincing evidence the conservator's decision is in accordance with either the conservatee's own wishes or best interest.

The trial court in the case before us, applying the clear and convincing evidence standard, found the evidence on both points insufficient and, thus, denied the conservator's request for authority to withhold artificial nutrition and hydration. The Court of Appeal, which believed the trial court was required to defer to the conservator's good faith decision, reversed. We reverse the decision of the Court of Appeal.

I. FACTS AND PROCEDURAL HISTORY

On September 29, 1993, Robert Wendland rolled his truck at high speed in a solo accident while driving under the influence of alcohol. The accident injured Robert's brain, leaving him conscious yet severely disabled, both mentally and physically, and dependent on artificial nutrition and hydration. Two years later Rose Wendland, Robert's wife and conservator, proposed to direct his physician to remove his feeding tube and allow him to die. Florence Wendland and Rebekah Vinson (respectively Robert's mother and sister) objected to the conservator's decision. This proceeding arose under the provisions of the Probate Code authorizing courts to settle such disputes. (Prob. Code, §§ 2355, 2359.)

Following the accident, Robert remained in a coma,

totally unresponsive, for several months. During this period Rose visited him daily, often with their children, and authorized treatment as necessary to maintain his health.

Robert eventually regained consciousness. . . .

After Robert regained consciousness and while he was undergoing therapy, Rose authorized surgery three times to replace dislodged feeding tubes. When physicians sought her permission a fourth time, she declined. She discussed the decision with her daughters and with Robert's brother Michael, all of whom believed that Robert would not have approved the procedure even if necessary to sustain his life. Rose also discussed the decision with Robert's treating physician, Dr. Kass, other physicians, and the hospital's ombudsman, all of whom apparently supported her decision. Dr. Kass, however, inserted a nasogastric feeding tube to keep Robert alive pending input from the hospital's ethics committee.

Eventually, the 20-member ethics committee unanimously approved Rose's decision. In the course of their deliberations, however, the committee did not speak with Robert's mother or sister. Florence learned, apparently through an anonymous telephone call, that Dr. Kass planned to remove Robert's feeding tube. Florence and Rebekah applied for a temporary restraining order to bar him from so doing, and the court granted the motion ex parte.

Rose immediately thereafter petitioned for appointment as Robert's conservator. In the petition, she asked the court to determine that Robert lacked the capacity to give informed consent for medical treatment and to confirm her authority "to withdraw and/or withhold medical treatment and/or life-sustaining treatment, including, but not limited to, withholding nutrition and hydration." Florence and Rebekah (hereafter sometimes objectors) opposed the petition. . . .

Robert's wife, brother and daughter recounted pre-accident statements Robert had made about his attitude towards life-sustaining health care. Robert's wife recounted specific statements on two occasions. The first occasion was Rose's decision whether to turn off a respirator sustaining the life of her father, who was near death from gangrene. Rose recalls Robert saying: "I would never want to live like that, and I wouldn't want my children to see me like that and look at the hurt you're going through as an adult seeing your father like that." On cross-examination, Rose acknowledged Robert said on this occasion that Rose's father "wouldn't want to live like a vegetable" and "wouldn't want to live in a comatose state." . . .

II. DISCUSSION

A. THE RELEVANT LEGAL PRINCIPLES

The ultimate focus of our analysis must be section 2355, the statute under which the conservator has claimed the authority to end the conservatee's life and the only statute under which such authority might plausibly be found. . . .

Effective July 1, 2000, the Health Care Decisions Law (Stats. 1999, ch. 658) gives competent adults extremely broad power to direct all aspects of their health care in the event they become incompetent. The new law permits a competent person to execute an advance directive about "any aspect" of health care. (§ 4701). Among other things, a person may direct that life-sustaining treatment be withheld or withdrawn under conditions specified by the person and not limited to terminal illness, permanent coma, or persistent vegetative state. A competent person may still use a power of attorney for health care to give an agent the power to make health care decisions (§ 4683), but a patient may also orally designate a surrogate to make such decisions by personally informing the patient's supervising health care provider. (§ 4711.) Under the new law, agents and surrogates are required to make health care decisions "in accordance with the principal's individual health care instructions, if any, and other wishes to the extent known to the agent." . . .

The ultimate focus of our analysis, as mentioned at the outset, must be section 2355, the statute under which the conservator claims the authority to end the conservatee's life. . . .

Historical evidence is lacking, however, that the Legislature . . . actually contemplated that the statute would be understood as authorizing a conservator to deliberately end the life of a conservatee by withholding artificially delivered food and water. Such au-

thority, if it indeed existed, would have been merely implicit, as a consequence of the statute's broad language. The claim that section 2355 conferred that authority was first considered and accepted in 1988 by the court in *Drabick*, 200 Cal.App.3d 185.

The *Drabick* court also read former section 2355 as severely restricting the role of courts in supervising conservators' treatment decisions. "[W]e do not believe," the court wrote, "that it is the [trial] court's role to substitute its judgment for the conservator's. Instead, when the conservator or another interested person has requested the court's approval the court should confine its involvement to ensuring that the conservator has made the type of decision for which the Probate Code expressly calls: a 'good faith' decision 'based on medical advice' whether treatment is 'necessary.' " (*Drabick*, 200 Cal.App.3d 185, 200, quoting former § 2355.) The required decision, the court explained, is the *conservator's* assessment of the conservatee's best interests. . . .

In 1990, the Legislature repealed and reenacted former section 2355 without change while reorganizing the Probate Code. But in 1999, section 2355 changed significantly with the Legislature's adoption of the Health Care Decisions Law (§ 4600 et seq., added by Stats. 1999, ch. 658). That law took effect on July 1, 2000, about four months after the Court of Appeal filed the opinion on review. Many of the new law's provisions, as already noted, are the same as, or drawn from, the Uniform Health-Care Decisions Act. (See Cal. Law Revision Com. Rep., at p. 49.) Section 2355, as a statute addressing medical treatment decisions, was revised to conform to the new law.

The main purpose of the Health Care Decisions Law is to provide "procedures and standards" governing "health care decisions to be made for adults at a time when they are incapable of making decisions on their own and [to] provide "mechanisms for directing their health care in anticipation of a time when they may become incapacitated." (Cal. Law Revision Com. Rep., at p. 6.) . . .

B. THE PRESENT CASE

This background illuminates the parties' arguments, which reduce in essence to this: The conservator has claimed the power under section 2355, as she interprets it, to direct the conservatee's health care providers to cease providing artificial nutrition and hydration. In opposition, the objectors have contended the statute violates the conservatee's rights to privacy and life under the facts of this case if the conservator's interpretation of the statute is correct.

1. The primary standard: a decision in accordance with the conservatee's wishes. The conservator asserts she offered sufficient evidence at trial to satisfy the primary statutory standard, which contemplates a decision "in accordance with the conservatee's . . . wishes. . . ." (§ 2355, subd. (a).) The trial court, however, determined the evidence on this point was insufficient. The conservator did "not [meet] her duty and burden," the court expressly found, "to show by clear and convincing evidence that [the] conservatee . . . , who is not in a persistent vegetative state nor suffering from a terminal illness would, under the circumstances, want to die." . . .

The objectors, in opposition, argue that section 2355 would be unconstitutional if construed to permit a conservator to end the life of a conscious conservatee based on a finding by the low preponderance of the evidence standard that the latter would not want to live. We see no basis for holding the statute unconstitutional on its face. We do, however, find merit in the objectors' argument. We therefore construe the statute to minimize the possibility of its unconstitutional application by requiring clear and convincing evidence of a conscious conservatee's wish to refuse life-sustaining treatment when the conservator relies on that asserted wish to justify withholding life-sustaining treatment. This construction does not entail a deviation from the language of the statute and constitutes only a partial rejection of the Law Revision Commission's understanding that the preponderance of the evidence standard would apply; we see no constitutional reason to apply the higher evidentiary standard to the majority of health care decisions made by conservators not contemplating a conscious conservatee's death. Our reasons are as follows:

At the time the Legislature was considering the present version of section 2355, no court had interpreted any prior version of the statute as permitting a conservator deliberately to end the life of a *conscious* conservatee. Even today, only the decision on review so holds. . . .

In amending section 2355 in 1999, neither the Legislature, nor the Law Revision Commission in its official report to the Legislature, alluded to the possibility that the statute might be invoked to justify withholding artificial nutrition and hydration from a conscious patient. The conservator sees evidence of specific legislative authority for such a decision in the findings that accompanied the Health Care Decisions Law, but we do not. . . .

One must acknowledge that the primary standard for decisionmaking set out in section 2355 does articulate what will in some cases form a constitutional basis for a conservator's decision to end the life of a conscious patient: deference to the patient's own wishes. This standard also appears in the new provisions governing decisions by agents and surrogates designated by competent adults. (§§ 4684, 4714). As applied in that context, the requirement that decisions be made "in accordance with the principal's individual health care instructions . . . and other wishes" (§ 4684) merely respects the principal-agent relationship and gives effect to the properly expressed wishes of a competent adult. Because a competent adult may refuse life-sustaining treatment (see *ante,* at p. 11 et seq.), it follows that an agent properly and voluntarily designated by the principal may refuse treatment on the principal's behalf unless, of course, such authority is revoked. (See, e.g., §§ 4682, 4689, 4695 [providing various ways in which the authority of an agent for health care decisions may be revoked or the agent's instructions countermanded].)

The only apparent purpose of requiring conservators to make decisions in accordance with the conservatee's wishes, when those wishes are known, is to enforce the fundamental principle of personal autonomy. The same requirement, as applied to agents and surrogates freely designated by competent persons, enforces the principles of agency. A reasonable person presumably will designate for such purposes only a person in whom the former reposes the highest degree of confidence. A conservator, in contrast, is *not* an agent of the conservatee, and unlike a freely designated agent cannot be presumed to have special knowledge of the conservatee's health care wishes. A person with "sufficient capacity . . . to form an intelligent preference" may nominate his or her own conservator (§ 1810), but the nomination is not binding because the appointment remains "solely in the discretion of the court" (§ 1812, subd. (a)). Furthermore, while statutory law gives preference to spouses and other persons related to the conservatee (*id.,* subd. (b)), who might know something of the conservatee's health care preferences, the law also permits the court in its sole discretion to appoint unrelated persons and even public conservators (*ibid.*). While it may be constitutionally permissible to assume that an agent freely designated by a formerly competent person to make all health care decisions, including life-ending ones, will resolve such questions "in accordance with the principal's . . . wishes" (§ 4684), one cannot apply the same assumption to conservators and conservatees (cf. § 2355, subd, (a)). For this reason, when the legal premise of a conservator's decision to end a conservatee's life by withholding medical care is that the conservatee would refuse such care, to apply a high standard of proof will help to ensure the reliability of the decision. . . .

In this case, the importance of the ultimate decision and the risk of error are manifest. So too should be the degree of confidence required in the necessary findings of fact. The ultimate decision is whether a conservatee lives or dies, and the risk is that a conservator, claiming statutory authority to end a conscious conservatee's life "in accordance with the conservatee's . . . wishes" (§ 2355, subd. (a)) by withdrawing artificial nutrition and hydration, will make a decision with which the conservatee subjectively disagrees and which subjects the conservatee to starvation, dehydration, and death. This would represent the gravest possible affront to a conservatee's state constitutional right to privacy, in the sense of freedom from unwanted bodily intrusions, and to life. While the practical ability to make autonomous health care decisions does not survive incompetence, the ability to perceive unwanted intrusions may. Certainly it is possible, as the conservator here urges, that an incompetent and uncommunicative but conscious conservatee might perceive the efforts to keep him alive as unwanted intrusion and the withdrawal of those efforts as welcome release. But the decision to treat is reversible. The decision to withdraw treatment is not. The role of a high evidentiary standard in such a case is to adjust the risk of error to favor the less perilous result. . . .

In conclusion, to interpret section 2355 to permit a conservator to withdraw artificial nutrition and hydration from a conscious conservatee based on a finding, by a mere preponderance of the evidence, that the conservatee would refuse treatment creates a serious risk that the law will be unconstitutionally applied in some cases, with grave injury to fundamental rights. . . .

III. CONCLUSION

For the reasons set out above, we conclude the superior court correctly required the conservator to prove, by clear and convincing evidence, either that the conservatee wished to refuse life-sustaining treatment or that to withhold such treatment would have been in his best interest; lacking such evidence, the superior court correctly denied the conservator's request for permission to withdraw artificial hydration and nutrition. We emphasize, however, that the clear and convincing evidence standard does not apply to the vast majority of health care decisions made by conservators under section 2355. Only the decision to withdraw life-sustaining treatment, because of its effect on a conscious conservatee's fundamental rights, justifies imposing that high standard of proof. Therefore, our decision today affects only a narrow class of persons: conscious conservatees who have not left formal directions for health care and whose conservators propose to withhold life-sustaining treatment for the purpose of causing their conservatees' deaths. Our conclusion does not affect permanently unconscious patients, including those who are comatose or in a persistent vegetative state (see generally *Conservatorship of Morrison*, 206 Cal.App.3d 304; *Drabick*, *supra*, 200 Cal.App.3d 185; *Barber*, 147 Cal.App.3d 1006), persons who have left legally cognizable instructions for health care (see §§ 4670, 4673, 4700), persons who have designated agents or other surrogates for health care (see §§ 4671, 4680, 4711), or conservatees for whom conservators have made medical decisions other than those intended to bring about the death of a conscious conservatee.

The decision of the Court of Appeal is reversed.

WERDEGAR. J.

WE CONCUR:

GEORGE, C.J.
KENNARD, J.
BAXTER, J.
CHIN, J.
BROWN, J.

The Moral Foundations of Public Policy on Physician-Assisted Death

DAN W. BROCK

Voluntary Active Euthanasia

Dan W. Brock was, until recently Charles C. Tillinghast, Jr., University Professor, professor of philosophy and biomedical ethics, and director of the Center for Biomedical Ethics at Brown University. He is a former staff philosopher on the President's Commission for the Study of Ethical Problems in Medicine. His books include *Life and Death: Philosophical Essays in Biomedical Ethics*, and (with Allen Buchanan) *Deciding for Others: The Ethics of Surrogate Decision Making*. Brock is currently at the National Institutes of Health (NIH).

In the recent bioethics literature some have endorsed physician-assisted suicide but not euthanasia. Are they sufficiently different that the moral arguments for one often do not apply to the other? A paradigm case of physician-assisted suicide is a patient's ending his or her life with a lethal dose of a medication requested of and provided by a physician for that purpose. A paradigm case of voluntary active euthanasia is a physician's administering the lethal dose, often because the patient is unable to do so. The only difference that need exist between the two is the person who actually administers the lethal dose—the physician or the patient. In each, the physician plays an active and necessary causal role.

In physician-assisted suicide the patient acts last (for example, Janet Adkins herself pushed the button after Dr. Kevorkian hooked her up to his suicide machine), whereas in euthanasia the physician acts last by performing the physical equivalent of pushing the button. In both cases, however, the choice rests fully with the patient. In both the patient acts last in the sense of retaining the right to change his or her mind until the point at which the lethal process becomes irreversible. How could there be a substantial moral difference between the two based only on this small difference in the part played by the physician in the causal process resulting in death? Of course, it might

From "Voluntary Active Euthanasia," *Hastings Center Report* 22, no. 2 (March/April 1992), 10–22 (edited). Reprinted by permission of the publisher.

be held that the moral difference is clear and important—in euthanasia the physician kills the patient whereas in physician-assisted suicide the patient kills him- or herself. But this is misleading at best. In assisted suicide the physician and patient together kill the patient. To see this, suppose a physician supplied a lethal dose to a patient with the knowledge and intent that the patient will wrongfully administer it to another. We would have no difficulty in morality or the law recognizing this as a case of joint action to kill for which both are responsible.

If there is no significant, intrinsic moral difference between the two, it is also difficult to see why public or legal policy should permit one but not the other; worries about abuse or about giving anyone dominion over the lives of others apply equally to either. As a result, I will take the arguments evaluated below to apply to both and will focus on euthanasia.

My concern here will be with *voluntary* euthanasia only—that is, with the case in which a clearly competent patient makes a fully voluntary and persistent request for aid in dying. Involuntary euthanasia, in which a competent patient explicitly refuses or opposes receiving euthanasia, and nonvoluntary euthanasia, in which a patient is incompetent and unable to express his or her wishes about euthanasia, will be considered here only as potential unwanted side-effects of permitting voluntary euthanasia. I emphasize as well that I am concerned with *active* euthanasia, not withholding or withdrawing life-sustaining treatment, which some commentators characterize as "passive euthanasia." . . .

THE CENTRAL ETHICAL ARGUMENT FOR VOLUNTARY ACTIVE EUTHANASIA

The central ethical argument for euthanasia is familiar. It is that the very same two fundamental ethical values supporting the consensus on patient's rights to decide about life-sustaining treatment also support the ethical permissibility of euthanasia. These values are individual self-determination or autonomy and individual well-being. By self-determination as it bears on euthanasia, I mean people's interest in making important decisions about their lives for themselves according to their own values or conceptions of a good life, and in being left free to act on those decisions. Self-determination is valuable because it permits people to form and live in accordance with their own conception of a good life, at least within the bounds of justice and consistent with others doing so as well. In exercising self-determination people take responsibility for their lives and for the kinds of persons they become. A central aspect of human dignity lies in people's capacity to direct their lives in this way. The value of exercising self-determination presupposes some minimum of decisionmaking capacities or competence, which thus limits the scope of euthanasia supported by self-determination; it cannot justifiably be administered, for example, in cases of serious dementia or treatable clinical depression.

Does the value of individual self-determination extend to the time and manner of one's death? Most people are very concerned about the nature of the last stage of their lives. This reflects not just a fear of experiencing substantial suffering when dying, but also a desire to retain dignity and control during this last period of life. Death is today increasingly preceded by a long period of significant physical and mental decline, due in part to the technological interventions of modern medicine. Many people adjust to these disabilities and find meaning and value in new activities and ways. Others find the impairments and burdens in the last stage of their lives at some point sufficiently great to make life no longer worth living. For many patients near death, maintaining the quality of one's life, avoiding great suffering, maintaining one's dignity, and insuring that others remember us as we wish them to become of paramount importance and outweigh merely extending one's life. But there is no single, objectively correct answer for everyone as to when, if at all, one's life becomes all things consid-

ered a burden and unwanted. If self-determination is a fundamental value, then the great variability among people on this question makes it especially important that individuals control the manner, circumstances, and timing of their dying and death.

The other main value that supports euthanasia is individual well-being. It might seem that individual well-being conflicts with a person's self-determination when the person requests euthanasia. Life itself is commonly taken to be a central good for persons, often valued for its own sake, as well as necessary for pursuit of all other goods within a life. But when a competent patient decides to forgo all further life-sustaining treatment then the patient, either explicitly or implicitly, commonly decides that the best life possible for him or her with treatment is of sufficiently poor quality that it is worse than no further life at all. Life is no longer considered a benefit by the patient, but has now become a burden. The same judgment underlies a request for euthanasia: continued life is seen by the patient as no longer a benefit, but now a burden. Especially in the often severely compromised and debilitated states of many critically ill or dying patients, there is no objective standard, but only the competent patient's judgment of whether continued life is no longer a benefit. . . .

Most opponents do not deny that there are some cases in which the values of patient self-determination and well-being support euthanasia. Instead, they commonly offer two kinds of arguments against it that on their view outweigh or override this support. The first kind of argument is that in any individual case where considerations of the patient's self-determination and well-being do support euthanasia, it is nevertheless always ethically wrong or impermissible. The second kind of argument grants that in some individual cases euthanasia may *not* be ethically wrong, but maintains nonetheless that public and legal policy should never permit it. The first kind of argument focuses on features of any individual case of euthanasia, while the second kind focuses on social or legal policy. In the next section I consider the first kind of argument.

EUTHANASIA IS THE DELIBERATE KILLING OF AN INNOCENT PERSON

The claim that any individual instance of euthanasia is a case of deliberate killing of an innocent person is, with only minor qualifications, correct. Unlike forgoing life-sustaining treatment, commonly understood as allowing to die, euthanasia is clearly killing, defined as depriving of life or causing the death of a living being. While providing morphine for pain relief at doses where the risk of respiratory depression and an earlier death may be a foreseen but unintended side effect of treating the patient's pain, in a case of euthanasia the patient's death is deliberate or intended even if in both the physician's ultimate end may be respecting the patient's wishes. If the deliberate killing of an innocent person is wrong, euthanasia would be nearly always impermissible.

In the context of medicine, the ethical prohibition against deliberately killing the innocent derives some of its plausibility from the belief that nothing in the currently accepted practice of medicine is deliberate killing. Thus, in commenting on the "It's Over, Debbie" case, four prominent physicians and bioethicists could entitle their paper "Doctors Must Not Kill."[1] The belief that doctors do not in fact kill requires the corollary belief that forgoing life-sustaining treatment, whether by not starting or by stopping treatment, is allowing to die, not killing. Common though this view is, I shall argue that it is confused and mistaken.

Why is the common view mistaken? Consider the case of a patient terminally ill with ALS disease. She is completely respirator dependent with no hope of ever being weaned. She is unquestionably competent but finds her condition intolerable and persistently requests to be removed from the respirator and allowed to die. Most people and physicians would agree that the patient's physician should respect the patient's wishes and remove her from the respirator, though this will certainly cause the patient's death. The common understanding is that the physician thereby allows the patient to die. But is that correct?

Suppose the patient has a greedy and hostile son who mistakenly believes that his mother will never decide to stop her life-sustaining treatment and that even if she did her physician would not remove her from the respirator. Afraid that his inheritance will be dissipated by a long and expensive hospitalization, he enters his mother's room while she is sedated, extubates her, and she dies. Shortly thereafter the medical staff discovers what he has done and confronts the son. He replies, "I didn't kill her, I merely allowed her to die. It was her ALS disease that caused her death." I think this would rightly be dismissed as transparent sophistry—the son went into his mother's room and

deliberately killed her. But, of course, the son performed just the same physical actions, did just the same thing, that the physician would have done. If that is so, then doesn't the physician also kill the patient when he extubates her? . . .

I have argued elsewhere that this alternative account is deeply problematic, in part because it commits us to accepting that what the greedy son does is to allow to die, not kill. Here, I want to note two other reasons why the conclusion that stopping life support is killing is resisted.

The first reason is that killing is often understood, especially within medicine, as unjustified causing of death; in medicine it is thought to be done only accidentally or negligently. It is also increasingly widely accepted that a physician is ethically justified in stopping life support in a case like that of the ALS patient. But if these two beliefs are correct, then what the physician does cannot be killing, and so must be allowing to die. Killing patients is not, to put it flippantly, understood to be part of physicians' job description. What is mistaken in this line of reasoning is the assumption that all killings are *unjustified* causings of death. Instead, some killings are ethically justified, including many instances of stopping life support.

Another reason for resisting the conclusion that stopping life support is often killing is that it is psychologically uncomfortable. Suppose the physician had stopped the ALS patient's respirator and had made the son's claim, "I didn't kill her, I merely allowed her to die. It was her ALS disease that caused her death." The clue to the psychological role here is how naturally the "merely" modifies "allowed her to die." The characterization as allowing to die is meant to shift felt responsibility away from the agent—the physician—and to the lethal disease process. Other language common in death and dying contexts plays a similar role; "letting nature take its course" or "stopping prolonging the dying process" both seem to shift responsibility from the physician who stops life support to the fatal disease process. However psychologically helpful these conceptualizations may be in making the difficult responsibility of a physician's role in the patient's death bearable, they nevertheless are confusions. Both physicians and family members can instead be helped to understand that it is the patient's decision and consent to stopping treatment that limits their responsibility for the patient's death and that shifts that responsibility to the patient. . . .

Suppose both my arguments are mistaken. Suppose that killing is worse than allowing to die and that withdrawing life support is not killing, although euthanasia is. Euthanasia still need not for that reason be morally wrong. To see this, we need to determine the basic principle for the moral evaluation of killing persons. What is it that makes paradigm cases of wrongful killing wrongful? One very plausible answer is that killing denies the victim something that he or she values greatly—continued life or a future. Moreover, since continued life is necessary for pursuing any of a person's plans and purposes, killing brings the frustration of all of these plans and desires as well. In a nutshell, wrongful killing deprives a person of a valued future, and of all the person wanted and planned to do in that future.

A natural expression of this account of the wrongness of killing is that people have a moral right not to be killed. But in this account of the wrongness of killing, the right not to be killed, like other rights, should be waivable when the person makes a competent decision that continued life is no longer wanted or a good, but is instead worse than no further life at all. In this view, euthanasia is properly understood as a case of a person having waived his or her right not to be killed.

This rights view of the wrongness of killing is not, of course, universally shared. Many people's moral views about killing have their origins in religious views that human life comes from God and cannot be justifiably destroyed or taken away, either by the person whose life it is or by another. But in a pluralistic society like our own with a strong commitment to freedom of religion, public policy should not be grounded in religious beliefs which many in that society reject. I turn now to the general evaluation of public policy on euthanasia.

WOULD THE BAD CONSEQUENCES OF EUTHANASIA OUTWEIGH THE GOOD?

The argument against euthanasia at the policy level is stronger than at the level of individual cases, though even here I believe the case is ultimately unpersuasive, or at best indecisive. The policy level is the place where the main issues lie, however, and where moral considerations that might override arguments in favor of euthanasia will be found, if they are found anywhere. It is important to note two kinds of disagreement about the consequences for public policy of permitting euthanasia. First, there is empirical or factual disagreement about what the consequences would be. This disagreement is greatly exacerbated by the lack of firm data on the issue. Second, since on any reasonable assessment there would be both good and bad consequences, there are moral disagreements about the relative importance of different effects. In addition to these two sources of disagreement, there is also no single, well-specified policy proposal for legalizing euthanasia on which policy assessments can focus. But without such specification, and especially without explicit procedures for protecting against well-intentioned misuse and ill-intentioned abuse, the consequences for policy are largely speculative. Despite these difficulties, a preliminary account of the main likely good and bad consequences is possible. This should help clarify where better data or more moral analysis and argument are needed, as well as where policy safeguards must be developed.

POTENTIAL GOOD CONSEQUENCES OF PERMITTING EUTHANASIA

What are the likely good consequences? First, if euthanasia were permitted it would be possible to respect the self-determination of competent patients who want it, but now cannot get it because of its illegality. . . .

One important factor substantially affecting the number of persons who would seek euthanasia is the extent to which an alternative is available. The widespread acceptance in the law, social policy, and medical practice of the right of a competent patient to forgo life-sustaining treatment suggests that the number of competent persons in the United States who would want euthanasia if it were permitted is probably relatively small.

A second good consequence of making euthanasia legally permissible benefits a much larger group. Polls have shown that a majority of the American public believes that people should have a right to obtain euthanasia if they want it.[2] No doubt the vast majority of those who support this right to euthanasia will never in fact come to want euthanasia for themselves. Nevertheless, making it legally permissible would reassure many people that if they ever do want euthanasia they would be able to obtain it. This reassurance would supplement the broader control over the process of dying given by the right to decide about life-sustaining treatment. . . .

A third good consequence of the legalization of euthanasia concerns patients whose dying is filled with severe and unrelievable pain or suffering. When there is a life-sustaining treatment that, if forgone, will lead relatively quickly to death, then doing so can bring an end to these patients' suffering without recourse to euthanasia. For patients receiving no such treatment, however, euthanasia may be the only release from their otherwise prolonged suffering and agony. This argument from mercy has always been the strongest argument for euthanasia in those cases to which it applies.[3]

The importance of relieving pain and suffering is less controversial than is the frequency with which patients are forced to undergo untreatable agony that only euthanasia could relieve. If we focus first on suffering caused by physical pain, it is crucial to distinguish pain that *could* be adequately relieved with modern methods of pain control, though it in fact is not, from pain that is relievable only by death.[4] For a variety of reasons, including some physicians' fear of hastening the patient's death, as well as the lack of a publicly accessible means for assessing the amount of the patient's pain, many patients suffer pain that could be, but is not, relieved.

Specialists in pain control, as for example the pain of terminally ill cancer patients, argue that there are very few patients whose pain could not be adequately controlled, though sometimes at the cost of so sedating them that they are effectively unable to interact with other people or their environment. Thus, the argument from mercy in cases of physical pain can probably be met in a large majority of cases by providing adequate measures of pain relief. This should be a high priority, whatever our legal policy on euthanasia—the relief of pain and suffering has long been, quite properly, one of the central goals of medicine. Those cases in which pain could be effectively relieved, but in fact is not, should only count significantly in favor of legalizing euthanasia if all reasonable efforts to change pain management techniques have been tried and have failed.

Dying patients often undergo substantial psychological suffering that is not fully or even principally the result of physical pain.[5] The knowledge about how to relieve this suffering is much more limited than in the case of relieving pain, and efforts to do so are probably more often unsuccessful. If the argument from mercy is extended to patients experiencing great and unrelievable psychological suffering, the numbers of patients to which it applies are much greater.

One last good consequence of legalizing euthanasia is that once death has been accepted, it is often more humane to end life quickly and peacefully, when that is what the patient wants. Such a death will often be seen as better than a more prolonged one. People who suffer a sudden and unexpected death, for example by dying quickly or in their sleep from a heart attack or stroke, are often considered lucky to have died in this way. We care about how we die in part because we care about how others remember us, and we hope they will remember us as we were in "good times" with them and not as we might be when disease has robbed us of our dignity as human beings. . . .

POTENTIAL BAD CONSEQUENCES
OF PERMITTING EUTHANASIA

Some of the arguments against permitting euthanasia are aimed specifically against physicians, while others are aimed against anyone being permitted to perform it. I shall first consider one argument of the former sort. Permitting physicians to perform euthanasia, it is said, would be incompatible with their fundamental moral and professional commitment as healers to care for patients and to protect life. Moreover, if euthanasia by physicians became common, patients would come to fear that a medication was intended not to treat or care, but instead to kill, and would thus lose trust in their physicians. This position was forcefully stated in a paper by Willard Gaylin and his colleagues:

> The very soul of medicine is on trial. This issue touches medicine at its moral center; if this moral center collapses, if physicians become killers or are even licensed to kill, the profession—and, therewith, each physician—will never again be worthy of trust and respect as healer and comforter and protector of life in all its frailty.

These authors go on to make clear that, while they oppose permitting anyone to perform euthanasia, their special concern is with physicians doing so:

> We call on fellow physicians to say that they will not deliberately kill. We must also say to each of our fellow physicians that we will not tolerate killing of patients and that we shall take disciplinary action against doctors who kill. And we must say to the broader community that if it insists on tolerating or legalizing active euthanasia, it will have to find nonphysicians to do its killing.[6]

If permitting physicians to kill would undermine the very "moral center" of medicine, then almost certainly physicians should not be permitted to perform euthanasia. But how persuasive is this claim? Patients should not fear, as a consequence of permitting *voluntary* active euthanasia, that their physicians will substitute a lethal injection for what patients want and believe is part of their care. If active euthanasia is restricted to cases in which it is truly voluntary, then no patient should fear getting it unless she or he has voluntarily requested it. (The fear that we might in time also come to accept nonvoluntary, or even involuntary, active euthanasia is a slippery slope worry I address below.) Patients' trust of their physicians could be increased, not eroded, by knowledge that physicians will provide aid in dying when patients seek it. . . .

A second bad consequence that some foresee is that permitting euthanasia would weaken society's commitment to provide optimal care for dying patients. We live at a time in which the control of health care costs has become, and is likely to continue to be, the dominant focus of health care policy. If euthanasia is seen as a cheaper alternative to adequate care and treatment, then we might become less scrupulous about providing sometimes costly support and other services to dying patients. Particularly if our society comes to embrace deeper and more explicit rationing of health care, frail, elderly, and dying patients will need to be strong and effective advocates for their own health care and other needs, although they are hardly in a position to do this. We should do nothing to weaken their ability to obtain adequate care and services.

This second worry is difficult to assess because there is little firm evidence about the likelihood of the feared erosion in the care of dying patients. There are at least two reasons, however, for skepticism about this argument. The first is that the same worry could have been directed at recognizing patients' or surrogates' rights to forgo life-sustaining treatment, yet there is no persuasive evidence that recognizing the right to refuse treatment has caused a serious erosion in the quality of care of dying patients. The second reason for skepticism about this worry is that only a very small proportion of deaths would occur from euthanasia if it were permitted. In the Netherlands, where euthanasia under specified circumstances is permitted by the courts, though not authorized by statute, the best estimate of the proportion of overall deaths that result from it is about 2 percent.[7] Thus, the vast majority of critically ill and dying patients will not request it, and so will still have to be cared for by physicians, families, and others. Permitting euthanasia

should not diminish people's commitment and concern to maintain and improve the care of these patients.

A third possible bad consequence of permitting euthanasia (or even a public discourse in which strong support for euthanasia is evident) is to threaten the progress made in securing the rights of patients or their surrogates to decide about and to refuse life-sustaining treatment.[8] This progress has been made against the backdrop of a clear and firm legal prohibition of euthanasia, which has provided a relatively bright line limiting the dominion of others over patients' lives. It has therefore been an important reassurance to concerns about how the authority to take steps ending life might be misused, abused, or wrongly extended.

Many supporters of the right of patients or their surrogates to refuse treatment strongly oppose euthanasia, and if forced to choose might well withdraw their support of the right to refuse treatment rather than accept euthanasia. Public policy in the last fifteen years has generally let life-sustaining treatment decisions be made in health care settings between physicians and patients or their surrogates, and without the involvement of the courts. However, if euthanasia is made legally permissible greater involvement of the courts is likely, which could in turn extend to a greater court involvement in life-sustaining treatment decisions. Most agree, however, that increased involvement of the courts in these decisions would be undesirable, as it would make sound decisionmaking more cumbersome and difficult without sufficient compensating benefits.

As with the second potential bad consequence of permitting euthanasia, this third consideration too is speculative and difficult to assess. The feared erosion of patients' or surrogates' rights to decide about life-sustaining treatment, together with greater court involvement in those decisions, are both possible. However, I believe there is reason to discount this general worry. The legal rights of competent patients and, to a lesser degree, surrogates of incompetent patients to decide about treatment are very firmly embedded in a long line of informed consent and life-sustaining treatment cases, and are not likely to be eroded by a debate over, or even acceptance of, euthanasia. It will not be accepted without safeguards that reassure the public about abuse, and if that debate shows the need for similar safeguards for some life-sustaining treatment decisions they should be adopted there as well. In neither case are the only possible safeguards greater court involvement, as the recent growth of institutional ethics committees shows.

The fourth potential bad consequence of permitting euthanasia has been developed by David Velleman and turns on the subtle point that making a new option or choice available to people can sometimes make them worse off, even if once they have the choice they go on to choose what is best for them.[9] Ordinarily, people's continued existence is viewed by them as given, a fixed condition with which they must cope. Making euthanasia available to people as an option denies them the alternative of staying alive by default. If people are offered the option of euthanasia, their continued existence is now a choice for which they can be held responsible and which they can be asked by others to justify. We care, and are right to care, about being able to justify ourselves to others. To the extent that our society is unsympathetic to justifying a severely dependent or impaired existence, a heavy psychological burden of proof may be placed on patients who think their terminal illness or chronic infirmity is not a sufficient reason for dying. Even if they otherwise view their life as worth living, the opinion of others around them that it is not can threaten their reason for living and make euthanasia a rational choice. Thus the existence of the option becomes a subtle pressure to request it.

This argument correctly identifies the reason why offering some patients the option of euthanasia would not benefit them. Velleman takes it not as a reason for opposing all euthanasia, but for restricting it to circumstances where there are "unmistakable and overpowering reasons for persons to want the option of euthanasia," and for denying the option in all other cases. But there are at least three reasons why such restriction may not be warranted. First, polls and other evidence support that most Americans believe euthanasia should be permitted (though the recent defeat of the referendum to permit it in the state of Washington raises some doubt about this support). Thus, many more people seem to want the choice than would be made worse off by getting it. Second, if giving people the option of ending their life really makes them worse off, then we should not only prohibit euthanasia, but also take back from people the right they now have to decide about life-sustaining treatment. The feared harmful effect should already have oc-

curred from securing people's right to refuse life-sustaining treatment, yet there is no evidence of any such widespread harm or any broad public desire to rescind that right. Third, since there is a wide range of conditions in which reasonable people can and do disagree about whether they would want continued life, it is not possible to restrict the permissibility of euthanasia as narrowly as Velleman suggests without thereby denying it to most persons who would want it; to permit it only in cases in which virtually everyone would want it would be to deny it to most who would want it.

A fifth potential bad consequence of making euthanasia legally permissible is that it might weaken the general legal prohibition of homicide. This prohibition is so fundamental to civilized society, it is argued, that we should do nothing that erodes it. If most cases of stopping life support are killing, as I have already argued, then the court cases permitting such killing have already in effect weakened this prohibition. However, neither the courts nor most people have seen these cases as killing and so as challenging the prohibition of homicide. The courts have usually grounded patients' or their surrogates' rights to refuse life-sustaining treatment in rights to privacy, liberty, self-determination, or bodily integrity, not in exceptions to homicide laws.

Legal permission for physicians or others to perform euthanasia could not be grounded in patients' rights to decide about medical treatment. Permitting euthanasia would require qualifying, at least in effect, the legal prohibition against homicide, a prohibition that in general does not allow the consent of the victim to justify or excuse the act. Nevertheless, the very same fundamental basis of the right to decide about life-sustaining treatment—respecting a person's self-determination—does support euthanasia as well. Individual self-determination has long been a well-entrenched and fundamental value in the law, and so extending it to euthanasia would not require appeal to novel legal values or principles. That suicide or attempted suicide is no longer a criminal offense in virtually all states indicates an acceptance of individual self-determination in the taking of one's own life analogous to that required for voluntary active euthanasia. The legal prohibition (in most states) of assisting in suicide and the refusal in the law to accept the consent of the victim as a possible justification of homicide are both arguably a result of difficulties in the legal process of establishing the consent of the victim after the fact. If procedures can be designed that clearly establish the voluntariness of the person's request for euthanasia, it would under those procedures represent a carefully circumscribed qualification on the legal prohibition of homicide. Nevertheless, some remaining worries about this weakening can be captured in the final potential bad consequence, to which I will now turn.

This final potential bad consequence is the central concern of many opponents of euthanasia and, I believe, is the most serious objection to a legal policy permitting it. According to this "slippery slope" worry, although active euthanasia may be morally permissible in cases in which it is unequivocally voluntary and the patient finds his or her condition unbearable, a legal policy permitting euthanasia would inevitably lead to active euthanasia being performed in many other cases in which it would be morally wrong. To prevent those other wrongful cases of euthanasia we should not permit even morally justified performance of it.

Slippery slope arguments of this form are problematic and difficult to evaluate.[10] From one perspective, they are the last refuge of conservative defenders of the status quo. When all the opponent's objections to the wrongness of euthanasia itself have been met, the opponent then shifts ground and acknowledges both that it is not in itself wrong and that a legal policy which resulted only in its being performed would not be bad. Nevertheless, the opponent maintains, it should still not be permitted because doing so would result in its being performed in other cases in which it is not voluntary and would be wrong. In this argument's most extreme form, permitting euthanasia is the first and fateful step down the slippery slope to Nazism. Once on the slope we will be unable to get off.

Now it cannot be denied that it is *possible* that permitting euthanasia could have these fateful consequences, but that cannot be enough to warrant prohibiting it if it is otherwise justified. A similar *possible* slippery slope worry could have been raised to securing competent patients' rights to decide about life support, but recent history shows such a worry would have been unfounded. It must be relevant how likely it is that we will end with horrendous consequences and an unjustified practice of euthanasia. How *likely* and *widespread* would the abuses and unwarranted extensions of permitting it be? By abuses, I mean the performance of euthanasia that fails to satisfy the conditions required for voluntary active euthanasia, for example, if the patient has been subtly pressured to accept it. By unwarranted extensions of policy, I mean

later changes in legal policy to permit not just voluntary euthanasia, but also euthanasia in cases in which, for example, it need not be fully voluntary. Opponents of voluntary euthanasia on slippery slope grounds have not provided the data or evidence necessary to turn their speculative concerns into well-grounded likelihoods.

It is at least clear, however, that both the character and likelihood of abuses of a legal policy permitting euthanasia depend in significant part on the procedures put in place to protect against them. I will not try to detail fully what such procedures might be, but will just give some examples of what they might include:

1. The patient should be provided with all relevant information about his or her medical condition, current prognosis, available alternative treatments, and the prognosis of each.
2. Procedures should ensure that the patient's request for euthanasia is stable or enduring (a brief waiting period could be required) and fully voluntary (an advocate for the patient might be appointed to ensure this).
3. All reasonable alternatives must have been explored for improving the patient's quality of life and relieving any pain or suffering.
4. A psychiatric evaluation should ensure that the patient's request is not the result of a treatable psychological impairment such as depression.[11]

These examples of procedural safeguards are all designed to ensure that the patient's choice is fully informed, voluntary, and competent, and so a true exercise of self-determination. Other proposals for euthanasia would restrict its permissibility further—for example, to the terminally ill—a restriction that cannot be supported by self-determination. Such additional restrictions might, however, be justified by concern for limiting potential harms from abuse. At the same time, it is important not to impose procedural or substantive safeguards so restrictive as to make euthanasia impermissible or practically infeasible in a wide range of justified cases.

These examples of procedural safeguards make clear that it is possible to substantially reduce, though not to eliminate, the potential for abuse of a policy permitting voluntary active euthanasia. Any legalization of the practice should be accompanied by a well-considered set of procedural safeguards together with an ongoing evaluation of its use. Introducing euthanasia into only a few states could be a form of carefully limited and controlled social experiment that would give us evidence about the benefits and harms of the practice. Even then firm and uncontroversial data may remain elusive, as the continuing controversy over what has taken place in the Netherlands in recent years indicates.[12]

THE SLIP INTO NONVOLUNTARY ACTIVE EUTHANASIA

While I believe slippery slope worries can largely be limited by making necessary distinctions both in principle and in practice, one slippery slope concern is legitimate. There is reason to expect that legalization of voluntary active euthanasia might soon be followed by strong pressure to legalize some nonvoluntary euthanasia of incompetent patients unable to express their own wishes. Respecting a person's self-determination and recognizing that continued life is not always of value to a person can support not only voluntary active euthanasia, but some nonvoluntary euthanasia as well. These are the same values that ground competent patients' right to refuse life-sustaining treatment. Recent history here is instructive. In the medical ethics literature, in the courts since Quinlan, and in norms of medical practice, that right has been extended to incompetent patients and exercised by a surrogate who is to decide as the patient would have decided in the circumstances if competent.[13] It has been held unreasonable to continue life-sustaining treatment that the patient would not have wanted just because the patient now lacks the capacity to tell us that. Life-sustaining treatment for incompetent patients is today frequently forgone on the basis of a surrogate's decision, or less frequently on the basis of an advance directive executed by the patient while still competent. The very same logic that has extended the right to refuse life-sustaining treatment from a competent patient to the surrogate of an incompetent patient (acting with or without a formal advance directive from the patient) may well extend the scope of active euthanasia. The argument will be, Why continue to force unwanted life on patients just because they have now lost the capacity to request euthanasia from us? . . .

Even if voluntary active euthanasia should slip into nonvoluntary active euthanasia, with surrogates acting for incompetent patients, the ethical evaluation is more complex than many opponents of euthanasia allow.

Just as in the case of surrogates' decisions to forgo life-sustaining treatment for incompetent patients, so also surrogates' decisions to request euthanasia for incompetent persons would often accurately reflect what the incompetent person would have wanted and would deny the person nothing that he or she would have considered worth having. Making nonvoluntary active euthanasia legally permissible, however, would greatly enlarge the number of patients on whom it might be performed and substantially enlarge the potential for misuse and abuse. As noted above, frail and debilitated elderly people, often demented or otherwise incompetent and thereby unable to defend and assert their own interests, may be especially vulnerable to unwanted euthanasia.

For some people, this risk is more than sufficient reason to oppose the legalization of voluntary euthanasia. But while we should in general be cautious about inferring much from the experience in the Netherlands to what our own experience in the United States might be, there may be one important lesson that we can learn from them. One commentator has noted that in the Netherlands families of incompetent patients have less authority than do families in the United States to act as surrogates for incompetent patients in making decisions to forgo life-sustaining treatment.[14] From the Dutch perspective, it may be we in the United States who are *already* on the slippery slope in having given surrogates broad authority to forgo life-sustaining treatment for incompetent persons. In this view, the more important moral divide, and the more important with regard to potential for abuse, is not between forgoing life-sustaining treatment and euthanasia, but instead between voluntary and nonvoluntary performance of either. If this is correct, then the more important issue is ensuring the appropriate principles and procedural safeguards for the exercise of decisionmaking authority by surrogates for incompetent persons in *all* decisions at the end of life. This may be the correct response to slippery slope worries about euthanasia. . . .

NOTES

1. Willard Gaylin, Leon R. Kass, Edmund D. Pellegrino, and Mark Siegler, "Doctors Must Not Kill," *JAMA* 259 (1988): 2139–40.

2. P. Painton and E. Taylor, "Love or Let Die," *Time*, 19 March 1990, pp. 62–71; *Boston Globe*/Harvard University Poll, *Boston Globe*, 3 November 1991.

3. James Rachels, *The End of Life* (Oxford: Oxford University Press, 1986).

4. Marcia Angell, "The Quality of Mercy," *NEJM* 306 (1982): 98–99; M. Donovan, P. Dillon, and L. Mcguire, "Incidence and

Characteristics of Pain in a Sample of Medical-Surgical Inpatients," *Pain* 30 (1987): 69–78.

5. Eric Cassell, *The Nature of Suffering and the Goals of Medicine* (New York: Oxford University Press, 1991).

6. Gaylin et al., "Doctors Must Not Kill."

7. Paul J. Van der Maas et al., "Euthanasia and Other Medical Decisions Concerning the End of Life," *Lancet* 338 (1991): 669–674.

8. Susan M. Wolf, "Holding the Line on Euthanasia," Special Supplement, *Hastings Center Report* 19, no. 1 (1989): 13–15.

9. My formulation of this argument derives from David Velleman's statement of it in his commentary on an earlier version of this paper delivered at the American Philosophical Association Central Division meetings; a similar point was made to me by Elisha Milgram in discussion on another occasion.

10. Frederick Schauer, "Slippery Slopes," *Harvard Law Re-view* 99 (1985): 361–83; Wibren van der Burg, "The Slippery Slope Argument," *Ethics* 102 (October 1991): 42–65.

11. There is evidence that physicians commonly fail to diagnose depression. See Robert I. Misbin, "Physicians Aid in Dying," *NEJM* 325 (1991): 1304–7.

12. Richard Fenigsen, "A Case against Dutch Euthanasia," Special Supplement, *Hastings Center Report* 19, no. 1 (1989): 22–30.

13. Allen E. Buchanan and Dan W. Brock, *Deciding for Others: The Ethics of Surrogate Decisionmaking* (Cambridge: Cambridge University Press, 1989).

14. Margaret P. Battin, "Seven Caveats Concerning the Discussion of Euthanasia in Holland," *American Philosophical Association Newsletter on Philosophy and Medicine* 89, no. 2 (1990).

JOHN D. ARRAS

Physician-Assisted Suicide: A Tragic View

John Arras is the Porterfield Professor of Biomedical Ethics, professor of philosophy, and director of the Undergraduate Program in Bioethics at the University of Virginia. He was for fourteen years a professor of bioethics at Montefiore Medical Center/Albert Einstein College of Medicine and adjunct professor of philosophy at Barnard College, Columbia University. A former member of the New York State Task Force on Life and Law, Dr. Arras is the editor (with Bonnie Steinbock) of *Ethical Issues in Modern Medicine, 4th ed.*, and *Bringing the Hospital Home: Ethical and Social Implications of High Technology Home Care*, and the author of numerous articles on bioethics.

For many decades now, the calls the PAS and euthanasia have been perennial lost causes in American society. Each generation has thrown up an assortment of earnest reformers and cranks who, after attracting their fifteen minutes of fame, inevitably have been defeated by the combined weight of traditional law and morality. Incredibly, two recent federal appellate court decisions suddenly changed the legal landscape in this area, making the various states within their respective jurisdictions the first governments in world history, excepting perhaps the Nazi regime in Germany, to officially sanction PAS. Within the space of

a month, both an eight-to-three majority of the United States Court of Appeals for the Ninth Circuit[1] on the West Coast, and a three-judge panel in the United States Court of Appeals for the Second Circuit,[2] in the Northeast, struck down long-standing state laws forbidding physicians to aid or abet their patients in acts of suicide. Within a virtual blink of an eye, the unthinkable had come to pass: PAS and euthanasia had emerged from their exile beyond the pale of law to occupy center stage in a dramatic public debate that eventually culminated in the United States Supreme Court's unanimous reversal of both lower court decisions in June 1997.[3]

Judge Reinhardt, writing for a majority of an *en banc* decision of the Ninth Circuit,[4] held that competent, terminally ill patients have a powerful "liberty

From Margaret P. Battin, Rosamond Rhodes, and Anita Silvers, *Physician Assisted Suicide: Expanding the Debate.* New York and London: Routledge 1998, 279–300. Footnotes renumbered.

interest," what used to be called a Constitutional right, to enlist the aid of their physicians in hastening death via prescriptions for lethal drugs.[5] He argued that, just as the right to privacy guarantees women the right to choose an abortion, this liberty interest protects a right to choose the time and manner of one's death.[6] . . .

Writing for the Second Circuit in striking down a similar New York statute, Judge Miner explicitly rejected the claim of the Second Circuit majority that a "substantive due process" right of PAS exists in the Constitution. While presciently conceding that the Supreme Court was unlikely to extend the boundaries of the so-called right to privacy, Judge Miner found nevertheless that the statute violated the equal protection clause of the Constitution. . . .

The Supreme Court has finally left little doubt about where it stands on these questions. In a set of majority and concurring opinions remarkable for their ideological restraint, compassion, and thoughtfulness, the various Justices have concluded that extant state laws barring PAS and euthanasia violate neither the Fourteenth Amendment protection of liberty nor the Fifth Amendment's due process provision.[8] While thus issuing a painful rebuke to the partisans of liberalization, each of the Justices tempered his or her final judgment with the recognition that their collective decision would by no means end public debate, but would rather displace it onto the agendas of the fifty state legislatures.

As a firm believer in patient autonomy, I find myself to be deeply sympathetic to the central values motivating the case for PAS and euthanasia; I have concluded, however, that these practices pose too great a threat to the rights and welfare of too many people to be legalized in this country at the present time. Central to my argument in this essay will be the claim that the recently overturned decisions of the circuit courts employ a form of case-based reasoning that is ill-suited to the development of sound social policy in this area. I shall argue that in order to do justice to the very real threats posed by the widespread social practices of PAS and euthanasia, we need to adopt precisely the kind of policy perspective that the circuit courts rejected on principle. Thus, this essay presents the case for a forward-looking, legislative approach to PAS and euthanasia, as opposed to an essentially backward-looking, judicial or constitutional approach. Although I suggest below that the soundest legislative

policy at the present time would be to extend the legal prohibition of PAS into the near future, I remain open to the possibility that a given legislature, presented with sufficient evidence of the reliability of various safeguards, might come to a different conclusion. . . .

OBJECTIONS TO PAS/EUTHANASIA

Opponents of PAS and euthanasia can be grouped into three main factions. One strongly condemns both practices as inherently immoral, as violations of the moral rule against killing the innocent. Most members of this group tend to harbor distinctly religious objections to suicide and euthanasia, viewing them as violations of God's dominion over human life.[9] They argue that killing is simply wrong in itself, whether or not it is done out of respect for the patient's autonomy or out of concern for her suffering. Whether or not this position ultimately is justifiable from a theological point of view, its imposition on believers and nonbelievers alike is incompatible with the basic premises of a secular, pluralistic political order.

A second faction primarily objects to the fact that physicians are being called upon to do the killing. While conceding that killing the terminally ill or assisting in their suicides might not always be morally wrong for others to do, this group maintains that the participation of physicians in such practices undermines their role as healers and fatally compromises the physician-patient relationship.[10]

Finally, a third faction readily grants that neither PAS nor active euthanasia, practiced by ordinary citizens or by physicians, are always morally wrong. On the contrary, this faction believes that in certain rare instances early release from a painful or intolerably degrading existence might constitute both a positive good and an important exercise of personal autonomy for the individual. Indeed, many members of this faction concede that should such a terrible fate befall them, they would hope to find a thoughtful, compassionate, and courageous physician to release them from their misery. But in spite of these important concessions, the members of this faction shrink from endorsing or regulating PAS and active euthanasia due to fears bearing on the social consequences of liberalization. This view is based on two distinct kinds of so-called "slippery slope" arguments. One bears on the inability to cabin PAS/euthanasia within the confines envisioned by its proponents; the other focuses on the likelihood of abuse, neglect, and mistake.

The first version of the slippery slope argument contends that a socially sanctioned practice of PAS would in all likelihood prove difficult, if not impossible, to cabin within its originally anticipated boundaries. Proponents of legalization usually begin with a wholesomely modest policy agenda, limiting their suggested reforms to a narrow and highly specified range of potential candidates and practices.[11] "Give us PAS," they ask, "not the more controversial practice of active euthanasia, for presently competent patients who are terminally ill and suffering unbearable pain." But the logic of the case for PAS, based as it is upon the twin pillars of patient autonomy and mercy, makes it highly unlikely that society could stop with this modest proposal once it had ventured out on the slope. As numerous other critics have pointed out, if autonomy is the prime consideration, then additional constraints based upon terminal illness or unbearable pain, or both, would appear hard to justify.[12] Indeed, if autonomy is crucial, the requirement of unbearable suffering would appear to be entirely subjective. Who is to say, other than the patient herself, how much suffering is too much? Likewise, the requirement of terminal illness seems an arbitrary standard against which to judge patients' own subjective evaluation of their quality of life. If my life is no longer worth living, why should a terminally ill cancer patient be granted PAS but not me, merely because my suffering is due to my "nonterminal" arterio-lateral sclerosis ("ALS") or intractable psychiatric disorder?[13]

Alternatively, if pain and suffering are deemed crucial to the justification of legalization, it is hard to see how the proposed barrier of contemporaneous consent of competent patients could withstand serious erosion. If the logic of PAS is at all similar to that of forgoing life-sustaining treatments, and we have every reason to think it so, then it would seem almost inevitable that a case soon would be made to permit PAS for incompetent patients who had left advance directives. That would then be followed by a "substituted judgment" test for patients who "would have wanted" PAS, and finally an "objective" test would be developed for patients (including newborns) whose best interests would be served by PAS or active euthanasia even in the absence of any subjective intent.[14]

In the same way, the joint justification of autonomy and mercy combine to undermine the plausibil-ity of a line drawn between PAS and active euthanasia. As the authors of one highly publicized proposal have come to see, the logic of justification for active euthanasia is identical to that of PAS.[15] Legalizing PAS, while continuing to ban active euthanasia, would serve only to discriminate unfairly against patients who are suffering and wish to end their lives, but cannot do so because of some physical impairment. Surely these patients, it will be said, are "the worst off group," and therefore they are the most in need of the assistance of others who will do for them what they can no longer accomplish on their own.

None of these initial slippery slope considerations amount to knock-down objections to further liberalization of our laws and practices. After all, it is not obvious that each of these highly predictable shifts (e.g., from terminal to "merely" incurable, from contemporaneous consent to best interests, and from PAS to active euthanasia), are patently immoral and unjustifiable. Still, in pointing out this likely slippage, the consequentialist opponents of PAS/euthanasia are calling on society to think about the likely consequences of taking the first tentative step onto the slope. If all of the extended practices predicted above pose substantially greater risks for vulnerable patients than the more highly circumscribed initial liberalization proposals, then we need to factor in these additional risks even as we ponder the more modest proposals.

THE LIKELIHOOD OF ABUSE

The second prong of the slippery slope argument argues that whatever criteria for justifiable PAS and active euthanasia ultimately are chosen, abuse of the system is highly likely to follow. In other words, patients who fall outside the ambit of our justifiable criteria will soon be candidates for death. This prong resembles what I have elsewhere called an "empirical slope" argument, as it is based not on the close logical resemblance of concepts or justifications, but rather on an empirical prediction of what is likely to happen when we insert a particular social practice into our existing social system.[16]

In order to reassure skeptics, the proponents of PAS/euthanasia concur that any potentially justifiable social policy in this area must meet at least the following three requirements.[17] The policy would have to insist: first, that all requests for death be truly voluntary; second, that all reasonable alternatives to PAS and active euthanasia must be explored before acceding to a patient's wishes; and, third, that a reliable system of reporting all cases must be establishes in order to effectively monitor these practices and respond to abuses. As a social pessimist on these matters, I believe, given social reality as we know it, that all three assumptions are problematic.

With regard to the voluntariness requirement, we pessimists contend that many requests would not be sufficiently voluntary. In addition to the subtly coercive influences of physicians and family members, perhaps the most slippery aspect of this slope is the highly predictable failure of most physicians to diagnose reliably and treat reversible clinical depression, particularly in the elderly population. As one geriatric psychiatrist testified before the New York Task Force, we now live in the "golden age" of treating depression, but the "lead age" of diagnosing it.[18] We have the tools, but physicians are not adequately trained and motivated to use them. Unless dramatic changes are effected in the practice of medicine, we can predict with confidence that many instances of PAS and active euthanasia will fail the test of voluntariness.

Second, there is the lingering fear that any legislative proposal or judicial mandate would have to be implemented within the present social system, one marked by deep and pervasive discrimination against the poor and members of minority groups. We have every reason to expect that a policy that worked tolerably well in an affluent community like Scarsdale or Beverly Hills might not work so well in a community like Bedford-Stuyvesant or Watts, where your average citizen has little or no access to basic primary care, let alone sophisticated care for chronic pain at home or in the hospital. There is also reason to worry about any policy of PAS initiated within our growing system of managed care, capitation, and physician incentives for delivering less care.[19] Expert palliative care no doubt is an expensive and time-consuming proposition, requiring more, rather than less, time spent just talking with patients and providing them with humane comfort. It is highly doubtful that the context of physician-patient conversation within this new dispensation of "turnstile medicine" will be at all conducive to humane decisions untainted by subtle economic coercion.

In addition, given the abysmal and shameful track record of physicians in responding adequately to pain and suffering, we also can confidently predict that in many cases all reasonable alternatives will *not* have been exhausted. Instead of vigorously addressing the pharmacological and psychosocial needs of such patients, physicians no doubt will continue to ignore, undertreat, or treat many of their patients in an impersonal manner. The result is likely to be more depression, desperation, and requests for physician-assisted death from patients who could have been successfully treated. The root causes of this predictable failure are manifold, but high on the list is the inaccessibility of decent primary care to over thirty-seven million Americans. Other notable causes include an appalling lack of training in palliative care among primary care physicians and cancer specialists alike; discrimination in the delivery of pain control and other medical treatments on the basis of race and economic status; various myths shared by both physicians and patients about the supposed ill effects of pain medications; and restrictive state laws on access to opioids.

Finally, with regard to the third requirement, pessimists doubt that any reporting system would adequately monitor these practices. A great deal depends here on the extent to which patients and practitioners will regard these practices as essentially *private* matters to be discussed and acted upon within the privacy of the doctor-patient relationship. As the Dutch experience has conclusively demonstrated, physicians will be extremely loath to report instances of PAS and active euthanasia to public authorities, largely for fear of bringing the harsh glare of publicity upon the patients' families at a time when privacy is most needed. The likely result of this predictable lack of oversight will be society's inability to respond appropriately to disturbing incidents and long-term trends. In other words, the practice most likely will not be as amenable to regulation as the proponents contend.

The moral of this story is that deeply seated inadequacies in physicians' training, combined with structural flaws in our healthcare system, can be reliably predicted to secure the premature deaths of many people who would in theory be excluded by the criteria of most leading proposals to legalize PAS. If this characterization of the status quo is at all accurate, then the problem will not be solved by well-meaning assurances that abuses will not be tolerated, or that patients will, of course, be offered the full range of palliative care options before any decision for PAS is ratified. . . .

We come now to the difficult task of assessing the capacity of various social policy approaches to address adequately all of the conflicting values implicated in this debate. This section shall contrast a forward-looking, policy-oriented legislative approach to the backward-looking, case-oriented judicial approach taken in the *Compassion in Dying* and *Vacco* cases. Before coming to that comparison, however, a crucial preliminary point must be noted. Central to any serious evaluation of competing policy approaches to PAS and euthanasia is the distinction between the morality of individual acts and the wisdom of social policy. Much of the debate in the popular media is driven by the depiction of especially dramatic and poignant instances of suffering humanity, desperate for release from the painful thrall of terminal illness. Understandably, many of us are prompted to respond: "Should such a terrible fate ever befall me, I certainly would not want to suffer interminably; I would want the option of an early exit and the help of my trusted physician in securing it." The problem, however, lies in getting from such compelling individual cases to social policy. The issue is not simply, "What should I want?" but rather, what is the best social policy, all things considered. Social pessimists warn that we cannot make this jump from individual case to policy without endangering the autonomy and the very lives of others, many of whom are numbered among our most vulnerable citizens.

A JUDGE-MADE POLICY BASED
ON CONSTITUTIONAL LAW

Appellate judges in the Ninth and Second Circuits authored powerful opinions giving constitutional protection to PAS for competent patients facing terminal illness. While these opinions fully vindicated patients' important stake in having a freely chosen and pain-free death, they seriously and fatally discounted the states' important interests in preventing the kinds of slippage and abuse catalogued above.

Dismissal of Social Consequences. The opinion of the Ninth Circuit, *Compassion in Dying,* authored by Judge Reinhardt, is particularly troubling with regard to the dismissal of social consequences. In response to the objection that legalizing PAS inevitably will prove "infinitely expansive," the court acknowledged the difficulty that it may be hard to distinguish the moral logic of PAS from that animating the call for direct physician-administered euthanasia. He further conceded that in some cases, patients will need the help of a physician in carrying out their choice of an autonomous and painless death. Instead of carefully weighing this sobering possibility in the balance, or asking whether this likelihood of slippage should make us hesitate in taking the first step onto the slope, the court immediately dismissed it as a problem for future cases, not this one, noting that, "here we decide only the issue before us."[20] For those who worry that direct euthanasia carried out by physicians might impose too great a risk in the current social climate, the dictum will prove less than comforting, especially in view of the judge's confession that "it [is] less important who administers the medication than who determines whether the terminally ill person's life shall end."[21]

Thus, although we have argued that this kind of forward-looking, policy-oriented perspective is crucial for adequately assessing the individual benefits and social risks involved in the proposal to legalize PAS, the judicial approach to the problem operates fully equipped with social blinders, and willfully dismisses the very real dangers lurking further down the slope, all in the name of individual rights. Indeed, at one point Judge Reinhardt implied that a refusal to contemplate such dangers is demanded by the judicial role itself.[22] To put it mildly and most charitably, this rights-oriented mind-set does not put us in a learning mode. When life and death are at stake, we need to base our social policy on a more comprehensive picture of the likely benefits and risks.

Judge Reinhardt's grasp of the clinical realities of depression and the ubiquitous absence of adequate pain control was no more impressive than the scope of his social vision. In response to the objection that the legalization of PAS eventually would lead physicians to treat requests to die in a routine and impersonal manner, Judge Reinhardt reassured us, in the face of massive evidence to the contrary, that "doctors would not assist a terminally ill patient to hasten his death as long as there were any reasonable chance of alleviating the patient's suffering or enabling him to live under tolerable conditions."[23] Judge Reinhardt's faith in professional and governmental regulations to ensure that all requests truly are voluntary (i.e., not due to depression), and free from the taint of untreated pain and suffering, is perhaps refreshing in the age of governmental regulation-bashing, but it is a naive and dangerous faith in all the same.

Equal Protection and the Fate of Responsible Regulation. The ability of a constitutional right to assisted suicide to provide adequately for safeguards against abuse, neglect, and mistake is especially problematic within the context of the Second Circuit's equal protection analysis in *Vacco*. That court's assertion of the moral and legal equivalence of withholding life-sustaining treatments, the provision of potentially death-hastening analgesics, and assisted suicide raised extremely troubling questions about the constitutionality of a wide variety of possibly effective regulations. The basic question is: If we have a constitutionally protected liberty interest in determining the time and manner of our deaths, then to what extent will various regulatory schemes cut too deeply into our personal choices?

We actually have seen this script played out before in the context of abortion law. Prior to *Roe v. Wade*, many states already had begun liberalizing their statutes to allow women to opt for abortion under specified conditions. One regulatory constraint that had been placed on women's choice in some jurisdictions was mandatory review by a hospital-based committee. Now, whether or not we think that such committee review was a good idea in the context of abortion—I do not think it was—it is still interesting to note that this regulatory mechanism, along with a host of others, was discarded unceremoniously by the Supreme Court in *Doe v. Bolton,*[24] the companion case to *Roe v. Wade*. In sum, the Court held that such mechanisms only serve to encumber the woman's choice, which really belongs to her (and perhaps also her doctor) alone.

Now, if the Second Circuit's equal protection analysis had prevailed, and had the Supreme Court come to see no cognizable legal or moral differences between "allowing to die" and assisted suicide, then presumably the regulatory mechanisms surrounding the two sets of practices would have been subjected to identical standards of moral analysis and judicial review. This kind of legally mandated parity would have had two likely consequences. First, all the paraphernalia of surrogate decision-making that currently surrounds decisions to forgo treatment would have been extended to PAS. Just as most states presently allow family or close friends to make life-and-death decisions for loved ones on the basis of so-called "substituted judgment" ("What would the patient have wanted?") or best-interests or reasonable-person determinations, so we would have to allow family members the same role in those cases in which suicide "would have been chosen" by the patient or "would have been" in his best interest. Obviously, this implication of the equal protection approach would have required proponents of PAS to bite a very large bullet indeed regarding the charge of indefinite expansion.

The second implication of the equal protection analysis is that a broad range of possibly helpful regulatory mechanisms, including waiting periods, committee review, second opinions, mandatory reporting, and perhaps even the requirement of terminal illness, might well have been swept aside in the name of individual liberty. Currently, we do not require these kinds of substantive and procedural constraints for most decisions to forgo life-sustaining treatments by competent, terminally ill patients. If, however, there is really no moral or legal difference between "allowing to die" and "assisting suicide"—if, as Judge Miner opines, adding PAS to our repertoire of choices would not add one iota of additional risk to individuals or society over and above those we already countenance—then encumbering the choice for PAS with all sorts of extra protective devices would seemingly lack constitutional validity. In sum, then, the equal protection analysis championed in the Second Circuit threatened precisely those braking mechanisms that arguably might make the slippery slope a far safer place on which to practice physician-assisted death.

The Conflation of Killing and Allowing to Die. Proceeding directly to the fulcrum of Judge Miner's analysis, we now consider the denial of a significant moral or legal difference between allowing a patient to die by means of forgoing life-sustaining treatments and assisting a patient in committing suicide. According to both circuit court opinions, there is no significant difference between withdrawing a ventilator, discontinuing a feeding tube, administering pain-killing but (potentially) life-shortening opioids, and prescribing a lethal dose of barbiturates.[25] In all these cases, the judges alleged, the intention is the same (i.e., to hasten death), the cause of death is the same (an *act* attributable to human agency), and the social risks of mistake and abuse are the same (e.g., misdiagnosis, undue pressure, etc.). Consequently, Judge Reinhardt concluded that PAS poses no greater threat to the state's interests in preventing suicide and in safeguarding the integrity of the medical profession than the already accepted practice of forgoing life-sustaining treatment. For identical reasons Judge Miner saw no point in a more restrictive public policy towards PAS and based his entire Constitutional argument upon the purported identity of the intentions and effects of these two social practices.[26]

Along with a majority of the Supreme Court, I wish to uphold, for purposes of social policy analysis, the distinction between forgoing treatment and assisting suicide. Although the boundaries between these two practices at times are admittedly quite fuzzy, overlooking relevant differences between them leads proponents of legalization to ignore the very real social risks inherent in the judicial approach to policy.[27]

Whatever the outcome of our long-standing conceptual skirmishes bearing on the "intrinsic" distinctions between PAS, direct euthanasia, and forgoing life-sustaining treatments, the crucial question remains whether any of the purported distinctions between these activities constitute important differences for purposes of social policy. As a slippery slope opponent of PAS and euthanasia, I have already conceded that individual acts involving either PAS or active euthanasia can be morally justified under certain circumstances. Having thus conceded that certain individual actions can be morally appropriate even when the intent is simply and unambiguously to end the patient's life, and even when "the cause" of death is simply and unambiguously attributable to the action of the physician, the crucial question is whether there are any remaining distinctions between allowing to die and actively killing (or assisting in a suicide) that might illuminate the negative policy implications of PAS and euthanasia.

Two points can be made in this connection. First, as the New York Task Force pointed out, the social consequences of not honoring requests to forgo treatment are very different from the consequences of failing to honor requests for PAS and euthanasia. When society fails to honor requests to prescribe or deliver a lethal dose, the results can admittedly be very onerous for individual patients. The patient may face a prolonged period of deterioration before death, with increased pain and decreased dignity, contrary to what they otherwise would have wished. It is important to note, however, that in many such cases there are alternatives to prolonged and painful deaths. Under the present legal regime it is still permissible for a patient to seek out effective and compassionate hospice care, to refuse further administration of life-sustaining treat-

ments, to request "terminal sedation" (inducing a loss of consciousness until death), and even to starve to death with the aid of a physician. It is also legal for an individual truly to take matters into his own hands and to kill himself, perhaps with the guidance of a popular "self-help" book. Finally, it is possible for many patients with good and trusting relationships with compassionate physicians to achieve their objectives within the bounds of private and discreet relationships, but without the cover and consolations of law.

By contrast, were society, systematically and as a matter of policy, to refuse to honor requests to forgo life-sustaining treatments in order to curb possible abuses, then everyone would have to submit to the imposition of unwanted and often invasive measures. Whereas the refusal to honor a request for PAS or direct euthanasia amounts to a refusal of a positive benefit or assistance, the imposition of medical treatment against one's will represents a violation of personal autonomy and physical integrity totally incompatible with the deepest meaning of our traditional respect for liberty. Such a refusal would entail the virtual imprisonment of the entire population of terminally ill and dying patients. While the failure to offer a deadly drug to a dying patient represents a failure of mercy requiring moral justification, the forced imposition of medical treatment against a patient's will arguably constitutes a trespass, or technically a legal battery, so profound that it simply cannot be justified, especially at the level of broad-gauged social policy.

Without trying to sound especially hyperbolical, we can say that the practice of forgoing treatment is by now so deeply embedded in our social and medical practices that a reversal of policy on this point would throw most of our major medical institutions into a state approaching chaos. The same cannot be said of a refusal to honor requests for PAS and euthanasia. Thus, while there may well be many overlapping similarities between withholding treatment and participating in PAS or euthanasia, their respective denial at the level of social policy would entail vastly different individual and social consequences. If our goal is to reduce the level of social risk surrounding all practices involving the treatment of incurable and/or dying patients, a blanket prohibition of PAS can arguably advance this goal without totally unacceptable moral, legal, and social consequences. The same cannot be said of a blanket prohibition of forgoing life-sustaining treatments.

The second point in this connection is that the practice of PAS and/or active euthanasia would be bound to implicate many more persons than the practice of forgoing treatment. While we should definitely worry about the possibility of error, neglect, and abuse in the context of allowing patients to die, it is at least somewhat comforting to realize that just about every patient in this category must be very badly off indeed. By the time that physicians discuss forgoing treatment with a patient or family, the patient is usually well into the process of dying.

With regard to PAS and euthanasia, however, we can expect that many candidates will be perfectly ambulatory and far from the dreaded scene of painful terminal illness depicted by advocates. Depending on how great the social slippage, this category may well come to encompass those with an incurable condition but who are not presently "terminal," such as persons in the early stages of HIV infection or Alzheimer's disease. It also may come to encompass patients suffering from prolonged and intractable depression who exhibit no other symptoms of physical illness. Although one important legislative proposal specifically excludes patients whose only symptoms are psychiatric in nature, this reluctance was likely motivated in no small measure by political considerations.[28] Once PAS or active euthanasia, or both, are firmly in place, however, it will be extremely difficult to withhold them from persons whose suffering is every bit as real but whose source is entirely psychological rather than physical. That, Judge Miner and many others would surely object, would constitute an invidious distinction and thus a form of unconstitutional discrimination against the mentally ill.

IF THE STATES ARE THE LABORATORY, WHAT'S THE EXPERIMENT?

Although the Ninth Circuit was prepared to grant that states have a legitimate interest in avoiding the possibly adverse social consequences of PAS, the court insisted that regulation, rather than prohibition, is the only constitutionally permissible means of so doing.[29] Toward that end, it would have assigned the challenging task of crafting appropriate regulations to the "laboratory of the states." In view of the very real possibility that the social and individual harms attendant upon the legalization of PAS eventually would prove disproportionate to their benefits, this division of labor between the judiciary and the state legislatures is

highly problematic. Had the Supreme Court affirmed the Ninth Circuit's reasoning in granting constitutional protection to the liberty interest in choosing death, states would have been deprived of their ability to put a stop to the widespread practice of PAS even if credible studies were to demonstrate that abuses were rampant and highly resistant to procedural safeguards. Short of a Constitutional amendment, there would have been no turning back had the right to PAS been guaranteed by either the due process or equal protection clauses.

Instead of putting ourselves into this precarious position, we should assign a different and more fundamental task to the laboratory of the states. Given the very real possibilities for extension and abuse of this liberty interest, state legislatures should be entrusted with the basic questions of whether, when, and under what circumstances such a risky social experiment should be attempted in the first place. State legislatures are in a better position than federal judges to study the social and clinical facts and come to a reasonable conclusion on the likely balance of individual benefit and social risks. Given the social and medical realities of this country, I would hope that most states would follow the lead of the New York Task Force in refusing to countenance the legalization and routinization of PAS at this time. However, even if some states do decide to run these risks as a social experiment, i.e., to determine for themselves on the basis of empirical evidence and moral judgment whether more good than harm will come from legalizing PAS, they would have the flexibility, absent rigidly defined constitutional mandates, both to impose very strict regulations and, if necessary, to stop the experiment cold in the face of disconcerting evidence of serious moral slippage. Such an approach is, I believe, much better suited to asking the relevant policy questions and taking appropriate and prudent action.

In addition to being safer, the legislative approach is also, at least potentially, much more democratic than the judicial, rights-based orientation. The legislature is the traditional site in this country for the resolution of most difficult and divisive questions of social policy, especially those marked by deep moral questions and highly troubling empirical uncertainties involving the lives and welfare of many citizens. A court-mandated solution to the question of PAS would, I believe, have secured a decisive and irrevocable victory for one side of this controversy before a thorough and robust public debate had taken place. One significant merit of a legislative approach is that, while it would not guarantee such a debate, it would at least be compatible with large-scale efforts at the state and local levels to foster a more democratically deliberative public dialogue on this matter. Such efforts could give citizens a chance to weigh the nature and value of the liberties at stake against the extent and probability of the social dangers posed by PAS. They could thus serve as a valuable *via media* between the judicial approach, which can often short circuit public debate, and decision-making by public referendum, which is more democratic in theory but often lacks an explicitly deliberative dimension that would allow citizens a deeper understanding of the issues involved before their legislatures took action.

TOWARD A POLICY OF PRUDENT (LEGAL) RESTRAINT AND AGGRESSIVE (MEDICAL) INTERVENTION

In contrast to the judicial approach, which totally vindicates the value of patient autonomy at the expense of protecting the vulnerable, my own preferred approach to a social policy of PAS and euthanasia conceives of this debate as posing essentially a "tragic choice." It frankly acknowledges that whatever choice we make, whether we opt for a reaffirmation of the current legal restraints or for a policy of legitimation and regulation, there are bound to be victims. The victims of the current policy are easy to identify: They are on the news, the talk shows, the documentaries, and often on Dr. Kevorkian's roster of so-called "patient." The victims of legalization, by contrast, will be largely hidden from view; they will include the clinically depressed eighty-year-old man who could have lived for another year of good quality if only he had been adequately treated, and the fifty-year-old woman who asks for death because doctors in her financially stretched HMO cannot, or will not, effectively treat her unrelenting, but mysterious, pelvic pain. Perhaps eventually, if we slide far enough down the slope, the uncommunicative stroke victim, whose distant children deem an earlier death to be a better death, will fall victim. There will be others besides these, many coming from the ranks of the uninsured and the poor. To the extent that minorities and the poor already suffer from the effects of discrimination in our healthcare system, it is reasonable to expect that any system of PAS and euthanasia will exhibit similar effects, such as failure to access adequate primary care, pain management, and psychiatric diagnosis and treatment. Unlike Dr. Kevorkian's "patients," these victims will not get their pictures in the papers, but they all will have

faces and they will all be cheated of good months or perhaps even years.

This "tragic choice" approach to social policy on PAS/euthanasia takes the form of the following argument formulated at the legislative level. First, the number of "genuine cases" justifying PAS, active euthanasia, or both, will be relatively small. Patients who receive good personal care, good pain relief, treatment for depression, and adequate psychosocial supports tend not to persist in their desire to die.

Second, the social risks of legalization are serious and highly predictable. They include the expansion of these practices to nonvoluntary cases, the advent of active euthanasia, and the widespread failure to pursue readily available alternatives to suicide motivated by pain, depression, hopelessness, and lack of access to good primary medical care.

Third, rather than propose a momentous and dangerous policy shift for a relatively small number of "genuine cases"—a shift that would surely involve a great deal of persistent social division and strife analogous to that involved in the abortion controversy— we should instead attempt to redirect the public debate toward a goal on which we can and should all agree, namely the manifest and urgent need to reform the way we die in America. Instead of pursuing a highly divisive and dangerous campaign for PAS, we should attack the problem at its root with an ambitious program of reform in the areas of access to primary care and the education of physicians in palliative care. . . .

CONCLUSION

Instead of conceiving this momentous debate as a choice between, on the one hand, legalization and regulation with all of their attendant risks, and on the other hand, the callous abandonment of patients to their pain and suffering, enlightened opponents must recommend a positive program of clinical and social reforms. On the clinical level, physicians must learn how to really listen to their patients, to unflinchingly engage them in sensitive discussions of their needs and the meaning of their requests for assisted death, to deliver appropriate palliative care, to distinguish fact from fiction in the ethics and law of pain relief, to diagnose and treat clinical depression, and finally, to ascertain and respect their patients' wishes for control regarding the forgoing of life-sustaining treatments. On the social level, opponents of PAS must aggressively promote major initiatives in medical and public education regarding pain control, in the sensitization of insurance companies and licensing agencies to issues of the quality of dying, and in the reform of state laws that currently hinder access to pain relieving medications.

In the absence of an ambitious effort in the direction of aggressive medical and social reform, I fear that the medical and nursing professions will have lost whatever moral warrant and credibility they might still have in continuing to oppose physician-assisted suicide and active euthanasia. As soon as these reforms are in place, however, we might then wish to proceed slowly and cautiously with experiments in various states to test the overall benefits of a policy of legalization. Until that time, however, we are not well served as a society by court decisions allowing for legalization of PAS. The Supreme Court has thus reached a sound decision in ruling out a constitutional right to PAS. As the Justices acknowledged, however, this momentous decision will not end the moral debate over PAS and euthanasia. Indeed, it should and hopefully will intensify it.

NOTES

1. *Compassion in Dying v. Washington,* 79 F. 3d 790, 838 (9th Cir. 1996).

2. *Quill v. Vacco,* 80 F. 3d 716, 731 (2nd Cir. 1996).

3. *Vacco, Attorney General of New York, et al. v. Quill et al.,* certiorari to the United States Court of Appeals for the second circuit, No. 95–1858. Argued January 8, 1997—Decided June 26, 1997. *Washington et al. v. Glucksberg et al.,* certiorari to the United States Court of Appeals for the ninth circuit, No. 96–110. Argued January 8, 1997—Decided June 26, 1997.

4. See *Compassion in Dying,* 79 F. 3d at 790.

5. Ibid., 816.

6. Ibid., 813–14.

7. *Vacco v. Quill,* 80 F. 3d 716, 724–25 (2nd Cir. 1996).

8. *Washington v. Glucksberg,* 117 Sup. Ct. 2258 (1997). *Vacco v. Quill,* 117 Sup. Ct. 2293 (1997).

9. For religious objections to suicide and euthanasia, see St. Thomas Aquinas, "Whether It Is Lawful to Kill Oneself," in Tom L. Beauchamp and Robert Veatch, eds., *Ethical Issues in Death and Dying,* 2nd ed. (1996), pp. 119–21.

10. Willard Gaylin et al., "Doctors Must Not Kill," *Journal of the American Medical Association* 259 (1988): 2139–40. See also David Orentlicher, "Physician Participation in Assisted Suicide," *Journal of the American Medical Association* 262 (1989): 1844–45.

11. See Christine Cassel et al., "Care of the Hopelessly Ill: Proposed Clinical Criteria for Physician-Assisted Suicide," *New England Journal of Medicine* 327 (1992): 1380–84 (approving of PAS but not of active euthanasia because it poses excessive social risks).

12. See Daniel Callahan, *The Troubled Dream of Life: Living With Mortality* (New York: Simon and Schuster, 1993). See also Yale Kamisar, "Against Assisted Suicide-Even a Very Limited Form," *University of Detroit-Mercy Law Review* 72 (1995): 735.

13. ALS also is known as Lou Gehrig's disease.

14. *In re Conroy,* 486 A. 2d 1209 (1985) (summarizing the logic of foregoing life-sustaining treatments).

15. Cassel et al., "Care of the Hopelessly Ill," 1380–84. See also Franklin G. Miller et al., "Regulating Physician-Assisted Death," *New England Journal of Medicine* 331 (1994): 199–23 (conceding the untenability of the previous distinction).

16. John Arras, "The Right to Die on the Slippery Slope," *Social Theory and Practice* 8 (1982): 285 (describing the "slippery slope" argument in favor of PAS).

17. See, e.g., Cassel et al., "Care of the Hopelessly Ill"; Miller et al., "Regulating Physician-Assisted Death"; Charles H. Baron et al., "Statute A Model State Act to Authorize and Regulate Physician-Assisted Suicide," *Harvard Journal of Legislation* 33 (1996): 1.

18. Dr. Gary Kennedy, Division of Geriatrics, Montefiore Medical Center, Albert Einstein College of Medicine, Testimony before the New York Task Force on Life and the Law.

19. Susan M. Wolf, "Physician-Assisted Suicide in the Context of Managed Care," *Duquesne Law Review* 35 (1996): 455.

20. *Compassion in Dying v. Washington,* 79 F. 3d 790, 830–32 (9th Cir. 1996).

21. *Compassion in Dying,* 79 F. 3d 832.

22. Ibid., 831.

23. Ibid., 827.

24. 410 U.S. 179 (1973).

25. *Quill v. Vacco,* 80 F. 3d 716, 729 (2nd Cir. 1996); see also *Compassion in Dying v. Washington,* 79 F. 3d 790, 822–24 (9th Cir. 1996).

26. *Quill v. Vacco,* 80 F. 3d 716, 729 (2nd Cir. 1996).

27. Dan Brock, "Voluntary Active Euthanasia," *Hastings Center Report* 22 (1992): 10. See also Brock, "Borderline Cases of Morally Justified Taking Life in Medicine," in Tom Beauchamp, ed., *Intending Death: The Ethics of Assisted Suicide and Euthanasia* (Upper Saddle River, NJ: Prentice Hall, 1996): 131–49.

28. Baron et al., "A Model State Act to Authorize and Regulate Physician-Assisted Suicide,'"11.

29. *Compassion in Dying v. Washington,* 79 F. 3d 790, 832–33, 836–37 (9th Cir. 1996).

Public Policy in the Netherlands on Physician-Assisted Death

HENK JOCHEMSEN AND JOHN KEOWN

Voluntary Euthanasia under Control? Further Empirical Evidence from the Netherlands

Henk Jochemsen is director of the Lindeboom Institute in the Netherlands and has held the Lindeboom Chair of Medical Ethics at the Free University in Amsterdam since 1998. He is a member of the Ethics Commission of the Federation of Associations of Patients with Congenital Disease and from 1992 to 1996 was a member of the Board of Administration of the European Association of Centres of Medical Ethics. Currently he is an Advisory Board member of the Center for Bioethics and Human Dignity and a member of the European editorial board of the journal *Ethics and Medicine*.

John Keown is senior lecturer in the Law and Ethics of Medicine at the University of Cambridge and a senior research fellow at Churchill College, Cambridge. He has served as a member of the Medical Ethics Committee of the British Medical Association and as a member of the board of the Human Values in Health Care Forum. Dr. Keown has also served as governor and vice-chairman of the Linacre Centre for Health Care Ethics, vice-chairman of the Centre for Bioethics and Public Policy, and manager of the Ver Heyden de Lancey Fund for Medico-Legal Studies at the University of Cambridge. His books include *Abortion, Doctors and the Law: Some Aspects of the Legal Regulation of Abortion in England from 1803 to 1982* and the edited collection *Euthanasia Examined: Ethical, Clinical and Legal Perspectives*.

INTRODUCTION

Worldwide, the euthanasia debate continues to intensity. In 1997, the Australian parliament voted to repeal euthanasia legislation in the Northern Territory and the US Supreme Court upheld the constitutionality of legislation prohibiting "physician-assisted suicide."[1] In deciding whether euthanasia or assisted suicide should be permitted in principle, and whether they can be controlled in practice, the experience of the Netherlands, where they have been officially tol-

erated and widely practised for well over a decade, is clearly of profound importance.

Nineteen ninety-one saw the publication of the results of an important survey, by Professor P.I. van der Maas, into end-of-life decision making by Dutch doctors in the year 1990.[2] Despite claims to the contrary by supporters of Dutch euthanasia, this survey helped to cast serious doubt on Dutch claims that their guidelines were sufficiently strict effectively to control the practice of voluntary euthanasia (the intentional termination of patients' lives at their request) and to prevent non-voluntary euthanasia (the intentional termination of the lives of patients incapable of making a request).

The survey disclosed the widespread practice of non-voluntary euthanasia; the use of euthanasia even

From *Journal of Medical Science* 25, no. 1 (February 1999), 16–21. Footnotes renumbered.

Table 1. End-of-Life Decisions by Doctors in the Netherlands, 1990–1995

	1990	1995
Deaths in the Netherlands	129000 (100%)	135500 (100%)
Requests for euthanasia	8900 (7%)	9700 (7.1%)
Euthanasia	2300 (1.8%)	3200 (2.4%)
Assisted suicide	400 (0.3%)	400 (0.3%)
Life-terminating acts without explicit request	1000 (0.8%)	900 (0.7%)
Intensification of pain and symptom treatment	22500 (17.5%)	20000 (14.8%)
a. Explicitly intended to shorten life	1350 (1%)	2000 (1.5%)
b. Partly intended to shorten life	6750 (5.2%)	2850 (2.1%)
c. Taking into account the probability that life will be shortened	14400 (11.3%)	15150 (11.1%)
Withdrawal/withholding treatment (incl. tube-feeding)	22500 (17.5%)	27300 (20.1%)
a. At the explicit request of the patient	5800 (4.5%)	5200 (3.8%)
b. Without the explicit request of the patient		
b1. Explicitly intended to short life	2670 (2.1%)	14200 (10.5%)
b2. Partly intended to shorten life	3170 (2.5%)	—
b3. Taking into account the probability that life will be shortened	10850 (8.4%)	7900 (5.8%)
Intentional termination of neonates		
a. Without withholding/withdrawing treatment	—	10.00
b. Withholding/withdrawing treatment plus administration of medication explicitly to shorten life	—	80.00
Assisted suicide of psychiatric patients	—	2–5

when doctors thought that palliative care was a viable alternative, and the common practice by doctors of illegally certifying euthanasia deaths as deaths by "natural causes" instead of reporting them, as required by the guidelines, to the authorities.[3]

In 1996, Van der Maas and Van der Wal published the results of an extensive survey into end-of-life decisions by Dutch doctors in the year 1995.[4] Do the results of this survey show any improvement in the degree of control over euthanasia?

I. THE SURVEY

The survey sought particularly to ascertain the incidence of intentional life-shortening by doctors; the extent to which they complied with their duty to report such cases (in accordance with a procedure dating from late 1990 which was given statutory force in June 1994), and the quality of their reporting. The main purpose of the reporting procedure is to provide for possible scrutiny of the intentional termination of life by doctors and to promote careful decision making in such cases. The most important quantitative data generated by the survey are reproduced in Table 1. . . .

1. EUTHANASIA AND ASSISTED SUICIDE

Between 1990 and 1995 the number of requests for euthanasia increased, as did the number of requests granted. Cases of euthanasia and assisted suicide rose from 2,700 cases in 1990 to 3,600 in 1995, or from 2.1% to 2.7% of all deaths.

According to the attending physicians, there were treatment alternatives in 17% of these cases but in almost all the patients did not want them. However, in 1994, the Dutch Supreme Court held that doctors should not hasten death whenever the alternative of palliative treatment was available, at least in cases of mental suffering and the ministers of justice and health, and the Royal Dutch Medical Association (KNMG), have decided that the same restriction should apply in cases of somatic suffering. The above cases appear, therefore, to have breached this guideline.

Life was shortened by one to four weeks in 31% of euthanasia cases and 45% of assisted suicides and by more than a month in 7% of cases of euthanasia and in 30% of assisted suicides.

Physicians stated that the main reason why patients requested euthanasia was "intolerable suffering without prospect of improvement" (74%), which has become the standard terminology to describe the seriousness of the condition required by the law. But the next most common reasons were "to prevent loss of dignity" (56%) and "to prevent further suffering" (47%). It must surely be doubted whether either of these reasons, by itself, satisfies the requirement of unbearable suffering.

Interestingly, one of the most important reasons for rejecting a request for euthanasia (cited by 35% of physicians) was the physician's opinion that the patient's suffering was not intolerable. This suggests that, despite the emphasis placed by the advocates of euthanasia on patient autonomy, the application of euthanasia is more a function of the *physician's judgment about the quality of the patient's life* than of respect for the patient's autonomy. This suggestion is fortified by the evidence about the extent to which Dutch doctors continue to terminate the lives of patients without an explicit request.

2. LIFE-TERMINATING ACTIONS WITHOUT EXPLICIT REQUEST

The survey confirms that the intentional shortening of patients' lives without explicit request remains far from uncommon. Nine hundred patients had their lives ended without explicit request in 1995, representing 0.7% of all deaths, only a slight decrease on the 0.8% so terminated in 1990. In other words, of the 4,500 (3,200 + 400 + 900) cases in which doctors admitted they actively and intentionally terminated life, one in five involved no explicit request.

The main reason for not discussing the issue with the patient was stated to be the patient's incompetence (due, for example, to dementia). But not all patients whose lives were terminated without an explicit request were incompetent. In 15% of cases where no discussion took place but could have, the doctor did not discuss the termination of life because the doctor thought that the termination of the patient's life was clearly in the patient's best interests.

Furthermore, in a third of the 900 cases, there had been a discussion with the patient about the possible termination of life, and some 50% of these patients were fully competent, yet their lives were terminated without an explicit request.

Moreover, in 17% of the 900 cases, treatment alternatives were thought to be available by the attending physician.

The physicians thought that life was shortened by

one to four weeks in 3% of cases but by more than a month in 6%. Finally, physicians had not discussed their action with a colleague in 40% of cases, with a close relative in 30% of cases, and with anyone at all in 5%.

3. INTENSIFICATION OF PAIN AND SYMPTOM TREATMENT

In 20,000 cases (according to the physician interviews) or 25,800 cases (according to the death certificate survey), palliative drugs were administered in doses which almost certainly shortened life. In some 2,000 of these cases the doctor explicitly intended, and in a further 2,850 cases, partly intended, to shorten life. The researchers estimate that the grey area between intending to alleviate pain and symptoms and intending to shorten life is about 2% of all deaths, the same as in 1990.

Where doctors administered palliative drugs partly in order to shorten life, they had discussed it with the patient in just over half of the cases (52%) and in only 36% of the cases was there an explicit request for life-shortening doses by the patient. The physicians stated that 86 patients (3%) with whom they had not discussed this treatment were fully competent. Moreover, in only 36% of the cases had the doctors consulted a colleague. Life was shortened by an estimated one to four weeks in 7% of cases but by more than a month in 1%.

4. WITHHOLDING/WITHDRAWING TREATMENT

In some 27,300 cases a treatment was withheld or withdrawn (in 5,200 cases at the patient's explicit request) taking into account a probable shortening of life.

However, in 18,000 of these cases (14,200 of which involved no explicit request by the patient) it was the physician's explicit intention to shorten life (though the survey does not state in how many cases the treatment was disproportionate, in which case doctors could, had they wished, have properly withdrawn it for that reason and without intending to shorten life.

In the majority of cases in which no discussion with the patient had taken place, the physicians stated that the patient was either incompetent or only partly competent. However, in 1% of these cases (140 patients) the physician considered the patient fully competent.

In cases where treatment was withheld or withdrawn with the explicit intent to shorten life, the physician estimated that life was shortened by one to seven days in 34% of cases, by one to four weeks in 18% and by more than a month in 9%.

5. NEONATES

The survey reports that over 1,000 newborns die in the Netherlands before their first birthday and estimates that the lives of about 15 are actively and intentionally terminated by doctors. The figure of 15 seems, however, a significant underestimate.

The survey shows that in ten cases (1%) doctors administered a drug with the explicit intention of shortening life. But it also reveals a further 80 cases in which, also with the explicit intention of shortening life, doctors administered a drug and withdrew or withheld a life-prolonging treatment. In total, therefore, it appears to have been the explicit intention of doctors to shorten the lives of 90 neonates, not 15.

Moreover, in no fewer than 41% of the 1,000 cases, treatment was withdrawn or withheld with the explicit intention of shortening life. In a significant proportion of these cases, life was terminated because the babies' lives were not thought bearable. Forty-five per cent of these babies expected to live more than four weeks, and some of them more than half a year.

In around a fifth of cases in which doctors intentionally withheld or withdrew treatment with the explicit purpose of shortening life because the baby's life was thought unbearable, there had been no discussion with the parents. Doctors said that in most cases this was because the situation was so clear that discussion was unnecessary or because there was no time, though these reasons are not elaborated.

Finally, doctors reported hardly any cases of the intentional shortening of neonatal life to the authorities.

6. ASSISTED SUICIDE OF PSYCHIATRIC PATIENTS

Based on the replies of psychiatrists in respect of the year 1995, the survey estimates that although some 320 psychiatric patients explicitly request assistance in suicide annually, only two to five are assisted to commit suicide by psychiatrists. Among psychiatrists who would never grant a request for assisted suicide on the basis of mental suffering (almost 1/3 of the respondents) "professional opinion" was cited by 88% as the most important reason. Only 2% of psychiatrists had ever assisted suicide.

This relatively restrictive approach of psychiatrists may owe not a little to the controversy generated by the case of Dr. Chabot, a psychiatrist criticised by a medical disciplinary court for assisting in the suicide of a 50-year-old woman who suffered grief after the loss of her two sons.

Disclosing statistics which support a restrictive approach, the survey also indicates that of those patients not assisted in suicide, 16% committed suicide without assistance by a physician and that, of those patients still living, 35% no longer wished for death and that the death wish in a further 10% had diminished.

7. CONSULTATION

The guidelines for permissible euthanasia and assisted suicide require the doctor, before agreeing to either, to engage in a formal consultation (consultatie), and not merely an informal discussion (overleg), with a colleague.

In cases of euthanasia and assisted suicide 92% of doctors had, according to the survey, discussed the case with a colleague. In 13% of these cases, however, the discussion did not amount to a formal consultation. Consultation took place, therefore, in 79% of cases. However, other figures in the survey suggest that consultation occurred in a significantly smaller percentage of cases. For the survey indicates that consultation occurred in 99% of reported cases but in only 18% of unreported cases and that almost 60% of all cases of euthanasia and assisted suicide were not reported, from which it seems that consultation occurred in only around half of all cases.

In the cases of life-termination without explicit request, a discussion occurred in 43% of cases but in 40% this did not amount to consultation. Consequently, there was no consultation in 97% of such cases.

Moreover, even when consultation did take place, it was usually with a physician living locally and the most important reasons given for consulting such a physician were his views on life-ending decisions and his living nearby: expertise in palliative care was hardly mentioned. Further, in the overwhelming majority of cases, the first doctor had made his mind up before consulting and the doctor consulted disagreed in only 7% of cases. In short, the requirement of consultation, even when it is satisfied, hardly operates as a rigorous check on decision making.

8. REPORTING

In 1995 41% of cases of euthanasia and assisted suicide were reported to the local medical examiner, as required by the reporting procedure. While this is an improvement on the figure of 18% reported in 1990, it means that a clear majority of cases, almost 60%, still go unreported. Moreover, the survey confirms that the legal requirements are breached more frequently in unreported cases, in which there is less often a written request by the patient, a written record by the doctor, or consultation by the doctor.

The most important reasons given by doctors for failing to report in 1995 were (as in 1990), the wish to avoid the inconvenience (for the doctor and/or the relatives) of an investigation by the authorities, and to avoid the risk of prosecution (though, as the consistently tiny number of prosecutions indicates, this risk is negligible). Thirty per cent of doctors stated that they did not report because they had failed to observe the requirements for permissible euthanasia and 12% because they considered euthanasia was a private matter between doctor and patient.

II. DISCUSSION

The second survey confirms at least three disturbing findings of the first survey.

1. INCIDENCE OF INTENTIONAL LIFE-SHORTENING WITH AND WITHOUT EXPLICIT REQUEST

Like the first survey, the second indicates a sizeable incidence of intentional life-shortening by Dutch doctors. Even adopting the unusually narrow Dutch definition of euthanasia as active, voluntary euthanasia there were no fewer than 3,200 cases in 1995 (2.4% of all deaths), an increase of almost a thousand on the 1990 total of 2,300 (1.8% of all deaths).

But if *all* cases in which doctors explicitly intended to shorten life (whether by act or omission, and whether with or without the patient's request) are included, the total rises steeply. Adding the cases of assisted suicide (400); life-termination without explicit request (900) and the intensification of pain and symptom treatment with the explicit intent to shorten life (2,000), the total more than doubles from 3,200 to 6,500.

And if to this number are added the cases of withholding or withdrawing treatment with the explicit intent to shorten life (18,000); cases in which neonates were intentionally terminated (90 cases) and psychiatric patients assisted in suicide (two to five cases), the total rises to over 24,500 cases.

2. EUTHANASIA AS AN ALTERNATIVE TO PALLIATIVE CARE

The survey's comment that "the quality of medical treatment near the end of life has improved" might not unreasonably be thought to display a certain complacency, particularly in a country which has some way to go in the provision of adequate palliative care. The high incidence of intentional life-shortening disclosed by the survey and the relative weakness of the reasons for euthanasia given in many cases by the doctors tend to suggest that euthanasia is not confined to cases of "last resort" and is at least sometimes used as an alternative to palliative care. The case of Dr. Chabot, in which the defendant doctor assisted a grieving woman, whom he did not consider to be physically or mentally ill, to kill herself, and in which the Supreme Court held that such suffering could indeed justify assisted suicide, illustrates the elasticity of the requirement of "unbearable suffering."

The survey confirms that, even when doctors believe that treatment alternatives are available, they not infrequently resort to euthanasia. The opinion of the Supreme Court, the ministers of justice and health, and the KNMG, that euthanasia is impermissible when treatment alternatives are available, even if the patient refuses them, has clearly not prevented its administration in such circumstances. In a move that would make the prospect of prosecution even more remote, the then minister of justice appeared to reverse her earlier position and instructed the attorneys general that the refusal by the patient of available treatment alternatives does not render euthanasia unlawful.

3. WIDESPREAD BREACH OF THE REQUIREMENT TO REPORT

Although 41% of cases (1,466) were reported in 1995 as opposed to 18% (486) in 1990, it remains true that in both years, as in every year in between, a clear majority of cases has gone unreported. There was, in short, no official control whatever over the majority of cases of euthanasia, assisted suicide or the termination of life without explicit request.

Nor should the alleged increase in reporting be accepted uncritically. First, the second survey records an increase in cases of euthanasia between 1990 and 1995 (900 cases) almost as large as the increase in cases reported (980 cases). Secondly, if the total of 6,500 cases of active, intentional life-shortening is used, then the proportion of unreported cases rises from 59% to 77%. On the total of 24,500 cases, the proportion unreported reaches 94%.

It will be recalled that the purpose of the reporting procedure is to allow for scrutiny of the intentional termination of life by doctors and to promote observance of the legal and professional requirements for euthanasia. The undisputed fact that a clear majority of cases (59% according to the survey, at least 77% on our calculations) still goes unreported, serves only to reinforce doubts about the ability of the procedure to fulfil its purpose and to undermine Dutch claims of effective regulation, scrutiny and control. Further, even those cases which *are* reported are reported by the doctor, and one may wonder whether the doctor's report is any more likely to disclose evidence of wrongdoing than is a tax return to disclose evidence of undeclared earnings.

CONCLUSIONS

With the publication of the first Van der Maas survey in 1991 it became clear that the so-called "strict safeguards" laid down in 1984 by the courts and the Royal Dutch Medical Association had largely failed. The survey cast doubt on central assurances which had been given by the advocates of voluntary euthanasia: that euthanasia would be performed only at the patient's explicit request and that doctors terminating life without request would be prosecuted for murder; that euthanasia would be used only in cases of "last resort" and not as an alternative to palliative care; and that cases would be openly reported and duly scrutinised. The Dutch reaction to the survey's findings was also revealing: the cases of nonvoluntary euthanasia it disclosed, far from being criticised, were largely condoned. In short, the survey indicated that, in less than a decade, the Dutch had slid down the slippery slope.

It is therefore surprising that an American commentator should observe that the similarity between the findings in respect of 1990 and 1995 shows that the Dutch are apparently *not* descending a slippery slope.[5] This observation quite overlooks the fact that the first survey showed that the descent had already occurred by 1990: the second survey, far from showing that there has been no *de*scent from 1984 to 1995 shows merely that there has been no significant *a*scent from 1990 to 1995.

The second survey is little more reassuring than the first. Dutch proponents of voluntary euthanasia claimed that tolerating voluntary euthanasia, subject to "safeguards," would allow it to be "brought into the open" and effectively controlled. As the valuable surveys by Van der Maas and Van der Wal disclose, and as several expert commentators have now concluded,[6] the reality is that a clear majority of cases of euthanasia, both with and without request, go unreported and unchecked. In the face of the undisputed fact that in a clear majority of cases there is not even an opportunity for official scrutiny, Dutch claims of effective regulation ring hollow.

REFERENCES AND NOTES

1. *Washington v. Glucksberg* (1997) 117 S Ct 2258; *Vacco v. Quill* (1997) 117 S Ct 2293.

2. Maas PJ van der *et al. Medische beslissingen rond het levenseinde.* s-Gravenhage: SDU Uitgeverij Plantijnstraat, 1991 (published in translation as *Euthanasia and other medical decisions concerning the end of life.* Amsterdam: Elsevier, 1992).

3. See for example Jochemsen H. Euthanasia in Holland: an ethical critique of the new law. *Journal of Medical Ethics* 1994;**20**:212; Keown J. Euthanasia in the Netherlands: sliding down the slippery slope? In: Keown J, ed. *Euthanasia examined.* Cambridge: Cambridge University Press, 1995: ch. 16.

4. Wal G van der, Maas PJ van der. *Euthanasie en andere medische beslissingen rond het levenseinde. De praktijk en de meldingsprocedure. (Euthanasia and other medical decision concerning the end of life. Practice and reporting procedure.)* Den Haag: SDU uitgevers, 1996.

5. See for example Angell M. Euthanasia in the Netherlands—good news or bad? *New England Journal of Medicine* 1996;**335**:1677.

6. See for example Gomez C. *Regulating death.* New York: Free Press, 1991; see reference 8: Hendin; see reference 3: Jochemsen; see reference 3; Keown.

JOHANNES J. M. VAN DELDEN

Slippery Slopes in Flat Countries—A Response

Johannes van Delden is a senior fellow at the Center for Bioethics and Health Law at Utrecht University in the Netherlands and a nursing home physician. Dr. van Delden serves as the Secretary of the International Association of Bioethics and was a principal investigator of the Remmelink Committee, which was established by the Dutch Government's Ministers of Justice and Public Health to investigate euthanasia in the Netherlands. His publications include (with Paul J. van der Maas and Loes Pijnenborg) "Changes in Dutch Opinions on Active Euthanasia," *Journal of the American Medical Association* and (with Paul J. van der Maas, Loes Pijnenborg, and C.W. Looman) "Deciding Not to Resuscitate in Dutch Hospitals," *Journal of Medical Ethics*.

I would like to . . . further the discussion by trying to analyse the Dutch situation in response to the points put forward by Jochemsen and Keown. . . .

Jochemsen and Keown have three major worries:

- the use of euthanasia even when doctors thought that palliative care was a viable alternative;
- the incidence of non-voluntary euthanasia;
- the underreporting of the euthanasia cases.

The reports that lead to these worries are not disputed, by either Jochemsen and Keown, or by me. Like them, I will use the term "euthanasia" in the Dutch way: euthanasia is the intentional ending of a patient's life at the patient's explicit request. My point, however, is that I think a more interesting analysis of the problem can be given than by repeating the ominous and incriminating slippery slope metaphor.

EUTHANASIA AND PALLIATIVE CARE

The Netherlands are often criticised for their presumed lack of palliative care. The existence of only very few hospices in the Netherlands, for example, is often interpreted as proof of a neglect of palliative care. Although much of this criticism is based on misunderstanding and much effort is made to improve

palliative care at present, Jochemsen and Keown are right when they say that the Netherlands "have some way to go in the provision of adequate palliative care." Which is, of course, also true for many other countries. But what does this mean for a moral evaluation of euthanasia?

By and large there appear to be three ways of dealing with the issue of euthanasia. The first is to reject it on the grounds that it is forbidden by the principle of respect for life. Proponents of this view often also claim that euthanasia is not necessary at all. They believe that by paying sincere and close attention to the person who requests euthanasia the "question behind the question" will surely be revealed to be something other than a request for death, and that with good palliative care extreme suffering need not remain unanswered. In this view euthanasia and palliative care are incompatible.

An alternative response to the euthanasia issue stresses the importance of compassion. From this point of view, respect for life is of paramount importance as is good palliative care. Sometimes however, supporters of this view admit that sometimes illness and dying come with such suffering that life is reduced to pointless surviving. If all other palliative measures fail, then euthanasia may be justified. The result of this view of euthanasia is the medicalisation of the end of life, since whether euthanasia is justifiable

From *Journal of Medical Ethics* 25, no. 1 (February 1999), 22–24. Footnotes renumbered.

becomes largely a matter of medical discretion.

These two responses appear to differ primarily in their answer to the question: "Does intractable excruciating suffering exist?" However, even palliative care specialists will state that, unfortunately, it does. The real difference therefore, will be whether one allows the principle of respect for life to be overridden by other considerations in special circumstances.

Most proposals to regulate euthanasia follow the second view. This is also true for the official legal position in the Netherlands where a conflict of the physician's duties is the basis for not prosecuting him or her, not the granting of a patient's right. There is no right to die in the Netherlands, nor is there an obligation for the physician to comply with the request of a competent patient to die even if certain conditions are met. From an official and legal point of view, therefore, euthanasia is only tolerated as a last resort.

The reality of the Dutch euthanasia practice, however, seems to be developing in another direction, with increasing emphasis on respect for patient autonomy. This could lead to a shift to a third approach in which euthanasia is seen as a choice. Some patients do not want to live through suffering and decline even if pain can be controlled. They want autonomously to decide about how and when to die and they want their relatives to remember them as they were when they were more or less healthy. They want to step out of life before the terminal phase really starts and they want a doctor to do the lethal work.

This development is reflected in the data produced in all major studies in the Netherlands. The first nationwide study of end-of-life decisions showed that pain hardly ever was the sole reason for requesting euthanasia.[1] In 1992 an independent study by Van der Wal showed that in 56% of cases of euthanasia, requests were made because patients thought suffering to be pointless and in 46% because they feared the decline.[2] And the 1996 report showed that many patients asked for euthanasia to prevent more suffering. . . .

One may also predict (as an aside) that this emphasis on patient autonomy will lead to a change in the medical circumstances in euthanasia cases. At this moment cancer is by far the predominant diagnosis. The shift towards autonomy-based decisions, however, will lead to an increase in the prevalence of situations characterised by a loss of autonomy (such as in dementia or after a stroke).

This emerging sense that one does have a right to die means that more palliative care does not necessarily lead to a decreasing incidence of euthanasia. From a sociological point of view one may be tempted to interpret the shift towards autonomy-based requests for euthanasia as a byproduct of a liberal society, with its emphasis on self-government, control and rational choice. A moral evaluation of this development, however, will depend largely on one's normative views. Jochemsen and Keown will presume that they can rest their case: their prediction of the slippery slope has come true. Others will say that more emphasis on patient autonomy fits perfectly into the process of emancipation of the patient that has been going on since the beginning of the 1970s. They might say that it is about time to start thinking about patient decisions concerning the end of life, instead of about medical ones.

THE CASES OF NON-VOLUNTARY EUTHANASIA

The cases of non-voluntary euthanasia, described both in the 1991 and the 1996 reports, created a new dimension in the Dutch euthanasia debate. Since the middle of the 1980s, this debate had been focused on euthanasia and assisted suicide with the explicit request of the patient as central feature. This in part had been a deliberate narrowing of the discussion because it was felt that consensus was greatest for these cases. The Dutch even changed their definition of euthanasia to mean only the cases in which there was an explicit request by the patient. Thus, a possibly justifying feature (the request) was turned into a necessary condition.

The description of the non-voluntary cases has broadened the discussion again. But what does their appearance in the reports mean? Does this prove the slippery slope? For many years Dutch commentators on euthanasia only talked about cases on request and non-voluntary cases only recently became known. Thus, the impression may have risen that the Dutch began with hastening the end of life on request and ended up with non-voluntary cases.

This, however, is not necessarily true. We simply do not know whether non-voluntary euthanasia occurred less or more often in the past. What we do know is that the occurrence of non-voluntary euthanasia did not increase in the Netherlands between 1991 and 1996, and also that its prevalence is much higher in another country (Australia), which did not slide down the slope by tolerating euthanasia for years and years.[3]

But even if they do not prove the existence of the slippery slope, the non-voluntary euthanasia cases do form a very serious problem. They are obviously not justified by the principle of respect for patient autonomy as in the third view described above, and therefore can only be tolerated (if at all) in extreme situations where life termination is really a last resort and non-voluntary euthanasia becomes "mercy-killing." It is very unlikely that this was the case in all cases described in the Dutch reports.

UNDERREPORTING

To accept euthanasia in an individual case is one thing, to accept it on a public policy level is quite something else. It is often argued that proposals to legalise euthanasia can never contain absolute safeguards.[4] I think this is true: there is no rule that cannot (and will not) be broken. By the way, this goes for the prohibition of drunk-driving as well. The question is whether this justifies a prohibition of euthanasia in an individual case. The Dutch tried to have it both ways by creating a public policy based on individual cases. The least one can say is that this resulted in an unsatisfactory situation of accepting and prohibiting at the same time. This created uncertainty and unclarity both for patients and physicians and probably contributed to some extent to the critical reports such as the one commented upon here.

Persuading the physician to bring euthanasia cases to the knowledge of the authorities is a problem for any euthanasia policy. The Dutch notification procedure helped to raise the notification rate to 41% in 1995.[5] ... The government has tried to diminish further the number of unreported cases by developing a new notification procedure, in which much of the assessment is done "outside of" the legal system. Since November 1, 1998, five regional multidisciplinary assessment committees have to advise the public prosecutor in all reported cases of euthanasia. The effect of this change in procedure is not clear yet.

Cuperus-Bosma et al. hope that reducing the role of the public prosecution will lead to fewer differences in assessment and more legal equality. However, one may ask why would these committees differ less in their assessment of cases. Their strength is their opportunity to communicate with the reporting physician in a decriminalised setting and, by so doing, influence practice. Uniformity should not be their main concern.

CONCLUSION

You cannot do ethics until you know the facts. Therefore, the need for empirical research in ethics is very clear. One of its tasks is to describe the morally relevant facts. Another task may be to verify empirical claims (as in the slippery slope argument and as in many consequentialist claims) and to provide insight into the effects of cultural differences on certain practices. Thus, facts provide the ethicist with the information she needs. However, facts will not settle a moral debate. When it comes to the euthanasia issue there is much to be learned from studies that the Dutch have performed. But the interpretation of these facts remains largely dependent upon our moral views. Not vice versa.

REFERENCES

1. Maas P.I. van der, Delden J.J.M. van, Pijnenborg L. *Euthanasia and other medical decisions concerning the end of life.* Amsterdam: Elsevier, 1992.

2. Wal G. van der, Eijk J.Th.M. van, Spreeuwenberg C. Euthanasia and assisted suicide. II. Do Dutch family doctors act prudently? *Family Practice* 1992;**9**:135–40.

3. Kuhse H., Singer P., Baume P., Clark M., Rickard M. End-of-life decisions in Australian medical practice. *Medical Journal of Australia* 1997;**166**:191–6.

4. Miles S., Pappas D., Koepp R. Considerations of safeguards proposed in laws and guidelines to legalize assisted suicide. In: Weir Robert E., ed. *Physician-assisted suicide.* Bloomington: Indiana University Press, 1997.

5. Wal G. van der, Maas P.J. van der. *Euthanasie en andere medische beslissingen rond het levenseinde.* Den Haag: SDU uitgevers, 1996: 57.

BERNARD GERT, CHARLES M. CULVER, AND K. DANNER CLOUSER

An Alternative to Physician-Assisted Suicide

Bernard Gert is the Stone Professor of Intellectual and Moral Philosophy at Dartmouth College and adjunct professor and psychiatry at Dartmouth Medical School. He is the editor of *Man and Citizen* (1972, 1991) by Thomas Hobbes, first author of *Morality and the New Genetics* (1996), and (with Charles M. Culver and K. Danner Clouser) *Bioethics: A Return to Fundamentals* (1997). He is also author of *Morality: Its Nature and Justification* (1998), a systematic work in ethical theory.

Charles Culver is a professor of medical education, director of Didactic Education, and chair of the Admissions Committee at Barry University. He is a psychiatrist who has coauthored (with Bernard Gert and K. Danner Clouser) *Bioethics: A Return to Fundamentals* (1997). Dr. Culver is also the coauthor of *Philosophy in Medicine: Conceptual and Ethical Problems in Medicine and Psychiatry* and editor of *Ethics at the Bedside*.

The late K. Danner Clouser was University Professor of Humanities at the Penn State College of Medicine from 1968 until his retirement in 1996. He was instrumental in building the first humanities department ever established at any medical school and was a pioneer in the newly emerging field of bioethics. His publications include (with Bernard Gert and Charles M. Culver) *Bioethics: A Return to Fundamentals* (1997) and *Teaching Bioethics: Strategies, Problems, and Resources*. His work was critically examined in a book edited by Loretta M. Kopelman, entitled *Building Bioethics: Conversations with Clouser and Friends on Medical Ethics*.

Two tasks are necessary in order to determine whether physician-assisted suicide should be legalized. The first is to clarify the meaning of the phrase "physician-assisted suicide" (PAS) so that one can be precise about what procedures are correctly specified by the phrase. The second task is to inquire into the moral acceptability of doctors' carrying out those procedures that are appropriately labeled as PAS. It is essential to settle the conceptual task before deciding about PAS's moral acceptability. Once conceptual matters are clarified and the moral acceptability of

PAS is determined, disagreements about the social consequences of legalizing PAS continue to make it an issue on which reasonable people can take either side. However, we shall show that awareness of an alternative to PAS, namely, the refusal of food and fluids, significantly weakens the arguments in favor of legalizing PAS.

It may seem odd to claim that there is a problem in clarifying what is meant by PAS. The prototypical example of PAS, and the way it is almost always practiced, is for a doctor to provide a lethal quantity of sedating medication to a patient who subsequently ingests it and dies. Everyone agrees that the doctor who carries out such an action has engaged in PAS. The conceptual problem arises not with the prototypical

From Margaret P. Battin, Rosamond Rhodes, and Anita Silvers, *Physician-Assisted Suicide: Expanding the Debate.* New York and London: Routledge, 1998, 182–202.

example but with the conceptual analyses that some philosophers and some courts have made in commenting on whether PAS is morally justified, or is legally sanctioned or forbidden. One philosopher, for example, has claimed that there is no morally significant difference between killing a patient (voluntary, active euthanasia; VAE) and helping a patient commit suicide (PAS).[1] One circuit court has argued that performing PAS is exactly the same as withdrawing life support and rendering palliative care as a patient dies.[2] Thus PAS has been identified both as the same as killing a patient (VAE) and the same as allowing a patient to die (voluntary, passive euthanasia; VPE). We believe that the three alternatives, 1) PAS; 2) killing a patient (VAE); and 3) allowing a patient to die (VPE), are quite distinct from one another conceptually and morally.

ACTIVE AND PASSIVE EUTHANASIA

To understand how PAS, VAE, and VPE differ, it is useful to begin with the distinction between VAE and VPE. A distinction between these two has traditionally been made and accepted both by clinicians and by philosophers. VAE is killing and, even if requested by a competent patient, is illegal and has been historically prohibited by the American Medical Association. VPE is "allowing to die" and, if requested by a competent patient, it is legally permitted and morally acceptable.

None of the standard attempts to describe the conceptual distinction between VAE and VPE have gained wide acceptance. These attempts have involved the following concepts and issues: 1) acts versus omissions, 2) stopping treatment (withdrawing) versus not starting treatment (withholding), 3) ordinary care versus extraordinary care, and 4) whether the patient's death is due to an underlying malady. However none of these four ways of making the distinction has any clear moral significance and all are inadequate because they all fail to appreciate the moral significance of the *kind of decision* the patient makes, in particular whether it is a request or a refusal.[3] It is this failure that leads to the mistaken conclusion that there is no morally significant distinction between VAE and VPE.

First, a terminological matter needs to be clarified. It is perfectly standard English to use the term "request" when talking about a refusal. Thus one can say that a patient requests that a treatment (such as ventilation) be stopped. The patient is, in fact, refusing continued use of the respirator. Unfortunately, this perfectly correct and common way of talking obscures

the crucial moral distinction between patients' refusals and requests. When combined with the use of the terms "choice" and "decision," which also can be applied to both requests and refusals, the language fosters the false conclusion that all patient decisions or choices, whether refusals or requests, generate the same moral obligation for physicians.

This confusion is compounded because the most common use of the terms "decision" and "choice" with regard to a patient involves neither refusals nor requests, but rather the patient's picking one of the options that her physician has presented to her during the process of informed consent. However, when dealing with patients who want to die, this most common use of "decision" or "choice" is not relevant. Rather a patient is either 1) refusing life-sustaining treatment (VPE), or 2) requesting that the physician kill her (VAE), or 3) requesting that the physician provide the medical means for the patient to kill herself (PAS). Thus talking of a patient's decision or choice to die can be extremely ambiguous. Furthermore, refusals of treatment and requests for treatment, whether or not death is a foreseeable result, have very different moral and legal implications.[4]

• • •

REFUSAL OF TREATMENT AND THE DUTIES OF A PHYSICIAN

Overruling a competent informed patient's rational refusal of treatment, including life preserving treatment, always involves depriving the patient of freedom, and usually involves causing him pain. No impartial rational person would publicly allow these kinds of paternalistic actions and so they are morally unacceptable. Since it is morally unacceptable to overrule the rational refusal of a competent informed patient, it cannot be the duty of a physician to do so. Theoretically, the situation does not change when lack of treatment will result in the patient's death, but as a practical matter, it does make a difference. Death is such a serious harm that it is never irrational to choose any other harm in order to prevent death. Even though it is sometimes rational to choose death over other harms, choosing death may be, and often is, irrational. Further, people are usually ambivalent about choosing death, often changing their minds several times, but death is permanent, and once it occurs, no further change of mind is possible.

The seriousness of death requires physicians to make certain that patients realize that death will result from failure to receive the life sustaining treatment. It also requires physicians to make sure a patient's desire to die is not due to suffering that can be relieved by palliative care. The physician also must make certain that a patient's desire to die, and hence his request to die, is not primarily the result of a treatable depression and, more generally, that a patient's unavoidable suffering is sufficient to make it rational for him to prefer death to continuing to live. When patients have terminal diseases, however, it is generally the case that when they want to die, it is rational for them to choose death. Further, although there is often some ambivalence, in our experience, their desire to die usually remains their dominant desire. When an informed competent patient makes a rational decision to stop life-prolonging treatment, a physician cannot have a duty to overrule his refusal of treatment, even though normally a physician has a duty to prevent death.

We have shown that physicians cannot have a duty to preserve the lives of their competent patients when those patients want to die and their desires are informed and rational. When prolonging a person's life requires unjustifiably depriving him of freedom, it is morally unacceptable to do so. We have thus established that physicians do not and cannot have a duty to prolong the lives of their patients when their patients have a rational desire to die. We are not suggesting that whenever a patient with a terminal disease makes any tentative suggestion that treatment be stopped, the physician should, with no question, immediately do so. It is part of the duty of a physician to make sure both that the refusal is rational and that it is the informed, considered, and noncoerced preference of the patient. When, however, it is clear that a patient really does want to die and the refusal is rational, then it is morally unacceptable for the physician to administer life prolonging treatment.

KILLING VERSUS ALLOWING TO DIE

Having shown that a physician does not have a duty to prolong the lives of patients who rationally prefer to die, the next issue to be settled is whether not treating such patients counts as killing them. If it does count as killing them, then the conclusions of the previous section may have to be revised. In the previous section not treating was taken as simply not prolonging the life of a competent patient when he rationally refuses treatment. However, not treating is sometimes correctly regarded as killing. If a physician turns off the respirator of a competent patient who does not want to die, with the result that the patient dies, the physician has killed him. The same is true if the physician discontinues antibiotics, or food and fluids. It may even count as killing if the physician refuses to start any of these treatments for his patient when the patient wants the treatment started and there is no medical reason for not starting it. Just as parents whose children die because of not being fed can be regarded as having killed their children, physicians who have a duty to provide life-saving treatment for their patients can be regarded as killing them if they do not provide that treatment. However, we have shown that a physician does not have a duty to provide life-saving treatment when a competent patient rationally refuses such treatment. Not treating counts as killing only when there is a duty to treat; in the absence of such a duty, not treating does not count as killing.[5]

If the patient refuses treatment and there is no duty to treat, then it does not make any moral difference whether the physician stops treating by an act, e.g., turning off the respirator, or an omission, e.g., not giving antibiotics. It also makes no moral difference whether the physician stops some treatment that has already started, e.g., turning off the respirator or discontinuing antibiotics, or simply does not start such treatment. . . .

STOPPING FOOD AND FLUIDS

. . . Since the point of dying sooner is to avoid the pain and suffering of a terminal illness, stopping only food while continuing fluids is not a good method of dying because it takes a long time, often more than a month. However, when fluids are also stopped, dying is much quicker; usually unconsciousness occurs within a week and death less than a week later. Further, contrary to what is widely assumed, dying because of lack of food and fluids is not physically unpleasant or painful if there is even minimal nursing care.[6] When there is no medical treatment keeping the patient alive, stopping food and fluids may be the best way of allowing a patient to die. It is usually painless, it takes long enough for the patient to have the opportunity to change his mind, but is short enough that significant relief from pain and suffering is gained. However, because of the psychological difficulties involved in a longer dying process, some patients may still prefer PAS to discontinuing food and fluids.

It may be thought that, if complying with a patient's refusal of treatment requires the physician to perform some identifiable act, e.g., turning off a respirator, which is the act that results in the patient's death, then regardless of what was said before, the doctor has killed the patient. This seems to have the support of the *Oxford English Dictionary* which says that to kill is simply to deprive of life. One may accept that a doctor is morally and legally required to turn off the respirator and thus is justified in killing her patient, but still maintain that she has killed him. Even those who accept the death penalty and hold that some prison official is morally and legally required to execute the prisoner do not deny that the official has killed the prisoner. Killing in self-defense is both morally and legally allowed, yet no one denies that it is killing. Similarly, one could agree that the doctor is doing nothing morally or legally unacceptable by turning off the respirator and even that the doctor is morally and legally required to do so, yet claim that in doing so the doctor is killing the patient.

If one accepts this analysis, then it might also seem plausible to say that an identifiable decision to omit a life-prolonging treatment, even if such an omission is morally and legally required, also counts as killing the patient. One could simply stipulate that doctors are sometimes morally and legally required to kill their patients, namely, when their action or omission is the result of a competent patient rationally refusing to start or to continue a life-prolonging treatment. Thus it would seem that the important point is that the doctor is morally and legally required to act as she does, not whether what she does is appropriately called killing. However, it is still significant whether such an action should be regarded as killing because having a too simple account of killing can cause numerous problems.

Many doctors do not want to regard themselves as killing their patients, even justifiably killing them. More importantly, all killing requires a justification or an excuse. If all the morally relevant features are the same, the justification or excuse that is not adequate for one way of killing will not be adequate for all other ways of killing either. Thus, if a justification is not publicly allowed for injecting a lethal dose of morphine, then it will not be publicly allowed for disconnecting the patient from the respirator. Since even advocates of VAE do not propose that doctors should ever be morally and legally required to kill their patients, even justifiably, doctors would not be required to comply with rational refusals of treatment by competent patients. It might even come to be thought justifiable to prohibit physicians from honoring the rational refusals of life-sustaining treatments of competent patients. Thus changing the way killing is understood (i.e., counting complying with a patient's rational refusal as killing him) would have unfortunate implications.

Those who favor legalizing VAE do not want to require doctors to kill their patients; they merely want to allow those doctors who are willing to kill, to do so. Similarly for PAS, no one has yet suggested that a doctor be required to comply with a patient's request for a lethal prescription. On the other hand, since doctors are morally and legally required to comply with a competent patient's rational refusal of life-sustaining treatment, complying with such a refusal has not been regarded as killing. Providing palliative care to a patient who refuses life-sustaining treatment is not morally controversial either. Killing a competent patient on his rational request or assisting him to commit suicide are morally controversial. No one claims that doctors are morally and legally required to do either. Thus it is clear that complying with a competent patient's rational refusal of treatment is not normally regarded as killing, nor does providing palliative care to such a patient count as assisting suicide.

Part of the problem is that insufficient attention is paid to the way in which the term "kill" is actually used. Killing is not as simple a concept as it is often taken to be. Killing is causing death, but what counts as causing death or any other harm is a complex matter. If the harm that results from one's action, or omission, needs to be justified or excused, then one is regarded as having caused that harm. Of course, causing harm often can be completely justified or excused, so that one can cause a harm and be completely free of any unfavorable moral judgment. So killing, taken as causing death, may be completely justified, perhaps even morally required.

All acts that are done in order to bring about someone's death count as causing the person's death, or killing them, for all such intentional actions need justification. Also, if the act which results in death is the kind of act which is morally unacceptable such as deceiving, breaking a promise, cheating, breaking the law, or neglecting one's duty, knowingly performing the act or omission needs justification and so counts as killing. For example, if I lie to someone, telling him that a mushroom that I know to be intensely poisonous is safe to eat, then if he eats the mushroom and dies, I have caused his death. Or if a child dies because her parents did not feed her, they have killed her, because parents have a duty to feed their children. This analysis shows why it is important to make clear that doctors have no duty to treat, or even feed, patients who refuse treatment or food. However, if one does not intend, but only knows, that one's act will result in someone's death, and the act is the kind of act that is morally acceptable, (such as giving a patient sufficient analgesia to control her severe pain) then even though this act results in the person's death, it may not count as causing his death.

When complying with the rational refusal of a competent patient, the doctor's intention is not to kill the patient, but rather to honor the patient's refusal even though she knows that the result will be that the patient dies. Even if the doctor agrees that it is best for the patient to die, her honoring that refusal does not count as intentionally causing his death. Of course, an individual doctor can want her patient to die, but her intention in these circumstances is not determined by whether she wants her patient to die. Rather, the intention is determined by what facts account for her deciding to act in one way rather than another. If she would cease treatment even if she did not want the patient to die and would not cease it if the patient had not refused such treatment, then her intention is not to kill the patient but to comply with the patient's refusal. Further, most doctors do not want to kill their patients, even if such actions were morally and legally justified, so clearly their intentions are simply to honor their patients' rational refusals. . . .

That our society does not regard death resulting from complying with a competent patient's rational refusal, even a refusal of food and fluids, as killing, is shown by the fact that almost all states have advance directives that explicitly require a physician to stop treatment, even food and fluids, if the patient has the appropriate advance directive. They also allow a presently competent patient to refuse treatment and food and fluids. None of these states allow a physician to kill a patient, under any circumstances. Most of these states do not even allow physicians to assist suicide, which strongly suggests that turning off a respirator, is not regarded even as assisting suicide when doing so is required by the rational refusal of a competent patient.

Thus, complying with a competent patient's rational refusal of treatment is not killing or assisting suicide, and it may even be misleading to say that a physician is allowing the patient to die. To talk of a physician allowing the patient to die suggests that the physician has a choice, that it is up to her to decide whether or not to save the patient's life. When a competent patient has rationally refused treatment, however, a physician has no choice. It is morally and legally prohibited to overrule the patient's refusal. The physician allows her patient to die only in the sense that it is physically possible for her to save her patient and she does not. Complying with the rational refusal of life-saving treatment by a competent patient is not merely morally acceptable, it is morally required. Overruling such a refusal is itself a morally unacceptable deprivation of freedom. . . .

IS THE REFUSAL OF LIFE-SUSTAINING TREATMENT SUICIDE?

If suicide is regarded simply as killing oneself, then the analysis of killing should apply to it in a fairly straightforward fashion. An action or an omission which is intended to result in the death of a patient and which does result in his death counts as killing. Therefore, one might argue that the refusal of treatment or of food and fluids that is intended by the patient to result in his own death and which does result in his death, should count as suicide. And if "assisting suicide" simply means doing those acts which help the person commit suicide, then physicians who provide palliative care to patients who are refusing life sustaining treatments are assisting suicide. Accepting this analysis would make providing palliative care to such patients a kind of assisted suicide.

However, it is not clear that the view that suicide is simply killing oneself should be accepted. Partly, this may be because "killing oneself" does not seem to need a justification or excuse as much as killing another person. This may be because our society, with some limitations, regards each person as allowed to do anything he wants to himself, as long as no one else is harmed. Indeed, it seems that any act which one does not intend but only knows will result in one's own death does not count as suicide. (It is only in an extended sense that someone who continues to smoke or drink or eat too much, when he knows that it may result in his death, could be said to be, slowly committing suicide.) It also seems that our society does not count as suicide any death that results from omissions, at least omissions stemming from rational decisions to omit or to stop treatment. Rather only those positive acts that are done in order to bring about one's own death immediately count as suicide, since those acts so closely resemble the paradigms of killing. Patients who take some pills to bring about their own death are committing suicide, but those who have the respirator removed or who refuse food and fluids are usually not regarded as committing suicide.[7]

This more complex analysis of suicide explains why the law has never regarded providing palliative care to those who are refusing treatment as assisting suicide. Even those states which explicitly forbid assisting suicide do not prohibit providing palliative care to those who are refusing treatment or food and fluids. Of course those who support legalizing PAS favor the simpler account of suicide because they can then claim that some PAS is already allowed, and hence that it is simply inconsistent not to allow other quicker and less painful suicides. That our society does not count refusals of treatment as suicide and hence does not count palliative care for patients who refuse treatment as assisting suicide is not intended by us as an argument against legalizing PAS. However, it does show that one argument for legalizing PAS, namely, that PAS is already allowed in the provision of palliative care for those who are refusing life-prolonging treatment, is based on a misunderstanding of how our society regards providing such palliative care.

Our argument places PAS much closer to VPE than to VAE, and so allowing PAS, one could argue, need not lead to allowing VAE. It is compatible with our analyses so far that one can either be for or against legalizing PAS. However, we believe that recognition of the option of refusing treatment or food and fluids makes much stronger the major argument against legalizing PAS, namely, that doing so will not have sufficient benefits to compensate for the risks involved. But we are also aware that different people can rank and weigh these benefits and risks differently. . . .

IS KILLING PATIENTS EVER JUSTIFIED?

Stopping food and fluids is often the best way of allowing a patient to die, but it may be claimed that killing is sometimes better. Given present knowledge and technology, one can kill a patient or allow a patient to kill herself absolutely painlessly within a matter of minutes. If patients have a rational desire to die, why wait several days or weeks for them to die; why not kill them or let them kill themselves quickly and

painlessly in a matter of minutes? We have provided no argument against allowing patients to kill themselves or even killing patients who want to die that applies to an ideal world where there are never any misunderstandings between people and everyone is completely moral and trustworthy. In such a world, if one could provide a patient with pills or inject the patient with appropriate drugs so that the patient dies painlessly and almost instantaneously, there would be no need to worry about the distinction between refusals and requests, or between killing, assisting suicide, and allowing to die. But in the real world, there are misunderstandings and not everyone is completely moral and trustworthy. In the real world no one even proposes that PAS or VAE be allowed without elaborate procedural safeguards, which almost always require at least two weeks. So, on a practical level, legalizing PAS or VAE would not result in a quicker death than simply complying with a refusal of food and fluids.

On our account, VPE is complying with the rational refusal of life-saving treatment or food and fluids by a competent patient. Since there is no duty to overrule a rational refusal by a competent patient, complying with this refusal does not count as killing. Further, failing to comply with such a refusal is itself morally prohibited, for it is an unjustified deprivation of the patient's freedom. Also, in some newer codes of medical ethics, e.g., that of the American College of Physicians, respecting patients' refusals is now listed as a duty. Physicians are not merely morally allowed to practice VPE, they are morally required to do so. VAE is killing; it is complying with the rational request of a competent patient to be killed. Although PAS is not killing, it does involve active intervention by the physician that is more than merely stopping treatment. It is not simply complying with a patient's desire to be left alone; it is providing the patient with some substance that causes his death, when one has no duty to do so.

VAE is killing and so needs to be justified. This contrasts quite sharply with VPE, and even with PAS, which may not even need to be morally justified. When a patient refuses treatment or food and fluids, it is not the complying with a patient's refusal but rather the overruling of the refusal that needs to be justified. But, as noted earlier, physicians may cause pain to their patients and be completely justified, because they do so at their patients' request, or at least with their consent, and do it in order to prevent what the patient takes to be a greater harm, e.g., disability or death. VAE could be regarded as no different than any other instance of a doctor being morally justified in doing a morally unacceptable *kind of act* with regard to a patient at the patient's request, in order to prevent what the patient takes to be a greater harm. In VAE the patient takes death to be a lesser harm than suffering pain and requests that the moral rule prohibiting killing be violated with regard to himself.

If causing pain can be justified, why is killing not justified when all of the other morally relevant features are the same? The answer is that killing needs a stronger justification because of a special feature of death that distinguishes it from all of the other serious harms. The special feature is that, after death, the person killed no longer exists and so cannot protest that he did not want to be killed. All impartial rational persons would advocate that violations against causing pain be publicly allowed when the person toward whom the rule is being violated rationally prefers to suffer that pain rather than suffer some other harm, e.g., disability or death. It is uncertain how many impartial rational persons would advocate that killing be publicly allowed when the person being killed rationally prefers to be killed rather than to continue to suffer pain. This uncertainty stems from taking seriously the two features that are essential to morality, the public character of morality and the fallibility of persons.

Causing pain with valid consent can be publicly allowed without any significant anxiety being caused thereby. Patients can usually correct a mistake rather quickly by ordering a stop to the painful treatment. Also physicians have a constant incentive to be careful not to cause pain by mistake, for patients will complain if they did not really want the pain caused. Killing, even with valid consent, being publicly allowed may create significant anxiety. Patients may fear that they will be mistakenly killed and that they will have no opportunity to correct that mistake. That a patient will not be around to complain if they are mistakenly killed removes a strong safeguard against mistaken violations. But it is not merely mistakes about which a patient would not be able to complain. If a physician tries to take advantage of legalized killing and intentionally kills a patient, complaint would not be possible. Taking advantage of causing pain being publicly allowed does not pose similar problems.

Legalizing PAS might prevent some pain and suffering that could not be prevented by greater education concerning refusing food and fluids, but it would also be likely to create significant anxiety and some unwanted deaths. Impartial rational persons can therefore disagree on whether they would advocate legalizing PAS. Once it is recognized that withholding food and fluids 1) can be painless; 2) usually results in unconsciousness in one week and death in two weeks; and 3) allows for patients to change their minds, the need for PAS significantly diminishes.

Unlike others who argue against legalizing PAS, we do not claim that PAS is in itself morally unacceptable, only that it may create a serious risk of unwanted deaths. Since impartial rational persons can rank these risks as outweighing the benefits of legalization, legalizing PAS is controversial. If the goal is to allow a patient to choose her own time of dying and also dying to be accomplished relatively painlessly, there seems to be little need for PAS. If patient refusal of treatment, including refusal of food and fluids, were not sufficient for a relatively quick and painless death for the overwhelming number of terminally ill patients, then we would favor PAS, although we would still have serious objections to VAE. However, since VPE, especially when this includes refusing food and fluids, is available together with appropriate palliative care, it seems far more difficult to justify controversial methods like PAS. The harms prevented by PAS are no longer the long term suffering of patients who have no other way to die, they are only the one week of suffering that may be present while the patient is refusing food and fluids, and this suffering can be almost completely controlled by appropriate palliative care. This is an excellent example of why the presence of an alternative is a morally relevant feature.

Given the alternative of refusing food and fluids, very little additional harm seems to be prevented by PAS. The presence of an alternative is a morally relevant feature and makes it questionable whether it has sufficient benefits to justify the risks involved in legalizing it. There are good reasons for believing that the advantages of refusing food and fluids together with adequate palliative care make it preferable to legalizing PAS. This is especially true in a multicultural society where doctors and patients sometimes do not even speak the same language. There are a small number of cases in which refusal of food and fluids might be difficult, but it is necessary to weigh the benefit to this relatively small number of people against the harm that might be suffered by a great number of people by the legalizing of PAS. . . .

SUMMARY

. . . We believe that the strongest argument against PAS is that, given the alternatives available, it does not provide sufficient benefit to individual patients to justify the societal risks. Patients already have the alternative of refusing treatment and food and fluids, and of receiving palliative care while they are refusing that treatment. If physicians were to educate patients about these matters and to make clear that they will support their choices and continue to care for them if they choose to refuse treatment, there might be little, if any, call for PAS. Because of the time involved, patients seem far less likely to be pressured into refusing treatment or food and fluids than they arc to avail themselves of PAS. There would also be far fewer opportunities for abuse. PAS provides less incentive to be concerned with palliative care. And finally, given the bureaucratic safeguards that most regard as necessary with PAS, death can come as soon or sooner with refusal of treatment or refusal of food and fluids than it would with PAS.[8]

A PRACTICAL PROPOSAL
FOR STATE LEGISLATORS

In order to avoid the serious societal risks of legalizing physician-assisted suicide, while still providing a method for allowing seriously ill patients to determine the timing of their deaths, we think that states should consider passing legislation based on language such as the following. This language is completely consistent with the statement of the United States Supreme Court that, "Just as a State may prohibit assisting suicide while permitting patients to refuse unwanted lifesaving treatment, it may permit palliative care related to that refusal, which may have the foreseen but unintended 'double effect' of hastening the patient's death."

If a competent patient is terminally ill or suffering from a condition involving severe chronic pain or serious permanent disability, that patient's refusal of treatment, or refusal or food and fluids, shall not count as suicide, even though the patient knows that death will result from not starting or from stopping that treatment. All physicians and other healthcare workers shall be informed that they are legally prohibited from overruling any rational refusal of a competent patient, including refusal of food and fluids, even though it is known that death will result. All patients will be in-

formed that they are allowed to refuse any treatment, or to refuse food and fluids, even though it is known that death will result, and that physicians and other healthcare workers are legally prohibited from overruling any such rational refusal by a competent patient.

Further, there shall be no prohibition placed upon any physician who provides pain relief in any form, in order to relieve the pain and suffering of the patient who has refused treatment, or food and fluids. In particular, providing pain medication shall not be considered as assisting suicide, and there shall be no liability for the physician who provides such pain medication for the purpose of relieving pain and suffering. The physician shall not provide such medication for the purpose of hastening the time of death, but is not prohibited from providing medication which is consistent with adequate pain relief even if he knows that such medication will hasten the time of death. Physicians are required to rigorously follow the accepted standards of medical practice in determining the competence of patients who refuse any treatment, or who refuse food and fluids, when they know that death will result from complying with that refusal.

NOTES

1. Dan W. Brock, "Voluntary Active Euthanasia," *Hastings Center Report* 22 (2): 10–22 (1992).

2. *Quill v. Vacco,* the U.S. Court of Appeals for the Second Circuit.

3. See James L. Bernat, Bernard Gert, and R. Peter Mogielnicki, "Patient Refusal of Hydration and Nutrition: An Alternative to Physician Assisted Suicide or Voluntary Euthanasia," *Archives of Internal Medicine* 153: 2723–28 (December 27, 1993).

4. See Bernard Gert, James L. Bernat, and R. Peter Mogielnicki, "Distinguishing between Patients' Refusals and Requests," *The Hastings Center Report* 24 (4): 13–15 (July–August 1994).

5. See K. Danner Clouser, "Allowing or Causing: Another Look," *Annals of Internal Medicine* 87: 622–24 (1977).

6. See Kathleen M. Foley, M.D., "The Relationship of Pain and Symptom Management to Patient Requests for Physician-Assisted Suicide," *Journal of Pain and Symptom Management* 6 (5): 289–297 (July 1991).

7. This view is not held by all. Some, especially those with religious views, regard refusing treatment and especially refusing food and fluids when treatment, or food and fluids would sustain life for a long time, as committing suicide. But this is not the prevailing view, nor is it the view that governs the legal classification of the act. However, a terminally ill patient who intentionally goes into the woods in order to stop eating and drinking, does so, and thereby dies, would be regarded by most as having committed suicide. For a sensitive analysis of the difficulty of formulating a precise definition of "suicide," see Tom L. Beauchamp, "Suicide" in Tom Regan, ed., *Matters of Life and Death,* 2nd ed. (New York: Random House, 1986), pp. 77–89.

8. See K. Danner Clouser, "The Challenge for Future Debate on Euthanasia," *The Journal of Pain and Symptom Management* 6 (5): 306–311 (July 1991).

TIMOTHY E. QUILL, BERNARD LO, AND DAN W. BROCK

A Comparison of Voluntarily Stopping Eating and Drinking, Terminal Sedation, Physician-Assisted Suicide, and Voluntary Active Euthanasia

Timothy Quill is associate chief of Medicine at the Genesee Hospital, a professor of medicine and psychiatry at the University of Rochester School of Medicine and Dentistry, and a primary care internist in Rochester, New York. He also directs the University of Rochester's Program for Biopsychosocial Studies. His publications include *Death and Dignity: Making Choices and Taking Charge* and *A Midwife Through the Dying Process: Stories of Healing and Hard Choices in Life.*

Bernard Lo is director of the Center for AIDS Prevention Studies Ethics Core and a professor of medicine and director of the Program in Medical Ethics at UCSF. He is a member of the Board of Health Sciences Policy, the Institute of Medicine, the Board of Directors of the American Society of Law, Medicine, and Ethics, and the National Bioethics Advisory Commission. His publications include (with A. Alpers) "Physician-Assisted Suicide in Oregon: A Bold Experiment," in *Resolving Ethical Dilemmas: A Guide for Clinicians* (2000).

Palliative care is the standard of care when terminally ill patients find that the burdens of continued life-prolonging treatment outweigh the benefits.[1–4] To better relieve suffering near the end of life, physicians need to improve their skills in palliative care and to routinely discuss it earlier in the course of terminal illness. In addition, access to palliative care needs to be improved, particularly for those Americans who lack health insurance. However, even the highest-quality palliative care fails or becomes unacceptable for some patients, some of whom request help hastening death. Between 10% and 50% of patients in programs devoted to palliative care still report significant pain 1 week before death.[1,5–7] Furthermore, patients request a hastened death not simply because of unrelieved pain, but because of a wide variety of un-relieved physical symptoms in combination with loss of meaning, dignity, and independence.[8,9]

How should physicians respond when competent, terminally ill patients whose suffering is not relieved by palliative care request help in hastening death? If the patient is receiving life-prolonging interventions, the physician should discontinue them, in accordance with the patient's wishes. Some patients may voluntarily stop eating and drinking (VSED). If the patient has unrelieved pain or other symptoms and accepts sedation, the physician may legally administer terminal sedation (TS). However, it is generally legally impermissible for physicians to participate in physician-assisted suicide (PAS) or voluntary active euthanasia (VAE) in response to such patient requests. The recent Supreme Court decisions that determined that there is no constitutional right to PAS placed great emphasis on the importance of relieving pain and suffering near the end of life.[10,11] The Court acknowledged the legal acceptability of providing pain relief, even to the point

From *Journal of the American Medical Association* 278, no. 23 (December 17, 1997), 2099–2104.

of hastening death if necessary, and left open the possibility that states might choose to legalize PAS under some circumstances.

In this article, we compare VSED, TS, PAS, and VAE as potential interventions of last resort for competent, terminally ill patients who are suffering intolerably in spite of intensive efforts to palliate and who desire a hastened death. Some clinicians and patients may find some of the differences between these practices to be ethically and psychologically critical, whereas others perceive the differences as inconsequential. We will define and compare the practices, examine underlying ethical justifications, and consider appropriate categories of safeguards for whichever practices our society eventually condones.

DEFINITIONS AND CLINICAL COMPARISONS

With VSED, a patient who is otherwise physically capable of taking nourishment makes an active decision to discontinue all oral intake and then is gradually "allowed to die," primarily of dehydration or some intervening complication.[12-14] Depending on the patient's preexisting condition, the process will usually take 1 to 3 weeks or longer if the patient continues to take some fluids. Voluntarily stopping eating and drinking has several advantages. Many patients lose their appetites and stop eating and drinking in the final stages of many illnesses. Ethically and legally, the right of competent, informed patients to refuse life-prolonging interventions, including artificial hydration and nutrition, is firmly established, and voluntary cessation of "natural" eating and drinking could be considered an extension of that right. Because VSED requires considerable patient resolve, the voluntary nature of the action should be clear. Voluntarily stopping eating and drinking also protects patient privacy and independence, so much so that it potentially requires no participation by a physician.

The main disadvantages of VSED are that it may last for weeks and may initially increase suffering because the patient may experience thirst and hunger. Subtle coercion to proceed with the process may occur if patients are not regularly offered the opportunity to eat and drink, yet such offers may be viewed as undermining the patient's resolve. Some patients, family members, physicians, or nurses may find the notion of "dehydrating" or "starving" a patient to death to be morally repugnant. For patients whose current suffering is severe and unrelievable, the process would be unacceptable without sedation and analgesia. If physicians are not involved, palliation of

symptoms may be inadequate, the decision to forgo eating and drinking may not be informed, and cases of treatable depression may be missed. Patients are likely to lose mental clarity toward the end of this process, which may undermine their sense of personal integrity or raise questions about whether the action remains voluntary.

Although several articles,[12,13] including a moving personal narrative,[14] have proposed VSED as an alternative to other forms of hastened death, there are no data about how frequently such decisions are made or how acceptable they are to patients, families, physician, or nurses.

With TS, the suffering patient is sedated to unconsciousness, usually through ongoing administration of barbiturates or benzodiazepines. The patient then dies of dehydration, starvation, or some other intervening complication, as all life-sustaining interventions are withheld.[15-18] Although death is inevitable, it usually does not take place for days or even weeks, depending on clinical circumstances. Because patients are deeply sedated during this terminal period, they are believed to be free of suffering.

It can be argued that death with TS is "foreseen" but not "intended" and that the sedation itself is not causing death.[15-18] The sedation is intended to relieve suffering, a long-standing and uncontroversial aim of medicine, and the subsequent withholding of life-sustaining therapy has wide legal and ethical acceptance. Thus, TS probably requires no change in the law. The recent Supreme Court decision gave strong support to TS, saying that pain in terminally ill patients should be treated, even to the point of rendering the patient unconscious or hastening death.[10,11] Terminal sedation is already openly practiced by some palliative care and hospice groups in cases of unrelieved suffering, with a reported frequency from 0% to 44% of cases.[1,6,7,15-20]

Terminal sedation has other practical advantages. It can be carried out in patients with severe physical limitations. The time delay between initiation of TS and death permits second-guessing and reassessment by the health care team and the family. Because the health care team must administer medications and monitor effects, physicians can ensure that the patient's decision is informed and voluntary before beginning TS. In addition, many proponents believe that it is appropriate to use TS in patients who lack decision-making capacity but appear to be suffering intolerably, provided that the patient's suffering is extreme and otherwise unrelievable, and the surrogate or family agrees.

Nonetheless, TS remains controversial[21–23] and has many of the same risks associated with VAE and PAS. Like VAE, the final actors are the clinicians, not the patient. Terminal sedation could therefore be carried out without explicit discussions with alert patients who appear to be suffering intolerably or even against their wishes. Some competent, terminally ill patients reject TS. They believe that their dignity would be violated if they had to be unconscious for a prolonged time before they die, or that their families would suffer unnecessarily while waiting for them to die. Patients who wish to die in their own homes may not be able to arrange TS because it probably requires admission to a health care facility. There is some controversy in the anesthesia literature about whether heavily sedated persons are actually free of suffering or simply unable to report or remember it.[24–26] In some clinical situations, TS cannot relieve the patient's symptoms, as when a patient is bleeding uncontrollably from an eroding lesion or a refractory coagulation disorder, cannot swallow secretions because of widespread oropharyngeal cancer, or has refractory diarrhea from the acquired immunodeficiency syndrome (AIDS). Although such patients are probably not conscious of their condition once sedated, their death is unlikely to be dignified or remembered as peaceful by their families. Finally, and perhaps most critically, there may be confusion about the physician's ethical responsibility for contributing to the patient's death.[21,22]

With PAS, the physician provides the means, usually a prescription of a large dose of barbiturates, by which a patient can end his or her life.[1,3,27] Although the physician is morally responsible for this assistance, the patient has to carry out the final act. Physician-assisted suicide has several advantages. For some patients, access to a lethal dose of medication may give them the freedom and reassurance to continue living, knowing they can escape if and when they choose.[28,29] Because patients have to ingest the drug by their own hand, their action is likely to be voluntary. Physicians report being more comfortable with PAS than VAE,[30–32] presumably because their participation is indirect.

Opponents of PAS believe that it violates traditional moral and professional prohibitions against intentionally contributing to a patient's death. Physician-assisted suicide also has several practical disadvantages. Self-administration does not guarantee competence or voluntariness. The patient may have impaired judgment at the time of the request or the act or may be influenced by external pressures. Physician-assisted suicide is limited to patients who are physically capable of taking the medication themselves. It is not always effective,[33,34] so families may be faced with a patient who is vomiting, aspirating, or cognitively impaired, but not dying. Patients brought to the emergency department after ineffective attempts are likely to receive unwanted life-prolonging treatment. Requiring physicians to be present when patients ingest the medication could coerce an ambivalent patient to proceed, yet their absence may leave families to respond to medical complications alone.

Physician-assisted suicide is illegal in most states, but no physicians have ever been successfully prosecuted for their participation.[3] Several studies have documented a secret practice of PAS in the United States. In Washington State, 12% of physicians responding to a survey had received genuine requests for PAS within the year studied.[8] Twenty-four percent of requests were acceded to, and over half of those patients died as a result. An Oregon study showed similar results.[35] Physician-assisted suicide is usually conducted covertly, without consultation, guidelines, or documentation. Public controversy about legalizing PAS continues in the United States. After narrow defeats of referenda in the states of Washington and California, an Oregon referendum was passed in 1994 that legalized PAS, subject to certain safeguards.[36] After a series of legal challenges, the Oregon legislature required that the referendum be resubmitted to the electorate this November before implementation, and it was repassed this November by a margin of 60% to 40%. The US Supreme Court ruled that laws in the states of Washington and New York prohibiting PAS were not unconstitutional, but the Court simultaneously encouraged public discussion and state experimentation through the legislative and referendum processes.[10,11,37,38]

With VAE, the physician not only provides the means, but is the final actor by administering a lethal injection at the patient's request.[1,3,25] As practiced in the Netherlands, the patient is sedated to unconsciousness and then given a lethal injection of a muscle-paralyzing agent like curare. For patients who are prepared to die because their suffering in intolerable, VAE has the advantages of being quick and effective. Patients need not have manual dexterity, the ability to swallow, or an intact gastrointestinal system. Voluntary active euthanasia also requires active and direct physician participation. Physicians can ensure the patient's competence and voluntariness at the time of the act, support the family, and respond to complications. The directness of the act makes the physician's moral responsibility clear.

On the other hand, VAE explicitly and directly conflicts with traditional medical prohibitions against intentionally causing death.[39] Although intended to relieve suffering, VAE achieves this goal by causing death. Furthermore, VAE could be conducted without explicit patient consent.[40,41] If abused, VAE could then be used on patients who appear to be suffering severely or posing extreme burdens to physician, family, or society, but have lost the mental capacity to make informed decisions.

The Netherlands is the only country where VAE and PAS are openly practiced, regulated, and studied, although the practices remain technically illegal. According to the Remmelink reports,[9,42,43] VAE accounts for 1.8% to 2.4% of all deaths, and PAS, another 0.2% to 0.4%. In 0.7% to 0.8% of deaths, active euthanasia was performed on patients who had lost the capacity to consent, raising concern about whether guidelines restricting VAE is competent patients can be enforced in practice.[44]

United States laws prohibiting VAE, however, are stricter than those governing PAS and more likely to be prosecuted. Physicians are also more reluctant to participate in VAE even if it were legalized.[30,31] Even less is known about the secret practice of VAE than of PAS in the United States. The recent Washington State study showed that 4% of physicians had received a genuine request for VAE within the year studied, and 24% of those responded by administering a lethal injection.[8] Voluntary active euthanasia was recently legalized in a province of Australia, but this legalization was subsequently reversed by the legislature.[45]

ETHICAL COMPARISONS BETWEEN THE PRACTICES

Many normative ethical analyses use the doctrine of double effect and the distinction between active and passive assistance to distinguish between currently permissible acts that may hasten death (forgoing life-sustaining treatment and high-dose pain medications) and those that are impermissible (PAS and VAE).[1,2,4,46,47] Both TS and VSED have been argued to be ethically preferable alternatives to PAS and VAE

on the basis of similar arguments.[12,13,16,19] In this section, we will critically examine these analyses. We also discuss the issues of voluntariness, proportionality, and conflict of duties, which may ultimately be more central to the ethical evaluation of these options. We suggest that there are more problems with the doctrine of double effect and the active/passive distinction than are ordinarily acknowledged and that TS and VSED are more complex and less easily distinguished ethically from PAS and VAE than proponents seem to realize. Our discussion in this section will be restricted to the potential ethical permissibility of these actions and not the public policy implications.

DOCTRINE OF DOUBLE EFFECT

When evaluating an action, the doctrine of double effect distinguishes between effects that a person intends (both the end sought and the means taken to the end) and consequences that are foreseen but unintended.[21,22,48,49] As long as the physician's intentions are good, it is permissible to perform actions with foreseeable consequences that it would be wrong to intend. In this view, intentionally causing death is morally impermissible, even if desired by a competent patient whose suffering could not otherwise be relieved. But if death comes unintentionally as the consequence of an otherwise well-intentioned intervention, even if foreseen with a high probability, the physician's action can be morally acceptable. The unintended but foreseen bad effect must also be proportional to the intended good effects.

The doctrine of double effect has been important in justifying the use of sufficient pain medications to relieve suffering near the end of life.[1,2,4,46,47] When high-dose opioids are used to treat pain, neither the patient nor the physician intends to accelerate death, but they accept the risk of unintentionally hastening death in order to relieve the pain. The doctrine of double effect has also been used to distinguish TS from PAS and VAE.[15,16,18,19] Relief of suffering is intended in all 3 options, but death is argued to be intended with PAS and VAE but is merely foreseen with TS. Yet to us it seems implausible to claim that death is unintended when a patient who wants to die is sedated to the point of coma, and intravenous fluids and artificial nutrition are withheld, making death certain.[21,22,50] Although the overarching intention of the sedation is to relieve the patient's suffering, the additional step of withholding fluids and nutrition is not needed to relieve pain, but is typically taken to hasten the patient's wished-for death. In contrast, when patients are similarly sedated to treat conditions like status epilepticus, therapies such as fluids and mechanical ventilation are continued with the goal of prolonging life.

According to the doctrine of double effect, intentionally taking life is always morally impermissible, whereas doing so foreseeably but unintentionally can be permissible when it produces a proportionate good. As applied to end-of-life medical decision making, the intentions of the physician are given more moral weight than the wishes and circumstances of the patient. An alternative view is that it is morally wrong to take the life of a person who wants to live, whether doing so intentionally or foreseeably. In this view, what can make TS morally permissible is that the patient gives informed consent to it, not that the physician only foresees but does not intend the patient's inevitable death.

The issue of intention is particularly complicated because the determination of what is intended by the patient or physician is often difficult to verify and because practices that are universally accepted may involve the intention to hasten death in some cases.[21,51] Death is not always intended or sought when competent patients forgo life support; sometimes patients simply do not want to continue a particular treatment, but hope nevertheless that they can live without it. But some patients find their circumstances intolerable, even with the best of care, and refuse further life support with the intent of bringing about their death. There is broad agreement that physicians must respect such refusals, even when the patient's intention is to die.[1–4,46,47,51] However, such practices are highly problematic when analyzed according to the doctrine of double effect.

THE ACTIVE/PASSIVE DISTINCTION

According to many normative ethical analyses, active measures that hasten death are unacceptable, whereas passive or indirect measures that achieve the same ends would be permitted.[1,2,4,46,47,52] However, how the active/passive distinction applies to these 4 practices remains controversial.[21,27] Voluntary active euthanasia is active assistance in dying, because the physician's actions directly cause the patient's death. Stopping life-sustaining therapies is typically considered passive assistance in dying, and the patient is said to die of the underlying disease no matter how proximate the physician's action and the patient's death. Physicians, however, sometimes experience stopping life-sustaining interventions as very active.[53] For example, there is nothing psychologically or physically passive about taking someone off a mechanical ventilator who is incapable of breathing on his or her own. Voluntarily stopping eating and drinking is argued to be a variant of stopping life-sustaining therapy, and the patient is said to die of the underlying disease.[12,13] However, the notion that VSED is passively "letting nature take its course" is unpersuasive, because patients with no underlying disease would also die if they stopped eating and drinking. Death is more a result of the patient's will and resolve than an inevitable consequence of his disease. Furthermore, even if the physician's role in hastening death is generally passive or indirect, most would argue that it is desirable to have physicians involved to ensure the patient is fully informed and to actively palliate symptoms.

Both PAS and TS are challenging to evaluate according to the active/passive distinction. Physician-assisted suicide is active in that the physician provides the means whereby the patient may take his or her life and thereby contributes to a new and different cause of death than the patient's disease. However, the physician's role in PAS is passive or indirect because the patient administers the lethal medication. The psychological and temporal distance between the prescribing and the act may also make PAS seem indirect and thereby more acceptable to physicians than VAE.[30–32] These ambiguities may allow the physician to characterize his or her actions as passive or indirect.[21,50]

Terminal sedation is passive because the administration of sedation does not directly cause the patient's death and because the withholding of artificial feedings and fluids is commonly considered passively allowing the patient to die.[15,16,19] However, some physicians and nurses may consider it very active to sedate to unconsciousness someone who is seeking death and then to withhold life-prolonging interventions. Furthermore, the notion that TS is merely "letting nature take its course" is problematic, because often the patient dies of dehydration from the withholding of fluids, not of the underlying disease.

The application and the moral importance of both the active/passive distinction and the doctrine of double effect are notoriously controversial and should not serve as the primary basis of determining the morality of these practices.

VOLUNTARINESS

We suggest that the patient's wishes and competent consent are more ethically important than whether the acts are categorized as active or passive or whether death is intended or unintended by the physician.[54–56] With competent patients, none of these acts would be morally permissible without the patient's voluntary and informed consent. Any of these actions would violate a competent patient's autonomy and would be both immoral and illegal if the patient did not understand that death was the inevitable consequence of the action or if the decision was coerced or contrary to the patient's wishes. The ethical principle of autonomy focuses on patients' rights to make important decisions about their lives, including what happens to their bodies, and may support genuinely autonomous forms of these acts.[27,52]

However, because most of these acts require cooperation from physicians and, in the case of TS, the health care team, the autonomy of participating medical professionals also warrants consideration. Because TS, VSED, PAS, and VAE are not part of usual medical practice and they all result in a hastened death, clinicians should have the right to determine the nature and extent of their own participation. All physicians should respect patients' decisions to forgo life-sustaining treatment, including artificial hydration and nutrition, and provide standard palliative care, including skillful pain and symptom management. If society permits some or all of these practices (currently TS and VSED are openly tolerated), physicians who choose not to participate because of personal moral considerations should at a minimum discuss all available alternatives in the spirit of informed consent and respect for patient autonomy. Physicians are free to express their own objections to these practices as part of the informing process, to propose alternative approaches, and to transfer care to another physician if the patient continues to request actions to hasten death that they find unacceptable.

PROPORTIONALITY

The principles of beneficence and nonmaleficence obligate the physician to act in the patient's best interests and to avoid causing net harm.[52] The concept of proportionality requires that the risk of causing harm must bear a direct relationship to the danger and immediacy of the patient's clinical situation and the expected benefit of the intervention.[52,57] The greater the patient's suffering, the greater risk the physician can take of potentially contributing to the patient's death, so long as the patient understands and accepts that risk. For a patient with lung cancer who is anxious and short of breath, the risk of small doses of morphine or anxiolytics is warranted. At a later time, if the patient is near death and gasping for air, more aggressive sedation is warranted, even in doses that may well cause respiratory depression. Although proportionality is an important element of the doctrine of double effect, proportionality can be applied independently of this doctrine. Sometimes a patient's suffering cannot be relieved despite optimal palliative care, and continuing to live causes torment that can end only with death.[58] Such extreme circumstances sometimes warrant extraordinary medical actions, and the forms of hastening death under consideration in this article may satisfy the requirement of proportionality. The requirement of proportionality, which all health care interventions should meet, does not support any principled ethical distinction between these 4 options.

CONFLICT OF DUTIES

Unrelievable, intolerable suffering by patients at the end of life may create for physicians an explicit conflict between their ethical and professional duty to relieve suffering and their understanding of their ethical and professional duty not to use at least some means of deliberately hastening death.[57,59] Physicians who believe they should respond to such suffering by acceding to the patient's request for a hastened death may find themselves caught between their duty to the patient as a caregiver and their duty to obey the law as a citizen.[58] Solutions often can be found in the intensive application of palliative care, or within the currently legitimized options of forgoing life supports, VSED, or TS. Situations in which VSED or TS may not be adequate include terminally ill patients with uncontrolled bleeding, obstruction from nasopharyngeal cancer, and refractory AIDS diarrhea or patients who believe that spending their last days iatrogenically sedated would be meaningless, frightening, or degrading. Clearly the physician has a moral obligation not to abandon patients with refractory suffering[60]; hence, those physicians who could not provide some or all of these options because of moral or legal reservations should be required to search assiduously with the patient for mutually acceptable solutions.

SAFEGUARDS

In the United States, health care is undergoing radical reform driven more by market forces than by commitments to quality of care,[61,62] and 42 million persons are currently uninsured. Capitated reimbursement could provide financial incentives to encourage terminally ill patients to hasten their deaths. Physicians' participation in hastening death by any of these methods can be justified only as a last resort when standard palliative measures are ineffective or unacceptable to the patient.

Safeguards to protect vulnerable patients from the risk of error, abuse, or coercion must be constructed for any of these practices that are ultimately accepted. These risks, which have been extensively cited in the debates about PAS and VAE,[39–41] also exist for TS and VSED. Both TS and VSED could be carried out without ensuring that optimal palliative care has been provided. This risk may be particularly great if VSED is carried out without physician involvement. In TS, physicians who unreflectively believe that death is unintended or that it is not their explicit purpose may fail to acknowledge the inevitable consequences of their action or their responsibility.

The typical safeguards proposed for regulating VAE and PAS[63–66] are intended to allow physicians to respond to unrelieved suffering, while ensuring that adequate palliative measures have been attempted and that patient decisions are autonomous. These safeguards need to balance respect for patient privacy with the need to adequately oversee these interventions. Similar professional safeguards should be considered for TS and VSED, even if these practices are already sanctioned by the law. The challenge of safeguards is to be flexible enough to be responsive to individual patient dilemmas and rigorous enough to protect vulnerable persons.

Categories of safeguards include the following.

1. Palliative care ineffective: Excellent palliative care must be available, yet insufficient to relieve intolerable suffering for a particular patient.

2. Informed consent: Patients must be fully informed about and capable of understanding their condition and treatment alternatives (and their risks and benefits). Requests for a hastened death must be pa-

tient initiated, free of undue influence, and enduring. Waiting periods must be flexible, depending on the nearness of inevitable death and the severity of immediate suffering.

3. Diagnostic and prognostic clarity: Patients must have a clearly diagnosed disease with known lethality. The prognosis must be understood, including the degree of uncertainty about outcomes (ie, how long the patient might live).

4. Independent second opinion: A consultant with expertise in palliative care should review the case. Specialists should also review any questions about the patient's diagnosis or prognosis. A psychiatrist should consult if there is uncertainty about treatable depression or about the patient's mental capacity.

5. Documentation and review: Explicit processes for documentation, reporting, and review should be in place to ensure accountability.

The restriction of any of these methods to the terminally ill involves a trade-off. Some patients who suffer greatly from incurable, but not terminal, illnesses and who are unresponsive to palliative measures will be denied access to a hastened death and forced to continue suffering against their will. Other patients whose request for a hastened death is denied will avoid a premature death because their suffering can subsequently be relieved with more intensive palliative care. Some methods (e.g., PAS, VAE, TS) might be restricted to the terminally ill because of current inequities of access, concerns about errors and abuse, and lack of experience with the process. Others (e.g., VSED) might be allowed for those who are incurably ill, but not imminently dying, if they meet all other criteria, because of the inherent waiting period, the great resolve that they require, and the opportunity for reconsideration. If any methods are extended to the incurably, but not terminally, ill, safeguards should be more stringent, including substantial waiting periods and mandatory assessment by psychiatrists and specialists, because the risk and consequences of error are increased.

We believe that clinical, ethical, and policy differences and similarities among these 4 practices need to be debated openly, both publicly and within the medical profession. Some may worry that a discussion of the similarities between VSED and TS on the one hand and PAS and VAE on the other may undermine the desired goal of optimal relief of suffering at the end of life.[40,41] Others may worry that a critical analysis of the principle of double effect or the active/passive distinction as applied to VSED and

TS may undermine efforts to improve pain relief or to ensure that patient's or surrogate's decisions to forgo unwanted life-sustaining therapy are respected.[67] However, hidden, ambiguous practices, inconsistent justifications, and failure to acknowledge the risks of accepted practices may also undermine the quality of terminal care and put patients at unwarranted risk.

Allowing a hastened death only in the context of access to good palliative care puts it in its proper perspective as a small but important facet of comprehensive care for all dying patients.[1-4] Currently, TS and VSED are probably legal and are widely accepted by hospice and palliative care physicians. However, they may not be readily available because some physicians may continue to have moral objections and legal fears about these options. Physician-assisted suicide is illegal in most states, but may be difficult, if not impossible, to successfully prosecute if it is carried out at the request of an informed patient. Voluntary active euthanasia is illegal and more likely to be aggressively prosecuted if uncovered. In the United States, there is an underground, erratically available practice of PAS and even VAE that is quietly condoned.

Explicit public policies about which of these 4 practices are permissible and under what circumstances could have important benefits. Those who fear a bad death would face the end of life knowing that their physicians could respond openly if their worst fears materialize. For most, reassurance will be all that is needed, because good palliative care is generally effective. Explicit guidelines for the practices that are deemed permissible can also encourage clinicians to explore why a patient requests hastening of death, to search for palliative care alternatives, and to respond to those whose suffering is greatest.[58,60,68-70]

REFERENCES

1. Foley K. M. Pain, physician-assisted suicide, and euthanasia. *Pain Forum*. 1995;4:163–178.

2. Council on Scientific Affairs, American Medical Association. Good care of the dying patient. *JAMA* 1996;275: 474–478.

3. Quill T. E.: *Death and Dignity: Making Choices and Taking Charge*. New York, NY: WW Norton & Co; 1993:1–255.

4. American Board of Internal Medicine End of Life Patient Care Project Committee. *Caring for the Dying: Identification and Promotion of Physician Competency*. Philadelphia, Pa: American Board of Internal Medicine; 1996.

5. Kasting G. A.: The nonnecessity of euthanasia. In: Humber J. D., Almeder R. F., Kasting G. A., eds. *Physician-Assisted Death*. Totowa, NJ: Humana Press; 1993:25–43.

6. Coyle N., Adelhardt J., Foley K. M., Portenoy R. K. Character of terminal illness in the advance cancer patient. *J Pain Symptom Manage*. 1990;5:83–93.

7. Ingham J., Portenoy R. Symptom assessment. *Hematol Oncol Clin North Am*. 1996;10:21–39.

8. Back A. L., Wallace J. I., Starks H. E., Pearlman R. A. Physician-assisted suicide and euthanasia in Washington State. *JAMA*. 1996;275:919–925.

9. vanderMaas P. J., van Delden J. J. M., Pijnenborg L. *Euthanasia and Other Medical Decisions Concerning the End of Life*. Amsterdam, the Netherlands: Elsevier, 1992.

10. *Vacco v. Quill*, 117 SCt 2293 (1997).

11. *Washington v. Glucksberg*, 117 SCt 2258 (1997).

12. Bernat J. L., Gert B., Mogielnicki R. P. Patient refusal of hydration and nutrition. *Arch Intern Med*. 1993;153:2723–2727.

13. Printz L. A. Terminal dehydration, a compassionate treatment. *Arch Intern Med* 1992;152:697–700.

14. Eddy D. M. A conversation with my mother. *JAMA*. 1994;272:179 181.

15. Cherney N. I., Portenoy R. K. Sedation in the management of refractory symptoms: guidelines for evaluation and treatment. *J Palliat Care*. 1994;10:31–38.

16. Truog R. D., Berde D. B., Mitchell C., Grier H.E. Barbiturates in the care of the terminally ill. *N Engl J Med*. 1991;327:1678–1681.

17. Enck R. E. *The Medical Care of Terminally Ill Patients*. Baltimore, Md: Johns Hopkins University Press; 1994.

18. Saunders C., Sykes N. *The Management of Terminal Malignant Disease*. 3rd ed. London, England: Hodder Headline Group; 1993:1–305.

19. Byock I. R. Consciously walking the fine line: thoughts on a hospice response to assisted suicide and euthanasia. *J Palliat Care*. 1993;9:25–58.

20. Ventrafridda B., Ripamonti C., DeConno F., et al. Symptom prevalence and control during cancer patients' last days of life. *J Palliat Care* 1990;6:7–11.

21. Brody H. Causing, intending, and assisting death. *J Clin Ethics*. 1993;4:112–117.

22. Billings J. A. Slow euthanasia. *J Palliat Care*. 1996; 12:21–30.

23. Orentlicher D. The Supreme Court and physician-assisted suicide: rejecting assisted suicide but embracing euthanasia. *N Engl J Med*. 1997;337:1236–1239.

24. Moerman N., Bonke B., Oosting J. Awareness and recall during general anesthesia: facts and feelings. *Anesthesiology*. 1993;79:454–464.

25. Utting J. E. Awareness: clinical aspects; consciousness, awareness, and pain. In: Rosen M, Linn JN. *General Anesthesia*. London, England: Butterworths; 1987:171–179.

26. Evans J. M. Patient's experience of awareness during general anesthesia; consciousness, awareness and pain. In: Rosen M, Linn JN. *General Anesthesia*. London, England: Butterworths; 1987:184–192.

27. Brock D. W. Voluntary active euthanasia. *Hastings Cent Rep*. 1992;22:10–22.

28. Quill T. E. Death and dignity. *N Engl J Med*. 1991; 324:691–694.

29. Rollin B. *Last Wish*. New York, NY: Warner Books, 1985.

30. Cohen J. S., Fihn S. D., Boyko E. J., et al. Attitudes toward assisted suicide and euthanasia among physicians in Washington State. *N Engl J Med*. 1994;331:89–94.

31. Bachman J. G., Alchser K. H., Koukas D. J., et al. Attitudes of Michigan physicians and the public toward legalizing physician-assisted suicide and voluntary euthanasia. *N Engl J Med.* 1996;334:303–309.

32. Duberstein P. R, Conwell Y., Cox C., et al. Attitudes toward self-determined death. *J Am Geriatr Soc.* 1995;43:395–400.

33. Preston T. A., Mero R. Observations concerning terminally-ill patients who choose suicide. *J Pharm Care Pain Symptom Control.* 1996;1:183–192.

34. Admiraal P. V. Toepassing van euthanatica (the use of euthanatics). *Ned Tijdschr Geneeskd.* 1995;139:265–268.

35. Lee M. A., Nelson H. D., Tilden V. P., Ganzini L., Schmidt T. A., Tolle S. W. Legalizing assisted suicide: views of physicians in Oregon. *N Engl J Med.* 1996;334:310–315.

36. Alpers A., Lo B. Physician-assisted suicide in Oregon: a bold experiment. *JAMA.* 1995;274:483–487.

37. *Compassion in Dying v Washington,* No. 94-35534, 1966 WL 94848 (9th Cir, Mar 6, 1996).

38. *Quill v. Vacco,* No. 95-7028 (2d Cir. April 9, 1996).

39. Gaylin W., Kass L. R., Pellegrino E. D., Siegler M. Doctors must not kill. *JAMA.* 1988;259:2139–2140.

40. Teno J., Lynn J. Voluntary active euthanasia: the individual case and public policy. *J Am Geriatr Soc.* 1991;39:827–830.

41. Kamisar Y. Against assisted suicide—even a very limited form. *Univ Detroit Mercy Law Rev.* 1995;72:735–769.

42. vanderMaas P. J, vanderWal G., Haverkate I., et al. Euthanasia, physician-assisted suicide and other medical practices involving the end of life in the Netherlands, 1990–1995. *N Engl J Med.* 1996;335:1699–1705.

43. van der Wal G., van der Maas P. J., Bosma J. M., et al. Evaluation of the notification procedure for physician-assisted death in the Netherlands. *N Engl J Med.* 1996;335:1706–1711.

44. Hendin H. Seduced by death. *Issues Law Med.* 1994;10:123–168.

45. Ryan C. J., Kaye M. Euthanasia in Australia: the Northern Territory rights of the terminally ill act. *N Engl J Med.* 1996;334:326–328.

46. President's Commission for the Study of Ethical Problems in Medicine and Biomedical and Behavioral Research. *Deciding to Forego Life-Sustaining Treatment: Ethical, Medical and Legal Issues in Treatment Decisions.* Washington, DC: US Government Printing Office; 1982.

47. The Hastings Center Report. *Guidelines on the Termination of Life-Sustaining Treatment and the Care of the Dying.* Briarcliff Manor, NY: Hastings Center, 1987.

48. Marquis D. B. Four versions of the double effect. *J Med Philos.* 1991;16:515–544.

49. Kamm F. The doctrine of double effect. *J Med Philos.* 1991:16:571–585.

50. Quill T. E. The ambiguity of clinical intentions. *N Engl J Med.* 1993;329:1039–1040.

51. Alpers A., Lo B. Does it make clinical sense to equate terminally ill patients who require life-sustaining interventions with those who do not? *JAMA.* 1997;277:1705–1708.

52. Beauchamp T. L., Childress J. F. *Principles of Biomedical Ethics.* 4th ed. New York, NY: Oxford University Press; 1994.

53. Edwards M. J., Tolle S. W. Disconnecting a ventilator at the request of a patient who knows he will die. *Ann Intern Med.* 1992;117:254–256.

54. Orentlicher D. The legalization of physician-assisted suicide. *N Engl J Med.* 1996;335:663–667.

55. Drickamer M. A., Lee Ganzini L. Practical issues in physician-assisted suicide. *Ann Intern Med.* 1997;126:146–151.

56. Angell M. The Supreme Court and physician-assisted suicide: the ultimate right. *N Engl J Med.* 1997;336:50–53.

57. de Wachter M. A. M. Active euthanasia in the Netherlands. *JAMA.* 1989;262:3316–3319.

58. Quill T. E., Brody R. V. 'You promised me I wouldn't die like this': a bad death as a medical emergency. *Arch Intern Med.* 1995;155:1250–1254.

59. Welie J. V. M. The medical exception: physicians, euthanasia and the Dutch criminal law. *J Med Philos.* 1992;17:419–437.

60. Quill T. E., Cassel C. K. Nonabandonment: a central obligation for physicians. *Ann Intern Med.* 1995;122:368–374.

61. Emanuel E. J., Brett A. S. Managed competition and the patient-physician relationship. *N Engl J Med.* 1993;329:879–882.

62. Morrison R. S., Meier D. E. Managed care at the end of life. *Trends Health Care Law Ethics.* 1995;10:91–96.

63. Quill T. E., Cassel C. K., Meier D. E. Care of the hopelessly ill: proposed criteria for physician-assisted suicide. *N Engl J Med* 1992;327:1380–1384.

64. Brody H. Assisted death. *N Engl J Med.* 1992;327:1284–1388.

65. Miller F. G., Quill T. E., Brody H., et al. Regulating physician-assisted death. *N Engl J Med.* 1994;331:119–123.

66. Baron C. H., Bergstresser C., Brock D. W., et al. Statute: a model state act to authorize and regulate physician-assisted suicide. *Harvard J Legislation* 1996;33:1–34.

67. Mount B., Flanders E. M. Morphine drips, terminal sedation, and slow euthanasia: definition and facts, not anecdotes. *J Palliat Care.* 1996;12:31–37.

68. Lee M. A., Tolle S. W. Oregon's assisted-suicide vote: the silver lining. *Ann Intern Med.* 1996;124:267–269.

69. Block S. D., Billings A. Patient requests to hasten death: evaluation and management in terminal care. *Arch Intern Med.* 1994;154:2039–2047.

70. Quill T. E., Doctor, I want to die: will you help me? *JAMA.* 1993;270:870–873.

SUGGESTED READINGS FOR CHAPTER 4

Angell, Marcia. "The Supreme Court and Physician-Assisted Suicide—the Ultimate Right." *New England Journal of Medicine* 336 (1997), 50–53.

Annas, George J., and Grodin, Michael, eds. *The Nazi Doctors and the Nuremberg Code.* New York: Oxford University Press, 1992.

Battin, Margaret P., Rhodes, Rosamond, and Silvers, Anita, eds. *Physician Assisted Suicide: Expanding the Debate.* New York, NY: Routledge, 1998.

Beauchamp, Tom L., ed. *Intending Death: The Ethics of Assisted Suicide and Euthanasia.* Upper Saddle River, NJ: Prentice-Hall, 1996.

Beauchamp, Tom L., and Veatch, Robert, eds. *Ethical Issues in Death and Dying.* Upper Saddle River, NJ: Prentice-Hall, 1997.

Beauchamp, Tom L., and Childress, James F. *Principles of Biomedical Ethics,* 5th ed. New York: Oxford University Press, 2001, chap. 4.

Bernat, James L., Gert, Bernard, and Mogielnicki, R. Peter. "Patient Refusal of Hydration and Nutrition: An Alternative to Physician-Assisted Suicide or Voluntary Active Euthanasia." *Archives of Internal Medicine* 153 (December 27, 1993), 2723–28.

Brock, Dan W. "A Critique of Three Objectives to Physician-Assisted Suicide." *Ethics* 109 (April 1999), 519–47.

———. "Death and Dying." In Robert M. Veatch, ed. *Medical Ethics,* 2d ed. Boston: Jones and Bartlett, 1997.

———. "Medical Decisions at the End of Life." In Helga Kuhse and Peter Singer, eds. *A Companion to Bioethics.* Malden, MA: Blackwell, 1998, 231–41.

Brody, Baruch A. *Suicide and Euthanasia: Historical and Contemporary Themes.* Dordrecht, Holland: Kluwer Academic Publishers, 1989.

Callahan, Daniel. "Pursuing a Peaceful Death." *Hastings Center Report* 23 (1993), 32–38.

———. *The Troubled Dream of Life: Living with Mortality.* New York: Simon & Schuster, 1993.

Cantor, Norman L. "Glucksberg, the Putative Right to Adequate Pain Relief, and Death with Dignity." *Journal of Health Law* 34 (2001), 301–33.

Caplan, Arthur, and Blank, Robert H, eds. *Compassion: Government Intervention in the Treatment of Critically Ill Newborns.* Totowa, NJ: Humana Press, 1992.

Cassel, Christine K. "Physician-Assisted Suicide: Are We Asking the Right Questions?" *Second Opinion* 18 (October 1992), 95–98.

Cavanaugh, Thomas A. "Currently Accepted Practices That Are Known to Lead to Death, and PAS: Is There an Ethically Relevant Difference?" *Cambridge Quarterly of Healthcare Ethics* 7 (Fall 1998), 375–81.

Dworkin, Ronald. *Life's Dominion: An Argument about Abortion, Euthanasia, and Individual Freedom.* New York: Knopf, 1993.

Dworkin, Gerald, Frey, Raymond G., and Bok, Sissela. *Euthanasia and Physician-Assisted Suicide: For and Against.* New York: Cambridge University Press, 1998.

Emanuel, Ezekiel J. "What Is the Great Benefit of Legalizing Euthanasia or Physician-Assisted Suicide?" *Ethics* 109 (April 1999), 629–42.

———, et al. "The Practice of Euthanasia and Physician-Assisted Suicide in the United States: Adherence to Proposed Safeguards and Effects on Physicians." *Journal of the American Medical Association* 280 (August 1998), 507–13.

Emanuel, Linda L., ed. *Regulating How We Die: The Ethical, Medical, and Legal Issues Surrounding Physician-Assisted Suicide.* Cambridge, MA: Harvard University Press, 1998.

Gert, Bernard, Culver, Charles M., and Clouser, K. Danner, *Bioethics: A Return to Fundamentals.* New York: Oxford, 1997, chaps. 11–12.

Glover, Jonathan. *Causing Death and Saving Lives.* New York: Penguin Books, 1977.

Gomez, Carlos. *Regulating Death: Euthanasia and the Case of the Netherlands.* New York: Free Press, 1991.

Gostin, Lawrence O. "Deciding Life and Death in the Courtroom: From *Quinlan* to *Cruzan, Glucksberg,* and *Vacco*—A Brief History and Analysis of Constitutional Protection of the 'Right to Die.' " *Journal of the American Medical Association* 278 (November 1997), 1523–28.

Kadish Sanford H. "Authorizing Death." In Jules Coleman, and Allen Buchanan, eds. *Harm's Way.* Cambridge: Cambridge University Press, 1993.

Kamm, Frances M. "Physician-Assisted Suicide, The Doctrine of Double Effect, and the Ground of Value." *Ethics* 109 (April 1999), 586–605.

Koop, C. Everett, and Grant, Edward R. "The 'Small Beginnings' of Euthanasia." *Journal of Law, Ethics & Public Policy* 2 (1986), 607–32.

Leenen, H. J. J., and Ciesielski-Carlucci, Chris. "*Force majeure* (Legal Necessity): Justification for Active Termination of Life in the Case of Severely Handicapped Newborns after Forgoing Treatment." *Cambridge Quarterly of Healthcare Ethics* 2 (Summer 1993), 271–74.

Lifton, Robert J. *The Nazi Doctors: Medical Killing and the Psychology of Genocide.* New York: Basic Books, 1986.

McMillan, Richard C., Engelhardt, H. Tristram, Jr., and Spicker, Stuart F., eds. *Euthanasia and the Newborn: Conflicts Regarding Saving Lives.* Dordrecht: D. Reidel, 1987.

Meier, Diane E., et al. "A National Survey of Physician-Assisted Suicide and Euthanasia in the United States." *New England Journal of Medicine* 338 (April 23, 1998), 1193–1201.

Meisel, Alan. *The Right to Die,* 2d ed. New York: John Wiley and Sons, 1995.

———, Jernigan, Jan C., and Youngner, Stuart J. "Prosecutors and End-of-Life Decision Making." *Archives of Internal Medicine* 159 (May 1999), 1089–95.

Miller, Franklin G., et al. "Regulating Physician-Assisted Death." *New England Journal of Medicine* 331 (1994), 119–23.

———, Fins, Joseph J., and Snyder, Lois. "Assisted Suicide Compared with Refusal of Treatment: A Valid Distinction?" *Annals of Internal Medicine* 132 (March 2000), 470–75.

New York State Task Force on Life and the Law. *When Death Is Sought: Assisted Suicide and Euthanasia in the Medical Context.* New York: New York State Task Force, 1994.

Orentlicher, David. "The Legalization of Physician Assisted Suicide: A Very Modest Revolution." *Boston College Law Review* 28 (1997), 443–75.

Perrett, Roy W. "Killing, Letting Die and the Bare Difference Argument." *Bioethics* 10 (1996), 131–39.

Quill, Timothy E. "Death and Dignity: A Case of Individualized Decision Making." *New England Journal of Medicine* 324 (March 7, 1991), 691–94.

———. *Death and Dignity: Making Choices and Taking Charge.* New York: W. W. Norton, 1993.

———, et al. "The Debate over Physician-Assisted Suicide: Empirical Data and Convergent Views." *Annals of Internal Medicine* 128 (April 1998), 552–58.

———, et al. "Palliative Treatments of Last Resort: Choosing the Least Harmful Alternative." *Annals of Internal Medicine* 132 (March 2000), 488–93.

———, and Byock, Ira R. "Responding to Intractable Terminal Suffering: The Role of Terminal Sedation and Voluntary Refusal of Food and Fluids: Position Paper." *Annals of Internal Medicine* 132 (March 2000), 408–14.

Rachels, James. "Active and Passive Euthanasia." *New England Journal of Medicine* 292 (January 9, 1975), 78–80.

———. *The End of Life: Euthanasia and Morality.* Oxford: Oxford University Press, 1986.

Regan, Tom, ed. *Matters of Life and Death,* 3d ed. New York: Random House, 1992.

Salem, Tania. "Physician-Assisted Suicide: Promoting Autonomy—or Medicalizing Suicide? *Hastings Center Report* 29 (May–June 1999), 30–36.

Schaffner, Kenneth F. "Recognizing the Tragic Choice: Food, Water, and the Right to Assisted Suicide." *Critical Care Medicine* 16 (October 1988), 1063–68.

Stead, William W., et al. "Terminal Dehydration as an Alternative to Physician-Assisted Suicide." [Letters and responses]. *Annals of Internal Medicine* 129 (December 1998), 1080–82.

Thomasma, David C. "When Physicians Choose to Participate in the Death of Their Patients." *Journal of Law, Medicine & Ethics* 24 (1996), 183–97.

———, and Graber, Glenn C. *Euthanasia: Toward an Ethical Social Policy.* New York: Continuum, 1990.

Truog, Robert, and Berde, Charles B. "Pain, Euthanasia, and Anesthesiologists." *Anesthesiology* 78 (February 1993), 353–60.

———, et al. "Barbiturates in the Care of the Terminally Ill." *New England Journal of Medicine* 327 (December 3, 1992), 1678–82.

Thomson, Judith Jarvis. "Physician-Assisted Suicide: Two Moral Arguments." *Ethics* 109 (April 1999), 497–518.

van Delden, Johannes J. M., et al. "The Remmelink Study: Two Years Later." *Hastings Center Report* 23 (1993), 24–27.

van der Maas, Paul J, et al. "Euthanasia and Other Medical Decisions Concerning the End of Life." *Lancet* 338 (1991), 669–74.

Velleman, J. David. "A Right to Self-Termination?" *Ethics* 109 (April 1999), 606–28.

Wanzer, S. H., et al. "The Physician's Responsibility toward Hopelessly Ill Patients: A Second Look." *New England Journal of Medicine* 320 (1989), 844–49.

Willems, Dick L., et al. "Attitudes and Practices Concerning the End of Life: A Comparison Between Physicians from the United States and from the Netherlands." *Archives of Internal Medicine* 160 (January 2000), 63–68.

Wolf, Susan. "Holding the Life on Euthanasia." *Hastings Center Report* 19 (1989), S13–S15.

BIBLIOGRAPHIES AND REFERENCE WORKS

Becker, Lawrence, and Becker, Charlotte, eds. *Encyclopedia of Ethics.* New York: Garland Publishing Inc., 1992.

Curran, William J., et al. *Health Care Law and Ethics.* New York: Aspen Law & Business, 1998. [Includes bibliographical references.]

Lineback, Richard H., ed. *Philosopher's Index.* Vols. 1–. Bowling Green, OH: Philosophy Documentation Center, Bowling Green State University. Issued quarterly. Also CD Rom.

National Library of Medicine (NLM) Gateway, http://gateway.nlm.nih.gov.

Reich, Warren, ed. *Encyclopedia of Bioethics,* 2d ed. New York: Macmillan, 1995.

Walters, LeRoy, and Kahn, Tamar Joy, eds. *Bibliography of Bioethics.* Vols. 1–. New York: Free Press. Issued annually.

7.
Eugenics and Human Genetics

INTRODUCTION

The last decade of the twentieth century and the first decade of this new century have been exciting times for human genetics. The detailed sequencing of the human genome will be completed in 2003, exactly fifty years after the discovery of the double helix by James Watson and Francis Crick. Parallel genome projects have already provided the genetic sequences for the fruit fly, a roundworm called *C. elegans,* a mustardlike plant named *Arabidopsis,* and at least sixty types of bacteria.[1] Within a year or two the mouse genome will also be sequenced.

These dramatic achievements of multiple genome projects will provide new understandings of health and disease, information about human evolution and migration, and, more controversially, insight into genetic factors in, or influences on, human behavior. The readings in this chapter explore two medical applications of new genetic knowledge: genetic testing and screening on one hand and human gene transfer aimed at treating disease (sometimes called *human gene therapy*) on the other. In a more speculative vein, the final readings in the chapter consider the moral arguments for and against enhancing human capabilities by genetic means.

While new scientific findings offer grounds for optimism about the future, some past attempts to apply genetic knowledge suggest that caution and vigilance may also be warranted. The initial readings in this chapter recount government-sponsored attempts to improve society by intervening in the reproductive decisions, or modifying the reproductive capacities, of human beings. The first of these eugenic programs emerged in the United States during the first half of the twentieth century. A second program, modeled in part on the U.S. experience and the writings of American eugenicists, was enacted in Germany when that country was governed by Adolf Hitler and the National Socialists. The extreme conclusion, and in some ways the logical outcome, of the German program was the Holocaust.

EUGENICS PROGRAMS IN THE TWENTIETH CENTURY

The definition of *eugenics* is controversial. One simple definition is that eugenics means "the study of human improvement by genetic means."[2] If this definition is accepted, one can discover eugenic proposals in writings as old as Plato's *Republic,* where selective breeding was proposed as a means of improving society.[3] The actual word *eugenics* was coined in 1883 by an English scientist, Francis Galton, who was a cousin of Charles Darwin. In his first major book, *Hereditary Genius,* published in 1869, and in later works Galton advocated a system of arranged marriages between men and women of distinction, with the aim of producing a group of gifted children and ultimately an improved British population.

In the eugenic programs of the twentieth century, the element of coercion by the state was added to the notion of eugenics as a social goal. The first systematic attempts to develop mandatory eugenic programs occurred in several states of the United States. The central aim of these programs was to prevent reproduction by people who were judged to be feeble-minded. The method by which this aim was to be achieved was involuntary sterilization. Daniel Kevles's essay chronicles the history of eugenic sterilization in the United States.

While several state courts struck down mandatory sterilization statutes as unconstitutional, the U.S. Supreme Court found Virginia's involuntary sterilization law to be compatible with the guarantees of the U.S. Constitution. Oliver Wendell Holmes wrote for the Supreme Court's majority and argued that if Carrie Buck's mother, Carrie herself, and Carrie's daughter were all feeble-minded, the state of Virginia was justified in attempting to prevent any further reproduction by Carrie Buck through involuntary sterilization. In Holmes's chilling words, "Three generations of imbeciles are enough." The full text of the court's 1927 *Buck v. Bell* decision is reprinted in this chapter. In his essay "Carrie Buck's Daughter" paleontologist Stephen Jay Gould critically examines the factual premises on which the Supreme Court based its decision.

The eugenic programs undertaken in several states of the United States were closely monitored by academics and policymakers in other parts of the world, and especially in Germany. There the method of mandatory sterilization was found to be compatible both with the academic field called "racial hygiene" and with the political agenda of the National Socialists. Jonathan Glover discusses the theory and practice of the Nazi sterilization program during the 1930s, when approximately 350,000 persons deemed unfit to reproduce were sterilized. As is well known, this sterilization effort was but an initial step on the road that led eventually to the extermination of "unworthy" individuals and groups in Nazi killing centers and concentration camps.[4]

THE HUMAN GENOME PROJECT

There can be no doubt that we live in the golden age of genetics, especially human genetics. Even before the 1950s, Gregor Mendel's classic work on various modes of inheritance was available as a framework for understanding how certain traits, like the colors of flowers, are transmitted from one generation to the next. However, Watson and Crick's discovery of the molecular structure of DNA in 1953 and the rapid advances made feasible by recombinant DNA techniques from the 1970s to the present have opened up entirely new possibilities for genetic diagnosis and therapy.

The genetic structure of human cells is incredibly intricate and complex. Within the nuclei of each human cell there are forty-six chromosomes. These chromosomes, in turn, are comprised of 30,000–50,000 genes plus intervening sequences; the function of the intervening sequences is not yet well understood. The simplest units into which the genes and intervening sequences can be analyzed are individual nucleotides or bases, designated by the familiar letters A, C, G, and T; two corresponding nucleotides form a base pair. It is estimated that each human cell contains approximately 3 billion base pairs.

Through the early years of the twenty-first century, we will witness an intensive international effort to complete the sequencing of the human genome and to achieve a better understanding of human genetic variation. Francis Collins and Victor McKusick, two leaders of human genetics and the human genome project, analyze the impact that current research is likely to have on medical diagnosis and treatment. They note that new genetic information will facilitate the more timely and precise diagnosis of human disease, as well as suggesting new approaches to treatment, whether through gene transfer or better targeted drug therapy. Collins and McKusick warn, however, that the same personal genetic information that provides medical benefits may expose individuals to new kinds of social and financial hazards, especially if such information is employed to sort people into risk categories.

In an essay that combines history with ethical and political analysis, James Watson describes the sequence of events that led a reluctant community of U.S. biomedical scientists to accept the importance of mapping and sequencing the human genome. As Watson notes with satisfaction, he insisted that a fixed percentage of the human genome project budget—initially 3 percent, later 5 percent—be set aside to the study the ethical, legal, and social implications of the project. The ELSI program, as it came to be known, has allowed philosophers, theologians, lawyers, social scientists, and clinicians to perform normative research on issues like those discussed in the current chapter. At the conclusion of his essay Watson predicts that behavioral genetics and genetic enhancement will become important topics as genetic knowledge continues to accrue. He argues that the main lesson to be drawn from the eugenic excesses of the past is that governments must be prevented from telling citizens what to do, and what not to do, in the genetic sphere.

Philosophers Allen Buchanan, Dan Brock, Norman Daniels, and Daniel Wikler have written an important book entitled *From Chance to Choice: Genetics and Justice.*[5] In the excerpt from this book reprinted here the authors extrapolate from current developments in human genetics to create five future scenarios—case studies that illustrate the moral dilemmas that may be faced by our children and grandchildren. Buchanan and colleagues focus primary attention on what they term *direct genetic interventions,* such as human gene transfer, and on a single *indirect genetic intervention*—the use of carefully tailored drugs designed to alleviate diseases caused (at least in part) by genetic factors. However, they also consider issues arising at the interface of human reproduction and genetics: preimplantation diagnosis and embryo selection, prenatal diagnosis, and the genetic screening of newborns. Rejecting both the public health model and the personal services model, Buchanan and his colleagues seek to develop a third approach to the public policy issues raised by genetic research. The authors' constructive proposal draws heavily on John Rawls's theory of justice and on a robust notion of equal opportunity that is indebted both to Rawls and to the writings of Norman Daniels on just health care.

European scholar Svante Pääbo considers possible nonmedical implications of the human genome project. The findings of this research will help us as humans to reconstruct our ancient history—that is, our sites of origin and the patterns of migration and conquest that have led to the current configuration of human ethnic groups and nations. At the same time, however, the genome project will reveal to what extent the human genome contains genes that are closely related to corresponding genes in "simple" organisms like the fruit fly and roundworms. Further research will also delineate more clearly the similarities and differences between humans and our closest nonhuman relatives, the great apes. In Pääbo's view, the fact that humans and chimpanzees show 99 percent similarity in their DNA sequences may raise intriguing questions about traditional notions of human uniqueness.

GENETIC TESTING AND SCREENING

As noted by Collins and McKusick, the human genome project will make more precise genetic *testing* possible. This type of testing will be applicable to the diagnosis of disease, or even a higher-than-average predisposition to develop a certain kind of disease later in life. However, as the science develops, more sophisticated types of genetic testing may also make possible the discovery of at least approximate correlations between genes (or small constellations of genes) and complex behavioral traits—for example, exceptional memory or specific personality characteristics.[6] The techniques of genetic testing can be employed at any of several stages in the human life cycle: between the time of in vitro fertilization and the time of embryo transfer (preimplantation diagnosis); after implantation but before birth (prenatal diagnosis); immediately after birth (newborn genetic testing); during childhood or adolescence; and in adulthood (for example, when reproductive decisions are being made). It is not yet clear whether the genetic testing of sperm and egg cells can be performed in ways that are both highly accurate and nondestructive to the cells being tested. Genetic *screening* involves the use of genetic testing in large populations—for example, all newborn infants.

The three essays in this section consider multiple dimensions of genetic testing and screening. Patricia Roche and George Annas assert that genetic information about oneself is almost uniquely personal and constitutes a kind of coded "future diary." In their view, individual genetic information should be shared with others only after the individual in question has been thoroughly counseled and has given his or her explicit consent to the release of the information. Roche and Annas advocate uniform federal legislation to protect genetic privacy in the United States. Canadian scholar Michael Burgess questions the exclusive focus on disclosure and consent that often characterizes discussions of genetic testing and screening. Burgess argues that an open-minded and wide-ranging consideration of genetic testing's potential benefits and harms is a necessary complement to respect for individual autonomy. In the final essay of this section Lainie Friedman Ross and Margaret Moon consider the moral justifications for the genetic testing of children. Their subtle analysis distinguishes between tests that confirm a probable diagnosis and tests that, with a higher or lower probability, can predict a future disease state even in an asymptomatic child. Ross and Moon also discuss the conditions under which mass newborn screening programs are morally justified. Like Burgess, they argue for a thoughtful, nuanced evaluation of both medical and psychosocial benefits and harms.

HUMAN GENE TRANSFER RESEARCH

In the history of medicine, diagnosis is often the necessary prelude to a cure. It thus seems likely that the capacity to identify genetic diseases and susceptibilities will provide new impetus for already existing efforts to develop ways to correct, or at least to compensate for, genetic defects. The general name usually given to these therapeutic initiatives is *gene therapy,* or, more broadly, *genetic intervention.*

A central distinction in any discussion of genetic intervention is the distinction between reproductive and nonreproductive cells, which are often called germ-line and somatic cells, respectively. Somatic cells, like skin or muscle cells, contain the full complement of forty-six chromosomes and cannot transmit genetic information to succeeding generations. In other words, the genetic information contained in somatic cells stops with us and is not passed on to our descendants. In contrast, germ-line cells, the egg and sperm cells, contain only twenty-three chromosomes and are capable of transmitting genetic information to our progeny in the next generation, as well as to their children and grandchildren.

A second important distinction in discussions of human genetic intervention is that between the cure or prevention of disease on one hand and the enhancement of human capabilities on the other. A genetic approach to the treatment of cystic fibrosis clearly would be regarded as gene therapy. In contrast, the attempt to increase stature or to improve the efficiency of long-term memory—in a child whose height or memory fall within the normal range—would probably be regarded by most observers as an effort to enhance capabilities rather than to cure disease. The two distinctions discussed in this and the preceding paragraph can be arrayed in the following two-by-two matrix:

	Somatic	Germ-line
Cure or prevention of disease	1	2
Enhancement of capabilities	3	4

In the late 1980s and early 1990s, the name generally applied to somatic-cell gene transfer to treat disease was gene therapy. This phrase had originally been suggested by scientists in 1970 as a less frightening alternative to the then-prevalent phrase *genetic engineering.*[7] However, the term *therapy* was potentially misleading because it tended to obscure the experimental character of human gene transfer. By 1995 at the latest, it had also become clear that human gene transfer would not immediately produce the dramatic therapeutic results that both scientists and the public had anticipated. Thus, in the late 1990s, several commentators recommended that the word *therapy* be replaced by the more neutral term *transfer* and that the entire phrase describing this technique include the word *research.*[8] The phrase *human gene transfer research* is therefore employed in this introduction as a more neutral and more accurate descriptor than *human gene therapy*.

By the end of 2001, more than 500 formal gene transfer protocols had been submitted to the National Institutes of Health for formal public review. Of these, approximately 475 studies were oriented toward the alleviation of disease. Almost two-thirds of the disease-oriented studies were conducted in human subjects who were afflicted with various kinds of cancers. Another 10 percent of the studies involved subjects with genetic disorders—for example, cystic fibrosis, a progressive disease of the lungs. Still other studies enlisted people with HIV infection or AIDS.

During the year 2000 the first clear-cut success occurred in human gene transfer research. Alain Fischer and his colleagues at the Necker Hospital in Paris, France, demonstrated decisive improvement in several children born with a genetically caused condition called "severe combined immunodeficiency."[9] David, the so-called boy in the bubble, had suffered from the same disease in the 1970s and early 1980s.[10] Fischer and his colleagues succeeded in transferring the gene that produces a missing enzyme into enough of the children's bone marrow cells to produce a clinical benefit that has now persisted for up to two and one-half years.[11] Gene-transfer researchers hope that this improvement will be permanent and that the children's immune systems will function normally into adulthood.

The three essays on human gene transfer research discuss several facets of this promising, but still very young, field. Ninkunj Somia and Inder Verma review the difficulties that researchers have encountered in attempting to create *vectors* for transporting genes into target cells. The authors summarize the characteristics of an ideal vector but reluctantly concede that no such vector currently exists. In his essay Theodore Friedmann describes the requirements for ethically acceptable, publicly accountable human gene transfer research. He tacitly acknowledges that the public oversight system for this field of research was weakened in 1997 and urges that the monitoring of serious adverse events in gene-transfer studies be enhanced. In Friedmann's view, researchers, universities, and companies should scrupulously avoid even the appearance of financial conflicts of interest in conducting such studies. Australian scholar Julian Savulescu reviews the tragic death of an 18-year-old young man, Jesse Gelsinger, in a gene-transfer study conducted at the University of Pennsylvania. After documenting numerous deficiencies in the way the Penn study was conducted, Savulescu goes on to argue that gene-transfer research in infants afflicted with life-threatening disorders can be morally justifiable if certain conditions are fulfilled.

GENETIC ENHANCEMENT

The last three selections in this chapter consider the more speculative possibility that in the future genetic technology will be employed to enhance human capabilities. In an adventuresome essay Jonathan Glover expresses dissatisfaction with at least some aspects of human nature as we know it. He also attempts to demolish several of the standard ethical objections to genetic enhancement. In the end Glover adopts a "principle of caution" and advocates a mixed system of public oversight for genetic enhancement—one that allows substantial leeway to parents in making decisions about the characteristics of their children while at the same time providing for a social check on possible parental excesses.

Jon Gordon's essay provides a reality check to current philosophical debates about human genetic enhancement. He points to the technical difficulties that have attended laboratory research aimed at enhancing nonhuman mammals and plants. In addition, Gordon argues that fears or claims about "controlling human evolution" through genetic enhancement techniques are grossly inflated, given the large number of unenhanced children that would be simultaneously produced through more traditional means. According to Gordon, unfounded hyperbole about the potential for genetic enhancement could have the unfortunate consequence of prompting panicked lawmakers to ban important kinds of basic laboratory research.

Without unconditionally rejecting genetic enhancement, philosopher Erik Parens questions whether the goals that proponents of enhancement seek to achieve are, on balance, worthwhile. Parens argues that enhancement seeks to replace change with stability and to substitute control or predictability for chance. In addition, he suggests that proposals for genetic enhancement tend toward utopianism. For Parens change, chance, and struggle are important—perhaps even essential—elements of the good life.

L. W.

NOTES

1. Russell F. Doolittle, "Microbial Genomes Multiply," *Nature* 416, no. 6882 (18 April 2002), 697–700.

2. *Encyclopedia Britannica,* Micropaedia, "Eugenics," 1989, 593.

3. Plato, *Republic,* III (410), IV, 456–61.

4. For the history of Nazi policies on the "unfit" and the "unworthy," see the following works: Robert Jay Lifton, *The Nazi Doctors: Medical Killing and the Psychology of Genocide* (New York: Basic Books, 1986); Robert N. Proctor, *Racial Hygiene: Medicine under the Nazis* (Cambridge, MA: Harvard University Press, 1988); Michael Burleigh and Wolfgang Wipperman, *The Racial State: Germany 1933–1945* (Cambridge: Cambridge University Press, 1991); and Michael Burleigh, *Death and Deliverance: "Euthanasia" in Germany 1900–1945* (Cambridge: Cambridge University Press, 1994).

5. Allan Buchanan et al., *From Chance to Choice: Genetics and Justice* (New York: Cambridge University Press, 2000).

6. For a primer on behavioral genetics, see Robert Plomin et al., *Behavioral Genetics,* 3d ed. (New York: W. H. Freeman, 1997).

7. LeRoy Walters, "Gene Therapy: Overview," in Thomas H. Murray and Maxwell J. Mehlman, eds., *Encyclopedia of Ethical, Legal, and Policy Issues in Biotechnology,* 2 vols. (New York: John Wiley and Sons, 2000), 336–42.

8. Larry R. Churchill et al., "Genetic Research as Therapy: Implications of 'Gene Therapy' for Informed Consent," *Journal of Law, Medicine, and Ethics* 26, no. 1 (Spring 1998), 38–47.

9. Marina Cavazzana-Calvo et al., "Gene Therapy of Severe Combined Immunodeficiency (SCID)-X1 Disease," *Science* 288, no. 5466 (28 April 2000), 627–29.

10. See LeRoy Walters and Julie Gage Palmer, *The Ethics of Human Gene Therapy* (New York: Oxford University Press, 1997), xiii–xvi.

11. Salima Hacein-Bey-Abina et al., "Sustained Correction of X-Linked Severe Combined Immunodeficiency by *ex vivo* Gene Therapy," *New England Journal of Medicine* 346, no. 16 (18 April 2002), 1241–43.

Eugenics Programs in the Twentieth Century

DANIEL J. KEVLES

Eugenics and Human Rights

Daniel Kevles is the Stanley Woodward Professor of History at Yale University. He has published extensively about the history of science in America; the interplay of science and society past and present; and scientific fraud and misconduct. His publications include *In the Name of Eugenics: Genetics and the Uses of Human Heredity* (Harvard University Press) and *The Baltimore Case: A Trial of Politics, Science, and Character* (Norton).

During the Nazi era in Germany, eugenics prompted the sterilisation of several hundred thousand people, then helped lead to antisemitic programmes of euthanasia and ultimately, of course, to the death camps. The association of eugenics with the Nazis is so strong that many people were surprised at the news several years ago that Sweden had sterilised around 60,000 people (mostly women) between the 1930s and 1970s. The intention was to reduce the number of children born with genetic diseases and disorders. After the turn of the century, eugenics movements—including demands for sterilisation of people considered unfit—had, in fact, blossomed in the United States, Canada, Britain, and Scandinavia, not to mention elsewhere in Europe and in parts of Latin America and Asia. Eugenics was not therefore unique to the Nazis. It could, and did, happen everywhere.

ORIGINS OF EUGENICS

Modern eugenics was rooted in the social darwinism of the late 19th century, with all its metaphors of fitness, competition, and rationalisations of inequality. Indeed, Francis Galton, a cousin of Charles Darwin and an accomplished scientist in his own right, coined the word eugenics. Galton promoted the ideal of improving the human race by getting rid of the "undesirables" and multiplying the "desirables." Eugenics began to flourish after the rediscovery, in 1900, of

Reprinted from the *British Medical Journal* 1999;319:435–438, with permission from BMJ Publishing Group. Copyright © 1999, the British Medical Association.

Mendel's theory that the biological make up of organisms is determined by certain factors, later identified with genes. The application of mendelism to human beings reinforced the idea that we are determined almost entirely by our "germ plasm."

Eugenic doctrines were articulated by physicians, mental health professionals, and scientists—notably biologists who were pursuing the new discipline of genetics—and were widely popularised in books, lectures, and articles for the educated public of the day. Publications were bolstered by the research pouring out of institutes for the study of eugenics or "race biology." These had been established in several countries, including Denmark, Sweden, Britain, and the United States. The experts raised the spectre of social degeneration, insisting that "feebleminded" people (the term then commonly applied to people believed to be mentally retarded) were responsible for a wide range of social problems and were proliferating at a rate that threatened social resources and stability. Feebleminded women were held to be driven by a heedless sexuality, the product of biologically grounded flaws in their moral character that led them to prostitution and producing illegitimate children. "Hereditarian" biology attributed poverty and criminality to bad genes rather than to flaws in the social corpus.

A DRIVE FOR SOCIAL IMPROVEMENT

Much of eugenics belonged to the wave of progressive social reform that swept through western Europe and North America during the early decades of the century. For progressives, eugenics was a branch of the drive for social improvement or perfection that many reformers of the day thought might be achieved through the deployment of science to good social ends. Eugenics, of course, also drew appreciable support from social conservatives, concerned to prevent the proliferation of lower income groups and save on the cost of caring for them. The progressives and the conservatives found common ground in attributing phenomena such as crime, slums, prostitution, and alcoholism primarily to biology and in believing that biology might be used to eliminate these discordances of modern, urban, industrial society.

Race was a minor subtext in Scandinavian and British eugenics, but it played a major part in the American and Canadian versions of the creed. North American eugenicists were particularly disturbed by the immigrants from eastern and southern Europe who had been flooding into their countries since the late 19th century. They considered these people not only racially different from but inferior to the Anglo-Saxon majority, partly because their representation among the criminals, prostitutes, slum dwellers, and feeble-minded in many cities was disproportionately high. Anglo-American eugenicists fastened on British data indicating that half of each generation was produced by no more than a quarter of married people in the preceding generation, and that the prolific quarter was disproportionately located among the "dregs" of society. Eugenic reasoning in the United States had it that if deficiencies in immigrants were hereditary and eastern European immigrants outreproduced natives of Anglo-Saxon stock, then inevitably the quality of the American population would decline.

POSITIVE AND NEGATIVE EUGENICS

Eugenicists on both sides of the Atlantic argued for a two pronged programme that would increase the frequency of "socially good" genes in the population and decrease that of "bad genes." One prong was positive eugenics, which meant manipulating human heredity or breeding, or both, to produce superior people; the other was negative eugenics, which meant improving the quality of the human race by eliminating or excluding biologically inferior people from the population.

In Britain between the wars, positive eugenic thinking led to proposals (unsuccessful ones) for family allowances that would be proportional to income. In the United States, it fostered "fitter family" competitions. These became a standard feature at a number of state fairs and were held in the "human stock" sections. At the 1924 Kansas Free Fair, winning families in the three categories—small, average, and large—were awarded a governor's fitter family trophy. "Grade A" individuals received a medal that portrayed two diaphanously garbed parents, their arms outstretched toward their (presumably) eugenically meritorious infant. It is hard to know exactly what made these families and individuals stand out as fit, but the fact that all entrants had to take an IQ test and the Wasserman test for syphilis says something about the organisers' views of necessary qualities.

Much more was urged for negative eugenics, notably the passage of eugenic sterilisation laws. By the late 1920s, sterilisation laws had been enacted in two dozen American states, largely in the middle Atlantic region, the Midwest, and California. By 1933, California had subjected more people to eugenic sterilisation than had all other states of the union combined. Similar measures were passed in Canada, in the provinces of British Columbia and Alberta. Almost everywhere they were passed, however, the laws reached only as far as the inmates of state institutions for the mentally handicapped or mentally ill. People in private care or in the care of their families escaped them. Thus, the laws tended to discriminate against poorer people and minority groups. In California, for example, the sterilisation rates of blacks and foreign immigrants were twice as high as would be expected from their representation in the general population.

SOCIETY BEFORE INDIVIDUAL RIGHTS

The sterilisation laws rode roughshod over private human rights, holding them subordinate to an allegedly greater public good. This reasoning figured explicitly in the US Supreme Court's eight to one decision, in 1927, in the case of Buck versus Bell, which upheld Virginia's eugenic sterilisation law. Justice Oliver Wendell Holmes, writing for the majority, averred: "We have seen more than once that the public welfare may call upon the best citizens for their lives. It would be strange if it could not call upon those who already sap the strength of the State for these lesser sacrifices, often not felt to be such by those concerned, in order to prevent our being swamped with incompetence. It is better for all the world, if instead of waiting to execute degenerate offspring for crime, or to let them starve for their imbecility, society can prevent those who are manifestly unfit from continuing their kind. The principle that sustains compulsory vaccination is broad enough to cover cutting the Fallopian tubes. . . . Three generations of imbeciles are enough."[1]

In Alberta, the premier called sterilisation far more effective than segregation and, perhaps taking a leaf from Holmes's book, insisted that "the argument of freedom or right of the individual can no longer hold good where the welfare of the state and society is concerned."[2,3]

Sterilisation rates climbed with the onset of the worldwide economic depression in 1929. In parts of Canada, in the deep south of the United States, and throughout Scandinavia, sterilisation acquired broad support. This was not primarily on eugenic grounds (though some hereditarian-minded mental health professionals continued to urge it for that purpose) but on economic ones. Sterilisation raised the prospect of reducing the cost of institutional care and of poor relief. Even geneticists who disparaged sterilisation as the remedy for degeneration held that sterilising mentally disabled people would yield a social benefit because it would prevent children being born to parents who could not care for them.

In Scandinavia, sterilisation was broadly endorsed by Social Democrats as part of the scientifically oriented planning of the new welfare state. Alva Myrdal spoke for her husband, Gunnar, and for numerous liberals like themselves when in 1941 she wrote, "In our day of highly accelerated social reforms the need for sterilization on social grounds gains new momentum. Generous social reforms may facilitate home-making and childbearing more than before among the groups of less desirable as well as more desirable parents. [Such a trend] demands some corresponding corrective."[4] On such foundations among others, sterilisation programmes continued in several American states, in Alberta, and in Scandinavia well into the 1970s.

EUGENICS UNDER FIRE

During the interwar years, however, eugenic doctrines were increasingly criticised on scientific grounds and for their class and racial bias. It was shown that many mental disabilities have nothing to do with genes; that those which do are not simple products of genetic make up; and that most human behaviours (including deviant ones) are shaped by environment at least as much as by biological heredity, if they are fashioned by genes at all. Science aside, eugenics became malodorous precisely because of its connection with Hitler's regime, especially after the second world war, when its complicity in the Nazi death camps was revealed.

All along, many people on both sides of the Atlantic had ethical reservations about sterilisation and were squeamish about forcibly subjecting people to the knife. Attempts to authorise eugenic sterilisation in Britain had reached their high water mark in the debates over the Mental Deficiency Act in 1913. They failed not least because of powerful objections from civil libertarians insistent on defending individual human rights. More than a third of the American states declined to pass sterilisation laws, and so did the eastern provinces of Canada. Most of the American states which passed the laws declined to enforce them, and British Columbia's law was enforced very little.

The opposition comprised coalitions that varied in composition. It came from mental health professionals who doubted the scientific underpinnings of eugenics and from civil libertarians, some of whom warned that compulsory sterilisation constituted "Hitlerisation." Sterilisation was also vigorously resisted by Roman Catholics—partly because it was contrary to church doctrine and partly because many recent immigrants to the United States were Catholics and thus disproportionately placed in jeopardy of the knife. For many people before the second world war, individual human rights mattered far more than those sanctioned by the science, law, and perceived social needs of the era.

The revelations of the holocaust strengthened the moral objections to eugenics and sterilisation, and so did the increasing worldwide discussion of human rights, a foundation for which was the Universal Declaration of Human Rights that the General Assembly of the United Nations adopted and proclaimed in 1948. Since then, the movement for women's rights and reproductive freedom has further transformed moral sensibilities about eugenics, so that we recoil at the majority's ruling in Buck versus Bell. History at the least has taught us that concern for individual rights belongs at the heart of whatever stratagems we may devise for deploying our rapidly growing knowledge of human and medical genetics.

NOTES

1. Buck v Bell [1927] 274 US 201–7.

2. Christian T. The mentally ill and human rights in Alberta: a study of the Alberta Sexual Sterilisation Act. Edmonton: Faculty of Law, University of Alberta, nd: 27.

3. McLaren A. Our own master race: eugenics in Canada, 1885–1945. Toronto: McClelland and Stewart, 1990.

4. Broberg G., Roll-Hansen N., eds. Eugenics and the welfare state: sterilization policy in Denmark, Sweden, Norway, and Finland. East Lansing: Michigan State University Press, 1996.

UNITED STATES SUPREME COURT

Buck v. Bell (1927)

Argued April 22, 1927. Decided May 2, 1927.

On Writ of Error to the Supreme Court of Appeals of the State of Virginia to review a judgment affirming a judgment of the Circuit Court for Amherst County directing the sterilization of an inmate of a Colony for Epileptics and Feeble Minded. Affirmed. . . .*

The facts are stated in the opinion.

Mr. I. P. Whitehead argued the cause and filed a brief for plaintiff in error:

The act of assembly of Virginia does not provide due process of law guaranteed by the 14th Amendment to the Constitution of the United States. . . .

The act of assembly of Virginia denies to the plaintiff and other inmates of the State Colony for Epileptics and Feebleminded the equal protection of the law guaranteed by the 14th Amendment to the Constitution of the United States. . . .

Mr. Aubrey E. Strode argued the cause and filed a brief for defendant in error:

The act affords due process of law. . . .

The act is a valid exercise of the police power.

The statute may be sustained as based upon a reasonable classification. . . .

MR. JUSTICE HOLMES delivered the opinion of the court:

This is a writ of error to review a judgment of the supreme court of appeals of the state of Virginia, affirming a judgment of the circuit court of Amherst county, by which the defendant in error, the superintendent of the State Colony for Epileptics and Feeble Minded, was ordered to perform the operation of sal-

pingectomy upon Carrie Buck, the plaintiff in error, for the purpose of making her sterile. 143 Va. 310, 51 A.L.R. 855, 130 S. E. 516. The case comes here upon the contention that the statute authorizing the judgment is void under the 14th Amendment as denying to the plaintiff in error due process of law and the equal protection of the laws.

Carrie Buck is a feeble minded white woman who was committed to the State Colony above mentioned in due form. She is the daughter of a feeble minded mother in the same institution, and the mother of an illegitimate feeble minded child. She was eighteen years old at the time of the trial of her case in the circuit court, in the latter part of 1924. An Act of Virginia approved March 20, 1924, recites that the health of the patient and the welfare of society may be promoted in certain cases by the sterilization of mental defectives, under careful safeguard, etc.; that the sterilization may be effected in males by vasectomy and in females by salpingectomy, without serious pain or substantial danger to life; that the Commonwealth is supporting in various institutions many defective persons who if now discharged would become a menace but if incapable of procreating might be discharged with safety and become self-supporting with benefit to themselves and to society; and that experience has shown that heredity plays an important part in the transmission of insanity, imbecility, etc. The statute then enacts that whenever the superintendent of certain institutions including the above named State Colony shall be of opinion that it is for the best interests of the patients and of society that an inmate under his care should be sexually sterilized, he may have the operation performed upon any patient afflicted with hereditary forms of insanity, imbecility, etc., on complying with the very careful provisions by which the act protects the patients from possible abuse.

*Editor's note: Some references to other court decisions are omitted or abbreviated.

From *United States [Supreme Court] Reports* 274 (1927), 200–08.

The superintendent first presents a petition to the special board of directors of his hospital or colony, stating the facts and the grounds for his opinion, verified by affidavit. Notice of the petition and of the time and place of the hearing in the institution is to be served upon the inmate, and also upon his guardian, and if there is no guardian the superintendent is to apply to the circuit court of the county to appoint one. If the inmate is a minor notice also is to be given to his parents if any with a copy of the petition. The board is to see to it that the inmate may attend the hearings if desired by him or his guardian. The evidence is all to be reduced to writing, and after the board has made its order for or against the operation, the superintendent, or the inmate, or his guardian, may appeal to the circuit court of the county. The circuit court may consider the record of the board and the evidence before it and such other admissible evidence as may be offered, and may affirm, revise, or reverse the order of the board and enter such order as it deems just. Finally any party may apply to the supreme court of appeals, which, if it grants the appeal, is to hear the case upon the record of the trial in the circuit court and may enter such order as it thinks the circuit court should have entered. There can be no doubt that so far as procedure is concerned the rights of the patient are most carefully considered, and as every step in this case was taken in scrupulous compliance with the statute and after months of observation, there is no doubt that in that respect the plaintiff in error has had due process of law.

The attack is not upon the procedure but upon the substantive law. It seems to be contended that in no circumstances could such an order be justified. It certainly is contended that the order cannot be justified upon the existing grounds. The judgment finds the facts that have been recited and that Carrie Buck "is the probable potential parent of socially inadequate offspring, likewise afflicted, that she may be sexually sterilized without detriment to her general health and that her welfare and that of society will be promoted by her sterilization," and thereupon makes the order. In view of the general declarations of the legislature and the specific findings of the court obviously we cannot say as matter of law that the grounds do not exist, and if they exist they justify the result. We have seen more than once that the public welfare may call upon the best citizens for their lives. It would be strange if it could not call upon those who already sap the strength of the state for these lesser sacrifices, often not felt to be such by those concerned, in order to prevent our being swamped with incompetence. It is better for all the world, if instead of waiting to execute degenerate offspring for crime, or to let them starve for their imbecility, society can prevent those who are manifestly unfit from continuing their kind. The principle that sustains compulsory vaccination is broad enough to cover cutting the Fallopian tubes. Jacobson v. Massachusetts, 197 U.S. 11. Three generations of imbeciles are enough.

But, it is said, however it might be if this reasoning were applied generally, it fails when it is confined to the small number who are in the institutions named and is not applied to the multitudes outside. It is the usual last resort of constitutional arguments to point out shortcomings of this sort. But the answer is that the law does all that is needed when it does all that it can, indicates a policy, applies it to all within the lines, and seeks to bring within the lines all similarly situated so far and so fast as its means allow. Of course so far as the operations enable those who otherwise must be kept confined to be returned to the world, and thus open the asylum to others, the equality aimed at will be more nearly reached.

Judgment affirmed.

MR. JUSTICE BUTLER dissents.

STEPHEN JAY GOULD

Carrie Buck's Daughter

Stephen Jay Gould (d. 2002) was Professor of Geology and Zoology at Harvard University. His main interests lay in palaeontology and evolutionary biology. He was a frequent and popular speak on the sciences. His published work included *The Mismeasure of Man* (Norton), *The Panda's Thumb: More Reflections in Natural History* (Norton), and *The Flamingo's Smile* (Norton).

The Lord really put it on the line in his preface to that prototype of all prescriptions, the Ten Commandments:

> ... for I, the Lord thy God, am a jealous God, visiting the iniquity of the fathers upon the children unto the third and fourth generation of them that hate me (Exod. 20:5).

The terror of this statement lies in its patent unfairness—its promise to punish guiltless offspring for the misdeeds of their distant forebears.

A different form of guilt by genealogical association attempts to remove this stigma of injustice by denying a cherished premise of Western thought—human free will. If offspring are tainted not simply by the deeds of their parents but by a material form of evil transferred directly by biological inheritance, then "the iniquity of the fathers" becomes a signal or warning for probable misbehavior of their sons. Thus Plato, while denying that children should suffer directly for the crimes of their parents, nonetheless defended the banishment of a personally guiltless man whose father, grandfather and great-grandfather had all been condemned to death.

It is, perhaps, merely coincidental that both Jehovah and Plato chose three generations as their criterion for establishing different forms of guilt by association. Yet we maintain a strong folk, or vernacular, tradition for viewing triple occurrences as minimal evidence of regularity. Bad things, we are told, come in threes. Two may represent an accidental association; three is a pattern. Perhaps, then, we should not wonder that our own century's most famous pronouncement of blood guilt employed the same criterion—Oliver Wendell Holmes's defense of compulsory sterilization in Virginia (Supreme Court decision of 1927 in *Buck v. Bell*): "three generations of imbeciles are enough."

Restrictions upon immigration, with national quotas set to discriminate against those deemed mentally unfit by early versions of IQ testing, marked the greatest triumph of the American eugenics movement—the flawed hereditarian doctrine, so popular earlier in our century and by no means extinct today ... that attempted to "improve" our human stock by preventing the propagation of those deemed biologically unfit and encouraging procreation among the supposedly worthy. But the movement to enact and enforce laws for compulsory "eugenic" sterilization had an impact and success scarcely less pronounced. If we could debar the shiftless and the stupid from our shores, we might also prevent the propagation of those similarly afflicted but already here.

The movement for compulsory sterilization began in earnest during the 1890s, abetted by two major factors—the rise of eugenics as an influential political movement and the perfection of safe and simple operations (vasectomy for men and salpingectomy, the cutting and tying of Fallopian tubes, for women) to replace castration and other socially unacceptable forms of mutilation. Indiana passed the first sterilization act based on eugenic principles in 1907 (a few states had previously mandated castration as a punitive measure for certain sexual crimes, although such laws were rarely enforced and usually overturned by judicial review). Like so many others to follow, it provided for sterilization of afflicted people residing in the state's "care," either as inmates of mental hospitals and homes for the feeble-minded or as inhabitants of prisons. Sterilization could be imposed upon those judged insane, idiotic, imbecilic, or moronic, and upon convicted rapists or criminals when recommended by a board of experts.

By the 1930s, more than thirty states had passed similar laws, often with an expanded list of so-called hereditary defects, including alcoholism and drug addiction in some states, and even blindness and deafness in others. These laws were continually challenged and rarely enforced in most states; only California and Virginia applied them zealously. By January 1935, some 20,000 forced "eugenic" sterilizations had been performed in the United States, nearly half in California.

No organization crusaded more vociferously and successfully for these laws than the Eugenics Record Office, the semiofficial arm and repository of data for the eugenics movement in America. Harry Laughlin, superintendent of the Eugenics Record Office, dedicated most of his career to a tireless campaign of writing and lobbying for eugenic sterilization. He hoped, thereby, to eliminate in two generations the genes of what he called the "submerged tenth"—"the most worthless one-tenth of our present population." He proposed a "model sterilization law" in 1922, designed

to prevent the procreation of persons socially inadequate from defective inheritance, by authorizing and providing for eugenical sterilization of certain potential parents carrying degenerate hereditary qualities.

This model bill became the prototype for most laws passed in America, although few states cast their net as widely as Laughlin advised. (Laughlin's categories encompassed "blind, including those with seriously impaired vision; deaf, including those with seriously impaired hearing; and dependent, including orphans, ne'er-do-wells, the homeless, tramps, and paupers.") Laughlin's suggestions were better heeded in Nazi Germany, where his model act inspired the infamous and stringently enforced *Erbgesundheitsrecht,* leading by the eve of World War II to the sterilization of some 375,000 people, most for "congenital feeble-mindedness," but including nearly 4,000 for blindness and deafness.

The campaign for forced eugenic sterilization in America reached its climax and height of respectability in 1927, when the Supreme Court, by an 8–1 vote, upheld the Virginia sterilization bill in *Buck v. Bell.* Oliver Wendell Holmes, then in his mid-eighties and the most celebrated jurist in America, wrote the majority opinion with his customary verve and power of style. It included the notorious paragraph, with its chilling tag line, cited ever since as the quintessential statement of eugenic principles. Remembering with pride his own distant experiences as an infantryman in the Civil War, Holmes wrote:

We have seen more than once that the public welfare may call upon the best citizens for their lives. It would be strange if it could not call upon those who already sap the strength of the state for these lesser sacrifices. . . . It is better for all the world, if instead of waiting to execute degenerate offspring for crime, or to let them starve for their imbecility, society can prevent those who are manifestly unfit from continuing their kind. The principle that sustains compulsory vaccination is broad enough to cover cutting the Fallopian tubes. Three generations of imbeciles are enough.

Who, then, were the famous "three generations of imbeciles," and why should they still compel our interest?

When the state of Virginia passed its compulsory sterilization law in 1924, Carrie Buck, an eighteen-year-old white woman, lived as an involuntary resident at the State Colony for Epileptics and Feeble-Minded. As the first person selected for sterilization under the new act, Carrie Buck became the focus for a constitutional challenge launched, in part, by conservative Virginia Christians who held, according to eugenical "modernists," antiquated views about individual preferences and "benevolent" state power. (Simplistic political labels do not apply in this case, and rarely in general for that matter. We usually regard eugenics as a conservative movement and its most vocal critics as members of the left. This alignment has generally held in our own decade. But eugenics, touted in its day as the latest in scientific modernism, attracted many liberals and numbered among its most vociferous critics groups often labeled as reactionary and antiscientific. If any political lesson emerges from these shifting allegiances, we might consider the true inalienability of certain human rights.)

But why was Carrie Buck in the State Colony and why was she selected? Oliver Wendell Holmes upheld her choice as judicious in the opening lines of his 1927 opinion:

> Carrie Buck is a feeble-minded white woman who was committed to the State Colony. . . . She is the daughter of a feeble-minded mother in the same institution, and the mother of an illegitimate feeble-minded child.

In short, inheritance stood as the crucial issue (indeed as the driving force behind all eugenics). For if measured mental deficiency arose from malnourishment, either of body or mind, and not from tainted genes, then how could sterilization be justified? If decent food, upbringing, medical care, and education might make a worthy citizen of Carrie Buck's daughter, how could the State of Virginia justify the severing of Carrie's Fallopian tubes against her will? (Some forms of mental deficiency are passed by inheritance in family lines, but most are not—a scarcely surprising conclusion when we consider the thousand shocks that beset us all during our lives, from abnormalities in embryonic growth to traumas of birth, malnourishment, rejection, and poverty. In any case, no fair-minded person today would credit Laughlin's social criteria for the identification of hereditary deficiency— ne'er-do-wells, the homeless, tramps, and paupers— although we shall soon see that Carrie Buck was committed on these grounds.)

When Carrie Buck's case emerged as the crucial test of Virginia's law, the chief honchos of eugenics understood that the time had come to put up or shut up on the crucial issue of inheritance. Thus, the Eugenics Record Office sent Arthur H. Estabrook, their crack fieldworker, to Virginia for a "scientific" study of the case. Harry Laughlin himself provided a deposition, and his brief for inheritance was presented at the local trial that affirmed Virginia's law and later worked its way to the Supreme Court as *Buck v. Bell*.

Laughlin made two major points to the court. First, that Carrie Buck and her mother, Emma Buck, were feebleminded by the Stanford-Binet test of IQ then in its own infancy. Carrie scored a mental age of nine years, Emma of seven years and eleven months. (These figures ranked them technically as "imbeciles" by definitions of the day, hence Holmes's later choice of words—though his infamous line is often misquoted as "three generations of idiots." Imbeciles displayed a mental age of six to nine years; idiots performed worse, morons better, to round out the old nomenclature of mental deficiency.) Second, that most feeble-mindedness resides ineluctably in the genes, and that Carrie Buck surely belonged with this majority. Laughlin reported:

> Generally feeble-mindedness is caused by the inheritance of degenerate qualities; but sometimes it might be caused by environmental factors which are not hereditary. In the case given, the evidence points strongly toward the feeble-mindedness and moral delinquency of Carrie Buck being due, primarily, to inheritance and not to environment.

Carrie Buck's daughter was then, and has always been, the pivotal figure of this painful case. I noted in beginning this essay that we tend (often at our peril) to regard two as potential accident and three as an established pattern. The supposed imbecility of Emma and Carrie might have been an unfortunate coincidence, but the diagnosis of similar deficiency for Vivian Buck (made by a social worker, as we shall see, when Vivian was but six months old) tipped the balance in Laughlin's favor and led Holmes to declare the Buck lineage inherently corrupt by deficient heredity. Vivian sealed the pattern—*three* generations of imbeciles are enough. Besides, had Carrie not given illegitimate birth to Vivian, the issue (in both senses) would never have emerged.

Oliver Wendell Holmes viewed his work with pride. The man so renowned for his principle of judicial restraint, who had proclaimed that freedom must not be curtailed without "clear and present danger"—without the equivalent of falsely yelling "fire" in a crowded theater—wrote of his judgment in *Buck v. Bell:* "I felt that I was getting near the first principle of real reform."

And so *Buck v. Bell* remained for fifty years, a footnote to a moment of American history perhaps best forgotten. Then, in 1980, it reemerged to prick our collective conscience, when Dr. K. Ray Nelson, then director of the Lynchburg Hospital where Carrie Buck had been sterilized, researched the records of his institution and discovered that more than 4,000 sterilizations had been performed, the last as late as 1972. He also found Carrie Buck, alive and well near Charlottesville, and her sister Doris, covertly sterilized under the same law (she was told that her operation was for appendicitis), and now, with fierce dignity, dejected and bitter because she had wanted a child more than anything else in her life and had finally, in her old age, learned why she had never conceived.

As scholars and reporters visited Carrie Buck and her sister, what a few experts had known all along became abundantly clear to everyone. Carrie Buck was a woman of obviously normal intelligence. For example, Paul A. Lombardo of the School of Law at the University of Virginia, and a leading scholar of *Buck v. Bell,* wrote in a letter to me:

As for Carrie, when I met her she was reading newspapers daily and joining a more literate friend to assist at regular bouts with the crossword puzzles. She was not a sophisticated woman, and lacked social graces, but mental health professionals who examined her in later life confirmed my impressions that she was neither mentally ill nor retarded.

On what evidence, then, was Carrie Buck consigned to the State Colony for Epileptics and Feeble-Minded on January 23, 1924? I have seen the text of her commitment hearing; it is, to say the least, cursory and contradictory. Beyond the bald and undocumented say-so of her foster parents, and her own brief appearance before a commission of two doctors and a justice of the peace, no evidence was presented. Even the crude and early Stanford-Binet test, so fatally flawed as a measure of innate worth . . . but at least clothed with the aura of quantitative respectability, had not yet been applied.

When we understand why Carrie Buck was committed in January 1924, we can finally comprehend the hidden meaning of her case and its message for us today. The silent key, again as from the first, is her daughter Vivian, born on March 28, 1924, and then but an evident bump on her belly. Carrie Buck was one of several illegitimate children borne by her mother, Emma. She grew up with foster parents, J. T. and Alice Dobbs, and continued to live with them as an adult, helping out with chores around the house. She was raped by a relative of her foster parents, then blamed for the resulting pregnancy. Almost surely, she was (as they used to say) committed to hide her shame (and her rapist's identity), not because enlightened science had just discovered her true mental status. In short, she was sent away to have her baby. Her case never was about mental deficiency; Carrie Buck was persecuted for supposed sexual immorality and social deviance. The annals of her trial and hearing reek with the contempt of the well-off and well-bred for poor people of "loose morals." Who really cared whether Vivian was a baby of normal intelligence; she was the illegitimate child of an illegitimate woman. Two generations of bastards are enough. Harry Laughlin began his "family history" of the Bucks by writing: "These people belong to the shiftless, ignorant and worthless class of anti-social whites of the South."

We know little of Emma Buck and her life, but we have no more reason to suspect her than her daughter Carrie of true mental deficiency. Their supposed deviance was social and sexual; the charge of imbecility was a cover-up, Mr. Justice Holmes notwithstanding.

We come then to the crux of the case, Carrie's daughter, Vivian. What evidence was ever adduced for her mental deficiency? This and only this: At the original trial in late 1924, when Vivian Buck was seven months old, a Miss Wilhelm, social worker for the Red Cross, appeared before the court. She began by stating honestly the true reason for Carrie Buck's commitment:

Mr. Dobbs, who had charge of the girl, had taken her when a small child, had reported to Miss Duke [the temporary secretary of Public Welfare for Albemarle County] that the girl was pregnant and that he wanted to have her committed somewhere—to have her sent to some institution.

Miss Wilhelm then rendered her judgment of Vivian Buck by comparing her with the normal granddaughter of Mrs. Dobbs, born just three days earlier:

It is difficult to judge probabilities of a child as young as that, but it seems to me not quite a normal baby. In its appearance—I should say that perhaps my knowledge of the mother may prejudice me in that regard, but I saw the child at the same time as Mrs. Dobbs' daughter's baby, which is only three days older than this one, and there is a very decided difference in the development of the babies. That was about two weeks ago. There is a look about it that is not quite normal, but just what it is, I can't tell.

This short testimony, and nothing else, formed all the evidence for the crucial third generation of imbeciles. Cross-examination revealed that neither Vivian nor the Dobbs grandchild could walk or talk, and that "Mrs. Dobbs' daughter's baby is a very responsive baby. When you play with it or try to attract its attention—it is a baby that you can play with. The other baby is not. It seems very apathetic and not responsive." Miss Wilhelm then urged Carrie Buck's sterilization: "I think," she said, "it would at least prevent the propagation of her kind." Several years later, Miss Wilhelm denied that she had ever examined Vivian or deemed the child feebleminded.

Unfortunately, Vivian died at age eight of "enteric colitis" (as recorded on her death certificate), an ambiguous diagnosis that could mean many things but may well indicate that she fell victim to one of the preventable childhood diseases of poverty (a grim reminder of the real subject in *Buck v. Bell*). She is therefore mute as a witness in our reassessment of her famous case.

When *Buck v. Bell* resurfaced in 1980, it immediately struck me that Vivian's case was crucial and that evidence for the mental status of a child who died at age eight might best be found in report cards. I have therefore been trying to track down Vivian Buck's school records for the past four years and have finally succeeded. (They were supplied to me by Dr. Paul A. Lombardo, who also sent other documents, including Miss Wilhelm's testimony, and spent several hours answering my questions by mail and Lord knows how much time playing successful detective in re Vivian's school records. I have never met Dr. Lombardo; he did all this work for kindness, collegiality, and love of the game of knowledge, not for expected reward or even requested acknowledgment. In a profession—academics—so often marred by pettiness and silly squabbling over meaningless priorities, this generosity must be recorded and celebrated as a sign of how things can and should be.)

Vivian Buck was adopted by the Dobbs family, who had raised (but later sent away) her mother, Carrie. As Vivian Alice Elaine Dobbs, she attended the Venable Public Elementary School of Charlottesville for four terms, from September 1930 until May 1932, a month before her death. She was a perfectly normal, quite average student, neither particularly outstanding nor much troubled. In those days before grade inflation, when C meant "good, 81–87" (as defined on her report card) rather than barely scraping by, Vivian Dobbs received A's and B's for deportment and C's for all academic subjects but mathematics (which was always difficult for her, and where she scored D) during her first term in Grade 1A, from September 1930 to January 1931. She improved during her second term in 1B, meriting an A in deportment, C in mathematics, and B in all other academic subjects; she was placed on the honor roll in April 1931. Promoted to 2A, she had trouble during the fall term of 1931, failing mathematics and spelling but receiving A in deportment, B in reading, and C in writing and English. She was "retained in 2A" for the next term—or "left back" as we used to say, and scarcely a sign of imbecility as I remember all my buddies who suffered a similar fate. In any case, she again did well in her final term, with B in deportment, reading, and spelling, and C in writing, English, and mathematics during her last month in school. This daughter of "lewd and immoral" women excelled in deportment and performed adequately, although not brilliantly, in her academic subjects.

In short, we can only agree with the conclusion that Dr. Lombardo has reached in his research on *Buck v. Bell*—there were no imbeciles, not a one, among the three generations of Bucks. I don't know that such correction of cruel but forgotten errors of history counts for much, but I find it both symbolic and satisfying to learn that forced eugenic sterilization, a procedure of such dubious morality, earned its official justification (and won its most quoted line of rhetoric) on a patent falsehood.

Carrie Buck died last year. By a quirk of fate, and not by memory or design, she was buried just a few steps from her only daughter's grave. In the umpteenth and ultimate verse of a favorite old ballad, a rose and a brier—the sweet and the bitter—emerge from the tombs of Barbara Allen and her lover, twining about each other in the union of death. May Carrie and Vivian, victims in different ways and in the flower of youth, rest together in peace.

JONATHAN GLOVER

Eugenics: Some Lessons from the Nazi Experience

Joanthan Glover is Professor of Ethics at King's College, University of London, and the Director of the Centre for Medical Law and Ethics. For many years, Jonathan was Fellow of New College, Oxford. During his years at Oxford, Jonathan gained the reputation of being an outstanding lecturer and tutor. He is currently working on the philosophy of mental illness, in particular the nature of psychopathology.

In one way, the existence of bioethics is very cheering. It is a fine thing that in our time there is so much ethical discussion about what we should do with the remarkable new developments in biology and medicine. But it is also hard not to be struck by the feeling that much work in bioethics is un-philosophical, in the sense of being unreflective on its own methods.

In particular, much of bioethics seems uncritically Cartesian in approach, in a way which makes the whole subject too easy. People writing about certain practical issues, for instance in medical ethics, often start off with principles which are taken to be self-evident. Or else there is a perfunctory attempt to explain why these are the appropriate principles and then practical conclusions are simply derived from them. Often the result is the mechanical application of some form of utilitarianism to various bioethical problems. Or, alternatively, there is a list of several principles about autonomy, beneficence, and so on, which is again mechanically applied.

What worries me about this approach is that it does not reflect real ethical thinking, which is a two-way process. We do not just start off with a set of axioms and apply them to particular cases. We also try to learn from experience. There is something to be said for a more empirical approach to bioethics. This involves not only looking at principles and thinking about what they imply. It involves also looking at particular experiences which, collectively, we have had, and seeing what can be learnt from them. Perhaps from these experiences we can learn something about the sorts of approach it would be a good idea to adopt. Sometimes these historical experiences can teach us a different, but still useful, lesson about the kinds of approach it would be a good idea not to adopt. That is one of the reasons for looking at the Nazi experiment in eugenics.

Before talking about the Nazi episode, it is worth mentioning a quite different case which might also be described as, in one sense, a kind of eugenics. In thinking about the Nazis, it is important to bear in mind how very different their concerns were from the motives which sometimes make people these days want to be able to choose to have one kind of child rather than another.

A letter was published in an English newspaper, the *Guardian*, a few years ago. It was at a time when there was a move to try to lower the time limit for legal abortion. Part of the aim of this proposal was to restrict the possibility of so-called "therapeutic abortion," since many of the tests for medical disorders would not give results by the proposed new time limit. Behind the proposal was an opposition to abortion on the "eugenic" grounds of wanting a child without disability, as opposed to one who had a disability.

Two parents wrote to the *Guardian* in these terms:

In December 1986 our newly born daughter was diagnosed to be suffering from a genetically caused disease

From John Harris and Søren Holm, eds., *The Future of Human Reproduction: Ethics, Choice, and Regulation* (Oxford: Clarendon Press, 1998). Reprinted with the permission of Oxford University Press.

called Dystrophic epidermolysis Bullosa (EB). This is a disease in which the skin of the sufferer is lacking in certain essential fibres. As a result, any contact with her skin caused large blisters to form, which subsequently burst leaving raw open skin that only healed slowly and left terrible scarring. As EB is a genetically caused disease it is incurable and the form that our daughter suffered from usually causes death within the first six months of life. In our daughter's case the condition extended to her digestive and respiratory tracts and as a result of such internal blistering and scarring, she died after a painful and short life at the age of only 12 weeks.

Following our daughter's death we were told that if we wanted any more children, there was a one-in-four probability that any child we conceived would be affected by the disease but that it was possible to detect the disease antenatally. In May 1987 we decided to restart our family only because we knew that such a test was available and that should we conceive an affected child the pregnancy could be terminated, such a decision is not taken lightly or easily . . .

We have had to watch our first child die slowly and painfully and we could not contemplate having another child if there was a risk that it too would have to die in the same way.

My reaction to this letter is one of complete sympathy with the parents' predicament and complete support for the decision that they took. Of course, this kind of decision raises very real questions. If you choose not to have a disabled child, there is a question about the impact on disabled people already alive, about what it does to the idea of equality of respect for the disabled. There is also an alarming slippery slope. How far should we go in choosing what kinds of people should be born? As soon as we start choosing at all, we enter a zone of great moral difficulty where there are important boundaries to be drawn.

But many people, when they think about this sort of issue, also have a feeling of horror and revulsion, linked in a vague way to the Nazi episode. Of course any morally serious person at our end of the twentieth century is bound to have reactions which are coloured by what the Nazis did. All the same, the Nazi episode is greatly misused in bioethics. People too readily reach for the argument that "the Nazis did this" and that therefore we should not. It is a poor case for eating meat that Hitler was a vegetarian. It is necessary to look and see precisely what the Nazis did, and to look a bit harder than people usually do at exactly what was wrong with what they did.

In the case of the decision not to have another child with EB, there are two issues. First, is choosing not to have a child with EB in itself a "eugenic" decision, in the objectionable way the Nazi policies were? Second, are we on a slippery slope, which may lead to objectionable Nazi-like policies?

It is worth making a brief mention of the parallel appeal to the Nazi example that is often made in the euthanasia debate. Here it is fairly obvious that the argument is used too crudely. The Nazi "euthanasia" programme (as the quotation marks indicate) was extraordinarily different from anything that other advocates of euthanasia support. The Nazi euthanasia programme was itself bound up with their ideas about eugenics. It was driven by a highly distinctive ideology. For them, it was not at all important to consider the interests of the individual person whose life was in question. Their project was one of tidying up the world, in the interest of what they called "racial hygiene."

The Nazi theorists were concerned with Darwinian natural selection. They were afraid that the "natural" selective pressures, which had functioned to ensure the survival of healthy and strong human beings, no longer functioned in modern society. Because of such things as medical care, and support for the disabled, people who in tougher times would have died were surviving to pass on their genes.

In the Nazi "euthanasia" programme, 70,723 mental patients were killed by carbon monoxide gas. The thinking behind this is not a matter of acting on the patients' wishes. Nor is it a matter of asking whether someone's life is such a nightmare for them that it is in their own interests that they should die. The thinking does not try to see things from the perspective of the individual person at all.

The bible of the Nazi "euthanasia" programme was a book by a lawyer, Karl Binding, and a psychiatrist, Alfred Hoche, called *Permission for the Destruction of Life Unworthy of Life*. In it, Karl Binding wrote: "The relatives would of course feel the loss badly, but mankind loses so many of its members through mistakes that one more or less hardly matters." That is very different from the agonized thought that goes into the decisions taken by doctors nowadays, when they wonder whether someone's life should be terminated. "One more or less hardly matters" is not the thinking behind the moral case for euthanasia.

The impersonal approach characteristic of the Nazi programme was expressed in 1939 in Berlin. Victor Brack chaired a meeting about who should be killed. The minutes report his remarks: "The number is arrived at through a calculation on the basis of a ratio of 1000 to 10 to 5 to 1. That means, out of 1000 people 10 require psychiatric treatment, of these 5 in residential form, and of these 1 patient will come out of the programme. If one applies this to the population of the Greater German Reich, then one must reckon with 65 to 75,000 cases. With this statement the question of who can be regarded as settled."[1]

This impersonal approach went all the way through the Nazi programme. A nurse described one of the first transports from the asylum of Jestetten in Württemberg: "The senior sister introduced the patients by name. But the transport leader replied that they did not operate on the basis of names but numbers. And in fact the patients who were to be transported then had numbers written in ink on their wrists, which had been previously dampened with a sponge. In other words the people were transported not as human beings but as cattle."[2]

We all know how the later murder of the Jews was preceded by transport in cattle trucks. Many of the people who ran the Nazis' so-called euthanasia programme moved to Poland to work in the extermination camps there. The ideology behind the murder of the Jews was a mixture of race hatred and the same racial hygiene outlook found in the euthanasia programme.

The ideology was one of racial purity. There was the idea that genetic mixing with other races lowered the quality of people. One of the great fathers of the Nazi eugenics movement was Dr. Eugen Fischer. Many years before, he had been to South Africa and in 1913 had published a study of people who he called "Rehoboth bastards." They were children of mixed unions between Boers and Hottentots. He reached the conclusion, on a supposedly scientific basis, that these children were, as he put it, "of lesser racial quality." He wrote that "We should provide them with the minimum amount of protection which they require, for survival as a race inferior to ourselves, and we should do this only as long as they are useful to us. After this, free competition should prevail and, in my opinion, this will lead to their decline and destruction."[3]

In 1933 Dr Fischer was made the new Rector of Berlin University. In his Rectoral Address he said: "The new leadership, having only just taken over the reins of power, is deliberately and forcefully intervening in the course of history and in the life of the nation, precisely when this intervention is most urgently, most decisively, and most immediately needed . . . This intervention can be characterized as a biological population policy, biological in this context signifying the safeguarding by the state of our hereditary endowment and our race." Fischer in 1939 extended this line of thinking specifically to the Jews. He said: "When a people wants to preserve its own nature it must reject alien racial elements. And when these have already insinuated themselves it must suppress them and eliminate them. This is self-defence."[4]

As well as belief in racial purity, there was the idea that in a given race only the "best people" should be encouraged to procreate. And the view was that those who are not "the best people" should be discouraged from having children, or even prevented from doing so. In 1934, one of the other fathers of the Nazi eugenics movement, Professor Fritz Lenz, said: "As things are now, it is only a minority of our fellow citizens who are so endowed that their unrestricted procreation is good for the race."[5] Fisher and Lenz, together with their colleagues, had perhaps more impact on the world than any other academics in the twentieth century. In 1923, Adolf Hitler, while confined in Landsberg prison, read their recently published textbook *Outline of Human Genetics and Racial Hygiene*. He incorporated some of its ideas in *Mein Kampf.*[6] These ideas influenced the Sterilization Law brought in when Hitler came to power in 1933. This made sterilization compulsory for people with conditions including schizophrenia, manic depression, and alcoholism.

This ideology is not one of the importance of the individual. There is a conception of the pure race and the biologically desirable human being. Reproductive freedom and individual lives are to be sacrificed to these abstractions. One medical model had great influence on the Nazis. It is an appalling medical model: the idea that in treating people who are "racially inferior," you are like the doctor who is dealing with a diseased organ in an otherwise healthy body. This analogy was put forward in a paper in 1940 by Konrad Lorenz, the very distinguished ethologist, now remembered for his work on aggression, and whose books on animals had an enormous charm. Lorenz wrote this:

There is a certain similarity between the measures which need to be taken when we draw a broad biological analogy between bodies and malignant tumours, on the one hand, and a nation and individuals within it who have become asocial because of their defective constitution, on the other hand . . . Fortunately, the elimination of such elements is easier for the public health position and less dangerous for the supra-individual organism, than such an operation by a surgeon would be for the individual organism.[7]

The influence in practice of this thinking can be seen very clearly in Robert Jay Lifton's book on the Nazi doctors. He quotes a doctor called Fritz Klein. Dr. Klein was asked how he would reconcile the appalling medical experiments he carried out in Auschwitz with his oath as a doctor. He replied: "Of course I am a doctor and I want to preserve life. And out of respect for human life, I would remove a gangrenous appendix from a diseased body. The Jew is the gangrenous appendix in the body of mankind."[8] This brings out the importance, not just of things people literally believe, but also of the imagery which colours their thinking. Dr Klein cannot literally have believed that Jews were a gangrenous appendix. It would be easier to think that the Nazis were all mad if they literally thought that.

The role of such imagery can be seen again in the way in which racism was given a biological justification. Appalling images likened Jews to vermin, or to dirt and disease. When all Jews were removed from an area, it was called "Judenrein"—clean of Jews. Hans Frank, talking about the decline of a typhus epidemic, said that the removal of what he called "the Jewish element" had contributed to better health in Europe. The Foreign Office Press Chief Schmidt said that the Jewish question was, as he put it, "a question of political hygiene."[9]

This kind of medical analogy was important in Nazi thinking. Hitler said, "The discovery of the Jewish virus is one of the greatest revolutions that have taken place in the world. The battle in which we are engaged today is of the same sort as the battle waged during the last century by Pasteur and Koch. How many diseases have their origin in the Jewish virus! . . . We shall regain our health only by eliminating the Jew."[10]

The medical analogies and the idea of racial hygiene were supplemented by the ideology of Social Darwinism. To study either Nazism or, further back, the origins of the First World War is to see how enormously more influential Social Darwinist ideas have been in our century than one would guess. Social Darwinist ideas were not confined to Germany. They originated in England. It would be unfair to blame Dar-win, who was a very humane person, for these ideas. They were developed by people like Francis Galton and Karl Pearson. Before the First World War, Karl Pearson said that the nation should be kept up to a high pitch of external efficiency by contest, chiefly by way of war with inferior races. The influence of Social Darwinism in Germany was partly the result of the Englishman Houston Stewart Chamberlain, who became an adopted German nationalist, holding that the Germans were a superior race.

Social Darwinism fuelled the naval arms race between Germany and Britain, a contest which helped to cause the First World War. Admiral Tirpitz thought naval expansion was necessary because, if Germany did not join the biological struggle between races, it would go under. When the danger of the arms race was obvious, the British Foreign Secretary, Sir Edward Grey, proposed a naval moratorium on both sides. The German Chancellor, Bethmann-Hollweg, rejected Grey's proposal: "The old saying still holds good that the weak will be the prey of the strong. When a people will not or cannot continue to spend enough on its armaments to be able to make its way in the world, then it falls back into the second rank . . . There will always be another and a stronger there who is ready to take the place in the world which it has vacated."[11]

Nazism emerged against this background of belief in life as a ruthless struggle for survival. According to Social Darwinism, victory goes to the strong, the tough, and the hard rather than to those who are gentle and co-operative. The Nazis took this up. They extolled struggle and the survival of the fittest. This led them to abandon traditional moral restraints. One Nazi physician, Dr Arthur Guett, said: "The ill-conceived 'love of thy neighbour' has to disappear . . . It is the supreme duty of the . . . state to grant life and livelihood only to the healthy and hereditarily sound portion of the population in order to secure . . . a hereditarily sound and racially pure people for all eternity."[12]

The Nazis also extolled hardness, which they thought led to victory in the struggle for survival. Hitler was proud of his own hardness. He said, "I am perhaps the hardest man this nation has had for 200 years."[13] The belief in hardness came partly from Nietzsche. He was contemptuous of English biologists, and so was predictably cool about Darwin. Despite this, Nietzsche was in certain respects a Social Darwinist. He too thought compassion for the weak was sentimental nonsense, and advocated struggle and hardness.

Hitler, an admirer of the darker side of Nietzsche, was also a Social Darwinist. One day at lunch he said, "As in everything, nature is the best instructor, even as regards selection. One couldn't imagine a better activity on nature's part than that which consists in deciding the supremacy of one creature over another by means of a constant struggle." He went on to express disapproval of the way "our upper classes give way to a feeling of compassion regarding the fate of the Jews who we claim the right to expel."[14]

This outlook influenced the people who worked in the Nazi eugenic and "euthanasia" programmes. They felt guilty about feelings of compassion, which they were taught were a weakness to overcome. One Nazi doctor involved in killing psychiatric patients as part of the "euthanasia" programme expressed this in a letter to the director of the asylum where he worked, explaining his reluctance to take part in murdering the children there. He wrote,

> I am very grateful for you willingly insisting that I should take time to think things over. The new measures are so convincing that I had hoped to be able to discard all personal considerations. But it is one thing to approve state measures with conviction and another to carry them out yourself down to their last consequences. I am thinking of the difference between a judge and an executioner. For this reason, despite my intellectual understanding and good will, I cannot help stating that I am temperamentally not fitted for this. As eager as I often am to correct the natural course of events, it is just as repugnant to me to do so systematically, after cold blooded consideration, according to the objective principles of science, without being affected by a doctor's feeling for his patient . . . I feel emotionally tied to the children as their medical guardian, and I think this emotional contact is not necessarily a weakness from the point of view of a National Socialist doctor . . . I prefer to see clearly and to recognise that I am too gentle for this work than to disappoint you later.[15]

This apology for his concern for his patients, his emotional tie to these children, as "not necessarily a weakness in a National Socialist doctor," shows how deeply ingrained this ideology was.

What lessons can be drawn from this grim episode? Any conclusions from this more empirical approach to ethics have to be tentative. There is always the danger of the mistake attributed to generals and strategists, of preparing for the previous war. There will not be an exact rerun of the Nazi episode, so we have to be flexible in learning from it.

The Nazi episode is evil on such a grand scale that any conclusions drawn from it are likely to seem puny by comparison with the events themselves. But it is worth not being deterred by this, and, at the risk of banality, trying to focus on some of the things we should guard against.

One conclusion may be that it is a mistake to let any system of belief, including a system of ethics, become too abstract. There are dangers in getting too far away from ordinary human emotional responses to people. The worry behind "racial hygiene," the worry about the consequences of removing "natural" evolutionary selective pressures, was a thought you did not have to be a very evil person to have. We see it as a misguided thought, but it is still one a morally good person might have had. The danger is to get hooked on an idea, such as this one, and then to follow it ruthlessly, trampling on all the normal human feelings and responses to individual people in front of you. This is a general danger in ethics. Even a humane outlook such as utilitarianism can do great harm when applied with ruthless abstraction.

Another lesson, in our time fortunately a platitude, is that we should not be thinking in terms of racial purity and of lesser racial quality. It is not at all clear what these phrases mean. They are woolly and muddled ideas, which are manifestly incredibly dangerous. (I mention this platitude because sometimes what was once a platitude stops being one. Who, a few years ago, would have thought it worth stating that "ethnic cleansing" should be utterly rejected?)

There is need for more thought about the answer to the claim about the necessity of replacing evolutionary selective pressures. All of us shudder when we see where this kind of thought led, but few do the thinking to find out exactly what is wrong with the arguments.

It is worth mentioning one thought about this. The fact that we can deal with some disorders, so that people with them are able to survive and have children who then may inherit the disorder, is supposed to be the problem. But, in the case of a disorder where people find their lives worth living, it is not a disaster if they pass on their genes. In the Stone Age, people with poor sight may have lost out in the evolutionary competition. Glasses and contact lenses are among the reasons why they now survive to have children. Their lives are not a disaster, and there is no reason why it is a disaster if their children inherit short-sightedness. To the extent that modern medicine makes possible, not just survival, but a decent quality of life, the supposed problem to which eugenics seemed to be the answer is not a real one.

Another lesson is the dangers of the group approach. The Nazis thought mainly in terms of nations and races. In decisions about who is to be born, decisions for instance about access to fertility treatment or about genetic screening, it is important to look first and foremost at those immediately involved: at the person who may be born and at the family. In the case of the kind of reproductive intervention where we are choosing the creation of one person rather than another, our central thought ought to be about what one kind of life or another would be like from the point of view of the person living it.

The case is like that of euthanasia. If we are to justify euthanasia at all, it has to be justified by saying either that a particular person wants not to go on living, or, where the person is past expressing any view, that their life must seem to them so terrible that it would be a kindness to kill them. We have to look at things from inside in taking these decisions. (Of course this is very difficult, which is a reason for extreme caution.)

It is utterly repugnant that "euthanasia" should be defended for instance on grounds of general social utility, such as the cost of keeping certain people alive. Killing on those grounds is not euthanasia, despite the Nazi attempt to hijack the term for such policies. People now sometimes ignorantly misuse the Nazi policy as though it were a knock-down argument against genuine euthanasia. Those of us who study what the Nazis really did tend to dislike this propagandist move. As with the casual use of "fascist" to describe political opponents, it makes light of something truly terrible, and leaves us without a vocabulary for the real thing. But the one place where the argument from Nazism really does apply is where killing the old or the sick or the insane to benefit other people is advocated.

In the same sort of way, I find repugnant the idea that decisions about the kind of children to be born should be made on grounds of general social utility.

Finally, there are issues about Social Darwinism. Rather few people these days hold Hitler's maniac racist views. But Social Darwinism may be a continuing danger. A crude interpretation of some claims in sociobiology could lend support to a renewed Social Darwinism. In mentioning this, I am not lending support to one crude reaction against sociobiology, a reaction which takes the form of denying any genetic contribution to the explanation of human behaviour. That sort of absolute denial is going to lose out in the intellectual debate. No doubt sometimes the evidence will suggest the existence of a genetic component. But, if people propose social policies supposed to follow from this, we need to look very hard at the supporting arguments. Claims about simple links between biology and social policy are often backed by very dubious arguments. And it is not just that the thinking is poor. The Nazi experience suggests that the conclusions may also be dangerous. The victims of the Nazis were not killed just by gas but also by beliefs, which can be poisonous too.

NOTES

1. Quoted in J. Noakes and G. Pridham, *Nazism, 1919–1945,* iii: *Foreign Policy, War and Racial Extermination: A Documentary Reader* (Exeter, 1988), 1010.

2. Quoted ibid. 1023–4.

3. Quoted in Benno Muller-Hill, *Murderous Science: Elimination by Scientific Selection of Jews, Gypsies, and Others, Germany 1933–1945,* trans. George R. Fraser (Oxford, 1988), 7–8.

4. Quoted ibid. 10, 12.

5. Quoted ibid. 10.

6. Cf. Robert N. Proctor, *Racial Hygiene: Medicine under the Nazis* (Cambridge, Mass.: Harvard University Press, 1988).

7. Quoted in Muller-Hill, *Murderous Science,* 14.

8. Quoted in Robert Jay Lifton, *The Nazi Doctors: A Study in the Psychology of Evil* (London, 1986), 16.

9. Quoted in Raul Hilberg, *The Destruction of the European Jews,* student edn. (New York, 1985), 287.

10. *Hitler's Table Talk, 1941–44,* introd. Hugh Trevor-Roper (Oxford, 1988), 332.

11. Quoted in Michael Howard, 'The Edwardian Arms Race', in Michael Howard, *The Lessons of History* (Oxford, 1993).

12. Quoted in Lifton, *The Nazi Doctors.*

13. Hitler, 8 Nov. 1940, quoted in J. P. Stren, *Hitler: The Fuhrer and the People,* 62.

14. *Hitler's Table Talk,* 396–7.

15. Noakes and Pridham, *Nazism, 1919–1945,* iii. 1014–15.

The Human Genome Project

FRANCIS S. COLLINS AND VICTOR A. MCKUSICK

Implications of the Human Genome Project for Medical Science

Francis S. Collin is the Director of the National Human Genome Research Institute and oversees the project aimed at mapping and sequencing all of the human DNA. In 1989 he helped to discover the CFTR gene, which is associated with cystic fibrosis.

Victor A. McKusick is Professor of Medical Genetics at the Johns Hopkins University. He has helped to introduce genetics into clinical medicine. His interests lie in the study and management of inherited diseases and predispositions.

Until recently, many physicians and other health care professionals considered medical genetics as the province of specialists in tertiary care medical centers, who spent their time evaluating unusual cases of mendelian disorders, birth defect syndromes, or chromosomal anomalies. Asked whether genetics was a part of their everyday practice, most primary care practitioners would say no. That is all about to change.

To be sure, there are numerous medical conditions found in children and adults that have a strong, indeed predominant, genetic basis. The continuously updated Online Mendelian Inheritance in Man (OMIM) lists many thousands of such conditions,[1] but offers a far too narrow view of the contribution of genetics to medicine. Except for some cases of trauma, it is fair to say that virtually every human illness has a hereditary component.[2] While common diseases, such as diabetes mellitus, heart disease, cancer, and the major mental illnesses, do not follow mendelian inheritance patterns, there is ample evidence from twin and pedigree studies over many decades showing that all of these disorders have important hereditary influences. In fact, for many common illnesses of developed countries, the strongest predictor of risk is family history.

The role of heredity in most diseases is thus not in itself a new revelation. But in the past, it was considered unlikely that much could be done with this information other than to guide medical surveillance based on careful family history taking. A sea change is now underway, and it is likely that the molecular basis for these hereditary influences on common illnesses soon will be uncovered. Even though on average the quantitative contribution of heredity to the etiological characteristics of diseases like diabetes mellitus or hypertension may be modest, uncovering the pathways involved in disease pathogenesis will have broad consequences, pointing toward possible environmental triggers as well. The implications for diagnostics, preventive medicine, and therapeutics will be profound.

GENETICS IN THE 20TH CENTURY

In the spring of 1900, 3 different investigators rediscovered Mendel's laws.[3] With Garrod's recognition of their application to human inborn errors of metabolism, the science of human genetics acquired a foundation. But it remained for Watson and Crick half a century later to uncover the chemical basis of heredity, with their elucidation of the double helical structure of DNA.[4] The role of RNA as a messenger and the genetic code that allows RNA to be translated to protein emerged over the next 15 years. This was followed by the advent of recombinant DNA technology in the 1970s, offering the ability to obtain pure preparations of a particular DNA segment. However, sequencing of DNA was difficult until Sanger and Gilbert independently derived methods of sequencing DNA in 1977.[5,6] (It is remarkable indeed that the Sanger dideoxy method for DNA sequencing remains the basic technology on which the genetic revolution is being built, albeit with major advances in automation of the analysis that have come along in the last 15 years.)

The use of variable DNA markers for linkage analysis of human disorders was set forth in 1980.[7] Mapping of disorders by linkage previously had been severely limited by the relatively small number of usable protein markers, such as blood groups. The notion that any mendelian disorder could be mapped to a chromosomal region caught the imagination of geneticists. An early and stunning success of this approach, the mapping of the Huntington disease gene to chromosome 4 in 1983, gave a burst of confidence to this adventurous new approach.[8] But the difficulty of going from a linked marker to the actual disease locus proved profoundly difficult. Years of work were required to map a candidate region and search for potential candidate genes, and many investigators in the 1980s longed for a more systematic approach to the genome.

At the same time, potential advances in mapping and sequencing technology led certain scientific leaders, particularly in the US Department of Energy, to propose the possibility of an organized effort to sequence the entire human genome. In the late 1980s much controversy raged about such proposals, with many in the scientific community deeply concerned that this was technologically impossible and likely to consume vast amounts of funding that might be taken away from other more productive hypothesis-driven research. But with the strong support of a panel of the National Academy of Sciences,[9] and the enthusiasm of a few leaders in the US Congress, the Human Genome Project (HGP) was initiated in the United States by the National Institutes of Health and the Department of Energy in 1990.[10]

THE HUMAN GENOME PROJECT

From the outset, it was realized that a detailed set of plans and milestones would be necessary for a project of this magnitude. The technology for carrying out

actual large-scale sequencing had not advanced to the point of being able to tackle the 3 billion base pairs of the human genome in 1990 nor were the necessary maps of the genome in hand to provide a scaffold for this effort.

Under the leadership of James Watson, it was decided to focus the first 5 years of the HGP on the development of genetic and physical maps of the human genome, which would themselves be of great value to scientists hunting for disease genes. The HGP also tackled mapping and sequencing of simpler model organisms, such as bacteria, yeast, the roundworm, and the fruit fly.[9–12] Considerable investments were made in improving technology. Perhaps the most unusual feature for a basic science enterprise, 3% to 5% of the budget was set aside from the outset for research on the ethical, legal, and social implications of this expected acceleration in obtaining genetic information about our species.[10] In the past, ethical, legal, and social analysis of the consequences of a scientific revolution often were relegated to other groups outside the scientific mainstream or lay dormant until a crisis developed. This time, the intention was to inspire a cohort of ethicists, social scientists, legal scholars, theologians, and others to address the coming dilemmas associated with increased knowledge about the genome, from social and legal discrimination on the basis of genetics to more philosophical issues such as genetic determinism.

The HGP has been international from the beginning. Although the United States made the largest investment, important contributions have been made by many countries, including Britain, France, Germany, Japan, China, and Canada. The original plan[9] called for completion of the sequence of the human genome by the year 2005, though there was limited confidence that this goal could be achieved. But one by one the intermediate milestones were accomplished. The HGP agreed at the outset to release all map and sequence data into the public domain. The availability of genetic and physical maps led to a considerable acceleration in the successful identification of genes involved in single gene disorders; while fewer than 10 such genes had been identified by positional cloning in 1990, that number grew to more than 100 by 1997.[13]

By 1996, the complete sequencing of several bacterial species and yeast led to the conclusion that it was time to attempt sequencing human DNA on a pilot scale. The introduction of capillary sequencing instruments and the formation of a company in the private sector promising to sequence the human genome for profitable purposes added further momentum to the effort. By 1999, confidence had gathered that acquiring the majority of the sequence of the 3 billion base pairs of the human genome could be attempted. In June 2000, both the private company and the international public sequencing consortium announced the completion of "working drafts" of the human genome sequence.

CURRENT RESEARCH FOCUS

Though the working draft of the human sequence represents a major milestone, a vast amount of additional work remains to be done to understand its function.

It is necessary to complete the sequence analysis by closing the gaps and resolving ambiguities. This finishing process already has been accomplished for chromosomes 21[14] and 22[15] and will be carried out for the remainder of the genome during the next 2 years.

The genomes of other organisms also will need to be sequenced. Probably the most powerful tool to identify the coding exons, as well as the regulatory regions, is a comparison of the sequence across different genomes. For that purpose, full-scale sequencing of the laboratory mouse genome already has been initiated, and the sequencing of the rat and zebrafish genomes will not be far behind. In both the public and private sectors, serious consideration is being given to the sequencing of other large vertebrate genomes, including the pig, dog, cow, and chimpanzee.

An intense effort is under way to develop a catalog of human variation. While human DNA sequences are 99.9% identical to each other, the 0.1% of variation is expected to provide many of the clues to the genetic risk for common illnesses.[16] A public-private partnership has formed to build this catalog of variants as quickly as possible and has identified more than 2 million of these single nucleotide polymorphisms. Of particular interest are those common variants that influence gene function.

Research Opportunities and Forecast: Genomics

Key research opportunities	Forecast
Define Complete List of All Human Genes and Proteins	Thousands of New Drug Targets for Heart Disease, Cancer, Diabetes, Asthma, etc
Define All Common Variants in the Genome, Determine Hereditary Factors in Virtually All Common Diseases, and Refine Technology for Low-Cost Genotyping	Individualized Preventive Medicine Based on Genetic Risk
	Pharmacogenomics to Improve Outcome of Drug Therapy
	Environmental Risk Factor Assessment Becomes Individual-Specific
Determine Regulatory Signals That Affect Expression of All Human Genes in Normal or Abnormal State	Therapies for Developmental Defects
	Precise Molecular Analysis of Malignancies, Guiding Choice of Therapy
Determine Structures of All Human Proteins, Using a Combination of Experimental and Computational Methods	"Designer Drugs" Based on Precise 3-Dimensional Information About Targets
Develop Safe and Effective Gene-Transfer Vectors for Many Different Tissues	Gene Therapy for Rare Single-Gene Disorders, and Some Common Ones
Vigorously Explore the Ethical, Legal, and Social Implications of Genome Research	Legal Safeguards Against Genetic Discrimination and Breaches of Privacy
	Effective Oversight of Clinical Application of Genetic Testing
	Mainstreaming of Genetics into the Practice of Medicine, With Achievement of "Genetic Literacy" Among Clinicians and Patients

A powerful set of technologies for studying gene expression is being developed and explored.[17] These methodologies, which allow analysis of the transcription of as many as 10000 genes in one experiment, make it possible to investigate the differences that occur between various tissue types and to explore the alterations in that expression pattern during disease. Such analyses have already been proved capable of identifying subtypes of certain malignancies that were identical by all other criteria.[18]

The same large-scale analysis strategies that have been applied so effectively to DNA and RNA also are being applied to proteins to characterize their structures, quantity, location in the cell, posttranslational modifications, and interaction partners.[19]

With the advent of these very large databases of information on sequence, variation, and expression, the field of computational biology is emerging as critically important to the future. Effective methods of sorting and analyzing the data will be required to glean biologically meaningful insights from the plethora of data.

The ethical, legal, and social implications research program has already fostered awareness of needs for intervention, particularly in the areas of privacy, genetic discrimination, guidelines for research, and education, and now focuses on the societal implications of increased information about human variation, in both medical and nonmedical situations.

THE 21ST CENTURY: CRITICAL ELEMENTS OF THE MEDICAL RESEARCH AGENDA

Obtaining the sequence of the human genome is the end of the beginning. As Knoppers has said, "As the radius of knowledge gets longer, the circumference of the unknown increases even more" (Bartha Knoppers, personal communication). For the full impact of advances in genetics to be felt in the practice of medicine, major challenges must be addressed.

Information about the human genome sequence and its variants must be applied to identify the particular genes that play a significant role in the hereditary contribution to common disease. This will be a daunting challenge. For a disease such as diabetes mellitus, 5 to 10 (or maybe more) genes are involved, each of which harbors a variant conferring a modest degree of increased risk. Those variants interact with each other and the environment in complex ways, rendering their identification orders of magnitude more difficult than

for single gene defects. Nonetheless, with the combination of careful phenotyping (so that different disorders are not inadvertently lumped together) and sampling genetic variants at high density across the genome, it should be possible to identify disease gene associations for many common illnesses in the next 5 to 7 years.[2,16] One should not underestimate, however, the degree of sophistication in clinical investigation that will be necessary or the need for development of more efficient genotyping technology, such as the use of DNA chips or mass spectrometry, to make this kind of genome-wide survey a reality.

An understanding of the major pathways involved in normal homeostasis of the human organism must be developed along with how those pathways are deranged in illness. Identification of each gene that harbors a high-risk variant will point toward a critical pathway for that illness. Many of those will come as a surprise, since the current molecular understanding of most common diseases is rather limited.

Efficient, high-volume methods will need to be developed and applied to the design of small-molecule drugs to modulate disease-related pathways in the desired direction. The pharmaceutical industry has been gearing up for this opportunity, and most companies now expect that the majority of future drug development will come from the field of genomics. With the application of methods that systematically combine chemical components into drugs and of high-volume assays for efficacy, it is expected that compounds can be efficiently identified that block or stimulate a particular pathway. A gratifying recent example is the development of the drug STI-571, which was designed to block the kinase activity of the bcr-abl kinase.[20] This protein is produced as a consequence of the translocation between chromosomes 9 and 22, a chromosome rearrangement that is characteristic of and central to the etiology of chronic myelogenous leukemia. STI-571 blocks the ability of the bcr-abl kinase to phosphorylate its unknown substrate and shows dramatic results in early clinical trials on patients with far advanced chronic myelogenous leukemia.

Along with the design of new drugs, genomics also will provide opportunities to predict responsiveness to drug interventions, since variation in those responses is often attributable to the genetic endowment of the individual. Examples have been identified where common variants in genes involved in drug metabolism or drug action are associated with the likelihood of a good or bad response. The expectation is that such correlations will be found for many drugs over the next 10 years, including agents that are already on the market. This field of pharmacogenomics promises to individualize prescribing practices.[21]

The field of gene therapy, having sustained a series of disappointments over the past few years, especially with the death of a volunteer in a gene therapy trial in the fall of 1999, has gone back to wrestling with the basic science questions of finding optimal methods for gene delivery.[22] While the optimism of the early 1990s about providing quick solutions to a long list of medical problems was probably never fully justified, it is likely that the development of safer and more effective vectors will ensure a significant role for gene therapy in the treatment of some diseases. There already have been promising reports of the application of gene therapy for hemophilia B[23] and severe combined immunodeficiency.[24]

GENETICS IN THE MEDICAL MAINSTREAM

The power of the molecular genetic approach for answering questions in the research laboratory will catalyze a similar transformation of clinical medicine, although this will come gradually over the course of the next 25 years (Figure).

By the year 2010, it is expected that predictive genetic tests will be available for as many as a dozen common conditions, allowing individuals who wish to know this information to learn their individual susceptibilities and to take steps to reduce those risks for which interventions are or will be available. Such interventions could take the form of medical surveillance, lifestyle modifications, diet, or drug therapy. Identification of persons at highest risk for colon cancer, for example, could lead to targeted efforts to provide colonoscopic screening to those individuals, with the likelihood of preventing many premature deaths.

Predictive genetic tests will become applicable first in situations where individuals have a strong family history of a particular condition; indeed, such testing is already available for several conditions, such as breast and colon cancers. But with increasing genetic information about common illnesses, this kind of risk assessment will become more generally available, and many primary care clinicians will become practitioners of genomic medicine, having to explain complex statistical risk information to healthy individuals who are seeking to enhance their chances of staying well. This will require substantial advances in the understanding of genetics by a wide range of clinicians.[25] The National Coalition for Health Professional Education in Genetics, an umbrella group of physicians, nurses, and other clinicians, has organized to help prepare for this coming era.

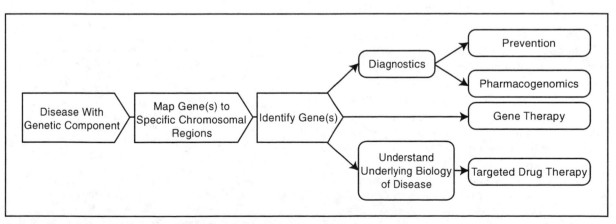

Figure.   Steps Involved in a Genetic Approach to the Diagnosis and Treatment of Disease.
The rate of progress for applying a genetic approach to the diagnosis and treatment of each disease will be different depending on the research investment and the degree of biological complexity underlying the disease. First, the gene variants contributing increased disease risk must be identified by family studies and/or case-control studies. Diagnostic opportunities may then come along rather quickly, but will be of greatest clinical usefulness once prevention measures are developed that have proven benefit to those at high risk. Some gene variants will also show clinically useful associations with drug responsiveness (pharmacogenomics). In general, full-blown therapeutic benefits from identification of gene variants will take longer to reach mainstream medicine. In some instances, the gene itself will be the drug (gene therapy), while in others, a sophisticated knowledge of the underlying disease mechanism, built upon genetics, may allow the design of targeted and highly effective drug therapy.

Another crucial step is the passage of effective federal legislation to outlaw the use of predictive genetic information in the workplace and in obtaining health insurance.[26,27] Numerous surveys have indicated that the public is deeply concerned about the potential for discrimination, and some individuals have forgone acquiring genetic information about themselves, since assurances cannot be currently provided about discriminatory misuse of the information. Although more than 2 dozen states have taken some action in this regard, a patchwork of different levels of protection across the United States is not satisfactory and this vexing problem must be dealt with effectively at the federal level.

By 2020, the impact of genetics on medicine will be even more widespread. The pharmacogenomics approach for predicting drug responsiveness will be standard practice for quite a number of disorders and drugs. New gene-based "designer drugs" will be introduced to the market for diabetes mellitus, hypertension, mental illness, and many other conditions. Improved diagnosis and treatment of cancer will likely be the most advanced of the clinical consequences of genetics, since a vast amount of molecular information already has been collected about the genetic basis of malignancy. By 2020, it is likely that every tumor will have a precise molecular fingerprint determined, cataloging the genes that have gone awry, and therapy will be individually targeted to that fingerprint.

Despite these exciting projections, certain tensions also will exist. Access to health care, already a major problem in the United States, will complicate these new advances, unless our medical care systems change in significant ways. Anti-technology movements, already active in the United States and elsewhere, are likely to gather momentum as the focus of genetics turns even more intensely on ourselves. Though the benefits of genetic medicine will be profound, there will be those who consider this advancement unnatural and dangerous. Efforts at public education need to start now to explain the potential benefits and to be honest about the risks.

In conclusion, this is a time of dramatic change in medicine. As we cross the threshold of the new millennium, we simultaneously cross a threshold into an era where the human genome sequence is largely known. We must commit ourselves to exploring the application of these powerful tools to the alleviation of human suffering, a mandate that undergirds all of medicine. At the same time, we must be mindful of the great potential for misunderstanding in this quickly developing field and make sure that the advancement of the social agenda of genetics is equally as vigorous as the medical agenda.

REFERENCES

1. National Center for Biotechnology Information. Online Mendelian Inheritance in Man. Available at: http://www.ncbi.nlm.nih.gov/omim/. Accessed November 30, 2000.

2. Collins F. S. Shattuck Lecture: medical and societal consequences of the Human Genome Project. *N Engl J Med.* 1999;341:28–37.

3. Henig R. M. *The Monk in the Garden.* New York, NY: Houghton Mifflin; 2000.

4. Watson J. D., Crick F. H. C. Molecular structure of nucleic acids. *Nature.* 1953;171:737–738.

5. Sanger F., Nicklen S., Coulson A. R. DNA sequencing with chain-terminating inhibitors. *Proc Natl Acad Sci U S A.* 1977;74:5463–5467.

6. Maxam A. M., Gilbert W. A new method for sequencing DNA. *Proc Natl Acad Sci U S A.* 1977;74:560–564.

7. Botstein D., White R. L., Skolnick M., Davis R. W. Construction of a genetic linkage map in man using restriction fragment length polymorphisms. *Am J Hum Genet.* 1980;32:314–331.

8. Gusella J. F., Wexler N. S., Conneally P. M., et al. A polymorphic DNA marker genetically linked to Huntington's disease. *Nature.* 1983;306:234–238.

9. National Research Council, Committee on Mapping and Sequencing the Human Genome. *Mapping and Sequencing the Human Genome.* Washington, DC: National Academy Press; 2000.

10. US Department of Health and Human Services and Department of Energy. *Understanding Our Genetic Inheritance. The U.S. Human Genome Project: The First Five Years.* Washington, DC: US Dept of Health and Human Services; 1990.

11. Collins F. S., Galas D. A new five-year plan for the U.S. Human Genome Project. *Science.* 1993;262:43–46.

12. Collins F. S., Patrinos A., Jordan E., Chakravarti A., Gesteland R., Walters L. New goals for the U.S. Human Genome Project: 1998–2003. *Science.* 1998;282:682–689.

13. Collins F. S. Positional cloning moves from perditional to traditional. *Nat Genet.* 1995;9:347–350.

14. Hattori M., Fujiyama A., Taylor T. D., et al. The DNA sequence of human chromosome 21. *Nature.* 2000;405:311–319.

15. Dunham I., Shimizu N., Roe B. A., et al. The DNA sequence of human chromosome 22. *Nature.* 1999;402:489–495.

16. Collins F. S., Guyer M. S., Chakravarti A. Variations on a theme: cataloging human DNA sequence variation. *Science.* 1997;278:1580–1581.

17. Lockhart D. J., Winzeler E. A. Genomics, gene expression and DNA arrays. *Nature.* 2000;405:827–836.

18. Bittner M., Meltzer P., Chen Y., et al. Molecular classification of cutaneous malignant melanoma by gene expression profiling. *Nature.* 2000;406:536–540.

19. Pandey A., Mann M. Proteomics to study genes and genomes. *Nature.* 2000;405:837–846.

20. Druker B. J., Lydon N. B. Lessons learned from the development of an abl tyrosine kinase inhibitor for chronic myelogenous leukemia. *J Clin Invest.* 2000;105:3–7.
21. Roses A. D. Pharmacogenetics and the practice of medicine. *Nature.* 2000;405:857–865.
22. Verma I. M. Gene therapy: beyond 2000. *Mol Ther.* 2000;1:493.
23. Kay M. A., Manno C. S., Ragni M. V., et al. Evidence for gene transfer and expression of factor IX in haemophilia B patients treated with an AAV vector. *Nat Genet.* 2000;24:257–261.
24. Cavazzana-Calvo M., Hacein-Bey S., de Saint Basile G., et al. Gene therapy of human severe combined immuno-deficiency (SCID)-X1 disease. *Science.* 2000;288:669–672.
25. Collins F. S. Preparing health professionals for the genetic revolution. *JAMA.* 1997;278:1285–1286.
26. Hudson K. L., Rothenberg K. H., Andrews L. B., Kahn M. J. E., Collins F. S. Genetic discrimination and health insurance: an urgent need for reform. *Science.* 1995;270:391–393.
27. Rothenberg K., Fuller B., Rothstein M., et al. Genetic information and the workplace: legislative approaches and policy challenges. *Science.* 1997;275:1755–1757.

JAMES D. WATSON

Genes and Politics

James D. Watson is the President of the Cold Spring Harbor Laboratory and shared the Nobel Prize for the discovery of the structure of DNA. He has been a member of the Harvard faculty and was the first Director of the National Center for Human Genome Research at the National Institutes of Health, where he helped to launch the Human Genome Project.

• • •

GENUINE HUMAN GENETICS EMERGES FROM RECOMBINANT DNA METHODOLOGIES

Long holding back the development of human genetics as a major science was the lack of a genetic map allowing human genes to be located along the chromosomes on which they reside. As long as conventional breeding procedures remained the only route to gene mapping, the precise molecular changes underpinning most human genetic diseases seemed foreordained to remain long mysterious. The key breakthrough opening a path around this seemingly insuperable obstacle came in the late 1970s when it was discovered that the exact sequence (order of the genetic letters A, G, T, and C) of a given gene varies from one person to another. Between any two individuals, roughly 1 in 1000 bases are different, with such variations most frequently occurring within the noncoding DNA regions not involved in specifying specific amino acids. Initially most useful were base differences (polymorphisms) which affected DNA cutting by one of the many just discovered "restriction enzymes" that cut DNA molecules within very specific base sequences.

Soon after the existence of DNA polymorphisms became known, proposals were made that they could provide the genetic markers needed to put together human genetic maps. In a 1980 paper, David Botstein, Ron Davis, Mark Scolnick, and Ray White argued that human maps could be obtained through studying the pattern through which polymorphisms were inherited in the members of large multigenerational families. Those polymorphisms that stay together were likely to be located close to each other on a given chromosome. During the next 5 years, two groups, one led by Helen Donis-Keller in Massachusetts, the other led by Ray White in Utah, rose to this challenge, both using DNA from family blood samples stored at CEPH (Centre d'Étude de Polymorphisme Humain), the mapping center established in Paris by Jean Dausset. By 1985, the mutant genes responsible for Huntington's disease and cystic fibrosis (CF) had been located on chromosomes 4 and 7, respectively.

By using a large number of additional polymorphic markers in the original chromosome 7 region implicated in CF, Francis Collins' group in Ann Arbor and L. C. Tsui's group in Toronto located the DNA segment containing the responsible gene. Its DNA sequence revealed that the CF gene coded for a large membrane protein involved in the transport of chloride ions. The first CF mutant they found contained three fewer bases than its normal equivalent and led to a protein product that was nonfunctional because of its lack of a phenylalanine residue.

THE HUMAN GENOME PROJECT: RESPONDING TO THE NEED FOR EFFICIENT DISEASE GENE MAPPING AND ISOLATION

Although the genes responsible for cystic fibrosis and Huntington's disease were soon accurately mapped using only a small number of DNA polymorphic markers, the genes behind many other important genetic diseases quickly proved to be much harder to map to a specific chromosome, much less assign to a DNA chromosomal segment short enough to generate hopes for its eventual cloning. All too obviously, the genes behind the large set of still very badly understood diseases like Alzheimer's disease, late-onset diabetes, or breast cancer would be mapped much, much sooner if several thousands more newly mapped DNA polymorphisms somehow became available. Likewise, the task of locating the chromosomal DNA segment(s) in which the desired disease genes reside would be greatly shortened if all human DNA were publicly available as sets of overlapping cloned DNA segments (contigs). And the scanning of such DNA segments to look for mutationally altered base sequences would go much faster if the complete sequence of all the human DNA were already known. However, to generate these importantly new resources for human genetics, major new sources of money would be needed. So, by early 1986, serious discussions began as to how to start, soon, the complete sequencing of the 3×10^9 [3 billion] base pairs that collectively make up the human genome (the Human Genome Project or HGP).

Initially, there were more scientific opponents than proponents for what necessarily would be biology's first megaproject. It would require thousands of scientists and the consumption of some $3 billion-like sums. Those disliking its prospects feared that, inevitably, it would be run by governmental bureaucrats not up to the job and would employ scientists too dull for assignment to this intellectually challenging research. Out of many protracted meetings held late in 1986 and through 1987, the argument prevailed that the potential rewards for medicine as well as for biological research itself would more than compensate for the monies the Human Genome Project would consume during the 15 years then thought needed to complete it. Moreover, completion of each of the two stages—the collection of many more mapped DNA markers and the subsequent ordering of cloned DNA segments into long overlapping sets (contigs)—would by themselves greatly speed up disease gene isolation.

Always equally important to point out, the 15 years projected to complete the Human Genome Project meant that its annual cost of $200 million at most would represent only 1–2% of the money spent yearly for fundamental biomedical research over the world. There was also the realization that some 100,000 human genes believed sited along their chromosomes would be much easier to find and functionally understand if genome sequences were first established for the much smaller, well-studied model organisms such as *Escherichia coli*, *Saccharomyces cerevisiae*, *Caenorhabditis elegans*, and *Drosophila melanogaster*. Thus, the biologists who worked with these organisms realized that their own research would be speeded up if the Human Genome Project went ahead.

The American public, as represented by their congressional members, proved initially to be much more enthusiastic about the objectives of the Human Genome Project than most supposedly knowledgeable biologists, with their parochial concerns for how federal monies for biology would be divided up. The first congressionally mandated monies for the Human Genome Project became available late in 1987, when many intelligent molecular geneticists still were sitting on the fence as to whether it made sense. In contrast, Congress, being told that big medical advances would virtually automatically flow out of genome knowledge, saw no reason not to move fast. In doing so, they temporarily set aside the question of what human life would be like when the bad genes behind so many of our major diseases were found. Correctly, to my mind, their overwhelming concern was the current horror of diseases like Alzheimer's, not seeing the need then to, perhaps prematurely, worry about the dilemmas arising when individuals are genetically shown at risk for specific diseases years before they show any symptoms.

GENOME ETHICS: PROGRAMS TO FIND WAYS TO AMELIORATE GENETIC INJUSTICE

The moment I began in October 1988 my almost 4-year period of helping lead the Human Genome Project, I stated that 3% of the NIH-funded component should support research and discussion on the Ethical, Legal, and Social Implications (ELSI) of the new resulting genetic knowledge. A lower percentage might be seen as tokenism, while I then could not see wise use of a larger sum. Under my 3% proposal, some $6 million (3% of $200 million) would eventually be so available, a much larger sum than ever before provided by our government for the ethical implications of biological research.

In putting ethics so soon into the Genome agenda, I was responding to my own personal fear that all too soon critics of the Genome Project would point out that I was a representative of the Cold Spring Harbor Laboratory that once housed the controversial Eugenics Record Office. My not forming a genome ethics program quickly might be falsely used as evidence that I was a closet eugenicist, having as my real long-term purpose the unambiguous identification of genes that lead to social and occupational stratification as well as to genes justifying racial discrimination. So I saw the need to be proactive in making ELSI's major purpose clear from its start—to devise better ways to combat the social injustice that has at its roots bad draws of the genetic dice. Its programs should not be turned into public forums for debating whether genetic inequalities exist. With imperfect gene copying always the evolutionary imperative, there necessarily will always be a constant generation of the new gene disease variants and consequential genetic injustice.

The issues soon considered for ELSI monies were far-ranging. For example, how can we ensure that the results of genetic diagnosis are not misused by prospective employers or insurers? How should we try to see that individuals know what they are committing themselves to when they allow their DNA to be used for genetic analyzing? What concrete steps should be taken to ensure the accuracy of genetic testing? And when a fetus is found to possess genes that will not allow it to develop into a functional human being, who, if anyone, should have the right to terminate the pregnancy?

From their beginnings, our ELSI programs had to reflect primarily the needs of individuals at risk of the oft tragic consequences of genetic disabilities. Only long-term harm would result in the perception of genetics as an honest science if ELSI-type decisions were perceived to be dominated either by the scientists who provided the genetic knowledge or by the government bodies that funded such research. And since women are even in the distant future likely to disproportionately share the burden of caring for the genetically disabled, they should lead the discussion of how more genetic knowledge is to come into our lives.

HUMAN HESITATIONS IN LEARNING THEIR OWN GENETIC FATE

With the initial distribution of American genome monies and the building and equipping the resulting genome centers taking 2 years, the Human Genome Project in its megaphase did not effectively start until the fall of 1990. Decisions to go ahead by funding bodies in the United States helped lead to the subsequent inspired creation of Genethon outside Paris by the French genetic disease charity, Association Française contre les Myopathies (AFM), as well as the building of the now immense Sanger Centre, just south of Cambridge, England, by the British medically oriented charity, the Wellcome Trust. Now effectively 7 years into its projected 15-year life, the Human Genome Project has more than lived up to its role in speeding up genetic disease mapping and subsequent gene cloning. It quickly made successful the search for the gene behind the fragile X syndrome that leads to severe mental retardation in boys preferentially affected by this sex-linked genetic affliction. The molecular defect found was an expansion of pre-existing three-base repetitive sequences that most excitingly increase in length from one generation to the next. The long mysterious phenomenon of anticipation, in which the severity of a disease grows through subsequent generations, was thus given a molecular explanation. Then at long last, in 1994, the gene for Huntington's disease was found. Its cause was likewise soon found to be the expansion of a repetitive gene sequence.

While the mapping to a chromosome per se of any disease gene remains an important achievement, the cloning of the disease gene itself is a bigger milestone. Thus, the 1990 finding by Mary Claire King that much hereditary breast cancer is due to a gene on chromosome 17 set off a big gene-cloning race. With that gene in hand, there was a chance that its DNA sequence would reveal the normal function of the protein it codes for. In any case, it gives its possessors the opportunity to examine directly the DNA from individuals known to be at risk for a disease to see whether they had the unwanted gene. Thus, when in 1993 the chromosome 17 breast cancer gene (BRCA1) was isolated by Myriad, the Utah disease gene-finding company, it could inform women so tested for BRCA1 whether or not they had the feared gene.

Initially, concerns were voiced that unbridled commercialization of this capability would all too easily give women knowledge they would not be psychologically prepared to handle. If so, the ethical way to prevent such emotional setbacks might be to regulate both how the tests were given and who should be allowed to be tested. I fear, however, that a major reason behind many such calls for regulation of genetic testing is the hidden agenda of wanting to effectively stop widespread genetic testing by making it so difficult to obtain. Now, however, calls for governmental regulation may fall on increasingly deaf ears. To Myriad's great disappointment, it appears that the great majority of women at 50% risk of being breast cancer gene carriers don't want to be tested. Rather than receive the wrong verdict, they seem to prefer living with uncertainty. Likewise, a very large majority of the individuals at risk for Huntington's disease are also psychologically predisposed against putting themselves at risk of possibly knowing of their genetic damnation.

Although we are certain to learn in the future of many individuals regretting that they subjected themselves to genetic tests and wishing they had been more forewarned of the potential perils of such knowledge, I do not see how the state can effectively enter into such decisions. Committees of well-intentioned outsiders will never have the intimate knowledge to assess a given individual's psychological need, or not, for a particular piece of scientific or medical knowledge. In the last analysis, we should accept the fact that if scientific knowledge exists, individual persons or families should have the right to decide whether it will lead to their betterment.

INARGUABLE EXISTENCE OF GENES PREDISPOSING HUMANS TO BEHAVIORAL DISORDERS

The extraordinarily negative connotation that the term eugenics now conveys is indelibly identified with its past practitioners' unjustified statements that behavioral differences, whether between individuals, families, or the so-called races, largely had their origins in gene differences. Given the primitive power of human genetics, there was no way for such broad-ranging assertions to have been legitimatized by the then methods of science. Even the eugenically minded psychiatrists' claims that defective genes were invariably at the root of their mental patients' symptoms were no more than hunches. Yet, it was by their imputed genetic imperfection that the mentally ill were first sterilized and then, being of no value to the wartime Third Reich, released from their lives by subsequent "mercy killings."

But past eugenic horrors in no way justify the "Not in Our Genes" politically correct outlook of many leftwing academics. They still spread the unwarranted message that only our bodies, not our minds, have genetic origins. Essentially protecting the ideology that all our troubles have capitalistic exploitative origins, they are particularly uncomfortable with the thought that genes have any influence on intellectual abilities or that unsocial criminal behavior might owe its origins to other than class or racially motivated oppression. Whether these scientists on the left actually believe, say, that the incidence of schizophrenia would seriously lessen if class struggles ended, however, is not worth finding out.

Instead, we should employ, as fast as we can, the powerful new techniques of human genetics to find soon the actual schizophrenia predisposing genes. The much higher concordance of schizophrenia in identical versus nonidentical twins unambiguously tells us that they are there to find. Such twin analysis, however, reveals that genetics cannot be the whole picture. Since the concordance rates for schizophrenia, as well as for manic-depressive disease, are more like 60%, not 100%, environmental predisposing factors must exist and, conceivably, viral infections that affect the brain are sometimes involved.

Unfortunately, still today, the newer statistical tricks for analyzing polymorphic inheritance patterns have not yet led to the unambiguous mapping of even one major schizophrenic gene to a defined chromosomal site. The only convincing data involve only the 1% of schizophrenics whose psychoses seemingly are caused by the small chromosome 22 deletions responsible also for the so-called St. George facial syndrome. Manic-depressive disease also has been more than hard to understand genetically. Only last year did solid evidence emerge for a major predisposing gene on the long arm of chromosome 18. This evidence looks convincing enough for real hopes that the actual gene involved will be isolated over the next several years.

Given that over half the human genes are thought to be involved in human brain development and functioning, we must expect that many other behavioral differences between individuals will also have genetic origins. Recently, there have been claims that both "reckless personalities" and "unipolar depressions" associate with specific polymorphic forms of genes coding for the membrane receptors involved in the transmission of signals between nerve cells. Neither claim now appears to be reproducible, but we should not be surprised to find some subsequent associations to hold water. Now anathematic to left-wing ideologues is the highly convincing report of a Dutch family, many of whose male members display particularly violent behavior. Most excitingly, all of the affected males possess a mutant gene coding for an inactive form of the enzyme monoamine oxidase. Conceivably having too little of this enzyme, which breaks down neurotransmitters, leads to the persistence of destructive thoughts and the consequential aggressive patterns. Subsequent attempts to detect in other violent individuals this same mutant gene have so far failed. We must expect someday, however, to find that other mutant genes that lead to altered brain chemistry also lead to asocial activities. Their existence, however, in no way should be taken to mean that gene variants are the major cause of violence. Nonetheless, continued denials by the scientific left that genes have no role in how people interact with each other will inevitably further diminish their already tainted credibility.

KEEPING GOVERNMENTS OUT OF GENETIC DECISIONS

No rational person should have doubts whether genetic knowledge properly used has the capacity to improve the human condition. Through discovering those genes whose bad variants make us unhealthy or in some other way unable to function effectively, we can fight back in several different ways. For example, knowing what is wrong at the molecular level should let us sometimes develop drugs that will effectively neutralize the harm generated by certain bad genes. Other genetic disabilities should effectively be neutralized by so-called gene therapy procedures restoring normal cell functioning by adding good copies of the missing normal genes. Although gene therapy enthusiasts have promised too much for the near future,

it is difficult to imagine that they will not with time cure some genetic conditions.

For the time being, however, we should place most of our hopes for genetics on the use of antenatal diagnostic procedures, which increasingly will let us know whether a fetus is carrying a mutant gene that will seriously proscribe its eventual development into a functional human being. By terminating such pregnancies, the threat of horrific disease genes continuing to blight many families' prospects for future success can be erased. But even among individuals who firmly place themselves on the pro-choice side and do not want to limit women's rights for abortion, opinions frequently are voiced that decisions obviously good for individual persons or families may not be appropriate for the societies in which we live. For example, by not wanting to have a physically or mentally handicapped child or one who would have to fight all its life against possible death from cystic fibrosis, are we not reinforcing the second-rate status of such handicapped individuals? And what would be the consequences of isolating genes that give rise to the various forms of dyslexia, opening up the possibility that women will take antenatal tests to see if their prospective child is likely to have a bad reading disorder? Is it not conceivable that such tests would lead to our devoting less resources to the currently reading-handicapped children whom now we accept as an inevitable feature of human life?

That such conundrums may never be truly answerable, however, should not concern us too much. The truly relevant question for most families is whether an obvious good to them will come from having a child with a major handicap. Is it more likely for such children to fall behind in society or will they through such affliction develop the strengths of character and fortitude that lead, like Jeffrey Tate, the noted British conductor, to the head of their packs? Here I'm afraid that the word handicap cannot escape its true definition—being placed at a disadvantage. From this perspective, seeing the bright side of being handicapped is like praising the virtues of extreme poverty. To be sure, there are many individuals who rise out of its inherently degrading states. But we perhaps most realistically should see it as the major origin of asocial behavior that has among its many bad consequences the breeding of criminal violence.

Only harm, thus, I fear will come from any form of society-based restriction on individual genetic decisions. Decisions from committees of well-intentioned individuals will too often emerge as vehicles for seeming to do good as opposed to doing good. Moreover, we should necessarily worry that once we let governments tell their citizens what they cannot do genetically, we must fear they also have power to tell us what we must do. But for us as individuals to feel comfortable making decisions that affect the genetic makeups of our children, we correspondingly have to become genetically literate. In the future, we must necessarily question any government which does not see this as its responsibility. Will it so not act because it wants to keep such powers for itself?

THE MISUSE OF GENETICS BY HITLER SHOULD NOT DENY ITS USE TODAY

Those of us who venture forth into the public arena to explain what Genetics can or cannot do for society seemingly inevitably come up against individuals who feel that we are somehow the modern equivalents of Hitler. Here we must not fall into the absurd trap of being against everything Hitler was for. It was in no way evil for Hitler to regard mental disease as a scourge on society. Almost everyone then, as still true today, was made uncomfortable by psychotic individuals. It is how Hitler treated German mental patients that still outrages civilized societies and lets us call him immoral. Genetics per se can never be evil. It is only when we use or misuse it that morality comes in. That we want to find ways to lessen the impact of mental illness is inherently good. The killing by the Nazis of the German mental patients for reasons of supposed genetic inferiority, however, was barbarianism at its worst.

Because of Hitler's use of the term Master Race, we should not feel the need to say that we never want to use genetics to make humans more capable than they are today. The idea that genetics could or should be used to give humans power that they do not now possess, however, strongly upsets many individuals first exposed to the notion. I suspect such fears in some ways are similar to concerns now expressed about the genetically handicapped of today. If more intelligent human beings might someday be created, would we not think less well about ourselves as we exist today? Yet anyone who proclaims that we are now perfect as humans has to be a silly crank. If we could honestly promise young couples that we knew how to give them offspring with superior character, why should we assume they would decline? Those at the top of today's societies might not see the need. But if your life is going nowhere, shouldn't you seize the chance of jump-starting your children's future?

Common sense tells us that if scientists find ways to greatly improve human capabilities, there will be no stopping the public from happily seizing them.

ALLEN BUCHANAN, DAN W. BROCK, NORMAN DANIELS, AND DANIEL WIKLER

From Chance to Choice: Genetics and Justice

Allen Buchanan is Professor of Philosophy at Duke University. He publishes primarily in bioethics and political philosophy and currently serves as a member of the Advisory Council for the Human Genome Research Institute on goals and funding priorities for genomic research. Among his books are *Ethics, Efficiency, and the Market* (Rowman & Littlefield) and (with Dan Brock) *Deciding for Others: The Ethics of Surrogate Decision Making* (Cambridge University Press).

Dan W. Brock is Charles C. Tillinghast, Jr. University Professor, Professor of Philosophy and Biomedical Ethics, and Director of the Center for Biomedical Ethics at Brown University. He is a former staff philosopher on the President's Commission for the Study of Ethical Problems in Medicine. His books include *Life and Death: Philosophical Essays in Biomedical Ethics* (Cambridge), and (with Allen Buchanan) *Deciding for Others: The Ethics of Surrogate Decision Making* (Cambridge).

Norman Daniels is Goldthwaite Professor of Philosophy at Tufts University and Professor of Medical Ethics at Tufts Medical School. He has written widely in the philosophy of science, ethics, political and social philosophy, and medical ethics. Among his books are *Seeking Fair Treatment: From the AIDS Epidemic to National Health Care Reform* (Oxford) and (with Donald Light and Ronald Caplan) *Benchmarks of Fairness for Health Care Reform* (Oxford). He is currently working on *Just Health*, a substantial revision and expansion of his earlier book *Just Health Care*.

Daniel Wikler is a professor in the Program in Medical Ethics in the Department of the History of Medicine, and in the Department of Philosophy at the University of Wisconsin-Madison. His research focuses on ethical issues in health care and population health, including international health. He has served as President of the International Association of Bioethics, and staff philosopher to the President's Commission for the Study of Ethical Problems in Medicine. He has also served on study commissions and advisory boards for the Institute of Medicine, the Office of Technology Assessment, and other health policy agencies.

CHALLENGES OF THE GENETIC AGE

A powerful alliance of government, business, and science is propelling society into a new era in which human beings will possess a much greater understanding of the most basic functions of all forms of life. With this understanding will come unprecedented control over living things, including ourselves. Scientific knowledge of how genes work will empower human beings to cure and prevent diseases. It may also let us shape some of the most important biological characteristics of the human beings we choose to bring into existence.

Reprinted with permission of the authors and publisher from *From Chance to Choice: Genetics and Justice* by Allen Buchanan, Dan W. Brock, Norman Daniels, and Daniel Wilker. Cambridge University Press, 2000, pp. 1–21. Copyright © 2000 Cambridge University Press.

No one knows the limits of our future powers to shape human lives—or when these limits will be reached. Some expect that at most we will be able to reduce the incidence of serious genetic diseases and perhaps ensure that more people are at the higher end of the distribution of normal traits. More people may have long and healthy lives, and perhaps some will have better memory and other intellectual powers. Others foresee not only greater numbers of people functioning at high levels, but the attainment of levels previously unheard of: lives measured in centuries, people of superhuman intelligence, humans endowed with new traits presently undreamt of. One thing, however, is certain: Whatever the limits of our technical abilities turn out to be, coping with these new powers will tax our wisdom to the utmost.

PREVIEWS OF PERPLEXITIES

Consider a few of the perplexities with which the genetic revolution is likely to confront us in the future.

SCENARIO 1: GENETIC COMMUNITARIANISM

A disaffected member of what the media refer to as a religious cult announces that the group is attempting to implement its vision of the good society by "mass producing" human embryos cloned from the group's leaders. He claims that the group has its own genetics lab and hopes to adapt for use on humans techniques for cloning embryos commonly employed in the commercial production of animals. Several members of Congress express outrage and urge that the government take action against the religious group. A spokesperson for the American Civil Liberties Union says that if we value reproductive freedom and freedom of religion, we must respect the right of religious communities to attempt to transmit their beliefs and way of life to future generations, whether by the traditional methods of teaching and indoctrination or by the application of genetic technology.

SCENARIO 2: PERSONAL CHOICE OR PUBLIC HEALTH CONCERN?

A single, inexpensive blood test for prospective parents can detect high risk for virtually all serious genetic disorders as well as a broad range of genetic susceptibilities for illnesses. An initiative is a foot to provide mass genetic screening using this test. A government commission examining the feasibility of this proposal notes that the program's cost-effectiveness depends on whether a sufficient number of those tested "act on the knowledge of positive results—that is, whether they choose to avoid conception of affected fetuses." An advocate of the mass screening program says "this is a public health matter; people should not be free to inflict avoidable diseases on their children, especially if we are ever to have an affordable health care system that provides coverage for everyone." An opponent replies that "genetic services of any kind are strictly a matter of personal choice—respect for reproductive freedom requires this. People must be free to act on the test results as they see fit; any program that will result in pressures that limit reproductive freedom would be unacceptable."

SCENARIO 3: THE QUEST FOR THE PERFECT BABY

Excerpt from the introduction to a dissertation in a history of medicine written in 2040:

In the 1990s, as in the preceding three decades, parents mainly practiced negative eugenics, using tests for major chromosomal defects such as Down syndrome and aborting "defective" fetuses. By 2020 the standards for acceptable babies had been raised: prospective parents routinely aborted fetuses that were otherwise healthy but that had genes that gave them a significantly higher than average risk of breast cancer, colorectal cancer, Alzheimer's dementia, or coronary artery disease. By 2030, the trend was toward even higher standards: Fetuses with any of a range of "undesirable" or "less than optimal" combinations of genes were routinely aborted, including those predicted not to be in the highest quintile with respect to intelligence or even height. Widespread use of these techniques by parents who could afford them began to raise the average level of health, physical strength and stature, and intellectual ability in the population, a trend encouraged by nationalist politicians. But the insistence of many parents that their child be in the upper quintile created a spiral in which no amount of genetic boost ever seemed enough.

SCENARIO 4: HEALTH CARE IN THE AGE OF GENETIC INTERVENTION

At a congressional hearing, Dr. Philip Jones testifies that the standard benefit package that all insurance companies are federally mandated to offer should be expanded to include what are popularly called "mood enhancer" drugs for all persons who have the "mild depression gene," even though these individuals do not usually meet existing criteria for having bipolar affective disorder. According to Jones, "What is important is whether clinical science can help people live better lives; the fact that a person's mood swings don't qualify as bipolar disorder isn't really important." A spokesperson for the National Association of Health Insurers protests, "Health care coverage stops where treatment for disease ends; there's a right to health care, but there's no right to be happy." Jones, shaking his head with a somewhat patronizing air, replies, "What we now know about the way genes affect the brain and hence the personality renders the distinction between psychiatric disorders and undesirable psychological conditions unimportant."

SCENARIO 5: THE GENETIC ENHANCEMENT CERTIFICATE

Katherine and Bill are applying for the same management position in a large firm. Included in Katherine's dossier is a genetic enhancement certificate from Opti-Gene, Inc. It certifies that the bearer has "benefited from cutting-edge genetic enhancement technology" and asserts that those who have had the package of services in question on average have fewer colds and other common respiratory infections, are less likely to suffer depression, and score higher on tests of memory skills. Bill, who cannot afford genetic enhancement, protests that "hiring on the basis of genetic enhancement is just as unfair as hiring on the basis of race or gender—it's a violation of equal opportunity and makes a travesty of the merit system." Katherine replies indignantly, "Merit means the position goes to the best candidate, and I am the best candidate, so what's the problem?"

THE NEED FOR SYSTEMATIC ETHICAL THINKING

Reflection on scenarios such as these prompts two sorts of self-doubt. We worry whether, like the sorcerer's apprentice, we will suffer the consequences of partial knowledge, overestimating our power to predict and control the causal chains we initiate through the application of our newfound knowledge. But we also worry about values. Even if we were more assured than we should be that our technical control will be complete, we would continue to wonder whether we will be able to distinguish between what we can do and what we ought to do. Do we have the ethical resources to use our genetic powers wisely and humanely? Or are we like hapless space-travelers embarking on an interstellar voyage equipped only with a pocket compass? Do existing ethical theories, concepts, and principles provide the materials for constructing more adequate instruments for moral navigation?

In the face of these doubts about whether our values will keep pace with our powers, there is an un-

fortunate tendency to rest content with inarticulate forebodings about the dangers of "playing God" when confronted with revelations of particular new genetic discoveries or technical breakthroughs. The admonition not to play God is useless, except as a general warning against hubris. It tells us nothing about how we should respond to any particular choice we may confront.

Something more is needed. A systematic vision of the moral character of the world we hope to be moving toward is required. The primary objective of this [essay], accordingly, is to make a contribution toward answering a single question: *What are the most basic moral principles that would guide public policy and individual choice concerning the use of genetic interventions in a just and humane society in which the powers of genetic intervention are much more developed than they are today?*

Accomplishing this will require responding to many other questions, among the most important of which are: What are the most important ethical problems to which greatly increased powers of genetic intervention will give rise? Are these new problems? How adequate are the resources of existing ethical theory to cope with them? And what sorts of ethical principles and distinctions are needed to help a society equipped with formidable powers of genetic intervention avoid the mistakes and evils of the eugenics movements of the late nineteenth and early to mid-twentieth centuries?

GENOMIC RESEARCH AND GENETIC INTERVENTION

THE HUMAN GENOME PROJECT AND RELATED GENETIC RESEARCH

Our knowledge of how genes function is growing at an almost imponderable rate. The Human Genome Project is ahead of schedule in achieving its goal of determining the sequence of the three million or so base pairs of nucleotides that make up the complete genetic material of a human being. Presumably the coming years will also bring a great expansion of our knowledge of how particular genes function. Almost daily, newspaper headlines proclaim startling and sometimes disquieting discoveries and feats of technological virtuosity, from the identification of a "fat gene" to the cloning of a sheep from an adult sheep's mammary cell. Eventually these advances will bear practical fruit: the ability to use knowledge of how genes function to intervene in significant ways in human life. The Human Genome Project, in part because of the impetus it has given to the rapid, worldwide sharing of information and technique, does much to guarantee that the stream of genetic knowledge will continue to increase in volume and speed.

Although it is the most highly publicized locus of research, the Human Genome Project does not stand alone. Many other projects for human genetic research are funded by the National Institutes of Health in the United States and by government agencies in other industrial countries. And private, commercial research efforts are increasingly capitalizing on the knowledge base provided by the Human Genome Project and other government-funded research and on the expertise of researchers in academic institutions, many of which are publicly funded. Although the research for this [essay] was funded by the program for Ethical, Legal, and Social Implications of the Human Genome Project of the National Institutes of Health, our concern is broader. We will speak generally of "human genomic research" or even more broadly of "advances in genetic knowledge," recognizing that the study of nonhuman organisms has contributed and will continue to contribute to an understanding of how genes function in human beings.

MODES OF GENETIC INTERVENTION

As a rough, initial categorization, modes of genetic intervention can first be divided into direct and indirect interventions. By "direct genetic interventions" we mean primarily two modes: gene therapy, in which normal or desirable genes are inserted into either somatic (body tissue) cells or germline cells (gametes—sperms or eggs—or embryos); and gene surgery, in which abnormal or undesirable genes are "switched off"—that is, deactivated so that they no longer produce their distinctive effects.

At present, gene therapy in human beings has been limited to somatic cells. For example, normal genes have been inserted into the bone marrow of patients who suffer from certain blood disorders due to the inability of their own genes to produce particular proteins. In the future, it is expected that gene therapy and gene surgery will be performed on human germline cells, with genes being inserted into or deactivated in gametes and embryos (fertilized eggs).

Gene therapy today involves the insertion of cloned normal genes—genes that occur naturally. Naturally occurring genes may come either from other human beings or from nonhuman animals. But it may eventually become possible to create new genes—that is, to synthesize new sequences of base pairs to produce effects that are not found in nature. Genes, after all, are just functionally significant sequences of base pairs.

From a technical standpoint, a fruitful combination of methods—at least for some conditions—would be to complement gene therapy on germline cells with gene surgery. The desirable gene would be introduced early enough in the gamete or embryo to replicate and keep reproducing throughout all the cells of the organism (rather than being inserted, decaying, and being reinserted into a particular tissue), and the undesirable gene would be "knocked out." Alternatively, recently isolated *totipotent* human embryo stem cells may eventually provide the ideal platform from which to develop a range of gene therapies. (A totipotent cell is one that can develop into any kind of tissue or organ, given the proper biochemical stimulation.)

In contrast to direct intervention, *indirect genetic intervention* means primarily genetic pharmacology and embryo selection. By *genetic pharmacology* we mean the use of knowledge about genes to design drugs that will either substitute for the chemical products that would be produced by a normal gene in an individual who has an abnormal one, augment the chemical products of normal genes or counteract the effects of an undesirable or abnormal gene (e.g., by disrupting the protein it produced; Lewontin 1997). Furthermore, someday novel sequences of base pairs—new genes synthesized in the laboratory—may produce drugs that will either ameliorate or prevent diseases, give individuals new desirable traits, or enhance desirable traits they already have or would have when they become fully developed. Embryo selection involves three main steps: "harvesting" embryos, subjecting them to DNA analysis, and implanting an embryo that possesses the preferred characteristics.

There is a third category of intervention that may be called genetic, though perhaps with some stretching of the term. It involves the application of knowledge about genes but without the use of either modifying genes, genetic pharmacology, or embryo selection. There are two subcategories: when genetic information is used in regard to reproductive decisions and when it is used to prevent or ameliorate genetically based diseases in an already existing individual. For convenience, we call the first group "reproductive genetic testing interventions" and the second "therapeutic genetic testing interventions."

BUCHANAN, BROCK, DANIELS, WIKLER   283

Reproductive genetic testing interventions are done in response to information revealed by genetic testing, where the testing is performed either on persons who intend to have children or, after conception has occurred, on the fetus. In one sense, the difference between these modes of genetic testing and embryo selection is not great: In the latter, testing is done on embryos rather than on prospective parents or fetuses.

If such a test reveals a risk of genetic disease or of some other undesirable condition, any of several steps may be taken to reduce or eliminate the risk. If it is determined that a woman is carrying a fetus with a genetic defect such as the chromosomal anomaly known as Down syndrome, she may elect to abort the fetus. If a couple undergoes carrier testing (by a blood test) and learns that they both carry a gene for cystic fibrosis or Tay-Sachs disease, they may choose not to have children, to have children by sperm or by egg donation, or to adopt. At present we lack the capacity to use gene therapy, gene surgery, or genetic pharmacology in any of these cases. The only way to reduce the risk of having a child with an abnormal or undesired genetic condition is to avoid having that child.

The second subcategory, therapeutic genetic testing intervention, has been widely practiced in the United States in the case of the hereditary metabolic disorder phenylketonuria (PKU) for more than 30 years. A blood test is performed on infants at birth. If it is positive for PKU, a special diet is used to avoid the buildup of an enzyme that causes brain damage.

The gene for another potentially lethal genetic disorder, hereditary hemochromatosis, or inherited excessive iron storage disease, was identified by a private genetic technology company in 1996. A blood test for the two mutations that cause the disease has just become available. The treatment for hemochromatosis, like that for PKU, is remarkably "low-tech," consisting of regular phlebotomies (bloodlettings) to deplete stored iron. Because hereditary hemochromatosis is by far the most common serious genetic disease in the United States (approximately 4 persons per 1,000 of the Caucasian population are homozygous, i.e., have two copies of the mutation, and 1 in 10 is heterozygous, i.e., has one copy), and because treatment is inexpensive and effective, some argue that testing for hemochromatosis should become the next mass genetic screening program in this country.

In addition, knowledge of how genes work will lead to greater knowledge of how genes interact with different environments. Increasingly, we can expect to identify subgroups of the population who have genetic characteristics that may call for special environments if their physical or cognitive development is to be maximized. Here, unlike with PKU and hemochromatosis, tailoring an environment to the special developmental needs of a genotypic subgroup of the population may not be a matter of offering a therapy to treat a disease.

For example, we already know that some children benefit from special environments for learning to read or do mathematics. It may well turn out that there are genetic markers that will help pick out those with special learning needs or special needs for nutrition if their cognitive development is to be maximized. (It is already known that the Tohono O'Odham Indians of southern Arizona and Sonora, Mexico, experience extraordinarily high rates of diabetes on a "normal" white American diet but not when they eat their traditional foods.) Intervening to tailor environments to the needs of genotypic groups may not be genetic intervention as ordinarily understood, yet it is intervention based on knowledge of how genes work in various environments.

. . . [We will focus] mainly on direct genetic interventions and genetic pharmacology, with much of what we say having direct implications for embryo selection as well. The reason for this focus is twofold: First, some of the most fundamental ethical issues arise most clearly in the case of direct genetic interventions and genetic pharmacology. Second, there is already considerable literature on ethical issues in both genetic testing reproductive interventions and genetic testing therapeutic interventions (Cook-Deegan 1994; Andrews et al. 1994; Russo and Cove 1995).

Our reason for giving genetic pharmacology equal billing with direct genetic interventions perhaps warrants explanation. When ethical issues arising from the new genetics are discussed in the popular media—and even in the bioethics literature—the focus is often on "genetic engineering," a phrase that evokes images of scientists splicing genes together to create new kinds of organisms. Nonetheless, genetic pharmacology is likely to be one of the most potent applications of genetic science in the immediate future. (Venture capitalists, including some of the largest pharmaceutical companies, appear to agree with this prediction.) "Engineering" human embryos, if it occurs at all, will probably happen only in the relatively distant future. Dramatic advances in genetic pharmacology are a much nearer and surer prospect. Another alternative to the embryo engineering is embryo selection. Like genetic pharmacology, it seems to be more likely to see extensive use in the nearer future.

THE SHADOW OF EUGENICS

Even the brightest aspirations of the new genetics are from time to time dimmed by the shadow of eugenics. The very term has been in such bad odor since the era of Nazi "racial hygiene" (Proctor 1988) that few people today wish to be associated with eugenics. Indeed, controversies over the new genetics often proceed as if the rival parties assume that if it can be shown that someone's views are "eugenic," they are thereby discredited. Much energy is then spent in trying to attach the label to an opponent or avoid being labeled a eugenicist.

Such exercises tend to be long on rhetoric and short on cognitive content. Attitudes toward eugenics are much like the common view of Marx's *Das Capital*—people know it is wrong though they know little about it—or, more charitably, like the attitude toward Freud's theory of the unconscious: "He was on to something, but he went too far."

At present, neither those who assert that the new genetics is infected by the evils of the old eugenics nor those who indignantly defend the new genetics' moral purity have made a convincing case. Two things are needed for the satisfactory resolution of this controversy: an ethical autopsy on the old eugenics and an examination of the ethical presuppositions and implications of the new genetics. . . .

To evaluate the charge that the new genetics is infected by the evils of eugenics, it is necessary to unearth the ethical assumptions that provide the best justifications currently available for pursuing genetic knowledge and for attempting to use this knowledge to intervene in human lives. As with the attempt to articulate the underlying values of the eugenics movement, our task here requires considerable reconstruction, because those who endorse the expansion of our genetic knowledge and powers of intervention rarely make their ethical assumptions explicit, and they certainly offer nothing like a developed ethical theory. . . .

• • •

TWO MODELS FOR GENETIC INTERVENTION

THE PUBLIC HEALTH MODEL

[We have identified] two quite different perspectives from which genetic intervention may be viewed. The first is what we call the public health model; the second is the personal choice model.

The public health model stresses the production of benefits and the avoidance of harms for groups. It uncritically assumes that the appropriate mode of evaluating options is some form of cost-benefit (or cost-effectiveness) calculation. To the extent that the public health model even recognizes an ethical dimension to decisions about the application of scientific knowledge or technology, it tends to assume that sound ethical reasoning is exclusively consequentialist (or utilitarian) in nature. In other words, it assumes that whether a policy or an action is deemed to be right is thought to depend solely on whether it produces the greatest balance of good over bad outcomes.

More important, consequentialist ethical reasoning—like cost-benefit and cost-effectiveness calculations—assumes that it is not only possible but permissible and even mandatory to aggregate goods and bads (costs and benefits) across individuals. Harms to some can be offset by gains to others; what matters is the sum. Critics of such simple and unqualified consequentialist reasoning, including ourselves, are quick to point out its fundamental flaws: Such reasoning is distributionally insensitive because it fails to take seriously the separateness and inviolability of persons.

In other words, as simple and unqualified consequentialist reasoning looks only to the aggregate balance of good over bad, it does not recognize fairness in the distribution of burdens and benefits to be a fundamental value. As a result, it not only allows but in some circumstances requires that the most fundamental interests of individuals be sacrificed in order to produce the best overall outcome.

Consequentialist ethical theory is not unique in allowing or even requiring that the interests of individuals sometimes yield to the good of all. Any reasonable ethical theory must acknowledge this. But it is unique in maintaining that in principle such sacrifice is justified whenever it would produce any aggregate gain, no matter how small. Because simple and unqualified consequentialism has this implication, some conclude that it fails to appreciate sufficiently that each individual is an irreducibly distinct subject of moral concern.

The public health model, with its affinity for consequentialist ethical reasoning, took a particularly troubling form among some prominent eugenicists. Individuals who were thought to harbor "defective germ plasm" (what would now be called "bad genes") were likened to carriers of infectious disease. While persons infected with cholera were a menace to those with whom they came into contact, individuals with defective germ plasm were an even greater threat to society: They transmitted harm to an unlimited line of persons across many generations.

The only difference between the "horizontally transmitted" infectious diseases and "vertically transmitted" genetic diseases, according to this view, was that the potential harm caused by the latter was even greater. So if measures such as quarantine and restrictions on travel into disease areas that infringed individual freedom were appropriate responses to the former, then they were even more readily justified to avert the greater potential harm of the latter. This variant of the public health model may be called the *vertical epidemic model*. Once this point of view is adopted and combined with a simple and unqualified consequentialism, the risks of infringing liberty and of exclusion and discrimination increase dramatically.

THE PERSONAL SERVICE MODEL

Today eugenics is almost universally condemned. Partly in reaction to the tendency of the most extreme eugenicists to discount individual freedom and welfare for the supposed good of society, medical geneticists and genetic counselors since World War II have adopted an almost absolute commitment to "nondirectiveness" in their relations with those seeking genetic services. Recoiling from the public health model that dominated the eugenics movement, and especially from the vertical disease metaphor, they publicly endorse the view that genetic tests and interventions are simply services offered to individuals—goods for private consumption—to be accepted or refused as individuals see fit.

This way of conceiving of genetic interventions takes them out of the public domain, relegating them to the sphere of private choice. Advocates of the personal service model proclaim that the fundamental value on which it rests is individual autonomy. Whether a couple at risk for conceiving a child with a genetic disease takes a genetic test and how they use the knowledge thus obtained is their business, not society's, even if the decision to vaccinate a child for common childhood infectious diseases is a matter of public health and as such justifies restricting parental choice.

The personal service model serves as a formidable bulwark against the excesses of the crude consequentialist ethical reasoning that tainted the application of the public health model in the era of eugenics. But it does so at a prohibitive price: It ignores the obligation to prevent harm as well as some of the most basic requirements of justice. By elevating autonomy to the exclusion of all other values, the personal service model offers a myopic view of the moral landscape.

In fact, it is misleading to say that the personal service model expresses a commitment to autonomy. Instead, it honors only the autonomy of those who are in a position to exercise choice concerning genetic interventions, not all of those who may be affected by such choices. . . . [T]his approach wrongly subordinates the autonomy of children to that of their parents.

In addition, if genetic services are treated as goods for private consumption, the cumulative effects of many individual choices in the "genetic marketplace" may limit the autonomy of many people, and perhaps of all people. Economic pressures, including requirements for insurability and employment, as well as social stigma directed toward those who produce children with "defects" that could have been avoided, may narrow rather than expand meaningful choice. Finally, treating genetic interventions as personal services may exacerbate inequalities in opportunities if the prevention of genetic diseases or genetic enhancements are available only to the rich. It would be more accurate to say, then, that the personal service model gives free reign to some dimensions of the autonomy of some people, often at the expense of others.

A THIRD APPROACH

Much current thinking about the ethics of genetic intervention assumes that the personal service model is not an adequate moral guide. However, the common response to its deficiencies is not to resurrect the public health model associated with eugenics. Instead, there is a tendency to assume the appropriateness of the personal service model in general and then to erect ad hoc—and less than convincing—"moral firebreaks" to constrain the free choices of individuals in certain areas. For example, some ethicists have urged that the cloning of human beings be strictly prohibited, that there be a moratorium or permanent ban on human germline interventions, or that genetic enhancements (as opposed to treatments of diseases) be outlawed. In each case the proposed moral firebreak shows a distrust of the unalloyed personal service model but at the same time betrays the lack of a systematic, principled account of why and how the choices of individuals should be limited.

[We] aim to avoid both the lack of attention to the moral equality, separateness, and inviolability of persons that afflicted the eugenics movement's public health model of genetic intervention and the narrow concern with autonomous individual choice that characterizes the personal service model. We argue that although respect for individual autonomy requires an extensive sphere of protected reproductive freedoms and hence a broad range of personal discretion in decisions to use genetic interventions, both the need to prevent harm to offspring and the demands of justice, especially those regarding equal opportunity, place systematic limits on individuals' freedom to use or not use genetic interventions.

We try to develop a systematic, defensible moral framework for choices about the use of genetic intervention technologies. Our view steers a course between a public health model in which individuals count only so far as what they do or what is done to them affects the genetic health of "society" and a personal service model in which the choice to use genetic interventions is morally equivalent to the decision to buy goods for private consumption in an ordinary market. Because our account locates the ethics of genetic intervention within the larger enterprise of ethical theorizing, it avoids the arbitrariness and lack of system of the moral firebreaks approach.

ETHICAL ANALYSIS AND ETHICAL THEORY

Although we discuss ethical principles for individuals, our focus more often than not is primarily on ethical principles for institutions. In most cases we try to refine, and sometimes reinterpret or modify, institutional ethical principles that are quite familiar. Prominent examples include the principle that the basic institutions in a society should ensure equal opportunity and the principle of individual self-determination (or autonomy). We also evaluate certain distinctions, such as that between positive and negative genetic interventions or between treatments and enhancements, that some have tried to elevate to the status of institutional ethical principles.

PRINCIPLES FOR INSTITUTIONS

One of the main results of our analysis is that a proper respect for individual self-determination in the realm of reproductive choices must recognize an asymmetry between institutional ethical principles and those for private individuals who are prospective parents: In general, parents should have considerably more latitude to use genetic interventions to shape their children than governments should have to shape their citizens. So even though our emphasis is on institutional ethical principles, determining their proper scope and limits requires an exploration of principles for individuals.

A comprehensive ethical theory—which we do not pretend to provide here—would include an account of virtues as well as principles. Our concern is not to attempt to provide a theory of the connection between ethical virtues and choices concerning the uses of genetic interventions. Nevertheless, some of what we say has direct and important implications for the sorts of virtues persons will need to have, both in their capacities as private individuals and as citizens concerned with public policy, in a society of heightened genetic powers. In particular, we have a good deal to say about the attitudes toward genetically based disabilities and the commitments to "the morality of inclusion" that members of such a society must exhibit if our new powers are to be used justly and humanely.

By way of partial preview, this much can be said about the institutional ethical principles we believe are most essential for a just and humane society equipped with robust capabilities for genetic intervention. As a first approximation, we can say that among the most important principles are those of justice and the prevention of harm. This is hardly surprising or controversial. Things become more complex and interesting as we explore different concepts of what justice requires and different understandings of what constitutes harm, and as we attempt to ascertain the scope and limits of the obligation to prevent harm.

JUSTICE

Following Rawls (1971, p. 3), we focus on the justice of basic social institutions and only by implication on the justice of particular policies or actions. We identify two main headings under which considerations of justice arise in a society of developed powers of ge-

One important conception of equal opportunity requires protection against limitations on individuals' opportunities imposed by racial, ethnic, religious, or gender discrimination. This principle, we argue, is important but incomplete. We opt for a somewhat more inclusive concept of equal opportunity—a version of what John Roemer has called a level playing field conception, of which Rawls's notion of fair equality of opportunity is the most prominent exemplar. Level playing field conceptions require efforts to eliminate or ameliorate the influence of some or all other social factors that limit opportunity over and above discrimination.

The most direct and compelling implication of this conception of the principle of equal opportunity lies in the domain of just health care. Here we adopt the main lines of Norman Daniels's theory of just health care, as developed in several books and a number of articles over the past 15 years. The core idea is that a just health care system should strive to remove barriers to opportunity that are due to disease. ("Disease" here is understood as any "adverse departures from normal species functioning.")

Regardless of how the term "genetic disease" is defined, the etiologies of many diseases include a genetic component. If just health care puts a premium on eliminating barriers to opportunity posed by disease, the question is not whether or in what sense a disease is genetic, but whether there is an intervention (genetic or otherwise) that can cure or prevent it. Thus the level playing field conception has direct implications for genetic intervention: In general, genetic intervention will be an important means of achieving equal opportunity, at least through its use to cure or prevent disease.

We also argue that equal opportunity, as an important principle of justice, has another bearing on genetic intervention. This principle can impose conditions on access to genetic interventions that go beyond the prevention or cure of disease. If, for example, it should ever become possible to enhance some normal desirable characteristics, a consistent commitment to equal opportunity might rule out an unrestricted market for the dissemination of the relevant technology, for if valuable enhancements were available only to the better-off, existing inequalities in opportunity might be exacerbated. Under such conditions, equal opportunity might require either making the enhance-

ments available to all, even those who cannot pay for them or preventing anyone from having them. How we respond to the fifth scenario sketched earlier—The Genetic Enhancement Certificate—will depend on whether justice requires constraints on unequal access to enhancement technologies.

A deeper and more perplexing question is whether equal opportunity may require or permit genetic interventions for the sake of preventing natural inequalities that do not constitute diseases. On the account we endorse, health care does not include everything of benefit that biomedical science can deliver. Health care, so far as it is a concern of justice, has to do only with the treatment and prevention of disease. However, we argue that some versions of the level playing field conception extend the requirements of equal opportunity, at least in principle, to interventions to counteract natural inequalities that do not constitute diseases.

The rationale for such an extension is straightforward: If one of the key intuitions underpinning a level playing field conception of equal opportunity is the conviction that people's opportunities should not be significantly limited due to factors that are wholly beyond their control, then it appears that equal opportunity may require the interventions to counteract the more serious opportunity-limiting effects of bad luck in the "natural lottery," regardless of whether the disadvantage conferred by a person's genes is a disease, strictly speaking, as in our fourth scenario (Health Care in the Age of Genetic Intervention).

Examples such as that of the person with the "mild depression gene" may pull one toward the conclusion that equal opportunity requires genetic interventions in such cases, even if the intervention is not treatment for a disease, for the same reason that equal opportunity requires efforts to counteract the effects of being born into a family of lower educational attainment. In both cases, it seems wrong that a person's opportunities should be limited by wholly undeserved and unchosen factors.

We will also see, however, that there are other interpretations of the level playing field conception that stop short of the conclusion that equal opportunity generally requires interventions to prevent natural disadvantages beyond the realm of disease. One such interpretation, which we believe to be Rawls's, does not hold that all undeserved disadvantages as such, including less desirable genetic endowments, require redress as a matter of justice. Instead, this understanding of equal opportunity only asserts that it is unjust to structure social institutions so as to base persons' entitlements to goods on their possession of natural advantages. According to this view, equal opportunity would not require intervention to prevent any and all instances in which an individual would have less desirable genetic endowments. Natural inequalities as such would not be problematic from the standpoint of justice. These alternative understandings of the level playing field conception of equal opportunity appear to have radically different implications for action: One seems to require what might be called genetic equality, the other does not. Thus, a satisfactory response to cases like our fourth scenario inevitably requires a sortie into the realm of ethical theorizing about the proper understanding and role of equality of opportunity in a theory of justice.

This divergence between different versions of the level playing field conception of equal opportunity provides the first illustration of one of the major aims of this [essay]: to explore how the prospects of genetic interventions with human beings challenge existing ethical theory. The challenge takes two distinct forms. First, the prospect of vastly increased powers of genetic intervention brings with it the inevitability of new choices, the contemplation of which stimulates us to articulate existing ethical theories in greater detail (in this case distinguishing different variants of level playing field theories of equal opportunity, which appear to have different practical implications). Second, by placing within human control features of our condition that we have heretofore regarded as given and unalterable (the fate assigned to us by the natural lottery), the prospect of genetic interventions forces us to rethink the boundary we have traditionally drawn between misfortune and injustice, and indeed between the natural and the social.

PREVENTING HARM

[W]e argue that the most straightforward and compelling case for developing and using genetic interventions is to fulfill one of the most basic moral obligations human beings have: the obligation to prevent harm. People have especially demanding obligations to prevent harm to their offspring, but through the agency of their political institutions, they also have obligations to prevent harm to others.

Taking seriously the potential of genetic interven-

tions to prevent harm pushes the limits of ethical theory in two ways: first, by forcing us to ascertain more precisely the scope and limits of the obligation to prevent harm; and second, by putting pressure on our very understanding of how harm is to be understood in ethical theory. Meeting the first challenge requires us to determine how the sometimes conflicting values of reproductive freedom and the obligation to prevent harm limit each other. Meeting the second requires us to take a stand on a fundamental question of ethical theory: whether behavior is subject to ethical evaluation only if it worsens or betters the condition of particular, individual persons. Some genetic interventions—those that prevent a genetic impairment by preventing an individual who would have the impairment from coming into existence—cannot be described as preventing harm, if a harm is a worsening of the condition of a particular individual. If the individual does not exist, then the intervention cannot worsen his condition.

In addition, our exploration of the obligation to prevent harm through genetic interventions calls into question common dogmas concerning "nondirective" genetic counseling and the right to refuse medical treatment in cases of "maternal/fetal" conflict—where a woman who intends to carry a fetus to term refuses treatment that would prevent a disability in the future child. Thus, whether it is morally permissible to require or at least encourage individuals to avoid a high risk of transmitting a genetic disease (Scenario 2: Personal Choice or Public Health Concern?) will depend in part on how the obligation to prevent harm is understood.

LIMITS ON THE PURSUIT OF "GENETIC PERFECTION"

Parents, of course, are typically not just concerned with preventing harm to their children; they want what is best for them. As the capability for genetic intervention increases, however, ethical issues arise concerning the proper expression of this benevolent parental impulse. [W]e distinguish between permissible and obligatory genetic enhancements, examine the social implications of some of the enhancements that parents might consider undertaking for their children, and argue that what Joel Feinberg has called the child's right to an open future places significant limitations on what it is permissible for parents to do in this regard.

We also distinguish between the ethical implications of the pursuit of improvements by individual parents and those that might be pursued by collectivities in the name of some communitarian vision of human perfection.... [We will] provide some of the distinctions and principles needed for a sound ethical response to the issues raised in the Genetic Communitarianism and The Quest for a Perfect Baby scenarios.

THE MORALITY OF INCLUSION

The dawning of the age of genetic intervention also pushes the limits of theories of justice in another way—by calling into question the manner in which the fundamental problem of justice is characteristically framed.

Theories of justice generally begin with the assumption that the most fundamental problem is how to distribute fairly the burdens and benefits of a society—understood as a single, cooperative framework in which all members are active and effective participants. This way of formulating the issue of justice overlooks two vital points: first, that increasingly human beings can exert some control over the character of the basic cooperative framework within which the most fundamental questions of fair distribution arise; and second, that the character of the most basic cooperative framework in a society will determine who is and who is not "disabled." In other words, what the most basic institutions for production and exchange are like will determine the capacities an individual must have in order to be an effective participant in social cooperation (Wikler 1983; Buchanan 1993, 1996).

But if the choice of a framework of cooperation has profound implications for whether some people will be able to participate effectively, there is a prior question of justice: What is required for fairness in the choice of a society's most basic and comprehensive cooperative scheme? Attempting to answer this question stimulates us to gain a deeper understanding of the very nature of disability.

[W]e distinguish genetic impairments from disabilities that have a genetic component, noting that whether or to what extent a genetic impairment results in disability depends on the character of the dominant cooperative framework and the kinds of abilities required for effective participation in it. We then argue that there is an important but often ignored obligation to choose a dominant cooperative framework that is inclusive—that minimizes exclusion from participation on account of genetic impairments. If obligations of inclusion are to be taken seriously, they too impose significant restrictions on the personal choice model for the ethics of genetic intervention.

Justice in the choice of cooperative schemes turns out to be complex, however. The obligation of inclusion is not the sole morally relevant factor, so it cannot be a moral absolute. There is also the morally legitimate interest that persons have in having access to the most productive, enriching, and challenging cooperative scheme in which they are capable of being effective participants. Where there are significant differences in persons' natural assets, the obligation of inclusion and this legitimate interest can come into conflict.

However this conflict is resolved, we argue, a just society of considerable powers of genetic intervention may require changes in both directions: genetic interventions to enable individuals to be effective participants in social cooperation who would not otherwise be able to, and efforts to design the structure of cooperation in ways that make it possible for more people to be effective participants. Appreciation of the problem of justice in the choice of cooperative schemes leads us to the conclusion that regardless of whether we choose to use genetic interventions to promote inclusiveness or refuse to do so, we are in a very real sense choosing who will and who will not be disabled.

· · ·

REFERENCES

Andrews, Lori B.; Fullerton, Jane E.; Holtzman, Neil A.; and Motulsky, Arno G., eds. *Assessing Genetic Risks: Implications for Health and Social Policy.* Washington, DC: National Academy Press, 1994.

Buchanan, Allen. "Genetic Manipulation and the Morality of Inclusion." *Social Philosophy and Policy* 13 (1996), 18–46.

Buchanan, Allen. "The Morality of Inclusion." *Social Philosophy and Policy* 10 (1993), 233–57.

Cook-Deegan, Robert. *The Gene Wars: Science, Politics, and the Human Genome.* New York: W. W. Norton and Co., 1994.

Lewontin, Richard C. "Science & 'The Demon-Haunted World': An Exchange." *New York Review of Books* (March 6, 1997), 51–2.

Proctor, Robert. *Racial Hygiene: Medicine Under the Nazis.* Cambridge, MA: Harvard University Press, 1988.

Rawls, John. *A Theory of Justice.* Cambridge, MA: Harvard University Press, 1971.

Russo, Enzo and Cove, David. *Genetic Engineering: Dreams and Nightmares.* Oxford, UK: W. H. Freeman/Spektrum, 1995.

Wikler, Daniel I. "Paternalism and the Mildly Retarded," in Rolf Sartorius, ed., *Paternalism.* Minneapolis: University of Minnesota Press, 1983, 83–94.

SVANTE PÄÄBO

The Human Genome and Our View of Ourselves

Svante Pääbo is one of the founding directors of the Max-Planck-Institute for Evolutionary Anthropology and Honorary Professor of Genetics and Evolutionary Biology at the University of Leipzig. He studies molecular evolution, with an emphasis on human history and origins. In particular, he works on the retrieval of DNA from archaeological and paleontological remains and comparative studies of genomes and gene expression in humans and the great apes.

Perhaps for the pragmatic biologist, the determination of the human genome sequence is a prosaic event—the delivery of a wonderfully powerful tool, but a tool nonetheless. For the general public, however, the human genome sequence is of enormous symbolic significance, and its publication [in] this issue[1] [of *Science*] and in this week's *Nature*[2] is likely to be greeted with the same awestruck feeling that accompanied the landing of the first human on the moon and the detonation of the first atomic bomb.

Why are certain achievements—the first lunar landing, atomic fission, the determination of the human genome sequence—imbued with such emblematic significance? The reason is, I believe, that they change how we think about ourselves. Landing a person on the moon gave us an extraterrestrial perspective on human life; atomic fission gave us the power to create enormous energy reserves and to extinguish all human life on Earth; and now the human genome sequence gives us a view of the internal genetic scaffold around which every human life is molded. This scaffold has been handed down to us from our ancestors, and through it we are connected to all other life on Earth.

How does the complete human genome sequence affect the way that we think about ourselves? Clearly, the availability of a reference human DNA sequence is a milestone toward understanding how humans have evolved, because it opens the door to large-scale comparative studies. The major impact of such studies will be to reveal just how similar humans are to each other and to other species.

The first comparisons will be between the human genome and distantly related genomes such as those of yeast, flies, worms, and mice. A glimpse of what this will show us comes from considering the fact that about 26,000 to 38,000 genes are found in the draft version of our own genome, a number that is only two to three times larger than the 13,600 genes in the fruit fly genome. Furthermore, some 10% of human genes are clearly related to particular genes in the fly and the worm. So, obviously, we share much of our genetic scaffold even with very distant relatives. The similarity between humans and other animals will become even more evident when genome sequences from organisms such as the mouse, with whom we share a more recent common ancestor, become available. For these species, both the number of genes and the general structure of the genome are likely to be very similar to ours. Although this has long been realized by insiders in the genetics community, the close similarity of our genome to those of other organisms will make the unity of life more obvious to everyone. No doubt the genomic view of our place in nature will be both a source of humility and a blow to the idea of human uniqueness.

However, the most obvious challenge to the notion of human uniqueness is likely to come from comparisons of genomes of closely related species. We already know that the overall DNA sequence similarity between humans and chimpanzees is about 99%.[3]

Reprinted with permission from *Science* 291 (16 February 2001), 1219–20. Copyright © 2001, American Association for the Advancement of Science.

When the chimpanzee genome sequence becomes available, we are sure to find that its gene content and organization are very similar (if not identical) to our own. Perhaps it is our subconscious discomfort with this expectation that explains the slowness with which the genomics community has embraced the idea of a chimpanzee genome project. Be that as it may, with most of the human genome sequence now complete, it will be easy to determine the chimpanzee sequence using the human sequence as a guide to assembly. The result is sure to be an even more powerful challenge to the notion of human uniqueness than the comparison of the human genome to those of other mammals.

Yet the few differences between our genome and those of the great apes will be profoundly interesting because among them lie the genetic prerequisites that make us different from all other animals. In particular, these differences may reveal the genetic foundation for our rapid cultural evolution and geographic expansion, which started between 150,000 and 50,000 years ago[4] and led to our current overbearing domination of Earth. The realization that one or a few genetic accidents made human history possible will provide us with a whole new set of philosophical challenges to think about.

Large-scale comparisons of human genomes from many individuals are now possible with the emergence of high-throughput techniques for DNA sequence determination. The general picture already apparent from such studies is that the gene pool in Africa contains more variation than elsewhere, and that the genetic variation found outside of Africa represents only a subset of that found within the African continent.[5] From a genetic perspective, all humans are therefore Africans, either residing in Africa or in recent exile.

In view of the sad part that race and ethnicity still play in most societies, concerns that genetic analyses of different human populations could be abused are appropriate. Fortunately, from the few studies of nuclear DNA sequences, it is clear that what is called "race," although culturally important, reflects just a few continuous traits determined by a tiny fraction of our genes. This tiny fraction gives no indication of variations at other parts of our genome. Thus, from the perspective of nuclear genes, it is often the case that two persons from the same part of the world who look superficially alike are less related to each other than they are to persons from other parts of the world who may look very different (see the figure p. 498).[6]

Although small segments of the genome—such as mitochondrial DNA and Y chromosomal DNA (which are inherited in an unusual way) or the few genes that encode visible traits (which may have been selected for)—show a pattern where the genes in a particular human population can be traced back to a single common ancestor, this is not the case for the vast majority of our genes. Indeed, one way in which we humans seem to differ from apes is that we have evolved with very little subdivision. This is surely because we are a young species (in evolutionary terms) and have a greater tendency for migration than many other mammals. I suspect, therefore, that genome-wide studies of genetic variation among human populations may not be so easy to abuse—in terms of using data as "scientific support" for racism or other forms of bigotry—as is currently feared. If anything, such studies will have the opposite effect because prejudice, oppression, and racism feed on ignorance. Knowledge of the genome should foster compassion, not only because our gene pool is extremely mixed, but also because a more comprehensive understanding of how our genotype relates to our phenotype will demonstrate that everyone carries at least some deleterious alleles. Consequently, stigmatizing any particular group of individuals on the basis of ethnicity or carrier status for certain alleles will be revealed as absurd.

From a medical standpoint, improved predictive capabilities provided by the identification of disease-associated alleles harbor great potential benefits but also problems. The benefits will come from using individualized risk assessment to modify the environmental and behavioral components of common diseases. Relatively minor measures implemented early in life may prove to be extremely effective in postponing or even preventing the onset of disease. But individualized risk assessment may come at the price of "genetic hypochondria," causing many to spend their lives waiting for a disease that may never arrive. Finally, increased medical predictive power obviously represents a societal challenge in terms of medical insurance, especially in countries that, unlike most Western European countries, are not blessed with health insurance systems that share risks in an equitable fashion among the whole population. Legislators in such countries would be wise to act now to counteract future temptations to "personalize" insurance risks. Later on, once powerful genetic diagnostic tests are in

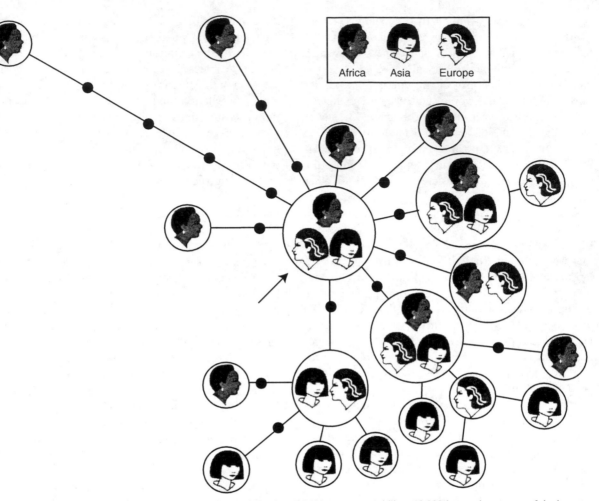

The global family. A network illustrating the relatedness of a series of DNA sequences within a 10,000-base pair segment of the human X chromosome sampled from 70 individuals worldwide. Identical DNA sequences found in people living on three different continents are illustrated by circles containing three faces; identical DNA sequences found in individuals from two continents are depicted as circles containing two faces; sequences that are found only among individuals inhabiting one continent are depicted as circles containing one face. A DNA sequence that is ancestral to all of the other sequences (arrow) is found in individuals from all continents. Black dots on the lines connecting the circles denote nucleotide substitutions in the DNA sequences. The network demonstrates that people from different continents often carry identical DNA sequences. Consequently, how a person looks gives little or no clue to what alleles he or she may carry at any particular locus. [Modified from (6)]

place, it will be hard to withstand pressure from the insurance lobby to prevent such legislation.

As we enter a genomic era in medicine and biology, perhaps the greatest danger I see stems from the enormous emphasis placed on the human genome by the media. The successes of medical genetics and genomics during the last decade have resulted in a sharp shift toward an almost completely genetic view of ourselves. I find it striking that 10 years ago, a geneticist had to defend the idea that not only the envi-

ronment but also genes shape human development. Today, one feels compelled to stress that there is a large environmental component to common diseases, behavior, and personality traits! There is an insidious tendency to look to our genes for most aspects of our "humanness," and to forget that the genome is but an internal scaffold for our existence.

We need to leave behind the view that the genetic history of our species is *the* history par excellence. We must realize that our genes are but one aspect of our history, and that there are many other histories that are even more important. For example, many people in the Western world feel a connection to ancient Greece, from which arose fundamental features of Western architecture, science, technology, and political ideals (such as democracy). Yet, at best a tiny fraction of the gene pool of the Western industrialized world came from the ancient Greeks. Obviously, this fact in no way diminishes the importance of ancient Greece. So it is a delusion to think that genomics in isolation will ever tell us what it means to be human. To work toward that lofty goal, we need an approach that includes the cognitive sciences, primatology, the social sciences, and the humanities. But with the availability of the complete human genome sequence now

at hand, genetics is in a prime position to play a prominent part in this endeavor.

REFERENCES

1. J. C. Venter *et. al.*, *Science* **291,** 1304 (2001).
2. International Human Genome Sequencing Consortium, *Nature* **409,** 860 (2001).
3. M.-C. King, A. C. Wilson, *Science* **188,** 107 (1975).
4. R. G. Klein, *The Human Career* (Univ. of Chicago Press, Chicago, IL, 1999).
5. L. B. Jorde, M. Bamshad, A. R. Rogers, *Bioessays* **20,** 126 (1998).
6. H. Kaessmann, F. Heissig, A. von Haeseler, S. Pääbo, *Nature Genet.* **22,** 78 (1999).

PATRICIA A. ROCHE AND GEORGE J. ANNAS

Protecting Genetic Privacy

George Annas is Edward R. Utley Professor and Chair, Health Law Department, Boston University Schools of Medicine and Public Health. He is the author or editor of a dozen books on health law and ethics, including *The Rights of Patients* (Humana Press); *American Health Law* (Little, Brown); and *Some Choice: Law, Medicine and the Market* (Oxford University Press). He has held a variety of regulatory positions including Chair of the Massachusetts Health Facilities Appeals Board, Vice-Chair of the Massachusetts Board of Registration in Medicine, and Chair of the Massachusetts Organ Transplant Task Force.

Patricia Roche is Assistant Professor in Health Law, Boston University School of Public Health. She has lectured on issues raised by for-profit medicine and the privacy implications of new technologies, particularly developments in genetics. She has practiced law in Massachusetts since 1989, concentrating in family law.

The simultaneous publication of two versions of the human genome could be an important impetus to take more seriously the legal, ethical and social policy issues at stake in human genome research.[1,2] There are many such issues, and the one that has caused the most public concern is that of genetic privacy. As DNA sequences become understood as information, and as this information becomes easier to use in digitized form, public concerns about internet and e-commerce privacy (regarding the security with which an individual's private details are protected) will merge with concerns about medical record privacy and genetic privacy. In this paper, we outline the key public policy issues at stake in the genetic privacy debate by reviewing generally medical privacy, by asking whether genetic information is like other medical information, and by outlining the current controversies over privacy in genetic research. We conclude with some public policy recommendations.

PRIVACY

Privacy is a complex concept that involves several different but overlapping personal interests. It encompasses informational privacy (having control over highly personal information about ourselves), relational privacy (determining with whom we have personal, intimate relationships), privacy in decision-making (freedom from the surveillance and influence of others when making personal decisions), and the right to exclude others from our personal things and places. In the United States, no single law protects all of these interests, and privacy law refers to the aggregate of privacy protections found in constitutions, statutes, regulations and common law.[3-9] Together, these laws reflect the value that US citizens place on individual privacy, sometimes referred to as "the right to be left alone" and the right to be free from outside intrusion, not as an end in itself, but as a means of enhancing individual freedom in various aspects of our lives. The centrality of individual freedom in Western societies is evident in the United States in state laws that establish a patient's right to make informed choices about treatment, that place an obligation on

Reprinted with permission from *Nature Reviews: Genetics* 2 (May 2001), 392–96. Copyright © 2001, Nature Publishing Group.

physicians to maintain patient confidentiality and that regulate the maintenance of medical records.

Privacy laws in the United States are fragmented because of the many sources of law, which includes the federal government and all 50 states. Legislative enactments are also often the result of negotiated agreements among segments of a diverse and often polarized society, rather than of a real consensus. This is perhaps most readily seen in the rules that govern highly sensitive and personal data in the United States. Unlike the approach of the European Data Protection Directive, which establishes similar rights and duties relative to different kinds of personal data (health and finance),[10] the United States has different rights and duties for personal information depending on the kind of information involved. Even for medical records, there are different rules that apply to the different types of information that they contain. For example, the United States has laws that govern generally medical record information,[11] as well as separate laws that govern specific types of medical information, such as HIV status,[12] substance-abuse treatment information[13] and mental health information.[14] New federal regulations apply the same privacy rules to all medical information except psychotherapy records.[9] Such exceptionalism has been criticized, and the primary argument against specific laws that are designed to protect genetic information is that such "genetic exceptionalism" would perpetuate the misconception that genetic information is uniquely private and sensitive.[15]

GENETIC PRIVACY

Is DNA-sequence information uniquely private or just like other sensitive information in an individual's medical record? If it is not unique, existing medical record confidentiality laws should be sufficient to protect genetic-sequence information, and no new laws would be needed. Those who support genetic exceptionalism (as we do) emphasize the distinguishing features of DNA-sequence information. The DNA molecule itself is a source of medical information and, like a personal medical record, it can be stored and accessed without the need to return to the person from whom the DNA was collected for permission. But DNA-sequence information contains information beyond an individual's medical history and current health status. DNA also contains information about an individual's future health risks, and in this sense is analogous to a coded "future diary."[16] As the code is broken, DNA reveals information about an individual's probable risks of suffering from specific conditions in the future. Our current obsession with genetic-sequence information means that it is likely to be taken more seriously than other information in a medical record that could also predict future risks, like high blood pressure or cholesterol levels. Information about the presence of proteins that specific genes might encode is also different from DNA-sequence information because the presence of certain proteins might change with time, and their levels, like cholesterol readings, can only be determined by retesting the patient personally. So, proteomics will not require new privacy rules, but rather the enforcement of existing privacy rules for medical records. DNA-sequence information might also contain information about behavioural traits that are unrelated to health status, although scepticism is called for in this area.[17]

Our use of the 'future diary' metaphor has been criticized as potentially perpetuating a mistaken view of genes as deterministic.[15] We understand this criticism, and also reject the idea that genes alone determine our future. Nevertheless, we continue to believe the future diary metaphor best conveys the private nature of genetic information itself. Our future medical status is not determined solely by genetics, any more than our past diaries are the only source for accurate information about our past (or even necessarily reflect it). DNA information, like a diary, however, is a uniquely private part of ourselves.

An individual's DNA can also reveal information about risks and traits that are shared with genetic relatives, and has been used to prove paternity and other relationships.[18] An individual's DNA has the paradoxical quality of being unique to that individual yet shared with others. Even if one believes that the DNA-sequence information extracted from an individual's DNA is no more sensitive than other medical information, this says nothing about the need to protect the DNA molecule itself. In this regard, we think it is useful to view the DNA molecule as a medical record in its own right. Having a DNA sample from an individual is like having medical information about the individual stored on a computer disk, except in this case the information is stored as blood or as other tissue samples. Like the computer disk, the DNA sequence can be "read" by the application of technology. So, regardless of the rules developed to control the use of genetic information when it is recorded in traditional paper and electronic medical records, separate rules are also needed to regulate the collection, analysis, storage and release of DNA samples themselves. This is because once a physician or researcher has a DNA sample, there is no practical need for further contact with the individual from whom the DNA was obtained, and DNA tests could be done on the stored sample (and thus on the individual) in their absence. Some of these tests might as yet be undeveloped but all will produce new genetic information about the individual.

DNA has also been culturally endowed with a power and significance exceeding that of other medical information.[19] Much of this significance is undoubtedly misplaced, but can be justified in so far as genetic information can radically change the way people view themselves and family members, as well as the way that others view them. The history of genetic testing, particularly in relation to rare monogenic diseases, such as Huntington disease, provides us with examples of this impact. Studies of individuals who have undergone testing in clinical settings show the changes in self-perception caused by positive, as well as negative, test results.[20,21] Individuals with a decreased risk of having a genetic disease have reported difficulty in setting expectations for their personal and professional lives in a more open-ended future. Adjustments seem to have been particularly difficult for those who have already made reproductive decisions based on the presumption that they were at high risk for developing a disease.[20] Consequently, it is good policy to provide genetic counselling before and after testing. And in the interests of protecting the privacy of children and adolescents, some institutions have also adopted a policy of refusing parental requests to test children for late-onset diseases when no medical intervention is available to prevent or alleviate the genetic condition.[22] Perhaps the principal reason why neither DNA-sequence information nor DNA samples themselves have been afforded special privacy protection is the strongly held view of many genetic researchers and biotechnology companies that privacy protections would interfere with their work. One court in the United States has addressed whether constitutional rights to privacy are implicated by genetic testing. In *Norman-Bloodsaw v. Lawrence Berkeley Laboratory,* employees of a research facility owned and operated by state and federal agencies alleged that non-consensual genetic testing by their employers violated their rights to privacy. Holding that the right to

privacy protects against the collection of information by illicit means, as well as unauthorized disclosures to third parties, the court stated, "One can think of few subject areas more personal and more likely to implicate privacy interests than that of one's health or genetic make-up."[23]

DNA RESEARCH AND PRIVACY

Now that the human genome has been sequenced, attention is shifting to research on genetic variation that is designed to locate genes and gene sequences with disease-producing or disease-prevention properties.[24] Some researchers have already taken steps to form partnerships and create large DNA banks that will furnish the material for this research.[25,26] Others want to take advantage of the large number of stored tissue samples that already exist.[27] In the United States, for example, the DNA of about 20 million people is collected and stored each year in tissue collections ranging from fewer than 200 to more than 92 million samples.[28] Collections include Guthrie cards, on which blood from newborns has been collected for phenylketonuria screening since the 1960s, paraffin blocks used by pathologists to store specimens, blood-bank samples, forensic specimens and the US military's bank of samples for use in identifying bodily remains.[28]

Several factors have contributed to the proliferation of DNA banking: the relative ease with which DNA can be collected, its coincidental presence in bodily specimens collected for other reasons and its immutability. Regardless of the original purposes for storing specimens, however, as the ability to extract information from DNA increases and the focus of research shifts to genetic factors that contribute to human diseases and behaviours, repositories that contain the DNA of sizeable populations can be "gold mines" of genetic information. So, it is not surprising that there is considerable interest on the part of biomedical researchers, companies that market genomic data and the pharmaceutical industry, to stake claims on these informational resources[29] and to exploit them for their own purposes.

Commercial enterprises, as well as academic researchers, have equally strong interests in making it relatively easy to access DNA samples that can be linked to medical records for research purposes. Representatives of these constituencies have been vocal in arguing that requirements for informed consent and the right to withdraw data from ongoing research projects (two aspects of genetic privacy) would greatly hamper their research efforts.[30] When US federal rules apply to such research—as is the case with federally funded projects and any projects related to obtaining approval from the US Food and Drug Administration to market drugs or devices—the local Institutional Review Board (IRB) must approve the research protocol. These boards should not waive basic federal research requirements on informed consent (nor exempt researchers from them) except when the IRB determines that the research will be conducted in such a way that the subjects cannot be personally identified.[31] If existing research rules were consistently and diligently applied perhaps we could confidently state that the privacy of research subjects is adequately protected.[32] Today, however, such confidence would be misplaced.[32]

These privacy and consent issues are not limited to the United States (Box 1). The most internationally discussed DNA-based project has been deCODE Genetics in Iceland, a commercial project that has been opposed by the Iceland Medical Association, among others, for "ethical shortcuts," such as "opt-out" provisions that presume an individual's consent (see below).[33–35] The deCODE project, which has been endorsed by two acts of the Iceland parliament, involves the creation of two new databases: the first containing the medical records of all Iceland citizens, and the second containing DNA samples from them (a third database, of genealogical records, already exists). deCODE intends to use these three databases in various combinations to identify genetic variations that could be of pharmaceutical interest. The chief ethical issues raised by this project are: first, the question of informed consent for inclusion of personal medical information in the database, which is at present included under the concept of presumed consent—this requires individuals to actively opt out of the research if they do not want their information in the database; second, informed consent for the inclusion of DNA in the DNA databank in an identifiable manner (whether encrypted or not, and no matter which entity holds the encryption key); and third, whether the right to withdraw from the research (including the right to withdraw both the DNA sample itself from the databank and all information generated about it) can be effectively exercised. Other issues include the security of the databases and community benefit from the research project itself.[35] Iceland is providing a type of ethical laboratory that will help identify the key issues involved in population-based genetic research, and might help to highlight why international privacy rules are desirable.

Box 1 Enterprises that raise challenging issues

- deCODE Genetics plans to computerize the patient records of the national health service of Iceland, and collect DNA samples from members of the population for genetic linkage analysis and association studies on common diseases. Results will be cross-referenced with information from publicly available genealogical information. Subscriptions to these databases are sold to researchers and information is entered into them on the basis of presumed consent.

- The UK Population Biomedical Collection, a joint initiative of the Medical Research Council and the Wellcome Trust, plans to focus on understanding the interactions between genes, environment and lifestyles in cancer and cardiovascular conditions. Their goal is to collect samples of up to 500,000 people and link these samples to an ongoing collection of the individuals' medical data. Investigators may be granted access to the results of genotyping, but not to the DNA samples.

- Ardais Corporation, a start-up biotechnology company that intends to enter into agreements with several major hospitals in the United States under which surgical patients will be asked for tissue that is left over from operations. These samples will be linked to records that detail the patient's medical history and family information. Tissue libraries and data will be licensed to researchers.

- Autogen Ltd, an Australian biotechnology firm that has secured exclusive rights to collect tissue samples and health data from the population of Tonga. The firm hopes to identify new disease-related genes and to aid the development of new drugs to prevent or treat common diseases, such as diabetes. It has pledged to abide by stringent ethical standards, to collect samples and data from individuals who voluntarily participate and to make the health database available to the Tongan people.

Although Icelanders themselves do not seem overly concerned with the adequacy of deCODE's plans to protect their personal privacy, other countries have not been as disposed to giving away the autonomy and privacy of their citizens so readily. Both Estonia and the United Kingdom, for example, have announced that their population-based DNA collections and research projects will contain strong consent and privacy-protection provisions.[36,37] The privacy problems inherent in large population-based projects could be avoided altogether by stripping DNA samples of their identifiers in a way that makes it impossible to link personal medical information with DNA samples (at least by using standard identifying methods). Of course, most researchers want to retain identifiers to do follow-up work or confirm diagnoses.[38] Such identification retention, however, puts individuals at risk of breach of confidentiality and invasion of privacy, and these risks are why both informed consent and strong privacy-protection protocols are ethically necessary for genetic research.[38] These considerations also apply to criminal DNA databases as even convicted felons have privacy rights.

Risks of disclosure of personal genetic information are so high that some prominent genetic researchers, including Francis Collins and Craig Venter, have suggested concentrating not on privacy rules, but rather on anti-discrimination legislation that is designed to protect individuals when their genetic information is disclosed, and when insurance companies, employers or others want to use that information against them.[39] We agree that anti-discrimination legislation is desirable, but it does not substitute for privacy rules that can prevent the genetic information from being generated in the first place without the individual's informed authorization.

This point is well illustrated by a law recently enacted in Massachusetts—a state with a population more than 20 times larger than the population of Iceland[40]—that has been mistakenly characterized in the US press as 'a sweeping set of genetic privacy protections.'[41] Under this new law, written informed consent is a prerequisite to predictive (but not diagnostic) genetic testing and to disclosing the results of such tests by entities and practitioners that provide health care. The law also limits the uses that insurers and employers can make of genetic information. However, it places no limitations on how researchers and biotechnology companies that engage in projects requiring the use of identifiable samples and identifiable genetic information conduct their activities. Apparently, those who drafted the statute believed that they need not be concerned about protecting research subjects because research with human subjects is regulated by the federal government, failing to recognize that many activities of genomic companies do not fall under the jurisdiction of the federal regulations.

POLICY RECOMMENDATIONS

We have argued in the past that a principal step to achieving genetic privacy would be the passage of a comprehensive federal genetic privacy law.[42,43] The primary purpose of such a law is to give individuals control over their identifiable DNA samples and the genetic-sequence information extracted from them. The model we suggest provides that individuals have a property interest in their own DNA—and that this property interest gives them control over it. Control could also, however, be obtained by requiring explicit authorization for the collection and use of DNA, including its research and commercial use. We believe that in the absence of authorization no one should know more about an individual's genetic make-up than that individual chooses to know themselves, and that an individual should also know who else knows (or will know) their private genetic information (see Box 2). Current US state laws at best offer some economic protections and a patchwork of genetic privacy protections. But existing state laws have significant gaps and inconsistently regulate those who engage in DNA banking and genetic research. Nevertheless, existing privacy laws provide models and a foundation that can be built on to protect genetic privacy and empower individuals in this genomic era. But until comprehensive federal legislation is passed in the United States, US citizens will have to rely on those who create and maintain DNA banks to design, implement and enforce self-imposed rules to protect individuals.

One proposal to deal with privacy issues and individual control over genetic information is to have DNA samples and medical records collected by a "third-party broker" of genetic information who would then, with the informed consent of the individual, make this information available to researchers in a coded form. A for-profit company, First Genetic Trust, has been formed in the United States to try out this model.[44] Individuals are solicited through the internet to participate in the Trust and all communication with those who participate, including consent to new studies, will take place over the internet. The purpose of

---

Box 2 Assessing genetic privacy

Laws or policies that purport to protect genetic privacy, at a minimum, should do the following:

- Recognize individual genetic rights particularly:
  - the right to determine if and when their identifiable DNA samples are collected, stored or analysed;
  - the right to determine who has access to their identifiable DNA samples;
  - the right to access to their own genetic information;
  - the right to determine who has access to their genetic information;
  - the right to all information necessary for informed decision-making about the collection, storage and analysis of their DNA samples and the disclosure of their private genetic information.
- Limit parental rights to authorize the collection, storage or analysis of a child's identifiable DNA sample so as preserve the child's future autonomy and genetic privacy.
- Prohibit unauthorized uses of individually identifiable DNA samples, except for some uses in solving crimes, determining paternity or identifying bodily remains.
- Prohibit disclosures of genetic information without the individual's explicit authorization.
- Strictly enforce laws and institutional policies.
- Provide accessible remedies for individuals whose rights are violated.
- Institute sufficient penalties to deter and punish violations.

---

the Trust is to assure individuals that no one would be able to use their DNA, or their personal medical information associated with it, without the individual's authorization. Some might criticize this approach as going too far in protecting participants, noting that consent is not generally necessary for IRB-approved research that does not involve identifiable data. Regardless of the fact that First Genetic Trust itself will not be engaged in research, as long as data held by the Trust can be linked to individuals, we think authorization should be required and that proposals such as this one are a step in the right direction.

Whether arrangements such as these will lead to significant public participation in genetic research remains to be seen. Despite the availability of tests for genes that predispose individuals to several diseases, including Huntington disease and some forms of breast and colon cancers, the number of people who choose to undergo clinical genetic testing has fallen far below the expectations of the companies that sell tests and of the physicians who believe their patients would benefit from them.[45] Why is the public, which is on the one hand fascinated with each advance in mapping the genome, the identification of particular genes and the possible association of a gene with particular human characteristics, simultaneously reticent to undergo genetic testing? Explanations that individuals give for avoiding genetic tests include fear of dis-

crimination, concern over the impact on family members, lack of effective treatments and preference for uncertainty about the future.[46,47] Privacy protections have little, if any, impact on attitudes towards the future. Nevertheless, by regulating the creation, maintenance and disclosure of information, they can reduce privacy risks and provide some reassurance to those who might not otherwise participate in genetic research or clinical testing.

Once individual interests in privacy and in being treated fairly on the basis of genetic information have been addressed, only property issues remain. Individuals can be thought of as having a property right in their DNA, including, among other things, the right to restrict others from "trespassing" on their property without permission.[42] One US state, Oregon, incorporated an individual's right of ownership of DNA into its laws in 1995.[48] Objections that this law would inhibit research in that state echoed objections that researchers and industry have made elsewhere to explicit and strict privacy rules.[49,50] Acknowledging property interests in DNA need not impede research any more than respect for individual privacy would. Conversely, individuals are free to grant property rights in their DNA to researchers, and are much more likely to do so if their privacy can be guaranteed (as it can be if identifiers are not retained).

DNA can rightly be seen as containing uniquely

personal, powerful and sensitive information about individuals and their families. Some individuals want to know as much of this information about themselves as possible, and might be willing to share this information with their families and others. Others would rather remain ignorant about their own genetic make-up, and thus their risks for future illnesses, or at least to keep others ignorant of such information. We believe that individual choices are best served by policies that place primary control over an individual's DNA and genetic information in the hands of individuals. We also believe privacy protections will prove as necessary for the future of genetic research and clinical applications as they will be for the future of e-commerce. We believe that the sooner that reasonable genetic privacy protections are in place, the better it will be for all of us.

NOTES

1. International Human Genome Sequencing Consortium. Initial sequencing and analysis of the human genome. *Nature* **409**, 860–921 (2001).

2. Venter J. C. *et al.* The sequence of the human genome. *Science* **291**, 1304–1351 (2001).

3. Miller, A. R. Personal privacy in the computer age. *Mich. Law Rev.* **67**, 1091–1296 (1968).

4. *Griswald v. Connecticut,* 381 US 479 (1965).

5. *Meyer v. Nebraska,* 262 US 390 (1923).

6. Privacy Act of 1974 (Pub. L. 93–579, December 31, 1974, 88 Stat. 1896).

7. Family Educational Rights and Privacy Act of 1974 (FERPA) (Pub. L. 93–380, Title V, § 513, August 21, 1974, 88 Stat. 571).

8. Right to Financial Privacy Act of 1978 (RFPA) (Pub. L. 95–630, Title XI, November 10, 1978, 92 Stat. 3697).

9. Standards for Privacy of Individually Identifiable Health Information, 50 Fed. Reg. 250 (2000).

10. Swartz. J. P. M. in *Genetic Secrets* (ed. Rothstein, M.) 392–417 (Yale Univ. Press, New Haven, Connecticut, 1997).

11. California Health & Safety Code sec. 120980 (West 2000).

12. Connecticut Gen. Stat. sec. 19a–583 (West 1999).

13. 42 US Code sec. 290-dd (West 2000).

14. Florida State sec. 394. 4615 (West 2000).

15. Murray, T. H. in *Genetic Secrets* (ed. Rothstein, M.) 60–76 (Yale Univ. Press, New Haven, Connecticut, 1999).

16. Annas, G. J. Privacy rules for DNA databanks. *J. Am. Med. Assoc.* **270**, 2346–2350 (1993).

17. Billings, P. R., Beckwith, J. & Alper, J. S. The genetic analysis of human behavior: a new era? *Social Sci. Med.* **35**, 227–238 (1992).

18. Marshall, E. Which Jefferson was the father? *Science* **283**, 153–154 (1999).

19. Nelkin, D. & Lindee, M. S. *The DNA Mystique: The Gene as a Cultural Icon* (W. H. Freeman, New York, 1995).

20. Huggins, M. *et al.* Predictive testing for Huntington disease in Canada: adverse effects and unexpected results in those receiving a decreased risk. *Am. J. Med. Genet.* **42**, 504–515 (1992).

21. DudokdeWit, A. C. *et al.* Distress in individuals facing predictive DNA testing for autosomal dominant late-onset disorders: comparing questionnaire results with in-depth interviews. *Am. J. Med. Genet.* **75**, 62–74 (1998).

22. American Society of Human Genetics and American College of Medical Genetics. Ethical, legal and psychological implications of genetic testing in children and adolescents: points to consider. *Am. J. Hum. Genet.* **57**, 1233–1241 (1995).

23. *Norman-Bloodsaw v. Lawrence Berkeley Laboratory,* 135 F. 3d 1260 (1998). At 1269.

24. Kaiser, J. Environment institute lays plans for gene hunt. *Science* **278**, 569–570 (1997).

25. Pollack, A. Company seeking donors for a 'gene trust'. *NY Times* A1 (August 1, 2000).

26. Karet, G., Boguslavsky, J. & Studt, T. Unraveling human diversity. *Drug Discovery Dev.* November/December, S5–S14 (2000).

27. Grody, W. W. Molecular pathology, informed consent, and the paraffin block. *Diagn. Mol. Pathol.* **4**, 155–157 (1995).

28. National Bioethics Advisory Commission. *Report on the Use of Human Biological Material in Research: Ethical Issues and Policy Guidance* (Bethesda, Maryland, 1999).

29. Pezzella, M. DNA databases take shape at firms on two coasts. *Biotechnol. Watch* (September 18, 2000) at 2000 WL 7388705.

30. Korn, D. in *Genetic Testing and the Use of Information* (ed. Long, G.) 16–83 (American Enterprise, Washington DC, 1999).

31. 46 CFR sec. 46. 101(b)(4) (2000).

32. Office of Inspector General US Department of Health and Human Services. *Institutional Review Boards: A Time for Reform* (Washington DC, 2000).

33. Greely, H. T. Iceland's plan for genomics research: facts and implications. *Jurimetrics* **40**, 153–191 (2000).

34. Jonantansson, H. Iceland's Health Sector Database: a significant head start in the search for the biological holy grail or an irreversible error? *Am. J. Law Med.* **26**, 31–67 (2000).

35. Annas, G. J. Rules for research on human genetic variation—lessons from Iceland. *N. Engl. J. Med.* **342**, 1830–1833 (2000).

36. Frank, L. Storm brews over gene bank of Estonian population. *Science* **286**, 1262–1263 (1999).

37. McKie, R. The gene collection. *Br. Med. J.* **321**, 854 (2000).

38. Clayton, E. W. *et al.* Informed consent for genetic research on stored tissue samples. *J. Am. Med. Assoc.* **274**, 1786–1792 (1995).

39. CBS News: *This Morning* 6/27/00, Federal Document Clearing House transcript at 2000 WESTLAW 6654407.

40. 2000 Massachusetts Acts Chapter 254.

41. Misha, R. New law gives genetic privacy protection. *Boston Globe* B2 (August 23, 2000).

42. Annas, G. J., Glantz, L. H. & Roche, P. A. *The Genetic Privacy Act and Commentary* (available by request from the Health Law Department, Boston University School of Public Health, Boston Mass. and at http://www.busph.bu.edu/Depts/HealthLaw/) (1995).

43. Roche, P. A., Annas, G. J. & Glantz, L. H. The genetic privacy act: a proposal for national legislation. *Jurimetrics* **37**, 1–11 (1996).

44. Marshall, E. Company plans to bank human DNA profiles. *Science* **291**, 575 (2001).

45. Kolata, G. Public slow to embrace genetic testing. *NY Times* 16, 1 (March 27, 1998).

46. Gettig, B. Survey reveals attitudes towards genetic testing. *The Marker* **10,** 6–7 (1997).

47. Hall, M. A. & Rich. S. S. Genetic privacy laws and patients fear of discrimination by health insurers: the view of genetic counselors. *J. Law Med. Ethics* **28,** 245–257 (2000).

48. Oregon Revised Statutes § 659. 715 (1998).

49. O'Neill, P. Researchers fight to get a piece of you. *Portland Oregonian* (July 11, 1999) at 1999 WESTLAW 5358096.

50. Rosenberg, R. Biotechnology: a study in data collection, genomics companies go abroad to obtain samples citing obstacles in the United States. *Boston Globe* D4 (November 1, 2000).

MICHAEL M. BURGESS

Beyond Consent: Ethical and Social Issues in Genetic Testing

Michael Burgess holds the Chair in Biomedical Ethics at the Centre for Applied Ethics and in the Department of Medical Genetics at the University of British Columbia. His current research activities concern ethical issues raised by genetic knowledge and technology. He has served on committees with the Management Committee of the Canadian Genetic Assessment and Technology Program and the American Society of Human Genetics.

INFORMED CONSENT promotes patient participation and AUTONOMY in health-care decisions by requiring the provision of information and recognizing that patients must voluntarily authorize interventions. In the case of genetic testing, genetic counselling provides the means to achieve informed consent. Genetic counselling explains the nature, usefulness and risks associated with genetic tests, and assures that participation in genetic testing is autonomous, or based on participants' understanding of the relevant information. Because informed consent is highly dependent on comprehension of information and good communication, genetic counselling provides excellent support, although evaluation of counselling is not well established and some researchers express concern about the ability of counsellors to be non-directive.[1–3]

However, genetic testing raises issues that cannot be managed through informed consent. To begin with, there might be few, if any, clinical benefits from genetic testing. As far as genetic counselling is concerned, the STANDARD OF PRACTICE is primarily directed at imparting understanding of possible test results, because the net benefit of a genetic test is often highly dependent on how much the participant values the information and what they want to do with it (Box 1). Genetic counselling also involves careful

---

Box 1 Possible benefits from tests

Clinical
- Avoidance of onset of disease
- Curative treatment due to timely and accurate diagnosis
- Avoidance of harms from inappropriate treatment or monitoring
- Symptomatic treatment

Psychological or social
- Relief from uncertainty
- Personal planning
- Improved well-being
- Fulfilment of patient wishes to be tested

Public health
- Decrease population morbidity and/or mortality from genetic disease
- Decrease population frequency of treatment-related morbidity or mortality

consideration of the social and psychological risks of genetic testing, but evolving social contexts, such as the workplace, the insurance industry and the family, shape whether and how these risks materialize. Genetic information produced by testing individuals also affects other family members, and those who share, or are perceived to share, a common genetic heritage.

Genetic testing therefore raises ethical issues that concern standard of practice, indeterminacy of risks and collective acceptability of risks and benefits. This article discusses each of these issues, indicating the extent to which informed consent addresses the ethical issues, and suggests fruitful avenues of research into the ethics of the social context of genetic practice.

GENETIC TESTING: A STANDARD OF PRACTICE

Because of the complexity of genetic information and its interpretation, genetic counselling has become a cornerstone of genetic research and clinical practice. Counsellors must explain the highly variable, and often changing, views about the relation between genetic test results and the associated conditions, as well as information about the conditions themselves and possible treatments or preventions.

One of the first and most influential studies of genetic testing for an adult onset disease was the predictive testing for Huntington disease. The concerns associated with predictive genetic testing[4,5] were managed in the Canadian multi-centre research protocol by requiring four pre-test and several post-test counselling sessions.[6] Although there were no definitive medical benefits in this instance, testing was felt to promote individual patient autonomy and emotional welfare. The conclusion of the Canadian study was that, with the provision of pre- and post-test counselling that included psychological assessments, genetic testing for Huntington disease did not pose unacceptable risks for consenting participants.[7] Clinical recommendations supporting genetic counselling of adults have been based on this research experience,[8] although in clinical practice and with other genetic tests, pre- and post-test counselling have become streamlined with little study of the effects of counselling itself or of modifications to clinical protocols.[9] The clinical availability of predictive testing for Huntington disease is based on the ethical assessment that the promotion of autonomy and the psychological and social benefits for people can jus-

tify the risks for those who want the test and undergo genetic counselling.

The case of Huntington disease illustrates the general trend for genetic testing to become the *de facto* standard of practice—available for those who wish to have the information once it is established that a genetic test can identify a genetic contribution to a disease. This is probably due to the low cost of the test, and the difficulty of justifying withholding the test on a clinical basis once it is established as accurate in the research context.[10,11] This emphasis on individual participant autonomy in the research setting might explain what some have referred to as "premature implementation" before establishing clinical benefit, particularly in the case of tests that are not predictive but that indicate an increase in disease susceptibility.[12]

There are, of course, genetic tests that direct clinical care. In the case of prenatal testing, the possibility of abortion as a clinical intervention does provide a clinical option with a clear outcome. A family history of colon cancer initiates invasive monitoring, and testing that eliminates a genetic contributor might reduce or eliminate the need for monitoring and the accompanying risks and discomforts. But, in many cases, the genetic information together with the choices that it provides to people are the primary benefits.

Providing access to a genetic test because it is accurate is different from evidence-based standards that are applied to other clinical interventions. These standards require that there is a measurable difference in clinical outcomes or population health measures for a test, screen or intervention to become the standard of practice. However, most genetic tests develop well in advance of effective interventions because of their usefulness in research. Many genetic tests are therefore available simply because they provide accurate information. This standard of practice does not protect patients from risks, but makes them responsible for evaluating whether the social and psychological risks are justified by the benefits. The historical association of genetics with eugenics has probably contributed to the vehemence with which patient autonomy and non-directive counselling have been asserted as the ethical standard for such assessments.[13]

Potential test participants cannot assume that there is benefit simply because genetic testing is offered as a clinical service. They have to evaluate for themselves whether the knowledge likely to result from the genetic test is beneficial. This poses an additional challenge to informed consent. It is not enough to provide information—patients must also be supported in evaluating their own responses and views of benefit. Policy decisions related to health-care insurance must also evaluate whether accurate genetic tests provide sufficient health benefits to justify coverage (and whether private and therefore unequal access constitutes a problem for justice in national health-care systems).[14] So it is not ethically sufficient to establish test accuracy and assure counselling and consent for test participants.

Participant evaluation of the benefits of testing engages a larger context than just the genetic counselling sessions. Media, marketing and some public enthusiasm for genetic testing and biotechnology in general will tend to raise participants' expectations of genetic testing.[15,16] Although the advent of preventive or ameliorating interventions will strengthen the benefits, the psychological and social risks will always be an important factor and make it difficult to consider genetic tests as being innocuous.

THE INDETERMINATE NATURE OF RISKS

Establishing the risks that are associated with genetic testing is also critical for both the standard of practice and for informed consent. In the absence of clear and dependable clinical benefits, the social and psychological risks might overwhelm the benefits. Even in cases for which there is clinical benefit from a particular test, the psychological and social risks should be disclosed in counselling, and there is a need for policies or regulation to minimize these risks. But evaluating the social and psychological risks (or benefits) that come from genetic testing and information is difficult. The same genetic information can pose harm or benefit owing to the highly variable nature of familial and social circumstances.

For example, a person told that they have not inherited the Huntington disease mutation might experience relief or increased responsibility for family members who are less fortunate. The experience of relief from being told that one is not at risk for a familial disease hardly needs explanation. But clinical reports, interviews and focus group discussions also describe the experiences of people receiving the same news whose relief is qualified by the misfortune of other family members, or who assume or are assigned caregiving responsibilities.[17] Whereas some people might experience caregiving roles as fulfilling and desirable, others find that their personal resources and social supports are inadequate, and describe their lives as still dominated by Huntington disease. Women receiving news that they have not inherited the mutation associated with breast cancer in their family certainly

will experience relief, although they might also feel an obligation to educate family members and to encourage others at risk to seek genetic testing. For some, this responsibility might be grasped with enthusiasm, but for others, familial responses will be marginalizing. Although genetic counselling might include discussion of familial responses to genetic information as well as sharing of test results within the family, it is unrealistic to expect genetic counsellors or individual test participants to be able to anticipate the actual familial responses and personal experiences. The unpredictability of familial and personal responses makes it difficult to assess the net benefit of genetic testing for any individual.

Another context that will shape the social and psychological effects of genetic testing is the work place. On the positive side, the identification of a genetic contributor to an environmental sensitivity can motivate an intervention to reduce exposure to the specific environmental agent (if it is readily alterable).[18] But increased susceptibility identified by a genetic test might also lead employers to discriminate against some people to minimize employees' sick time. Liability, disability and life insurance create incentives for employers to increase scrutiny of those with genetic-based susceptibilities to minimize overhead costs or legal risks. It is not the genetic information itself that poses the risk, but individual and social system responses.[19,20]

Although confidentiality of health-care records could reduce some discriminatory uses of genetic testing information, it is controversial whether mere disclosure of the risks and the current privacy regulations for genetic information are adequate.[21,22] The privacy issue is particularly problematic for insurance policies, because insurance contracts are based on the sharing of medical information to assess risk and to establish proportionate or market-related premiums.[23–26] It is controversial whether broad social policy to restrict the insurance industry's access to genetic information is necessary to protect fair access to insurance,[27] despite strong international pressures either to restrict access or to require the provision of basic levels of insurance without scrutiny of medical records.[28–31] The various uses of genetic information in these social contexts emphasize the need to identify, evaluate and regulate for possible discrimination.

The occurrence of social and psychological effects,

and whether they are experienced as harms or benefits, is sensitive to many factors such as individual resources, family support, supportive social services, insurance company policies and social attitudes. Although informed consent must explain that these broader social contexts are relevant to assessing the effects of genetic testing, the actual effects remain unpredictable owing to the complexity and variability of social systems. Whenever genetic testing provides a definitive response to a pressing clinical problem, these more abstract concerns appropriately recede into the background. But when genetic tests provide primarily social or psychological benefits, these social contexts are critical for assessing whether the anticipated benefits will materialize, and whether the harms will be justified. Such an assessment is inevitably part of informed consent. But the genetic counselling must clearly articulate uncertainty about the harms and benefits of genetic testing.

Ethical evaluations of genetic tests must assess the social and psychological effects of testing and consider the actual and possible responses of social systems. Although informed consent and genetic counselling might disclose or discuss these ethical dimensions for the test candidate, they must not be construed as adequate to manage these risks. The social context is beyond the control of geneticists and participants; neither can be held responsible for deciding whether to expose the participant to effects that are essentially unstable and not universally experienced as good or bad. Ultimately, the acceptance of genetic testing in society must be accompanied by investment in social research that will identify social system responses, provide ethical and social analyses and alternatives for reform.

EFFECTS ON NON-CONSENTING PERSONS

Genetic testing produces information that is familial and not only individual. A participant's genetic test for an inherited mutation reveals whether they received the mutation from their parents, whether their siblings might have inherited the mutation, and whether their children could inherit it. The previous discussion of the subjectivity of non-clinical benefit established that the same test result could be beneficial or harmful, or some mix of the two, and that consent depended on the evaluation of the individual. But the model of consent presumes that harms and benefits can be isolated to consenting persons. Therefore,

the combination of the familial effects of genetic testing and individual authorization of the acceptance of risks and benefits seems to entail the impractical requirement that every family member, for whom the test participant's information might have relevance, should provide consent before the participant is tested. The usual compromise is to suggest to a test candidate that he or she discuss the testing possibilities with family members, and, whenever possible, to first counsel and test potential carriers, such as parents. If the persons most likely to be affected by one family member's test are already tested, then the effects on the rest of the family will be minimized. But even if family members insist on their "right not to know," the presumption of the ethical sufficiency of informed consent for clinical services makes it difficult to justify refusing genetic testing to the consenting person.

The effects of genetic testing on groups larger than families are probably most familiar with inherited disease related to minorities or religious communities. Tay-Sachs disease, sickle cell anaemia and specific mutations associated with breast and ovarian cancers are the best-known examples. In these instances, historical reproductive and immigration patterns have preserved a degree of genetic homogeneity in ethno-cultural communities, which makes the genetic contributions to some diseases easier to identify in these groups. Such communities are therefore attractive as research populations. It is important to recognize that the frequency of a condition in a specific population might not be higher than in the general population, but that the reduced heterogeneity makes it easier to search for meaningful genetic variations.[32] And it is this same association of heritage, race or social group with the identification of genetic risk that can lead to stigmatization of ethnic populations as genetically 'defective.'[33]

Informed consent of individual ethno-cultural COMMUNITY members is wholly inadequate for authorizing the acceptability of the risks of stigmatization for the entire group.[34,35] Even if there are collective benefits likely to accrue from the clinical testing of individuals or from research, consent from individual community members cannot authorize the acceptability of the effects to the community. Although researchers might sometimes seek authoritative acceptance by leaders, even this approach begs important ethical questions about the representativeness of leadership and heterogeneity of moral beliefs and judgments within communities.[36] The authority of leadership might, in some cases, require consent processes that encourage independence and strong confidentiality to leave room for people to refuse to participate.[37] Despite some views that if ethics gets in the way of science and benefits then the ethics should be examined,[38] there is considerable recognition that some kind of collective acceptability of research must be negotiated with identified populations.[39]

Untested and non-consenting members of disease-related charitable organizations and patient support groups can also experience the effects of genetic testing of persons within their group. For instance, a complex genetic disease might have several genetic components that interact with each other and with the environment in which the disease is manifested. Understanding these genetic components might differentiate between those who would benefit from one form of intervention rather than another, or show that environmental contributors can be controlled to avoid disease in some subset of the affected population. But characterization of the disease as genetic could lead to insurance discrimination for the entire population. Some persons with the disease who lack the social and financial resources so relevant to a sense of empowerment might assume fatalism with respect to the disease, avoiding possibly ameliorating measures. Affected persons might be stigmatized for not avoiding the environmental contributors. These are the effects on the population that result from a genetic understanding of disease and, as such, are the result of individuals' consent to genetic research on their own disease. Contrary to some attempts to extend informed consent to groups, the collective acceptability of research,[40] or its justifiability in the case of diverse opinion, requires detailed negotiation and specific ethical assessments.[41]

BEYOND CONSENT

Individualized ideas about autonomy and informed consent are a part of the CULTURE of bioethics in Western health-care practice and politics. Cultural studies indicate that the concept of culture should not be understood as a set of beliefs that explain the behaviour of others,[42] but instead as the nest of practices and assumptions that underlie everyday practice for all people, however diverse. Cultural dimensions shape what is considered desirable research for researchers, granting agencies, health-care systems and commercial enterprises, as well as for families, "ethnic groups" and groups organized around fund raising and research for particular diseases. In other words, the development of genetic testing as well as the trend towards genomic science are themselves cultural phenomena that can be understood as being made possible and supported by particular cultural views.[43]

The orientation towards accurate knowledge as a benefit independent of clinical relevance is a part of the culture of science and is promoted by a tradition that emphasizes individual autonomy. Resorting to the individual to assess net benefit in the face of ambiguity is a feature of liberal political philosophy. Contemporary bioethics tends to support the insulation of scientists, institutions and commercial producers from responsibility for social contexts in which scientific knowledge is used, without suggesting alternative responsible parties. Social research and explicit discussion of the culture of research, commercialization, and risk-orientated health education allow the wider public to participate in meaningful discussions about technology and health policy,[44–46] a critical but often neglected feature of democracy in this area.

Clinical research and health policy analysis must return to an evaluation of the clinical and non-clinical benefits related to the standard of practice. The current *ad hoc* addition of genetic tests to the standard of practice merely because they provide accurate genetic information is not justifiable. This is particularly true as social and psychological effects cannot be adequately described or predicted. Some of the most important research related to genetic testing has to do with the use of genetic information and ideas of inheritance in social institutions, ranging from the family to whole communities. Finally, as the social effects of genetic and inheritance information are better described, it will be vital to establish collaborative research with communities and other groups who have collective interests in the effects of research on themselves.

GLOSSARY

Autonomy The capacity to be rational and self-directing. Autonomy creates the possibility of moral responsibility, and is therefore accorded strong ethical protection in bioethics.
Community Communities usually share some element of value or practice that provides cohesiveness despite considerable heterogeneity. Aggregates might be identified as having a common feature, such as a disease, but lack any social cohesiveness. Disease-related groups might move from being an aggregate to a community as they organize activities around their common features.
Culture Culture is constituted by the practices and assumptions that underlie a group's everyday activities, and is typically heterogeneous and constantly evolving.

Informed consent A doctrine intended to assure patient participation in health-care decisions. It requires that the recommended and alternative interventions be explained, together with their harms and benefits. Authorization of treatment is based on comprehension of this information and voluntary agreement.

Standard of practice Historically rooted in clinical practice, the standard of practice is the service or intervention that is recognized by the relevant group of health professionals as appropriate care. The move to evidence-based standards of practice evaluates whether the benefits of a new intervention outweigh the possible harms.

NOTES

1. Rapp, R. Chromosomes and communication: the discourse of genetic counseling. *Med. Anthrop. Quart.* **2,** 143–157 (1988).

2. Lippman, A. in *The Future of Human Reproduction* (ed. Overall, C.) 182–194 (The Women's Press, Toronto, 1989).

3. Clarke, A. Is non-directive genetic counseling possible? *Lancet* **338,** 998–1001 (1991).

4. Farrer, L. A. Suicide and attempted suicide in Huntington disease: implications for preclinical testing of persons at risk. *Am. J. Med. Genet.* **24,** 305–3111 (1986).

5. Kessler, S. & Bloch, M. Social system responses to Huntington disease. *Family Processes* **28,** 59–68 (1989).

6. Fox, S., Bloch, M., Fahy, M. & Hayden, M. R. Predictive testing for Huntington disease: description of a pilot study in British Columbia. *Am. J. Med. Genet.* **32,** 211–216 (1988).

7. Benjamin, C. M. *et al.* and the Canadian collaborative groups for predictive testing for Huntington disease. Proceed with care: direct predictive testing for Huntington disease. *Am. J. Hum. Genet.* **55,** 606–617 (1994).

8. Quaid, K. A. Presymptomatic testing for Huntington disease: recommendations for counseling. *Am. J. Med. Genet.* **39,** 347–354 (1992).

9. Biesecker, B. B. & Marteau, T. M. The future of genetic counseling: an international perspective. *Nature Genet.* **22,** 133–137 (1999).

10. DeGrazia, D. The ethical justification for minimal paternalism in the use of the predictive test for Huntington's disease. *J. Clin. Ethics* **2,** 219–228 (1991).

11. Burgess, M. M. & Hayden, M. R. Patients' rights to laboratory data: trinucleotide repeat length in Huntington disease. *Am. J. Med. Genet.* **162,** 6–9 (1996).

12. Koenig, B. *et al.* Genetic testing for BRCA1 and BRCA2; recommendations of the Stanford program in genomics, ethics and society. *J. Women's Health* **7,** 531–545 (1998).

13. Kerr, A. & Cunningham-Burley, S. On ambivalence and risk: reflexive modernity and the new human genetics. *Sociology* **34,** 283–304 (2000).

14. Burgess, M. M. in *The Commercialization of Genetics Research: Ethical, Legal, and Policy Issues* (eds Caulfield, T. A. & Williams-Jones, B.) 181–194 (Kluwer Academic/Plenum Publishers, New York, 1999).

15. Nelkin, D. & Lindee, M. S., *The DNA Mystique: The Gene as a Cultural Icon* (New York: Freeman, 1995).

16. Harper, P. S. Direct marketing of cystic fibrosis carrier screening: commercial push or population need? *J. Med. Genet.* **32,** 249–250 (1995).

17. Huggins, M. *et al.* Predictive testing for Huntington disease in Canada: adverse effects and unexpected results in those receiving a decreased risk. *Am. J. Med. Genet.* **42,** 508 (1992).

18. Vineis, P. & Schulte, P. A. Scientific and ethical aspects of genetic screening of workers for cancer risk: the case of *N*-acetyltransferase phenotype. *J. Clin. Epidemiol.* **48,** 189–197 (1995).

19. MacDonald, C. & Williams-Jones, B. Ethics and genetics: susceptibility testing in the workplace. *J. Business Ethics* [35 (2002), 235–41.]

20. Lemmens, T. What about your genes? Ethical, legal and policy dimensions of genetics in the workplace. *Politics and the Life Sciences* **16,** 57–75 (1997).

21. Working Group on Ethical, Legal and Social Implications of Human Genome Research. *Genetic Information and Health Insurance. Report of the Task Force:* (National Institutes of Health, Bethesda, Maryland, 1993).

22. Abbott, A. Israel split on rights to genetic privacy. *Nature* **394,** 214 (1998).

23. McGleenan, T., Weising, U. & Ewald, F. (eds) *Genetics and Insurance* (Springer, New York, 1999).

24. NIH-DOE Working Group on Ethical, Legal, and Social Implications of Human Genome Research. *Genetic Information and Health Insurance* (Human Genome Project, Washington DC, 1993).

25. Lemmens, T. & Bahamin, P. in *Socio-Ethical Issues in Human Genetics* (ed. Knoppers, B. M.) 115–275 (Les Editions Yvons-Blais Inc., Cowansville, Quebec, 1998).

26. Greely, H. T. in *The Code of Codes: Scientific and Social Issues in the Human Genome Project* (eds Kelves, D. J. & Hood, L.) 274–280 (Harvard Univ. Press, Cambridge, Massachusetts, 1992).

27. McGleenan, T. & Wiesing, U. in *Genetics and Insurance* (eds McGleenan, T. *et al.*) 116–117 (Springer, New York, 1999).

28. Murray, T. Genetics and the moral mission of health insurance. *Hastings Center Report* **22,** 12–15 (1992).

29. Wilkie, T. Genetics and insurance in Britain: why more than just the Atlantic divides the English-speaking nations. *Nature Genet.* **20,** 119–121 (1998).

30. Dutch Health Council. *Genetics, Science & Society* (Dutch Health Council, The Hague, 1989).

31. Sandberg, P. Genetic information and life insurance: a proposal for an ethical European policy. *Social Sci. Med.* **40,** 1549–1559 (1995).

32. Collins, F. cited in Wadman, M. News: Jewish leaders meet NIH chiefs on genetic stigmatisation fears. *Nature* **392,** 851 (1998).

33. Editorial. Privacy matters. *Nature Genet.* **19,** 207–208 (1998).

34. Weijer, C., Goldsand, G. & Emanuel, E. J. Protecting communities in research: current guidelines and limits of extrapolation. *Nature Genet.* **23,** 275–280 (1999).

35. Weijer, C. Protecting communities in research: Philosophical and pragmatic challenges. *Cam. Q. Health Ethics* **8,** 501–513 (1999).

36. Burgess, M. M. & Brunger, F. in *The Governance of Health Research involving Human Subjects* (ed. McDonald, M.) 141–175 (Law Commission of Canada, Ottawa, 2000). Also see http://www.lcc.gc.ca/en/themes/gr/hrish/macdonald/macdonald.pdf

37. Foster, M. W., Berensten, D. & Carter, T. H., A model agreement for genetic research in socially identifiable populations. *Am. J. Hum. Genet.* **63,** 696–702 (1998).

38. Scheuermann, R. H. & Picker, L. J. Letter to the editor. *Nature* **392,** 14 (1998).

39. Council for International Organizations of Medical Sciences (CIOMS) *International Ethical Guidelines for Biomedical Research Involving Human Subjects* (CIOMS, Geneva, 1993).

40. Weijer, C., Goldsand, G. & Emanuel, E. J. Protecting communities in research: current guidelines and limits of extrapolation. *Nature Genet.* **23,** 275–280 (1999).

41. Burgess, M. M. & Brunger, F. in *The Governance of Health Research involving Human Subjects* (ed. McDonald, M.) 14–175 (Law Commission of Canada, 2000). Also see http://www.lcc.gc.ca/en/papers/macdonald/macdonald.pdf

42. Stephenson, P. in *A Cross-Cultural Dialogue on Health Care Ethics* (eds Coward, H. & Ratanakul, P.) 68–91. (Wilfrid Laurier Univ. Press, 1999).

43. Brunger, F. & Bassett, K. *Culture and Genetics in Socioethical Issues in Human Genetics* (ed. Knoppers, B. M.) 30–34 (Les Editions Yvon Blais Inc., Cowansville, Quebec, 1998).

44. Sclove, R. E. *Democracy and Technology* (The Guilford Press, New York, 1995).

45. Kerr, A:, Cunningham-Burley, S. & Amos, A. The new genetics and health: Mobilizing lay expertise. *Public Understanding of Science* **7,** 41–60 (1998).

46. Kerr, A., Cunningham-Burley, S. & Amos, A. Drawing the line: an analysis of lay people's discussions about the new genetics. *Public Understanding of Science* **7,** 113–133 (1998).

LAINIE FRIEDMAN ROSS AND MARGARET R. MOON

Ethical Issues in Genetic Testing of Children

Lainie Friedman Ross is Assistant Director at the MacLean Center for Clinical Medical Ethics at the University of Chicago. She has published widely on ethical issues in the field of pediatrics. Her most recent book is *Children, Families and Health Care Decision Making* (Clarendon Press).

Margaret R. Moon is the Senior Vice President and the Ethics and Medical Director of Doctors Community Healthcare Corporation. Her main interests lie in medical risk management and clinical ethics. In the past she held a dual appointment as Assistant Professor of Pediatrics and Medical Education and Director of the Clinical Ethics Service at the University of Illinois, Chicago.

Clinical genetics is an integral part of pediatrics. Genetic diseases are common in childhood: as many as 53 per 1000 children and young adults can be expected to have diseases with an important genetic component.[1] This rate increases to 79 per 1000 if congenital anomalies are included.[1] In addition, 12% to 40% of all pediatric hospitalizations are for genetic diseases and birth defects.[2–4] Despite its importance in primary care pediatrics, genetics has maintained its subspecialty status. Newborn screening for genetic diseases is the only aspect of genetics that has been incorporated as routine pediatric practice.[5]

Reprinted by permission of the authors and the publisher from the *Archives of Pediatrics and Adolescent Medicine* 154 (September 2000), 873–79. Copyright © 2000, American Medical Association.

The Human Genome Project is expanding knowledge of the genetic basis of disease at an incredible rate, and one by-product has been the development of new technology that makes widespread genetic testing feasible. Because there are not enough geneticists or genetic counselors to provide adequate counseling, primary care physicians will need to increase their knowledge about genetics and become the frontline providers of some of these services.[6] However, many primary care pediatricians are currently ill prepared to provide genetic counseling.[7–10] Even beyond the necessary medical knowledge, the development of new genetic technology raises ethical and social policy concerns that further challenge the primary care physician.[11,12]

The goal of this article is to help prepare pediatricians to respond to the ethical and policy challenges raised by the new genetics. Recent developments in genetics do not necessarily create new ethical concerns, but they highlight how social, political, and economic factors affect the implementation, use, and regulation of new biotechnologies. The ethical implications of these decisions need to be explored at the macro and micro levels. At the macro level, we examine the current policies and consensus statements regarding genetic testing of children, although our main focus is to provide pediatricians with a framework with which to interpret genetic testing in their own practice. Specifically, we examine the ethical issues raised in 3 clinical scenarios: (1) diagnostic genetic testing, (2) population-based genetic screening, and (3) carrier identification. The decision-making process is also described by 3 decision trees.

ETHICS OVERVIEW

To date, the Human Genome Project's greatest successes have been in gene discovery and the development of commercial genetic tests; gene therapy is still in an early experimental stage. Genetic testing of children can occur for a variety of reasons and in a variety of contexts, each of which raises a myriad of ethical questions, particularly with respect to consent and confidentiality.

Traditionally in pediatric medicine, parents are presumed to be best suited to make decisions for their children. Various arguments have been made to support parental control over medical decision making for minor children.[13–15] First, parents are presumed to have the child's best interests at heart, because they naturally care deeply for their children and because they are in a position to know the child best. Second, for parents to fulfill the responsibilities of child rearing, they need significant leeway in how they rear their children. This includes control over decisions about medical care, provided that the parents and their decisions are neither abusive nor neglectful. In part, this parental discretion is supported by the fact that many of the financial and emotional consequences of these decisions will be borne most heavily by the child and his or her parents. Third, society has an interest in supporting the family as the primary child-rearing institution. To do so requires that families be afforded a wide degree of privacy and freedom from governmental intrusion.

One constraint on parental control lies in our evolving understanding of children's autonomy and their role in the informed consent process. Historically, health care providers have downplayed the child's capacity for decision making, but the current attitude is to give greater weight to the child's developing decision-making capacity[16,17] and future autonomy.[18] We rely on parents to make decisions for their children while remaining open to the possibility that the child may have something important to add. However, parental autonomy is not and should not be absolute. The American Academy of Pediatrics argues that there are some situations in which parents should not be empowered to consent on their child's behalf and other situations in which the child's dissent ought to be binding.[16] Although the American Academy of Pediatrics does not make specific reference to genetic services, there are some genetics cases in which the parents' and child's interests may be in conflict. Evaluating parental requests requires finding the appropriate balance between the child's present and future needs and interests with the interests and needs of the families.[19–22]

Part of what makes genetics unique, however, is that knowledge about one family member might have great significance for other family members. To view decisions about genetic testing in the context of a single patient ignores the relationships and obligations that individuals have to those with whom they are genetically related because genetic information often applies to families as much as to individuals.[23,24] Confidentiality of genetic information requires clarification: confidentiality for whom and from whom? This is even more complex in pediatrics because of the role of the parents in the consent process.

In this article, we focus on the question of when genetic testing should be performed on children. Issues pertaining to the appropriate roles for parents and children in the consent process are addressed in another article.[25]

GENETIC SERVICES

TESTING HIGH-RISK CHILDREN

High-risk children are those who are symptomatic or are members of a family at high risk for a known genetic trait or disease.

Genetic testing is least controversial when an individual patient has some identifiable symptom or some specific risk factor that is best diagnosed via genetic testing. The use of genetic testing for confirming clinical diagnoses is indistinguishable from other therapeutic medical tests. The differential diagnosis of a child born with weak muscle tone and a large tongue includes the genetic condition of Down syndrome and the nongenetic condition of hypothyroidism; the former is tested by chromosomal analysis, the latter by endocrine function. The differential diagnosis of a child who has failure to thrive and chronic recurrent upper respiratory tract infections includes cystic fibrosis (CF), an autosomal recessive genetic condition, and acquired immunodeficiency syndrome, a nongenetic condition. In the symptomatic child, human immunodeficiency virus infection may be determined by Western blot or polymerase chain reaction testing (depending on the child's age and maternal antibody status), whereas CF can be diagnosed by measuring sweat chloride levels or by genetic mutational analysis. None of these tests are medically controversial in a symptomatic child provided that adequate consent is obtained.

If a patient has an extra chromosome 21 or 2 CF mutations, the clinician can conclude that the patient has Down syndrome or CF, respectively: the genetic test results confirm the clinical diagnoses. There is little controversy in these genetic tests when performed postnatally to provide appropriate clinical services for the affected child and family.

Contrast such tests with presymptomatic genetic testing used to identify disease in a currently healthy person known to be at risk. Testing for the genes for retinoblastoma or Huntington disease (HD) represent 2 such conditions. Both are autosomal dominant conditions, meaning that there is a 50% probability that an offspring of an affected adult (either symptomatic or presymptomatic) will inherit the gene. Both conditions are virtually 100% penetrant, which means that all individuals with the gene will become symptomatic. In hereditary retinoblastoma, most children present in the first year of life.[26] About 40% of retinoblastoma cases are familial, related to a mutation of a tumor suppressor gene on chromosome 13. Identification allows for targeted surveillance by frequent ophthalmologic examinations to minimize disease morbidity and mortality. The genetic test prevents unnecessary harm because it allows targeting of at-risk children in at-risk families. Children found to be positive for the gene are followed up with frequent ophthalmologic examinations (often under general anesthesia) to try to detect the disease early; children found to be negative for the gene are able to avoid frequent examinations. Without the test, all children in an at-risk family would have to undergo frequent ophthalmologic examinations. The genetic test optimizes treatment by enabling clinicians to focus on truly at-risk children and to avoid unnecessary medical surveillance of low-risk children from high-risk families.

In contrast, childhood onset of HD accounts for less than 5% of all affected individuals.[27] The value of testing children is to minimize uncertainty, to allow a person to incorporate positive or negative status as part of his or her self-concept, and to allow for better lifetime planning.[28,29] The risks to the child who has a positive test result are the potentially serious psychosocial sequelae that this information has on his or her relationships and interactions within the family, school, potential employers, and even with oneself.[28,29] The child who has a negative test result might also experience serious psychosocial sequelae ranging from survivor guilt to the possible social ostracization that occurs when one is perceived as different from siblings and parents.[28,29]

In retinoblastoma and HD, the tests are targeted to populations known to be at risk. The difference, however, is that there are preventive measures and treatments available for children with retinoblastoma, whereas there are neither preventive measures nor treatments that can minimize the morbidity of HD. Most genetic conditions are similar to HD in that they are currently untreatable, and diagnostic testing often offers no clear medical benefit to the patient. This does not mean that testing is necessarily harmful; rather, the calculation of benefit and risk will focus on psychosocial factors.

Retinoblastoma and HD are atypical genetic diseases in that they are almost 100% penetrant. Most genes and associated genetic tests, however, only identify an increased susceptibility, and their expression is widely variable, even within the same family. The probabilistic nature of genetic information adds further complexity to the ethical issues, in part because physicians and patients have a hard time understanding uncertainty and using such information in the decision-making process.[8–10,30] *BRCA1* testing for inheritable breast cancer exemplifies the point. A positive test result for the *BRCA1* gene identifies an increased risk of developing breast or ovarian cancer before age 65 years. In women of Ashkenazi Jewish ancestry with a positive family history, the probability can be as high as 85%.[31] Presymptomatic genetic diagnosis can offer some medical benefit for adult women, who can choose to undergo prophylactic mastectomy and oophorectomy, thereby reducing their chances of disease.[32] But there are currently no preventive measures appropriate for children or adolescents. Individuals who undergo testing for *BRCA1* and *BRCA2*, however, must understand that the gene is neither necessary nor sufficient for the development of breast cancer. *BRCA1* and *BRCA2* account for less than 10% of all breast cancers.[31] Even if a person has one of these inherited genetic predispositions, the fact is that the *BRCA1* mutation is only the first step in the development of breast or ovarian cancer. A "second hit," probably nongenetic, is required for a tumor to develop.[33–35] The nature of the second hit is not well specified, but a significant number of women with the *BRCA1* mutation avoid it.

Individuals who are not members of high-risk families can also test positive for *BRCA1* and *BRCA2*. Although they also have an increased risk of breast cancer compared with the general population, the risk is much lower than for members of high-risk families.[31,36] Parents might want to test their children for these genes because of family history, heightened awareness through an ill friend, or a community educational program. These parents need to know that presymptomatic genetic testing in low-risk families is often difficult to interpret. False-positive screening results might create a lasting burden of worry; alternatively, false-negative screening results might provide undue reassurance. As such, parents who request genetic testing of children for *BRCA1* need extensive counseling about what the test can and cannot do and how the results only provide information about increased or decreased disease susceptibility. A positive test result does not predict whether the disease will affect a particular individual, and it cannot predict at what age it might present, how aggressive the cancer might be, or whether it will be susceptible to standard chemotherapy.

For parents to interpret the risks and benefits of a particular genetic test, they need to understand the differences in (1) genetic testing in a child who is symptomatic, (2) genetic testing for the presence of a virtually 100% penetrant gene that has not yet expressed itself, and (3) genetic testing to determine increased susceptibility to a particular disease. The calculation of risks and benefits must take into account the technological quality of the test, its predictive value, its reliability, and its validity. Genetic technology is developing rapidly and is being introduced into the clinical setting early such that the actual quality of

a test cannot be taken for granted and must be factored into decision making.[7,37,38]

The first step in helping parents calculate the risks and benefits is to delineate the possible medical benefits, if any, of genetic testing. Genetic testing that determines the cause of a child's symptoms has obvious medical benefits if treatments are available; and even if treatments are not available, the diagnosis can serve to prevent unnecessary additional workup. Genetic testing that diagnoses a presymptomatic child or a child with a genetic predisposition also has medical benefits when preventive or therapeutic measures are available at an early stage. But for most other genetic testing, there are no medical benefits. Even when genetic testing offers medical benefits, it is accompanied by and must be balanced with the possible medical risks created by false-negative and false-positive results.[7,39]

The next step is to consider the psychosocial benefits and risks. Empirical data on the emotional and psychosocial benefits and risks are inadequate and hard to come by. These issues are further complicated by the long time lag between genetic testing and diagnosis in childhood vs disease presentation in adulthood. The potential psychosocial benefits are (1) family uncertainty about the future can be reduced; (2) planning for the future can be more practical; and (3) parental expectations for the child's future can be more "realistic."[28,29] The potential psychosocial risks include (1) the possibility of stigmatization associated with genetic abnormality, even in the absence of phenotypic abnormality; (2) the potential for inhibiting parent-child bonding; (3) disruption of normal family relationships because of guilt on the part of parents or on behalf of the unaffected siblings (so-called survivor guilt); (4) the potential for a variation of the "vulnerable child syndrome"; and (5) modification of parental expectations (often subconsciously).[28,29] Little empirical data are available about how parents quantify the risks and benefits of presymptomatic and susceptibility testing in their children or how these children develop in contrast to their peers who were not diagnosed in childhood.

Other risks that must be incorporated into decisions about genetic testing include risks of discrimination related to genotypic abnormalities, even if the condition is not 100% penetrant, and concerns about the long-term privacy of genetic information. As a society, we are only in the early stages of understanding the relationship of genotype-phenotype correlation and the interaction of various genotypes with the environment. But this has not stopped different institutions from using this information in a discriminatory manner.[40–42]

Given that a risk-benefit analysis of most genetic tests will not yield an easy or obvious decision, pediatricians must learn to help their families navigate this decision-making process. Figure 1 summarizes a basic algorithm for decisions about genetic testing for children with known risk factors or symptoms. Genetic tests performed on children with symptoms or known risk factors that have immediate medical benefit to the child are ethically noncontroversial, despite the potential for psychosocial disruption. As medical benefits become less available, genetic testing becomes more controversial. The decision, however, whether to test a child will also take into account the psychosocial benefits and risks of testing for the child and the family. Although the values of the family are paramount, the pediatrician can help the family by ensuring that the whole range of possible scenarios is examined and that the family considers all of the possible implications and repercussions of testing.

The importance of the psychosocial analysis must not be underestimated. In many ways, the medical benefit of genetic testing in pediatric patients is the simple question. More important and more difficult to know is the impact of testing, both immediate and long-term, on the child and family. Although some would argue that all requests for genetic tests that do not offer obvious and immediate medical benefit should be refused, we do not. It is conceivable that the psychosocial benefit of a test, even a test that has little or no medical benefit, might be decisive for a particular family. We believe that pediatricians need to work with families to ensure that they understand what the test does and does not offer and to ensure that the family has considered all the potential consequences and repercussions such information might have on the child during childhood and adulthood as well as on the family unit. Although we would tend to discourage parents from pursuing genetic information that offers no medical benefit, we realize that parents, not clinicians, must ultimately decide what is in the child's best interest. This includes weighing medical and nonmedical factors, many of which the pediatrician might not be cognizant of for this particular family in its particular circumstances.

GENETIC SCREENING

Genetic screening, in contrast to genetic testing, refers to testing whole populations for disease, usually without regard to particular risk factors. Population-based screening of children is most commonly done in the newborn period but can be done at other stages. Newborn screening is performed for a variety of medical conditions, both genetic and nongenetic. For example, thyroid disease, a nonmendelian condition, is included in all newborn state screens,[5] and the National Institutes of Health and the American Academy of Pediatrics recommend universal newborn screening for hearing loss in children that might or might not be genetic in origin.[43,44] Beyond the newborn period, it is also recommended that pediatricians screen targeted populations of children for lead[45,46] and tuberculosis.[47]

Newborn screening is an integral part of pediatrics. The list of genetic diseases varies by state, but screening for phenylketonuria, hemoglobinopathies, and galactosemia is nearly universal in the United States.[5] In 1994, the Institute of Medicine (IOM) recommended that population-based (newborn) screening programs fulfill 3 criteria: (1) there is a clear indication of benefit to the newborn, (2) a system is in place to confirm the diagnosis, and (3) treatment and

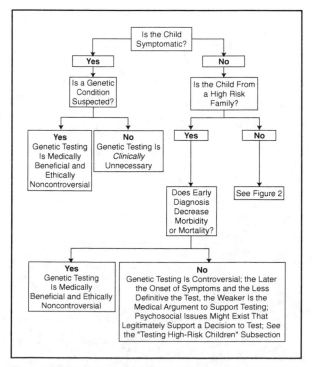

Figure 1.   Genetic testing in high-risk children (i.e., children who have symptoms or are from a high-risk family).

follow-up are available for affected newborns. Additional criteria to justify screening whole populations include (1) that the condition is frequent and severe enough to be a public health concern; (2) that the condition causes a known spectrum of symptoms; and (3) that the screening test is simple and reliable, with low false-positive and false-negative rates.[11]

Medical data show that newborn screening for most conditions included in state screens is beneficial in reducing morbidity and mortality. In that regard, we support such testing, although we are against the current policy that mandates such testing without parental consent. We support parental consent because it gives authority to the parents, who are the appropriate surrogate decision-makers for their children.[39,48] Through the consent process, the parents would be informed about the conditions for which testing is offered, why follow-up might be necessary, and why follow-up should be done early. Currently, parental consent is sought in Maryland only, where fewer than 1 parent in 1000 refuses testing for their newborns.[49] Although this creates a possibility that an affected child will not be screened, the probability is much lower than the chance of missing an affected child because of a false-negative test result or because the specimen was inadequate or lost.[50]

An even more serious challenge for the future, however, is to evaluate carefully all new proposals for population-based screening programs, and not to institutionalize programs that do not meet, at minimum, the criteria enumerated by the IOM. Historically, newborn screens have not fulfilled these criteria at the time of implementation. For example, when newborn screening for sickle cell disease was first initiated, there was no known benefit to presymptomatic diagnosis.[11] Now that penicillin prophylaxis has been shown to reduce morbidity and mortality, newborn screening for sickle cell disease is a paradigm case of justifiable universal screening,[51] but that does not justify its earlier implementation. Even today, governments continue to test for conditions for which newborn testing has not been shown to benefit the newborn. For example, 2 states in the United States screen for CF despite the fact that data do not show that early initiation of therapy changes the course of disease.[52,53] In some countries, children are tested for Duchenne muscular dystrophy although there are no known early treatments.[54] The justification is to educate couples about their future reproductive risks.

Early diagnosis can benefit the affected child because it will avoid unnecessary workup when symptoms develop. However, early diagnosis might place the child at risk because the parents might now view their healthy-appearing child as ill or even doomed and might bond poorly or otherwise neglect him or her. We believe that the expansion of universal newborn testing to these conditions is not warranted because the risks to the child, and possibly to the family, might outweigh the benefits.

On the other hand, there may be some genetic conditions that might not warrant universal screening because the cost of the test is too great or the cost-benefit analysis on a universal basis does not justify it. This does not mean, however, that genetic testing for this condition should never be offered. If there are identifiable groups who may be at increased risk for whom early diagnosis can decrease morbidity and mortality (eg, maple syrup urine disease in the Amish population or Gaucher disease in the Ashkenazi Jewish population), the medical benefits may support screening in these targeted populations. Even in low-risk communities, parental requests for specific genetic testing of their newborn may be justifiable. For example, we believe that parental anxiety alone may justify genetic testing, particularly when the condition is treatable. Parents who seek broad-spectrum testing of their newborn, however, need to be counseled that even the exclusion of a large number of genetic and nongenetic conditions does not promise a healthy child.

Our recommendations for universal screening are summarized in Figure 2, where we point out that,

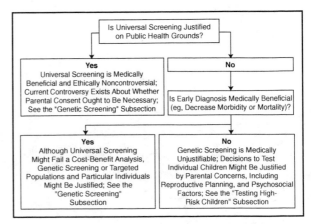

Figure 2. Genetic screening and testing in low-risk children (i.e., children who are asymptomatic and are from a low-risk family).

even when universal screening cannot be justified from a medical cost-benefit analysis, screening targeted populations or testing particular children may still be ethically permissible. Again, the final determination will depend on the psychosocial benefit-risk calculation made by the parents with appropriate counseling.

IDENTIFICATION OF CARRIER STATUS

All individuals carry several recessive genes that would prove lethal to a fetus if it received a double dose.[55] We all carry other recessive genes that are not lethal in the homozygous state but cause serious diseases. Carriers of recessive genes are often asymptomatic and unaware that they carry particular genes. For most recessive genetic traits, being a carrier confers no known medical morbidity. As such, tests to identify carrier status are not intended to provide a medical benefit to the patient, but they serve to provide information that may be important for reproductive decisions.

Carrier testing is most often done in the prenatal setting. Sometimes, however, carrier status is determined incidentally. For example, every child with a quantifiable amount of hemoglobin S on newborn screening in the United States is retested. Hemoglobin electrophoresis determines whether they are homozygous (sickle cell anemia) or heterozygous (sickle cell trait) for hemoglobin S. Currently, parents in the United States are told if their child is a carrier. This disclosure is not without controversy: the IOM recommends that parents not be told their child's trait status.[11] The IOM's justification is that the information has no clinical relevance but solely reproductive relevance, for which the child has a right to privacy and a right not to know.[11] We disagree with the IOM's recommendation insofar as it implies that the state has more right to information about a child than does his or her parents. Parents who receive such information need appropriate counseling to understand the distinction between clinical and reproductive relevance of this information so that they do not erroneously treat their child as "diseased" and can counsel their child effectively. Nevertheless, we also believe that there is a need for longitudinal research to determine the impact such knowledge has on children and adolescents and their families during the life cycle so that any policy changes can be based on empirical analysis of harms and benefits.

If informing parents of trait status when the information is determined incidentally is controversial,

even more controversial is whether parents electively can request to test their children for carrier status. Often the interest is prompted by the diagnosis of a sibling or other relative with the disease.[56] We consider the possible scenarios and the framework with which to respond in Figure 3.

The arguments in favor of honoring the parents' requests are that being informed of carrier status in childhood might make it easier to accept that status and incorporate it into one's personal identity[57]; that it might be useful for other family members[58]; and that parents, not the state, are in a better position to decide if the benefits of knowledge outweigh the risks for a particular child.[25] The main arguments for refusing a parental request for carrier state testing are that it frustrates the child's right not to know as an

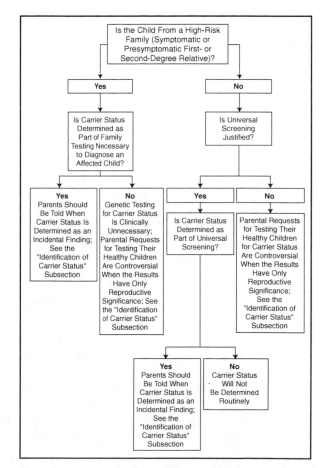

Figure 3. Genetic testing for carrier status (i.e., an autosomal recessive or sex-linked condition in which the carrier status confers no or minimal risk of morbidity or mortality but is important for reproductive decisions).

adult, it fails to respect the child's right to confidential reproductive knowledge, it may adversely impact the child's self-concept, and it may expose the child to unwarranted genetic discrimination. There is also concern that parental misunderstanding of test results will lead to treating the child who is a carrier as an ill or potentially ill child.[57]

Although we would neither encourage nor recommend carrier testing of children solely for informational purposes, we would not want to make a blanket prohibition of such testing in children. Rather, we are willing to respect parental requests, following appropriate counseling, on the grounds that they know what is best for the child and the family. Again, the importance of longitudinal research on the impact of such knowledge over the life cycle cannot be underestimated. Pediatricians need this information to help counsel families who request carrier testing of their children. In fact, we would be willing to reconsider our position if research found that knowledge of carrier status caused more harm than benefit for most children during the life cycle.

CONCLUSIONS

There are many different flavors of genetic testing: testing can be targeted or universalized in statewide screening programs; testing may uncover disease risk for which treatments may or may not exist or it may uncover information that has relevance only in the reproductive context; and testing may yield results of varying predictive value. Genetic testing is complicated because knowledge about one family member can have significant impact on other family members. This is further complicated in pediatrics because the decisions can have lifelong repercussions for the individual who did not consent himself or herself to this testing. Further research on the psychosocial and ethical implications of genetic information is needed to ensure that policies are designed that meet our needs as individuals and as members of families, communities, and society-at-large. In addition, primary care pediatricians need to familiarize themselves with the scientific and the psychosocial data regarding genetic services to better serve children and their families.

REFERENCES

1. Baird P. A., Anderson T. W., Newcombe H. B., Lowry R. B. Genetic disorders in children and young adults: a population study. *Am J Hum Genet.* 1988;42:677–93.

2. Hall J. G., Powers E. K., McIlvaine R. T., Ean V. H. The frequency and financial burden of genetic disease in a pediatric hospital. *Am J Med Genet.* 1978;1:417–436.

3. Scriver C. R., Neal J. L., Saginur R., Clow A. The frequency of genetic disease and congenital malformation among patients in a pediatric hospital. *CMAJ.* 1973;108:1111–1115.

4. Yoon P. W., Olney R. S., Khoury M. J., Sappenfield W. M., Chavez G. F., Taylor D. Contributions of birth defects and genetic diseases to pediatric hospitalizations: a population-based study. *Arch Pediatr Adolesc Med.* 1997;151:1096–1103.

5. American Academy of Pediatrics, Committee on Genetics. Newborn screening fact sheet. *Pediatrics.* 1996;98: 473–501.

6. Holtzman N. A. Primary care physicians as providers of frontline genetic services. *Fetal Diagn Ther.* 1993;8(suppl 1):213–219.

7. Holtzman N. A. *Proceed With Caution: Predicting Genetic Risks in the Recombinant DNA Era.* Baltimore, Md: The Johns Hopkins University Press; 1989.

8. Hofman K. J., Tambor E. S., Chase G. A., Geller G., Faden R. R., Holtzman N. A. Physicians' knowledge of genetics and genetic tests. *Acad Med.* 1993;68:625–632.

9. Giardiello F. M., Brensinger J. D., Petersen G. M., et al. The use and interpretation of commercial APC gene testing for familial adenomatous polyposis. *N Engl J Med.* 1997; 336:823–827.

10. Rowley P. T., Loader S., Levenkron J. C., Phelps C. E. Cystic fibrosis carrier screening: knowledge and attitudes of prenatal care providers. *Am J Prev Med.* 1993;9:261–266.

11. Andrews L., Fullarton J., Holtzman N., Motulsky A., eds. *Assessing Genetic Risks: Implications for Health and Social Policy.* Washington, DC: National Academy Press; 1994.

12. Marteau T., Richards M., eds. *The Troubled Helix: Social and Psychological Implications of the New Human Genetics.* New York, NY: Cambridge University Press; 1996.

13. Buchanan A., Brock D. *Deciding for Others: The Ethics of Surrogate Decision Making.* New York, NY: Cambridge University Press; 1990.

14. Blustein J. *Parents and Children: The Ethics of the Family.* New York, NY: Oxford University Press Inc; 1982.

15. Ross L. F. *Parents, Children, and Health Care Decision Making.* Oxford, England: Oxford University Press; 1998.

16. American Academy of Pediatrics, Committee on Bioethics. Informed consent, parental permission, and assent in pediatric practice. *Pediatrics.* 1995;95:314–317.

17. Alderson P., Montgomery J. *Health Care Choices: Making Decisions With Children.* London, England: Institute for Public Policy Research; 1996.

18. Feinberg J. The child's right to an open future. In: Aiken W., LaFollette H., eds. *Whose Child? Children's Rights, Parental Authority, and State Power.* Totowa, NJ: Littlefield, Adams & Co; 1980:124–153.

19. Sharpe N. F. Presymptomatic testing for Huntington disease: is there a duty to test those under the age of eighteen years? *Am J Med Genet.* 1993;46:250–253.

20. Patenaude A. F. The genetic testing of children for cancer susceptibility: ethical, legal and social issues. *Behav Sci Law.* 1996;14:393–410.

21. Cohen C. B. Wrestling with the future: should we test children for adult-onset genetic conditions? *Kennedy Inst Ethics J.* 1998;8:111–130.

22. Davis D. S. Genetic dilemmas and the child's right to an open future. *Rutgers Law J.* 1997;28:549–592.

23. American Society of Human Genetics Social Issues Subcommittee on Familial Disclosure. ASHG statement: professional disclosure of familial genetic information. *Am J Hum Genet.* 1998;62:474–483.

24. Deftos L. J. The evolving duty to disclose the presence of genetic disease to relatives. *Acad Med.* 1998;73:962–968.

25. Ross L. F. Genetic testing of children: who should consent? In: Burley J., Harris J., eds. *A Companion to Genethics: Ethics and the Genetic Revolution.* Oxford, England: Blackwell Publishers; 2000. Companions to Philosophy Series.

26. Birch J. M. Genes and cancer. *Arch Dis Child.* 1999;80:1–3.

27. Baraitser M. Huntington's chorea. In: Baraitser M., ed. *The Genetics of Neurological Disorders.* Oxford, England: Oxford Medical Publications; 1990:308–323.

28. American Society of Human Genetics Board of Directors and American College of Medical Genetics Board of Directors. ASHG/ACMG report: points to consider: ethical, legal and psychosocial implications of genetic testing in children and adolescents. *Am J Hum Genet.* 1995; 57:1233–1241.

29. Report of a Working Party of the Clinical Genetics Society (UK). The genetic testing of children. *J Med Genet.* 1994;31:785–797.

30. Davison C. Predictive genetics: the cultural implications of supplying probable futures. In: Marteau T., Richards M., eds. *The Troubled Helix: Social and Psychological Implications of the New Human Genetics.* Cambridge, England: Cambridge University Press; 1996:317–330.

31. Burke W., Daly M., Garber J., et al. Consensus statement: recommendations for follow-up care of individuals with an inherited predisposition to cancer, II: *BRCA1* and *BRCA2. JAMA.* 1997;277:997–1003.

32. Hartmann L. C., Schaid D. J., Woods J. E., et al. Efficacy of bilateral prophylactic mastectomy in women with a family history of breast cancer. *N Engl J Med.* 1999;340:77–84.

33. Armitage P., Doll R. A two-stage theory of carcinogenesis in relation to the age distribution of human cancer. *Br J Cancer.* 1957;11:161–169.

34. Ashley D. J. B. The two "hit" and multiple "hit" theories of carcinogenesis. *Br J Cancer.* 1969;23:313–328.

35. Knudson A. G. Hereditary cancer: two hits revisited. *J Cancer Res Clin Oncol.* 1996;122:135–140.

36. Malone K. E., Daling J. R., Thompson J. D., O'Brien C. A., Francisco L. V., Ostrander E. A. *BRCA1* mutations and breast cancer in the general population. *JAMA.* 1998;279:922–929.

37. Task Force on Genetic Testing. *Promoting Safe and Effective Genetic Testing in the United States: Final Report.* Baltimore, Md: The Johns Hopkins University Press; 1998.

38. Holtzman N. A., Murphy P. D., Watson M. S., Barr P. A. Predictive genetic testing: from basic research to clinical practice. *Science.* 1997;278:602–605.

39. Paul D. Contesting consent: the challenge to compulsory neonatal screening for PKU. *Perspect Biol Med.* 1999;42:207–219.

40. Billings P. R., Kohn M. A., de Cuevas J., Beckwith J., Alper J. S., Natowicz M. R. Discrimination as a consequence of genetic testing. *Am J Hum Genet.* 1992;50:476–482.

41. Duster T. *Backdoor to Eugenics.* New York, NY: Routledge; 1990.

42. Draper E. *Risky Business: Genetic Testing and Exclusionary Practices in the Hazardous Workplace.* New York, NY: Cambridge University Press; 1991.

43. NIH Consensus Statement. Early identification of hearing impairment in infants and young children. *NIH Consens Statement.* 1993;11:1–24.

44. American Academy of Pediatrics Joint Committee on Infant Hearing. Joint Committee on Infant Hearing 1994 position statement. *Pediatrics.* 1995;95:152–156.

45. American Academy of Pediatrics. Lead poisoning from screening to primary prevention. *Pediatrics.* 1993;92: 176–183.

46. Centers for Disease Control. *Preventing Lead Poisoning in Young Children.* Atlanta, Ga: US Dept of Health and Human Services; 1991.

47. American Academy of Pediatrics, Committee on Infectious Diseases. Update on tuberculosis skin testing of children. *Pediatrics.* 1996;97:282–284.

48. Annas G. J. Mandatory PKU screening: the other side of the looking glass. *Am J Public Health.* 1982;72:1401–1403.

49. Faden R., Chwalow J., Holtzman N. A., Horn S. D. A survey to evaluate parental consent as public policy for neonatal screening. *Am J Public Health.* 1982;72:1347–1352.

50. Holtzman N. A., Leonard C. O., Farfel M. R. Issues in antenatal and neonatal screening and surveillance for hereditary and congenital disorders. *Annu Rev Public Health.* 1981; 2:219–251.

51. Consensus Conference. Newborn screening for sickle cell disease and other hemoglobinopathies. *JAMA.* 1987; 258:1205–1209.

52. Genetic testing for cystic fibrosis. *NIH Consens US Statement.* 1997;15:1–37.

53. Wald N. J., Morris J. K. Neonatal screening for cystic fibrosis. *BMJ.* 1998;316:40–45.

54. Bradley D. M., Parsons E. P., Clarke A. J. Experience with screening newborns for Duchenne muscular dystrophy in Wales. *BMJ.* 1993;306:357–360.

55. Lee J. K., Lascoux M., Nordheim E. V. Number of lethal equivalents in human populations: how good are the previous estimates? *Heredity.* 1996;77:209–216.

56. Balfour-Lynn I., Madge S., Dinwiddie R. Testing carrier status in siblings of patients with cystic fibrosis. *Arch Dis Child.* 1995;72:167–168.

57. Fanos J. H. Developmental tasks of childhood and adolescence: implications for genetic testing. *Am J Med Genet.* 1997;71:22–28.

58. Bowman J. E. Genetics and African Americans. *Seton Hall Law Rev.* 1997;27:919–937.

THEODORE FRIEDMANN

Principles for Human Gene Therapy Studies

Theodore Friedmann is Professor of Pediatrics and Whitehill Professor of Biomedical Ethics at the University of California, San Diego (UCSD) and Director of the UCSD Program in Human Gene Therapy. He was one of the first to publish on the need for gene therapy for human disease. He is currently Chair of the NIH Recombinant DNA Advisory Committee.

The human gene therapy community finds itself struggling with technical and policy problems arising from several recently publicized adverse events in human gene therapy studies. The current discussion was catalyzed by the tragic death of Jesse Gelsinger, an 18-year-old patient with ornithine transcarbamylase (OTC) deficiency who died, apparently as a direct result of the experimental gene therapy studies being carried out by investigators at the University of Pennsylvania in Philadelphia and the National Children's Medical Center in Washington, DC.

Preliminary public review of the events leading to the tragedy in the Philadelphia OTC study was presented at a recent public meeting of the Recombinant DNA Advisory Committee (RAC) of the Office of Biotechnology Activities (OBA) of the National Institutes of Health. An ongoing Food and Drug Administration (FDA) investigation has already resulted in a compulsory hold of indefinite duration being placed on gene therapy studies at the Institute for Human Gene Therapy at the University of Pennsylvania and a voluntary hold on at least one other academic institution until possible deficiencies can be corrected. One commercially sponsored study was placed on temporary hold but now has been resumed. Additional inquiries by the involved universities, the Advisory Committee to the Director of the NIH, the United States Senate, and the executive branch are under way.

These events suggest that the gene therapy community has not fully succeeded in developing mechanisms to ensure the highest possible quality of clinical research. The intention of this discussion is to derive lessons from the preliminary information available and to reexamine the principles that constitute the foundation of clinical research in gene therapy.

HUMAN EXPERIMENTATION REQUIRES CAREFUL PATIENT SELECTION AND PROTECTION

Human disease and therapy are, eventually, best studied in human subjects. Codes of medical ethics recognize the importance of appropriate human studies, as long as they rest on strong basic and preclinical science and voluntary informed consent by patients. To be truly "informed," a patient's consent must be based on current and complete information of the procedures and their potential risks and benefits.

The patient population with potentially the most to gain in the Philadelphia OTC study, patients with the neonatal lethal form of the disease, were justifiably included in the initial study design. However, investigators were advised by their institutional review board (IRB) and medical ethics consultants that phase I experiments (in which dose and safety are being tested) would be ethically unacceptable in these infants because of the danger of implying a potential benefit to desperate parents. The next-best study population was used instead—less severely affected older patients from whom informed consent and meaningful data might be more readily obtained. There is debate in the medical ethics community whether this decision to exclude desperately ill newborns was appropriate. The quandary of patient selection in this case underscores this general dilemma in medical ethics and the unrealistic degree to which we have come to expect therapeutic results in phase I studies.

HUMAN EXPERIMENTATION INVOLVES RISKS

Human experimental studies, genetic or otherwise, are "experimental" precisely because the results are not known beforehand. Preclinical studies sometimes indicate adverse outcomes that can be readily avoided. In other instances, adverse results are found, only in retrospect, to have been foreshadowed by clues during early testing that investigators were neither alert nor wise enough to appreciate. In still other studies, adverse outcomes could not have been predicted in animals and limited human trials. Preclinical studies did not predict the discovery that the diet medication fen-phen is associated with potentially life-threatening cardiac valvular damage. Likewise, the recent withdrawal from the market by the FDA of a rotavirus vaccine came only after large-scale human experience with the vaccine.

ADVERSE RESULTS DO NOT INVALIDATE THE RATIONALE OF GENE THERAPY

Apparent "failures" in early phaseI/II or even phase III studies do not necessarily indicate a therapeutic wild-goose chase. Because gene therapy is highly experimental and many patients are desperately ill, serious adverse events and even deaths will occur. It is vital to understand the reasons for unexpected results or clinical failures to allow the development of corrected procedures and improved experimental methods. For example, problems with polio vaccines due to persistence of live disease-causing poliovirus in incompletely inactivated preparations and the presence of SV40 in the vaccine were identified early, corrected, and used to develop improved programs.

The development of gene therapy is similar to vaccine and drug development. Drug development is difficult and expensive, and gene therapy will not be simpler. The pharmaceutical industry, more mature and experienced than the gene therapy community, devotes enormous research and financial resources to studies of the biodistribution, pharmacological properties, stability, and metabolic properties of a potential new drug, as well as the physiological, immunological, and teratogenic effects on the host. Despite such care, because of the enormous complexity of hu-

man physiology and disease, and because even the most extensive animal data do not always faithfully predict responses in humans, adverse clinical responses have occurred and will again. The same understanding of pharmacokinetics and mechanisms has not been available for gene therapy trials. Some clinical applications have simply outstripped scientific understanding of the disease model or the properties of the vectors, resembling an army too far ahead of its supply lines. Despite clinical urgency, there is a need to develop a similar degree of rigor for gene transfer agents as for small molecule therapeutics or viral vaccines.

Despite the caveats regarding the need for better knowledge, the search for optimum methods should not paralyze attempts to use available tools to conduct clinical research studies. To make progress, one must accept the limitations of knowledge and simultaneously use available information to ease suffering and to continue research into improvements in technology.

INFORMED CONSENT IS CRUCIAL TO PATIENT PROTECTION

The single most important mechanism for ensuring patient protection from inherent risks of clinical experiments, unrealistic expectations, and potential conflicts of interest of the investigator is accurate and full disclosure of potential risks and benefits and a well-executed informed consent process. For gene therapy studies, the FDA and RAC review the adequacy of locally approved informed consent procedures during the protocol approval process. The FDA concluded that there were deficiencies in the informed consent process in the OTC study that resulted in incomplete disclosure of all potential risks to the subjects or their families. Additional troublesome public revelations of potential lapses in quality control and in patient protection have been made for other gene therapy studies.

Exaggerated expectations and potential conflicts of interest of investigators pose additional problems to the informed consent process. In 1995, an NIH advisory committee chaired by Stuart Orkin and Arno Motulsky criticized the gene therapy community for its overly optimistic public portrayal of gene therapy experiments and for unsubstantiated claims for efficacy.[1] There is still too ready a tendency by some in the gene therapy community to exaggerate potential benefits at the expense of full disclosure of potential risks. If that tendency is the result of optimism, it is at least unfortunate and should be guarded against. If it was determined that risks were intentionally omitted or misstated, appropriate sanctions by the gene therapy community and oversight bodies should be applied.

DEALING WITH FINANCIAL CONFLICT OF INTEREST

The issue of conflicts of interest is magnified by the very large role that biotechnology and pharmaceutical industries have come to play in gene therapy. In many cases, academic investigators have had to forge commercial collaborations to implement clinical studies because of the high costs (production and testing of a gene vector usually exceeds several hundred thousand dollars). Although commercial interactions have facilitated clinical studies, they have also introduced corporate financial interests and investigator economic conflicts. Therefore, at minimum, involved investigators should disclose direct commercial ties in the informed consent process. Those investigators with direct financial interest in the study outcome should recuse themselves from patient selection, the informed consent process, and study direction.

IMPROVEMENTS ARE NEEDED IN REVIEW AND REGULATION

During the early phase of clinical studies of human gene transfer, the RAC played a major role by providing an avenue for public evaluation of the scientific basis and patient protection aspects of a proposed study. The FDA shared responsibility for oversight of gene therapy studies through its traditional regulatory function of ensuring safety and efficacy. In 1997, in response to an advisory committee report to the NIH director, the FDA assumed the principal regulatory and oversight responsibility for gene therapy proposals, and the RAC was given the function of catalyzing public awareness and understanding of the issues of gene therapy. It also retained a secondary responsibility to determine whether studies submitted to the FDA utilized technological concepts and tools so novel that they required further public review.

An important difference between the RAC and FDA processes is that the RAC reviews of proposals and adverse-event reporting are public and open, whereas FDA is required by statute to carry out these functions privately and without provision for public disclosure. In a field as immature and filled with public interest and concern as gene therapy, more, rather than less, public review seems desirable. A cohesive mechanism must be developed in which primary regulatory control stays with the appropriate regulatory agency—the FDA—but which more effectively takes advantage of the advisory role of the RAC or a RAC-like body and also uses the RAC as a conduit for public discussion and disclosure before protocol approval. It is encouraging that discussions are under way between the RAC, FDA, and NIH through the Advisory Committee to the NIH director on potential mechanisms to provide this kind of process.

GENE THERAPY TRIALS REQUIRE IMPROVED MONITORING

For the field to progress, investigators must have more ready access to the clinical experience in other studies, and it is therefore particularly encouraging that the OBA has reaffirmed its intention to develop a gene therapy database that will make the occurrence and nature of adverse events available online to other gene therapy investigators.[2] Such a database can only succeed if investigators report their adverse events, and disclosure is useful only if mechanisms exist to collate, evaluate, and promulgate such information.

The existence of widely different reporting requirements has contributed to uncertainty and, quite probably, to deficiencies in reporting. The FDA requires that serious, unexpected, or related events be reported to the agency within 7 days if there is a patient death, or within 15 days for other serious adverse events. All other events are to be included in annual reports.[3] The words "serious," "unexpected," and "related" allow room for interpretation by investigators and study sponsors; the NIH requirements are less flexible. It is therefore possible, as the oversight agencies and several investigators have recently discovered, to be in compliance with the FDA requirements but not with the NIH guidelines. The NIH has recently proposed strengthening its reporting requirements through amendments of the NIH guidelines in which the definition of adverse events is clarified, and there is notification that such reports may not contain any confidential trade secrets or commercial and financial information.[4] The NIH has also notified all federally supported institutions to review their policies and procedures to ensure that they are in compliance with reporting requirements.[5] The FDA has stated that it will notify the RAC of the receipt of all adverse events in a gene therapy study.[6]

CONCLUSIONS

Scientific and policy problems in gene therapy studies, together with the explosive growth of clinical studies, challenge the academic gene therapy community, commercial biotechnology and pharmaceutical firms, regulatory agencies, and professional societies such as the American Society of Human Gene Therapy to work together to improve current practices and infrastructures. Announcements of new initiatives for FDA and NIH that would require earlier review of researcher's plans for monitoring safety and quarterly meetings to promote communication are encouraging developments. Further critical steps toward that goal would include RAC determination of the need for full public evaluation of protocols before investigational new drug (IND) assignment by FDA and IRB approval; the development of a single, uniform mechanism for reporting adverse events to the RAC, FDA, and other relevant agencies; establishment by OBA of its proposed public database of all adverse events; and nonparticipation of investigators with financial interests in study outcomes in patient selection, the informed consent process, and direct management of clinical studies. While there is need for improvements, there is also much to celebrate—major technical advances that promise imminent proof that the lives of patients can eventually be made better by gene therapy.

REFERENCES AND NOTES

1. S. Orkin and A. Motulsky, www.nih.gov/news/panelrep.html, 7 December 1995.
2. Testimony of A. Patterson, www4.od.nih.gov/oba/patterson2-00.pdf, 2 February 2000.
3. FDA Manual of Regulatory Standard Operating Procedures and Policies, www.fda.gov/cber/regsopp/91101.htm; www.fda.gov/cber/regsopp/91102.htm; and www.fda.gov/cber/ind/21cfr312.pdf.
4. Minutes of RAC meeting, 5 September 1999, www4.od.nih.gov/oba/9%2D99pro.htm.
5. Letter from A. Patterson to federally funded institutions, 22 November 1999.
6. Letter from K. Zoon to Investigational New Drug Sponsors and Principal Investigators, www.fda.gov/cber/ltr/gt110599.htm, 5 November 1999.

NIKUNJ SOMIA AND INDER M. VERMA

Gene Therapy: Trials and Tribulations

Ninkunj Somia was formerly a research associate at the Salk Institute working with Inder Verma. He is currently an Assistant Professor at the University of Minnesota. His research interests lie in gene therapy, and in particular, the targeting of retroviral vectors to specific cell types. More recently he has been developing novel uses for these vectors in the area of functional genomics.

Inder Verma is Professor and Co-Director of the Laboratory of Genetics at the Salk Institute, as well as Adjunct Professor of Biology at the University of California, San Diego. He has published extensively on the molecular basis for oncogenesis and on human gene therapy.

The basic concept of gene therapy is disarmingly simple—introduce the gene, and its product should cure or slow down the progression of a disease. Encompassed within this idea are a number of goals, including the treatment of both inherited and acquired disease. This approach requires a technology capable of gene transfer in a wide variety of cells, tissues and whole organs, but the delivery vehicles needed to ferry genetic material into a cell still represent the "Achilles heel" of gene therapy. An ideal vector should have the attributes outlined in Box 1. At present, not all of these attributes can be found in any one vector, although distinct classes of vector have different combinations of attributes.

The vectors available now fall into two broad categories—the non-viral and viral vectors. Non-viral vectors include naked DNA and LIPOSOMES.[1] Although non-viral vectors can be produced in relatively large amounts, and are likely to present fewer toxic or immunological problems, they suffer from inefficient gene transfer at present. Furthermore, expression of the foreign gene is transient. Given the need, in many diseases, for sustained and often high-level expression of the transgene, viral vectors are the most suitable vehicles for efficient gene delivery. . . .

• • •

IMMUNE RESPONSE: THE BANE OF GENE THERAPY

The biggest challenge facing all viral vectors is the immune response of the host. The host defence mechanism functions at both the cellular level, by generating cytotoxic T cells, and at the humoral level, by generating antibodies to viral proteins. Cellular immunity eliminates the transduced cells, whereas humoral immunity precludes the repeat administration of the vector because the subsequent antibody response will be boosted by MEMORY CELLS.[5,6] The host immune system may also recognize the transgene product as foreign, and induce both cellular and humoral immunity.[7]

To minimize the cellular response, most vectors have been designed to prevent the synthesis of viral proteins following transduction. However, adenoviral vectors present a unique problem, because even the inactivated recombinant adenoviral vectors can elicit potent cytotoxic T-cell responses against viral proteins.[6] Therefore it is difficult to see how gutless vectors, which still require the full complement of viral structural proteins for efficient transduction, can bypass this host immune response. The humoral response is also most pertinent to adenoviral vectors because they do not integrate, and so suffer loss by cell

---

Box 1 Properties of the ideal gene therapy vector

Easy production

The vector should be easy to produce at high titre on a commercial scale. This consideration stems from the wide range of cell numbers that must be transduced—from a handful of stem cells capable of reconstituting the entire haematopoietic repertoire to 10^{11} or more cells to infect 5–10% of the liver. For widespread use, the vector should be amenable to commercial production and processing (such as concentration technology for delivery in small volumes), and should have a reasonable shelf-life for transport and distribution.

Sustained production

The vector, once delivered, should be able to express its genetic cargo over a sustained period or expression should be regulable in a precise way. Different disease states have different requirements (for example, regulated expression in diabetes and lifetime expression in haemophilia).

Immunologically inert

The vector components should not elicit an immune response after delivery. A humoral antibody response will make a second injection of the vector ineffective, whereas a cellular response will eliminate the transduced cells.

Tissue targeting

Delivery to only certain cell types is highly desirable, especially where the target cells are dispersed throughout the body (such as in the haematopoietic system), or if the cells are part of a heterogeneous population (such as in the brain). It is also important to avoid certain cells, such as dendritic cells, the "professional" antigen-presenting cells of the body, because of their role in mediating the immune response. Cell or tissue-targeted vectors present a great challenge, but also offer rich dividends for gene therapy approaches.

Size capacity

The vector should have no size limit to the genetic material it can deliver. The coding sequence of a therapeutic gene can vary from 350 base pairs for insulin, to over 12,000 base pairs for dystrophin. Furthermore, addition of appropriate regulatory sequences may be required for efficient transduction and expression of the foreign genetic material.

Replication, segregation or integration

The vector should allow for site-specific integration of the gene into the chromosome of the target cell, or should reside in the nucleus as an episome that will faithfully divide and segregate on cell division. Site-specific integration is a very desirable attribute because it eliminates the uncertainty of random integration into the host chromosome, and endogenous regulatory regions will control its expression under physiological conditions. The ability of the vector to be maintained as an episome could make the genetic elements independent of local chromatin environments, but faithful replication and segregation is needed if the vector is to be effective in systems such as stem cells.

Infection of dividing and non-dividing cells

As large numbers of cells (such as neurons, hepatocytes and myocytes) are postmitotic, vectors capable of efficiently transducing non-dividing cells are very desirable.

---

division and by DNA degradation, necessitating a repeat infection with the vector. The host raises neutralizing antibodies against viral proteins, thereby precluding any further infection. As there are scores of adenoviral SEROTYPES, one strategy to overcome this problem might be to use different serotypes.[3,7]

Retroviral, lentiviral and AAV [adeno-associated-viral] vectors do not seem to suffer from cytotoxic-T cell responses. It could be that the vectors are completely replication-defective, and that the incoming viral proteins do not elicit a cytotoxic T-cell response.

Alternatively, the titres of at least the recombinant retro- or lentiviral vectors tested so far might not be sufficiently high to elicit an immune response. Antibody responses are also less of a concern, as retro- and lentiviral vectors integrate into the host genome and may not require subsequent transduction. Furthermore, for vectors engineered with the VSVG [vesicular stomatitis virus glycoprotein] protein, there are several strains of VSV that have different serotypes.[8] Antibodies to AAV-based vectors have been detected, which has prevented transduction by a second injection of the vector,[9] but this may also be overcome by using another serotype of AAV.[10]

Why some vectors are more immunogenic than others is a matter of considerable interest, and early hints indicate that antigen-presenting DENDRITIC CELLS may be important. In contrast to AAV-based vectors, it seems that adenoviral vectors efficiently transduce dendritic cells.[11] The route of administration also influences the immunological outcome,[12] and there is the question of pre-immunity in the host. Over 70% of the population may be carrying antibodies to adenovirus and AAV. What function might these pre-existing antibodies have in the efficiency of transduction or the toxicity of viral vectors? Are there sites in the body where the humoral response can be bypassed by the introduced vectors? Finally, the transgene itself may be highly immunogenic, particularly in hosts in which the transgene product was never made, due to either complete gene deletion or aberrant expression.[13] So, the gene therapy strategy in such hosts will also require the induction of TOLERANCE. Ultimately, individual patients may well require a therapeutic regimen tailored to their specific pathology, in the context of a genetic background that influences their immune response.

THE GELSINGER TRAGEDY

Jesse Gelsinger was barely 18 years old when he became the first patient to die in a Phase I gene therapy clinical trial. Although many patients have experienced severe adverse effects and even death during Phase I safety and toxicity studies, Jesse was the first patient in whom death could be directly attributed to the vector—an adenoviral vector.

Jesse suffered from deficiency of ornithine transcarbamylase (OTC), a metabolic enzyme required to break down ammonia. The total lack of this enzyme leads to death shortly after birth, owing to a build-up of ammonia. The partial presence of enzyme activity also leads to an accumulation of ammonia, but can be controlled by drugs and dietary intake. The aetiology of the disease, its associated morbidity, and the need for rapid production of the enzyme suggested that transient production of OTC by adenoviral vectors could extend the lifespan of OTC-deficient newborns, to allow implementation of a drug and dietary regime.[14]

The Phase I trial consisted of a study in which a cohort of patients with partial OTC activity were given escalating doses of second-generation (deleted for the *E1* and *E4* genes) adenoviral vectors. Jesse was in the last cohort, receiving up to 6×10^{13} recombinant adenoviruses particles containing the *OTC* gene. Within hours of intra-hepatic administration, he began to experience severe complications and died two days later. What went wrong? Was too much virus infused? Perhaps not, as another patient getting the same dose of the same vector did not suffer the same consequences. Were Jesse's adenoviral antibody titres higher? Again, there is no clear answer, as other patients with higher antibody titres did not have the same reaction. Perhaps there were other mitigating causes, like other viral infections or higher levels of ammonia before vector transduction. Are the animal models really reliable? Should we be screening patients for genetic variations, as immune responses are so heterogeneous? These are just some of the questions that have been raised, and several expert committees are now in the process of defining and refining new measures for gene therapy trials.

THE FIRST SUCCESSES

The field of gene therapy also has cause to celebrate. Alain Fischer and colleagues in Paris have successfully treated three young babies (1–11 months old), who suffer from a fatal form of severe combined immunodeficiency (SCID) syndrome.[15] SCID-X1 is an X-linked disorder characterized by an early block in T- and natural killer (NK) cell differentiation, due to mutations of the gene encoding the γC cytokine receptor subunit common to several interleukin receptors. A mutation in the γC subunit leads to disruption of signals required for growth, survival and differentiation of lymphoid progenitor cells.

Haematopoietic stem cells from the patients were transduced *ex vivo* with a recombinant mouse leukaemia viral vector containing the γC receptor gene and infused back into the young patients. After ten months, γC transgene expression in T- and NK cells was detected in the patients but, more importantly, T-, B- and NK-cell counts and function were comparable to those of age-matched controls. To all appearances, the recipients are clinically cured, and the fantastic promise of gene therapy is realized. Some concerns remain: only ten months of data are available, and expression of the transgene may be "shut-off." Also, very few patients have been treated so far. It remains to be seen if this approach will work for other diseases, because the success with SCID-X1 is probably owing to the strong selective advantage provided to the transduced lymphoid progenitors. Only those haematopoietic cells that express the γC receptor subunit can survive and differentiate. In earlier trials of SCID patients suffering from adenosine deaminase deficiency (ADA), PEG–ADA (a protein preparation with enzymatic activity) was administered to the patients in addition to the vector expressing the *ADA* gene. This may have prevented the selective advantage observed in the successful French trial.[16–18] The use of modified MLV [murine leukemia virus] vectors and the extensive manipulation of the stem cells (use of cytokines to stimulate cell proliferation) before transduction are a testimony to the continuous and incremental progress made in the field. We believe that with the availability of lentiviral vectors capable of transducing resting stem cells, the efficiency of transduction will improve even further.[19,20]

Haemophilia (A and B) is another excellent model system for gene therapy because the deficient protein does not have to be provided from its normal cellular source. Therefore, several vectors have been designed that transduce a range of cells to produce and secrete factor IX protein. Both the factor IX knockout mice and haemophilic dogs have turned out to be extremely beneficial pre-clinical model systems.[13,21,22] Further model systems will continue to be useful for pre-clinical studies, and promising results have recently been obtained in a mouse model of β-thalassaemia.[23] In another exciting human study, Kathryn High and colleagues at the University of Pennsylvania have treated several haemophilia B (factor IX-deficient) patients in a Phase I clinical trial with AAV vectors that contain the human *factor IX* gene.[2] The recombinant vector was injected intramuscularly, and preliminary results indicate that factor IX protein can be found in the serum of a patient. Although the levels of the factor IX protein expected to be produced by the low doses of injected AAV are not curative,[2] the treated patients did show some clinical benefits. No factor IX inhibitors were found, but neither could they be expected, because very low amounts of factor IX were being secreted. This is still a preliminary study, but nevertheless it bodes well for success in treating haemophilia.

THE NEXT PHASE

It was not long ago that the "battlecry" of the gene therapy community was "titres, titres, titres." Then it switched to "delivery, delivery, delivery," and now it is "expression, expression, expression." We have the appropriate titres of desirable vectors for delivering genes to patients. The emphasis now is on efficiency, safety and duration of expression. The issue of safety will always remain predominant, and the trend is to generate "minimal vectors" carrying the least amount of viral information needed for successful transduction.

Significant progress in vector development is occurring in the area of tissue- or cell-specific expression. . . .

• • •

PERSPECTIVES

The last two decades have witnessed the birth of the field of gene therapy, which has generated great hopes and great hypes. The promise of influencing the outcome of a vast array of diseases, ranging from birth defects to neurological disorders and from cancer to infectious diseases, although far-reaching, is not beyond reach. With the completion of the sequence of the human genome, over 50,000 genes will be available to the practitioners of gene therapy. The potential benefits for human health are vast, so how can the biomedical community move forward to realize this potential?

Geneticists will continue to identify the genetic contribution to disease. Virologists will generate safe and efficient viral vectors, and molecular biologists will help to design vectors capable of cell- and tissue-specific expression of the foreign genes carried by the transducing vectors. Immunologists will work out ways to prevent unwanted immunological consequences of the delivery vehicles and their cargo. Cell biologists will devise ways to facilitate gene transfer to various tissues and will take the lead in identifying stem cells. Clinicians will carry out clinical trials on humans with the best vectors that the scientists can supply. To achieve successful gene therapy, all branches of biology will have to contribute to this endeavour.

Society has an enormous stake in science, and scientists have an obligation not to promise more than they can deliver. Gene therapy is a young science that has undergone extreme scrutiny in the recent past. It is our responsibility to assure the public that the patient's health and welfare is of paramount concern. Adherence to accepted guidelines is incumbent on all investigators participating in clinical trials, and those wilfully violating the recommended practices will have to pay the consequences. The field of gene therapy has also been rocked by charges of conflict of interest, an area relatively new in biomedical science. Harmonized guidelines need to be put in place to allay the public's concern of real or perceived conflicts of interest. The science of gene therapy has many hurdles ahead, but they are surmountable.

GLOSSARY

Liposomes Artificial lipid vesicles. Liposomes fuse with the cell membrane to deliver their contents, such as DNA for gene therapy.

Episomes DNA molecules that are maintained in the nucleus without integrating into the chromosomal DNA.

Transduction The introduction of a gene into a target cell by a viral vector.

Haematopoiesis The programme of cellular differentiation leading to the formation of blood cells.

Memory cells Immune cells that are primed, after an initial exposure to an antigen, to make rapid response to subsequent exposure to the same antigen.

Serotypes Antigenically distinct forms that elicit different antibody responses by the immune system.

Dendritic cells These cells present antigen to T cells, and stimulate cell proliferation and the immune response.

Tolerance The lack of an immune response to a specific foreign protein.

NOTES

1. Li, S. & Huang, L. Nonviral gene therapy: promises and challenges. *Gene Ther.* **7,** 31–34 (2000).

2. Kay, M. A. *et al.* Evidence for gene transfer and expression of *factor IX* in haemophilia B patients treated with an AAV vector. *Nature Genet.* **24,** 257–261 (2000).

Gives the first hints of successful gene therapy in haemophilia B patients by using recombinant adeno-associated viral vectors. Expression of transduced *factor IX* could be detected in one patient.

3. Shenk, T. in *Fields Virology* (eds Fields B. N., Knipe D. M. & Howley P. M.) 2111–2148 (Lippincott-Raven, Philadelphia, 1996).

4. Morral, N. *et al.* Administration of helper-dependent adenoviral vectors and sequential delivery of different vector serotype for long-term liver-directed gene transfer in baboons. *Proc. Natl. Acad. Sci. USA* **96,** 12816–12821 (1999).

5. Dai, Y. *et al.* Cellular and humoral immune responses to adenoviral vectors containing *factor IX* gene: tolerization of *factor IX* and vector antigens allows for long-term expression. *Proc. Natl Acad. Sci. USA* **92,** 1401–1405 (1995).

6. Kafri, T. *et al.* Cellular immune response to adenoviral vector infected cells does not require *de novo* viral gene expression: implications for gene therapy. *Proc. Natl Acad. Sci. USA* **95,** 11377–11382 (1998).

Even physically inactivated adenoviral particles can generate a cytotoxic T-cell response, raising concerns about adenoviral vectors as suitable tools for long-term gene therapy.

7. Tripathy. S. K., Black, H. B., Goldwasser, E. & Leiden, J. M. Immune responses to transgene-encoded proteins limit the stability of gene expression after injection of replication-defective adenovirus vectors. *Nature Med.* **2,** 545–550 (1996).

8. Wagner, R. R., & Rose, J. K. in *Fields Virology* (eds Fields, B. N., Knipe D. M. & Howley, P. M.) 1121–1136 (Lippincott–Raven, Philadelphia, 1996).

9. Chirmule, N. *et al.* Humoral immunity to adeno-associated virus type 2 vectors following administration to murine and non-human primate muscle. *J. Virol.* **74,** 2420–2425 (2000).

10. Halbert, C. L., Rutledge, E. A., Allen, J. M., Russell, D. W. & Miller, A. D. Repeat transduction in the mouse lung by using adeno-associated virus vectors with different serotypes. *J. Virol.* **74,** 1524–1532 (2000).

11. Fields, P. A. *et al.* Role of vector in activation of T cell subsets in immune responses against the secreted transgene product *factor IX. Mol. Ther.* **1,** 225–235 (2000).

12. Xiao, W. *et al.* Route of administration determines induction of T-cell-independent humoral responses to adeno-associated virus vectors. *Mol. Ther.* **1,** 323–329 (2000).

13. Wang, L., Takabe, K., Bidlingmaier, S. M., III, C. R. & Verma, I. M. Sustained correction of bleeding disorder in hemophilia B mice by gene therapy. *Proc. Natl Acad. Sci. USA* **96,** 3906–3910 (1999).

14. Scriver, C. R. S., Beaudet, A. L., Sly, W. S. & Valle, D. V. (eds) *The Metabolic Basis of Inherited Disease* (McGraw-Hill, New York, 1989).

15. Cavazzana-Calvo, M. *et al.* Gene therapy of human severe combined immunodeficiency (SCID)-XI disease. *Science* **288,** 669–672 (2000).

The first definitive example of successful gene therapy, in three children suffering from SCID-XI. The haematopoietic stem cells from the patients were transduced by recombinant retroviruses expressing the γc-subunit, which is common to many interleukin receptors.

16. Kohn, D. B. *et al.* T lymphocytes with a normal *ADA* gene accumulate after transplantation of transduced autologous umbilical cord blood CD34$^+$ cells in ADA-deficient SCID neonates. *Nature Med.* **4,** 775–780 (1998).

17. Blaese, R. M. *et al.* T lymphocyte-directed gene therapy for ADA-SCID; initial trial results after 4 years. *Science* **270,** 475–480 (1995).

18. Bordignon, C. *et al.* Gene therapy in peripheral blood lymphocytes and bone marrow for ADA-immunodeficient patients. *Science* **270,** 470–475 (1995).

19. Miyoshi, H., Smith, K. A., Mosier, D. E., Verma, I. M. & Torbett, B. E. Transduction of human CD34$^+$ cells that mediate long-term engraftment of NOD/SCID mice by HIV vectors. *Science* **283,** 682–686 (1999).

20. Guenechea, G. *et al.* Transduction of human CD34$^+$ CD38$^-$ bone marrow and cord-derived SCID-repopulating cells with third-generation lentiviral vectors. *Mol. Ther.* **1,** 566–573 (2000).

References 19 and 20 show successful long-term transduction of human haematopoietic stem cells by lentiviral vectors, without the use of agents such as growth factors and cytokines.

21. Snyder, R. O. *et al.* Persistent and therapeutic concentrations of human factor IX in mice after hepatic gene transfer of recombinant AAV vectors. *Nature Genet.* **16,** 270–276 (1997).

22. Wang, L., Nichols, T. C., Read, M. S., Bellinger, D. A. & Verma, I. M. Sustained expression of therapeutic level of *factor IX* in hemophilia B dogs by AAV-mediated gene therapy in liver. *Mol. Ther.* **1,** 154–158 (2000).

23. May, C. *et al.* Therapeutic haemoglobin synthesis in thalassaemic mice expressing lentivirus-encoded human-globin. *Nature* **406,** 82–86 (2000).

JULIAN SAVULESCU

Harm, Ethics Committees and the Gene Therapy Death

Julian Savulescu is Director of the Ethics Program at the Murdoch Institute at the Royal Children's Hospital. He helped to establish the Oxford Institute for Ethics and Communication in Health Care Practice. Journals in which he has published include the *British Medical Journal*, *Bioethics*, and the *Journal of Medical Ethics*. His research interests encompass consent, advance directives, research ethics and resource allocation.

The recent tragic and widely publicised death of Jesse Gelsinger in a gene therapy trial has many important lessons for those engaged in the ethical review of research. One of the most important lessons is that ethics committees can give too much weight to ensuring informed consent and not enough attention to minimising the harm associated with participation in research. The first responsibility of ethics committees should be to ensure that the expected harm associated with participation is reasonable.

Jesse was an 18-year-old man with a mild form of ornithine transcarbamylase (OTC) deficiency, a disorder of nitrogen metabolism. His form of the disease could be controlled by diet and drug treatment. On September 13 1999 a team of researchers lead by James Wilson at the University of Pennsylvania's Institute for Human Gene Therapy (IHGT) injected 3.8×10^{13} adenovirus vector particles containing a gene to correct the genetic defect. He was the eighteenth and final patient in the trial. The virus particles were injected directly into the liver. He received the largest number of virus particles in a gene therapy trial.[1] Four days later he was dead from what was probably an immune reaction to the virus vector. This was the first death directly attributed to gene therapy. It resulted in worldwide publicity, an independent investigation, the Federal Drug Administration (FDA) suspending all trials at the IHGT, an FDA, and a senate subcommittee investigation.

At a special public meeting at the National Institutes of Health (NIH) in December 1999, James Wilson, also the director of the IHGT, said they still did not understand fully what had gone wrong.[2] Even though a massive dose had been used, only 1% of transferred genes reached the target cells. (None of the patients in the trial showed significant gene expression. Art Caplan, the University of Pennsylvania's outspoken bioethicist, is reported to have said: "if you cured anyone from a Phase 1 trial, it would be a miracle" and "there was never a chance that anyone would benefit from these experiments."[3]) Wilson claimed the death was the result of an anomalous response. Jesse's bone marrow had very low levels of red blood cell precursors, which probably predated the experiment. This may have reflected another genetic defect or a parvovirus infection. While most gene therapists at the meeting agreed that Jesse's response was unusual, some claimed it was foreseeable, given the ability of adenovirus to elicit an immune response and the high dose employed.[2]

The death also resulted in a wrongful death lawsuit which alleged[3]:

- that members of the IHGT team and others were careless, negligent and reckless in failing to adequately evaluate Jesse's condition and eligibility. Jesse had an ammonia level 30%-60% higher than the eligibility criterion stated in the protocol approved by the FDA;
- that the adenovirus vector was unreasonably dangerous;

- that storage of the vector for 25 months led researchers to underestimate its potency;
- that a conflict of interest existed. Researchers and members of the University of Pennsylvania held patents covering several aspects of the technology employed. Wilson and colleagues also hold equity holdings in Genovo, the private sector biotechnology collaborator in the project. These conflicts of interest were alleged to have not been disclosed to the participant;
- that researchers failed to notify the FDA of adverse events in prior patients and animals.

The lawsuit also named Art Caplan, director of the University of Pennsylvania's Bioethics Center. It was also suggested but not explicitly alleged that Caplan had a conflict of interest because his centre was funded by Wilson's department. The complaint also drew attention to Caplan's intervention to persuade Wilson and others to use older participants who could consent (but who had a mild form of the disease) rather than newborns who could not consent (but had an otherwise lethal form of the disease).[3]

Other concerns related to this trial have included[4]:

- Researchers continued to increase the dose despite signs of toxicity in other patients;
- Volunteers were recruited by direct appeal on a patient advocacy website which described "very low doses" and "promising results." Such appeals had been rejected by federal officials as being coercive.
- The original consent reviewed publicly by the NIH mentioned that monkeys had died from the treatment but the final version did not mention that.
- The NIH's Recombinant DNA Advisory Committee (RAC) discussed the potential for lethal liver inflammation related to this experiment in December 1995, after reviewing toxicity results in rhesus monkeys and the death of one monkey from an extremely high dose of a first-generation vector. They recommended administration through a peripheral vein rather than directly into the liver. Food and Drug Administration regulators were concerned about infection of reproductive cells (germ line modification) and made researchers go back to direct liver injection.[1]

In February 2000, at a separate hearing, Paul Geisinger, Jesse's father, asserted:

1. that his son had not been told important preclinical evidence of toxicity (including the deaths of monkeys);
2. that his son was led to believe that his participation would be clinically beneficial, despite this being a Phase 1 trial where no benefit was envisaged.[5]

James Wilson while acting as director of the IHGT, was also involved in several clinical trials and basic research. Judith Rodin, the University of Pennsylvania's president and William Danceforth, the lead author of an independent report into Jesse's death, said that Wilson was "overloaded."[6] The IHGT has been downsized and no longer conducts clinical trials. The Department of Health and Human Services has said it intends to introduce laws which will fine researchers up to $250,000 and instructions up to one million dollars for failing to meet new stricter standards.[6]

INTERSTING INSIGHTS

This experiment yields many interesting insights into the problems related to ethics review of research in general. But there is perhaps one lesson which is more important than all the others. Research ethics review is concerned primarily with two goals: ensuring that the expected harm involved in participation is reasonable and that participants give valid consent. The requirement to give valid consent has led many in the research ethics community to suggest that non-therapeutic research on incompetent patients is unethical. This trial illustrates *par excellence* the increasing and mistaken tendency of ethics committees to give too much weight to consent and to fail to give sufficient attention to protecting participants from harm.

One simple justification for conducting this trial in adults with the mild form of the disease rather than severely affected newborns goes like this. "There are serious risks including a risk of death associated with participation in this trial. Since the risks are significant, it is better that the trial be conducted on humans who consent to those risks rather than on those who cannot consent."

However, it is important to distinguish between the *chance* of a bad outcome occurring and *expected harm.* Expected harm is the probability of a harm occurring multiplied by the magnitude of that harm. Being harmed by an intervention is being made worse off than one would otherwise have been if that intervention had not been performed.

Consider an illustration using a quality adjusted life year (QALY) approach. Let's assume for simplicity's sake that the only harm in this experiment was death from the virus vector. Let's assign a value of 1 to perfect health and 0 to death. Jesse's existing quality of life was less than perfect, but still acceptable. Let's say it was 0.8. Assume that he would have lived another 50 years. Assume that the risk of the gene therapy killing him was small—1/10,000 (this is a conservative estimate: Jesse's death was the first death in nearly 400 gene therapy trials involving over 4000 patients).[7] That means that the expected harm of Jesse participating was $0.8 \times 50/10,000 = 40/10,000 = 0.004$ quality adjusted life year. This is a very small expected harm.

Now compare this to the expected harm that severely affected newborns would experience. Imagine that a newborn boy, who is already very likely to die of his disease, dies as a result of a similar gene therapy trial. Has he been harmed? He is not worse off than he would otherwise have been, since he would have died if the trial had not been conducted. He would have died of the severe form of the underlying disease. The magnitude of the expected harm to adult participants with milder forms of this disease was significantly greater than to newborns with the severe form of the disease.

Put simply, Jesse had something to lose while the seriously affected newborn did not. Even though the expected harm to Jesse prior to commencing the trial may have been small, why prefer a small expected harm to no harm? There is no good reason, regardless of whether someone is prepared to consent. It is irrational to prefer more harm to less harm.

The ethics committee which persuaded Wilson and colleagues to invite adults to participate either:

1. misunderstood the nature of expected harm and/or ethics committees' responsibilities in evaluating it, or
2. (more likely) gave greater weight to consent than to expected harm.

Attempting to draw lessons from Jesse's death, Friedmann, director of the Program in Human Gene Therapy at the University of California, stated: "The single most important mechanism for ensuring patient protection from inherent risks of clinical experiments, unrealistic expectations, and potential conflicts of interest of the investigator is accurate and full disclosure of potential risks and benefits and a well-executed informed consent process."[8]

Fine rhetoric but probably false. In Jesse's case, there were allegedly significant omissions in the consent process, allegedly involving failure to disclose relevant risks and conflicts of financial interest. But would these have made a difference? Jesse understood the trial would not cure him and there was a small chance it could hurt him. But, as his father said: "He wanted to help the babies. . . . My son had the purest intent." Indeed, strong intentions. He attempted to enrol when he was 17 but had to return when he turned 18 and was eligible.[7] Even if Jesse Gelsinger would not have participated if disclosure had been more frank, someone would have. (After all, one healthy person offered his own heart when Barney Clark received the first artificial heart!) The key to research review is not only consent, but a responsible objective evaluation of the reasonableness of harm in research.[9]

There are complex issues about whether this trial should have been conducted on human beings at all. But if it was justified, it would have been better to conduct it on newborns with the severe form of the disease. Sometimes it is better that an incompetent person participate in research than a competent person who can consent. Consent is important. But the fact that a human being is not able to consent should not paralyse ethics committees. It is a mistake to give more weight to consent than to expected harm. Ethics committees must make an evaluation of the expected harm and whether less harmful avenues should be pursued.

REFERENCES

1. Lehrman S. Virus treatment questioned after gene therapy death. *Lancet* 1999;**401**:517–8.
2. Marshall E. Gene therapy death prompts review of adenovirus vector. *Science* 1999; **286**: 2244–5.
3. Fox J. L. Gene-therapy death prompts broad civil lawsuit. *Nature Biotechnology* 2000;**18**: 1136.
4. Nelson D., Weiss R. Is Jesse's death a stain on the new science? *The Age* 1999 Dec 5: news section: 1.
5. Walters L. "Gene therapy: overview." In: Murray T., Mehlman MJ, eds. *Encyclopedia of ethical, legal and policy issues in biotechnology.* New York: Wiley, 2000: 341.
6. Smaglik P. Clinical trials end at gene therapy institute. *Nature* 2000; **405**: 497.
7. Verma I. M. A tumultuous year for gene therapy. *Molecular Therapy* 2000; **2**: 415–6.
8. Friedmann T. Principles for human gene therapy studies. *Science* 2000;**287**:2163–5.
9. Savulescu J. Safety of participants of non-therapeutic research must be ensured. *British Medical Journal* 1998;**16**:891–2.

JONATHAN GLOVER

Questions about Some Uses of Genetic Engineering

There is a widespread view that any project for the genetic improvement of the human race ought to be ruled out: that there are fundamental objections of principle. The aim of this discussion is to sort out some of the main objections. It will be argued that our resistance is based on a complex of different values and reasons, none of which is, when examined, adequate to rule out in principle this use of genetic engineering. The debate on human genetic engineering should become like the debate on nuclear power: one in which large possible benefits have to be weighed against big problems and the risk of great disasters. The discussion has not reached this point, partly because the techniques have not yet been developed. But it is also partly because of the blurred vision which fuses together many separate risks and doubts into a fuzzy-outlined opposition in principle.

1. AVOIDING THE DEBATE ABOUT GENES AND THE ENVIRONMENT

In discussing the question of genetic engineering, there is everything to be said for not muddling the issue up with the debate over the relative importance of genes and environment in the development of such characteristics as intelligence. One reason for avoiding that debate is that it arouses even stronger passions than genetic engineering, and so is filled with as much acrimony as argument. But, apart from this fastidiousness, there are other reasons.

The nature-nurture dispute is generally seen as an argument about the relative weight the two factors have in causing differences within the human species: "IQ is 80 per cent hereditary and 20 per cent environmental" versus "IQ is 80 per cent environmental and 20 per cent hereditary." No doubt there is some approximate truth of this type to be found if we consider variations within a given population at a particular time. But it is highly unlikely that there is any such statement which is simply true of human nature regardless of context. To take the extreme case, if we could iron out all environmental differences, any residual variations would be 100 per cent genetic. It is only if we make the highly artificial assumption that different groups at different times all have an identical spread of relevant environmental differences that we can expect to find statements of this kind applying to human nature in general. To say this is not to argue that studies on the question should not be conducted, or are bound to fail. It may well be possible, and useful, to find out the relative weights of the two kinds of factor for a given characteristic among a certain group at a particular time. The point is that any such conclusions lose relevance, not only when environmental differences are stretched out or compressed, but also when genetic differences are. And this last case is what we are considering.

We can avoid this dispute because of its irrelevance. Suppose the genetic engineering proposal were to try to make people less aggressive. On a superficial view, the proposal might be shown to be unrealistic if there were evidence to show that variation in aggressiveness is hardly genetic at all: that it is 95 per cent environmental. (Let us grant, most implausibly, that such a figure turned out to be true for the whole of humanity, regardless of social context.) But all this would show is that, within our species, the distribution of genes relevant to aggression is very uniform.

It would show nothing about the likely effects on aggression if we use genetic engineering to give people a different set of genes from those they now have.

In other words, to take genetic engineering seriously, we need take no stand on the relative importance or unimportance of genetic factors in the explanation of the present range of individual differences found in people. We need only the minimal assumption that different genes could give us different characteristics. To deny *that* assumption you need to be the sort of person who thinks it is only living in kennels which make dogs different from cats.

2. METHODS OF CHANGING THE GENETIC COMPOSITION OF FUTURE GENERATIONS

There are essentially three ways of altering the genetic composition of future generations. The first is by environmental changes. Discoveries in medicine, the institution of a National Health Service, schemes for poverty relief, agricultural changes, or alterations in the tax position of large families, all alter the selective pressure on genes.[1] It is hard to think of any social change which does not make some difference to who survives or who is born.

The second method is to use eugenic policies aimed at altering breeding patterns or patterns of survival of people with different genes. Eugenic methods are "environmental" too: the difference is only that the genetic impact is intended. Possible strategies range from various kinds of compulsion (to have more children, fewer children, or no children, or even compulsion over the choice of sexual partner) to the completely voluntary (our present genetic counselling practice of giving prospective parents information about probabilities of their children having various abnormalities).

The third method is genetic engineering: using enzymes to add to or subtract from a stretch of DNA.

Most people are unworried by the fact that a side-effect of an environmental change is to alter the gene pool, at least where the alteration is not for the worse. And even in cases where environmental factors increase the proportion of undesirable genes in the pool, we often accept this. Few people oppose the National Health Service, although setting it up meant that some people with genetic defects, who would have died, have had treatment enabling them to survive and reproduce. On the whole, we accept without qualms that much of what we do has genetic impact. Controversy starts when we think of aiming deliberately at genetic changes, by eugenics or genetic engineering.

I want to make some brief remarks about eugenic policies, before suggesting that policies of deliberate intervention are best considered in the context of genetic engineering.

Scepticism has been expressed about whether eugenic policies have any practical chance of success. Medawar has pointed out the importance of genetic polymorphism: the persistence of genetically different types in a population.[2] (Our different blood groups are a familiar example.) For many characteristics, people get a different gene from each parent. So children do not simply repeat parental characteristics. Any simple picture of producing an improved type of person, and then letting the improvement be passed on unchanged, collapses.

But, although polymorphism is a problem for this crudely utopian form of eugenics, it does not show that more modest schemes of improvement must fail. Suppose the best individuals for some quality (say, colour vision) are heterozygous, so that they inherit a gene A from one parent, and a gene B from the other. These ABs will have AAs and BBs among their children, who will be less good than they are. But AAs and BBs may still be better than ACs or ADs, and perhaps much better than CCs or CDs. If this were so, overall improvement could still be brought about by encouraging people whose genes included an A or B to have more children than those who had only Cs or Ds. The point of taking a quality like colour vision is that it may be genetically fairly simple. Qualities like kindness or intelligence are more likely to depend on the interaction of many genes, but a similar point can be made at a higher level of complexity.

Polymorphism raises a doubt about whether the offspring of the three "exceptionally intelligent women" fertilized by Dr. Shockley or other Nobel prize-winners will have the same IQ as the parents, even apart from environmental variation. But it does not show the inevitable failure of any large-scale attempts to alter human characteristics by varying the relative numbers of children different kinds of people have. Yet any attempt, say, to raise the level of intelligence, would be a very slow affair, taking many generations to make much of an impact. This is no reason for preferring to discuss genetic engineering. For the genetic engineering of human improvements, if it becomes possible, will have an immediate effect, so we will not be guessing which qualities will be desirable dozens of generations later.

There is the view that the genetic-engineering techniques requires will not become a practical possibility. Sir MacFarlane Burnet, writing in 1971 about using genetic engineering to cure disorders in people already born, dismissed the possibility of using a virus to carry a new gene to replace a faulty one in cells throughout the body: "I should be willing to state in any company that the chance of doing this will remain infinitely small to the last syllable of recorded time."[3] Unless engineering at the stage of sperm cell and egg is easier, this seems a confident dismissal of the topic to be discussed here. More recent work casts doubt on this confidence.[4] So, having mentioned this skepticism, I shall disregard it. We will assume that genetic engineering of people may become possible, and that it is worth discussing. (Sir MacFarlane Burnet's view has not yet been falsified as totally as Rutherford's view about atomic energy. But I hope that the last syllable of recorded time is still some way off.)

The main reason for casting the discussion in terms of genetic engineering rather than eugenics is not a practical one. Many eugenic policies are open to fairly straightforward moral objections, which hide the deeper theoretical issues. Such policies as compulsory sterilization, compulsory abortion, compelling people to pair off in certain ways, or compelling people to have more or fewer children than they would otherwise have, are all open to objection on grounds of overriding people's autonomy. Some are open to objection on grounds of damage to the institution of the family. And the use of discriminatory tax- and child-benefit policies is an intolerable step towards a society of different genetic castes.

Genetic engineering need not involve overriding anyone's autonomy. It need not be forced on parents against their wishes, and the future person being engineered has no views to be overridden. (The view that despite this, it is still objectionable to have one's genetic characteristics decided by others, will be considered later.) Genetic engineering will not damage the family in the obvious ways that compulsory eugenic policies would. Nor need it be encouraged by incentives which create inequalities. Because it avoids these highly visible moral objections, genetic engineering allows us to focus more clearly on other values that are involved.

(To avoid a possible misunderstanding, one point should be added before leaving the topic of eugenics. Saying that some eugenic policies are open to obvious moral objections does not commit me to disapproval of all eugenic policies. In particular, I do not want to be taken to be opposing two kinds of policy. One is genetic counselling: warning people of risks in having children, and perhaps advising them against having them. The other is the introduction of screening-programmes to detect foetal abnormalities, followed by giving the mother the option of abortion where serious defects emerge.)

Let us now turn to the question of what, if anything, we should do in the field of human genetic engineering.

3. THE POSITIVE-NEGATIVE DISTINCTION

We are not yet able to cure disorders by genetic engineering. But we do sometimes respond to disorders by adopting eugenic policies, at least in voluntary form. Genetic counselling is one instance, as applied to those thought likely to have such disorders as Huntington's chorea. This is a particularly appalling inherited disorder, involving brain degeneration, leading to mental decline and lack of control over movement. It does not normally come on until middle age, by which time many of its victims would in the normal course of things have had children. Huntington's chorea is caused by a dominant gene, so those who find that one of the parents has it have themselves a 50 per cent chance of developing it. If they do have it, each of their children will in turn have a 50 per cent chance of the disease. The risks are so high and the disorder so bad that the potential parents often decide not to have children, and are often given advice to this effect by doctors and others.

Another eugenic response to disorders is involved in screening-programmes for pregnant women. When tests pick up such defects as Down's syndrome (mongolism) or spina bifida, the mother is given the possibility of an abortion. The screening-programmes are eugenic because part of their point is to reduce the incidence of severe genetic abnormality in the population.

These two eugenic policies come in at different stages: before conception and during pregnancy. For this reason the screening-programme is more controversial, because it raises the issue of abortion. Those who are sympathetic to abortion, and who think it would be good to eliminate these disorders will be sympathetic to the programme. Those who think abortion is no different from killing a fully developed human are obviously likely to oppose the programme. But they are likely to feel that elimination of the disorders would be a good thing, even if not an adequate justification for killing. Unless they also disapprove of contraception, they are likely to support the genetic-counselling policy in the case of Huntington's chorea.

Few people object to the use of eugenic policies to eliminate disorders, unless those policies have additional features which are objectionable. Most of us are resistant to the use of compulsion, and those who oppose abortion will object to screening-programmes. But apart from these other moral objections, we do not object to the use of eugenic policies against disease. We do not object to advising those likely to have Huntington's chorea not to have children, as neither compulsion nor killing is involved. Those of us who take this view have no objection to altering the genetic composition of the next generation, where this alteration consists in reducing the incidence of defects.

If it were possible to use genetic engineering to correct defects, say at the foetal stage, it is hard to see how those of us who are prepared to use the eugenic measure just mentioned could object. In both cases, it would be pure gain. The couple, one of whom may develop Huntington's chorea, can have a child if they want, knowing that any abnormality will be eliminated. Those sympathetic to abortion will agree that cure is preferable. And those opposed to abortion prefer babies to be born without handicap. It is hard to think of any objection to using genetic engineering to eliminate defects, and there is a clear and strong case for its use.

But accepting the case for eliminating genetic mistakes does not entail accepting other uses of genetic engineering. The elimination of defects is often called "negative" genetic engineering. Going beyond this, to bring about improvements in normal people, is by contrast "positive" engineering. (The same distinction can be made for eugenics.)

The positive-negative distinction is not in all cases completely sharp. Some conditions are genetic disorders whose identification raises little problem. Huntington's chorea or spina bifida are genetic "mistakes" in a way that cannot seriously be disputed. But with other conditions, the boundary between a defective state and normality may be more blurred. If there is a genetic disposition towards depressive illness, this seems a defect, whose elimination would be part of negative genetic engineering. Suppose the genetic disposition to depression involves the production of lower levels of an enzyme than are produced in normal people. The negative programme is to correct the genetic fault so that the enzyme level is within the range found in normal people. But suppose that within "normal" people also, there are variations in the enzyme level, which correlate with ordinary differences in [the] tendency to be cheerful or depressed. Is there a sharp boundary between "clinical" depression and the depression sometimes felt by those diagnosed as "normal"? Is it clear that a sharp distinction can be drawn between raising someone's enzyme level so that it falls within the normal range and raising someone else's level from the bottom of the normal range to the top?

The positive-negative distinction is sometimes a blurred one, but often we can at least roughly see where it should be drawn. If there is a rough and ready distinction, the question is: how important is it? Should we go on from accepting negative engineering to accepting positive programmes, or should we say that the line between the two is the limit of what is morally acceptable?

There is no doubt that positive programmes arouse the strongest feelings on both sides. On the one hand, many respond to positive genetic engineering or positive eugenics with Professor Tinbergen's though: "I find it morally reprehensible and presumptuous for anybody to put himself forward as a judge of the qualities for which we should breed" [*Guardian*, 5 March, 1980].

But other people have held just as strongly that positive policies are the way to make the future of mankind better than the past. Many years ago H. J. Muller expressed this hope:

And so we foresee the history of life divided into three main phases. In the long preparatory phase it was the helpless creature of its environment, and natural selection gradually ground it into human shape. In the second—our own short transitional phase—it reaches out at the immediate environment, shaking, shaping and grinding to suit the form, the requirements, the wishes, and the whims of man. And in the long third phase, it will reach down into the secret places of the great universe of its own nature, and by aid of its ever growing intelligence and cooperation, shape itself into an increasingly sublime creation—a being beside which the mythical divinities of the past will seem more and more ridiculous, and which setting its own marvellous inner powers against the brute Goliath of the suns and the planets, challenges them to contest.[5]

The case for positive engineering is not helped by adopting the tones of the mad scientist in a horror film. But behind the rhetoric is a serious point. If we decide on a positive programme to change our nature, this will be a central moment in our history, and the transformation might be beneficial to a degree we can now scarcely imagine. The question is: how are we to weigh this possibility against Tinbergen's objection, and against other objections and doubts?

For the rest of this discussion, I shall assume that, subject to adequate safeguards against things going wrong, negative genetic engineering is acceptable. The issue is positive engineering. I shall also assume that we can ignore problems about whether positive engineering will be technically possible. Suppose we have the power to choose people's genetic characteristics. Once we have eliminated genetic defects, what, if anything, should we do with this power? . . .

4. THE VIEW THAT OVERALL IMPROVEMENT IS UNLIKELY OR IMPOSSIBLE

There is one doubt about the workability of schemes of genetic improvement which is so widespread that it would be perverse to ignore it. This is the view that, in any genetic alteration, there are no gains without compensating losses. On this view, if we bring about a genetically based improvement, such as higher intelligence, we are bound to pay a price somewhere else: perhaps the more intelligent people will have less resistance to disease, or will be less physically agile. If correct, this might so undermine the practicability of applying eugenics or genetic engineering that it would be hardly worth discussing the values involved in such programmes.

This view perhaps depends on some idea that natural selection is so efficient that, in terms of gene survival, we must already be as efficient as it is possible to be. If it were possible to push up intelligence without weakening some other part of the system, natural selection would already have done so. But this is a naive version of evolutionary theory. In real evolutionary theory, far from the genetic status quo always being the best possible for a given environment, some mutations turn out to be advantageous, and this is the origin of evolutionary progress. If natural mutations can be beneficial without a compensating loss, why should artificially induced ones not be so too?

It should also be noticed that there are two different ideas of what counts as a gain or a loss. From the point of view of evolutionary progress, gains and losses are simply advantages and disadvantages from the point of view of gene survival. But we are not compelled to take this view. If we could engineer a genetic change in some people which would have the effect of making them musical prodigies but also sterile, this would be a hopeless gene in terms of survival, but this need not force us, or the musical prodigies themselves, to think of the changes as for the worse. It depends on how we rate musical ability as against having children, and evolutionary survival does not dictate priorities here.

The view that gains and losses are tied up with each other need not depend on the dogma that natural selection *must* have created the best of all possible sets of genes. A more cautiously empirical version of the claim says there is a tendency for gains to be accompanied by losses. John Maynard Smith, in his paper on "Eugenics and Utopia,"[6] takes this kind of "broad balance" view and runs it the other way, suggesting, as an argument in defence of medicine, that any loss of genetic resistance to disease is likely to be a good thing: "The reason for this is that in evolution, as in other fields, one seldom gets something for nothing. Genes which confer disease-resistance are likely to have harmful effects in other ways: this is certainly true of the gene for sickle-cell anaemia and may be a general rule. If so, absence of selection in favour of disease-resistance may be eugenic."

It is important that different characteristics may turn out to be genetically linked in ways we do not yet realize. In our present state of knowledge, engineering for some improvement might easily bring some unpredicted but genetically linked disadvantage. But we do not have to accept that there will in general be a broad balance, so that there is a presumption that any gain will be accompanied by a compensating loss (or Maynard Smith's version that we can expect a compensating gain for any loss). The reason is that what counts as a gain or loss varies in different contexts. Take Maynard Smith's example of sickle-cell anaemia. The reason why sickle-cell anaemia is widespread in Africa is that it is genetically linked with resistance to malaria. Those who are heterozygous (who inherit one sickle-cell gene and one normal gene) are resistant to malaria, while those who are homozygous (whose genes are both sickle-cell) get sickle-cell anaemia. If we use genetic engineering to knock out sickle-cell anaemia where malaria is common, we will pay the price of having more malaria. But when we eradicate malaria, the gain will not involve this loss. Because losses are relative to context, any generalization about the impossibility of overall improvements is dubious.

Unlike various compulsory eugenic policies, genetic engineering need not involve any interference with decision by couples to have children together, or with their decisions about how many children to have. And let us suppose that genetically engineered babies grow in the mother's womb in the normal way, so that her relationship to the child is not threatened in the way it might be if the laboratory or the hospital were substituted for the womb. The cruder threats to family relationships are eliminated.

It may be suggested that there is a more subtle threat. Parents like to identify with their children. We are often pleased to see some of our own characteristics in our children. Perhaps this is partly a kind of vanity, and no doubt sometimes we project on to our children similarities that are not really there. But, when the similarities do exist, they help the parents and children to understand and sympathize with each other. If genetic engineering resulted in children fairly different from their parents, this might make their relationship have problems.

There is something to this objection, but it is easy to exaggerate. Obviously, children who were like Midwich cuckoos, or comic-book Martians, would not be easy to identify with. But genetic engineering need not move in such sudden jerks. The changes would have to be detectable to be worth bringing about, but there seems no reason why large changes in appearance, or an unbridgeable psychological gulf, should be created in any one generation. We bring about environmental changes which make children different from their parents, as when the first generation of children in a remote place are given schooling and made literate. This may cause some problems in families, but it is not usually thought a decisive objection. It is not clear that genetically induced changes of similar magnitude are any more objectionable.

A related objection concerns our attitude to our remoter descendants. We like to think of our descendants stretching on for many generations. Perhaps this is in part an immortality substitute. We hope they will to some extent be like us, and that, if they think of us, they will do so with sympathy and approval. Perhaps these hopes about the future of mankind are relatively unimportant to us. But, even if we mind about them a lot, they are unrealistic in the very long term. Genetic engineering would make our descendants less like us, but this would only speed up the natural rate of change. Natural mutations and selective pressures make it un-

likely that in a few million years our descendants will be physically or mentally much like us. So what genetic engineering threatens here is probably doomed anyway. . . .

[6.] RISKS AND MISTAKES

Although mixing different species and cloning are often prominent in people's thoughts about genetic engineering, they are relatively marginal issues. This is partly because there may be no strong reasons in favour of either. Our purposes might be realized more readily by improvements to a single species, whether another or our own, or by the creation of quite new types of organism, than by mixing different species. And it is not clear what advantage cloning batches of people might have, to outweigh the drawbacks. This is not to be dogmatic that species mixing and cloning could never be useful, but to say that the likelihood of other techniques being much more prominent makes it a pity to become fixated on the issues raised by these ones. And some of the most serious objections to positive genetic engineering have wider application than to these rather special cases. One of these wider objections is that serious risks may be involved.

Some of the risks are already part of the public debate because of current work on recombinant DNA. The danger is of producing harmful organisms that would escape from our control. The work obviously should take place, if at all, only with adequate safeguards against such a disaster. The problem is deciding what we should count as adequate safeguards. I have nothing to contribute to this problem here. If it can be dealt with satisfactorily, we will perhaps move on to genetic engineering of people. And this introduces another dimension of risk. We may produce unintended results, either because our techniques turn out to be less finely tuned than we thought, or because different characteristics are found to be genetically linked in unexpected ways.

If we produce a group of people who turn out worse than expected, we will have to live with them. Perhaps we would aim for producing people who were especially imaginative and creative, and only too late find we had produced people who were also very violent and aggressive. This kind of mistake might not only be disastrous, but also very hard to "correct" in subsequent generations. For when we suggested sterilization to the people we had produced, or else corrective genetic engineering for *their* offspring, we might find them hard to persuade. They might like the way they were, and reject, in characteristically violent fashion, our explanation that they were a mistake.

The possibility of an irreversible disaster is a strong deterrent. It is enough to make some people think we should rule out genetic engineering altogether, and to make others think that, while negative engineering is perhaps acceptable, we should rule out positive engineering. The thought behind this second position is that the benefits from negative engineering are clearer, and that, because its aims are more modest, disastrous mistakes are less likely.

The risk of disasters provides at least a reason for saying that, if we do adopt a policy of human genetic engineering, we ought to do so with extreme caution. We should alter genes only where we have strong reasons for thinking the risk of disaster is very small, and where the benefit is great enough to justify the risk. (The problems of deciding when this is so are familiar from the nuclear power debate.) This "principle of caution" is less strong than one ruling out all positive engineering, and allows room for the possibility that the dangers may turn out to be very remote, or that greater risks of a different kind are involved in *not* using positive engineering. These possibilities correspond to one view of the facts in the nuclear power debate. Unless with genetic engineering we think we can already rule out such possibilities, the argument from risk provides more justification for the principle of caution than for the stronger ban on all positive engineering. . . .

DECISIONS

Some of the strongest objections to positive engineering are not about specialized applications or about risks. They are about the decisions involved. The central line of thought is that we should not start playing God by redesigning the human race. The suggestion is that there is no group (such as scientists, doctors, public officials, or politicians) who can be entrusted with decisions about what sort of people there should be. And it is also doubted whether we could have any adequate grounds for basing such decisions on one set of values rather than another. . . .

1. NOT PLAYING GOD

Suppose we could use genetic engineering to raise the average IQ by fifteen points. (I mention, only to ignore, the boring objection that the average IQ is al-

ways by definition 100.) Should we do this? Objectors to positive engineering say we should not. This is not because the present average is preferable to a higher one. We do not think that, if it were naturally fifteen points higher, we ought to bring it down to the present level. The objection is to our playing God by deciding what the level should be.

On one view of the world, the objection is relatively straightforward. On this view, there really is a God, who has a plan for the world which will be disrupted if we stray outside the boundaries assigned to us. (It is *relatively* straightforward: there would still be the problem of knowing where the boundaries came. If genetic engineering disrupts the programme, how do we know that medicine and education do not?)

The objection to playing God has a much wider appeal than to those who literally believe in a divine plan. But, outside such a context, it is unclear what the objection comes to. If we have a Darwinian view, according to which features of our nature have been selected for their contribution to gene survival, it is not blasphemous, or obviously disastrous, to start to control the process in the light of our own values. We may value other qualities in people, in preference to those which have been most conducive to gene survival.

The prohibition on playing God is obscure. If it tells us not to interfere with natural selection at all, this rules out medicine, and most other environmental and social changes. If it only forbids interference with natural selection by the direct alteration of genes, this rules out negative as well as positive genetic engineering. If these interpretations are too restrictive, the ban on positive engineering seems to need some explanation. If we can make positive changes at the environmental level, and negative changes at the genetic level, why should we not make positive changes at the genetic level? What makes this policy, but not the others, objectionably God-like?

Perhaps the most plausible reply to these questions rests on a general objection to any group of people trying to plan too closely what human life should be like. Even if it is hard to distinguish in principle between the use of genetic and environmental means, genetic changes are likely to differ in degree from most environmental ones. Genetic alterations may be more drastic or less reversible, and so they can be seen as the extreme case of an objectionably God-like policy by which some people set out to plan the lives of others.

This objection can be reinforced by imagining the possible results of a programme of positive engineering, where the decisions about the desired improvements were taken by scientists. Judging by the literature written by scientists on this topic, great prominence would be given to intelligence. But can we be sure that enough weight would be given to other desirable qualities? And do things seem better if for scientists we substitute doctors, politicians or civil servants? Or some committee containing businessmen, trade unionists, academics, lawyers and a clergyman?

What seems worrying here is the circumscribing of potential human development. The present genetic lottery throws up a vast range of characteristics, good and bad, in all sorts of combinations. The group of people controlling a positive engineering policy would inevitably have limited horizons, and we are right to worry that the limitations of their outlook might become the boundaries of human variety. The drawbacks would be like those of town-planning or dog-breeding, but with more important consequences.

When the objection to playing God is separated from the idea that intervening in this aspect of the natural world is a kind of blasphemy, it is a protest against a particular group of people, necessarily fallible and limited, taking decisions so important to our future. This protest may be on grounds of the bad consequences, such as loss of variety of people, that would come from the imaginative limits of those taking the decisions. Or it may be an expression of opposition to such concentration of power, perhaps with the thought: 'What right have *they* to decide what kinds of people there should be?' Can these problems be side-stepped?

2. THE GENETIC SUPERMARKET

Robert Nozick is critical of the assumption that positive engineering has to involve any centralized decision about desirable qualities: "Many biologists tend to think the problem is one of *design,* of specifying the best types of persons so that biologists can proceed to produce them. Thus they worry over what sort(s) of person there is to be and who will control this process. They do not tend to think, perhaps because it diminishes the importance of their role, of a system in which they run a "genetic supermarket," meeting the individual specifications (within certain moral limits) of prospective parents. Nor do they think of seeing what limited number of types of persons people's choices would converge upon, if indeed there would be any such convergence. This supermarket system has the great virtue that it involves no centralized decision fixing the future human type(s)."[7]

This idea of letting parents choose their children's

characteristics is in many ways an improvement on decisions being taken by some centralized body. It seems less likely to reduce human variety, and could even increase it, if genetic engineering makes new combinations of characteristics available. (But we should be cautious here. Parental choice is not a guarantee of genetic variety, as the influence of fashion or of shared values might make for a small number of types on which choices would converge.)

To those sympathetic to one kind of liberalism, Nozick's proposal will seem more attractive than centralized decisions. On this approach to politics, it is wrong for the authorities to institutionalize any religious or other outlook as the official one of the society. To a liberal of this kind, a good society is one which tolerates and encourages a wide diversity of ideals of the good life. Anyone with these sympathies will be suspicious of centralized decisions about what sort of people should form the next generation. But some parental decisions would be disturbing. If parents chose characteristics likely to make their children unhappy, or likely to reduce their abilities, we might feel that the children should be protected against this. (Imagine parents belonging to some extreme religious sect, who wanted their children to have a religious symbol as a physical mark on their face, and who wanted them to be unable to read, as a protection against their faith being corrupted.) Those of us who support restrictions protecting children from parental harm after birth (laws against cruelty, and compulsion on parents to allow their children to be educated and to have necessary medical treatment) are likely to support protecting children from being harmed by their parents' genetic choices.

No doubt the boundaries here will be difficult to draw. We already find it difficult to strike a satisfactory balance between protection of children and parental freedom to choose the kind of upbringing their children should have. But it is hard to accept that society should set no limits to the genetic choices parents can make for their children. Nozick recognizes this when he says the genetic supermarket should meet the specifications of parents "within certain moral limits." So, if the supermarket came into existence, some centralized policy, even if only the restrictive one of ruling out certain choices harmful to the children, should exist. It would be a political decision where the limits should be set.

There may also be a case for other centralized

restrictions on parental choice, as well as those aimed at preventing harm to the individual people being designed. The genetic supermarket might have more oblique bad effects. An imbalance in the ratio between the sexes could result. Or parents might think their children would be more successful if they were more thrusting, competitive and selfish. If enough parents acted on this thought, other parents with different values might feel forced into making similar choices to prevent their own children being too greatly disadvantaged. Unregulated individual decisions could lead to shifts of this kind, with outcomes unwanted by most of those who contribute to them. If a majority favour a roughly equal ratio between the sexes, or a population of relatively uncompetitive people, they may feel justified in supporting restrictions on what parents can choose. (This is an application to the case of genetic engineering of a point familiar in other contexts, that unrestricted individual choices can add up to a total outcome which most people think worse than what would result from some regulation.)

Nozick recognizes that there may be cases of this sort. He considers the case of avoiding a sexual imbalance and says that "a government could require that genetic manipulation be carried on so as to fit a certain ratio."[8] He clearly prefers to avoid governmental intervention of this kind, and, while admitting that the desired result would be harder to obtain in a purely libertarian system, suggests possible strategies for doing so. He says: "Either parents would subscribe to an information service monitoring the recent births and so know which sex was in shorter supply (and hence would be more in demand in later life), thus adjusting their activities, or interested individuals would contribute to a charity that offers bonuses to maintain the ratios, or the ratio would leave 1:1, with new family and social patterns developing." The proposals for avoiding the sexual imbalance without central regulation are not reassuring. Information about likely prospects for marriage or sexual partnership might not be decisive for parents' choices. And, since those most likely to be "interested individuals" would be in the age group being genetically engineered, it is not clear that the charity would be given donations adequate for its job.[9]

If the libertarian methods failed, we would have the choice between allowing a sexual imbalance or imposing some system of social regulation. Those who dislike central decisions favouring one sort of person over others might accept regulation here, on the grounds that neither sex is being given preference: the aim is rough equality of numbers.

But what about the other sort of case, where the working of the genetic supermarket leads to a general change unwelcome to those who contribute to it? Can we defend regulation to prevent a shift towards a more selfish and competitive population as merely being the preservation of a certain ratio between characteristics? Or have we crossed the boundary, and allowed a centralized decision favouring some characteristics over others? The location of the boundary is obscure. One view would be that the sex-ratio case is acceptable because the desired ratio is equality of numbers. On another view, the acceptability derives from the fact that the present ratio is to be preserved. (In this second view, preserving altruism would be acceptable, so long as no attempt was made to raise the proportion of altruistic people in the population. But is *this* boundary an easy one to defend?)

If positive genetic engineering does become a reality, we may be unable to avoid some of the decisions being taken at a social level. Or rather, we could avoid this, but only at what seems an unacceptable cost, either to the particular people being designed, or to their generation as a whole. And, even if the social decisions are only restrictive, it is implausible to claim that they are all quite free of any taint of preference for some characteristics over others. But, although this suggests that we should not be doctrinaire in our support of the liberal view, it does not show that the view has to be abandoned altogether. We may still think that social decisions in favour of one type of person rather than another should be few, even if the consequences of excluding them altogether are unacceptable. A genetic supermarket, modified by some central regulation, may still be better than a system of purely central decisions. The liberal value is not obliterated because it may sometimes be compromised for the sake of other things we care about.

3. A MIXED SYSTEM

The genetic supermarket provides a partial answer to the objection about the limited outlook of those who would take the decisions. The choices need not be concentrated in the hands of a small number of people. The genetic supermarket should not operate in a completely unregulated way, and so some centralized decisions would have to be taken about the restrictions that should be imposed. One system that would answer many of the anxieties about centralized decision-making would be to limit the power of the decision-makers to one of veto. They would then only check departures from the natural genetic lottery, and so the power to bring about changes would not be given to them, but spread through the whole population of potential parents. Let us call this combination of parental initiative and central veto a "mixed system." If positive genetic engineering does come about, we can imagine the argument between supporters of a mixed system and supporters of other decision-making systems being central to the political theory of the twenty-first century, parallel to the place occupied in the nineteenth and twentieth centuries by the debate over control of the economy.[10]

My own sympathies are with the view that, if positive genetic engineering is introduced, this mixed system is in general likely to be the best one for making decisions. I do not want to argue for an absolutely inviolable commitment to this, as it could be that some centralized decision for genetic change was the only way of securing a huge benefit or avoiding a great catastrophe. But, subject to this reservation, the dangers of concentrating the decision-making create a strong presumption in favour of a mixed system rather than one in which initiatives come from the centre. And, if a mixed system was introduced, there would have to be a great deal of political argument over what kinds of restrictions on the supermarket should be imposed. Twenty-first-century elections may be about issues rather deeper than economics.

If this mixed system eliminates the anxiety about genetic changes being introduced by a few powerful people with limited horizons, there is a more general unease which it does not remove. May not the limitations of one generation of parents also prove disastrous? And, underlying this, is the problem of what values parents should appeal to in making their choices. How can we be confident that it is better for one sort of person to be born than another?

4. VALUES

The dangers of such decisions, even spread through all prospective parents, seem to me very real. We are swayed by fashion. We do not know the limitations of our own outlook. There are human qualities whose value we may not appreciate. A generation of parents might opt heavily for their children having physical or intellectual abilities and skills. We might leave out a sense of humour. Or we might not notice how important to us is some other quality, such as emotional warmth. So we might not be disturbed in advance by the possible impact of the genetic changes on such a quality. And, without really wanting to do so, we might stumble into producing people with a deep coldness. This possibility seems one of the worst imaginable. It is just one of the many horrors that could be blundered into by our lack of foresight in operating the mixed system. Because such disasters are a real danger, there is a case against positive genetic engineering, even when the changes do not result from centralized decisions. But this case, resting as it does on the risk of disaster, supports a principle of caution rather than a total ban. We have to ask the question whether there are benefits sufficiently great and sufficiently probable to outweigh the risks.

But perhaps the deepest resistance, even to a mixed system, is not based on risks, but on a more general problem about values. Could the parents ever be justified in choosing, according to some set of values, to create one sort of person rather than another?

Is it sometimes better for us to create one sort of person rather than another? We say "yes" when it is a question of eliminating genetic defects. And we say "yes" if we think that encouraging some qualities rather than others should be an aim of the upbringing and education we give our children. Any inclination to say "no" in the context of positive genetic engineering must lay great stress on the two relevant boundaries. The positive-negative boundary is needed to mark off the supposedly unacceptable positive policies from the acceptable elimination of defects. And the genes-environment boundary is needed to mark off positive engineering from acceptable positive aims of educational policies. But it is not clear that confidence in the importance of these boundaries is justified. . . .

NOTES

1. Chris Graham has suggested to me that it is misleading to say this without emphasizing the painful slowness of this way of changing gene frequencies.

2. *The Future of Man* (The Reith Lectures, 1959), London, 1960, chapter 3; and in "The Genetic Improvement of Man," in *The Hope of Progress*, London, 1972.

3. *Genes, Dreams and Realities*, London, 1971, p. 81.

4. "Already they have pushed Cline's results further, obtaining transfer between rabbit and mouse, for example, and good expression of the foreign gene in its new host. Some, by transferring the genes into the developing eggs, have managed to get the new genes into every cell in the mouse, including the sex cells; those mice have fathered offspring who also contain the foreign gene." Jeremy Cherfas: *Man Made Life*, Oxford, 1982, pp. 229–30.

5. *Out of the Night,* New York, 1935. To find a distinguished geneticist talking like this after the Nazi period is not easy.

6. John Maynard Smith: *On Evolution,* Edinburgh, 1972; the article is reprinted from the issue on "Utopia" of *Daedalus, Journal of the American Academy of Arts and Sciences,* 1965.

7. *Anarchy, State and Utopia,* New York, 1974, p. 315.

8. Op. cit., p. 315.

9. This kind of unworldly innocence is part of the engaging charm of Nozick's dotty and brilliant book.

10. Decision-taking by a central committee (perhaps of a dozen elderly men) can be thought of as a "Russian" model. The genetic supermarket (perhaps with genotypes being sold by TV commercials) can be thought of as an "American" model. The mixed system may appeal to Western European social democrats.

JON W. GORDON

Genetic Enhancement in Humans

Jon W. Gordon is Professor of Obstetrics and Gynecology, Geriatrics and Human Genetics at the Mount Sinai School of Medicine. He has authored more than 100 articles and book chapters on the subjects of gene transfer and reproductive biology. He has also served on numerous government committees that consider the ethics of gene transfer, including the NIH Recombinant DNA Advisory Committee.

Dramatic advances in gene transfer technology since the early 1980s have prompted consideration of its use in humans to enhance phenotypic traits. The notion that genetic modification could confer special advantages on an individual has generated excitement. Controversial issues surround this prospect, however. A practical concern is determining how to ensure equal access to such advanced medical technologies. There has also been speculation that genetic enhancement might affect human evolution, and philosophical objections have been raised, based on the belief that to intervene in such fundamental biological processes is to "play God." Although such philosophical questions cannot be resolved through data analysis, we nevertheless have the tools in hand to objectively assess our state of progress. We can also assess the impact that promulgation of such technology might have on human evolution and formulate sensible guidelines for developing policies governing human genetic enhancements.

DEFINING GENETIC ENHANCEMENT

Some experts have argued that "enhancement" can have different meanings depending on the circumstances. For example, when a disease is common, the risk for developing the disorder may be considered the norm, and genetic alleviation of that risk might be regarded as a form of enhancement.[1] This kind of semantic gamesmanship is misleading. The obvious public concern does not relate to improvement of traits for alleviation of deficiencies or reduction of disease risk, but to augmentation of functions that without intervention would be considered entirely normal. To raise the athletic capabilities of a schoolyard basketball player to those of a professional or to confer the talents of Chopin on a typical college music professor is the sort of genetic enhancement that many find troublesome. The experts in the gene transfer field should acknowledge the distinction in order to avoid causing public distrust and undermining the deliberative process.

Another important distinction is that between genetic changes that are heritable and those that cannot be genetically transmitted. At the present time, gene transfer approaches that involve the early embryo are far more effective than somatic cell gene therapy methodologies. Embryo gene transfer affords the opportunity to transform most or all cells of the organism and thus overcomes the inefficient transformation that plagues somatic cell gene transfer protocols. Moreover, the commonly used approaches to embryo gene insertion—pronuclear microinjection[2] and transfection of embryonic stem cells[3]—are associated with stable, high expression of donor DNA. Typically, however, genetic changes introduced into the embryo extend to the gametes and are heritable.

Scenarios can be constructed wherein introduced genes could be deleted from germ cells or early embryos derived from the treated individual. For example, transferred genes could reside on artificial chromosomes that could be deleted by activating a recombinase that induced recombination of the chromosome ends.[1] Such approaches, however, are currently only speculative. Germline gene transfer has already succeeded in several animal species. Because of this and the general belief that voluntary abstention from germline modification in humans is unlikely, a candid discussion of genetic enhancement must include the possibility that changes introduced will be transmitted to offspring.

THE STATE OF THE ART

Animal experiments thus far have attempted to improve what are intuitively regarded as "simple" traits such as growth rate or muscle mass. Efforts to genetically improve the growth of swine have involved insertion of transgenes encoding growth hormone.[4,5] Nevertheless, despite the fact that growth hormone transgenes are expressed well in swine, increased growth does not occur.[4,5] Although the transgenic animals fortuitously have less body fat,[5] these unexpected benefits cannot be extrapolated to human clinical protocols. Before a human embryo is treated with recombinant DNA, we must know exactly what we are doing.

Another spectacular failed attempt at enhancement resulted from efforts to increase muscle mass in cattle. When expressed in mice, the avian c-*ski* gene, the cellular counterpart of the retroviral v-*ski* oncogene, induced massive muscle hypertrophy.[6] This prompted efforts to produce cattle expressing a c-*ski* transgene. When gene transfer was accomplished, the transgenic calf initially exhibited muscle hypertrophy, but muscle degeneration and wasting soon followed. Unable to stand, the debilitated animal was killed.[7]

Why did these enhancement experiments fail? For clues, it is useful to compare modern-day gene transfer technology with the more traditional approach to genetic engineering: selective breeding. Selective breeding maximizes the reproductive efficiency of individuals that exhibit desired characteristics. The selection strategy is oblivious to the number of genes responsible for generating the phenotype. Swine selected for rapid growth may consume more food, produce more growth hormone, respond more briskly to endogenous growth hormone, divert proteins toward somatic growth, and possess skeletal anatomy that allows the animal to tolerate increased weight. Dozens or perhaps hundreds of genes may influence these traits, but in selective breeding, favorable alleles at all loci can simultaneously be selected. In contrast, gene transfer selects one relevant locus and attempts to improve it in isolation. It is little wonder that this approach, albeit potentially powerful and efficient, is more chancy, and has, despite more than 10 years of effort, failed to yield even one unequivocal success. Greater success has been achieved in genetic enhancement of plants, which are more easily manipulated genetically and reproductively; for example, see note 8.

Given the inherent limitations of the gene transfer approach to enhancement, discussion of extending such procedures to humans is scientifically unjustified. We clearly do not yet understand how to accomplish controlled genetic modification of even simple phenotypes. Where more complex traits such as intelligence are concerned, we have no idea what to do, and in fact we may never be able to use gene transfer for enhancement of such phenotypes. A useful way to appreciate the daunting task of manipulating intelligence through gene transfer is by considering the fact that a single cerebellar Purkinje cell may possess more synapses than the total number of genes in the human genome. There are tens of millions of Purkinje cells in the cerebellum, and these cells are involved in only one aspect of brain function: motor coordination. The genome only provides a blueprint for formation of the brain; the finer details of assembly and intellectual development are beyond direct genetic control and must perforce be subject to innumerable stochastic and environmental influences.

GENETIC ENGINEERING AND HUMAN EVOLUTION

Some have suggested that genetic enhancement and related reproductive technologies now give us the power to control human evolution. This solemn pronouncement is totally without scientific foundation. The evolution of the human species may be understood as a nonrandom change in allelic frequencies resulting from selective pressure. The change progresses over generations because individuals with specific patterns of alleles are favored reproductively. If new alleles were introduced by gene transfer, the impact on the species would be negligible. Every month worldwide approximately 11 million babies are born. The addition of one genetically modified individual could not significantly affect gene frequencies. Moreover, if the "enhanced" individual had his or her first child at the age of 20, then 2,640,000,000 unengineered children would be born during the interval between the birth and procreation of the gene recipient. Even if 1000 successful gene transfers were performed per year, a number not likely to be achieved in the foreseeable future, those newborns would constitute only 1/132,000 of all live births. Thus, any effort to enhance the human species experimentally would be swamped by the random attempts of Mother Nature.

Finally, there is no certainty that genetically enhanced individuals would have greater biological fitness, as measured by reproductive success. A genius or great athlete who has no children has no biological fitness as defined in evolutionary theory. For these reasons, neither gene transfer nor any of the other emerging reproductive technologies will ever have a significant impact on human evolution.

DEVELOPING POLICY

If we accept the notion that genetic enhancement is not practicable in the near future, what policies should we develop concerning the use of such technology? The decision to undertake any form of invasive medical intervention immediately renders the treatment subject a patient who has a right to informed consent as well as to protection from unjustifiably dangerous medical manipulation. Our inability to predict the consequences of an attempt at genetic enhancement makes informed consent impossible, and current knowledge from animal experiments tells us that embryo gene transfer is unsafe: The common approach of pronuclear microinjection is characterized by random integration of donor DNA, a lack of control of the number of gene copies inserted, significant rearrangements of host genetic material, and a 5 to 10% frequency of insertional mutagenesis.[9] Homologous

recombination[10] in embryonic stem cells overcomes many of these shortcomings, but human embryonic stem cell transfection would necessarily be followed by nuclear transfer into enucleated oocytes. Because nuclear transfer in at least two animal models is associated with a low birth rate and a very high rate of late pregnancy loss or newborn death,[11] this procedure is also unsafe. The risks are so high and the documented efficacy is so low for gene transfer that it could not compare favorably to straightforward prenatal diagnosis even when a compelling need for therapy exists, as in cases of genetic disease. The use of gene transfer for elective purposes such as enhancement would stray far beyond the limits of acceptable medical intervention.

To attempt genetic enhancement with extant methods would clearly be medically unacceptable, but attempts to ban gene transfer legally could be a cumbersome approach to limiting its clinical use. Verification of compliance would be difficult. The diverse resources required for gene transfer necessitate that the procedure be carried out in facilities equipped for in vitro fertilization. Direct inspection would be required to uncover gene transfer procedures in such facilities. This would impose on the privacy of patients undergoing accepted assisted reproduction procedures such as sperm injection. Moreover, gene transfer can be easily concealed; in the case of pronuclear microinjection, only a few seconds are needed to complete the process. Legal restrictions can also be easily avoided by performing the procedure outside the area of jurisdiction.

Finally, and perhaps most important, broad legal restrictions incur the risk of limiting invaluable research. Exemplifying this problem is the current overly broad ban on federal funding for experiments with human embryos. The recent derivation of human embryonic stem cells from preimplantation embryos[12] has created important new research opportunities, accompanied by pressure to provide federal funds for the work. This pressure has led to the odd situation in which federal funds will likely be allowed for research with embryonic stem cells but not for manipulating human embryos to produce embryonic stem cell lines. If, as a society, we feel compelled to make a statement against genetic enhancement, we need not enact anticipatory legislation. Instead we can evaluate such manipulations as we would any other invasive clinical procedure. If we require that gene transfer be accompanied by informed consent, that it have a reasonable possibility of succeeding, that its cost not be excessive, that it have acceptable side effects and toxicities, that it not be accompanied by a burdensome requirement for long-term follow-up evaluation, and that it compare favorably with other treatment options, we will currently reject the procedure on all counts as medically unethical. Were entities such as the National Bioethics Advisory Commission or Congress to make such statements formally, no responsible physician would attempt genetic enhancement. Irresponsible use of technology can never be stopped, even by legislation.

Fear of genetic manipulation may encourage proposals to limit basic investigations that might ultimately lead to effective human gene transfer. History has shown that effort is far better spent in preparing society to cope with scientific advances than in attempting to restrict basic research. Gene transfer studies may never lead to successful genetic enhancement, but they are certain to provide new treatment and prevention strategies for a variety of devastating diseases. No less significant is the potential for this research to improve our understanding of the most complex and compelling phenomenon ever observed—the life process. We cannot be expected to deny ourselves this knowledge.

REFERENCES

1. G. Stock and J. Campbell, Eds., *Summary Report, Engineering the Human Germline Symposium* (University of California, Los Angeles, 1998).

2. J. W. Gordon *et al., Proc. Natl. Acad. Sci. U.S.A.* **77,** 7380 (1980); J. W. Gordon and F. H. Ruddle, *Science* **214,** 1244 (1981); F. Costantini and F. E. Lacy, *Nature* **294,** 92 (1981); R. L. Brinster *et al., Cell* **27,** 223 (1981).

3. M. J. Evans and M. H. Kaufman, *Nature* **292,** 154 (1981); G. R. Martin, *Proc. Natl. Acad. Sci. U.S.A.* **78,** 7634 (1981); S. L. Mansour, K. R. Thomas, M. R. Capecchi, *Nature* **336,** 348 (1988); S. Thompson *et al., Cell* **56,** 313 (1989).

4. V. G. Pursel *et al., Vet. Immunol. Immunopathol.* **17,** 303 (1987).

5. C. A. Pinkert, E. J. Galbreath, C. W. Yang, L. J. Striker, *Transgenic Res.* **3,** 401 (1994); M. B. Solomon *et al., J. Anim. Sci.* **72,** 1242 (1994).

6. P. Sutrave, A. M. Kelly, S. H. Hughes, *Genes Dev.* **4,** 1462 (1990).

7. R. A. Bowen *et al., Biol. Reprod.* **50,** 664 (1994).

8. K. J. Kramer and S. Muthukrishnan, *Insect. Biochem. Mol. Biol.* **27,** 887 (1997).

9. R. D. Palmiter and R. L. Brinster, *Annu. Rev. Genet.* **20,** 465 (1986); J. W. Gordon, *Int. Rev. Cytol.* **115,** 171 (1989).

10. O. Smithies, R. G. Grett, S. S. Boggs, M. A. Koralewski, R. S. Kucherlapati, *Nature* **317,** 230 (1981).

11. I. Wilmut *et al., ibid.* **385,** 810 (1997); T. Wakayama, A. C. F. Perry, M. Zucotti, K. R. Johnson, R. Yanagimachi, *ibid.* **394,** 369 (1998).

12. M. J. Shamblott *et al., Proc. Natl. Acad. Sci. U.S.A.* **95,** 13726 (1998); J. A. Thomson *et al., Science* **282,** 1145 (1998).

ERIK PARENS

The Goodness of Fragility: On the Prospect of Genetic Technologies Aimed at the Enhancement of Human Capacities

Erik Parens is the Associate for Philosophical Studies at the Hastings Center, a bioethics think tank in Garrison, New York. He has published extensively on the ethical and social questions raised by biotechnological advances; he is also editor of *Enhancing Human Traits: Ethical and Social Ramifications* (Georgetown University Press) and coeditor of *Prenatal Genetic Testing and the Disability Rights Critique* (Georgetown University Press).

Currently, genetic technology cannot be used to significantly enhance human capacities. Although, for instance, genetically engineered bovine somatotropin (BST) is now used to enhance the milk production of cows, no one suggests an analogous enhancement of humans. And while human growth hormone (hGH) has been administered to enhance the stature of children who are not hGH deficient, it is not clear whether the procedure has worked (White 1993).

Yet if it is true that humans cannot now significantly enhance their capacities with genetic technology, it is also true that they always have sought to enhance their capacities with whatever means have been available. For example, we enhance our intellectual capacities with education, our bodily capacities with exercise, and our capacity to attract sexual partners with a variety of cosmetic techniques. From this I infer two things: (1) that it would make no sense to argue that the enhancement of human capacities is, in itself, a bad thing; and (2) that when genetic technology gets to the point where enhancement is possible, there will be a powerful drive to employ it.

Indeed, there seems to be no reason why, in principle, the gene-therapy techniques used to replace defective genes with "healthy" ones could not be used to replace healthy genes with "enhanced" or "better"

ones.[1] Nor is there any reason why, in principle, the genetic-engineering techniques used to make products that the body cannot make could not be used to make more of a product that the body already makes.

If today, a drug like fluoxetine (Prozac) can enhance the capacity of a significant minority of users to compete in a consumer society by raising the level of the neurotransmitter serotonin (Kramer 1993; Sherman 1994), then there is reason to think that genetic technology will be able to enhance human capacities in similarly significant ways.[2] Indeed, a recent issue of *Science* reports on researchers who generated mice that lacked the gene for one of the serotonin receptors (5-HT_{1B}) (Saudou et al. 1994). As one might predict from fluoxetine's ability to increase serotonin levels in humans by inhibiting the reuptake of serotonin, the researchers found that the aggressiveness of the mice was increased. While these researchers clearly did not have in mind the significant minority of fluoxetine users whose competitiveness is enhanced by increased levels of serotonin, they apparently did have in mind the possibility of using genetic technology to achieve the same therapeutic effect that drugs like fluoxetine have. Furthermore, although enhancing the aggressiveness of mice is a long way from enhancing the competitiveness of humans with genetic technology, such enhancements no longer seem the stuff of science fiction.

Given the apparently enduring desire of humans to enhance their capacities, and given the likelihood that

Reprinted by permission from *Kennedy Institute of Ethics Journal* 5 (June 1995), 141–53. Copyright © 1995 by the Johns Hopkins University Press.

new genetic technologies will at some point enable us to enhance our capacities in significant and perhaps unprecedented ways, now is the time for society to begin thinking about how far it ought to go in this regard.[3] While there are good and self-evident reasons to go in the direction of such enhancements, a chief aim of this essay is to reflect on some good and less evident reasons why our society ought to exercise extreme caution as it contemplates such a move.

Urging caution with respect to genetic enhancement is nothing new (see, e.g., President's Commission 1982; Davis and Englehardt 1983; Anderson, 1989; Walters 1991). But the problem does not admit of a neat solution. It is, rather, the sort of problem that requires ongoing engagement. My attempt to engage it will take the form of the following question: Will we, in some of our attempts to enhance humans, inadvertently improverish them by reducing what I will call their fragility.[4] Before beginning to answer this question, I want to make three preliminary points.

First, my use of the term "fragility" might seem strange. When I say that we are fragile creatures, I mean that we are creatures subject to change and to chance. In this essay I attempt to reflect upon what life would be like if we could significantly reduce the change and chance to which we—creatures whose forms are largely determined by the genetic hand dealt us by nature—have hitherto been subject.

Second, I am not trying to argue that genetic technology aimed at enhancement could rid life of fragility. Even if human beings were to become uniformly beautiful, marvelously tempered, hugely healthy, and massively smart, there still would be plenty of change and chance for everyone to be subject to. I am merely exploring that might be lost if, to an unprecedented extent, we could reduce our vulnerability to change and chance.

Finally, I am not making the unconditional or absolute claim that we ought never to use genetic technology to enhance human beings. Nor am I attempting to provide an algorithm that we could simply apply when faced with the prospect of a given technology. Rather, I am attempting to articulate a series of considerations that ought to be factored into any decision about whether to go ahead with a given technology aimed at enhancement. I undertake to articulate these considerations because, given the potential for prodigious benefits, we might overlook them. In the end, I will speculate about what besides benevolence inclines us to overlook such considerations as

we contemplate the use of technologies aimed at the enhancement of human capacities.

THE DESIRE TO REDUCE CHANGE

One of the easiest ways to begin appreciating what is valuable about fragility is to think about the pleasure we take in our experience of some forms of the beautiful. Consider the ordinary experience of beholding other organisms—such as flowers. The intensity of one sort of pleasure we receive from beholding flowers depends decisively on their transience, on the fact that they undergo change. Crucial ingredients in our pleasure are our anticipation of the blossoming and our anxiety about, and memory of, its passing.

That the blossom comes into being and passes away may be a source of anxiety—but it is an anxiety that heightens our pleasure: this flower, in this form, is here but for a few, beautiful days. It may even be that this "little" anxiety in the face of the flower's coming into being and passing away is an occasion for our reflection upon the "great" anxiety we experience in the face of our own mortality. Though we often turn away from anxiety, both little and great, doing so is to turn away from an important part of being human and thus is to impoverish our experience.

The goodness of this sort of fragility receives one of its most beautiful expressions in the poetry of Wallace Stevens:

> Is there no change of death in paradise?
> Does ripe fruit never fall? Or do the boughs
> Hang always heavy in that perfect sky,
> Unchanging, yet so like our perishing earth,
> With rivers like our own that seek for seas
> They never find, the same receding shores
> That never touch with inarticulate pang? . . .
> Death is the mother of beauty. . . .[5]

If there is no change in paradise, then, according to Stevens, neither is there beauty of a fundamental sort.

If the attempt to reduce our subjection to change could affect for the worse our experience of some forms of the beautiful, it could do the same for our experience of caring and being cared for.[6] Suppose enhancement technology were aimed at removing the difficulties of aging, thereby altering our conception and experience of, for example, relationships between the generations. Given that figuring out how to care for a burgeoning elderly population is one of our most pressing social problems, it might, at first glance, seem quite wonderful if we could, say, enhance the capacities of ninety-five-year-olds so that they could act and feel like twenty-five-year-olds.

Furthermore, while we're thinking about trying to reduce the time spent on the elderly members of our society, we could also think about trying to reduce the time spent on the young. We could, I suppose, strive to discover an "acceleration hormone"—a hormone aimed at making children grow faster. Much money and energy would be saved if we could compress not only old age, but childhood too. I can well imagine the complaint that I have created a straw man. After all, children are sweet; no one would make such a proposal. But what about accelerating adolescence? No one ever claimed that adolescents are sweet; moreover, adolescence is a time of pain and danger to the people undergoing it, as well as to the rest of us. Compressing this difficult period could significantly reduce pain and the expenditure of valuable social resources.

I assume that one reason no one would assent to my modest proposal is that we think that we ought to caringly respond to the pain of adolescence rather than engineer a way around it. There is a point beyond which the reduction of our subjection to some sorts of change costs too much. Though it would be naive to forget just how burdensome the need for care can be to both the giver of care and the receiver, it would be equally naive to forget that the shared recognition and acceptance of human neediness can be profoundly valuable. That is, I take it to be valuable for us to recognize and accept our nature, and neediness is a constituent of that nature.

Further, as I will discuss more fully below, when we consider whether to proceed with a given technology aimed at enhancement, we ought to consider whether that technology threatens to reduce the great diversity of human forms. Given what appears to be a deep human tendency to fear and hate the different, we ought to be especially vigilant about promoting technologies that could—by engineering sameness—collude with that tendency. At the point where a given enhancement technology diminishes difference across the life span, where it promises to make us all look and act more alike, the good that is diversity across the life span is threatened.

In a word, before we attempt to enhance human beings by reducing their subjection to change—before attempting to reduce their fragility—we ought to consider how such attempts would affect the good that is our experience of some forms of the beautiful, the good that is relationships of care, and the good that is diversity across the life span.

THE DESIRE TO REDUCE CHANCE

Let me invite you now to think about the pleasure we take in our experience of some human excellences. Why is it, for example, that our knowledge of a runner's use of steroids diminishes our pleasure in his or her performance? Why is it that watching Ben Johnson run does not give track fans the same sort of pleasure as watching, say, Carl Lewis? Part of the reason is no doubt simply a sense of fairness: Johnson has an unfair, steroid-induced advantage. I want to suggest, however, that something subtler is at work as well. Part of our experience of the particular excellence of a winning runner resides in our intuition that this performance is the result of an extraordinary combination of human effort and chance. It could have been otherwise, and it almost always is, but this time a human being ran 100 meters in well under 10 seconds. To reduce the role of chance—to alter with steroids the hand that nature dealt the runner—is to diminish, if not ruin, our experience of this form of excellence.

Sport is neither the only, nor the most significant, area of human endeavor where chance plays a crucial role. When we speak of equal opportunity, for example, we mean that within the constraints of those gifts that come to people from the natural lottery, we give each an equal opportunity to compete. When there no longer is a natural lottery such as we have understood is heretofore, when what we are depends not upon the hand nature dealt us, but—even more than now—upon the hand our parents bought us, then concepts such as equal opportunity will have to undergo fundamental transformations.[7]

It is predictable, for example, that an even larger chasm will open between the rich who can afford enhancement treatment and the poor who cannot. This prediction rests on the assumption that enhancement treatment will be distributed unevenly, according to people's ability to pay. But let us change the assumption. What would happen if resources were not limited and enhancement treatment were available to all? At first glance, it might seem that nothing could be lost; it might seem that, finally, we had discovered how to make humankind happier. Reducing the chance to which humans are subject in the natural lottery might seem like a brilliant way to end the competitiveness and resentment that are the root of clashes in the kindergarten and on the battlefield. Imagine: Everyone could be porcelain-skinned, blond, blue-eyed, straight, tall, small-waisted, big-chested, smart, and nice. Nobody would have to have skin too dark anymore. Nobody would have to have hair too kinky anymore. Nobody would have to be gay. Nobody would be too short. Nobody would have too big a nose or too small a chest. Nobody would be too mean or too nice. Everybody would be just right (see Fielder 1985).

If society could in fact enhance away the "imperfections" resulting from chance, it could, once again, reduce one of its most pressing burdens: the burden of responding to the needs of those who are marginalized because they do not possess the specifications deemed valuable. And once again the questions arise: Would it be a good thing to reduce the diversity—to diminish the difference—that results from our subjection to chance? Would it be a good thing to reduce the need to respond to the vulnerability of others that results from our subjection to chance? For the reasons offered above in the context of attempting to reduce our subjection to change, my tentative answers to those questions are clear.

Just as I suggested that it is in exuberant moments—of imagining how much better life might be if we could rid it of change—that we forget about the goodness of change, so in exuberant moments we forget about the goodness of chance.[8] When we are carried away by our benevolent desires to reduce the suffering of vulnerable people and, less benevolently, their cost to society, we forget that the vulnerability of others not only burdens us (though it surely does so), but also elicits from us the awesome capacity to care for others. Although—and I cannot be too emphatic about this—it would be a profound mistake to romanticize the need to care for vulnerable others and the need of vulnerable others to be cared for, it would be equally mistaken to ignore the goodness that those relationships can possess.[9]

THE DESIRE FOR PARADISE

In my attempt to articulate the considerations that ought to be factored into any decision to implement a given technology aimed at enhancement, there operates an as-yet unarticulated premise involving a particular conception of the proper relationship between humans and the rest of the natural world. Indeed it seems that significantly different conceptions of the value and the meaning of human life—profoundly different conceptions of our proper relationship to

ourselves and to the rest of the natural world—are at work in the argument between those who tend to favor enhancement technologies and those who tend to be critical of them. I would like now to suggest one way to begin thinking about that difference.

Those who tend to favor genetic enhancement proceed from a conception of the relationship between humans and the rest of the world much like that of Francis Bacon. Bacon's project to conquer and control nature is relentlessly commented upon, yet one element of the project is often forgotten. Bacon thinks that his project has a divine sanction; in *The New Organon* (I, cxxix), for instance, he writes that the human race has a "right over nature which belongs to it by divine bequest." Consistent with his Calvinism, Bacon believes, as one scholar succinctly puts it, that "the mission of science [is] to repair the damage done by the Fall of Man and to restore man to his original glory" (Finch 1963, p. xiii).[10]

It goes without saying that Bacon's project has benefited humankind enormously. It does not, however, go without saying that Bacon's project is embedded in a very particular conception of the proper relationship between humans and the rest of nature. In fact, we are so embedded in Bacon's conception that it does not seem particular to us at all. Medicine, for example, has been one of the greatest beneficiaries of that project's success. When Ronald Munson and Lawrence Davis (1992) argue in this journal that medicine ought to employ germ-line therapy for the treatment of disease, they speak as if the aim of medicine were self-evident. Like Bacon, they proceed as if the Western biomedical conception were ordained by God. Because the aim of medicine is self-evident for Munson and Davis, the only remaining problem is to find the means to achieve it. As they write, "The basic standard of evaluation [for medicine] must be practical or instrumental success with respect to its specific aim." What, in their view is the aim of medicine? It is to achieve "control over the factors affecting health. . . . [Knowledge] is important to medicine because it leads to control" (Munson and Davis 1992, p. 155). Given that control is the aim, and given that germ-line therapy "is the most effective form of control," they conclude that medicine has a prima facie duty to employ germ-line therapy.

Although the view that the proper relationship between humans and the rest of the world is one of control is so entrenched as to seem self-evident, there are alternative perspectives: certainly many feminists, environmentalists, and peoples from different cultures have articulated such views. But people in the bioethical conversation also have attempted to articulate an alternative vision; Hans Jonas is one such person.

Whereas Bacon proceeds from the assumption that the mission of science is to repair the damage done by the Fall of Man and to restore Man to his original glory, Jonas—to translate his thought into theological terms—proceeds from the assumption that leaving Paradise did not constitute a Fall at all, but rather marked the beginning of peculiarly difficult and good human life. Whereas Bacon thinks that creation needs restoration to a former state of perfection, Jonas thinks that creation is owed preservation in its altogether "imperfect" state. Whereas Bacon thinks that nature is ours to use in whatever ways conduce to our desires, Jonas thinks that because nature is in an important sense not ours—"being [is] strictly on loan" (1992, p. 36)—we ought not so to use it.[11]

The archenemy of the Baconian project—death—is of course the ultimate form of fragility. Whereas, according to Bacon, death is the enemy and life extension is medicine's "noblest goal" (Amundsen 1978, p. 27), according to Jonas, death is both a "bitter burden" and a "blessing." Following Heidegger, Jonas (1992, p. 36) writes of death: "only in confrontation with ever-possible not-being could being come to feel itself, affirm itself, make itself its own purpose." For Jonas, death is not an accidental part of life that we ought to try to overcome, but rather is an essential part of life, the goodness of which we need to try to understand.

Those who seek to understand the goodness of death—that ultimate form of fragility—hope that we are the sort of animals who can decide that, although technologies aimed at enhancement might gratify both pedestrian and noble desires, we won't go ahead with some of those technologies because to do so would be to lose too much that makes life good. As valuable as the human capacity for self-transformation and control of the world is, the human capacity to relinquish control and to resist the desire for transformation is equally valuable. We are the animals that can ask: When does that marvelous capacity to manipulate and control the world, when does that marvelous and peculiarly human capacity to change ourselves, go too far?

With respect to genetic technology, we can begin

by saying that it goes too far when—in an attempt to establish paradise on earth—it threatens the good that is the pleasure we take in some forms of the beautiful and excellent, or when it threatens the good that is some relationships of care, or when it threatens the good that is the diversity of human forms. When we ask whether it makes a difference if we figure out when our capacity to manipulate and control the world and ourselves has gone too far, we might think about what that capacity has wrought, in the last forty years, on the diversity of life forms on this planet.

Since Watson and Crick discovered the double helix in 1953, the world's population has more than doubled and its economic activity has more than quadrupled (Kennedy 1993, p. 97). According to an appeal sent to Latin American presidents by Gabriel Garcia Marquez and others, "By the year 2000 three-quarters of America's tropical forests may have been felled and 50 percent of their species lost forever" (Kennedy 1993, p. 100). Thus, it is possible that in approximately the same time it will have taken us to garner the knowledge necessary to diminish the diversity of human forms by making ourselves more alike, we also will have reduced by one-half the diversity of other animal forms in some places.[12]

It seems to me that it would be profoundly tragic if the virtue that is our capacity for self-transformation became a vice. It would be profoundly tragic and paradoxical if what Nietzsche calls "the unfixed animal"—due to its capacity for change and its desire for perfection—were to "fix itself" (see Jonas 1974, p. 153).

Let me emphasize: It would be cruel, if not stupid, to suggest that we ought never to use genetic technology to heal the sick. It probably would be foolish to suggest that technology ought never to be used for the enhancement of human beings. So too would it be foolish to forget that without the desire to control and master the world there would be no desire to control and master ourselves.[13] My suggestion has not been that we should figure out a way to extirpate our desire to control and alter ourselves and the world; rather, it has been simply that we should think more deeply about how attempts at control and alteration that truly enhance life are different from those that impoverish it. It may be that thinking more deeply about that difference will entail rethinking some basic beliefs about our proper relationship to ourselves and the rest of nature.

To paraphrase the Czech novelist, Milan Kundera, whose native country has been subjected to relentless political violence in the name of establishing Paradise on earth, "Humankind's longing for Paradise is humankind's longing not to be human." No less than the nobility, we should remember the peril of that longing.

NOTES

1. I am keenly aware that, given the extent to which concepts such as health and enhancement are socially constructed, the distinction between treatment aimed at health and treatment aimed at enhancement is highly contestable. For an account of the reasonableness of the distinction, see Normal Daniels (1992).

2. Although Prozac's effectiveness is correlated with altered serotonin levels, research suggests that increased serotonin is a necessary, but not sufficient, cause for the effects now associated with Prozac. Nonetheless, my point remains: if we can enhance behavior with a drug like Prozac, it stands to reason that we can do the same with genetic technology.

3. It seems to me that we should respond to the prospect of genetic enhancement (somatic and germ-line) as Nelson Wivel and LeRoy Walters respond to the prospect of germ-line treatment aimed at the prevention of disease: "Because the readily identifiable technical problems necessarily consign germ-line gene modification to the relatively distant future, a discussion of the ethical issues might be viewed as an exercise in the abstract. . . . It [nonetheless] would, in our view, be a useful investment of time and energy to continue and in fact to intensify the public discussion . . . *even though the application of this new technology to humans is not likely to be proposed in the near future*" (Wivel and Walters 1993, p. 537, emphasis added).

4. Always in the background for me will be the words of Martha Nussbaum (1986, p. 2), "Human excellence is seen . . . in the Greek poetic tradition . . . as something whose very nature it is to be in need, a growing thing in the world that could not be made invulnerable and keep its own peculiar fineness."

5. My attention was first called to Stevens's "Sunday Morning" by Leon Kass's essay "Mortality and Morality: The Virtues of Finitude" (1985).

6. For the dangers of such "care talk," see Adrienne Asch (1993).

7. Concerning the implications of the genetic technologies for (1) our concept of equality of opportunity, (2) our conception of humans as responsible agents, and (3) our conception of normality, see Dan Brock (1992).

8. See Hans Jonas (1985, p. 500): "The random nature of the sexual process is both the irreplaceable blessing and the inescapable burden of our lot. . . ."

9. See Bruce Jennings, Daniel Callahan and Arthur Caplan (1988, p. 15): "The provision of care and social support for persons with chronic illness by temporarily well and able-bodied citizens reflects an acknowledgment of the links that join the sick and the well, the young and the old in a community of common humanness and vulnerability."

10. See also Charles Taylor's discussion of the Calvinist desire to "clean up the human mess" (Taylor, 1989, pp. 227–28).

11. Though here I am contrasting Jonas's world view with the Calvinist one, the respect in which Jonas's view is commensurate with much of Christian thought is clear.

12. This desire to McDonaldize the world—to reduce the diversity of animate and inanimate forms—is as deep as it is demanding of our attention. Benjamin R. Barber's (1992) "Jihad vs. McWorld" is pertinent. For a closely related argument, see James V. Neel (1993, p. 127): "The elucidation of the precise nature of our genetic material, four billion years in evolving, occurred only 40 years ago. Despite the incredible advances in molecular genetics, we still have a very limited knowledge of the anatomy of our DNA, but even less understanding of how it transacts its excruciatingly complex business. Right now the ecosystem is reeling under the impact of an intellectual arrogance which assumed unbridled license to perturb that system. We are a part of that ecosystem, the last frontier, so to speak. Is there any informed person who, surveying the current evidence of the profound consequences of precipitous human action, believes we are now ready for a serious consideration of how to mold ourselves genetically?"

13. Similarly, it would be foolish to suggest that Bacon and his contemporary followers are without awe or reverence for nature; there are, however, "reverences" or "awes" with different emphases. See Renée Fox's discussion of the difference between the awe Barbara McClintock brings to the study of molecular biology and the awe Albert Claude brings to it (Fox 1989, pp. 190–94).

REFERENCES

Amundsen, Darrel W. 1978. The Physician's Obligation to Prolong Life: A Medical Duty without Classical Roots. *Hastings Center Report* 8 (4): 23–30.

Anderson, W. French, 1989. Human Gene Therapy: Why Draw a Line? *Journal of Medicine and Philosophy* 14: 681–93.

Asch, Adrienne. 1993. Abused or Neglected Clients—Abusive or Neglectful Service Systems? In *Ethical Conflicts in the Management of Home Care*, ed. Rosalie A. Kane and Arthur L. Caplan, pp. 113–21. New York: Springer Publishing Co.

Barber, Benjamin R. 1992. Jihad vs. McWorld. *Atlantic Monthly* (March): 53–65.

Brock, Dan. 1992. The Human Genome Project and Human Identity. *Houston Law Review* 29 (1): 7–22.

Daniels, Norman. 1992. Growth Hormone Therapy for Short Stature: Can We Support the Treatment/Enhancement Distinction? *Growth: Genetics & Hormones* 8 (Supplement 1): 46–48.

Davis, Bernard D., and Engelhardt, H. Tristram, Jr. 1984. Genetic Engineering: Prospects and Recommendations. *Zygon* 19: 277–80.

Fielder, Leslie A. 1985. The Tyranny of the Normal. In *Which Babies Shall Live?*, ed. Thomas H. Murray and Arthur L. Caplan, pp. 151–60. Clifton, NJ: Humana Press.

Finch, Henry LeRoy, ed. 1963. *The Complete Essays of Francis Bacon*. New York: Washington Square Press.

Fox, Renée. 1989. *The Sociology of Medicine: A Participant Observer's View*. Englewood Cliffs, NJ: Prentice-Hall.

Jennings, Bruce; Callahan, Daniel; and Caplan, Arthur. 1988. Ethical Challenges of Chronic Illness. *Hastings Center Report* 18 (1, Special Supplement): 1–16.

Jonas, Hans. 1974. Biological Engineering—A Preview. In *Philosophical Essays: From Ancient Creed to Technological Man*, ed. Hans Jonas, pp. 141–67. Englewood Cliffs, NJ: Prentice-Hall.

———. 1985. Ethics and Biogenic Art. *Social Research* 52: 491–501.

———. 1992. The Burden and Blessing of Mortality. *Hastings Center Report* 22 (1): 34–40.

Kass, Leon. 1985. Mortality and Morality: The Virtues of Finitude. In *Toward a More Natural Science*, ed. Leon Kass, pp. 299–317. New York: The Free Press.

Kennedy, Paul. 1993. *Preparing for the Twenty-First Century*. New York: Random House.

Kramer, Peter D. 1993. *Listening to Prozac*. New York: Viking.

Munson, Ronald, and Davis, Lawrence H. 1992. Germ-Line Therapy and the Medical Imperative. *Kennedy Institute of Ethics Journal* 2: 137–58.

Neel, James V. 1993. Germ-Line Gene Therapy: Another View. *Human Gene Therapy* 4: 127–28.

Nussbaum, Martha. 1986. *The Fragility of Goodness*. New York: Cambridge University Press.

President's Commission for the Study of Ethical Problems in Medicine and Biomedical and Behavioral Research. 1982. *Splicing Life: The Social and Ethical Issues of Genetic Engineering with Human Beings*. Washington, DC: U.S. Government Printing Office.

Saudou, Frédéric; Amara, Djamel Aït; Dierich, Andrée; et al. 1994. Enhanced Aggressive Behavior in Mice Lacking 5-HT$_{1B}$ Receptor. *Science* 265: 1875–78.

Sherman, Carl. 1994. Depression's Complex, Tangled Biologic Roots. *Clinical Psychiatry News* 22 (2): 3, 15.

Taylor, Charles. 1989. *Sources of the Self: The Making of the Modern Identity*. Cambridge: Harvard University Press.

Walters, LeRoy. 1991. Human Gene Therapy: Ethics and Public Policy. *Human Gene Therapy* 2: 115–22.

White, Gladys. 1993. Human Growth Hormone: The Dilemma of Expanded Use in Children. *Kennedy Institute of Ethics Journal* 3: 401–9.

Wivel, Nelson A., and Walters, LeRoy. 1993. Germ-Line Gene Modification and Disease Prevention: Some Medical and Ethical Perspectives. *Science* 262: 533–38.

SUGGESTED READINGS

GENERAL ISSUES

Andrews, Lori B., et al. "Genetics and the Law." *Emory Law Journal* 39 (1990), 619–853. Symposium.

Asch, Adrienne, and Geller, Gail. "Feminism, Bioethics, and Genetics." In Susan M. Wolf, ed., *Feminism and Bioethics: Beyond Reproduction*. New York: Oxford University Press, 1996, 318–50.

Annas, George J., and Elias, Sherman, eds. *Gene Mapping: Using Law and Ethics as Guides*. New York: Oxford University Press, 1992.

Bankowski, Zbigniew, and Capron, Alexander Morgan, eds. *Genetics, Ethics, and Human Values: Human Genome Mapping, Genetic Screening and Gene Therapy*. Geneva: Council for International Organizations of Medical Sciences, 1990.

Davis, Bernard D., ed. *The Genetic Revolution: Scientific Prospects and Public Perceptions*. Baltimore: Johns Hopkins University Press, 1991.

Evans, John H. *Playing God?: Human Genetic Engineering and the Rationalization of Public Bioethical Debate*. Chicago: University of Chicago Press, 2002.

Fletcher, Joseph. *The Ethics of Genetic Control: Ending Reproductive Roulette*. Garden City, NY: Anchor Books, 1974.

Frankel, Mark S., and Teich, Albert, eds. *The Genetic Frontier: Ethics Law, and Policy*. Washington, DC: American Association for the Advancement of Science, 1994.

Fukuyama, Francis. *Our Posthuman Future: Consequences of the Biotechnology Revolution*. New York: Farrar, Straus and Giroux, 2002.

Gert, Bernard, et al. *Morality and the New Genetics: A Guide for Students and Health Care Providers*. Boston: Jones and Bartlett, 1996.

Greely, Henry T. "Human Genome Diversity Project." In Thomas H. Murray and Maxwell J. Mehlman, eds., *Encyclopedia of Ethical, Legal, and Policy Issues in Biotechnology*. 2 vols. New York: John Wiley & Sons, 2000, 552–66.

Harris, John. *Clones, Genes, and Immortality: Ethics and the Genetic Revolution*. New York: Oxford University Press, 1998.

House of Commons, Select Committee on Science and Technology. *Human Genetics: The Science and Its Consequences* (Third Report). 4 vols. London: Her Majesty's Stationery Office, 1995. (HC41.)

Hubbard, Ruth, and Wald, Elijah. *Exploding the Gene Myth*. Boston: Beacon Press, 1993.

Kitcher, Philip. *The Lives to Come: The Genetic Revolution and Human Possibilities*. New York: Simon & Schuster, 1996.

Krimsky, Sheldon. *Biotechnics and Society: The Rise of Industrial Genetics*. Westport, CT: Praeger, 1991.

Kristol, William, and Cohen, Eric, eds. *The Future Is Now: America Confronts the New Genetics*. New York: Rowman & Littlefield, 2002.

Mahowald, Mary B., et al. "The New Genetics and Women." *Milbank Quarterly* 74 (1996), 239–83.

McGee, Glenn. *The Perfect Baby: A Pragmatic Approach to Genetics*. Lanham, MD: Rowman and Littlefield, 1997.

———. "Parenting in an Era of Genetics." *Hastings Center Report* 27 (March–April 1997), 16–22.

Nelkin, Dorothy, and Lindee, M. Susan. *The DNA Mystique: The Gene as a Cultural Icon*. New York: Freeman, 1995.

Ramsey, Paul. *Fabricated Man: The Ethics of Genetic Control*. New Haven: Yale University Press, 1970.

Rifkin, Jeremy. *The Biotech Century: Harnessing the Gene and Remaking the World*. New York: Penguin Putnam, 1998.

Suzuki, David, and Knudtson, Peter. *Genethics: The Clash between the New Genetics and Human Values*. Rev. updated ed. Cambridge, MA: Harvard University Press, 1990.

Tong, Rosemarie. "Feminist and Nonfeminist Perspectives on Genetic Screening, Diagnosis, Counseling, and Therapy." In Rosemarie Tong, ed., *Feminist Approaches to Bioethics: Theoretical Reflections and Practical Applications*. Boulder, CO: Westview Press: 213–42, 268–71.

U.S. Congress, Office of Technology Assessment. *New Developments in Biotechnology—Background Paper: Public Perceptions of Biotechnology*. Washington, DC: U.S. Government Printing Office, May 1987.

Wachbroit, Robert. "Genetic Determinism, Genetic Reductionism, and Genetic Essentialism." In Thomas H. Murray and Maxwell J. Mehlman, eds., *Encyclopedia of Ethical, Legal, and Policy Issues in Biotechnology*. 2 vols. New York: John Wiley & Sons, 2002, 352–56.

Walters, LeRoy. "Human Genetic Intervention and the Theologians: Cosmic Theology and Casuistic Analysis." In Lisa Sowle Cahill and James F. Childress, eds., *Christian Ethics: Problems and Prospects*. Cleveland: Pilgrim Press, 1996, 235–49.

Weir, Robert F., Lawrence, Susan C., and Fales, Evan, eds. *Genes and Human Self-Knowledge: Historical and Philosophical Reflections on Modern Genetics*. Iowa City, IA: Iowa University Press, 1994.

Wasserman, David T. "Behavioral Genetics, Human." In Thomas H. Murray and Maxwell J. Mehlman, eds., *Encyclopedia of Ethical, Legal, and Policy Issues in Biotechnology*. 2 vols. New York: John Wiley & Sons, 2000, 117–27.

Wolf, Susan M. "Beyond 'Genetic Discrimination'; Toward the Broader Harm of Geneticism." *Journal of Law, Medicine and Ethics* 23 (1995), 345–53.

Zweiger, Gary. *Transducing the Genome: Information, Anarchy, and Revolution in the Biomedical Sciences.* New York: Mc-Graw-Hill, 2001.

EUGENICS PROGRAMS IN THE TWENTIETH CENTURY

Adams, Mark B., ed. *The Wellborn Science: Eugenics in Germany, France, Brazil, and Russia.* New York: Oxford University Press, 1990.

Allen, Garland E. "Is a New Eugenics Afoot?" *Science* 294 (2001), 59–61.

———. "The Social and Economic Origins of Genetic Determinism: A Case History of the American Eugenics Movement, 1900–1940, and Its Lessons for Today." *Genetica* 99 (1997), 77–88.

American Society of Human Genetics, Board of Directors. "Eugenics and the Misuse of Genetic Information to Restrict Reproductive Freedom." *American Journal of Human Genetics* 64 (1999), 335–38.

Barondess, Jeremiah A. "Medicine against Society: Lessons from the Third Reich." *Journal of the American Medical Association* 276 (1996), 1657–61.

Biesold, Horst. *Crying Hands: Eugenics and Deaf People in Nazi Germany.* Washington DC: Gallaudet University Press, 1999.

Burleigh, Michael, and Wippermann, Wolfgang. *The Racial State: Germany 1933–1945.* Cambridge: Cambridge University Press, 1991.

Carlson, Elof Axel. *The Unfit: A History of a Bad Idea.* Woodbury, NY: Cold Spring Harbor Laboratory Press, 2000.

China, People's Republic of. "Presidential Decree No. 33 of 27 October 1994 Promulgating the Law of the People's Republic of China on the Protection of Maternal and Child Health." *International Digest of Health Legislation* 46, no. 1 (1995), 39–42.

Dikötter, Frank. *Imperfect Conceptions: Medical Knowledge, Birth Defects, and Eugenics in China.* New York: Columbia University Press, 1998.

———. "Race Culture: Recent Perspectives on the History of Eugenics." *American Historical Review* 103 (1998), 467–78.

Dowbiggin, Ian Robert. *Keeping America Sane: Psychiatry and Eugenics in the United States and Canada, 1880–1940.* Ithaca, NY: Cornell University Press, 1997.

Dubow, Saul. *Scientific Racism in Modern South Africa.* New York: Cambridge University Press, 1995.

Duster, Troy. *Backdoor to Eugenics.* New York: Routledge, Chapman and Hall, 1990.

Field, Martha A., and Sanchez, Valerie A. *Equal Treatment for People with Mental Retardation: Having and Raising Children.* Cambridge, MA: Harvard University Press, 2001.

Gallagher, Nancy L. *Breeding Better Vermonters: The Eugenics Project in the Green Mountain State.* Hanover, NH: University Press of New England, 1999.

Galton, David J. and Galton, Clare J. "Francis Galton: and Eugenics Today." *Journal of Medical Ethics* 24 (1998), 99–105.

Gillham, Nicholas Wright. *A Life of Sir Frances Galton: From African Exploration to the Birth of Eugenics.* New York: Oxford University Press, 2001.

Haller, Mark H. *Eugenics: Hereditarian Attitudes in American Thought.* New Brunswick, NJ: Rutgers University Press, 1963.

Hesketh, Therese, and Zhu, Wei Xiang. "Maternal and Child Health in China." *British Medical Journal* 314 (1997), 1898–1900.

Kerr, Anne and Shakespeare, Tom. *Genetic Politics: From Eugenics to Genome.* Cheltenham, UK: New Clarion Press, 2002.

Kevles, Daniel J. "Eugenics: I. Historical Aspects." in Warren Thomas Reich, ed., *Encyclopedia of Bioethics.* Rev. ed. New York: Simon & Schuster Macmillan, 1995, 765–70.

———. *In the Name of Eugenics: Genetics and the Uses of Human Heredity.* Cambridge, MA: Harvard University Press, 1995.

King, David S. "Preimplantation Genetic Diagnostic and the 'New' Eugenics." *Journal of Medical Ethics* 25 (1999), 176–82.

Kline, Wendy. *Building of a Better Race: Gender, Sexuality, and Eugenics From the Turn of the Century to the Baby Boom.* Berkeley, CA: University of California Press, 2001.

Kühl, Stefan. *The Nazi Connection: Eugenics, American Racism, and German National Socialism.* New York: Oxford University Press, 2002.

Lappé, Marc. "Eugenics: II. Ethical Issues." In Warren Thomas Reich, ed., *Encyclopedia of Bioethics.* Rev. ed. New York: Simon & Schuster Macmillan, 1995, 770–77.

Larson, Edward J. *Sex, Race, and Science: Eugenics and the Deep South.* Baltimore, MD: Johns Hopkins University Press, 1996.

Lifton, Robert J. *The Nazi Doctors: Medical Killing and the Psychology of Genocide.* New York: Basic Books, 2000.

Ludmerer, Kenneth M. *Genetics and American Society: A Historical Appraisal.* Baltimore: Johns Hopkins University Press, 1972.

Lynn, Richard. *Eugenics: A Reassessment.* Westport, CT: Greenwood, 2001.

McGee, Glenn, and Magus, David. "Eugenics, Ethics." In Thomas H. Murray and Maxwell J. Mehlman, eds., *Encyclopedia of Ethical, Legal, and Policy Issues in Biotechnology.* 2 vols. New York: John Wiley & Sons, 2000, 199–204.

Micklos, David, and Carlson, Elof. "Engineering American Society: The Lesson of Eugenics." *Nature Reviews: Genetics* 1 (2000), 153–58.

Neri, Demetrio. "Eugenics." In *Encyclopedia of Applied Ethics.* vol. 2. San Diego, CA: Academic Press, 1998, 161–73.]

Neumann-Held, Eva M. "Can It Be a 'Sin' to Understand Disease? On 'Genes' and 'Eugenics' and an 'Unconnected Connection.' " *Medicine, Health Care and Philosophy* 4 (2001), 5–17.

Nies, Betsy Lee L. *Eugenic Fantasies: Racial Ideology in the Literature and Popular Culture of the 1920's.* New York: Routledge, 2001.

Paul, Diane B. *Controlling Human Heredity, 1865 to the Present.* Atlantic Highlands, NJ: Humanities Press International, 1995.

———. *The Politics of Heredity: Essays on Eugenics, Biomedicine, and the Nature-Nurture Debate.* Albany, NY: State University of New York Press, 1998.

Pearson, Veronica. "Population Policy and Eugenics in China." *British Journal of Psychiatry* 167 (1995), 1–4.

Pernick, Martin S. *The Black Stork: Eugenics and the Death of "Defective" Babies in American Medicine and Motion Pictures Since 1915.* New York: Oxford University Press, 1999.

———. "Eugenics and Public Health in American History." *American Journal of Public Health* 87 (1997), 1767–72.

Proctor, Robert N. "Genomics and Eugenics: How Fair Is the Comparison?" In George J. Annas and Sherman Elias, eds., *Gene Mapping: Using Law and Ethics as Guides.* New York: Oxford University Press, 1992, 75–93.

———. *Racial Hygiene: Medicine under the Nazis.* Cambridge, MA: Harvard University Press, 1988.

Rafter, Nicole Hahn. *Creating Born Criminals.* Urbana, IL: University of Illinois Press, 1998.

Reilly, Philip R. "Eugenic Sterilization in the United States." In Aubrey Milunsky and George J. Annas, eds., *Genetics and the Law III.* New York: Plenum Press, 1985, 227–241.

———. Eugenics, Ethics, Sterilization Laws." In Thomas H. Murray and Maxwell J. Mehlman, eds., *Encyclopedia of Ethical, Legal, and Policy Issues in Biotechnology.* 2 vols. New York: John Wiley & Sons, 2000, 204–14.

———. *The Surgical Solution: A History of Involuntary Sterilization in the United States.* Baltimore: Johns Hopkins University Press, 1991.

Roll-Hansen, Nils, and Broberg, Gunnar, eds. *Eugenics and the Welfare State: Sterilization Policy in Denmark, Sweden, Norway, and Finland.* East Lansing, MI: Michigan State University Press, 1996.

Romeo-Casabona, Carlos M. "Health and Eugenics Practices: Looking towards the Future." *European Journal of Health Law* 5 (1998), 241–60.

Selden, Steven. *Inheriting Shame: The Story of Eugenics and Racism in America,* New York: Teachers College Press, 1999.

Smith, J. David, and Nelson, K. Ray. *The Sterilization of Carrie Buck.* Far Hills, NJ: New Horizon Press, 1989.

Sofair, Andre N., and Kaldjian, Lauris C. "Eugenic Sterilization and a Qualified Nazi Analogy: The United States and Germany, 1930–1945." *Annals of Internal Medicine* 132 (2000), 312–19.

Stepan, Nancy Leys. *The Hour of Eugenics: Race, Gender, and Nation in Latin America.* Ithaca, NY: Cornell University Press, 1996.

Thomson, Mathew. *Problem of Mental Deficiency: Eugenics and Social Policy in Britain.* New York, Oxford University Press, 1998.

Wachbroit, Robert. "What Is Wrong with Eugenics?" In Edward Erwin, Sidney Gendin, and Lowell Kleiman, eds., *Ethical Issues in Scientific Research.* New York: Garland, 1994, 329–36.

Weindling, Paul. *Health, Race, and German Politics between National Unification and Nazism, 1870–1945.* Cambridge: Cambridge University Press, 1989.

Zenderland, Leila. *Measuring Minds: Henry Herbert Goddard and the Origins of American Intelligence Testing.* New York: Cambridge University Press, 1997.

THE HUMAN GENOME PROJECT

Andrews, Lori B., et al., Institute of Medicine, Committee on Assessing Risks. *Assessing Genetic Risks: Implications for Health and Social Policy.* Washington, DC. National Academy Press, 1994.

Balint Peter J., ed. *The Human Genome Project and Minority Communities: Ethical, Social, and Political Dilemmas.* Westport, CT: Greenwood, 2000.

Bishop, Jerry E., and Waldholz, Michael. *Genome: The Story of the Most Astonishing Scientific Adventure of Our Time—The Attempt to Map All the Genes in the Human Body.* New York: Simon & Schuster, 1990.

Bloom, Barry R., and Trach, Dang Duc. "Genetics and Developing Countries." *British Medical Journal* 322 (2001), 1006–1007.

Boyle, Philip J., et al. "Genetic Grammar: 'Health,' 'Illness,' and the Human Genome Project." *Hastings Center Report* 22 (July–August 1992; Supplement), S1–S20.

Brock, Dan W. "The Human Genome Project and Human Identity." In Robert F. Weir, Susan C. Lawrence, and Evan Fales, eds., *Genes and Human Self-Knowledge: Historical and Philosophical Reflections on Modern Genetics.* Iowa City: Iowa University Press, 1994: 18–33.

Buchanan, Allen, et al. *From Chance to Choice: Genetics and Justice.* New York: Cambridge University Press, 2000.

Cantor, Charles R. "How Will the Human Genome Project Improve Our Quality of Life?" *Nature Biotechnology* 16 (1998), 212–13.

Capron, Morgan Alexander. "Which Ills to Bear? Reevaluating the 'Threat' of Modern Genetics." *Emory Law Journal* 39 (1990), 665–96.

Clayton, Ellen W. "Through the Lens of the Sequence." *Genome Research* 11 (2001), 659–64.

Collins, Francis S. "Medical and Ethical Consequences of the Human Genome Project." *Journal of Clinical Ethics* 2 (1991), 260–67.

———. "Ahead of Schedule and under Budget: The Genome Project Passes Its Fifth Birthday." *Proceedings of the National Academy of Sciences* 92 (1995), 10821–23.

———. "Contemplating the End of the Beginning." *Genome Research* 11 (2001), 641–43.

———; Guyer, Mark S.; and Chakravarti, Aravinda. "Variations on a Theme: Cataloging Human DNA Sequence Variation." *Science* (1997), 1580–81.

Cook-Deegan, Robert M. *The Gene Wars: Science, Politics, and the Human Genome.* New York: W. W. Norton, 1993.

———. "Genome Mapping and Sequencing." in Warren Thomas Reich, ed., *Encyclopedia of Bioethics.* Rev. ed. New York: Simon & Schuster Macmillan, 1995, 1011–20.

Ganten, Detlev. "James D. Watson at the Congress of Molecular Medicine." *Journal of Molecular Medicine* 75 (1997), 615–17.

Glasner, Peter, et al., eds. *Genetic Imaginations: Ethical, Legal and Social Issues in Human Genome Research.* Aldershot, Hampshire, UK: Ashgate, 1998.

Green, Eric D., and Chakravarti, Aravinda. "The Human Genome Sequence Expedition: View from the 'Base Camp.' " *Genome Research* 11 (2001), 645–51.

Hanna, Kathi E. "The Ethical, Legal, and Social Implications Program of the National Center for Human Genome Research: A Missed Opportunity?" In Ruth Ellen Bulger, Elizabeth Meyer Bobby, and Harvey F. Fineberg, eds. Institute of Medicine, Committee on the Social and Ethical Impacts of Developments in Biomedicine. *Society's Choices: Social and Ethical Decision Making in Biomedicine.* Washington, DC: National Academy Press, 1995, 432–57.

Hedgecoe, Adam M. "Genome Analysis." In Ruth Chadwick, ed., *Encyclopedia of Applied Ethics.* San Diego, CA: Academic Press, 1998, 463–70.

Holtzman, Neil A. "Putting the Search for Genes in Perspective." *International Journal of Health Services* 31 (2001), 445–61.

Institute of Physics. "The Human Genome Project—What's the Public Got to Do with It?" *Public Understanding of Science* 8 (1999), 153–59.

Juengst, Eric T. "Respecting Human Subjects in Genome Research: A Preliminary Policy Agenda." In Harold Y. Vanderpool, ed., *The Ethics of Research Involving Human Subjects: Facing the Twenty-First Century.* Frederick, MD: University Publishing Group, 1996, 401–29.

———. "Self-Critical Federal Science? The Ethics Experiment within the U.S. Human Genome Project." *Social Philosophy and Policy* 13 (1996), 63–95.

Kaveny, M. Cathleen. "Jurisprudence and Genetics." *Health Progress* (March–April 2001), 43–47, 78.

Kevles, Daniel J., and Hood, Leroy, eds. *The Code of Codes: Scientific and Social Issues in the Human Genome Project*. Cambridge, MA: Harvard University Press, 1993.

Koonin, Steven E. "An Independent Perspective on the Human Genome Project." *Science* (1998), 36–37.

Lapham, E. Virginia, et al. "Genetic Discrimination: Perspectives of Consumers." *Science* 274 (1996), 621–24.

Lenoir, Noelle. "UNESCO, Genetics, and Human Rights." *Kennedy Institute of Ethics Journal* 7 (1997), 31–42.

Lewontin, Richard C. *It Ain't Necessarily So: The Dream of the Human Genome and Other Illusions*. New York: New York Review of Books, 2001.

McKusick, Victor A. "The Human Genome Project: Plans, Status, and Applications in Biology and Medicine." In George J. Annas and Sherman Elias, eds., *Genome Mapping: Using Law and Ethics as Guides*. New York: Oxford University Press, 1992, 18–42.

Mehlman, Maxwell J. and Botkin, Jeffrey R. *Access to the Genome: The Challenge of Equality*. Washington, DC: Georgetown University Press, 1998.

Meslin, Eric M., Thomson, Elizabeth J., and Boyer, Joy T. "The Ethical, Legal, and Social Implications Research Program at the National Human Genome Research Institute." *Kennedy Institute of Ethics Journal* 7 (1997), 291–98.

Murray, Thomas H., Rothstein, Mark A., and Murray, Robert F. Jr., eds. *The Human Genome Project and the Future of Health Care*. Bloomington and Indianapolis, IN: Indiana University Press, 1996.

National Research Council. *Mapping and Sequencing the Human Genome*. Washington, DC: National Academy Press, 1988.

Olson, Maynard V. "The Human Genome Project." *Proceedings of the National Academy of Sciences* 90 (1993), 4338–44.

Peters, Ted, ed. *Genetics: Issues of Social Justice*. Cleveland, OH: Pilgrim Press, 1998.

Ridley, Matt. *Genome: The Autobiography of a Species in 23 Chapters*. New York: HarperCollins, 2000.

Rosenberg, Alexander. "The Human Genome Project: Research Tactics and Economic Strategies." *Social Philosophy and Policy* 13 (1996), 1–17.

Rothman, Barbara Katz. *The Book of Life: A Personal and Ethical Guide to Race, Normality, and the Implications of the Human Genome Project*. Boston, MA: Beacon Press, 2001.

———. *Genetic Maps and Human Imaginations: The Limits of Science in Understanding Who We Are*. New York: W. W. Norton, 1998.

———. "Of Maps and Imaginations: Sociology Confronts the Genome." *Social Problems* 42 (1995), 1–10.

Rothstein, Mark A., ed. *Legal and Ethical Issues Raised by the Human Genome Project*. Houston, TX: University of Houston, Health Law and Policy Institute, 1991.

Rowen, Lee, Mahairas, Gregory, and Hood, Lee. "Sequencing the Human Genome." *Science* 278 (1997), 605–607.

Sloan, Philip R., ed. *Controlling Our Destinies: The Human Genome Project from Historical, Philosophical, Social, and Ethical Perspectives*. Notre Dame, IN: University of Notre Dame Press, 1997.

United Nations Educational, Scientific, and Cultural Organization. *Universal Declaration on the Human Genome and Human Rights*. Paris: UNESCO, 1997.

U.S. Congress, Office of Technology Assessment. *Mapping Our Genes—The Genome Projects: How Big, How Fast?* Washington, DC: U.S. Government Printing Office, April 1988.

Venter, J. Craig, et al. "Shotgun Sequencing of the Human Genome." *Science* 280 (1998), 1540–42.

Wade, Nicholas. *Life Script: How the Human Genome Discoveries Will Transform Medicine and Enhance Your Health*. New York: Simon & Schuster, 2001.

Watson, James D. *A Passion for DNA: Genes, Genomes, and Society*. Woodbury, NY: Cold Spring Harbor Laboratory Press, 2000.

———, et al. *The Human Genome*. New York: Palgrave Macmillan, 2001.

Weiss, Kenneth M. "In Search of Human Variation." *Genome Research* 8 (1998): 691–97.

World Health Organization, Advisory Committee on Health Research. *Genomics and World Health*. Geneva: World Health Organization, 2002.

GENETIC TESTING AND SCREENING, GENETIC INFORMATION

AAAS-ABA National Conference of Lawyers and Scientists and AAAS Committee on Scientific Freedom and Responsibility. *The Genome, Ethics, and the Law: Issues in Genetic Testing*. Washington, DC: American Association for the Advancement of Science, 1992.

Advisory Committee on Genetic Testing. *Code of Practice and Guidance on Human Genetic Testing Services Supplied to the Public*. London: Her Majesty's Stationery Office, 1997.

American Medical Association, Council on Ethical and Judicial Affairs, "Use of Genetic Testing by Employers." *Journal of the American Medical Association* 266 (1991), 1827–30.

Anderlik, Mary R., and Pentz, Rebecca D. "Genetic Information, Legal, Genetic Privacy Laws." In Thomas H. Murray and Maxwell J. Mehlman, eds., *Encyclopedia of Ethical, Legal, and Policy Issues in Biotechnology*. 2 vols. New York: John Wiley & Sons, 2000, 456–68.

Anderlik, Mary R. "Genetic Information, Legal, Genetics and the Americans with Disabilities Act." In Thomas H. Murray and Maxwell J. Mehlman, eds., *Encyclopedia of Ethical, Legal, and Policy Issues in Biotechnology*. 2 vols. New York: John Wiley & Sons, 2000, 468–78.

Andre, Judith, et al. "On Being Genetically 'Irresponsible.'" *Kennedy Institute of Ethics Journal* 10 (2000), 129–46.

Andrews, Lori B. *Future Perfect: Confronting Decisions about Genetics*. New York: Columbia University Press, 2001.

———, et al. Institute of Medicine, Committee on Assessing Genetic Risks. *Assessing Genetic Risks: Implications for Health and Social Policy*. Washington, DC: National Academy Press, 1994.

Annas, George J. "The Limits of State Laws to Protect Genetic Information." *New England Journal of Medicine* 345 (2001), 385–88.

Association of British Insurers. *Genetic Testing: ABI Code of Practice*. London: ABI, 1997.

Bartels, Dianne M., LeRoy, Bonnie S., and Caplan, Arthur L., eds. *Prescribing Our Future: Ethical Challenges in Genetic Counseling*. New York: Aldine De Gruyter, 1993.

Biesecker, Barbara Bowles. "Reproduction, Ethics, The Ethics of Reproductive Genetic Counseling: Nondirectiveness." In

Thomas H. Murray and Maxwell J. Mehlman, eds., *Encyclopedia of Ethical, Legal, and Policy Issues in Biotechnology.* 2 vols. New York: John Wiley & Sons, 2000, 977–983

Billings, Paul R., ed. *DNA on Trial: Genetic Identification and Criminal Justice.* Plainview, NY: Cold Spring Harbor Laboratory Press, 1992.

———, et al. "Discrimination as a Consequence of Genetic Testing." *American Journal of Human Genetics* 50 (1992), 476–82.

Bobinski, Mary Anne. "Genetic Information, Legal, ERISA Preemption, and HIPAA Protection." In Thomas H. Murray and Maxwell J. Mehlman, eds., *Encyclopedia of Ethical, Legal, and Policy Issues in Biotechnology.* 2 vols. New York: John Wiley & Sons, 2000, 427–40.

Botkin, Jeffrey R. "Reproduction, Law, Wrongful Birth, and Wrongful Life Actions." In Thomas H. Murray and Maxwell J. Mehlman, eds., *Encyclopedia of Ethical, Legal, and Policy Issues in Biotechnology.* 2 vols. New York: John Wiley & Sons, 2000, 996–1003.

Burke, Wylie, et al. "Recommendations for Follow-Up Care for Individuals with an Inherited Predisposition to Cancer. I. Hereditary Nonpolyposis Colon Cancer. Cancer Genetics Studies Consortium." *Journal of the American Medical Association* 277 (1997), 915–19.

Chadwick, Ruth, et al., eds. *The Ethics of Genetic Screening.* New York: Kluwer Academic Publishers, 1999.

———, et al. "Euroscreen 2: Towards Community Policy on Insurance, Commercialization and Public Awareness." *Journal of Medicine and Philosophy* 26 (2001), 263–72.

Clark, A. J. J., et al. *The Genetic Testing of Children.* Philadelphia, PA: Coronet Books, 1997.

Clayton, Ellen Wright. "Genetic Testing in Children." *Journal of Medicine and Philosophy* 22 (1997), 233–51.

———. "Genetic Testing Is Different." *Journal of Health Politics, Policy and Law* 26 (2001), 457–64.

Cunningham, George S. "Genetic Information, Legal, Regulating Genetic Services." In Thomas H. Murray and Maxwell J. Mehlman, eds., *Encyclopedia of Ethical, Legal, and Policy Issues in Biotechnology.* 2 vols. New York: John Wiley & Sons, 2000, 478–83.

DeGrazia, David. "The Ethical Justification for Minimal Paternalism in the Use of the Predictive Test for Huntington's Disease." *Journal of Clinical Ethics* 2 (1991), 219–28.

Doherty, Peter and Sutton, Agneta, eds. *Man-Made Man: Ethical and Legal Issues in Genetics.* Portland, OR: Four Courts Press, 1997.

Evans, James P., et al. "The Complexities of Predictive Genetic Testing." *British Medical Journal* 322 (2001), 1052–56.

Giannelli, Paul, Hoffman, Sharona, Wagner, Wendy. "Genetic Information, Law, Legal Issues in Law Enforcement DNA Databanks." In Thomas H. Murray and Maxwell J. Mehlman, eds., *Encyclopedia of Ethical, Legal, and Policy Issues in Biotechnology.* 2 vols. New York: Johns Wiley & Sons, 2000, 413–26.

Gostin, Larry. Genetic Discrimination: The Use of Genetically Based Diagnostic and Prognostic Tests by Employers and Insurers." *American Journal of Law and Medicine* 17 (1991), 109–44.

Grodin, Michael A., et al. "Susceptibility Genes and Neurological Disorders." *Archives of Neurology* 57 (2000), 1569–74.

Hoedemaekers, Rogeer, ten-Have, Henk, and Chadwick, Ruth. "Genetic Screening: A Comparative Analysis of Three Recent Reports." *Journal of Medical Ethics* 23 (1997), 135–41.

Holtzman, Neil A. *Proceed with Caution: Predicting Genetic Risks in the Recombinant DNA Era.* Baltimore: Johns Hopkins University Press, 1989.

———, and Watson, Michael S., eds. *Promoting Safe and Effective Genetic Testing in the United States: Final Report of the Task Force on Genetic Testing.* Baltimore, MD: Johns Hopkins University Press, 1998.

———, and Shapiro, David. "Genetic Testing and Public Policy." *British Medical Journal* 316 (1998), 852–56.

———, et al. "Predictive Genetic Testing: From Basic Research to Clinical Practice." *Science* 278 (1997), 602–605.

Huang, Anny. "Genetic Information, Legal, FDA Regulation of Genetic Testing." In Thomas H. Murray and Maxwell J. Mehlman, eds., *Encyclopedia of Ethical, Legal, and Policy Issues in Biotechnology.* 2 vols. New York: Johns Wiley & Sons, 2000, 441–55.

Hudson, Kathy L., et al. "Genetic Discrimination and Health Insurance: An Urgent Need for Reform." *Science* 270 (1995), 391–93.

Juengst, Eric T. "Genetic Information, Ethics, Family Issues." In Thomas H. Murray and Maxwell J. Mehlman, eds., *Encyclopedia of Ethical, Legal, and Policy Issues in Biotechnology.* 2 vols. New York: Johns Wiley & Sons, 2000, 390–96.

Kass, Nancy F. "The Implications of Genetic Testing for Health and Life Insurance." In Mark A. Rothstein, ed. *Genetic Secrets.* New Haven: Yale University Press, 1997, 299–316.

Koenig, Barbara A., et al. "Genetics Testing for BRCA1 and BRCA2: Recommendations of the Stanford Program in Genomics, Ethics, and Society." *Journal of Women's Health* 7 (1998), 531–45.

Knoppers, Bartha M. "Cancer Genetics: A Model for Multifactorial Conditions?" *Medicine and Law* 20 (2001), 177–82.

Laurie, Graeme. *Genetic Privacy: A Challenge to Medico-Legal Norms.* New York: Cambridge University Press, 2002.

Lerman, Caryn, et al. "BRCA1 Testing in Families with Hereditary Breast-Ovarian Cancer: A Prospective Study of Patient Decision Making and Outcomes." *Journal of the American Medical Association* 275 (1996), 1885–92.

Lippman, Abby. "Prenatal Genetic Testing and Screening: Constructing Needs and Reinforcing Inequities." *American Journal of Law and Medicine* 17 (1991), 15–50.

Long, Clarisa, ed. *Genetic Testing and Use of Information.* Washington, DC: The American Enterprise Institute for Public Policy Research, 1999.

Marshall, Eliot. "Fast Technology Drives New World of Newborn Screening." *Science* 294 (2001), 2272–74.

Marteau, Theresa M., and Crooyle, Robert T. "Psychological Responses to Genetic Testing." *British Medical Journal* 316 (1998), 693–96.

Matthews, Anne L. "Genetic Counseling." In Thomas H. Murray and Maxwell J. Mehlman, eds., *Encyclopedia of Ethical, Legal, and Policy Issues in Biotechnology.* 2 vols. New York: Johns Wiley & Sons, 2000, 342–52.

Naser, Curtis, and Alpert, Sheri. "Genetic Information, Ethics, Ethical Issues in Tissue Banking and Human Subject Research in Stored Tissues." In Thomas H. Murray and Maxwell J. Mehlman, eds., *Encyclopedia of Ethical, Legal, and Policy Issues in Biotechnology.* 2 vols. New York: Johns Wiley & Sons, 2000, 363–89.

National Academy of Sciences, Committee on DNA Technology in Forensic Science. *DNA Technology in Forensic Science.* Washington, DC: National Academy Press, 1992.

National Research Council, Committee for the Study of Inborn Errors of Metabolism. *Genetic Screening: Programs, Principles and Research*. Washington, DC: National Academy of Science, 1975.

Natowicz, Marvin R., Alper, Jane K., and Alper, Joseph S. "Genetic Discrimination and the Law." *American Journal of Human Genetics* 50 (1992), 465–75.

Neitzel, Heidemarie, et al., eds. *The New Genetics: From Research into Health Care: Social and Ethical Implications for Users and Providers*. New York: Springer-Verlag, 2001.

Nelkin, Dorothy, and Tancredi, Laurence. *Dangerous Diagnostics: The Social Power of Biological Information*. Chicago, IL: University of Chicago Press, 1994.

New York State Task Force on Life and the Law. *Genetic Testing and Screening in the Age of Genomic Medicine*. New York: The Task Force, November 2000.

Nuffield Council on Bioethics. *Genetic Screening: Ethical Issues*. London: The Council, 1993.

Organization for Economic Cooperation and Development (OECD) Staff. *Genetic Testing: Policy Issues For the New Millenium*. Organization for Economic Cooperation and Development, 2001.

Pagon, Roberta A., et al. "Genetic Testing." *Western Journal of Medicine* 174 (2001), 344–47.

Parens, Erik, Asch, Adrienne, and Powell, Cynthia. "Reproduction, Ethics, Prenatal Testing and the Disability Rights Critique." In Thomas H. Murray and Maxwell J. Mehlman, eds., *Encyclopedia of Ethical, Legal, and Policy Issues in Biotechnology*. 2 vols. New York: Johns Wiley & Sons, 2000, 957–69.

Peterson, James C. *Genetic Turning Points: The Ethics of Human Genetic Intervention*. Grand Rapids: William B. Eerdmans, 2001.

Powers, Madison. "Genetic Information, Ethics, Privacy and Confidentiality: Overview." In Thomas H. Murray and Maxwell J. Mehlman, eds., *Encyclopedia of Ethical, Legal, and Policy Issues in Biotechnology*. 2 vols. New York: John Wiley & Sons, 2000, 405–13.

———. "Privacy and the Control of Genetic Information." In Mark S. Frankel, and Albert Teich, eds., *The Genetic Frontier: Ethics, Law, and Policy*. Washington, DC: American Association for the Advancement of Science, 1994, 77–100.

Quaid, Kimberly A. "Genetic Information, Ethics, Informed Consent to Testing and Screening." In Thomas H. Murray and Maxwell J. Mehlman, eds., *Encyclopedia of Ethical, Legal, and Policy Issues in Biotechnology*. 2 vols. New York: Johns Wiley & Sons, 2000, 397–405.

Robertson, John A. "Ethical and Legal Issues in Preimplantation Genetic Screening." *Fertility and Sterility* 57 (1992), 1–11.

———. "Genetic Selection of Offspring Characteristics." *Boston University Law Review* 76 (1996), 421–82.

Rothman, Barbara Katz. *The Tentative Pregnancy: Prenatal Diagnosis and the Future of Motherhood*. New York: Viking Penguin, 1986.

Rothenberg, Karen H. "Genetic Information and Health Insurance: State Legislative Approaches." *Journal of Law, Medicine, and Ethics* 23 (1995), 312–19.

———, and Thomson, Elizabeth J., eds. *Women and Prenatal Testing. Facing the Challenges of Genetic Technology*. Columbus, OH: Ohio State University Press, 1994.

———, et al. "Genetic Information and the Workplace: Legislative Approaches and Policy Challenges." *Science* 275 (1997), 1755–57.

Rothstein, Mark A., ed. *Genetic Secrets: Protecting Privacy and Confidentiality in the Genetic Era*. New Haven: Yale University Press, 1997.

Shi, Michael M., and Bleavins, Michael R. "Pharmacogenetics." In Thomas H. Murray and Maxwell J. Mehlman, eds., *Encyclopedia of Ethical, Legal, and Policy Issues in Biotechnology*. 2 vols. New York: Johns Wiley & Sons, 2000, 880–88.

Smith, David H., et al. *Early Warning: Cases and Ethical Guidance for Presymptomatic Testing in Genetic Diseases*. Bloomington, IN: Indiana University Press, 1998.

Takala, Tuija. "Who Should Know about Our Genetic Makeup and Why? *Western Journal of Medicine* 175 (2001), 260–63.

Tauer, Carol A. "Genetic Testing and Discrimination." *Health Progress* (March–April 2001), 48–53, 71.

———. "Personal Privacy and the Common Good." *Health Progress* (March–April 2001), 36–42, 78.

Testart, Jacques. "The New Eugenics and Medicalized Reproduction." *Cambridge Quarterly of Healthcare Ethics* 4 (1995), 304–12.

Thomson, Elizabeth J., et al., eds. *Genetics and Public Health in the Twenty-First Century: Using Genetic Information to Improve Health and Prevent Disease*. New York: Oxford University Press, 2000.

U.S. Congress, Office of Technology Assessment. *Cystic Fibrosis and DNA Tests: Implications of Carrier Screening*. Washington, DC: U.S. Government Printing Office, August 1992.

———. *Genetic Monitoring and Screening in the Workplace*. Washington, DC: U.S. Government Printing Office, October 1990.

———. *Genetic Witness: Forensic Uses of DNA Tests*. Washington, DC: U.S. Government Printing Office, July 1990.

U.S. President's Commission for the Study of Ethical Problems in Medicine and Biomedical and Behavioral Research. *Screening and Counseling for Genetic Conditions*. Washington, DC: U.S. Government Printing Office, February 1983.

Welch, Charles A. "Sacred Secrets—The Privacy of Medical Records." *New England Journal of Medicine* 345 (2001), 371–72.

Wertz, Dorothy C., and Fletcher, John C., eds. *Ethics and Human Genetics: A Cross-Cultural Perspective*. Berlin and New York: Springer-Verlag, 1989.

Whitehouse, Peter J. and Post, Stephen G., eds. *Genetic Testing for Alzheimer Disease: Ethical and Clinical Issues*. Baltimore, MD: Johns Hopkins University Press, 1998.

Wolf, Susan M. "Beyond 'Genetic Discrimination': Toward the Broader Harm of Geneticism." *Journal of Law, Medicine and Ethics* 23 (1995), 345–53.

Xin, Mao, and Wertz, Dorothy C. "China's Genetics Services Providers' Attitudes towards Several Ethical Issues: A Cross-Cultural Survey." *Clinical Genetics* 52 (1997), 100–109.

Zallen, Doris Teichler. *Does It Run in the Family? A Consumers Guide to DNA Testing for Genetic Disorders*. Piscataway, NJ: Rutgers University Press, 1997.

HUMAN GENE TRANSFER RESEARCH

AND GERM-LINE GENETIC INTERVENTION

Ackerman, Terrence F. and Nienhuis, Arthur W., eds. *Ethics of Cancer Genetics and Gene Therapy*. Totowa, NJ: Humana Press, 2001.

Agius, Emmanuel, et al., eds. *Germ-Line Intervention and Our Responsibilities to Future Generations, Vol. 55*. New York: Kluwer Academic Publishers, 1998.

Anderson, W. French. "Human Gene Therapy." *Science* 256 (1992), 808–13.

————. "Human Gene Therapy." *Nature* 392 Supplement (1998), 25–30.

————. "Excitement in Gene Therapy." *Human Gene Therapy* 12 (2001), 1483–84.

Billings, Paul R., et al. "Human Germline Gene Modification: A Dissent." *Lancet* 353 (1999), 1873–75.

Bonnicksen, Andrea A. "Gene Therapy, Ethics, and International Perspectives." In Thomas H. Murray and Maxwell J. Mehlman, eds., *Encyclopedia of Ethical, Legal, and Policy Issues in Biotechnology*. 2 vols. New York: Johns Wiley & Sons, 2000, 275–85.

Boylan, Michael, and Brown, Kevin E. *Genetic Engineering: Science and Ethics on the New Frontier*. Upper Saddle River, NJ: Pearson Education, 2001.

Clark, William R. *The New Healers*. New York: Oxford University Press, 1999.

Fletcher, John C., and Anderson, W. French. "Germ-Line Gene Therapy: A New Stage of Debate." *Law, Medicine and Health Care* 20 (1992), 26–39.

————, and Richter, Gerd. "Human Fetal Gene Therapy: Moral and Ethical Questions." *Human Gene Therapy* 7 (1996), 1605–14.

Fowler, Gregory, Juengst, Eric T., and Zimmerman, Burke K. "Germ-Line Gene Therapy and the Clinical Ethos of Medical Genetics." *Theoretical Medicine* 10 (1989), 151–65.

Frankel, Mark S., and "Facing Inheritable Genetic Modifications." *Science* 292 (2001), 1303.

————. *Human Inheritable Genetic Modifications: Assessing Scientific, Ethical, Religious, and Policy Issues*. Washington, DC: American Association for the Advancement of Science, 2000.

Friedmann, Theodore, ed. *The Development of Human Gene Therapy*. New York: Cold Spring Harbor Laboratory Press, 1999.

————. "The Evolution of Public Review and Oversight Mechanisms in Human Gene Transfer Research: Joint Roles of the FDA and NIH." *Current Opinion in Biotechnology* 12 (2001), 304–307.

————. *Gene Therapy: Fact and Fiction in Biology's New Approaches to Disease*. Woodbury, NY: Cold Spring Harbor Laboratory Press, 1994.

Gura, Trisha. "After a Setback, Gene Therapy Progresses . . . Gingerly." *Science* 291 (2001), 1692–97.

Hedgecoe, Adam M. "Gene Therapy." In Ruth Chadwick, ed. *Encyclopedia of Applied Ethics*. San Diego, CA: Academic Press, 1998, 383–90.

High, Katherine A. "Gene Therapy: A 2001 Perspective." *Haemophilia* 7 (2001), suppl. 1, 23–27.

Juengst, Eric T., ed. "Human Germ-Line Engineering." *Journal of Medicine and Philosophy* 16 (1991), 587–694. Thematic issue.

Kaji, Eugene H., and Leiden, Jeffrey M. "Gene and Stem Cell Therapies." *Journal of the American Medical Association* 285 (2001), 545–50.

Knight, Jonathan. "Biology's Last Taboo." *Nature* 413 (2001), 12–15.

Lyon, Jeff. *Altered Facts: Gene Therapy and the Retooling of Human Life*. New York: W. W. Norton, 1996.

McKenny, Gerald P. "Gene Therapy, Ethics, Religious Perspectives." In Thomas H. Murray and Maxwell J. Mehlman, eds., *Encyclopedia of Ethical, Legal, and Policy Issues in Biotechnology*. 2 vols. New York: Johns Wiley & Sons, 2000, 300–311.

Nelson, Robert. "Gene Therapy, Ethics, Germ Cell Gene Transfer." In Thomas H. Murray and Maxwell J. Mehlman, eds., *Encyclopedia of Ethical, Legal, and Policy Issues in Biotechnology*. 2 vols. New York: Johns Wiley & Sons, 2000, 292–300.

Nichols, Eve K., and Institute of Medicine, National Academy of Sciences. *Human Gene Therapy*. Cambridge, MA: Harvard University Press, 1988.

Pollack, Andrew. "Gene Therapy's Focus Shifts from Rare Illness." *New York Times*, August 4, 1998, p. F1.

Proctor, Robert N. "Genomics and Eugenics: How Fair Is the Comparison?" In George J. Annas and Sherman Elias, eds., *Gene Mapping: Using Law and Ethics as Guides*. New York: Oxford University Press, 1992, 75–93.

Resnik, David B. *Human Germ-Line Therapy: Scientific, Moral and Political Issues*. Georgetown, TX: Landes Bioscience, 1999.

Ross, Gail, et al. "Gene Therapy in the United States: A Five-Year Status Report." *Human Gene Therapy* 7 (1996), 1781–90.

Simon, Jurgen W., et al. *Interdisciplinary Approaches to Gene Therapy: Legal, Ethical, and Scientific Aspects*. New York: Springer, 1997.

Stock, Gregory, and Campbell, John eds. *Engineering the Human Germline: An Exploration of the Science and Ethics of Altering the Genes We Pass to Our Children*. New York: Oxford University Press, 2000.

Szebik, Imre, and Glass, Kathleen C. "Ethical Issues of Human Germ-Cell Therapy: A Preparation for Public Discussion." *Academic Medicine* 76 (2001), 32–38.

Tauer, Carol A. "Gene Therapy, Ethics, Gene Therapy for Fetuses and Embryos." In Thomas H. Murray and Maxwell J. Mehlman, eds., *Encyclopedia of Ethical, Legal, and Policy Issues in Biotechnology*. 2 vols. New York: Johns Wiley & Sons, 2000, 285–292.

Thompson, Larry. *Correcting the Code: Inventing the Genetic Cure for the Human Body*. New York: Simon & Schuster, 1994.

U.K. Department of Health, Gene Therapy Advisory Committee. "Guidance on Making Proposals to Conduct Gene Therapy Research on Human Subjects." *Human Gene Therapy* 12 (2001), 711–20.

U.S. President's Commission for the Study of Ethical Problems in Medicine and Biomedical and Behavioral Research. *Splicing Life: A Report on the Social and Ethical Issues of Genetic Engineering with Human Beings*. Washington, DC: U.S. Government Printing Office, November 1982.

Walters, LeRoy. "Ethical Issues in Human Gene Therapy." *Journal of Clinical Ethics* 2 (1991), 267–74.

————. "Human Gene Therapy: Ethics and Public Policy." *Human Gene Therapy* 2 (1991), 115–22.

Walters, LeRoy. "Gene Therapy: Overview." In Thomas H. Murray and Maxwell J. Mehlman, eds., *Encyclopedia of Ethical, Legal, and Policy Issues in Biotechnology*. 2 vols. New York: Johns Wiley & Sons, 2000, 336–42.

————, and Palmer, Julie G. "Germ-Line Gene Therapy." *The Ethics of Human Gene Therapy*. New York: Oxford University Press, 1997, 60–98.

————, and Palmer, Julie Gage. *The Ethics of Human Gene Therapy*. New York: Oxford University Press, 1997.

Willgoos, Christine. "FDA Regulation: An Answer to the Questions of Human Cloning and Germline Gene Therapy." *American Journal of Law & Medicine* 27 (2001), 101–24.

Wivel, Nelson A. "Gene Therapy, Ethics, Somatic Cell Gene Therapy." In Thomas H. Murray and Maxwell J. Mehlman, eds., *Encyclopedia of Ethical, Legal, and Policy Issues in Biotechnology*. 2 vols. New York: Johns Wiley & Sons, 2000, 310–21.

Wivel, Nelson A., and Walters, LeRoy. "Germ-Line Gene Modification and Disease Prevention: Some Medical and Ethical Perspectives." *Science* 262 (1993), 533–38.

GENETIC ENHANCEMENT

Cole-Turner, Ronald. "Do Means Matter? Evaluating Technologies of Human Enhancement." In Erik Parens, ed., *Enhancing Human Traits: Ethical and Social Implications*. Washington, DC: Georgetown University Press, 1998, 151–61.

Daniels, Norman. "Normal Functioning and the Treatment-Enhancement Distinction." *Cambridge Quarterly of Healthcare Ethics* 9 (2000), 309–22.

Engelhardt, Tristram H. "Germ-Line Genetics Engineering and Moral Diversity: Moral Controversies in a Post-Christian World." *Social Philosophy and Policy* 13 (1996), 47–62.

Gardner, William. "Can Human Genetic Enhancement Be Prohibited?" *Journal of Medicine and Philosophy* 20 (1995), 65–84.

Glover, Jonathan. *What Sort of People Should There Be?* New York: Penguin Books, 1984.

Juengst, Eric T. "Can Enhancement Be Distinguished from Prevention in Genetic Medicine?" *Journal of Medicine and Philosophy* 22 (1997), 125 42.

———. "Human Enhancement Uses of Biotechnology, Ethics, The Ethics of Enhancement." In Thomas H. Murray and Maxwell J. Mehlman, eds., *Encyclopedia of Ethical, Legal, and Policy Issues in Biotechnology*. 2 vols. New York: Johns Wiley & Sons, 2000, 503–07.

McKenny, Gerald. "Human Enhancement Uses of Biotechnology, Ethics, Therapy vs. Enhancement." In Thomas H. Murray and Maxwell J. Mehlman, eds., *Encyclopedia of Ethical, Legal, and Policy Issues in Biotechnology*. 2 vols. New York: Johns Wiley & Sons, 2000, 507–15.

Mehlman, Maxwell J. "Human Enhancement Uses of Biotechnology, Law, Genetic Enhancement, and the Regulation of Acquired Genetic Advantages. In Thomas H. Murray and Maxwell J. Mehlman, eds., *Encyclopedia of Ethical, Legal, and Policy Issues in Biotechnology*. 2 vols. New York: Johns Wiley & Sons, 2000, 515–27.

Muller, Hermann J. "The Guidance of Human Evolution." *Perspectives in Biology and Medicine* 3, (1959), 1–43.

Parens, Erik, ed. *Enhancing Human Traits: Ethical and Social Implications*. Washington, DC: Georgetown University Press, 1998.

Resnik, David B. "The Moral Significance of the Therapy-Enhancement Distinction in Human Genetics." *Cambridge Quarterly of Healthcare Ethics* 9 (2000), 365–77.

Scully, Jackie Leach, and Rehmann-Sutter, Christoph. "When Norms Normalize: The Case of Genetic 'Enhancement.' " *Human Gene Therapy* 12 (2001), 87–95.

Shapiro, Michael H. "Human Enhancement Uses of Biotechnology, Policy, Technological Enhancement, and Human Equality. In Thomas H. Murray and Maxwell J. Mehlman, eds., *Encyclopedia of Ethical, Legal, and Policy Issues in Biotechnology*. 2 vols. New York: Johns Wiley & Sons, 2000, 527–48.

Stock, Gregory. *Redesigning Humans: Our Inevitable Genetic Future*. Boston, MA: Houghton Mifflin, 2002.

Wachbroit, Robert. "Human Enhancement Uses of Biotechnology: Overview." In Thomas H. Murray and Maxwell J. Mehlman, eds., *Encyclopedia of Ethical, Legal, and Policy Issues in Biotechnology*. 2 vols. New York: Johns Wiley & Sons, 2000, 549–52.

Walters, LeRoy, and Palmer, Julie G. "Enhancement Genetic Engineering." *The Ethics of Human Gene Therapy*. New York: Oxford University Press, 1997, 99–142.

Whitehouse, Peter J., and Marling, Cynthia R. "Human Enhancement Uses of Biotechnology, Ethics, Cognitive Enhancement." In Thomas H. Murray and Maxwell J. Mehlman, eds., *Encyclopedia of Ethical, Legal, and Policy Issues in Biotechnology*. 2 vols. New York: Johns Wiley & Sons, 2000, 485–91.

GENE PATENTS

Brody, Baruch A. "Protecting Human Dignity and the Patenting of Human Genes." In Audrey R. Chapman, ed., *Perspectives on Genetic Patenting*. Washington, DC: American Association for the Advancement of Science, 1999, 111–26.

Chapman, Audrey R., ed. *Perspectives on Genetic Patenting*. Washington, DC: American Association for the Advancement of Science, 1999.

Cole-Turner, Ronald. "Patents and Licensing, Ethics, Organizations with Prominent Positions on Gene Patenting." In Thomas H. Murray and Maxwell J. Mehlman, eds., *Encyclopedia of Ethical, Legal, and Policy Issues in Biotechnology*. 2 vols. New York: Johns Wiley & Sons, 2000, 834–44.

Cook-Deegan, Robert M. and McCormack, Stephen J. "Patents, Secrecy, and DNA." *Science* 293 (2001), 217.

Doll, John J. "The Patenting of DNA." *Science* (1998), 689–90.

Gilbert, Penny X. and Walter, Claire. "Patents and the Human Genome Project—New Claims for Old?" *Trends in Biotechnology* 19 (2001), 49–52.

Grisham, Julie. "New Rules for Gene Patents." *Nature Biotechnology* 18 (2000), 921.

Guenin, Louis M. "Patents, Ethics, Human Life Forms." In Thomas H. Murray and Maxwell J. Mehlman, eds., *Encyclopedia of Ethical, Legal, and Policy Issues in Biotechnology*. 2 vols. New York: Johns Wiley & Sons, 2000, 866–80.

Heller, Michael A., and Eisenberg, Rebecca S. "Can Patents Deter Innovation? The Anticommons in Biomedical Research." *Science* (1998), 698–701.

Hermerén, Göran. "Patents and Licensing, Ethics, International Controversies." In Thomas H. Murray and Maxwell J. Mehlman, eds., *Encyclopedia of Ethical, Legal, and Policy Issues in Biotechnology*. 2 vols. New York: Johns Wiley & Sons, 2000, 817–25.

Hoedemaekers, Rogeer. "Commercialization, Patents and Moral Assessment of Biotechnology Products." *Journal of Medicine and Philosophy* 26 (2001), 273–84.

———. "Human Gene Patents: Core Issues in Multi-layered Debate." *Medicine, Health Care and Philosophy* 4 (2001), 211–21.

Jones, Philip B. C. "Patentability Requirements for Genes and Proteins: Perspectives from the Trilateral Patent Offices." *Journal of BioLaw and Business* 3 (2000), 5–15.

Katz, Dana, and Merz, Jon F. "Patents and Licensing, Policy, Patenting of Inventions Developed with Public Funds." In Thomas H. Murray and Maxwell J. Mehlman, eds., *Encyclopedia of Ethical, Legal, and Policy Issues in Biotechnology*. 2 vols. New York: Johns Wiley & Sons, 2000, 854–66.

Lui, Jacqueline. "Patenting Biotechnology Inventions in China." *Nature Biotechnology* 19 (2001), 83–84.

Poste, George. "The Case for Genomic Patenting." *Nature* 378 (1995), 534–36.

Resnik, David B. "DNA Patents and Human Dignity." *Journal of Law, Medicine and Ethics* 29 (2001), 152–65.

———. "The Morality of Human Gene Patents." *Kennedy Institute of Ethics Journal* 7 (1997), 43–61.

Svatos, Michele. "Patents and Licensing, Ethics, Ownership of Animal, and Plant Genes." In Thomas H. Murray and Maxwell J. Mehlman, eds., *Encyclopedia of Ethical, Legal, and Policy Issues in Biotechnology*. 2 vols. New York: Johns Wiley & Sons, 2000, 844–54.

Yanai, Itai. "Brave New Patents: The Law of DNA Worship." *Journal of BioLaw and Business* 4 (2001), 27–33.

BIBLIOGRAPHIES

Goldstein, Doris Mueller. *Bioethics: A Guide to Information Sources*. Detroit: Gale Research Company, 1982. See under "Genetic Intervention."

Lineback, Richard H., ed. *Philosopher's Index*. Vols. 1– . Bowling Green, OH: Philosophy Documentation Center, Bowling Green State University. Issued quarterly. See under "Genetic Engineering" and "Genetics."

Walters, LeRoy, and Kahn, Tamar Joy, eds. *Bibliography of Bioethics*. Vols. 1– . Washington, DC: Kennedy Institute of Ethics, Georgetown University. Issued annually. See under "Eugenics," "Gene Therapy," "Genetic Counseling," "Genetic Intervention," "Genetic Screening," and "Genome Mapping."

WORLD WIDE WEB RESOURCES

Kennedy Institute of Ethics Georgetown University: National Information Resource on Ethics and Human Genetics, *Scope Notes* (http://www.georgetown.edu/research/nrcbl/nirehg/scope.htm

National Library of Medicine: PubMed (http://www.ncbi.nlm.nih. gov/PubMed/)

National Library of Medicine: LocatorPlus (http:///locatorplus.gov/)

University Microfilms: Periodical Abstracts (http://www.umi. com/proquest)